Also by Robert Lacey

Majesty
The Kingdom
Ford: The Men and the Machine

LITTLE
MAN

Meyer Lansky, police mug shot, March 1928.

LITTLE MAN

Meyer Lansky and the Gangster Life

ROBERT LACEY

Little, Brown and Company

Boston   Toronto   London

LIBRARY OF CONGRESS CATALOGING-IN-PUBLICATION DATA

Lacey, Robert.
    Little man: Meyer Lansky and the gangster life / by Robert Lacey.
    — 1st ed.
        p.   cm.
    Includes bibliographical references and index.
    ISBN 0-316-51168-4
    1. Lansky, Meyer, 1902–   . 2. Criminals — United States —
Biography.   3. Mafia — United States — History — 20th century.
I. Title.
HV6248.L25L33   1991
364.1'092 — dc20
[B]   91-18324

            10 9 8 7 6 5 4 3 2 1

                        RRD-VA

            Published simultaneously in Canada by
            Little, Brown & Company (Canada) Limited

        PRINTED IN THE UNITED STATES OF AMERICA

For my children,
Sasha, Scarlett, and Bruno

DODGE PARK KENNEL CLUB

FLAMINGO HOTEL

Omaha

Council
Bluffs

Las Vegas

Los Angeles

THE BEVERLY CLUB

EL CORTEZ HOTEL

GRAN CASINO NACIONAL

G.W. WARD

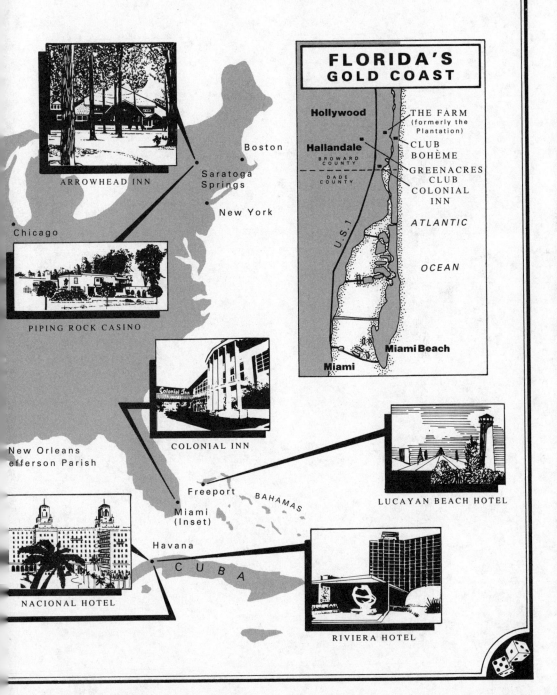

Casinos & Carpet Joints

THE WORLD OF MEYER LANSKY

ARROWHEAD INN

Boston

Saratoga Springs

New York

Chicago

PIPING ROCK CASINO

FLORIDA'S GOLD COAST

Hollywood

THE FARM
(formerly the
Plantation)

Hallandale

CLUB
BOHÈME

BROWARD
COUNTY

GREENACRES
CLUB

DADE
COUNTY

COLONIAL
INN

ATLANTIC

U.S. 1

OCEAN

Miami Beach

Miami

COLONIAL INN

New Orleans
Jefferson Parish

LUCAYAN BEACH HOTEL

Freeport

BAHAMAS

Miami
(Inset)

Havana

NACIONAL HOTEL

C U B A

RIVIERA HOTEL

Contents

LITTLE MAN

Godfather, Retired

MEYER LANSKY walked into the Miami Beach Public Library several mornings every week, a short, rather slight man, who kept himself to himself.

"Mild mannered," remembers the librarian. "Very pleasant. He was never pushy in any way."[1]

When he picked himself out a book, it was a work of history, usually, or a biography of some sort, seldom fiction. If a book was important and a little difficult, it appealed to Meyer Lansky the more. In his later years, he came to sample the philosophers.[2]

"He was always a great reader," remembers Joseph Varon, who became Meyer Lansky's lawyer in the early 1950s. "He brought me a book once when I was in the hospital — a book of economics. 'This is just marvelous,' he said. I had to stop on the second page. I couldn't understand a word of it."[3]

It was the hallmark of Meyer Lansky that he was always trying to improve himself, forever striving to tighten up his mind that notch or two more. The thinking man's gangster. Bugsy Siegel and Joe Adonis, his partners in the 1940s, loved him for it. "That Meyer!"

The details of the interviews, documents, and other evidence upon which this book is based can be found in the reference section in the back of the book.

3

they would marvel, chewing over his cleverness, his love of figures, the way he did sums in his head as a form of recreation. Why, he even had his own private tutor in math![4] Then, lowering their voices, they would pay tribute to what had to be Meyer Lansky's ultimate achievement — the very crowning touch.

"Can you believe it? He's a member of the Book-of-the-Month Club!"[5]

Meyer Lansky was a little man — five foot four and a half, according to the FBI.[6]

"Five foot three," says Gerry "Mad Dog" Coyle, a croupier who worked in several of Lansky's casino operations. "He was a very little guy — seriously small. He was not an inch over five foot three."[7]

Close scrutiny of Meyer Lansky's heels revealed a definite lift[8] — nothing vulgar, or flamenco-dancer-like, but a stacking which could only betray the wish to stretch things in the direction of five foot five. His light gray socks matched his light gray trousers. His wrinkle-free shirt was always in a harmonious tone of blue, white, or gray, and he wore it on the outside of his pants, dropping in straight suspension from the profile of his paunch, which was by no means excessive, the roundness appropriate for a gentleman of his age. In 1974, Meyer Lansky was seventy-two years old.

From the library, Meyer Lansky would walk a few yards across a sun-baked patch of grass to Wolfie's (proprietor, Wolfie Cohen), on the corner of Collins Avenue and Twenty-first Street.

It is a route that is trodden to this day. Wolfie's, a pink-painted temple to the glories of bagels and smoked whitefish, is one of the basic points of reference on Miami Beach. Daily in January and February — and on almost any Sunday morning throughout the year — the lines spill out onto the sidewalk fifty yards or more, their destinations neatly segregated: parties of two, parties of three or more, counter seats only. Brunch at Wolfie's would be no fun without half an hour's wait.

In the moist, mushroomy air of an off-season morning, Meyer Lansky would not have to wait. His friends were already at the table, coffee steaming. Hymie Lazar, Yiddy Bloom, Benny Sigelbaum, Meyer's brother, Jake. They were short and old and neat, just as he was — except, perhaps, when it came to the shortness department and brother Jake. Jake Lansky was quite a large man — five foot eight — the bigger and baggier of the two brothers since anyone could remember.

It was a daily ritual, this gathering over the coffee and cake.[9] Meyer Lansky did some of the best deals of his life in deli booths, the bowl of pickles on the table, the ashtray filling up with butts. The morning "meet" over coffee and Danish was the daily partners' conference, where the progress of existing business was checked upon, and where new business got done.

By the mid-1970s, however, Meyer and his friends considered themselves retired. They were slowing down a bit, so they spent much of their time together reminiscing, testing each other's memories for fun, a trivial pursuit of their own devising, the subject categories heavy with remembrances that were particular to them. What was the number of the amendment that ended Prohibition? Did Estes Kefauver have a middle name?[10]

If they disagreed on the facts, someone was dispatched across the grass to the reference shelves of the library — and great was the merriment if it was discovered that Meyer had got his answer wrong. He was supposed to be the one with all the answers in his head.

These old friends laughing and gossiping round their basket of pastries had all, in their time, had their brushes with the law, and they survived by staying sharp. But Meyer, they would acknowledge, was the sharpest of all of them — the one who was blessed with something really special up top.

The comedian Jackie Mason had a joke about it. All those Italians with broad shoulders and dark glasses? he would ask. How could they possibly have created something like the Mafia — unless they had a Jew to show them how?

"Meyer Lansky? He's their Henry Kissinger."[11]

According to the FBI, Lucky Luciano was the first of the modern Mafia chieftains,[12] and Meyer Lansky was Lucky Luciano's right-hand man. Meyer was Lucky's partner and friend in the early 1930s, when Luciano was trying to leaven the traditional Sicilian way of doing things with some current business theory and practice. So if Meyer served as Lucky's one-man think tank in those formative years, then he has a fair claim to be considered one of the architects of modern organized crime.

Meyer Lansky was the man through whom the U.S. Navy went in 1942 when naval intelligence wanted underworld help to combat the U-boats operating off Long Island. Then the navy turned to him again in 1943, when it was wondering how the Italian Mafia's cousins in America might be able to help with the forthcoming invasion of Sicily.

Lansky was the key man in 1946 and 1947, providing some of the financing to help Bugsy Siegel get started in Las Vegas, the most profitable piece of business diversification that the Mob ever did — and if Bugsy had only run his business the way that Meyer did, he might not have ended up dead in Beverly Hills, a set of bullets in his head.

In the 1950s it was Meyer Lansky who fixed things with President Batista so that big-time gambling could start up in Cuba. Moe Dalitz, Santo Trafficante, Jr., George Raft — gangsters real and cinematic went down to Havana, and it was Meyer who did the best deal of all, raising his twenty-one-story, mosaic-covered Riviera Hotel, with its pool and egg-shaped casino, beside the Caribbean.

In the 1960s Meyer's friends and partners were busy in the Bahamas and in London — and most of all in Las Vegas — skimming the tables in the last, happy fling before the big corporations moved in. The money went offshore, via Canada or the Bahamas, often ending up in Switzerland, a process which gangland folklore gave Meyer the credit for devising. He was said to be the prophet of the voguish new gospel of money laundering, and he was profiled at length in the *Wall Street Journal,* which quoted unnamed federal agents who set his worth at $300 million.[13]

When FBI agents raided the New Jersey operations room of the Lucchese crime family, a back area of the Hole in the Wall luncheonette, in Newark, in the mid-1980s, they found two black-and-white icons on the wall: a photograph of Al Capone and, alongside it, a photograph of Meyer Lansky — the twin patron saints.[14]

Capone stood for all the traditional violence and toughness of U.S. urban crime — the machine gun in the violin case, the menace that lies at the heart of gangster appeal. Meyer Lansky stood for the brains, the sophistication, the funny money — the sheer cleverness of it all.

After a two-year trial, the Luccheses all got off.[15]

Through his very specialized abilities, Meyer Lansky became his own version of the great American success story: the poor boy who made it to the top, the very top in his own field. He chose his business, and he prospered in it, as a bright boy can hope to prosper in the land of the free.

He did not, perhaps, quite win respectability in the process. But he did secure acceptance, and in a rather particular form. At the high holidays, the fund-raisers would come calling.

"Money for Israel? You did not have to ask Meyer Lansky twice," remembers Shepard Broad, mayor of Bay Harbor Islands, and, since World War II, one of the most eminent Jewish activists on Miami Beach. "Not like some. He was always waiting for me in the lobby, ready with the check."[16]

A check? Not cash in a brown envelope? Meyer Lansky paid his taxes — some of them — and he was careful to document his deductions properly. He was a faithful contributor to WPBT-TV, the local public television station,[17] sending in his check like all the other inhabitants of Miami and Miami Beach who enjoyed noncommercial news coverage and wildlife documentaries.

That was what gave the achievement of Meyer Lansky real flavor. Not the millions of dollars that the world presumed he was worth, nor the hard, sinister power that Meyer Lansky had been part of, back in the days of Lucky Luciano and the contract killers of Murder, Inc. But to finish up here in south Florida in the ranks of all the other retired accountants, finally free to hang his shirt outside his trousers with the rest of them, to enjoy the condo on Collins, the doorman's salute, the homage of the fund-raisers, the greetings of his neighbors as he walked his dog along the palm trees in the sun.

When visiting reporters came to town, the crime desk of the *Miami Herald* liked to drive them over to Collins Avenue to cruise amongst the Cadillacs so they could photograph him, the notorious Meyer Lansky caught in the act of walking his dog.

It was not that he stood out in any way. The power of the image was that he looked just like anybody else. The magazine features usually described him as looking like a tailor or a violin teacher. The difference was that none of the other retired accountants, tailors, or violin teachers who patronized public television and the Miami Beach library in the mid-1970s, who drank their coffee in Wolfie's or took the air along Collins Avenue, were followed, at fifty yards' distance, by an unmarked surveillance car containing plainclothes police.[18]

In May 1951, Senator Estes Kefauver named Meyer Lansky as one of the principal partners in the crime syndicate dominating New York and the eastern half of the United States.[19] The nationwide inquiries of Kefauver's Senate Crime Committee marked the beginning of modern America's horror and fascination with organized crime, and from 1951 onward Meyer Lansky was the target of law enforcement inquiries of every sort. The Immigration and Naturalization Service examined his past, trying to get him deported. The Internal Revenue Service scrutinized his tax returns, hoping to catch him as it had snared Al Capone in the days of Prohibition. The Federal Bureau of Investigation followed him everywhere, listening to his phone calls and bugging his home and the hotel rooms in which he stayed.

When they got him into court, however, Meyer Lansky would often claim illness — ulcers, emphysema, a poor heart — as a reason for delaying his case. So one day, in the mid-1970s, Sergeant David Green, of the Dade County Public Safety Department, decided to find out just how frail the ganglord really was.

Green was part of an undercover inquiry into illegal bookmaking and betting in Miami Beach. Hymie Lazar and Benny Sigelbaum, Lansky's friends from Wolfie's, were among his targets, and one morning, driving down Collins Avenue, Green caught sight of Lansky walking in the opposite direction.

The policeman made a U-turn, drove up ahead of Lansky to a parking lot, and went into hiding. Green was in his Hell's Angel undercover mode. More than six feet tall, 260 pounds in weight, with long hair, a greasy beard, and a lurid T-shirt, he was "a pretty horrible-looking person," as he himself cheerfully admits.[20]

Green found himself a perch beside and a few feet above the sidewalk, and as Meyer Lansky came abreast of him, the policeman suddenly jumped down with a thud, flapping his arms and letting out a bloodcurdling "Grrrrr!"

"It would have scared anybody," remembers Green. "But he just backed up calmly, put his hand in his pocket like he had a knife, and kind of lifted his other hand. 'What do you want?' he said.

"'How ya' doing?' I said. 'I guess you own the planet, don't you?'

"He said, 'Who are you?' And I said, 'I'm Green, from Dade Public Safety.'

"'Oh,' he said. 'You're Green.' I had put some of his associates in jail for bookmaking, you see. So I guess he knew who I was.

"I said, 'I'm probably not going to get you in your lifetime, or in my lifetime, but I'm gonna keep on truckin'.'"

"You want anything else from me, Green?" Meyer Lansky asked — and he went on his way, quite unruffled.

"He was just cold blooded," remembers Green. "There wasn't an ounce of fear in his eyes."[21]

The young policeman had wanted to scare Meyer Lansky, but it was Lansky who had given him something to think about — the cold, hard eyes, quite unmoved, that would stop anyone dead in their tracks. You could understand why, when people got to talking about organized crime in the 1970s, they used to call Meyer Lansky the Chairman of the Board.

When the telephone rang in the New York apartment of Lee Strasberg, actor, in December 1974, it was breakfast time, and Strasberg was lying in bed. *The Godfather, Part II* had recently received its premiere in New York, and in the weeks since then several million people had been introduced to the Chairman of the Board as depicted by this venerable and venerated drama teacher turned film star.

To avoid legal complications, Lee Strasberg's character had not been given the name Meyer Lansky. The character was called Hyman Roth. But this Hyman Roth — the principal, and sinister, addition to the overwhelmingly Italian cast of characters established in the original *Godfather* movie — was Jewish, he functioned as the respected, almost academic éminence grise of gambling from Nevada to Havana, and he claimed to be living "in retirement" in Miami Beach.

"Michael," breathed Lee Strasberg at one point to Al Pacino's character, Michael Corleone, adapting a line picked up and much publicized by the FBI in the early sixties after they had bugged a hotel room occupied by Meyer Lansky. "We're bigger than U.S. Steel!"

Strasberg, father of the Method school of acting in the United States — the inspiration of actors from Marlon Brando to Marilyn Monroe — had gone back to his own roots to distill the essence of Meyer Lansky on the screen. Born in eastern Europe, Lee Strasberg had come to America via Ellis Island when his parents fled the pogroms of the czar. He had grown up on Manhattan's Lower East Side, a few blocks from Grand Street, where the young Meyer Lansky was graduating to street crime.[22] So the history, the advancing years, the fragility, the Jewishness, these were part of him already.

To this Lee Strasberg added the figures: whenever he walked onto the set of *Godfather II*, he started doing sums in his head — quite complicated calculations. And he also added the secret: keeping things close, Strasberg decided, was where the power of Meyer Lansky lay. So as Anna Strasberg, Lee Strasberg's young, second wife, went on location with her husband, she had found a distance developing as Lee got into his part, becoming more and more Lansky, less and less Strasberg.

When the phone rang that morning, it was Anna Strasberg who answered. The caller had a deep voice, firm and rather persuasive. He did not say he was Meyer Lansky.

"He didn't have to. I knew. He said, 'Lee Strasberg?'

"I said, 'Lee — for you.' "[23]

The Strasbergs each had their own phone, on the same line, on either side of the bed, so Anna Strasberg was able to listen in on the conversation that followed.

"He said, 'You did good.' And Lee said, 'Thank you, I tried.' And Lee said, 'How are you?' And he said, 'Ah . . .' "

Meyer Lansky had obviously been doing his own research into the life and character of Lee Strasberg, because he started inquiring after the health of the actor's young wife, and of Strasberg's two sons by her. How were the young men?

"Lee said, 'They're a handful. They're four and five, and you know . . .'

"And *he* said, 'Now, why couldn't you have made me more sympathetic? After all, I am a grandfather.' He didn't say it rough. He said it almost with a sense of humor.

" 'After all, I *am* a grandfather.' "[24]

The deep voice on the phone was flesh and blood seeking contact with the celluloid image, intrigued to be the catalyst for such artistry and imagination. But Meyer Lansky, famous gangster, also wanted to remind the famous actor that there was a difference between the exotic imaginings of the outside world and the truth about his life as he actually lived it.

In 1948 the film critic Robert Warshow remarked on how the average American reckoned that he or she knew all about gangsters, but that this knowledge depended, in reality, almost entirely on what people had seen at the movies. Gangsters, wrote Warshow, had come to form part of the everyday, psychic experience of being an American, but rare was the American man or woman who had ever met a gangster in real life, let alone got to know one with any intimacy.[25]

At the height of his notoriety, Meyer Lansky was reckoned to be, and was targeted by the U.S. Justice Department as, the biggest gangster in the United States — a dangerous lawbreaker of extraordinary power. He was identified as the Mafia's banker, the boss of the National Crime Syndicate, the head of the Combination — the Chairman of the Board.

All these job descriptions were symbolic, attempts from the outside to interpret the strange and secretive subculture that Meyer Lansky inhabited. He experienced his own criminal career in one fashion. Trying to make sense of it, the world experienced it in another. So this book is one gangster's story. But its purpose is also to examine the myths, the legends — and, sometimes, the sheer fantasy — that America has woven around the reality of the gangster life.

Part One

The Gangster Life

1

"Little Child, Close Your Eyes. If God Will, You'll Be a Rabbi"

MEYER is a Jewish name. It has no equivalent among the names of other faiths or races. It is thought to have originated in the second century, with a rabbi whose writings won him a special following, and who became known as Rabbi Mei'or — the Bringer of Light. In the course of time, Mei'or became Mei'er, which is usually rendered in modern English as Meyer. It is pronounced with a long *i,* as in "hire" or "shire."[1]

Not being biblical, the name Meyer has no ambiguity about it, ethnically speaking. It is not like David or Joseph or Abraham — Old Testament names which are taken by Christians and Jews alike. Being called Meyer does not afford a Jew much camouflage in a Gentile society.

Ninety years ago, in a long-established and religiously educated Jewish community in eastern Europe, a mother and father who called their firstborn son Meyer did so in celebration of the symbolism and history that was attached to the name. Their little Meyer was a bringer of light to them — and, if the name stood for anything at all, it must also have been the hope that he would, in the course of his life, prove to be a bringer of light to others.

❖   ❖   ❖

The precise date of Meyer Lansky's birth is not known. He was born Meyer Suchowljansky sometime around 1902 in the town of Grodno, on the gray, windswept borderlands of Russia and Poland. There have been periods of history when Grodno lay on the Russian side of the border, at other times it has been Polish or even German. In the years leading up to the First World War the Russians ruled the area, so Meyer Suchowljansky spent the first decade of his life as a subject of Nicholas II, the last of the czars.

Grodno was a predominantly Jewish town. Nearly 70 percent of its forty thousand or so inhabitants were Jewish, according to the census of 1887.[2] Jews owned the main factories and businesses. They ran the market that operated not far from the Russian Orthodox cathedral.[3] There were more than forty synagogues, a Jewish poorhouse and orphanage, a Jewish theater and hospital. Almost everyone spoke Yiddish.[4]

The Gentiles of Grodno tended to have homes on the outskirts of the town,[5] leaving the center to the Jews who lived in and over their shops. Work stopped every Friday night, the Sabbath eve, and the streets grew quiet as families gathered for the *Shabbes* meal, father in velvet skullcap, mother in black silk and pearls, the whole family savoring the glow of the candles, the calm moments of communion — the warm sense that, while it was hard, it was very good to be a Jew.[6]

The Suchowljanskys were middle class. As Meyer Lansky later remembered it, his grandfather Benjamin was a businessman of some standing who owned a house on one of the streets that ran between the castle and the marketplace.[7] To the doorpost was nailed a small box containing a parchment inscribed with biblical verses, a mezuzah, the proud sign that this was a Jewish home:

"Thou shalt bind the words of the Lord for a sign upon thy door."[8]

Meyer Suchowljansky reached the age of nine or ten living in this stone townhouse with his younger brother, Jacob, his father and mother, Max and Yetta, and his paternal grandparents, Benjamin and Basha Suchowljansky.

Meyer Lansky idolized his grandfather Benjamin. All through his life, he would hark back to the things his grandfather taught him — the ordeals of Jewish history, the promise of Palestine. It was the custom in the synagogues of eastern Europe that those who gave most generously to Jewish causes should sit in the places of honor, in the front rows of the congregation. A man was judged by how much of his substance he was prepared to donate to the community, and Meyer Lansky remembered his grandfather as a generous and respected man.[9] It was Grandfather Benjamin who first took Meyer to the *cheder,* the religious school where the little boy learned his prayers and the Hebrew alphabet from tattered old Bibles and prayerbooks.

Cheder is Hebrew for room, and it became the word for these schools because the school in communities like Grodno's was often just a room in the home of the rabbi. With one stove for warmth, and plain wooden benches to sit upon, pupils were crammed side by side, all wearing cloth caps, and rocking slightly as they chanted their lessons together.

Orthodox Judaism does not place undue emphasis on hellfire and damnation, nor are children specially pressured to search their souls for sin. But the priorities of a *cheder* education were anything but material. Read, read, read. Study, study, study. These were the objectives of school — and of life itself. The brightest graduates of Orthodox Jewish education were not directed by their teachers toward business, but toward the revered calling of the rabbi.

"My little child, close your eyes," mothers crooned over the cradle of their sons. "If God will, you'll be a rabbi."[10]

A young man who was a scholar of the Torah could easily find a well-to-do girl to marry, and he could count on being subsidized by her proud family while he devoted his time to study.[11]

Grodno had many such young men. Aspiring scholars would travel hundreds of miles to the town to sit at the feet of one of Grodno's several teaching rabbis. They would cluster around his home, black hatted and thin bearded, debating points and jostling each other in the muddy streets, giving the place something of the atmosphere of a university town.

At the time of Meyer Suchowljansky's birth, however, the warm and textured life created by the Jews in the five centuries they had lived in Grodno was coming under threat. With the accession of Czar Alexander III in 1881, the dark undertow of anti-Semitism that tugged around all the Jewish communities of eastern Europe had been channeled into official form. New laws prohibited Jews from buying rural land, from freely attending university, from changing their names to non-Jewish ones — and from 1894 onward, all Jewish identity passes were marked with the word "Jew."[12]

Most disturbing of all, the czarist government actually condoned pogroms and demonstrations against Jews, blaming them on Jewish exploitation of ordinary Russians. When Meyer Suchowljansky was four or five, there was trouble in the nearby town of Bialystok, and Jews fled by the hundred to Grodno with stories of rape and murder.

"The worst time . . . was always at Easter and the Passover," Meyer Lansky later recalled. He remembered the menace of Russian peasants swaggering into town, pushing old Jews around and molesting women.[13] An uncle of his, he related, got in the way of some cossacks, and had his whole arm severed.[14]

Grodno was one of the first — and one of the comparatively few — eastern European communities where the Jews met this sort of violence with violence. They formed a self-defense organization, hiding weapons in their homes. They practiced shooting in the woods — and their targets included the policemen who abetted their persecutors. In September 1906, Grodno's Jewish partisans assassinated the Russian district commander of police who had presided over the troubles at Bialystok. He had come to Grodno, and his presence there at the time of the Jewish holidays seemed suspicious.[15]

Two years later another senior official, the Bialystok chief of police, turned up in Grodno at the same time of year. The Jew who tried to shoot him died in prison.[16]

Grodno's sturdiness seems to have earned it some reprieve from the worst excesses of anti-Semitism, but the odds were not on its side. After centuries creating a world for themselves on this bare, gray edge of Europe, Jews had to wonder how much longer they could remain in a society that treated them with such contempt. Meyer Suchowljansky was born into a community that was questioning its future and was searching for new directions.

One option was Zionism — asylum in the Promised Land. As early as 1851 a Grodno kolel, or religious community, had been established in Jerusalem. By 1902 it had spread to form a little township outside the walls,[17] some two thousand Grodno Jews who were anything but rich, but who believed that their long and dangerous journey had brought them treasure beyond price.

The other option was America, a different style of Promised Land. Some forty thousand Jews had emigrated there in the 1870s from eastern Europe,[18] and as anti-Semitic pressures mounted in Russia in the following decades, they proved the forerunners of the massive and momentous migration which was to transfer several million Jews from Russia and eastern Europe to the distant, and very different, challenge of the United States.

America or Palestine? Meyer Suchowljansky heard his family

debate the alternatives — which, either way, could only mean the breakup of the life they had created together in Grandfather Benjamin's reassuring home between the castle and the marketplace.

The old man was for the Holy Land.

"L'shono habo'o biY'rusholayim," his grandson remembered him saying — "Next year in Jerusalem!"[19]

After a lifetime of insult at the hands of Gentiles, Grandfather Benjamin could not bring himself to believe in the United States. "What for America?" he remonstrated with Meyer's father. "There will be other ghettos there."[20] It was a Jew's duty to go to Palestine, he argued — and he went. Grandfather Benjamin died in Jerusalem, his duty done, almost as soon as he arrived, on September 10, 1910, to be buried on the Mount of Olives. His wife, Basha, who had traveled with him, died one month later, and was buried beside him.

Respected for his generosity to the community, Grandfather Benjamin had not left Grodno with much. The old couple used up whatever money they had brought from Russia on the journey. So their graves were paid for by the community of Grodno living in Jerusalem.[21]

"Even now I sometimes wake up in the middle of the night," Meyer Lansky said of his grandfather when he was himself an old man, "feeling the warmth of his personality surrounding me."[22]

Max Suchowljansky, Meyer's father, retained his confidence in America. He set off alone in 1909 on the arduous journey by land and ship, and within two years he had saved enough for his wife and children to join him. So sometime around the age of ten, the young Meyer Suchowljansky said good-bye to Grodno — the danger and the sense of rootedness, the would-be rabbis and the muddied streets. But there was a part of him that never left.

The journey did not get off to a good start. In the bewilderment of the freight cars, the quarantine stations, and the endless waiting in lines, Yetta Suchowljansky handed over the money for her own and her two sons' steamship tickets to a Jew she met who offered to help — and whom she never saw again.[23] They were entering a different world.

The betrayal was redeemed by one of the welfare associations established by the Jewish communities that lay along the emigrant route from western Russia, a charity house.[24] While living in the hostel, the two little boys were taken away and lodged separately from their mother, though, as Meyer Lansky later remembered, it was his mother who cried most at this. Meyer felt that he should not let his feelings show.

"I knew it was my duty to protect her."[25]

The Suchowljanskys were eventually helped to find passage from the Latvian port of Libau on the S.S. *Kursk*,[26] a recently commissioned vessel of the Russian-American Line.[27] Meyer felt sick for much of the journey — though this, again, was something that he hid from his mother and younger brother.

"I felt ashamed," he said, "for the people who lay in their bunks and were sick and didn't do anything about it. I didn't want anybody to see me in the same condition." In defiance of his mother's orders, the youngster would go up secretly to the main deck when he felt ill, would put his head through the railings and vomit straight into the ocean.[28]

On April 8, 1911, after more than two weeks at sea, they reached Ellis Island[29] — a pungent, white-tiled ordeal of queuing and prodding and chalking on clothes. *H* meant a possible heart defect. *X* meant suspected mental weakness.[30]

The Suchowljanskys passed all the medical tests, but they ran into a problem with the immigration inspection. It seems from Meyer Lansky's American school records that his mother regarded August 28 as his birthday,[31] and she later told him, by one account, that he had been ten years old when the family landed at Ellis Island.[32] If this was the case, then she presumably considered August 28, 1900, to be the date of birth of her elder child.

But Meyer was not recorded at Ellis Island as a ten-year-old. Whatever Yetta Suchowljansky managed to explain in all the strain and confusion of the echoing immigration hall, frightened Yiddish being translated into official English, her elder son, Meyer, was credited by the immigration authorities with being just eight years old. Noted throughout his life for his short stature, he cannot have looked a very credible ten-year-old. Two years were knocked off his age with a stroke of the immigration officer's pen — and, as the magazine writers later liked to tell it, he was also assigned July 4 as his birthday. Made in America.

The final part of this story, unfortunately, is not true. The Ellis Island authorities listed America's new recruits by their age in years alone, with no precise day or month of birth being requested or recorded. The list of alien passengers arriving on the S.S. *Kursk* from Libau on April 8, 1911, records "Yenta" Suchowljansky, female, married, housewife, not able to read or write, a Hebrew from Grodno, Russia, as being thirty years old. Her children, Meyer and Jacob, are listed as eight and six years old, respectively, with no date of birth specified. The fourth of July entered the picture sometime later.[33]

Meyer Lansky's New World birthday was to be a source of some pride to him in adult life. He observed it solemnly, never saw the funny side. Depending on your point of view, it sat uneasily or quite suitably with his reputation as the mastermind of American organized crime. But either way, it started his life in America on an ambiguous note. The myth of Meyer Lansky's birthday was evident. The facts were not.

Max Suchowljansky had a home waiting for his family in Brownsville, a low-budget area of Brooklyn which had proved attractive to garment manufacturers seeking cheap labor away from Manhattan. Max Suchowljansky had saved up the money to get his family to America by working as a Brownsville garment presser.[34]

Arriving in Brownsville in the spring of 1911 from Jewish eastern Europe, the young Meyer Lansky found himself in a community that was remarkably similar to the one he had just left. In Brownsville, reported one contemporary observer, "Jews could live as in the old country. . . . Jews there didn't work on the Sabbath."[35] The clean tablecloth came out on Friday night. The cracked dishes were put away,[36] and a surprising number of poor households found the cents to pay the Gentile child, the "*Shabbes* goy," whom the Orthodox brought in to perform the domestic tasks proscribed to them on the Sabbath.[37] A computation based on the children absent from public elementary school in Brownsville on Yom Kippur 1914 set the Jewish population at 102,000[38] — more than twice as many Jews as there had been in Grodno.

Yet if Meyer Lansky found the Yiddish street cries of Pitkin Avenue, Brownsville's main thoroughfare, comparatively familiar, Brooklyn Public School 84 was not. No more lessons with a dozen friends in a rabbi's back parlor, but a melee of several hundred streetwise young strangers running up and down the stone staircases of an overcrowded municipal palace of learning. Meyer and his brother, Jake, were admitted to PS 84 in Brownsville on April 26, 1911, less than three weeks after they had first landed in America.

Books and articles about Meyer Lansky have generally assumed that he fashioned the American version of his long Polish surname for himself when he embarked on his career of lawbreaking in his late teens. But his school record card shows him registered from the start as plain Lansky, not Suchowljansky. His brother's record card shows the same. The boys' father had evidently decided already to commit himself and his family to their new homeland — Jewish surnames being, in any case, a Gentile invention, the more-or-less willing expression of their holder's betrothal to society.*

Meyer Lansky was an excellent student. New York schools in these years made no special provision for children who arrived in class not speaking English. Newcomers were put into the first grade and they had to make the best they could of the elementary exercises designed for American children speaking their native language.[39]

"Our teachers were strict," remembered Lansky. "They didn't tolerate nonsense." The boy clearly thrived on the challenge. "I loved school," he said later.[40]

Meyer Lansky's record card at PS 84 and PS 165, to which he and Jake transferred at the beginning of 1912, shows a long string of A's broken by only a B-plus and a B-minus.† Meyer's grades for conduct were equally exemplary — one B-plus and nine straight A's.[41]

Starting in grade one, Meyer was moved up to grade two after just one full semester, and he kept on jumping upward, covering two grades every year. By June 1914, Meyer had reached the sixth grade, little more than three years after he had started school.

Dr. Saul Badanes, the principal of Public School 84 when the Lansky brothers started there, was one of the first Jewish headmasters in Brownsville, and he was a pioneer in several respects. He noticed how his pupils in the early grades were often discouraged by the old-fashioned techniques of teaching arithmetic. So he developed fresh, vivid ways to make numbers concrete and simple for little children.

---

*Until the nineteenth century, most European Jews were known by their father's name — David son of Benjamin, et cetera — in the Middle Eastern tradition maintained by many Arabs to this day. Then the increasingly sophisticated civil services of Germany and eastern Europe began requiring Jews to bear surnames in the Gentile style. On or after arrival in the United States, the newcomers frequently Americanized their surnames, unrecognizably so, in the case of many film stars and entertainers. In the second half of the twentieth century, these surnames have often been modified yet again when their bearers have moved to Israel.

†These grades were not allocated by subject, but were total, consolidated grades covering all work for the whole term. Each report card contained a column headed "Not proficient in." This column was blank on Meyer's card. On the card of Lansky, Jacob, reading and spelling were each marked in this column three times.

The Badanes System of Primary Arithmetic became the basis of a series of primers and teachers' manuals for the first grades all over Brooklyn, and it served as Meyer Lansky's introduction to the joy of figures.[42]

"We had a lot of arithmetic," he later remembered. Meyer also recalled spelling, geography, chemistry, and science. "We learned a lot of History from Roman to American," he wrote in a memoir whose spelling and syntax might well have been criticized by his grammar teacher. "We learned to recite Gettysberg address by memory and much more poems of American Poets."[43]

Lansky also learned Shakespeare, and sixty years later, when making notes for a projected book about his life, there was one play in particular that he remembered. "Was able," he wrote, "to recite Merchant of Venice by memory."[44]

The first home of the Lansky family was at 33 Chester Street, Brownsville, in the crowded tenement section at the back of Pitkin Avenue, a hotbed of freethinkers and socialists. Agitators shouted their slogans and passed out handbills among the shoppers at the street market. Nearby on Amboy Street in 1916, Margaret Sanger was to earn thirty days in jail for daring to open America's first birth control clinic, her response to the overcrowding and hardship of the area.[45]

In later years, Meyer Lansky was to characterize himself as a liberal Democrat, and he stuck by the label even when his own particular version of private enterprise had raised him far above the ranks of the have-nots.

"If you were born into poverty as I was," he told the journalist Harold Lavine in Havana during the early days of the Castro revolution, "you'd be a liberal Democrat too."[46]

In 1912 the Lanskys moved seven blocks south of Pitkin to 894 Rockaway Avenue.[47] The building stands to this day, a three-story, redbrick, walk-up tenement over a shop, its facade topped off by an ornate cornice. A metal fire escape runs diagonally across the front.

We do not know which floor the Lansky family lived on, but the tenement apartments are all the same — stuffed in tightly, two per story, each apartment virtually identical to the others, and each, to the modern eye, impossibly cramped and confined. It is as if someone had attempted to construct a home inside a railway boxcar. Thin plywood divisions partition off the spaces: a couple of bedrooms

little more than eight by eight feet, a narrow sitting area (which people called a lounge),[48] and the kitchen containing stove, zinc bath,
and dining table, with the toilet directly off it.

It was not an environment which offered much privacy, but
Brownsville in those days was a comparatively rural area — "mostly
farms and open field," Meyer later remembered.[49] There were cows
grazing in the fields not far from Rockaway Avenue, and one of the
regular errands for Brownsville children was to take the family's
white enamel milk can to the dairy and get it filled — fresh milk,
warm and foaming, almost straight from the cow.[50]

Reunited in America, Max and Yetta started a second family —
three little girls, Rose, Lena, and Esther.[51] Rose and Lena died young,
but Esther survived to become, in subsequent years, an admiring sister and a loyal champion of her elder brothers, Meyer and Jake.

"I was much devoted to my parents," Meyer Lansky later recalled,
slipping a little between his tenses. "All the family is devoted to one
another. There were periods that food was just enough to exist. We
had hard times. Regardless of good times or bad times, we had
love."[52]

But not enough money. In the autumn of 1914, the Lansky family
moved out of Brownsville, traveling into Manhattan to settle in the
Lower East Side of New York — by no means a step up in the world.
Families who made it in Brownsville usually moved north to the leaf-
iness of the Bronx, or south toward Brighton Beach and the sea.

Meyer Lansky knew that the move was in the wrong direction.
"The East Side was crowded and mostly poor," he was to recall,[53]
with a disdain that reflected on his father's inability to do any better
for his family.

Max Suchowljansky never quite made it in any endeavor. He was
a hardworking man, gentle and dutiful, toiling long hours in the
sweatshops of the garment industry to give his children a good start
in America. But his efforts never, somehow, won him the gratitude
or respect of his elder son.

Meyer did not like to talk about his father. There was an emptiness there. It was as if the boy who had hidden his tears and his
seasickness had accorded himself a certain primacy during the father-
less months in Russia and on the journey to America, and had never
quite yielded up that sovereignty. In his eyes, he was the true companion and protector of his mother.

"Even as a little boy," he told the Israeli journalist Uri Dan, "I
remember swearing to myself that when I grew up I'd be very rich,

and I'd make sure that for the rest of her days my mother had only the best."[54]

There was no place for a father in this scenario. For a senior male role model, Meyer Lansky turned to the safe and hallowed memory of Grandfather Benjamin, dead in Jerusalem, and successful in the accomplishment of his own particular life's goal. It was his grandfather whom Meyer always venerated, and he seems to have considered his father a failure by comparison — something of a fool to have worked so hard all his life for so little reward.

This was less than fair to Max Lansky, who had, at the least, got his family out of Russia and off to a fresh start. But it was an indication of how, in his new American life, Max's son Meyer felt driven to select a different and more adventurous path from the safe and straight course that had been taken by his father.

2

Growing Up on
Grand Street

I was about 11 yrs. old," Meyer Lansky remembered, "when we moved to Manhattan."[1]

The Lanskys' new home was a tenement at 546 Grand Street, a little more than a mile from City Hall and the Athenian pillars of Wall Street. In 1914 the Lower East Side of New York was a fierce, teeming world — the pushcarts, the peddlers, the hydrants spraying on summer streets, the ships at the piers, and the great metal bridges. Number 546 Grand was a five-story brick building faced with a spiderwork of fire escapes,[2] and the Lanskys' apartment was even more cramped and airless than the one in Brownsville.

"Hot in summer, cold in winter," recalled Meyer in later life. He did not spend much time at home. "I joined a library as soon as we moved to Manhattan."[3]

The two libraries that lay closest to 546 Grand Street were ten minutes' walk away, on either side of East Broadway. On the right stood the Seward Park branch of the New York Public Library system, a towering chateau of redbrick and limestone whose construction had been paid for by the steel magnate Andrew Carnegie.[4] The Seward Park Library catered to young Jewish readers with Yiddish versions of American classics like *Huckleberry Finn*. There was a special children's room on the second floor, and in summer you could study high above the street in the clean, cool shade of its roof reading terrace.[5]

"I loved History, Biographys, sports and mechanical magazines and books," remembered Meyer, "als [also] the natural resources."[6]

Straight across from the Seward Park Library, and equally imposing, rose the red sandstone facade of the Educational Alliance, a settlement house built in the last decades of the previous century by subscription among New York's established Jewish communities.[7] By 1914, the reading rooms of the Educational Alliance were famous as a means of escape, the first step up the ladder for the tens of thousands of Jews who lived in the impoverished tenements all around.

Together, the Educational Alliance and the Seward Park Library were the focus of a little cultural complex on East Broadway. Each organized its own programs of self-improvement, and dotted around them were the private "night high schools" where earnest young immigrants worked to convert their education into professional qualifications.[8]

Today there is a photographic hall of fame which hangs in the lobby of the Educational Alliance — a gallery of Jews of Meyer Lansky's generation who came through its doors on their way to a distinguished life: David Sarnoff, the broadcaster and founder of NBC; Eddie Cantor, the entertainer; Jan Peerce, the opera star. There are influential rabbis (A. Hillel Silver), eminent jurists and lawyers (Louis J. Lefkovitz, attorney general of New York State), concert pianists and conductors, artists and industrialists, doctors, scientists, and journalists — pillars of the community, every one, their portraits composing an inspiring mosaic of persistence and achievement.

They are glowing testimonials to the Jewish talent for betterment against the odds, and a tribute to the country which, unlike any other on earth, offered such opportunities to the poor and unwashed. But there were other opportunities which America offered to the enterprising young immigrant in the early decades of this century — and other temptations.

"If you walk along Grand Street on any night in the week during the winter months," reported the social reformer Belle Lindner Israels in 1909, "the glare of lights and the blare of music strikes you on every side. It might be an esplanade at Dreamland."[9]

In Brownsville the enticements of Coney Island had lain at the end of a trip down Ocean Parkway to the sea. Now, in the autumn of 1914, Max Lansky had brought his family to an area where, alongside the libraries and reading rooms, there was a fair representation of Coney Island right on their doorstep. Just a few blocks away from 546 Grand Street was some of the most colorful and disreputable street life in New York.

"On sunshiny days the whores sat on chairs along the sidewalks," Michael Gold was later to write in his vivid and moving memoir of Lower East Side life, *Jews Without Money*. "They sprawled indolently, their legs taking up half the pavements. People stumbled over a gauntlet of whores' meaty legs. The girls gossiped and chirped like a jungle of parrots. Some knitted shawls and stockings. . . . Others chewed Russian sunflower seeds. . . . They called their wares like pushcart pedlars. At five years I knew what it was they sold."[10]

"It is better to stay away from Allen, Chrystie and Forsyth streets if you go walking with your wife, daughter, or fiancee," cautioned the *Jewish Daily Forward* in 1898. "There is an official flesh trade in the Jewish quarter."[11]

The flesh, and the trade, were almost entirely Jewish.[12] The whores were Jewish girls, and their pimps were Jewish too, often young and quite recently off the boat. Nor was Jewish crime confined to prostitution. In 1907, a Jewish reformatory, the Hawthorne School, was opened to cope with the problem of young Jewish street thieves and pickpockets.[13] The loan sharks of the Lower East Side were known as shylocks, while the crime of arson was popularly referred to as Jewish lightning, humorous magazines featuring cartoon characters with names like Blazenheimer and Burnupski. Insurance companies routinely declined to accept coverage of applicants whose names ended in *-sky* or *-ski*.[14]

Something had gone awry. The Jews of eastern Europe were noted for their respect for the law, editorialized the *New York Evening Post*, in September 1908. "But those who follow the trend of Jewish life in this country are not at all sure that this boasted ethical pre-eminence . . . stands unimpaired."[15]

Was there some sort of infection in the American air? Being streetwise, getting in on a gang — these were all options which, to a dismaying number of newcomers, went along with learning good English or changing their name.

"Lawlessness has been and is one of the most distinctive American traits," declared James Truslow Adams. "There seems to me plenty of evidence to prove that the immigrants were made lawless by America, rather than America made lawless by them."[16]

Rabbi Judah Magnes felt the answer lay in looking back to the world from which most of New York's Jews had just come. There had been comparatively little crime in the ghettos and Jewish villages of eastern Europe, reasoned the rabbi, because of the sense of community and the shared values that prevailed there. This same sense of communal self-discipline should be generated in New York, and in February 1909, Magnes helped bring about the creation of the Kehillah (literally, "community" in Hebrew/Yiddish), an organization which started its work by sending out agents to document vice and crime in the Lower East Side.[17] Their reports added up to a veritable yellow pages of wickedness — and they revealed a particular concentration of wrongdoing around Grand Street.

At numbers 311, 321, and 345 Grand were the "dancing academies," where gentlemen could hire a private dancer for more than dancing lessons. At 267, 410, 468, and 488 Grand there were gambling joints, and at 270 there was a cigar store which, like virtually every other cigar store in the neighborhood, made its real money not from tobacco, but from taking illegal bets. The cigar store was where you went to put your money on horses, baseball — almost anything.[18]

Parallel to Grand Street, and one block over, ran Broome Street, where the two Lansky brothers went to school, Jake to PS 110, Meyer to PS 34. These were two towering stone academies in the style of PS 165 in Brownsville; PS 110 proclaimed its identity with a wise-looking owl carved in stone and perched over the main entrance.

But only a block or so down Broome Street were establishments of a different color. At 248 Broome, reported Kehillah agent Abraham Shoenfeld, was a gambling joint (a "stuss parlor") that was notorious as a center where thieves went to fence stolen goods. There were five saloons which were the habitual resorts of "thieves, cadets [pimps], gangmen, gunmen, and prostitutes," while number 249 was a disorderly house run by Jenny Morris, a lady known as Jenny the Factory on account of her considerable size and work capacity.[19]

The reports of the Kehillah's agents presented a colorful cast of characters. Here was Jenny the Factory, the madam of Broome Street, with Harry Morris, her husband and pimp. Here were Benny Greenie and Harry Goldberg, pickpockets, Bobby Mendelsohn, pimp, Charlie

Auerbach, a pimp who doubled as a *shtarke* — a strong-arm man — and countless other wiseguys.

"Wiseguy" has become something of a vogue word in recent years. It was popularized in 1985 by Nicholas Pileggi's compelling book of that title. But the currency of "wiseguy" as a term for a small-time criminal goes back at least as far as January 5, 1915, when it appeared in one of the Kehillah's reports by Abraham Shoenfeld to Judah Magnes, describing the type of character who hung out in the joints that Shoenfeld was investigating.*

One specialty of the wiseguy was the running of street-corner crap games — and it was craps that first drew Meyer Lansky into the world that offered a venturesome boy such alluring alternatives to the reading rooms of the Educational Alliance and the Seward Park Library.

The essence of craps is to stake your money, bet after bet, on the combinations formed by two dice when they fall. Betting on a 7 is the safest wager, since there are six different ways in which a 7 can be thrown (6 and 1, 5 and 2, 4 and 3, 3 and 4, 2 and 5, 1 and 6). Betting on 2 (1 and 1) or 12 (6 and 6), by comparison, means putting your money on a long shot. The odds on any number's being thrown, from 2 to 12, can be expressed mathematically, and as Meyer Lansky watched the wiseguys play, bouncing their dice along the sidewalks of the Lower East Side, he found that he had an uncanny knack for calculating the odds.

Lansky could look at a crap game and sum it up in figures. It made sense to him, it had a shape of its own. One player throws the dice in craps, trying to make a particular score, or "point." Onlookers bet, as if at a horse race, for or against the chances of the shooter making his point, and as the probabilities ebbed and flowed, the young A student discovered that he could chart the progress of the game in his head, as the best gamblers can, in terms of the odds.

There was always chance — the arbitrary and fatal element of risk — and that, of course, could never be defeated. But an understanding of the odds showed when the shooter had a fair chance of making his point, or when the probabilities were that he would "crap out."

Meyer Lansky was snared by his own cleverness. Whether it was

---

*Other modern-sounding terms that appear in the Kehillah reports for the years 1909–1915 include pimp, punk, creep, rat, cop, dick, broad, mol, sucker, john, fink, fence, graft, dough, coke, stool-pigeon, squealer, strong-arm-guy, stick-up-guy, and cat-house.[20]

the Badanes System of Primary Arithmetic, or the peculiar adding
machine of a mind with which he was born, Meyer felt sure he could
tell, as he looked over the shoulders of the players crouched on the
sidewalk, which way the odds were swinging. The figures left him no
alternative. He had to put down his money.

When Meyer Lansky got home from school on a Friday night, his
mother always had a job for him — to take the *cholent* to the baker's. It was a weekly ritual, the baking of the *cholent* — pronounced
with a short *o* as in "tolerant" — a bean, beef, and barley stew tra-
ditionally prepared for the Sabbath midday meal in the ghettos and
villages of Jewish Russia. "The French have Cassoulet. We have
Tcholent," proclaims a proud sign in the window of Abe Lebewohl's
Second Avenue Kosher Delicatessen in modern Manhattan. With its
Fiddler on the Roof connotations, the *cholent* today enjoys a certain
nostalgic chic.

In the early decades of this century, however, it was the public sign
of a household that was less than fully Americanized. Mothers cut
up the ingredients and gave the stew its first cooking on a Wednesday
or Thursday. Leaving the dish to stand for a day or so made a crucial
contribution to its flavor. Then, as work stopped on Friday, the *cholent* was borne through the streets — as it had been for centuries in
eastern Europe — to be placed in the oven of the local baker, along
with all the other *cholent* pots of the neighborhood.

Following the Saturday synagogue service next morning, and after
more than twelve hours of gentle simmering, the *cholent* was
retrieved in all its warmth and fragrance, to be hurried back home
and enjoyed as the rich, meaty, labor-free high point of the Sabbath — after which every adult in the household fell asleep.[21]

Meyer Lansky was proud to be chosen by his mother for the *cholent* detail, and he later recalled one particular expedition in his early
teens, when the family was living on Grand Street. Together with the
cold pot of stew, his mother would entrust him with five cents, the
rent that the baker charged for space on his oven shelf, and on this
particular Friday young Meyer decided he would turn a profit on the
nickel.

His way to the baker's led down Delancey Street, where the ramp
of the Williamsburg Bridge hit land on the Lower East Side. Noisy
and bustling, Delancey was one of the principal thoroughfares of the
Lower East Side. Every square foot of the sidewalk was rented

out[22] — to pushcarts, prostitutes, and to gamblers and cardsharps who hunched over their crap games, betting nickels and dimes as the shooters tried to make their points.

On Friday nights the shooters had their pay packets to gamble. The piles of nickels and dimes on the sidewalk looked like a fortune to Meyer. It seemed so easy to put one coin down and to walk away with two. But the young teenager walked away with nothing. He lost his nickel on the very first throw — and he was left holding his cold pot of stew. For hours, Meyer later recalled, he wandered the streets in total despair. Then he went home to his mother, placed the unde-livered *cholent* on the table, and confessed.

The nickel she had given him had been her last. His mother burst into tears, swaying from side to side, not saying anything. But it was lunchtime the next day that Meyer was to remember all his life, when the Lanskys got home from the synagogue — the silent reproach of his family, the cold, empty table, the Sabbath without its centerpiece.

The lesson that the young Meyer Lansky drew from this episode was not that he had been a fool to gamble. He knew that all the nickels and dimes that he had seen on the sidewalk had gone into some-body's pocket. His mistake had been to lose.

"To tell the truth," he was later to confess, "I was genuinely con-cerned at the way I had upset my family. But what troubled me more than anything else was the fact that I had lost that money."[23] In the weeks that followed the loss of his five cents, Meyer was to spend still more hours on the sidewalks of Delancey Street, studying the gamblers. He sensed that there must be some added dimension beyond the mathematical framework of odds and possibilities which he had already worked out, and he watched until he found it.

The secret, he came to see, lay in the way in which the game was organized. A new player would join the group, an outsider — a sucker with money to spend — and to start with, somehow, the dice would roll his way. Winning small sums, the newcomer would be enticed by his success to gamble more and more, until he put down a major stake — all his winnings, perhaps, or his week's earnings — and it was at that point that he lost everything.

As a variation, when the onlookers on the sidewalk kept their hands firmly in their pockets, unwilling to bet, an apparent outsider might step forward and put money down on bets on which he did not lose. To the contrary, this outsider would win handsomely, since the crapshooters knew — and Meyer Lansky came to know, as he grew familiar with all the faces up and down Delancey Street — that this "outsider" was not an outsider at all. He was a part of the play, a shill who was gambling with the bank's money and was being allowed to pile up winnings in order to draw the real suckers and their money into the game.

It was the classic sting, as old and obvious as the shell game. It depended on cheating, on the use of shaved or weighted dice whose numbers the dice-throwers could predict, and it was not, perhaps, surprising that a boy should have fallen for it — the first time, at least. What was extraordinary was how fully grown men, who knew, presumably, all about cardsharps and con men, could fall for the ploy with such regularity. As young Meyer watched passerby after passerby get sucked into the sidewalk games by the prospect of easy money, he absorbed his first lesson in human gullibility — and he also saw the way to make back his lost nickel.

One fateful Sabbath evening, he stopped beside a crap game on Delancey for a second time with his mother's pot of stew in his hands, and once again he put down his money. This time, however, he was not gambling, for he had identified a shill who was about to place a come-on bet. Meyer Lansky waited until the last moment before the banker threw the dice. Then swiftly the boy put his own nickel down on the same bet.

"I saw the banker give me a black look," he later recalled.[24] But the crapshooter would have aroused the suspicions of the crowd if he had refused Meyer's wager.

Meyer Lansky went home that evening with an extra nickel in his pocket — and next day his family ate a warm lunch after shul.

Meyer Lansky's sidewalk defeat and victory taught him a lesson he never forgot. "There's no such thing as a lucky gambler," he liked to say. "There are just the winners and the losers. The winners are those who control the game."[25]

In the weeks that followed, Meyer toured the crap games of the Lower East Side, putting down a nickel here, a nickel there. He was careful only to bet where he could identify a shill, and then prudently to move on before he himself could be recognized.

The boy never gambled with his mother's money again. He did not need to. He built up his own private bankroll of winnings, which he stored in a hole he had made in the corner of his mattress.

Meyer was still going to school, and he was continuing to get good grades. Through his twelfth, thirteenth, and fourteenth birthdays, he was racking up as many A's and B-pluses at PS 34, Manhattan, as he had in Brownsville.[26] To please his mother, and as a sort of homage to Grandfather Benjamin, Meyer kept going to *cheder* for religious instruction, until he was Bar Mitzvah at the age of thirteen. He still loved going to the library.[27] The young man was, in many respects, the perfect immigrant student, ambitious and hardworking.

But Meyer Lansky was also pursuing another life, a secret existence, with very different values and objectives. His trophy cupboard was the mattress in which he stowed his bankroll of crap game winnings. His dream world was occupied by shooters and points, by odds and margins and winning percentages — the joy of figures translated to the sidewalks of Delancey.

Meyer Lansky remembered the first time he got to know Benjamin Siegel. Benny was fighting at the time. Two rival bunches of craps players had got into a scuffle over street-corner territory, and somehow a gun had fallen to the ground. A good-looking boy rushed forward to retrieve it, a boy who was four or five years younger than Meyer.[28] Just as the boy's hand closed around the weapon, there came the sound of police whistles in the street.

The gun's owner turned on the young thief, menacing. As the sound of the police whistles grew closer, the combatants started to make their escape. But the boy with the gun was in a world of his own. He was raising the revolver slowly, carefully, taking deliberate aim at the assailant from whom he had claimed his prize. It was at this point that Meyer Lansky intervened.

"You're crazy," Meyer later remembered shouting, grabbing the boy's arm and forcing him to drop the gun.[29] As the two boys ran to safety, dodging around the pushcarts and vendors of the street market, the older attempted to pass on some basic street knowledge to the younger, explaining the danger he had been running in letting the police see him with a weapon.

Benjamin Siegel was neither grateful nor impressed.

"I needed that gun," he said.[30]

Benjamin Siegel was to become one of Meyer Lansky's best friends. Violent and irrational, generous and charming, Benny Siegel shivered with an exuberance and vitality that Meyer found difficult to generate on his own account. His smile was devastating, his rages quite mesmeric.

Lansky was a studious and introverted character. His hours in the library were the measurement of that. But Meyer the brainbox had another side — the daring that had led him to test his skills against the crapshooters of Delancey Street, and it was this side of his character that was drawn toward Benjamin Siegel.

Benny was the youngest and wildest of a group of boys who lived around Grand Street and who became friends with Meyer Lansky in the years between 1914 and 1920. There was Meyer's own brother, Jake — broad, slow, and loyal. He liked to be known as Jack. There was another Meyer, Meyer Wassell, a pupil at PS 34 who had a similar preference: he wanted to be known as Mike.[31] Samuel Levine, a freckle-faced boy from Houston Street, was nicknamed Red.[32] Irving Sandler, a cousin of the Lansky boys, was nicknamed Tabbo.[33] Joseph "Doc" Stacher was the fat boy that every gang needs. Short and boastful, Joe Stacher shared Meyer's fondness for craps, and he had no hesitation in claiming to be the better player.[34]

Jack, Mike, Red, Tabbo, and Doc. Meyer Lansky was to spend his life in a world of nicknames and buddies. He loved the easy camaraderie that was the essence of a gang. Studious and detached though Meyer could be, he enjoyed male fellowship, and it was one of his talents to win the trust of his cronies. No one who knew Meyer Lansky as a friend ever had a bad word to say about him. Among his own he was a trouper, a good companion — and when it came to the mechanics of group relations, Meyer also had the ability, rare at any age, to mediate and settle differences through intelligence and reason.

Meyer was one of the few people who could handle Benny Siegel and help him function in a group. When Benny got angry, he glowed incandescent. *Chaye* was the Yiddish word for someone like Benjamin Siegel — "untamed." He was so hotheaded, people said that he was crazy. Somebody said that he was crazy as a bedbug — and that, according to East Side folklore, was how he got his nickname, Bugsy Siegel.

Bugs and Meyer, brawn and brain. It became their trademark. The two boys were opposites. Benny was flashy where Meyer was quiet, impulsive where Meyer was shy and reflective. Benny favored checked jackets — good, strong, houndstooth plaid. Nobody could ever quite remember what Meyer had been wearing. So that was how the story went. Bugsy was the strong-arm man. Meyer was the thinker — and as the years went by, these contrasting stereotypes became more fixed.

In reality, however, Benjamin Siegel was quite a clever fellow.

Pathological when angry, he also knew how to wheel and deal very successfully. The young Meyer Lansky, for his part, could be as rough and tough as any other kid who had grown up on Grand Street. Meyer Lansky never walked away from a fight. That was how he met Lucky Luciano.

It was a bitterly cold New York day, Meyer later remembered, and he was walking on his own through the snow.

"The Jews," as he later explained when describing the ethnic neighborhoods of the Lower East Side, "were locked in between Italians and Irish."[35]

Chinatown lay to the west, Little Italy slightly to the north of it. Meyer Lansky was walking along Hester Street, which runs parallel to Grand, when suddenly he found himself surrounded by a gang of young Italians.[36]

Their leader was a Sicilian in his late teens, strong and stocky, with dark, curly hair, full lips, and thick, menacing eyebrows. He would have been more handsome if he had not had such bad acne. Salvatore Lucania — known to his friends as Charlie, and later to a wider public as Lucky Luciano — had come to America with his parents in 1906, when he was nine, and he was just starting to pick out his route through American society after the fashion of Meyer Lansky. He was taking shortcuts.

One of these was a protection racket preying on solitary Jews — who, the young Sicilian found, did not usually fight back. Lucania and his gang would corral their victim and extort tribute under the threat of a beating or some alternative humiliation.

But Salvatore Lucania found he had taken on no ordinary little Jewish boy. Meyer Lansky was small, and he was hopelessly outnumbered, but he was not paying one cent in tribute to any Italian.

"Go fuck yourself," said Meyer Lansky.[37]

The stories of this first youthful encounter between two of the legends of American organized crime have grown in the telling. Paragraphs of colorful dialogue have imaginatively detailed the trading of insults — and the affection which, apparently, swelled within the heart of the young Lucania for this plucky, diminutive Jew. "We both had a kind of instant understanding," Luciano later explained, according to one version. "It was something that never left us."[38]

This is a fair enough paraphrase of the relationship that came to exist in later years between the adult Luciano and Meyer Lansky. Meyer had met another tough guy — the other great friendship of his life. Meyer Lansky and Charlie Lucania were two rough, enterprising teenagers, both at the very bottom of the heap. Each was bright enough to see that they had more to gain as allies than from jostling over street-corner rights — and, as Meyer later remembered it, they found their first field for cooperative action in the trouble being generated by their mutual neighbors, the Irish.

"The Irish boys would stop Jews in the street," Lansky later remembered. "They'd strip them to see if they had really been circumcised. They would spit on Jews and pull their beards."[39]

A generation or so longer on Manhattan and a couple of rungs higher up the immigrant ladder, the Irish looked down on the more recently arrived Jews and Italians, and they had connections. "Whenever there was a fight between Irish and Italians, or an incident involving Irish with Jews," Lansky later recalled to Uri Dan, "the cops would always take the side of the Irish."[40]

Lansky and Lucania brought their respective Jewish and Italian gangs together to fight against the gangs formed by Irish boys, and in later years, Meyer liked to compare this mutual alliance to the way that the Jews in Grodno had fought back against their Russian persecutors.

"I never got on my knees for any Christian," he proudly told the Israeli historian Robert Rockaway in the 1970s.[41]

There is a sense in which criminals never grow up. Teenagers quite routinely get into fights and break the law, then mature, realizing the error of their ways. It is the inability to identify or admit wrongdoing that defines the criminal mentality — comparing Manhattan's street-corner gang alliances to the Jewish defense groups in Grodno, for example, and not seeing the difference.

"We were beaten up daily by the Irish boys," Meyer Lansky told Yoram Alroy, his lawyer in Israel, when he was nearly seventy years old. "And we had the choice. We could run away, or we could fight back — and fighting back meant everything connected with that."[42]

That was not the choice, in fact. Many Lower East Side Jews lived proud, independent lives without once getting into sidewalk confrontations with Italian or Irish anti-Semites. Others who did encounter insult returned it physically or verbally without making ethnic warfare their way of life.

It was a question of perspective. For all his intelligence, the teenage Meyer Lansky had too much Benny Siegel in his head. His wise-beyond-his-years, adult mind was capable of cold analysis. But Meyer was equally a child, mesmerized by the quick dividend promised by the nickel bet or the punch on the nose. Gambling in the sidewalk crap games, feuding with the Irish, making friends who could not raise their sights above the blind alleys of ancient insult, Meyer Lansky was getting drawn into the mechanics of street crime and gang culture — and he could not, or would not, see this for what it was.

Meyer Lansky left school a few weeks short of his fifteenth birthday.[43] He graduated from the eighth grade, the stage at which most of his contemporaries finished their full-time education. Many of his friends went into the garment trade, but Max Lansky wanted better for his son, and this was one thing upon which father and son agreed.

The *shmattes* business* — or "the great needle industry" as its proponents preferred[44] — was the principal source of employment on the Lower East Side. Garment racks and bundles of unfinished clothing shuttled busily through the streets, lending the whole area the air of one enormous sweatshop. Men, women, and children slaved over sewing machines and flatirons in factories, in workshops, out on fire escapes, and in their own homes — a grinding, insecure, thankless existence.

"I'll never let you do that," Meyer's father, Max, told his son. "You'll die young from the tailor's disease" — consumption, or tuberculosis.[45]

Working long hours away from home as a garment presser, Max Lansky had had little opportunity to provide direction to the development of his bright and independent elder son. But when it came to a first job for his boy, the father had definite ideas, and he made a real effort. It was the age of the machine. The automobile and the internal combustion engine were the wave of the future. Through a relative, Max Lansky got his son started among the elite of mechanics and machinists, working in a tool-and-die shop.[46]

"I started at 10¢ an hour 52 hours a week," Meyer Lansky later remembered.[47] This was a considerable improvement on slavery as a presser in the garment trade, but it was not the work for which Meyer Lansky really felt himself qualified.

"I wanted to continue my education," he declared later. "I had a great desire for learning. I wanted to study engineering. Circumstances didn't permit."[48]

At critical junctures throughout his life, Meyer Lansky would use his humble origins as an alibi for his failure to make it in the world

---

*From the Polish *szmata*, a rag or piece of cloth.

of the conventional and the law-abiding. Sometimes he would blame his family's poverty, sometimes his Jewishness. Usually he would blame both.

He would have liked to become a doctor or a lawyer, he told Joseph "Yoskeh" Sheiner, an Israeli friend he made in later life. But there was no money to pay for his studies — and besides, he explained to Yoskeh, he came from a background that was considered "third class." The professions were closed to Jews like him, he said, in the years when he was growing up.[49]

This was simply untrue. It was difficult for a Jew — particularly a Jew who was newly arrived from eastern Europe — to penetrate the American professional establishment in the early decades of this century. But it was by no means impossible. Jews who finished their conventional education, like Meyer Lansky, at any stage before twelfth grade would work all day at their jobs in factories, garages, or shops, and would then spend much of their wages on the night classes and tutorials sold by the night schools around the Educational Alliance on East Broadway.

The route was arduous, but it was clearly defined. Students would toil through the syllabus set by the New York Board of Regents to move up through the grades to the equivalent of high school graduation. Every year they would take their Regents exams, then move on to City College, where books and tuition were free, and where poor New Yorkers had been earning college degrees and qualifications since 1849.[50]

By 1917, when America entered the First World War — the year in which Meyer Lansky left school — some 70 percent of City College's two thousand or so free students were Jewish.[51] If Meyer had been truly determined to become an engineer, a doctor, or a lawyer, he could have followed the path taken by so many of the young men and women who ended up with their photographs on the walls of the Educational Alliance — all born "third class," poor, and Jewish as he was. All that Meyer Lansky had to provide from his own resources was intelligence and the long-term view necessary to motivate sustained effort. But while he quite clearly possessed the first, in the second respect he was singularly lacking.

The foreman at the tool-and-die shop where he started work used to praise his dexterity. "You have golden hands," he would tell Meyer. "In twenty years, you'll be a professional worker and make good money. You'll earn a dollar an hour."[52]

A dollar an hour in twenty years' time seemed a laughable objective for a boy who reckoned he already knew how to make a dollar in a few minutes, with a throw of the dice. At the age of fourteen, Meyer Lansky had little interest in the rewards that the conventional world might offer when he eventually reached his twenties or thirties. He was thinking about now. Seeing nothing to aspire to in the dutiful, put-upon figure of his father, young Meyer was studying the clever-looking men with their snap-brimmed hats and their sharp-looking suits, the lords of the sidewalk who peeled off bills from fat rolls of dollars — the wiseguys.

John Barth, a small-time crook who Americanized his name to Barrett, and who worked in the same tool-and-die shop as Meyer Lansky in the years 1917 and 1918, later recalled his workmate's apprenticeship — the one that took place in the evenings, after his day at the tool-and-die shop was over. Meyer went to work, Barrett recalled, in a crap game that operated in the upper room of a saloon a few blocks north of Grand, at the junction of Essex and Rivington streets. The bosses of the game were Yudie and Willie Albert, brothers who operated a number of gambling establishments in the area, and the position that the brothers assigned Meyer, according to Barrett, was that of lookout and "strong-arm man." Meyer was earning his pocket money as a *shtarke*.[53]

Daniel Ahearn, an Irish acquaintance of both Barrett and Meyer Lansky, described an occasion when he and Lansky were hanging out at a Russian bar on Allen Street. They met a union organizer there who was recruiting strong-arm guys. The union was having trouble with a factory at Peekskill, thirty miles up the Hudson River, to the north of New York. Scabs were sleeping in the factory to frustrate union pickets' attempts to shut the factory down. So the union official gave Ahearn and Lansky the name of the "main mechanic, a Jewish person" and his home address in Brooklyn.[54]

"If we get rid of him," they were told, "it will slow up the production."[55]

Ahearn and Lansky went to work:

"We trailed this guy," recalled Ahearn, "went on the train with him, but we lost him in the shuffle at Grand Central, getting off. But we had his address. We beat him out there. We went in a cab. He lived in the Williamsburg section. He lived in this house, and we stayed on the other side of the street, and naturally, when we saw him getting out of the cab — there were some people standing in front of the building — we didn't want to take a chance going over there to hurt him. We figured we would catch him in his house."

When the coast was clear, Ahearn crossed the street with Lansky.

"I knocked on the door and a woman responded . . . and she said 'Who do you want? Who is there?'

"I says, 'Telegram.' So she opened the door.

"When she opened the door I pushed it right in and I went right into their apartment and Meyer started going to work on the male there. That was the mechanic. . . .

"[Lansky] had a pipe in his hand. . . . He hit [the mechanic]. The man went down."[56]

Daniel Ahearn remembered that he and Lansky were paid for their work and were commended by the union organizer.[57] The mechanic was not in a fit state to go back to the factory at Peekskill. The two young thugs worked for nine months or more on similar jobs, according to Ahearn, "going into factories, breaking up machines, throwing acid on goods, and assaulting them workers, them scabs."[58]

They also operated as a team at a number of local crap games, said Ahearn, "to keep order, be on the lookout in case they crash us, the cops, and so forth." Sometimes they would carry guns. "We were paid a salary and 10 percent of the winnings after all the overhead was taken care of."[59]

Ahearn claimed to have committed several burglaries with Lansky, breaking into lofts in their neighborhood and fencing the stolen goods. He was arrested in 1919 after one such expedition, on which, he said, Meyer did not join him, and he was sent to Elmira for fifteen months[60] — the start, for Ahearn, of a long and varied career behind bars.

Daniel Ahearn's memories of his youthful escapades with Meyer Lansky formed a major part of the case which the U.S. Justice Department brought against Meyer in the 1950s in the hope of canceling his American citizenship. Meyer fiercely disputed the accuracy of Ahearn's recollections, and in cross-examination, Meyer's lawyer, Moses Polakoff, was able to demonstrate a number of inconsistencies in Ahearn's testimony.[61] Ahearn was serving a fifteen-to-thirty-year prison term when he testified against his old friend, more than thirty years after the event, and he freely admitted the hope that his testimony might help his chances of parole.

But the contemporary — and quite indisputable — records of the Magistrates' Court for the First District of Manhattan suggest that

Meyer Lansky, tool-and-die apprentice, was more than tough enough to have moonlighted as a *shtarke* in a gambling joint or to have wielded a length of pipe on behalf of a labor union ready to pay for some illicit muscle.

Docket 9208 for October 25, 1918, describes a Meyer Lansky of 484 Grand Street, male, sixteen, white, born in Russia, arrested that day by Officer Hughes and appearing in front of Chief Magistrate McAdoo on a charge of felonious assault (case dismissed).[62]

Less than a month later, on November 15, 1918, Lansky's name appears again, under docket 1054, arrested this time by Officer Weiss, and appearing in front of Magistrate Mancuso on a charge of disorderly conduct (annoyance), on which charge Lansky was found guilty and fined two dollars.[63]

Two things distinguish these arrests from the hundreds of other cases recorded in the meticulous copperplate script of the court ledger. Still only in his midteens, Meyer Lansky was one of the youngest offenders in the volume for the months September 1918 to April 1919. And in each of the two cases, the first of them alleging assault, the second arraigning Lansky for disorderly and annoying conduct, the complainant was a woman.

In adult life Meyer Lansky had a reputation for being gracious and rather gentle toward women. There is little evidence to sustain the suggestion of violence which is conveyed, prima facie, by assault and annoyance complaints brought against him at the age of sixteen, within a matter of weeks, by two different women.

The addresses given by the complainants, Lena Freedman, of 395 Madison Street, and Sarah Ginsburg, of number 370, provide an alternative explanation. Madison Street was a center of prostitution. The women sat in their windows there as brazenly as the whores on Allen, Forsyth, or Chrystie streets. They employed local boys to hand out their calling cards on the surrounding streets — which included Grand Street. Madison ran into Grand a block or so from the Lanskys' tenement.

So either Meyer Lansky was, at the age of sixteen, crudely attempting to force his unwanted attentions upon innocent women or, more probably, since women from Madison Street were seldom innocent, he was attempting to impose himself upon Lena Freedman and Sarah Ginsburg in another fashion. He was trying to become their pimp.

Pimping was a common occupation for enterprising young Jewish males on the Lower East Side. It was not usually looked on as a full-time occupation. But it was a stage in the evolution of a wiseguy to have a couple of girls in tow, to appear with them in bars and hangouts, to enjoy their services — and to enjoy a proportion of their income. It was one of several revenues which might well include a share in a crap game, plus some strong-arm work on the side — the useful additions to regular wages which helped a young fellow pay for good suits, a smart hat, a velvet collar on the overcoat. The ultimate objective was to build these various free-lance enterprises to a point where you could become your own master and break free from the constricting tie of regular employment.

Meyer Lansky accomplished this ambition before he was twenty. In January 1920 the Volstead Act brought Prohibition to America, an unparalleled new source of revenue for street-corner wiseguys, and Meyer seized his opportunity like thousands of others, Benny Siegel and Charlie Lucania among them. In 1921, after little more than three years as a mechanic, Meyer gave up his work at the tool-and-die shop.[64] For good. He never worked for anyone again — and he was never again employed in a conventional "job."

In later years Lansky was to look back proudly on his working start in a basic and practical trade. As a husband and father, he would hold up the example of his humble beginnings in the tool-and-die shop — the long hours and the low wages, the grease and the overalls. When at the gas station, he liked to stand over the mechanic who checked his oil and water, supervising the man's activities with a little more officiousness than the situation, perhaps, really called for.[65]

Meyer Lansky would not deign, however, to lean under the hood himself. Not in a $300 suit.[66] Proud to have started out his working life in a tool-and-die shop, he was prouder still to have escaped from it.

3

"A Gray Rat, Waiting for His Cheese"

PROHIBITION made Meyer Lansky a full-time gangster, and it offered the same career to hundreds of others. At midnight on January 15, 1920, the Volstead Act* put America's law-abiding breweries and distilleries out of business, thus surrendering a billion-dollar industry to men who had no objection to breaking the law.

Prohibition also strengthened the connections between the lawbreaker and U.S. politics, since the profits from the newly illegal sector of the national economy created a vast and lively pool of wealth to tempt police, magistrates, and public officials. This unholy liaison was a long-established component of American public life, but the "noble experiment" breathed new vigor into the relationship.

As the teenage Meyer Lansky had stood watchfully on the curbsides of the Lower East Side, studying the gamblers, he had acquired an understanding which went beyond the mechanics of any particular

---

*Prohibition did not technically deny the right of any American to consume alcohol. It directed its ban rather at the alcohol supplier. On January 16, 1919, the Eighteenth Amendment to the U.S. Constitution outlawed "the manufacture, sale, or transportation of intoxicating liquors," and one year later the Volstead Act, named after Republican congressman Andrew Volstead of Minnesota, put the Eighteenth Amendment into effect. Prohibition was eventually repealed by the Twenty-first Amendment, ratified on December 5, 1933.

game. He saw how the wiseguy controlled the action along his own designated piece of curb — but as the weeks went by, the boy also observed other men who would stand in the background, watching.

These men were not there all the time. They would come and just watch. They would appear without warning, and stand there discreetly. The banker of the crap game knew who they were, and if there was not much action on the sidewalk, he would go over and talk to them. He would take money from his pockets and hand it over. Figures would be jotted down in little books.

But this was no ordinary business transaction, for there was a certain menace about these well-dressed and wary onlookers. On one occasion, young Meyer saw a banker getting beaten up by his collector and by a couple of thugs who accompanied him. The banker took his punishment without complaining, and the collector went on his way.[1]

What Meyer Lansky had been watching was clearly not some haphazard and uncoordinated street-corner enterprise. He was witness to a network of some sort, a series of connections by which money and cunning were combined with an underpinning of violence to produce regular profit.

Observing similar activities from his own, rather different point of view, Abraham Shoenfeld, agent of the Kehillah, had come to a similar conclusion. "The gangster is a tool," he wrote in a thoughtful memorandum to Rabbi Judah Magnes in 1915. Shoenfeld's investigations and reports for the Kehillah had helped put dozens of street gamblers and lawbreakers out of business. But for every wrongdoer who disappeared, six seemed to spring up in his place — and the original culprits were soon back on the street again, as if nothing had happened.[2]

A particularly frustrating example of this process was to be found at 267 Grand Street, where Fat Al Levy ran one of the Lower East Side's most luxurious and profitable gambling houses, the Down Town Merchants Club. Abraham Shoenfeld had monitored the activities of this totally illegal casino with mounting exasperation. There was auction pinochle, poker, and stud poker played for large sums of money. Part of the premises was set up as a horse parlor — a full-scale bookmaker's shop where odds were listed on chalkboards, and where cash bets were taken on races whose results could already, by that date, be transmitted directly from the track by telephone. The club's private crap game was played for some of the highest stakes in town.[3]

Shoenfeld compiled a thick dossier on the barefaced illegality of the casino at 267 Grand — the comings and goings of paperhangers who rendered the premises even more luxurious, the activities of Fat Al Levy, the principal partner and operator, and also the character of the membership, which comprised some notable figures in the local establishment: Abraham Harawitz, a lawyer and former assemblyman, Louie Rosenberg, a clothier, Louie Friedel, a Republican district leader, and Harry Bloom, a cigar manufacturer.[4]

What irked Shoenfeld about the Down Town Merchants Club was that he could not get the place closed. He sent monthly reports to Judah Magnes which were passed on promptly to the authorities. But Fat Al Levy's casino remained curiously immune to all complaints and requests for action — the precise nature of its immunity being most potently explained by the presence of the uniformed policemen from the local precinct who took turns standing outside the door every day.

Here, in the heart of Grand Street, New York City, was the special twist to the American system, the secret of how so many seemingly undoable things got done. Fat Al Levy's was the curbside crap game writ large, with one additional element, the dimension which kept profit recurring, and which even managed to cloak illegality with a certain appearance of respectability: the payoff.

Abraham Shoenfeld wrote pained and indignant memoranda to Rabbi Magnes about 267 Grand. Meyer Lansky, in the fullness of time, went into business with Al Levy.[5]

The first use of the word "gangster" in the English language has been traced back to April 10, 1896, three days after organized gangs of hoodlums had done battle on behalf of rival candidates in a Chicago municipal election.

"The gangster may play all kinds of pranks with the ballot box," declared the *Columbus* (Ohio) *Evening Dispatch* in its disapproving comments on the events in Chicago, "but in its own good time the latter will get even by kicking the gangster into the gutter."[6]

In his earliest known appearance on the printed page, the gangster was clearly defined as a man of violence, a member of a gang. But he was also, in some way, rather more than any other thug. He had a curious immunity — a license, even. Parading his muscle in an open and organized fashion on behalf of candidates for municipal office — would-be public servants — the gangster constituted a challenging reversal to the ordinary rules of law and behavior.

At the turn of the twentieth century, America's major cities were so many boomtowns, garish and unscrupulous, and their politics reflected that. Chicago's 1896 battles at the polling places demonstrated the appetite with which the city's rival political machines sought the profit and patronage that went with municipal power. In New York City, there was less overt violence, but no less corruption, thanks to the supremacy long enjoyed by one particular political machine, the notorious Tammany Hall.

Formed shortly after the American Revolution, Tammany was originally a patriotic, social fraternity like a number of others, taking its name from a legendary Indian chief, Tammany, of the Delaware tribe. The fraternity organized itself, Elk-like, into chapters, or "tribes," with names like Eagle, Otter, and Panther, and its network of clubhouses and ward workers came to constitute an electoral machine that could virtually guarantee power to its candidates. Tammany worked through the Democratic party in New York City, and for most of the nineteenth century New York's mayors, aldermen, and assemblymen — along with the magistrates and policemen they appointed — owed their positions to the lobbying and support of the Tammany organization.[7]

Tammany's power and corruption were the objects of frequent attack by its opponents and by political reformers. In 1894, State Senator Clarence Lexow showed how the city's gambling houses paid the Tammany-appointed police up to $300 a month to stay in business, and how brothels paid even more.[8] There was a price list, according to the *New York Times* in 1900 — $150 a month for a thriving crap game, $1,000 a month for a large gambling house.[9] In 1932, Judge Samuel Seabury discovered that upward of 4,000 persons were arraigned every year in New York magistrates' courts for illegal bookmaking — but that fewer than 175 of them were ever held for trial.[10]

These were flagrant examples of the way in which New York's lawbreakers could systematically purchase immunity through Tammany's politicians and through the police chiefs and magistrates that they appointed. The fraternity's local clubhouses were classic examples of that basic unit of old-time American urban politics, the "smoke-filled room."

But reformers who waxed indignant at the name of Tammany did their cause a misservice in suggesting that New York's wicked ways were explicable in terms of one particular pressure group of greedy and unscrupulous men. Tammany had simply proved itself the clever-

est organization at exploiting the spoils of power in a city where
everything was for sale.

The man who most totally mastered the New York system of power
and profit in the early decades of the twentieth century was Arnold
Rothstein, the first urban criminal to attain — and in his lifetime —
the mythic status that America had already bestowed on frontier
thugs like Jesse James and Billy the Kid. A decade before Al Capone
became famous — and before Prohibition spawned similar racketeer
princes in half a dozen of the great cities — Arnold Rothstein had
provided the archetype of what came to be known in America as
organized crime.

Charming and debonair, with quiet good looks and shiny, slicked-
down hair, the public Rothstein played a restrained, Jewish version
of the great American gentleman gambler in the tradition of Saratoga's Richard Canfield. Rothstein emulated Canfield by running a successful string of racehorses. He had a grand home on Fifth Avenue,
and a smart office on West Fifty-seventh Street. He had a weakness
for show girls which completed the playboy image. But there was a
sinister and mysterious side to him as well.

Arnold Rothstein was the inspiration for Scott Fitzgerald's Meyer
Wolfsheim in *The Great Gatsby* — the dark eminence whose financial backing and "gonnegtions" are revealed at the end of the novel
to have been the basis for Jay Gatsby's mysterious prosperity. For
Damon Runyon, Arnold Rothstein provided the quicksilver in
Nathan Detroit, and he was also the model for the character who
features in several of Runyon's Broadway short stories as The Brain:
"Nobody knows how much dough The Brain has, except that he
must have plenty."[11]

Rothstein's fortune was based on a gambling and bookmaking
empire which started on Manhattan and later spread out of town to
Saratoga Springs in upstate New York. Heavily dependent on payoffs
to Tammany, Rothstein's business ran into temporary difficulties in
July 1912, when Herman Rosenthal, the proprietor of an illegal
Manhattan gambling house, was shot dead by gunmen working to
the orders of a corrupt police lieutenant. Rosenthal had threatened
to expose the policeman's taking of bribes.

In *The Great Gatsby*, Scott Fitzgerald describes Meyer Wolfsheim / Arnold Rothstein dining with Herman Rosenthal on the
night that Rosenthal was shot down. "Don't let that waiter take
away my coffee!" says Rosenthal defiantly to Meyer Wolfsheim as he

walks out to certain death — the original and classic gangster tableau in American literary fiction.[12]

Rothstein was a fixer — a "shtadlan" in the words of the *Jewish Daily Forward*,[13] which, like the rest of the Jewish press, followed his activities with a mixture of shame and pride. A creature of the smoke-filled room, Rothstein was the first Jew to win significant influence with Tammany, deploying his charm and money to win the friendship of bosses like "Big Tim" Sullivan and, later, the mayor of New York, Jimmy Walker. The politician who needed funds or votes, the garment trade boss anxious for a deal with the union, a theatrical producer in search of an angel — all went to Arnold Rothstein.

By 1919, Rothstein's fame was so great that he was credited with being the evil genius behind the notorious throwing of the World Series by the Chicago White Sox — though the evidence of the case clearly shows that Rothstein neither devised the swindle nor financed it. His reputation was such that the professional gamblers who arranged the fraud used his name to impress the players — and a legend was born which endures to this day.[14]

With the Volstead Act and the coming of Prohibition, Rothstein's business empire developed a new and even more profitable dimension, and he became the first of the bootleg tycoons. He arranged to have high-quality liquor purchased in England and smuggled into the United States, then distributed to the restaurants, nightclubs, and gambling clubs in which he already had a financial interest.

It was not Rothstein's style, however, to administer such schemes himself. He looked around New York for bright young wiseguys he could bankroll. He would put up the money. They would take the risks. And one of the first rising entrepreneurs whom Arnold Rothstein chose to back was a short, shy, tough young man from the Lower East Side — Meyer Lansky.

Meyer Lansky had met Rothstein at the Bar Mitzvah of the son of mutual friends in Brooklyn.[15] "The Brain" represented the very pinnacle of the underworld career which Meyer had begun to construct for himself, and fifty years later there was still a little wonder in his recollection of his first contact with the great man.

"He invited me to dinner at the Park Central Hotel, and we sat talking for six hours. It was a big surprise to me. Rothstein told me quite frankly that he had picked me because I was ambitious and 'hungry'."[16]

Rothstein had an eye for criminal talent. His money and "gonneg-

tions" helped provide a start up the ladder for a whole generation of
fledgling gangsters: Charlie Luciano, Jack "Legs" Diamond, Dutch
Schultz, Waxey Gordon,* Abner "Longy" Zwillman, and an intelligent young Italian, Francesco Castiglia, who had Americanized his
name while giving it a helpful touch of Irish — Frank Costello.[17]

As Rothstein became a newspaper celebrity, crime reporters wrote
about his "empire" of corruption and criminal enterprise as if it were
a monolithic organization. Rothstein was popularly viewed as an
underground czar — "the J. P. Morgan of the underworld," heading
an integrated hierarchical machine that could be compared to J. P.
Morgan's banking and financial empire.

But the essence of organized crime as perfected by Arnold Rothstein was not structural organization as the conventional world knew
it. It was, rather, the absence of structure. His office on West Fifty-
seventh Street dealt strictly with the legal side of his activities — his
real estate investments, his Broadway shows, his racehorses. It would
have been folly to allow a lawbreaker, or any evidence of his criminal
activities, through his office doors. When it came to his partnerships
with protégés like Meyer Lansky in the 1920s, Arnold Rothstein
built up a series of self-contained deals which were sealed with a
handshake and recorded in the head.

This was not the integrated empire of a czar or a J. P. Morgan.
Such comparisons failed to grasp the secrecy and nimbleness essential
for success in organized crime. Rothstein's attorney, William J. Fal-
lon, the "great mouthpiece" who represented the leading racketeers
of the period, understood it better. His client, he said, was "a man
who dwells in doorways. . . . A gray rat, waiting for his cheese."[18]

Rothstein put Meyer Lansky in one doorway, Charlie Luciano in
another. The rats who ran quickest got cheese for Rothstein and
cheese for themselves as well. Those who got caught, got caught —
but their failure did not threaten anyone else. Each of Rothstein's
deals was separate, flexible, and detached. His protégés and partners
might operate individually or together. It was a question of what
worked. Fueled by the riches of Prohibition in the 1920s, Arnold
Rothstein set new and historic standards in the development of organized crime in America. But the secret of his organization was the
lack of it.

*   *   *

*Dutch Schultz's real name was Arthur Flegenheimer. Waxey Gordon was originally
called Irving Wexler.

Meyer Lansky's front for his activities as a full-time, professional bootlegger was a car and truck rental business based in a garage on Cannon Street in the Lower East Side. Benny Siegel was one of his partners,[19] together with a tough little friend of Benny's, Moe Sedway.[20]

Meyer's time in the tool-and-die shop had not gone to waste. There was good money to be made from a legitimate car and truck rental business on Manhattan in the 1920s. Car rental rates started at fifteen dollars a day, as compared to six dollars for a single room in the Waldorf-Astoria.[21]

"Rothstein taught us that mass production of cars would revolutionize many things in America," Lansky later said. "I realized myself how important it could become in our particular kind of business."[22]

Efficient bootlegging depended on efficient transportation. The Lansky-Siegel garage on Cannon Street was an ideal front for the transfer and shipment of liquid and illegal cargoes. Moe Sedway supervised the liquor trucks that pulled in there quite openly.[23] Bugs and Meyer rented out their vehicles without asking embarrassing questions, and they paid friends to be drivers if they had deliveries of their own to make. Red Levine, Meyer's freckle-faced chum from his Grand Street days, was one of these chauffeur-rumrunners.[24]

Charlie Luciano was Meyer's partner in a number of his bootlegging ventures. The Jewish and Italian communities lay side by side in Manhattan, and their speakeasies consumed the same sorts of liquor. There were obvious economies of scale in using the same network to supply both markets.[25]

There were two routes by which bootleg liquor came by sea into the New York area. Foreign-registered cargo ships would anchor just outside American territorial waters, twelve miles offshore, and high-speed motorboats would sneak out under cover of darkness to what became known as Rum Row, loading up and returning to one of the dozens of little harbors and inlets along the coast of Long Island and the Jersey shore. But it was also possible, with the right contacts, to bring cargoes of liquor directly into the New York waterfront, then get them unloaded and trucked away as if they were legitimate. This was less dramatic, but it was more businesslike, and it was the way that Charlie Luciano preferred.

The original basis of Meyer and Charlie's business lay in their own Lower East Side neighborhoods, where they could reach comfortable accommodations with their customers, competitive suppliers — and the police. There was a curbside exchange at the junction of Kenmare and Mulberry streets, where liquor traders waited to take orders. Two blocks away in their precinct house, the police looked the other way.[26] According to Meyer's tool-and-die friend, John Barrett, Meyer and Benny Siegel had a speakeasy on Broome Street, and another at the corner of Goerck and Lewis. Meyer also did business, Barrett said, with Mike Reardon, a longshoreman who operated an illegal bar at the corner of Mangin and Grand.[27]

Alongside his bootlegging, Meyer maintained and developed his involvement in the gambling business, graduating from *shtarke* work, as he built up his capital, to running and owning his own games. It was usual to have drink available to complement the craps, so when Meyer sold liquor to his gambling customers, he was making money two ways, and as his businesses developed, he looked around for partners and helpers he could trust.

Brother Jake had left school to go into the fur trade. It was the better end of the garment business. But as Meyer's bootlegging and gambling enterprises developed, Jake Lansky forsook furs, as Meyer had forsaken tool-and-die work, to become the principal partner and lieutenant of his elder brother.

There was no way that Jake Lansky was as sharp as Benny Siegel or Charlie Luciano. "Jake had a way of chewing on his cigar," said a friend. "He would beetle up his eyebrows, so you thought there must be a lot going on inside there — when, actually, it was pretty dead."[28]

But Jake Lansky had loyalty to offer. He was one of nature's lieutenants, and he loved his brother. Jake's life revolved around seeing and talking to Meyer every morning. He did not have Meyer's nimbleness with figures, but he learned to run a crap game, to keep an eye out for any cheating by the shooters — or by the banker, who was supposed to be Meyer's man.

The two brothers made a sort of headquarters for themselves in a private room at the back of Ratner's kosher restaurant on Delancey Street. Jake went there almost daily. It was the beginning of the coffee shop partners' meetings, sorting out business over the Danish pastries and the bowls of warty green pickles. The brothers would meet for breakfast, often with Ben Siegel, gossiping, laughing, comparing notes, checking to see if anything untoward had happened the previous night, going through the details for the coming day.

It was Meyer's habit to stagger his breakfast throughout the morning in a succession of little meals: some lox (Nova was not salty enough), a portion of corned beef, and then, perhaps, toward lunchtime, a tongue sandwich, middle slice — the fatty cut. He did not drink much coffee, but he did chain-smoke enthusiastically, as did all his friends — three-pack-a-day smokers to a man.[29]

Their life was business, but their way of doing business was fun. Concocting deals over the sugar shaker, parading their latest hat or coat or diamond stickpin — their profit and pleasure were stitched together into a lifestyle which offered them more than any conventional business career. No nine-to-five or paper clips for Meyer Lansky and his friends. The Ratner's management knew that these sharp and swaggering young men had to be engaged in something illicit. But the Lansky brothers were good customers, and they treated the waiters well.[30]

In a world without filing cabinets, Meyer Lansky's genius turned out to be the ability to act as a human cash register and ledger book in the succession of shifting partnerships and deals which were the essence of the bootlegging business. He could keep all the calculations in his head: the at-source cost, the allowances to be made for transport and protection, the profit margin — and, most important of all, the share-out among his partners.

Criminals, high and low, are risk takers and deal makers — and fairly short-term deal makers at that. It is the prospect of a bonanza, or some share in one, that draws them to crime. Why suffer the hazards of a life outside the law for the tyranny of a routine pay packet?

Criminal life is, thus, a succession of deals. The average modern wiseguy has, typically, four or five deals in the air at any one time.[31] They are partnerships, in varying combinations, that he has put together with his own immediate contacts, with the members of other criminal rings, and, from time to time, with a recruit from the straight world — a truck driver, perhaps, who is willing to look the other way when his load gets hijacked. It is a matter of individual enterprise, and the share-out at the end of it — payday — is the measure of how successful any particular deal has been.

The problem is that most criminals cannot handle the share-out. They lack the skills — the sheer, basic brainpower — to juggle all the figures in their head without resorting to pen and paper, which creates evidence, and thus the risk of incrimination.

Worse, they are congenitally dishonest. They are greedy. So they tell their partners clumsy tales of unanticipated expenses, of some policeman or lawyer who had to be paid off, and everyone goes home with less money in his pocket than he had been counting on. That is when the brooding starts, the reflection that leads to quarrels, to violence — to killing, even.

But there was never any killing over the deals in which Meyer Lansky was involved. With Meyer, somehow, there were never any nasty surprises. No one felt he had been shortchanged. As deal followed deal, and as the sums kept turning out right, his partners came to trust his calculations. They came back for more — and, as is the way with partners who have come to know and rely on each other over a period of time, they got better at what they were doing together.

Meyer was clever, and Meyer was straight. That was his ultimate cleverness, in the kingdom of cheats and shortcut takers.

"I listened and read about men in all kinds of endeavor," he later explained. "The men who mostly went to the top were men with integrety [sic]."[32]

In a flawed world, peopled by flawed characters, Meyer Lansky could deliver accuracy and probity, the honest bedrock without which no false adventure could hope to succeed.

It helped that he was not a greedy man. Meyer did not have the loud, expensive tastes for which his friends Charlie and Benny were soon to become bywords. "No money would rule me," he later said.[33]

Meyer Lansky could see the danger of becoming hostage to his own appetites. The proud and controlled little boy had grown into a tightly controlled adult. This made for personal repression. But it also made for business efficiency — and running a business efficiently was what provided Meyer Lansky with his ultimate job satisfaction. Closemouthed throughout his life on the details of his money and how he made it, Meyer could not resist, fifty years later, waxing lyrical to the Israeli journalist Uri Dan on how well he had run his bootlegging business.

"To cut costs and increase efficiency, we chartered our own ships to bring the Scotch across the Atlantic," he said. "I must say in all modesty that we ran things well. . . . By the middle twenties we were running the most efficient international shipping business in the world."[34]

This boast conjures up the image of offices full of shipping clerks, with Meyer Lansky striding up and down the aisles. The very opposite was the case. Meyer Lansky stayed in Ratner's. True to the example of Arnold Rothstein, his organization lay in the absence of structure. He operated at long distance — the phone call to the person who mattered, the money to the right pair of hands. Meyer kept the paperwork in his own head, and if he did require the services of anyone else, he insisted that they should do the same.

"Trust your memory," he used to say. "Keep your business in your hat."[35]

Meyer worked out strict rules for the men who drove his liquor consignments: no loud clothes, no fighting or showing off. Picking steady, reliable characters and instilling morale into men whose nature was not to be disciplined, Lansky displayed the management skills that were to be part of his business success throughout his life.

"We paid more than anyone else, and paid in cash," he told Uri Dan. "It's remarkable how loyal people will be when you look after them as well as we did. We gave them incentives and rewards for good work. When they came up with useful proposals, we praised them and lined their pockets."[36]

As a serious distributor whose deliveries could be relied upon, Meyer dealt with liquor dealers some distance from New York. In Cleveland he made friends with Morris Barney "Moe" Dalitz and his partners, who ran bootlegging and illegal gambling in several corners of Ohio.[37] He also did business with entrepreneurs who were to become giants in the liquor industry after the end of Prohibition — Samuel Bronfman, a Russian Jew who had settled in Canada and was building what became the Seagram liquor company,[38] and Lewis Rosensteil, later the architect of Schenley Distilleries.

"We were in business like the Ford Motor Company," said Meyer of his bootlegging activities in the 1920s. "Shooting and killing was an inefficient way of doing business. Ford salesmen didn't shoot Chevrolet salesmen. They tried to outbid them."[39]

In the spring of 1928 Meyer Lansky was the subject of two photographs, both taken on the same occasion, and by the same photographer. One was taken from the side, a portrait that showed Meyer relaxed and somewhat rumpled, his eyes looking away from the camera. Without the focus of his dark and direct gaze, you notice other features — his nose and lips, which are rather fine and sharp, his slightly weak chin. Meyer is hatless, off duty, leaning backward a bit, at ease with himself. With his hair neatly trimmed, his smart tie, and his expensive, dark overcoat, Meyer Lansky looks the very picture of the rising executive — a successful young Ford or Chevrolet salesman.

But this picture of the twenty-five-year-old Meyer Lansky was not a business portrait — not in the conventional sense, at least, for it was taken by a photographer of the New York City Police Department. It was one of two mug shots, one full-face and one profile, taken, along with fingerprints, in March 1928. Somehow, inadvertently, the photographer's side view had chanced to capture Meyer in repose. But the full-face portrait showed another Meyer Lansky.

Seen from the front, the suspect is staring straight into the camera, angry and defiant, obviously infuriated to be caught. It could be the picture of a totally different man. Now Meyer is wearing his hat, snap-brimmed, gangster-style, pulled down in a hard, straight line across the top of his eyes. He is sitting up, giving the fierce, blank stare that could chill a man to the marrow, the intimidating look that threatens pain, disfigurement — you scarcely dare guess what.

This was the other side of Meyer — and it was the other side of the American gangster. The gangster might enjoy his political dimension, the odd and fascinating immunity from ordinary rules that he purchased through his "business" activities. But he rested his business on a far more basic bottom line, the fact that he was willing to hurt and maim and kill people.

The system was fascinating to analyze — the payoffs, the recurring profit, all the wickedness and ingenuity embraced by those oddly passionless words, "organized crime." But the violence was the ultimate fascination, the dimension that made the gangster really special — the fact that at any time, on a whim, the gun could come out, his arm could be raised in your direction, and BOOM!

Meyer Lansky liked to talk learnedly in later life about the limitations of violence. "It's always much better not to shoot if you can help it," he said. "It's better to use reason — or if that fails, threats."[40] He lectured on the subject, developing a minor philosophy of intimidation — the applied use of fear without the need to resort to anything so messy, irrational, and inefficient as bloodshed itself.

But threats only work if people believe that you may implement them, and Meyer Lansky's record provided him with that rather particular credibility. His contrasting police mug shots were taken in 1928 after he had been arrested on charges of attempted homicide.

Daniel Ahearn, Meyer's companion on his expedition to deal with the union-busting foreman from the factory in Peekskill, was there when it happened. Ahearn had been in and out of jail and courtrooms through the 1920s. In the winter of 1927–28 he was out again, mixing with his Lower East Side friends, Meyer, Ben Siegel, John Barrett, and Red Levine, and involved in an adventure which nearly led to murder.

Lansky, Siegel, and Levine suspected Barrett of not playing them straight. So to teach him a lesson, they drove with him out of town, pushed him out of the car, and then used him for target practice as he fled for safety into the darkness.

"He started running through the field — he was a hell of a runner, this guy — and they started firing at him," Ahearn later related. He said that he got the story straight from Lansky. "They hit him four times." Ahearn thought there was an Italian in the car with Lansky, Siegel, and Levine.[41]

Ahearn got personally involved when it was discovered that Barrett had been admitted to a hospital with his wounds. Ahearn had a score of his own to settle with Barrett, and so, according to a statement sworn by Ahearn in 1957, Lansky said to him: "I'll tell you what, here's a good idea: Let's go down to Mott Street. I know some ginzo down there, and we can get a juiced-up chicken. . . . His wife knows I was in the car, I can't give him the chicken, but you could pull the gag and give him the chicken. . . ." By "juiced-up" Ahearn meant poisoned.

"So," said Ahearn in his statement, "we went down to Mott Street and we got this chicken, which was juiced-up. I will admit it, I was hot for Barrett at the time. . . . And I met his wife, Grace, I believe her name was. . . . I says, 'Seeing you are going to the hospital to see him, here, give him this and don't even tell him it's from me. Surprise him. . . .' So she took the chicken and she headed for the hospital. . . . I met her later and she started calling me all kinds of names . . . because when . . . he asked her, 'Who gave you the chicken?' [she told him]. He took the chicken and winged it out of the window."[42]

It sounds a fanciful story — the moving target practice, the "juiced-up" chicken. But the ledger of the Long Island City Magistrates' Court, Fifty-ninth Precinct, for the early months of 1928 shows a Meyer Lansky, and a Samuel Levine, arrested on March 6, 1928, in the company of an Italian, Joseph Benzole. The trio were charged with felonious assault on John Barrett, of 433 Grand Street, New York City.[43]

Detective Joseph P. Heinrich, the arresting officer in the case, later testified that he had interviewed John Barrett twice — once when Barrett was first admitted to the hospital, and a second time a few weeks later.

On the first occasion, right after his wounding, Barrett had had no hesitation in naming Meyer Lansky and his cronies as his assailants, said the detective. Barrett had described a gathering that evening at the home of Louis "Lepke" Buchalter, a notorious *shtarke* who organized muscle and intimidation in the garment trade. There had been an argument over a warehouse robbery, said Barrett, and the suggestion that Barrett had talked to the police. The shooting had occurred after they all left Lepke's place, driving away from his home.[44]

A few weeks later, however, by the time he had recovered from his wounds and was fit enough to testify in court, John Barrett had undergone a striking change of heart. Now he was scared, according to Detective Heinrich.[45] Barrett declined to sign a complaint against Meyer Lansky, and he refused to take the stand to testify against him. For lack of evidence, the charges against Lansky, Levine, and Benzole were dismissed.

Asked about this incident in later years, Meyer Lansky suffered memory loss to rival that of John Barrett — though most people, innocent or guilty, would have little difficulty recalling the experience of being arrested and arraigned on a shooting charge at the age of twenty-five.

"I never had any business with him," Meyer said. He admitted that he had known John Barrett. "But," he insisted, "I had no reason to act against him — and certainly not to shoot him."[46]

It was such a long time ago. Kids got up to funny things. Daniel Ahearn was an Irishman, a storyteller.[47] Meyer's memory stayed vague and cloudy until his interviewer, Uri Dan, got onto the mechanics of Prohibition and the liquor business. Then the details all started coming back — the picture of the clever young businessman, giving orders to the shipping departments, handling his partners with aplomb, and generally making his way in the world with professionalism and skill.

It was a much clearer image, somehow, than the picture that never made it to court in March 1928 — the rancor of a vengeful young hoodlum, leaning and laughing out of the window of a car, letting loose with live bullets in the direction of a man running like a hunted animal into the darkness of a winter night.

In the thirteen years between October 1918 and November 1931, Meyer Lansky's name featured seven times as a defendant in the records of the New York City magistrates' courts.[48] His first two appearances were on his teenage charges of annoying women — on one of which he was fined two dollars — and his third appearance was scarcely that of a big-time hoodlum. In 1924, Lansky was arraigned in traffic court and was fined four dollars for speeding.[49]

In 1928, Meyer's name was listed for the fourth and fifth times, in the felonious assault case against John Barrett, which did not finally proceed, and in another similar assault case a few days later, which seems to have been a genuine case of mistaken identity. The police were struck by the similarity between the Barrett shooting and another, unsolved case which had involved shooting from a car, but they could bring no evidence against Meyer Lansky. So this fifth case, like the Barrett case, was dismissed.[50]

Meyer's sixth court appearance was with Benjamin Siegel in January 1929. The two men faced charges under the Public Health Act, legislation which was often deployed against drug offenders. That case was also dismissed. Meyer's only serious conviction came in his seventh and final appearance — a $100 fine for violation of the Volstead Act in November 1931, two years before Prohibition ended.

It would be interesting, since we know that Lansky was making his living throughout these Prohibition years by breaking the law, to discover more of the circumstances of the seven court cases that were brought against him — the nature of the police evidence, the statements made, the witnesses called. But the truth about them will never be known, for sometime around June 1936, the New York City Police Department threw out almost all of its nonactive case files. The investigative notes on Lansky's indictments — and on tens of thousands of others — were destroyed, leaving nothing but the bare records of arrest dates, charges, and disposition of cases, effectively wiping the slate clean for large numbers of Prohibition offenders — and more important, perhaps, for large numbers of New York City policemen as well.[51]

When questioned in later years about his youthful roster of arrests, Meyer Lansky would talk vaguely of youthful indiscretion and police victimization, and would point to his impressive acquittal record — four out of seven — as the vindication of his innocence. But his fellow wiseguys, bootleggers, and crap game operators drew a different lesson, the beginning of what became a legend: clever Meyer!

On the evening of Sunday, November 4, 1928, Arnold Rothstein was doing business as usual at his favorite table in Lindy's. The deli-restaurant served as his headquarters on Seventh Avenue, as well as

the social center for the colorful cast of characters with which
Damon Runyon peopled his short stories, later the basis for the musical *Guys and Dolls*.

A phone call came through for Mr. Rothstein, and after he took
it, Rothstein hurried out onto Seventh Avenue, heading toward Fifty-
sixth Street and the Park Central Hotel. Asked later about the possible content of the phone call, Abe Scher, Lindy's night cashier, testified that he had no idea what The Brain might have said.

"The way he talks, you can stand beside him and not hear anything," Scher told the police, in an interesting example of the *Guys
and Dolls* historical present being used by a real-life Broadway character. "Besides, who listens?"[52]

Later that evening, the body of Arnold Rothstein was found crumpled on the floor beside the servants' entrance to the Park Central
Hotel. He had been shot in the belly. Two days later, The Brain died
in the hospital, having resolutely declined to give the police the slightest idea of who shot him, or why.[53]

"I'm not talking," he told Detective Patrick Flood, before lapsing
into a coma. "You stick to your trade and I'll stick to mine."[54]

Arnold Rothstein had lived mysteriously, and his death was of a
piece with that. But as detectives investigated his murder, it became
clear that he was not the victim of a gangland killing for power or
territory. Arnold Rothstein was almost certainly killed because of
personal gambling debts that he was refusing to pay.[55]

The death of The Brain demonstrated how even the most elevated
gangster and fixer was not immune to the basic rules of the game.
Those who lived by violence died by violence, particularly if, like
Rothstein, they suffered from some personal flaw — in his case, a
weakness for gaming with high money stakes.

Investigators rushed eagerly to examine Rothstein's documents
and personal effects, hopeful they might discover the secrets of his
organized crime edifice, and that they might bring its activities to a
halt. They were to be disappointed in both respects.

The investigations following Rothstein's murder uncovered corruption extending, via a number of Tammany figures, to the mayor
of New York himself, Jimmy Walker, and these disclosures led, eventually, to Walker's disgrace and resignation in 1932.

But the only evidence of organization uncovered was in the world
of the straight and the ostensibly respectable — city government
offices, party machines. The mayor of New York might fall, but not
a single criminal went to jail as a result of any evidence that Arnold

Rothstein left behind, because Rothstein had no criminal organization to be uncovered. The strength of all his many separate partnerships and deals lay in their separateness. The failure of one did not jeopardize the others. The Brain was dead, but the other gray rats went on getting their cheese.

Charles "Lucky" Luciano believed in business. His ambitions focused on whatever made a dime, and his ethical system flowed from that. Noticing, as a bright eighteen-year-old, the number of drug addicts living in his neighborhood around East Tenth Street, the young Salvatore Lucania had purchased a half-bottle of opium and went round dispensing it to them, selling the drug by the measure. The bottle lasted ten days, and with his profits the budding entrepreneur bought another.[56]

Charlie had been on his third bottle when he was caught and sentenced to eight months in reform school. Arrested again for selling heroin five years later, he avoided jail by leading the narcotics agents to a stash of drugs in a Mulberry Street basement, and by providing information which helped get several rival drug dealers sent away.[57] Meyer Lansky's closest Italian friend was not noted for his sentiment — and this was to provide the keynote of the style with which, in the years after the death of Arnold Rothstein, Charlie Luciano cut his way through the convoluted world of Italian American crime.

The Black Hand, the Camorra, the Mafia, the Unione Siciliano — outsiders used many words to try to interpret the patterns of lawbreaking in the Italian communities of early twentieth-century America. As in the Lower East Side's Jewish communities, the "service crimes" of prostitution and illegal gambling — crap games, bookmaking, numbers — provided the steadiest sources of illegal income, supplemented by more obviously criminal activities like thievery. But the Little Italys around America had an additional specialty — the backroom still which produced low-cost, high-kick alcohol — and this gave the Italians a niche of their own in the business of Prohibition.

Conspiracy and secrecy are necessary in any criminal activity, but they loomed particularly large in the style of America's early immigrants from Italy. Joining together in legal or illegal fellowship, newly arrived Italian Americans showed a fondness for oaths and initiation rituals — finger-prickings, candles, and male-bonding rites which could be traced back to the clans and hill villages of the old country. They also brought from Europe an almost feudal sense of hierarchy, doing homage to *padrones* — elders or bosses who cultivated the old traditions.

"I was much like a squire in the service of a knight," wrote Joseph Bonanno of his apprenticeship, as a young man, to his *padrone,* Salvatore Maranzano, who, like Bonanno, hailed originally from the town of Castellammare del Golfo at the western tip of Sicily.[58]

Salvatore Maranzano had built up a profitable business collecting and distributing the product of Little Italy's illegal stills, and he had also developed a network of contacts by which, following Congress's 1921 curb on immigration, young Italians could be smuggled into America. Maranzano used his Castellammarese connections to place his protégés in jobs all over the East, from New York City to Buffalo, thus further enhancing his patriarchal status and strengthening the pattern of obligation which earned him that particularly Italian commodity — "respect."[59]

Charlie Luciano had been born in Sicily, but he spoke little Sicilian. The Americanizing of his name from Salvatore Lucania was the sign of where his priorities lay. Looking for profit where he could find it, Charlie knew it made sense to deal in the illegal economy of the Italian community. But he was tone deaf to the music which a Joseph Bonanno found in the clan loyalties of the old way.

"Lucky lived in two worlds," wrote Bonanno. "He lived among us, the men of the old Tradition; but he also lived in a world apart from us, among a largely Jewish coterie whose views of life and of moneymaking were alien to ours."[60]

Meyer Lansky, chief partner and confidant in the coterie, made clear how alien that view was. "They were so honorable," said Meyer, looking back with scorn on the feudings of the so-called Honored Society, "that no one in the Mafia ever trusted anyone else."[61]

By the early months of 1931, vendettas between New York's rival Italian factions were starting to produce open warfare — stabbings, shootings, and even bodies in the streets of Brooklyn and the Lower East Side.

Joe Bonanno loved it, watching his *padrone,* Maranzano, oil his weapons and weigh out gunpowder and pellets on the night before battle. "He performed the loading of the shotgun shells," Bonanno related, "as if it were a sacred ritual."[62]

Charlie Luciano was less impressed. The newspaper stories of street-corner violence were not good for business, and one day in the spring of 1931 he went to pay a visit to Salvatore Maranzano.

According to Bonanno, who was present at the meeting, Luciano offered to bring an end to the current hostilities by arranging the liquidation of Maranzano's archrival and war enemy, Giuseppe Masseria, "Joe the Boss."[63]

"I didn't know much about Luciano," wrote Bonanno, "who up to then had operated independently with his associate Meyer Lansky."[64]

A few weeks later Joe the Boss was dead, cut down by gunmen while waiting for a late lunch at the Nuova Villa Tammaro Restaurant on Coney Island on April 15, 1931.[65] Charlie Luciano was able to take over Little Italy's profitable lotteries rackets, which had been run by Masseria, while Maranzano could move in on the dead boss's bootlegging.

But the killing did not bring peace. Salvatore Maranzano was a man with ambitions. His favorite reading matter was said to be books about Julius Caesar,[66] and that seemed a fair indication of how his thinking ran. Not content with being a *capo* — a boss — Maranzano wanted to be the *capo di tutti capi* — the boss of all bosses. In the weeks following his rival's killing, he summoned a conclave of New York's Italian crime figures, extending the invitation to gang chieftains from as far away as Buffalo. They met at a Catskills resort hotel near Wappingers Falls, where Maranzano had a farm, seventy-five miles up the Hudson River from New York.[67]

Joseph Bonanno was close to Maranzano, and he loved him dearly, but his description of his patron's behavior at the meeting was of a man with delusions of grandeur. Maranzano had hired a plane to circle the hotel and had armed it, he told the assembled company, with bombs and machine guns. Throughout the meeting, the drone of the engine could be heard as the plane circled menacingly overhead.[68]

More threatening still, according to Bonanno, Maranzano began the meeting by identifying those who had been loyal to him in his recent battles with Masseria and those whom he considered "dishonest."[69] Publicly, he included Luciano among his friends, but it was not long before Charlie developed the suspicion that Maranzano had plans to do away with the dangerous young man who had helped him dispose of his rival, Masseria.

Luciano decided to strike first.[70] On September 10, 1931, less than six months after the killing of Joe Masseria, Salvatore Maranzano was shot down by four gunmen who had gained entry to his office over Grand Central Station by claiming to be police officers.

The assassins were never caught, but underworld lore has it that they were Jewish hitmen, organized on Luciano's behalf by Ben Siegel and Meyer Lansky. Dutch Schultz's bodyguard, Abe "Bo" Weinberg, later asserted that he was one of the shooting party.[71] According to Joseph Valachi, Red Levine was another of the killers.[72] It would certainly have been difficult for armed Italians to walk unchallenged into the inner sanctum of the untrusting Maranzano.

We do not know the details of the counsel that Meyer Lansky gave his friend Charlie Luciano in the tense maneuverings which led to the death of Salvatore Maranzano in September 1931. The only solid evidence of their being together in these years came when they were photographed in Chicago in April 1932, probably on a bootlegging business trip. Surprised by an enterprising detective in the company of Paul "The Waiter" Ricca, one of Capone's successors, Meyer and Charlie were lined up in front of the camera in their best hats and overcoats. Charlie managed a slight smile, but Meyer did not look amused one bit. Both men were then released.[73]

Meyer himself always avoided commenting on whether his closeness to Luciano extended beyond advice to the provision of practical help — and this could be because there is no statute of limitations on murder. It was Meyer's style to stay discreetly in the background, a shadowy presence whose influence with Luciano was mistrusted by Charlie's fellow Italians, and by Maranzano in particular.[74] But Meyer was no puppetmaster pulling the strings.

"Luciano was his own man," remembers Moses Polakoff, who was lawyer to both Lansky and Luciano in the 1930s.[75]

There was something instinctive about the trust and understanding that the two friends shared. "They would just look at each other," Benny Siegel once said to Doc Stacher, with more than a hint of jealousy, "and you would know that a few minutes later, one would say what the other was thinking."[76]

Having served their apprenticeship under Rothstein's umbrella, Meyer Lansky and Charlie Luciano had developed a very similar vision of how to carry on their business — the profitable and self-sustaining system of illegal enterprise that the world has come to know as organized crime — and that vision was to be reflected in the patterns of crime which emerged from New York's Italian gang wars.

It is important to understand, however, what those patterns were. Most popular accounts of the Castellammarese Wars have lent the episode a national dimension, telling the story of how the killing of Maranzano in New York provided the signal for a massive, countrywide purge, in the days that followed, of other old-time Italian-Sicilian gang leaders — the so-called Mustache Petes — who were killed by the dozen in cities across America.[77]

"At the very same time when Maramanenza [*sic*] was knocked off . . . there was about ninety guineas knocked off all over the country," claimed Bo Weinberg in the earliest printed version of this tale.[78] Much repeated by criminals and crime writers both, with the number of victims ranging from a few dozen to nearly a hundred, this story of what one writer called a "painstakingly executed mass extermination"[79] has come to be seen as one of the turning points in the modern history of organized crime — most recently in April 1988, in testimony which the FBI presented to the U.S. Senate.

"Following the death of Salvatore Maranzano," noted the FBI's "Chronological History of La Cosa Nostra," updated to 1987, "a wave of gangland slayings, known as the 'Sicilian Vespers,' swept the country."[80]

In 1985, Dr. Alan Block published the results of a systematic study of newspapers in eight major American cities in the two weeks before and the two weeks following September 10, 1931, the date of Maranzano's killing. Most of the newspapers carried some account of the shooting in the office above Grand Central Station, but in all the column inches devoted to crime and violence, there were only three reports of similar gang- or racketeer-linked killings — two in Newark and one in Pittsburgh.[81] On October 15, 1931, a date outside Dr. Block's survey period, Joe Ardizonne, a Los Angeles hoodlum, disappeared, presumed murdered.[82]

Four killings do not make a purge. The tale of the latter-day Sicilian Vespers is a classic example of how, in organized crime history, an easy and dramatic conspiracy theory can, through frequent repetition, come to replace reality. And this particular myth has been responsible for the fostering of two major fallacies about organized crime in America.

The first is that the early 1930s saw America's gangsters become overwhelmingly Italian. This makes no allowance for the flourishing in New York City, throughout this period and beyond, of Dutch Schultz, Lepke Buchalter, Jake "Gurrah" Shapiro, and Benny Siegel — four tough Jews who were responsible for more deaths between them than Lucky Luciano and all the *padrones* in the Castellammarese Wars.

Nor were the tough Jews confined to New York. Across the river in New Jersey were Doc Stacher and Abner "Longy" Zwillman. In

Philadelphia, there was Harry Stromberg. St. Paul–Minneapolis boasted Kid Cahn (Isadore Blumenfeld), his brother, Yiddy Bloom, and the Berman brothers, Davie and Chickie. In Cleveland there were Moe Dalitz and his partners Sam Tucker, Louis Rothkopf, and Morris Kleinman — bootleggers and illegal gamblers who did better business than any Italian.[83] In Chicago, the trial and downfall of Al Capone in the autumn of 1931 was followed by the emergence of several non-Italians, among them Jake "Greasy Thumb" Guzik, Capone's Jewish accountant, and Murray "The Camel" Humphreys, who came originally from Wales.[84]

The second, and still more deeply rooted misconception fostered by the legend of Lucky Luciano's nationwide purge, is that American organized crime can be seen as a closely integrated, almost corporate syndicate, operating in every corner of the country, one word in New York getting instant action in Chicago or in San Francisco. Salvatore Maranzano had edged in this direction in the summer of 1931, when he attempted to extend his authority beyond the confines of New York City and to become some sort of northeastern "boss of bosses" — but the purpose and effect of Charlie Luciano's intervention was to achieve the very opposite.

"Luciano . . . mainly wanted to be left alone to run his enterprises," explained Joe Bonanno. "He was not trying to impose himself on us as had Masseria. Lucky demanded nothing from us."[85]

It was Arnold Rothstein's principle of the gray rats being unconfined by structure, free to scavenge for themselves and to pursue profit as opportunity and their aptitudes led them. Gang leaders might meet together from time to time for sit-downs at which they would sort out disputes over territory and common threats to their welfare. But the fundamental rule was live and let live — laissez-faire, the unstructured, free-market principle on which the country's legitimate business had long been founded.

This had already become the pattern in the Italian communities of such cities as Milwaukee, Cleveland, Dallas, and Detroit, where a new generation of American-reared and American-thinking toughs had risen to power in the late 1920s. In the years 1932–36 there were similar leadership changes in the Italian gangs of Pittsburgh, Kansas City, and Philadelphia.[86]

Myths are often attempts to explain complicated phenomena in simple terms, and it seems likely that the legend of the modern Sicilian Vespers took its life from these upheavals in different parts of the country — disturbing and often violent local power struggles in which the old-style *padrones* were supplanted, city by city, by younger rivals or successors. "That was the time," said Bo Weinberg, "when we Americanized the mobs."[87]

Operating in New York, Meyer Lansky and Charlie Luciano provided the most dramatic and visible examples of this new generation of criminal entrepreneurs whose self-governing, profit-oriented partnerships were to constitute American organized crime for the next half-century. But Meyer and Charlie did not invent or impose the change. They were part of it.

4

"*There Was Never Anything*
We Wanted"

SOMETIME in the late 1920s, Meyer Lansky fell in love. Now approaching the age of thirty, Meyer was looking to settle down — and, rather against the odds, his friend Benny Siegel was moving in the same direction.

Bugs and Meyer operated their bootlegging garage on Cannon Street as partners, and they joined forces for their romantic adventures as well. In 1927 they started going out with two Lower East Side girls, Anne Citron and Esther Krakower, an elegant pair of friends who had known each other since childhood, and whose families both came from Jewish eastern Europe. Esther was Benny's date. Anne Citron was Meyer's.

The foursome kept each other company for the best part of two years.[1] Anne and Esther were similar in looks and style — dark haired and strong featured. Meyer and Benny were a well-polished double act, and they knew how to give a girl a good time. The two men had plenty of cash in their pockets — which meant new cars, smart clothes, admission to the most fashionable restaurants.

The girls were under no illusion as to where the money came from. Anne Citron knew that the garage which Meyer ran with Benny was a front for illegal enterprises, but it did not bother her greatly. She took some pride in the fact that her boyfriend made his living from what she liked to describe as a "clean fingernail" occupation.[2]

A photograph survives of Anne Citron in these days — a young face that stares out of the frame with a knowing half-smile. Anne is wearing a satin dressing gown, Hollywood siren–style, leaning forward alluringly, with the stub of a cigarette between the fingers of her right hand. Even in the age of jazz and cocktails, her pose tells you this is no shy, retiring Jewish girl. As with his choice of male friends, Meyer had gone for someone who was more outgoing than he was.

Anne livened Meyer up. Esther quieted Benny down. Dashing, handsome, and well aware of it, Benny Siegel was notorious for his womanizing. But the Bug became calmer, somehow, under the influence of Esther Krakower — and Meyer helped with the process. Meyer was the only male whose opinion mattered much to Benny. When Meyer and Anne decided to get married in the spring of 1929, Ben and Esther did the same. Meyer and Benny each acted as the other's best man.[3]

The months preceding the two marriages were a flurry of activity. Meyer had fallen behind on the formalities of getting himself naturalized as an American, and his brushes with the law could have disqualified him from citizenship.[4] But when he went for his naturalization interview in 1928, he did not declare his five arrests to that date, and the immigration authorities made no inquiries of their own.[5] "NCR" — no criminal record — noted the examiner on Meyer's papers. The citizenship, and the marriage, could go ahead,[6] and in May 1929 Meyer drove his young bride up through the spring greenery to Canada.[7]

"I remember my honeymoon as a wonderful time," Meyer Lansky later said. "In those days, when you traveled 100 miles by car, it was something worth talking about."[8]

A few weeks short of nine months later, on January 15, 1930, Anne Lansky gave birth to the couple's first child — a bright and alert little boy, a trifle on the small side, like his father. The young parents gave their son the names Bernard and Irving, after relatives, but they soon had their own pet name for him — Buddy.[9]

Buddy Lansky was a cheerful child, equable and good-tempered for a baby. Yet after six months or so, it seemed to Anne Lansky that her son was not developing quite as rapidly as other children of his age. Buddy had trouble sitting up. He was slow with crawling, and the problem became more obvious when he reached the walking stage.

Moses Polakoff, Meyer's lawyer, who was also a family friend, remembers how the baby would never get to its feet. Whenever Polakoff came round to visit the Lanskys, he would see little Buddy on the floor, happy, healthy, and smiling — and always crawling.[10]

Buddy Lansky was three years old before he was able to walk in a jerky and uncertain fashion,[11] and by then Anne and Meyer had found out the truth. Their firstborn son was physically retarded, and he would always remain so. Buddy was a cripple.

The diagnosis of the doctors who examined Buddy Lansky as a baby was cerebral palsy, a condition afflicting the links between the brain and the motor nerves. Doctors who examined Buddy in later years suggested that his problem stemmed more probably from some damage to his spinal cord while in the womb or at birth, since, unlike the typical palsy sufferer, Buddy enjoyed speech and mental faculties that remained sharp throughout his life.[12] Inside his disobedient body, Bernard Irving Lansky had the lively mind of his father.

Meyer Lansky did not react well to illness or disability. It embarrassed him. Meyer liked to feel that he was in control of things, and if he sensed that this was not the case, he would just withdraw from the situation. Throughout his life, he had difficulty dealing with the reality of his son's disability.

Buddy was told a story which came to haunt him in his later years — that his father's first reaction to the news of his son's disability was to walk out on his wife and spastic child. Meyer just went away, Buddy was told, vanishing from the world for days in an effort to escape this imperfection which had settled in his life.[13]

As an adult, Buddy could never bring himself to ask his father directly about the truth of this tale. But it fitted so well, it seemed to Buddy, with all he knew about his father. Meyer Lansky had feelings, deep, personal emotions that boiled to the surface on rare occasions. But Meyer found it difficult to express them. He bottled things up. The movements of his heart were his own personal secret — even from the people who had stimulated them, and whom they most concerned.

Meyer Lansky liked to get things worked out ahead of time, and this is how he dealt, eventually, with Buddy's illness. Meyer went to the library and made himself an expert on cerebral palsy, then set about finding the doctors who knew how to treat it. From New York to California, Meyer Lansky traveled and telephoned in 1931 and 1932 to track down the leading authorities on the treatment of the condition.

He took his wife and baby with him, the young family making a pilgrimage of hospitals in search of help. When he heard of an Austrian orthopedic surgeon who had developed some new techniques, he had the doctor brought over to New York.[14] The Lanskys went down to Hot Springs, Arkansas, where Owney Madden, the one-time backer of New York's Cotton Club, presided over a curious southern enclave of hot mineral bath therapies and luxurious, illegal resort casinos. Neither the Austrian doctor nor the waters of Hot Springs, Arkansas, had the answer.

Expense was no object. Meyer Lansky wanted the best for his son. Channeling the right amount of money to the right pair of hands was how he had fixed most things in his life to date. It would be difficult, but he was sure that somehow it would work for Buddy.

Anne and Meyer Lansky started their married life in a modest rented apartment in Brooklyn. Soon after Buddy's birth, they moved to the Upper West Side of Manhattan, to an apartment at Ninety-ninth and Broadway, and then they moved on, a year or so after that, to the Majestic at Seventy-second and Central Park West, one of the grandest of the apartment blocks overlooking Central Park.[15]

Meyer Lansky did not live with the ostentation of Charlie Luciano, who was lording it at the Waldorf-Astoria in these years. But the Majestic was superior enough. It attracted several of the stars of the new medium of radio, Walter Winchell among them.[16] For Anne and Meyer Lansky to rent in the same building as America's most famous broadcaster and gossip columnist showed a certain aplomb.

The impulse for style came from the young Mrs. Lansky. One of the things that had drawn Anne Citron to Meyer was his spending power, and she knew how to make the most of it. When Anne Lansky and her friend Esther Siegel hit Fifth Avenue, they had the capacity to inflict significant damage.

"Ooooh," remembered Buddy Lansky of his mother. "Did she know how to spend!"[17]

One of their favorite shopping spots was Wilma's on Fifty-seventh Street, between Fifth and Madison. Anne and Esther would shuttle in and out of the changing booths, often accompanied by Florence

Alo, the wife of Vincent Alo, an Italian who was one of Luciano's friends and partners, and who had become a friend of Meyer's.[18] Vincent Alo was known as Jimmy Blue Eyes.

Anne Lansky, Esther Siegel, and Flo Alo all used the same interior decorator. Ada Hector worked with her sister, Vivian, out of an apartment on Madison Avenue, and she was known for her high-quality work.[19] She was big on wallpaper. When you walked into a room done by Ada Hector, the wallpaper told you plainly how much money had been spent.

When you walked into the Lanskys' apartment in the Majestic, what struck you first was the light bouncing off the greenery of Central Park. Living on the third floor, they looked down on it all through the treetops. The sitting room featured a deep, comfortable sofa, a couple of loveseats, Ada Hector's wallpaper, and a large Grandway piano. Meyer's den was a library with wood paneling, a wide desk, and lots of books — a big atlas, the *Book of Knowledge,* and a complete set of *Encyclopaedia Britannica.*[20]

In the closet by the door Meyer kept a wooden hat block on which sat one of his pearl-gray, black-banded Cavanaugh hats. In his bedroom closet sat another wooden hat block, with an identical hat placed carefully upon it to preserve its shape.[21]

Lansky was a meticulous dresser. He bought his shirts — white on white, and usually silk — off the rack from Sulka. His suits were from Maurice. His ties were by Countess Mara. When Meyer Lansky bought one of an item, he bought three or four more, and he hung them all up neatly, side by side, in his bedroom closet. Also in his closet, he had a safe which was bolted into the floor. Inside the safe he kept money, papers, and a gun.[22]

In September 1932 Anne Lansky gave birth to a second child, another son, and this baby turned out to be normal and healthy. Anne and Meyer named him Paul. Around the same time, they also made contact with a doctor who could offer some hope for little Buddy — Dr. Carruthers, a Boston specialist who was developing new techniques for the treatment of spastic children. Meyer and Anne decided to shift their family headquarters to Boston.

The Lanskys kept on their apartment in the Majestic overlooking Central Park. Meyer's business was centered in New York. But he had come to treat Buddy's disability as a priority. Whatever his initial panic, getting his elder son put to rights had become a quest around which Meyer was prepared to make quite considerable adjustments.

In 1933 the family decamped to their new home near Boston Common, a third-floor apartment in a stolid, modern block on the corner of Beacon Street and Embankment Road. They had a terrace to the rear, and a view of the Charles River and the Hatch Shell, the open-air auditorium on the Esplanade famous for its summer evening concerts.[23]

The therapies that three-year-old Buddy Lansky had to suffer were severe. At home he had to wear leg braces, and at Dr. Carruthers's clinic at Children's Hospital he had to spend long hours stretched out and tied down to boards.[24]

"He went through hell," Meyer later remembered. "I used to feel so sorry for him."[25]

Since Meyer had to be away from Boston for much of the week doing business, Buddy's chief companion became his mother. There was a streak of nervousness running through the Citron family, and Anne's own nerves had been quite badly frayed by the ordeal of her elder son's disability. But the challenge drew something extra from her, and Anne Lansky was a good mother. When it came to her children, she seemed able to draw on extra resources. She had endless patience. She would sit with her son for long hours when he was confined to bed, trying to take his mind off the pain of his leg braces by reading him stories and playing games like go fish and checkers.

Anne Lansky was not domesticated, however. "My mother couldn't boil water," Buddy remembered.[26]

Down in New York, Anne Lansky had amassed maids and nannies like dresses from Wilma's, and the same went for Boston. The running of the apartment at 100 Beacon Street depended on a cook and also on a Filipino butler, Tommy, who, in the absence of Meyer, did some of the things for Buddy that fathers are supposed to do.[27] It was Tommy who took Buddy Lansky to his first baseball game — the Boston Braves versus the New York Giants at Braves Field[28] — carrying the child to his seat so that Buddy did not have to struggle painfully up the steps, as he was supposed to. Dr. Carruthers's therapy was quite strict, relying on a good measure of self-help from the patient.

Facially, the two Lansky boys, Buddy and Paul, resembled their father, with the wide, monkey grin and the inviting eyes of Meyer's private and more approachable face. Neither of them was very tall. But they were both overflowing with energy, and as they grew up, they became quite mischievous little boys. One weekend when their father and mother were out together, Paul and Buddy started playing around in their parents' bathroom, washing their clothes in the toilet and squirting water at each other with their mother's douche, a cumbersome rubber contraption which they happened to let fall from the window at the very moment their parents returned home.[29]

This is the only time in his life that Buddy Lansky could remember being hit by his parents — but it was his mother who administered the punishment. When, on another occasion, Buddy was caught swearing, it was his mother who, in traditional fashion, washed out his mouth with soap.[30] Meyer would get angry with his sons from time to time, threatening the direst consequences. But the boys soon discovered that Dad seldom followed through on his threats. The man with the eyes — the professor of intimidation — was putty in the hands of his children.

Meyer even seemed, in some ways, to connive at his two sons' indiscipline. Anne believed that the children should have liver for supper at least once a week, but the two boys hated it. So they would wait until their mother had given the day's menu to the cook, then slip into the kitchen and order changes to the items that they did not like. When Meyer heard about that, he just laughed. He thought it showed great enterprise.[31]

As he moved to and fro between Boston and New York, Meyer was out of touch with his family for much of the time. But the lack of contact that mattered was emotional. In material terms, Meyer Lansky was a generous father. He bought his children the best of everything — toys and presents, construction kits, a huge, authentic electric train set — just as, quite frugal himself, he provided the money to support the spending of his wife. He knew, somehow, what he was supposed to do.

But when it came to himself, Meyer found it more difficult to give. His commitment to his crippled son could hardly be doubted, but he could not communicate his feelings in any direct fashion — and he never had enough time. Buddy remembered his father's giving him a Monopoly set and never once playing the game with him. When it came to real treats, and to the fun of doing something with a grown-up, Meyer's sons looked to Tommy, the butler, or to their mother's elder brother, Jules — Uncle Julie — who was in the Citron family produce and grocery business.

When Buddy was in New York, Uncle Julie, who did not yet have children of his own, would take his nephew to Giants games, where the chirpy and gregarious little cripple made something of an impression with the occupants of the surrounding box seats. One night,

Buddy stayed at home, and Julie Citron took his brother-in-law, Meyer, to the ballpark instead. But the evening got off to an uneasy start for Meyer when the neighbors in the box seats greeted Julie with the question, "Where's your son tonight?"[32]

"He was a good father," said Buddy Lansky, "as far as giving us everything. I mean, there was never anything we wanted. . . ."[33]

In the late 1930s, Isabel Schlossman, newly graduated from nursing school, was hired as a special nurse to look after Yetta, Mrs. Max Lansky. Meyer's mother had had eye surgery, and she had to remain in the hospital, lying quietly in bed with her eyes covered, for the best part of two weeks. There was ample staff available in the hospital, but Meyer wanted his mother to be cared for by her own, private, full-time nurse.

Meyer came to the hospital to visit his mother almost every day. He would sit by her bedside for long hours, talking and listening intently. As he left, he would always take the young nurse aside and ask if she could suggest anything that would make her patient more comfortable.[34]

"He showed much compassion," says Isabel Schlossman.[35]

At the end of the two weeks, Meyer asked Isabel to accompany his mother home, and to continue caring for her until she was thoroughly recovered. So every morning, just as Meyer's sister, Esther, was leaving for work, Isabel would arrive at the Max Lanskys' apartment on Ocean Parkway near Prospect Park, Brooklyn — it was "most elegantly furnished," she remembers, "in fine taste."[36]

Max Lansky himself was now an old man — tall, straight, rather handsome, and nattily dressed, with a cane. He was long retired. His savings as a garment presser could not have sustained the fashion in which he and Yetta now lived, in quite a classy part of Brooklyn, with a maid.[37] It was the two Lansky boys who kept their parents in such style.

Meyer maintained his regular visits to his mother, coming down from Manhattan to Brooklyn almost daily. His arrival was always something of a relief for Isabel, who did not know much Yiddish, but who struggled gamely to read out to her patient the daily letters in the "Bintel Brief," Abraham Cahan's popular advice column in the *Jewish Daily Forward.*

Meyer would get into deep conversation with his mother. From time to time, he would pick up the phone and call his children so that they could talk to their grandmother, long distance.[38] Isabel

Schlossman had no reason to think that this rather shy and dutiful son was anything other than a respectable businessman. Meyer Lansky's name had never been in the newspapers.

"He was a taciturn, soft-spoken, almost bashful man, as I observed him," says Isabel Schlossman today.[39]

What struck the young nurse most was the closeness between mother and son. Ill though she was, Yetta clearly played the role of matriarch in the household, and Meyer responded to her strength. Yetta thought the world of her clever elder boy, and Meyer responded to that affection. He put his mother on a pedestal.

In later years, Meyer was to settle his mother, with Jake's help, in a comfortable retirement apartment near the sea in Hollywood, Florida. He kept up his regular visits whenever he was there, making sure that the grandchildren did their duty, and that, as Yetta grew frailer, her doctors and nurses gave her the very best in medical care.[40]

Yetta Lansky was to die in June 1959, poor in sight in her later years, but very rich in the affection of her two sons — and of her elder son, in particular. Meyer had made good on his childhood vow that, for the rest of her days, his mother should have only the best.

Meyer Lansky's relationship with his father was not such a warm and happy matter. Max Lansky had never been reconciled to his elder son's way of life — Meyer's giving up of his steady job at the tool-and-die shop, the cash and danger of the crap games and the bootlegging. Max could not take pride in a son who made his living from breaking the law — and he did not try to hide his disappointment.[41]

"My grandfather," remembered Buddy, "disliked everything that my father did."[42]

It was not just that Meyer had thrown up the honest career that his father had taken some trouble to arrange. Meyer had also taken advantage of his younger brother's loyalty to lure Jake outside the law, making Jake, to all intents and purposes, his accomplice. Max Lansky, with his old-fashioned mustache and his old-fashioned values, found himself the father of a couple of wiseguys.

The conflict expressed itself in terms of Jewishness and the grandchildren. To his father's displeasure, Meyer was not bringing up his boys with any sense of their roots. There was bacon in the Meyer Lansky household, and the Gentile ritual of gift-giving was much enjoyed every December 25 — around a tall, decorated Christmas tree.

The Christmas tree shocked even the Citrons, who were a comparatively easygoing clan. "You don't like it?" said Anne when her mother remonstrated at the presence of the tree. "Go home!"[43]

Little Buddy Lansky only found out that he was Jewish — and what kosher food tasted like — when he went to his grandparents' for Passover. Neither he nor his brother, Paul, was Bar Mitzvahed, and the first time that either boy saw the inside of a temple was at their aunt Esther's wedding in the late 1930s. The rabbi in his beard and costume looked ridiculous to them.

"Why don't you get a shave?" called out Buddy, cheekily. The Lansky boys spent the rest of the ceremony outside.[44]

Max Lansky was particularly upset by Meyer's failure to send Buddy and Paul to *cheder* for religious instruction. The boys were wild and unruly. Grandma Citron, on the other side of the family, could not cope with them at all. When they came to stay with her, she was forever phoning the family grocery business in hysterics, so that Julie Citron would have to leave work to rescue her.[45]

Max Lansky felt that the boys needed roots. He argued frequently with Meyer about it. The discipline of the *cheder* would do the boys good. There was value to the tradition. It was what turned boys into men. But Max's arguments fell on deaf ears. Meyer was anxious for Buddy to take extra math lessons. But religion?

The disagreement was quite common in transplanted families of Meyer and Max Lansky's generations, the conflict between the New World and the Old getting entangled in the tensions between father and son.

Arnold Rothstein's father, Abraham, a respectable garment manufacturer, used to reprove Arnold for not following the example of his elder brother, Harry, who had taken *cheder* seriously. "I'm an American," shrugged Arnold. "Let Harry be a Jew."[46]

So far as Meyer Lansky was concerned, his Jewishness was a handicap he had had to fight to overcome. His own success had come, in his view, from his adventurous pursuit of the American way — in singular contrast to the path chosen by his father, an exploited drone in the garment industry, who had profited nothing from his adherence to the traditions of the old country.

The gap between father and son was never closed. Max Lansky was to die in 1939,[47] when Meyer was thirty-seven years old.

The Jewish tradition is for a son to remember his father every year on the anniversary of his death, lighting a candle and saying a prayer. But it was a tradition that Meyer Lansky chose not to keep, just as

he was disinclined to discuss his father when conversation got round
to his own childhood and his past.

Meyer never said anything that was directly disrespectful of his
father's memory. That was not his way. But it is, perhaps, difficult
for a son to feel great pride and affection for a father who never felt
great pride in him.

5

"Gambling Pulls at the Core of a Man"

FEDERAL Prohibition ended on December 5, 1933 — a chance for America to go straight. It was also a chance for individual bootleggers to wipe the slate clean and to make a fresh start.

On November 25, 1933, just ten days before Prohibition ended, Meyer Lansky became a partner in the Molaska Corporation, Inc., a company formed to supply dehydrated, powdered molasses to the about-to-be-reborn distilling industry.[1] Meyer's coinvestors included two of Cleveland's more successful bootleggers, Moe Dalitz and Sam Tucker, as well as Meyer's own father-in-law, Moses Citron, who served as the company's assistant treasurer.

Molaska had all the hallmarks of a shrewd and forward-looking investment. Powdered molasses was an inexpensive supplement to sugar in the distilling process, and the Molaska Corporation was using new production techniques to get in on the ground floor of what promised to be a boom business after the repeal of the Volstead Act. Here was a profitable opportunity for Meyer Lansky to go "legit."

But bootlegging in America did not end with Prohibition. The "drys," who defended Volstead to the end, finally surrendered on the promise that stiff taxes would be levied on alcohol once it was relegalized. These taxes stimulated a lively traffic in the production and smuggling of contraband, untaxed liquor, and this was the promising new market in which the Molaska Corporation chose to deal: the supply of raw material for illegal, post-Prohibition distilling.

In the early months of 1935, agents of the Bureau of Alcohol and Tobacco raided factories in Zanesville, Ohio, and in Elizabeth, New Jersey, to discover vast illegal distilleries which were using Molaska molasses as a staple of their production process. The Zanesville plant was a major facility. It had the capacity to produce as many as twenty thousand bottles of 190-proof alcohol per day — the largest illegal distillery ever discovered by the Bureau of Alcohol and Tobacco. The plant at Elizabeth, New Jersey, was not much smaller.[2]

In later life, Meyer Lansky would eye the success of apparently respectable businessmen like Samuel Bronfman and Lewis Rosensteil, liquor magnates who had laid the foundations of their fortunes during Prohibition.

"Why is Lansky a 'gangster,'" he complained to Uri Dan in the 1970s, "and not the Bronfman and Rosensteil families?"[3]

Both Bronfman and Rosensteil peddled illegal liquor during the years of Prohibition, but after 1933 each man made a point of striking out for the high road in his own respective fashion. They never became saints, but they saw a corner to turn and they turned it.[4]

If Meyer Lansky ever saw that turning point, he chose not to take it. He did not become a legal liquor distributor. Nor did he capitalize on his car and truck rental experience — a golden business opportunity, as it turned out. Only just entering his thirties, Meyer Lansky had grown accustomed to doing things the crooked way. In the course of their investigations, the agents of the Alcohol and Tobacco tax division unearthed evidence connecting Meyer and his partners with no fewer than eight different illicit stills.[5]

Within weeks of the raids on Zanesville and Elizabeth, however, the Molaska Corporation declared bankruptcy,[6] and the various federal and local agents investigating the cases were never able to link the distilleries directly with the partners in the defunct company. Meyer's father-in-law, Moses Citron, was quite a crafty businessman, and it was his lawyer, Aaron Sapiro, who had structured Molaska's confusing web of front men and hidden investments.[7] The investigators could lay their hands on nothing solid, and Meyer Lansky was able to skip unscathed from the wreckage.

The Molaska adventure demonstrated Meyer Lansky's continuing mastery of subterfuge and the quick profit — the sharp, easy, clever way of doing business. But the world had changed in 1933, and the newly law-abiding careers of Samuel Bronfman and Lewis Rosensteil suggested that the old, sharp, easy way was no longer necessarily the cleverest.

One autumn day in the mid-1930s, when the Lanskys were living in New York, Meyer had telephoned Anne to let her know that he would not be home for dinner that night. She should not bother to prepare any food for him, he said. He phoned her again, later in the day, to repeat the message, and he made at least one more call which gave her the same news.

So Anne Lansky was surprised that evening, at dinnertime, when her husband turned up at the apartment in the company of his brother, Jake, and another friend. All that Anne had to offer the unexpected arrivals was a few lamb chops — and the conversation of her mother, Grandma Citron, who had come round to keep her company.

It was not the hospitality that Meyer Lansky had envisioned for his guests, and he lost his temper. He was rude to his mother-in-law, then started quarreling with Anne, seizing a hot potato from a dish. In his anger, Meyer flung the hot potato at his wife, hitting her in the eye.[8]

Looking back in later years, Anne Lansky set 1933 as the time when her marriage started to lose its first bloom. It was a time of strain and readjustment, for 1933 was the year when Prohibition ended, and that meant an end to much of Meyer's income as well. When Anne's elder brother, Jules — Uncle Julie — happened to run into Meyer on Delancey Street around this time, and casually asked his brother-in-law how he was doing, he discovered that he had struck a sore spot.

"I'm not making any money," Meyer replied, with uncharacteristic bluntness, complaining to Julie that he was having to get by on "ten thousand a year."[9]

Ten thousand dollars — some $160,000 in early 1990s' terms[10] — struck Julie Citron as a very comfortable sum indeed. But it was less than Meyer Lansky needed, with his homes in New York and Boston, the bills for Buddy's therapy, the comfort of his retired parents, and his wife's shopping habit to support. The Molaska Corporation might have kept Meyer's income flowing, but it had rapidly proved an almost disastrous dead end.

So Meyer Lansky was driven back to the expertise with which he had won his very first illegal nickel. Like Charlie and Benny, Meyer had kept his crap games going throughout the bootlegging years, and the end of Prohibition brought him back to his primary virtuosity — his original love, which he was now to pursue steadily for the rest of his life.

From 1933 onward, Meyer Lansky could most accurately be defined as a "gambler," the somewhat confusing American legal term for someone who makes his living from organizing games of chance — as opposed to the person who wagers and plays, and who is, technically, a "bettor." In 1933, the statutes of every state of the Union, bar Nevada, prohibited gambling. So in pursuing his vocation as a gambler, Meyer Lansky was continuing to direct his career toward the wrong side of the law.

Meyer had learned the basics of his craft in the crap games of the Lower East Side, and as his games attracted better players and higher stakes, he had graduated to rub shoulders with the likes of Fat Al Levy.[11] New York's gamblers and bettors were a relatively small fraternity in the 1920s and 1930s. Most of the action took place in floating crap games and pickup rooms, which were organized individually and which found themselves niches ranging from the back rooms of bars to suites in the grandest hotels on Manhattan. It was a fragmented series of worlds, scattered and secretive. But once a year, everyone gathered together for a month of open license — gambling included — when they boarded the train and headed north up the Hudson Valley to Manhattan's annual summer camp, the August racing season at Saratoga Springs, New York.

It was the therapeutic qualities of Saratoga's sulfur baths and waters that first drew visitors to the little spa town, 30 miles north of Albany and 190 miles north of Manhattan. The racetrack opened in 1863. Southern grandees forsook their plantations for the summer season, and they brought north the casino games that they had learned to enjoy on the Mississippi riverboats. By the 1890s, the casinos of Saratoga in their month of summer glory rivaled those of Europe's most glamorous spas. Monte Carlo was the Saratoga Springs of the French Riviera. Saratoga's two principal hotels on the main street, the Grand Union and the United States, were the two largest hotels in the world.

The first great casinos of Saratoga Springs were presided over by John Morrissey, the onetime prizefighter who, with the help of Tammany Hall, became both a congressman and a prominent New York City gambling boss in the later decades of the nineteenth century.

Morrissey paid off Saratoga's local political bosses, then transported his Manhattan dealers and croupiers out to the country each summer. By the early 1920s, it was Arnold Rothstein who brought out his table crews on a similar basis — and it was under the umbrella of Arnold Rothstein in the 1920s that aspiring young wiseguys like Meyer Lansky and Lucky Luciano first came to Saratoga.[12]

In Saratoga, as everywhere else, Rothstein worked through loose and flexible partnerships. He had to have at least one local partner who could arrange the fix with the local political machines. Then Rothstein needed specialists to take care of the dining room and entertainment, along with the individual gambling games and tables in his casino. It was through running franchises inside Rothstein's Saratoga casinos that Meyer Lansky and Lucky Luciano graduated from crap games to greater things.[13]

Saratoga in the month of August was a community given up to chance in all its forms. From seven in the morning the clubhouse served breakfast at the track, where the dedicated student of form could study the horses in whose performance he would be investing later. He could work up an appetite for lunch with a massage and scrubdown in the fierce-smelling but therapeutic atmosphere of the sulfur baths. And then there were the afternoon races, a blur of dust, betting slips, racing silks, and soiled dollar bills changing hands in vast quantities. The gothic green-and-white wooden grandstands of Saratoga were the setting for some of the most elegant and formal racing in America.

The last race was over by six P.M., and then the action shifted out of town to institutions that were as particular to Saratoga as their sulfurous bath parlors: the "lake houses," exotic and mysterious pleasure palaces that lay out in the woods surrounding Saratoga Lake. The Arrowhead Inn, the Piping Rock, the Brook, Riley's, Newman's — they were so many rambling manor houses, each with its own dining room, dance floor, and gaming salon. Every August, racegoers and owners went out to Saratoga's lake houses to play and wager in an ambience of fine wine, excellent food, and some of the most spectacular floor shows to be seen anywhere in America.

Saratoga's month of summer indulgence operated on the basis of bribery and corruption, but it was bribery with a sense of style, while the corruption bore something of the character of a community chest. Down in Manhattan, Tammany Hall and the political clubs were special-interest groups which operated, in many respects, at the expense of the city as a whole. Out in the foothills of the Adirondacks, the payoff bore a more dispersed and bucolic character, and almost everybody got in on the act.

The lake houses existed to soak the rich visitors, not the local poor. It was almost impossible, in fact, for a local — poor or otherwise — to get into a casino, which, in every lake house, was housed in a separate building, or in a part of the building which could be easily and obviously sealed off from the restaurant, bar, and dance floor. The fiction was that the lake houses were no more than high-class dining and entertainment establishments. So if busybodies or reformers made enough fuss, the police might arrange an inspection — with appropriate advance notice — and then report that they had seen no gambling on the premises.

Saratoga's political bosses — Dr. Arthur J. Leonard, a Democrat, in town, and Jim Leary, a successful lawyer who ran the Republican machine out in Saratoga County — were not so crass as to accept any payoffs directly from the lake houses, nor from any other of the enterprises that generated so much illegal cash in the month of August. Rather, they used the track, the horse parlors, and the out-of-town casinos as sources of patronage and reward for party and personal loyalty. Republican farmers were given guaranteed contracts for the supply of milk, eggs, and meat, and there were several hundred part-time jobs to be filled, from dishwashers to hat-check girls.[14]

There were also the no-show jobs. Loyal party supporters, and the sons of supporters, were told to report for "work" to such-and-such casino on a particular evening. They would receive their pay packet and be told to come back a week later for the next installment. Relatives of local police officers — and in some cases, the officers themselves — were specially favored for this sort of retainer.

Almost everyone got rich when the casinos came to town — and the lake house operators were particularly careful to ensure that the local charities and churches received their fair share. The Redemptorist Fathers of St. Clement's Church ran their fund-raising bazaar every year in the month of August. The food was catered by the lake houses' gourmet chefs, and the bingo stall was operated by gentlemen whose mastery of the numbers patter was polished with most evident expertise. The highlight of the afternoon was entertainment by one or more of the acts currently appearing beside the lake — Sophie Tucker, Hildegarde, the comedy duo Cross and Dunn.[15] The good fathers could not believe their luck. They had the best church bazaar in America.

The Saratoga lake house, part speakeasy, part gentlemen's club, was where Meyer Lansky learned to put together the components that make a class casino. The lake houses were plush and stylish, and they were, above all, reputable. The Saratoga Bar Association held its annual dinner at Newman's.[16] The scions of America's greatest names and fortunes drove out of town to stroll into the lake houses as unashamedly as if they were entering church, and it was the ability to attract these customers, the high rollers, that made for a successful August.

"Gambling," said Meyer Lansky at the age of sixty-nine, "pulls at the core of a man."[17]

Meyer was looking back on a career spent in the rattle, click, and murmur of the gaming room — the green felt, the dark wood, the glamorous, brightly colored chips. He was talking of the players, the men with their eyes and their hearts fixed on the table, losing themselves, and hoping to find something else in their contest with the dice or card or wheel. But Meyer Lansky could have been talking about himself, for it was in the course of his Saratoga summers that he discovered he was made to run casinos.[18]

The foundation of it all was the figures — the margins of advantage on which a casino's profits are based.[19] On a mechanical game like roulette, the house has a 2.7 percent advantage when the wheel has one zero. In craps, the house advantage depends on the bet — 1.4 percent on "pass," and from 2.6 percent to 5.2 percent on "field," depending on the layout of the table. In modern Las Vegas, the more tourist-oriented casinos of the Strip take an average of 5.3 percent from the crap tables, while the odds in the purist crap games in the downtown casinos are laid out to take only 2.6. The only casino game in which the player has an even chance of winning, and can actually hope to get a slight edge on the house, is blackjack (vingt-et-un, twenty-one) — provided that the player has the ability to "count" the cards, keeping track of them in his head. For this reason, it is the custom of many casinos to ban card counters when they detect them. A good blackjack player who does not count yields an advantage, on average, of 0.75–1.5 percent to the house.[20]

All these figures compound into different statistics as players wager and rewager their stakes. There are good nights and bad nights, and the house needs a large enough bankroll to tide it through the times when the games are running the wrong way. Meyer Lansky was proud to have bankrolled losses of up to $100,000 a night.[21] But over the weeks, the percentages come home to the last decimal place, and, given cost control, the difference between good business and bad business is simply turnover.

Running a casino is an art form all its own: the ability to conjure up the glamour and escapism that will entice others to wager — the illusion that money is not really money — while retaining your own workaday, bedrock restraint, the ruthless sense of business to make sure that the cash ends up in your pocket. Meyer Lansky had the sense of style, and he also had the discipline.

One lesson he had learned in the crap games of the Lower East Side was that the principal ingredient for long-term gaming success is not flashiness but probity. It is easy to fix a roulette wheel or to rig a game of craps — as Meyer himself had had the game rigged against him, as a boy, on the sidewalk of Delancey. But such tricks can only yield temporary dividends. The moment that serious players sniff the slightest suspicion that the games are rigged against them, they will go elsewhere, and the word spreads quickly. A crap game or a casino can be dead in a matter of hours, and once dead, it stays dead. So, as with his bootlegging, Meyer Lansky found himself in an illegal enterprise where enduring success depended on being honest.

"Everyone who came into my casino," Meyer later said with pride, "knew that if he lost his money it wouldn't be because he was cheated."[22]

Honesty in a casino, however, is a relative concept. Winning a big bet is like pulling off a successful crime. The bottom line in gambling is the desire for reward without effort, and casinos attract every class of adherent to that seductive quest — on both sides of the table. Running a good casino thus revolves around containment of the cheating which may come from any direction, and particularly from the casino's own employees. It is a special sort of man who is drawn to work long hours through the night, dealing cards and raking dice for hourly wages, while hundreds of thousands of dollars pass through his hands. Cheating on the part of a dealer can range from palming chips and cash, to contriving the success of an accomplice at the table, who is ostensibly a player.

Meyer Lansky had studied such tricks in the crap games of the Lower East Side, and over the years he had come to know the dealers he could trust. As well as setting the momentum of a game, the dealers are in charge of the money, and they must have the ability to calculate, in fractions of a second, how many chips should be pushed out to the winners — and to get that sum right. If they shortchange a player, he will soon let them know about it. If they give him too much, he is not likely to make so much fuss.

Lansky paid a salary plus commission to the men that he hired for the month in Saratoga — their wages, plus a percentage of the "drop" on their table every night.[23] The percentage made them watch themselves, and it encouraged them to watch each other. Meyer's dealers came to form teams, cohesive little groups that were linked by mutual professionalism and trust.

American gaming in the 1990s is a mass-market business. The casinos of modern Las Vegas and Atlantic City depend on the endless drip of quarters into the maw of their flashing slot machines. In the 1930s, serious gaming and serious business were done at the tables by a small and relatively exclusive group of wealthy players. Winning their wary and demanding patronage was the challenge facing an operator like Meyer Lansky, and August by August through the 1930s, his business quietly grew.

Meyer operated his gambling as he had operated his bootlegging, in joint-venture partnerships in which his main role was to organize the money and the share-out. By the years before the Second World War, he was part of a partnership running one of the most successful casinos in the woods beside Saratoga Lake — the Piping Rock, a long, low, raffish establishment with something of a Moorish character. Its pale apricot stucco walls were studded with covered balconies and plaited wood mashrebeeyahs. There was a porte cochère where you might almost have expected a Rudolph Valentino to leap from the back of his Arabian steed. Uniformed parking jockeys dealt with the parade of Packards and Cadillacs which drove out from town every night.

Meyer's principal partners in the Piping Rock were Frank Costello, who brought out the chefs, maître d', and engraved silverware from his Manhattan club, the Copacabana,[24] and Joe Adonis, the handsome, fleshy operator of New Jersey's most successful gambling joints. Adonis brought his table crews — and his most prosperous clients — north to Saratoga in August, and Meyer invited his own best customers up from Manhattan. As front man, the trio enlisted a local businessman, Francis Tierney, whose name went on the paperwork as the official licensee, and whose job it was to arrange the fix.[25]

The traditional Saratoga recipe for attracting money onto the gaming tables had been for swashbuckling impresarios to preside personally over their casinos as so many ringmasters, meeting and greeting and slapping on the back. But this was not Meyer Lansky's style. Careful and cautious, he stayed in the background.

"Inconspicuous is the word," says a crap dealer who worked for him in these years. "You didn't even know he was there, and when he was there, he looked like nothing."[26]

In the limited documentation summarizing the details of the Piping Rock partnership, Meyer Lansky's name was not even on the record. He had his own share placed in the name of his brother, Jake.[27]

Such reticence was the norm among the gamblers who moved into Saratoga every August in the 1930s. Arnold Rothstein had operated high profile, running his own racehorses on the Saratoga track. But his successors were more discreet. In 1935, the inquiring new money magazine *Fortune* went to Saratoga Springs to analyze the town's curious, once-a-year holiday economy, from the tidy sums that the Whitneys and Vanderbilts spent on their horses, to the activities of the rooming-house hookers. Investigating these ladies, and Saratoga's other groups of furtive itinerants, *Fortune* identified the lake houses and the gambling that went on there. But the magazine could not come up with the names of any owners or partners, only managing a passing reference to the presence in town that summer of Charlie Luciano, whom they described as "Capone's numbers man."[28]

Fortune did well to get that close. Lucky Luciano, Frank Costello, Joe Adonis, and Meyer Lansky were not at all anxious for the notoriety that they later attained, and the magazine's ill-informed picture of Luciano as an underling of Capone is a reminder of just how little was generally known, as late as August 1935, about these rather unusual men and the ways in which they made their money.

With the repeal of the Volstead Act, America hoped it might have rid itself of the urban gangster. Crime, as popularly perceived, took on a more dashing, Robin Hood face, thanks to the escapades of the automobile bandits — John Dillinger, Machine Gun Kelly, Baby Face Nelson, Pretty Boy Floyd, Bonnie and Clyde — the wave of motorized cowboys who enlivened the gloom of the Depression by giving local banks the treatment many people thought they deserved. Marauding adventurers who made no pretense at trying to work inside society, the automobile bandits represented crime that was anything but "organized."

The dramatic pursuit of these picaresque, numbered "public ene-mies" made national heroes of J. Edgar Hoover and his agents, the G-men of the FBI. The cross-country car chases and the unfailingly successful shoot-outs in which they ended were Hollywood brought to real life, crime as people quite like to experience it: thrilling with-out being threatening, and defeated reassuringly, with no loose ends.

But the gangsters had not gone away. The illegal economies of America's cities had been powerfully reinforced by bootlegging's prof-its and by the corruption that they fostered, and five years before Prohibition came to an end it was possible to see the future pattern emerging.

"Racketeering," the *Daily Express* informed its British readers in September 1928, "is the new word that has been coined in America to describe the big business of organised crime."[29]

The use of "racket" to define a scheme yielding money by illegal or improper means went back to the early 1800s, but it was in the late 1920s that America's newspapers and magazines seized on the word to bring it into popular parlance.[30] Extortion and the threat of violence were identifying characteristics of any racket. So was an ele-ment of self-sustaining, almost functional profit, and by the early years of the Depression, the term was generally used to sum up all that was nefarious, corrupt, and frightening about life in the big city: "the rackets."

There were the fresh produce rackets. New York's meat, fish, and perishable fruit and vegetable trades all operated in networks that linked the waterfront, the food markets, and the hotel and restaurant business. At the mercy of labor and handling delays, they paid tribute at every connection, not least to the teamsters on whose trucks they depended.

"Racketeering is a new word," said Frederick Kernochan, chief justice of the New York Court of Special Sessions, to a Senate com-mittee investigating rackets in 1933, "but what they do is old."[31]

New York's garment industry supported some of the most vicious rackets of all. Lepke Buchalter and Gurrah Shapiro were hired as *shtarkes* by the garment unions to do battle with management strike-breakers, and they exerted that muscle most effectively. But they also strong-armed their way into the ownership of rag trade firms as the price of guaranteeing their new partners labor peace, later deploying their hired toughs to do the same in the bakery and flour-trucking industries.

Charlie Luciano concentrated on what could be classified as the service rackets: bookmaking, numbers, prostitution, some narcotics smuggling.[32] Benny Siegel ran crap games and also made book. Frank Costello's line was slot machines — one-armed bandits — along with a share in the business of New York's largest bookmaker, Frank Erickson. Meyer Lansky's niche was as a crap-game and casino specialist, and he remained the master of the share-out — in the deals that he approved of, at least.

Meyer steered himself scrupulously clear of Charlie's involvement in prostitution and drugs. They lay on the other side of a barrier that he would not cross. "I haven't ever dealt in narcotics," he told the New York newspaper editor Paul Sann in 1975, with a mixture of pride and distaste. "I dislike people dealing in it."[33]

Being cronies did not mean having to invest in everything together. By a selective morality which he shared with Frank Costello, Meyer Lansky was happy to stay friends with Charlie Luciano and to do business with him in "clean" rackets, like gambling. But when it came to drugs and hookers, Charlie was on his own. Costello and Lansky both worked within a wary etiquette which exploited the tolerance that society extended them, while also sensing the limits beyond which that tolerance would not go.

There was a similar etiquette when it came to violence. Lepke and Gurrah routinely enforced their power with beatings and killings. It was an integral part of their business, fully justifying the unforgettable title bestowed on them by Harry Feeny, of the New York World Telegram — "Murder, Inc."[34]

Charlie Luciano used violence in a less frequent, almost political sense. He owed his position to the killings of Masseria and Maranzano. But service rackets like numbers, gambling, and bookmaking generally avoided any more violence than was necessary — the exception to this rule being Benny Siegel, who got into a fight whenever he possibly could.

Meyer Lansky and Frank Costello saw themselves as standing back one step further still. Costello had started off a young street tough like Meyer, but both men were now anxious to forget those days. Frank and Meyer both reckoned they had learned to get what they wanted in business without the necessity of hurting people — and when it came to attracting legitimate high rollers to a Saratoga lake house, violence and criminality were the very last impressions they needed to convey.

By the mid-1930s, the boys no longer met at Ratner's. They had moved uptown to grander surroundings — the Waldorf Apartments at the Waldorf-Astoria Hotel. "Charlie and Ben lived for a while in the Waldorf," Meyer later remembered. "I often visited Ben and his family there."[35] Other tenants at the Waldorf Apartments in these years included former president Herbert Hoover.[36]

Luxuriating in their suites or in the Waldorf's Norse Grill, Charlie Luciano and Benny Siegel were impressive proof of how well the rackets could pay. Frank Costello and his tall, plump bookmaking partner, Frank Erickson, liked to start off their day in the Waldorf with a shave and manicure in the mirrored opulence of the barbershop. There were leather seats by the door, and the barbershop became an informal headquarters.

"We sort of met there mornings," Meyer recalled. "I spoke often about gambling to both Franks, Charlie, and Ben."[37]

Staying within the boundaries that prudence suggested to him, Meyer saw nothing to be ashamed of in the gaming rackets that he made his own. "I chose my role the same way as any businessman chooses his role," he later said.[38]

Meyer had identified and was seizing his profit in the gray area between what society defined as illegal and what it tolerated as necessary. As Walter Lippmann said: "The underworld performs many services that respectable members of society call for."[39]

Lippmann was talking of service racketeering, but the same could be said, socially and economically, of racketeering as a whole. The racketeer was sometimes violent, and he was invariably illicit, but he made things possible. Bringing together the connections by which America's exploding urban communities could get themselves supplied and organized, smoothing the relations between labor and management, the rackets were the grease that enabled the machinery of a big city like New York to keep functioning.

In the aftermath of the stock market crash, however, and several years into the Depression, the people of New York did not see things in this way. As living got harder, the racketeer was no longer envied or admired as the facilitating middleman. He was the symbol of all that was going wrong in a complex, frightening, and increasingly impersonal world — and his political accomplices paid the price. In September 1932, Mayor Jimmy Walker resigned, compromised by the proof of payoffs and by the suspicion of his links to Arnold Rothstein.

In 1929, Fiorello La Guardia had been defeated when he ran against Walker and Tammany on the Rothstein issue. Four years later, La Guardia was swept into office on a wave of reformist sentiment, and the new mayor promptly appointed a new police commissioner, Lewis J. Valentine, an upright officer who had actually been demoted in Tammany days for his ardor in pursuing corruption.[40]

La Guardia's most memorable statement of intent was to pile more than a thousand slot machines onto a barge in October 1934 and to set about demolishing them with a sledgehammer. Many of these one-armed bandits belonged to Frank Costello, and they had been seized from bars, clubhouses, and fraternities which had been operating for years under the protection of Tammany. The bumptious little mayor flung them cheerfully into the waters of Long Island Sound.[41]

Thirty-three years old, humorless, fierce and uncompromising, Thomas E. Dewey was the most immediate consequence of New York's new political climate for Meyer Lansky, Lucky Luciano, and their friends. In the summer of 1935, Dewey was appointed the city's special prosecutor, with responsibility for rackets. La Guardia had won the mayoralty in 1933, but Tammany had managed to hold on to the district attorney's office. So Dewey was made special prosecutor to bypass the district attorney. His brief was to attack the very people that Tammany would not touch.

Dewey later traced his horror of gangsters to the election day late in the 1920s when, freshly arrived from Owosso, Michigan, he had volunteered for polling-place duty as a Republican party worker on 110th Street. His Democrat-Tammany counterparts turned out to be a menacing gang of hoodlums in the pay of Dutch Schultz, and the young Dewey had watched helpless as they escorted bogus voters and double-voters in and out of the polling place all day with the open connivance of the police.[42]

At eight-thirty on the evening of July 30, 1935, in the first days of his appointment as special prosecutor, Dewey broadcast an appeal to the people of New York. The city, he proclaimed, had fallen victim to "organized gangs of low-grade outlaws who lack either the courage or the intelligence to earn an honest living." There was scarcely a household in New York which did not suffer from their depredations, paying a tribute that was "levied by force and collected by fear." The power exercised by racketeers on the waterfront, in the city's food markets and bakeries, and in enterprises like the garment trade represented, he said, "a huge, unofficial sales tax" by which the honest subsidized the corrupt.[43]

Salvation, Dewey stated, lay in New York's own hands. Racketeers "succeed only so long as they can prey upon the fears and weaknesses of disorganized or timid witnesses." The new special prosecutor appealed to his listeners to stand up and make a difference. "If you have evidence of organized crime," he concluded, "bring it to us. . . . The rest is our job. We will do our best."[44]

The public response was overwhelming. In a single month, three thousand New Yorkers jostled and queued to get into Dewey's office on the fourteenth floor of the Woolworth Building, where earnest young law school graduates noted their complaints and information on five-by-eight-inch cards.*

Dewey had no difficulty deciding on his first target — Dutch Schultz. By 1935, the former Arthur Flegenheimer occupied a place in America's demonology comparable to that of Capone in Chicago half a dozen years earlier. Controlling one of New York's most prosperous numbers rackets, photographed frequently, complete with entourage, on champagne-drenched tours of his protected restaurants, and spectacularly fixing one trial which had seemed certain to bring him to justice, Dutch Schultz had made himself the nation's number-one racketeer, the man that Thomas E. Dewey just had to get.

It was the underworld that got Schultz first. On the night of October 23, 1935, two gunmen strode into the back room of the Palace Bar and Chop House in Newark, New Jersey, where Schultz was dining in the company of two bodyguards and Otto "Abbadabba" Berman, the legendary accountant of his numbers racket. They shot all four men dead — or almost dead in the case of Schultz himself. The Dutchman lingered on for twenty hours while detectives sat by his hospital bedside trying to make sense of his final, oddly poetic ramblings: "I want harmony, oh, mamma, mamma. . . . It is confused and it says no. A boy has never wept, nor dashed a thousand kim . . . ."[46]

---

*More than two thousand lawyers applied for the twenty jobs on Dewey's legal staff. Of the twenty he selected, fourteen had graduated from either Harvard or Columbia law school, seven were Republicans, six were Democrats, and the remainder "Fusionists" or Independents. The oldest was forty, the youngest twenty-five, and half of them were Jews. In the 1930s, Jews were still admitted to the Ivy League schools in limited quotas, and New York's established law firms operated on a similar basis, if they admitted any Jews at all.[45]

What Schultz was trying to say, and who gave the order to kill him, have never been determined. The two hit men never talked.[47] At the time, the murder was interpreted as the culling of an erratic rogue elephant by tougher, fitter males in the herd, and Police Commissioner Valentine told the press who he thought Schultz's successors would be.

"The new combination," he told the New York Times, "consists of gangs headed by six notorious racketeers: Charles (Lucky) Luciana, Charles (Buck) Siegel, Meyer Lansky, Louis (Lefty) Buckhouse, Jacob (Gurrah) Shapiro, and Abe (Longy) Zwillman, the last one of Newark."[48]

The commissioner's several mistakes of names and spelling suggested that the police knew less about the new "combination" than they claimed. But the names were enough. Newspapers dubbed the newly defined gangster elite the Big Six, and Thomas Dewey had a fresh set of targets to aim at. His five-by-eight cards had already thrown up the name of Lucky Luciano, and in June 1936, the thirty-four-year-old special prosecutor went for his man on a charge of compulsory prostitution.

Dewey's evidence was tenuous, and it depended heavily on the testimony of one streetwalker, a heroin addict known as "Cokey" Flo Brown, who told her story after she had been kept incarcerated, and drugless, for several days. Cokey Flo would have sworn to absolutely anything to get fresh supplies, argued Luciano's counsel derisively.

But Cokey Flo stood up well under nearly nine hours of cross-examination, and the jury chose to believe her story of Luciano's seeking to organize Manhattan's streetwalkers, through partners and underlings, into a businesslike combine. She described a meeting in a Chinese restaurant in which, she said, Luciano talked of organizing prostitution efficiently, "the same as the A&P"[49] — the chain of stores that was revolutionizing grocery and produce retailing with its new concept, the supermarket.

Dewey made much of Luciano's ostentatious lifestyle, the luxurious suites that he occupied in the Barbizon Plaza and the Waldorf-Astoria, getting himself personally serviced by a cluster of the prostitutes involved in the case — with disappointing results, according to one of them.[50]

"I gave to them. I never took," said Luciano, expressing a positive pride in his predilection for paid sex.[51]

The gangster boss made a poor impression when he took the stand, trying to parry Dewey's thrusts with inelegant asides, and getting caught by the special prosecutor in a number of crude deceptions.

Discussing the case in later years, Meyer Lansky always maintained that his friend was the victim of a fix. The girls were coerced, Meyer said, and their evidence only showed that Charlie was in the background of the racket.[52]

That was probably the case. But the evidence also revealed a man whose appetites had overwhelmed his judgment. Luciano had been a fool to invite women he scarcely knew to his apartment — while his concept of organizing whores off the shelf, A&P-style, suggested that, forgetting the lesson of Maranzano, he had succumbed to a dangerous grandiosity. The supermarket fantasy and the image of the hookers parading through the Waldorf did not prove Dewey's charge of compulsory prostitution, but they were enough to persuade the jury that New York would be a better place with Charles "Lucky" Luciano safely behind bars.

The trial of Lucky Luciano was the making of Thomas E. Dewey. At the age of thirty-four, the fierce-eyed special prosecutor with the bottlebrush mustache was an idol to millions, the first man to strike a blow against the evils of racketeering. Thomas E. Dewey was a real-life Dick Tracy, the original gangbuster, cheered whenever his image appeared on the newsreels.* In November 1937, Dewey had no difficulty winning election as New York district attorney, the beginning of what proved a glittering political career. Three times governor of New York, Dewey twice secured the Republican nomination for the presidency, and was to come within a whisker of defeating Harry Truman in 1948.

The fame was contagious. The hookers who had been the special prosecutor's key witnesses were invited to Hollywood, where they played themselves in one of the several instant movies that were

---

*Generations reared on the legend of "The Untouchables" might believe that the original gangbuster was Eliot Ness, the fearless foe of Al Capone in Chicago in the years 1929 to 1932. But Ness's team of seven incorruptible detectives did little more than harass Capone and his fellow bootleggers, while, quite independently, the IRS did the real job of bringing the gangster to court and convicting him. In the 1930s, Eliot Ness was scarcely known outside Chicago and Cleveland, where he became public safety director in 1935. He did not become an American hero until after his death, when the television series (which premiered in 1959) made him one.

based on the case, while Lucky Luciano himself became a national figure in the great and wicked gangster tradition — entering the pantheon with Rothstein, Capone, and Dutch Schultz even as he went to jail to start a thirty-to-fifty-year sentence. Little known previously outside his own, shadowy circle, Charlie was made famous by his downfall.

Meyer Lansky did not seek that kind of fame — or any other. The presence of his name on Commissioner Valentine's list marked his first appearance in the newspapers, while his own view that Charlie's conviction was rigged carried with it the lesson that Thomas E. Dewey would stop at nothing to convict any man who got in his sights. New York City was not, for the moment, a very comfortable place to stay.

But there were other corners of America where the fix still survived — and, thanks to his developing interests in the casino business, Meyer Lansky was now getting involved in a racket that actually functioned better out of town.

6

The Carpet Joints

THE colorful excesses of Prohibition from 1920 to 1933 — the speakeasies, the shoot-outs, the boats shuttling to and from Rum Row — are well established in the American folk memory. People have an awareness, too, of the maneuverings of the late 1940s in the Nevada desert, when outlaws and legalized gambling came together to create the neon empire of Las Vegas.

But there was a period in between, something of a forgotten era — more than a decade and a half from 1933 to the years after the Second World War — when the characteristics of the speakeasy and the Nevada casino were combined on the outskirts of cities all over America into a format which represented glamour, fun, and wickedness to a whole generation. This gaming roadhouse went by the name of the carpet joint, and it was in America's carpet joints of the 1930s and 1940s that Meyer Lansky rounded out his vocation as a gambler.

Modeled on the Saratoga lake house, the carpet joint was an upgrading of the more venerable and familiar sawdust joint with its rough-and-ready crap game in the back of a saloon or pool parlor. The carpet demonstrated the superior tone of the establishment, and there were embellishments to match: a uniformed doorman, an unctuous maître d' — the trimmings of a respectable restaurant or nightclub.

But a joint remained a joint, for all that — and the wickedness was part of the fun. Prohibition left America with a taste for disregarding laws that interfered with personal pleasure, and the illegal element of the carpet joint — the gambling — capitalized on that. The carpet joint's gaming tables — housed, as in Saratoga, discreetly separate from the rest of the establishment — subsidized the ingredients of the great American roadhouse night out: a good dinner, some dancing, and a Copacabana-style floor show that featured a magician, a comedian, and a big-name entertainer, the whole package topped and tailed by a chorus line of a dozen or so leggy beauties, generally known by a name that ended in *-ettes*.

As with the Saratoga lake house, the operation of the carpet joint depended on the fix, and for this reason it was usually situated across the state or county line from the conurbation which provided its principal clientele. Going to a gambling roadhouse involved a drive, often across a river — and invariably "across the line" — to a smaller, and usually more rural, community where the local police and politicians were more-or-less silent partners in the deal.

"Crossing the line" was made possible by the considerable rights and powers vested in America's individual states — and in the cities, counties, and townships within those states. Abortion, divorce, the death penalty, the color of car license plates — the practicalities of American daily life, great and small, were, and still are, regulated in state capitals, not in Washington, D.C.

The most striking example of crossing the line in the New York area was Ben Marden's Riviera, a nightclub-casino which operated every summer in Fort Lee, Bergen County, New Jersey, immediately across the George Washington Bridge. It was no longer possible, in the age of La Guardia and Dewey, for Manhattan gamblers to operate in fixed locations in the style of Al Levy's Down Town Merchants Club. So players and merrymakers made their way to the spot on Broadway where limousines were waiting to drive customers over the river to Ben Marden's white Art Deco pillbox, perched on the crest of the Palisades. A rolling roof opened up on fine summer nights for dancing beneath the stars, and upstairs was the gaming room — two blackjack tables, three crap tables, and six roulette wheels, all operating in plain sight of Manhattan.[1]

Lying on the west bank of the Hudson River, Bergen County became the particular asylum of gamblers who operated in New Jersey but who made their money from the population of New York. Meyer Lansky's Saratoga partner Joe Adonis ran phenomenally successful cash crap games in the Barn, a rough-hewn club a mile or so down the road from Ben Marden's Riviera,[2] and the business headquarters of Manhattan's major bookmakers were all situated in New Jersey. You could meet Frank Erickson most mornings in the Waldorf barbershop on Park Avenue, but if you wanted to lay a bet with him, you would phone one of his switchboard operators on the other side of the river.

New York's reformers fretted at the safe haven that Bergen County offered to lawbreakers less than a mile from the city. But elsewhere in America many communities quietly welcomed the transplanting of illegality outside their limits. It suited the respectable citizens of Cincinnati for conventioneers and visitors to base themselves in their wholesome metropolis, then go across the river to the sin bins of Covington and Newport, Kentucky. Omaha, Nebraska, had Council Bluffs, Iowa. New Orleans had Jefferson Parish.

In each of these locations — and in several dozen more across America — a car ride transported you to a world where normal rules did not apply. When Americans chuckled at Claude Rains, the police chief in *Casablanca,* who expressed horror at the possibility that there might be gambling at Rick's Bar, then quietly pocketed his own winnings from the tables, it was not the hypocrisies of the Middle East they were smiling at.

The Ricks who operated the carpet joints that sprang up around America from 1933 onward were former speakeasy owners, for the most part. In Houston, Texas, there was Benny Binion, who packed a gun, cowboy-style. At the Mounds, in Cleveland, the host was Thomas Jefferson "Black Jack" McGinty. In Hot Springs, Arkansas, Owney Madden — a former operator, with Ben Marden, of New York's Cotton Club in the 1920s — paraded the gaming rooms like a Rothstein in retirement.

Lacking his own local base outside Manhattan, Meyer Lansky lagged behind these rollicking characters. He did his business in Saratoga every August. In 1936, he went down to Fort Worth for the Texas Centennial Exhibition, running a slot machine arcade there with his brother, Jake.[3] He went into partnership with Bill Syms, the owner of a New Jersey dog track. It took time for Meyer to find a niche — and when he did, he had others to thank for paving the way.

Julian Kaufman was a speculator. He got his nickname from some enterprising dealing on the Chicago produce marts, when he cornered the potato market. He was a bookmaker, and he also ran a crap game in Chicago until a change of administration removed the officials who were in his pocket. That was when Potatoes Kaufman decided to look for winter business in south Florida.

Southern Florida was as close to frontier territory as you could get in the America of the 1920s and early 1930s. Until 1924, it even had its own band of outlaws, the Ashley gang, who made a living robbing banks and then retreating to the safety of the Everglades. The railway had not reached Miami till 1896, only a few years before it reached Nevada, and the process of civilization had proved erratic.

The Florida land boom of the early 1920s took on gold rush proportions as easterners rushed south to speculate on property in the sun. But then came the disastrous hurricane of 1926, which swept across Florida, as across any other Caribbean sandbar. The hurricane devastated the plaster-and-cinder-block dream developments of the southeast coast from Coral Gables to Boca Raton. Not for the first or last time, you could hardly give away real estate in Florida — and things got still worse with the crash and the Great Depression.

Florida reverted to being backwoods country. Palm Beach and Miami derived some brief winter comfort from those visitors rich enough to keep up the traditions of the January-to-March season. But these were rare islands of affluence in a sea of mosquitoes and sand fleas. Small-time farmers scratched a living from tomatoes and fruit which they carried to the railheads, where they haggled with the packers who loaded the produce cars of the trains going north, while, here and there, dotting the landscape, you might find the occasional office of a die-hard real estate agent, forlornly peddling the promise of Opa-Locka, the Moorish city, or the faded glamour of Hollywood-by-the-Sea.*

It was in this depressed yet faintly Wild West atmosphere that Potatoes Kaufman decided he would have a shot at opening a gambling saloon. The location he selected was not promising, at first sight. The "city" of Hallandale† was an impoverished farming community of a few hundred families, situated on the southern border of

---

*Hollywood, Florida, which was to become the home of Jake Lansky and of Jimmy Alo — and of Meyer Lansky, for a while — was briefly prospected as a center of movie production. D. W. Griffith shot *Idol Dancer* in the area in 1919, a few years before the city was incorporated. But filmmakers soon discovered that, unlike its California namesake, Hollywood, Florida, could not offer year-round shooting. In the days before air conditioning, south Florida summers were intolerable.

†Hallandale was named after Luther Halland, a real estate promoter of Swedish origin, who brought many Scandinavians to settle in the area in the late 1890s.

Broward County, halfway between Miami and Fort Lauderdale. Hallandale's only visitors during the season were the "fruit tramps" — itinerant pickers who arrived for the tomato harvest every spring, and who shacked up, for a dollar a night, in a fly-blown local rooming house, the Collins Hotel.[4]

But the no-man's-land location of Hallandale proved the secret of its success. Desperate for income of any sort, its inhabitants were as willing to bend the law as were the inhabitants of other across-the-line corners of America. Potatoes Kaufman struck up a partnership with a Broward bookmaker, Frank Shireman, who held the local outlet of the racing wire — the telegraphed sports results service — and he made another connection with a genial Fort Lauderdale gambler, Claude Litteral, who, lacking one of his arms, was known, predictably, as the One-Armed Bandit.

In the early months of 1936, Kaufman and his local partners ran their wire into a tomato-packing shed not far from the crossroads where U.S. 1, then a dusty, unpaved laterite highway, hit the Dade-Broward county line. They put up blackboards, loudspeakers, and ladders, filling part of the shed with all the paraphernalia of a horse parlor, the bookmaking equivalent of a speakeasy. They set out another area with roulette wheels and crap tables to create a rough-and-ready casino, and the third part of their establishment was laid out as a bingo hall.

Kaufman named his enterprise the Plantation, and it was going full-swing by the early spring of 1936. Horse bettors came to wager at the Plantation in the afternoons, and after dark the crap tables did reasonable business. But it was bingo, the lottery game popularized by the cinemas of the period on "B" movie nights, that really drew the crowds. Kaufman started offering big prizes — as much as $3,000 on the main game of the evening, enough money to buy a Cadillac or three Packards.[5]

The visitors flocked up over the line from Dade County — and from Miami Beach, in particular — eager to stake two dollars a card. The Plantation's bingo area could not hold them. They spilled across the crap tables and the horse parlor. Before long, the rough, sandy parking area around the former packing shed was jammed solid with cars every night, their occupants feverishly marking their cards with numbers called out by bullhorn from the main building. It was the most exciting thing to hit Hallandale in its modest forty-year history.

Then Potatoes Kaufman had a visitor — Vincent Alo, the spare, lean husband of Anne Lansky's friend Flo Alo. Jimmy Blue Eyes, as

Alo was universally known, was an Italian American, a friend and partner of Charlie Luciano — and, as such, a friend and partner of Meyer Lansky.

Meyer and Jimmy had known each other since the early days. They were a couple of Lower East Side boys. Their relationship was interrupted for a period after 1923, when Jimmy Blue Eyes did time in Sing Sing on a robbery conviction.[6] But when he came out, their friendship resumed, and, with Charlie Luciano in prison, Jimmy Blue Eyes became Meyer's closest Italian friend.

Frank Costello could be pompous. Joe Adonis was cripplingly vain. But Meyer and Jimmy Blue Eyes had the same restrained taste in business and pleasure.[7] They admired and respected each other — and their wives were good friends. In 1936, Jimmy Blue Eyes was moving, in a low-profile fashion, to set up his own numbers, book-making, and gambling operations in the voids left by Dutch Schultz and Charlie Luciano. When Jimmy worked with Meyer, he repre-sented the muscle, and it was as the muscle that he approached Pota-toes Kaufman in 1936 with an offer that Potatoes could hardly refuse.

What Potatoes needed, Jimmy Blue Eyes suggested, was a part-ner — several partners, in fact. Kaufman had struck on a situation in Hallandale which had enormous potential, but now he needed capital and expertise to develop it: a bigger bankroll, some new games, some new gaming houses, and perhaps — who could tell? — even a little extra protection?[8]

Julian Kaufman was a prudent gambler. He believed in spreading his risks. He decided to say yes to Jimmy Blue Eyes, surrendering a share in his existing business for a share in the larger enterprise that his new partners promised to create. He received an immediate div-idend. An action group of local vigilantes had brought an injunction against the Plantation as a public nuisance, and had managed to secure a judgment which was legally and permanently attached to the title deeds of the property, specifically prohibiting gambling on the premises. Expensive lawyers had taken the case to appeal without success.

Meyer Lansky studied the injunction, which was not susceptible to the normal mechanism of the payoff. Carpet joints survived on the willingness of the local police and community to look the other way, and on the complications and effort it took for anyone else to get involved. Once an injunction had been granted prohibiting gambling on the premises, the gaming house would have to cease operations on that particular parcel of land.

That particular parcel of land. . . . Meyer Lansky looked at the title deeds to the Plantation. Several parcels of land were involved, and the Plantation only stood on one of them. So next season the Plantation was no more — while standing magically on the adjacent plot was a building that looked identical, and which went under the name of the Farm.[9]

The building looked identical because it was. The same rough packing shed had been shifted bodily sideways onto a plot of land that was injunction-free. The new Farm was just as vulnerable to closure as the old Plantation, however, if the same group of citizens chose to seek another injunction, so Meyer Lansky applied to Hallandale the lessons of community relations that he had learned in Saratoga. During the months preceding the reopening, his operations manager, brother Jake, supervised the handouts: to the Benevolent and Protective Order of Elks, to the Fort Lauderdale Shrine Club, to the Hollywood Fishing Tournament, to the South Florida Children's Hospital — more than two dozen local organizations began receiving generous and helpful donations from the new owners of the bingo parlor near the crossroads on U.S. 1.[10] When the Plantation turned Farm opened in its new location in December 1936, there were no more complaints, injunctions, or action committees of unhappy citizens.

The new Farm featured bingo as usual, a beefed-up gaming room with some of Meyer's best men from Saratoga, Jake Lansky in the cashier's cage — and a dining room. In its opening season under Potatoes Kaufman, the Plantation had served drinks but no dinner. It had been a gambling joint at its most basic — more sawdust than carpet. But Meyer Lansky had learned the importance of providing his customers with good food. Once they stepped outside for supper they would stop gambling — and they might not come back. So in its reincarnation as the Farm, the old Plantation had new kitchens, and the services of a decent team of chefs.

Nothing, however, could overcome the bare and essentially barnlike decor of the former tomato-packing shed. So when the gambling crowds came back for later seasons on the Dade-Broward county line, they discovered that the Farm was no longer the only establishment catering to their business. There was the Beach Club, the 204 Club, and a variety of horse parlors offering fixed odds and the latest from the wire. Grandest of all, there was Ben Marden's Colonial Inn, a plush new carpet joint, almost worthy to be called a casino, with a decor of burgundy, gold, and white, and floor shows with all the éclat that Marden had made his trademark at his Riviera on the cliffs overlooking the Hudson.

Ben Marden had tried to open up the previous winter in West Palm Beach, but he had found his way blocked by Colonel E. R. Bradley, who had his own casino on the island of Palm Beach, and who brooked no competition.[11] So Marden came south to Broward, to open his Colonial Inn under the more accommodating umbrella of Meyer Lansky and Jimmy Blue Eyes.

Each of the Hallandale clubs — including the Colonial Inn — was run by a partnership in which Jimmy Alo and Meyer Lansky had some sort of participation, either in their own names, or through others. Jake Lansky held shares in the Plantation/Farm, as well as in the Beach Club, and also in a partnership called Miller and Lansky, Ike Miller being the operator of a small crap game near Fort Lauderdale which called itself the "It" Club.[12] Jimmy Blue Eyes ran a bookie joint in the Hollywood Yacht Club in partnership with Ben Siegel's friend Moe Sedway.[13]

As in Saratoga, each partnership contained the local element responsible for the fix — in Broward County, it was Frank Shireman, Claude Litteral, or one of their associates — and there was also a judicious sprinkling of high-profile outsiders like Ben Marden, who were known for their involvement in carpet joints in other corners of America. One of these was George Sadlo from Texas, a jovial and much-loved character who was reputed to have learned his gambling while running Mexican casinos in partnership with Pancho Villa, and who was also credited with having worked out how to lift craps off the sidewalk and turn it into a green-baize table game.[14]

Gamblers like Marden and Sadlo encouraged their personal high-rolling clients to travel to Florida for winter gambling in a setting they could trust, and they also contributed to the local credit data network. If a high roller turned up in one of the Hallandale establishments wanting to purchase chips by check in any large amount, it was unlikely that Messrs. Sadlo, Marden, Lansky, and Alo would not have heard of him between them, and that they would not know how many thousand dollars he could safely be advanced.

The clients became more numerous with each succeeding season. By the end of the 1930s, America was on her feet again. The economy was on the upswing, and the benefits of that were obvious in what was now the country's foremost winter playground — the Gold Coast of southeast Florida. In 1929, there had been only a dozen or so hotels on Miami Beach. By 1939, there were several hundred, and a good proportion of their guests took the taxis and limousines that shuttled the ten miles northward to Hallandale.

It was a gambler's paradise. Meyer's friend and New Jersey partner Bill Syms had opened a dog track in Hollywood in 1936. In 1939, the Gulfstream racetrack opened in Hallandale, with avenues of royal palms and a lake to rival Hialeah's. Even as the visitors approached the county line, they could see the lights twinkling, the Hallandale roadhouses and horse parlors boldly advertising their attractions.

The Farm, the Beach Club, Ben Marden's Colonial Inn — you could take your pick: high-stakes craps for cash, more leisurely roulette, or the bingo games with the bullhorn blaring out across the parking lot. You could not see better floor shows on Broadway. Paul Whiteman, Sophie Tucker, Harry Richman, Joe E. Lewis — the big names all added Hallandale to their annual circuit of dates. Here in the sandy wasteland of the Dade-Broward line in the late 1930s was a winter Saratoga where the season lasted three months, a veritable wellspring of dollars enriching Meyer Lansky and his partners — a little Las Vegas before its time.

It was swift and practical justice that they dispensed in the city of Hallandale, Florida, at the end of the 1930s:

> Case No. 499: Arthur Bean. Disturbing the Peace: To Wit: Begging in the white section of town after dark. Sex: M Color: C[olored]. . . . September 11, 1939. Fined $25.00 and cost of court. Sentence stayed for a period of 1 year, providing defendant leave town within 30 minutes.[15]

Hallandale's municipal court was presided over by H. L. Chancey, the municipal judge who was also the city's mayor, and the record of his judgments survives to this day in the old courthouse, in a gilt-embossed, leather-bound ledger.[16]

Most of the cases dealt with such matters as fighting, profane language, or the installation of sanitary privies, and the fines the court levied were quite small — $5 to $10, $25 at the most. Then suddenly, at the end of January 1941, the prices in the ledger doubled.

An unprecedented entry for $60 shows Joe Price, a white male, charged with disorderly conduct — "$60 bond forfeit for nonappearance." On February 10, 1941, a Joseph Sawyer forfeits $50 for the same offense, and Sawyer is back again two weeks later, forfeiting a further $50. On March 14 and March 31, Hugh Pender, another double nonappearer, also forfeits $50 twice.[17]

In the course of these two early spring months in 1941, the leather-bound ledger of the little municipal court shows the community making as much money from the "disorderly conduct" and subsequent nonappearance of Price, Sawyer, Pender, and two other bond-forfeiters as it made from all its routine cases put together.

The city of Hallandale was levying its own municipal betting tax. Messrs. Price, Sawyer, and Pender were bookies and gamblers. The forfeiting of their bonds was Hallandale's way of raising an assessment on their business, and as the number and size of the city's various gambling joints increased, so did the fines — $500, $1,000, $1,500 even, by the late 1940s.[18]

It became a ritual. Every Monday morning during the winter season, the Hallandale clerk of the court would solemnly take note of the gambling house representatives arraigned before him on charges of disorderly conduct — the precise nature of the disorderliness not being specified. Each would lodge his bond, in cash, and each would be given notice to appear later that week to hear the charge against him. On his failure to appear, the cash that he had lodged would be duly forfeit to the court.

"We filled up the treasury in the winter months," remembers Joseph Varon, who was Hallandale's city attorney in the late 1940s, "and by the end of the summer, we were running low. So in September, we would get a loan of ten thousand dollars from the bank to tide us over until the casinos opened again."[19]

Aid to impoverished municipalities — it was the ultimate in Meyer Lansky's program of community handouts. But it was not unique to Hallandale. In the early 1940s, Meyer was invited to the other side of America, to Council Bluffs, Iowa, on a similar errand of mercy.

Council Bluffs was an across-the-line enclave that lay on the other side of the Missouri River from Omaha, Nebraska — a distant prairie outpost, with its neighboring enclave of Carter Lake, for gamblers and entertainers on the carpet-joint circuit.

In 1937, Council Bluffs had been the site of a failed attempt to stage a "Centennial Exhibition," an Iowa version of the fashionable trade fairs of the 1930s, and the city fathers had been left with an empty exhibition park — the Dodge Park Fairgrounds — plus a deficit of some $12,000 owed to more than sixty local creditors.

On May 17, 1941, Bill Syms and Meyer Lansky signed a contract with the Council Bluffs Board of Park Commissioners. They agreed to pay the board $1,000 per week for the rent of the Dodge Park Fairgrounds, undertaking to operate greyhound racing there for at least five weeks per year for five years, and they also agreed to build a track and small stadium, which would become the property of the city when the lease was over.[20]

A use for the old fairgrounds, and retirement of the municipal debt. In the summer of 1941, the Dodge Park Kennel Club rose rapidly on the eastern bank of the Missouri, looking out across the river at the outskirts of Omaha. The track opened for racing in July, and business was brisk from the start. With a municipal contract, and operating on city park land, Meyer Lansky and Bill Syms could hardly offer routine parimutuel betting, but what they organized was just as good. When spectators arrived for the opening of the Dodge Park Kennel Club, they found an array of cashiers' windows and clerks behind them who offered "investors" the chance to buy "options" in the dogs running in every race.

If your dog won, your option in the animal increased in value, and you could sell your option back to the track for a profit — which happened to correspond exactly to the payout you would have received under a parimutuel betting system. If your dog lost, then your option was worthless, and you lost your money.[21]

On the basis of this system, Meyer Lansky and Bill Syms's Dodge Park Kennel Club operated most profitably for eight weeks in the summer of 1941, eight and a half weeks in 1942, and for more than twelve weeks in 1943.[22] The $12,000 debt to the creditors of the Centennial Exhibition was paid off in Dodge Park's second season, and from that point the weekly payments that the track made to the municipality went to fill up the treasury of Council Bluffs — an officially sanctioned betting levy in a town where betting was officially illegal.

Meyer Lansky was a lawbreaker, and his decision to break the law was conscious and deliberate. He could make no excuses. But there was also a sense in which his career, at times, was less his own creation than an accommodation to the ways of his adopted country, and to the rough-and-ready style in which America had chosen to create herself.

* * *

In 1938, Meyer Lansky took his gambling services to Cuba.[23] Fulgencio Batista, the handsome young sergeant who had made himself the strongman of Cuban politics five years earlier, wanted to boost the country's gaming revenues. Before the Depression, Havana's two casinos that were associated with Oriental Park, the city's racetrack, had been meccas for rich American winter visitors. But now both the track and the casinos were doing badly, and it was Meyer Lansky's job to help put them straight.

The problem was partly the Depression — but mainly the cheating. Oriental Park was a beautiful racetrack, with lush, tropical vegetation and a stage-set lake that was fringed with clouds of pink flamingos. It was the model for Hialeah and the other later tracks of Florida. By the time Batista seized power in 1933, however, Oriental Park had a poor reputation in the racing world — crooked stewards, races fixed, horses that were hyped or nobbled. American owners were becoming less and less inclined to risk their better thoroughbreds on the sea voyage to Havana, while no sensible bettor would chance his money with the track's bookies or with the local, Cuban casino dealers.

In January 1937, a new decree had transferred the bulk of Cuba's gambling operations from civil to military control,[24] but the revenues had not lived up to Fulgencio Batista's expectations. So Lou Smith, the respected operator of several successful horse and dog tracks in New England, was offered a contract to clean up and operate the racing at Oriental Park. Smith — who, Meyer later recalled, "had no idea how to run a casino"[25] — passed on the job of cleaning up the track's two casinos to his friend Meyer Lansky.

Lou Smith was one of a group of New England friends that Meyer had made through bootlegging and gambling. Joe Linsey had served time for an infringement of the Volstead Act. He was in the dog track business. Ben Gaines, born Ginsberg, was a hotelier. Moving to Boston for the sake of Buddy's medical treatment in the early 1930s had strengthened Meyer's links with the fraternity.

When Lou Smith arrived at Oriental Park, he took firm control. He installed a Bahr mechanical starting gate and a photo-finish machine. To rein in favoritism, he replaced the local stewards with his own men. He initiated a program of drug tests for the horses,[26] and he brought down Frank Erickson from New York to straighten out the bookmaking.

The new, reformed winter schedule of racing at Oriental Park went well. William K. Vanderbilt came. So did the actress Eleanor

Powell and Sonja Henie, the ice skater. Opinion in the Jockey Club, the exclusive heart of the Oriental Park complex, was that racing in Havana was fair again.

So was the gambling. Meyer Lansky had brought his own pit crews down with him to replace the Cubans in the plush little casino room at the track. In the evenings, after the races, the outfit would move over to the Gran Casino Nacional, a classic, Grecian-looking nightclub set in a garden of fountains and marble statues in Marianao, not far away.

To run the crap tables, Meyer signed up Al Levy, of the Down Town Merchants Club. Levy was quite old by now, but he remained a brand name for New York bettors. To mark the opening of the reformed casino, Levy and Lansky worked out a ceremony — the presentation of the "Golden Ticket." They welcomed Colonel Batista to a special reception, and Al Levy presented the dictator with his own complimentary "key" to the casino.[27]

It was a happy and successful winter. Meyer had not been very keen when Lou Smith first asked him to handle the casino side of his Oriental Park contract,[28] but he discovered that he liked Havana. He brought Anne and the two boys, Buddy and Paul, down to spend a month or so with him.

It was Meyer's first experience operating gambling in an open and legal fashion, with no need for protection payments or for quasi-legal subterfuges, and he liked it. Meyer was hardly an impartial witness, but he could not see any evidence of the woes that gambling's opponents liked to cite against its legalization in America.

"If Socrates and Plato had trouble defining what morality was," he said later, talking of these days, "how can people come along, just like that, and lay down that gambling is immoral?"[29]

Hallandale, Saratoga Springs, Council Bluffs, and Cuba — twenty years after he had quit the tool-and-die shop, Meyer Lansky had begun to achieve his own style of eminence in his own chosen field. Viewed from the vantage point of the late 1930s, his years of bootlegging — with his attempt to continue bootlegging after Prohibition — could be seen as a dead end. Meyer's first instinct as a teenager for the odds of the crap game had been the right way to go. Numbers were his magic. As Meyer approached his fortieth birthday, he found himself a private math teacher, Mr. Miller, a tall, bespectacled man who gave him tutorials in the apartment that Miller shared on the Upper East Side with two smelly Afghan hounds.[30]

Together, the gangster and the mathematician played numbers games.

Meyer's success and sense of achievement had a happy impact on his marriage. He was able to spend more time with Anne and the children, and in December 1937 Anne Lansky gave birth to a third child, strong and healthy like Paul — a little girl whom her parents named Sandra.

Meyer started a summer tradition of renting a holiday home for the family on the Jersey shore — the best time, Buddy Lansky remembered, that his family ever spent together. For several years in the late 1930s and on into the early 1940s, his father rented a cottage in one or another of the little towns — Deal, Allenhurst, Long Branch — that run along the New Jersey coast a hundred miles or so south of New York.[31]

Buddy did not have the balance or the strength in his legs to ride a bicycle. So Meyer bought him a large tricycle, which gave the boy independence. Buddy remembered the thrill of being able to ride his tricycle down to the beach on his own to pick up an ice cream soda from a drugstore. There were excursions in Meyer's car, a long black Oldsmobile 98, and games of catch and baseball — though Meyer would not let Buddy play for long. The boy teetered around in heavy, black, Victorian-looking orthopedic boots, and Meyer was worried about his elder son toppling over and getting hurt.[32]

There were other children to play with — the Siegel daughters, the Adonis kids, and the young Stachers — since Meyer's New York friends rented homes in the same area, and his New Jersey friends were not far away. The fathers gathered together for games of cards in the evening, playing gin rummy for a penny a point, and getting feverishly excited over their minuscule stakes. Joe Adonis, Doc Stacher, and Longy Zwillman were the visitors that Buddy remembered, along with Gerry Catena, a partner of Zwillman and Adonis in various New Jersey gambling ventures.[33]

Uncle Ben was the grown-up to whose arrival Buddy looked forward most of all. Benjamin Siegel was spending a lot of time out in California. He was running floating crap games in the private homes of the famous movie moguls, ferocious bettors to a man. He made book at the Santa Anita track, and he also had interests in California's variations on the carpet joint — the gambling ships that moored just outside U.S. territorial waters. When Uncle Ben arrived back every summer, loud and laughing, to see his children on the Jersey shore, it meant extra trips and fun for all the kids — and a lot more noise from the gin rummy room.[34]

In later years, Buddy Lansky read books and articles which said that his father, Ben Siegel, Joe Adonis, and the others had together constituted the membership of the "National Crime Syndicate" in the years before World War II. Buddy wondered what that title meant.[35] Gambling was certainly a crime, and if a syndicate was a group of businessmen who knew each other and who worked together — in partnerships or, when alone, without interfering in each other's territories — then Meyer Lansky and his circle were clearly that.

But to Buddy, they were just Dad and his friends all sitting down around the gin rummy table, laughing and joking together in the cigarette smoke, and making a great deal of fuss if they won or lost five bucks.

7

"I'll Help You. It's Patriotism"

GEORGE RAFT liked to tell the tale of the time his friend Benny Siegel nearly wiped out Joseph Goebbels. Hitler's propaganda chief was visiting Italy, according to Raft, in the company of Hermann Göring. The two Nazi potentates were installed in the Villa Madama in Rome, the home of Count Carlo Difrasso and of his wife, Dorothy, a freewheeling lady who had met Benny Siegel in Hollywood. The countess and the gangster were enjoying a grand and reckless affair.

Countess Difrasso happened to bring Siegel to Rome at the same time the two Nazis were there. Siegel did not like what he had heard about Nazi anti-Semitism, and when he discovered how close he happened to be to Hitler's henchmen, he became apoplectic. He announced his intention of liquidating them both.

"You can't do that!" protested the countess.

"Sure I can," replied the gangster. "It's an easy set-up."[1]

According to Raft, Siegel was only dissuaded from his homicidal course when the countess pointed out the dire consequences that would ensue for her husband. But for the rest of his days, Ben Siegel liked to claim he had had it in his power to alter the course of World War II.

* * *

Meyer Lansky started his own war against fascism quite early in the 1930s. The rise to power of Hitler in Germany stimulated the growth in America of pro-Nazi groups — the Brown Shirts, the Silver Shirts, the German-American Bund, and the Friends of the New Germany — all of whom organized rallies and marches which took on an increasingly anti-Semitic tone.

"We Jews now have to demonstrate a little more militancy," Judge Nathan Perlman said to Lansky in 1935.[2]

Nathan Perlman was a former Republican congressman who had just been appointed to the New York bench of magistrates by Mayor La Guardia. Perlman was not the type who would normally have had dealings with gangsters,[3] but he was active in many Jewish causes, among them the then-radical cause of Zionism. Dangerous times called for dangerous measures.[4]

Meyer Lansky had no shortage of tough friends. So he rounded them up, and they added their strength to the quite numerous bands of activists who went round New York disrupting pro-Nazi meetings in the mid-1930s. Lansky earned quite a name for it. One day Walter Winchell phoned him to pass on details of a pro-Hitler meeting in Yorkville, the German neighborhood in northeast Manhattan.[5]

"We got there that evening," Meyer later recalled, "and found several hundred people dressed in their brown shirts. The stage was decorated with a swastika and pictures of Hitler. . . . There were only about fifteen of us, but we went into action."[6] Lansky's volunteers threw firecrackers and started fights, so that the meeting degenerated into chaos.[7] Fritz Kuhn, America's foremost Nazi, had been scheduled to speak, but the audience did not get to hear his remarks.

"Walter Winchell thanked me later for breaking up the meeting," remembered Meyer. "I told him he didn't have anything to thank me for — and that he'd given me the wrong address, in any case. . . . I never believed that a Jew should expect thanks for acting on behalf of the Jewish interest."[8]

Meyer Lansky liked to tell this tale in later life as testimony to the solidity of his Jewishness. But even as Meyer was breaking up Nazi meetings in the mid-1930s, he was also arguing bitterly with his father, rejecting old Max Lansky's wish that his grandsons, Paul and Buddy, should go to *cheder,* and be Bar Mitzvahed. Being Jewish, it seemed, only aroused pride in Meyer Lansky if it involved aggression and violence. The little Jew going to shul in his skullcap was not an object of respect. The little Jew who beat up Nazis was.

This conflict was the flaw line through Meyer's entire life. In the mid-1930s he was pursuing his studies with his math tutor, Mr. Miller, and he was as much of a reader as ever. It gave Meyer deep satisfaction to be considered an intellectual — someone who had power in his head. But in his heart, the power that counted with Meyer Lansky came from being tough.

In the first three months of war following Pearl Harbor, the United States and its allies lost more than 120 merchant ships to German U-boats in the waters off the American coast.[9] Not a single U-boat was sunk in retaliation, and the German submarines seemed able to operate with impunity, as if they were getting help of some sort — fuel, food, intelligence — from German agents or sympathizers along the shore.

The suspicion of enemy infiltration deepened in February 1942, when the French liner *Normandie,* at anchor in the Hudson River and being converted into a high-speed troopship, caught fire spectacularly. The great liner burnt out and capsized at her moorings — the largest vessel destroyed in the war to that date.[10]

Subsequent inquiry was to make clear that the loss of the *Normandie* was the consequence of incompetence and of grossly inadequate fire precautions.[11] But at the time, the humiliating disaster, bottom-up in the heart of Manhattan, prompted rumors and suspicions that the sinking was the result of sabotage. America was on the defensive in these first months of the war. People had no idea where the enemy might be.

The investigative section of U.S. Naval Intelligence in the New York area was called B-3, and it was headed by Lieutenant Commander Charles Radcliffe "Red" Haffenden, a bluff and bulky naval reserve officer in his early fifties. Haffenden reveled in his role as a spymaster, puffing on his pipe, Sherlock Holmes–style, and tinkering with impressive gadgets — in his case, a Dictaphone with a large speaking horn, into which he would whisper his letters and memoranda conspiratorially.

Red Haffenden had more than 150 agents dispersed around New York,[12] and in the early months of 1942 he set them to investigate who might be giving help to the enemy — starting on the waterfront and with the fishing fleets which went in and out of the harbor every day. But as the agents began trying to talk to the longshoremen and to the largely Italian fishermen, they hit unexpected resistance. The waterfront, they discovered, was a world of its own.

"It was part of their being," explained Lieutenant Maurice P. Kelly, one of B-3's agents, talking of the longshoremen. "They just refused to talk to anybody, war effort or no war effort. They didn't know whether it interfered with somebody who was running the pier, and until such time as they got definite orders to cooperate, it was a different situation. . . . They didn't know. They didn't see him. They didn't know the guy you were inquiring about."[13]

The navy was getting a crash course in how New York worked. As Red Haffenden pondered the problem, it became obvious to him that B-3 needed inside help, and for that navy intelligence turned to Frank S. Hogan, the new district attorney of New York.

Hogan had just succeeded Thomas E. Dewey, who was moving up for his successful first run at the governorship of New York, and the new district attorney was happy to help, putting Haffenden straight in touch with the head of his rackets bureau, Murray I. Gurfein. Gurfein — who, like Hogan, was a former aide of Dewey's — had been investigating the rackets in and around the waterfront, and he had one immediate source to suggest: the racketeer boss of the Fulton Street Fish Market, Joseph "Socks" Lanza.

Joe "Socks" Lanza was the classic labor racketeer, the elected head of Local 16975 of the United Seafood Workers, who negotiated pay raises for his members while also taking payoffs from the fish markets' employers to keep those pay increases within limits.[14] Nestling on the waterfront, a mile south of Grand Street, the pungent stalls and alleys of the Fulton Fish Market were the center of New York's wholesale fish business. As on the waterfront, money in the right hands — along with the use of violence — was the way that things got done, and Murray Gurfein had been able to nail down enough solid evidence to bring seven counts of extortion and conspiracy against Lanza at the beginning of 1941.[15]

Approached by Gurfein through his attorney, the racketeer was happy to meet and help Commander Haffenden, and within days, thanks to Lanza's contacts, Haffenden's agents were up and down the coast on fishing boats, pulling used flares and significant debris out of the water. Through Lanza, the navy's men also made contact with numerous seamen and captains who promised to supply B-3 with news of any suspicious goings-on.

After less than a month, however, Socks Lanza found himself running into difficulties. Gurfein's racketeering indictments were a matter of public knowledge. A number of valuable contacts had spurned Lanza's inquiries on B-3's behalf, not trusting his motives — and the

U-boat toll, meanwhile, mounted. Forty-seven more merchantmen were sunk off the Atlantic coast in the months of April and May 1942, and the toll continued to rise, bringing the total of ships sunk off the eastern sea frontier in the first six months of the war to a horrifying 272.[16] Uncounted hundreds of sailors were losing their lives.

As navy intelligence put more pressure on Lanza to come up with information, he had to confess himself defeated. Someone bigger was needed, he said, someone whose contacts extended beyond the fishing industry. That man, Lanza suggested, had to be Charles "Lucky" Luciano, who had been in prison since 1936, but who was "still respected by the underworld."[17]

Haffenden broached the idea with Murray Gurfein, who took it in turn to his boss, Frank Hogan. Given the circumstances, the district attorney did not find the idea so extraordinary. Hogan suggested that Gurfein should contact Moses Polakoff, one of Luciano's attorneys.

Polakoff's reaction, when Gurfein approached him on Haffenden's behalf at the end of April 1942, was not encouraging. "I told him," Polakoff later remembered, "that I did not know Luciano well enough to broach the subject to him on my own."[18]

But Polakoff told Gurfein that he did know someone, "who I had confidence in, and whose patriotism, or affection for our country, irrespective of his reputation, was of the highest, and I would like to discuss the matter with this person first before I committed myself."[19]

Later that afternoon, Polakoff telephoned Gurfein, suggesting a breakfast meeting the following day at the Longchamps Restaurant on West Fifty-eighth Street, between Fifth and Sixth avenues.[20] In the morning, Gurfein picked up Polakoff in a taxi on Central Park West, and the two men drove together to the Longchamps, where they found waiting for them a short, dark, neat individual, of whom Gurfein had heard, but whom he had never met. Moses Polakoff introduced the head of the rackets bureau to Meyer Lansky.[21]

Meyer Lansky had put his name down for war work sometime before Pearl Harbor. He registered with his Selective Service Board, filling in his form like a man who was anxious to see action.

In response to the questions about his education, Meyer had to admit that he had got no further than eighth grade. But he pointed out that he was taking private tuition in math, and he also made it clear that he was prepared to play quite a humble role in the war

Above and right: The earliest known photographs of Meyer Lansky, taken in the 1920s. *Below:* Lansky's Brooklyn school record card.

DEPARTMENT OF EDUCATION.						PUPIL'S RECORD. *Vac. '11*							CITY OF NEW YORK			

Name *Lansky* *Meyer* Family — Born *8-28-02* Mo.-Da.-Yr. — Emp. Cert. No. *968* 7B Geog.
Parent *Max* — Special Aptitudes
Attended ____ days from 13th birthday to end of term

No.	Street	Fl.	No.	Street	Fl.	No.	Street	Fl.	No.	Street	Fl.	No.	Street	Fl.
33	Chester St.													
894	Rockaway													
546	Grand St.													

School	Bor.	Date Entered	Class	Present	Abs.	Late	Con.	Wt.	Not proficient in	School	Bor.	Date Entered	Class	Present	Abs.	Late	Con.	Wt.	Not proficient in
New																			
P.S. 26		4-28-11	1B−3	45	1	0	A	A											
"	"	6-30-11	1B3	91	2	0	a	a											
"	"	1-31-12	2A3	19	0	0	a	a											
165	"	3/1/12	2A6	72	7	0	a	a											
"	"	3/28/12	3A.c	42½	1½	0	a	a											
"	"	9/1/12	3B.²	44	0	1	a	B−											
"	"	1/31/13	4A²	89	9	0	a	a											
"	"	6/27/13	5A.¹	80	14	1	a	a											
"	"	1-30-14	5B²	93	6	1	a	a											
"	"	6/30/14	6B¹	37	11	0	B+	B+											
No.		11-30-16		×	3	f	man												

Mug shots from the files of the
New York City Police Department,
1928–1939.

Charles "Lucky" Luciano

Benjamin "Bugsy" Siegel

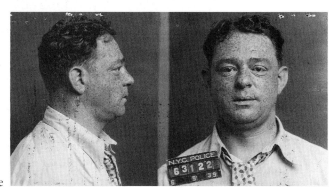

Samuel "Red" Levine

Moe Sedway

Frank Costello

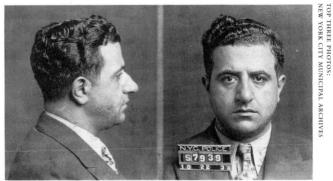

Albert Anastasio/Anastasia

Jacob "Gurrah" Shapiro

Meyer Lansky

Dark eminence of organized crime: Arnold Rothstein, shortly before his death in 1928.

High-stakes gambler Joe Adonis in 1937.

"The Dutchman," Arthur Flegenheimer, aka Dutch Schultz (left), with lawyer, April 1935.

Boss of Murder, Inc.: Louis "Lepke" Buchalter, November 1939.

When August came, the high rollers flocked to the lake houses of Saratoga Springs, New York, where Meyer Lansky learned how to run a stylish casino. *Right:* Advertisement for the Arrowhead Inn, August 14, 1941. *Below:* The Piping Rock Casino, August 1934.

Meyer's brother-in-law, Jules
Citron, in Sloppy Joe's Bar,
Havana. With him, his sister,
Anne Citron Lansky (right),
and Ruthie Cohen, a friend.

Moses Citron, Lansky's
father-in-law and partner in
the ill-fated Molaska venture.

Anne Citron, Lansky's first wife, at the time of their marriage, May 1929.

Detained for questioning by the Chicago Police Department, April 19, 1932 (left to right): Paul "The Waiter" Ricca, Sylvester Agoglia, Charles "Lucky" Luciano, Meyer Lansky, John Senna, Harry Brown.

Cleaning up New York: Mayor Fiorello La Guardia dumping confiscated slot machines and firearms into Long Island Sound, October 1934.

effort. Asked to describe the job for which he might best be fitted, he wrote, "machinist, lathe shaper, or drill press,"[22] noting his years of experience in the tool-and-die shop.*

Only a few months away from his fortieth birthday, Meyer Lansky was more than a dozen years over the age of military eligibility. His draft board did not call on his services. So when Moses Polakoff contacted him at the end of April 1942, Meyer's reaction was positive.

"I'll help you," he said. "It's patriotism."[26]

By the time Meyer got to the Longchamps Restaurant to meet Gurfein and Polakoff next day, he had tried to think through some of the practical aspects of the problem. "We had to be very careful in making any moves," Polakoff later recalled Meyer's cautioning the two attorneys, "because, at the time, Mussolini appeared to be popular with some Italians in New York."[27]

Could they trust Luciano? Gurfein wanted to know.

"I felt we could," Lansky recalled. "Yes, I felt we could. His whole family was here, his mother and father and two brothers and sisters with children; and I said, 'Of course, I would like to go up and see him and ask him.' I felt that he would respond."[28]

The three men moved on from breakfast to the Hotel Astor on Times Square, where Red Haffenden kept an office to meet the under-cover contacts that he could not invite to naval intelligence's head-quarters at Church Street, Manhattan.[29]

"Mr. Haffenden told us where we were weak," remembered Meyer. "Where he felt the government needs lots of assistance such as the waterfront, pertaining to loaders of ships, employees on the docks. . . . He wanted people that could be of assistance in that way, so that nothing is brought out to any submarines. . . . He was afraid that they were getting fuel out."[30]

Dannemora prison, to which Charlie Luciano had been sent to serve his thirty-to-fifty-year sentence, lay in the remote and chilly northern corner of New York State, near the Canadian border, and

---

*Meyer Lansky's eagerness to serve his country was not unusual among his peers. His friend Doc Stacher managed to get enrolled, taking great delight in the $300 military uniforms which he had specially tailored around his rather squat frame.[23] Moe Dalitz, the Cleveland bootlegger, entered the service as a private and left as a captain.[24] Dave Berman of Minneapolis[25] and Charles Barron of Chicago, bootleggers and gamblers both, were turned down for service by their draft boards. So they went north to Canada, enrolled under false names, and joined the fighting forces of the British Empire. Barron, who worked with Meyer Lansky in Cuba for a period in the 1950s, was respectfully referred to in his circle as "Colonel" Barron for the rest of his life.

both Polakoff and Lansky had expressed their unhappiness at the
long and complicated journey. Could Luciano not be moved, they
suggested, to Sing Sing, a simple drive, thirty miles north of Manhattan? Gurfein and Haffenden thought that the idea made good
sense.

But John A. Lyons, the New York State commissioner of correc-
tions, whom Gurfein approached a few days later, did not agree.
Luciano's appearance in Sing Sing would provoke gossip, thought
Lyons, and it would be difficult for his meetings with people like
Lansky to go unremarked there. Great Meadow, the state's un-
prison-looking prison at Comstock, sixty miles north of Albany,
would be a more appropriate venue. So on May 12, 1942, Luciano
was moved to Comstock.[31]

Three days later, on May 15, 1942, Commissioner Lyons sent
Comstock's warden, Vernon A. Morhous, a letter marked "PER-
SONAL & CONFIDENTIAL":

> Dear Warden:
>   This is to advise you that I have granted permission to Mr.
> Meyer Lansky to visit and interview Inmate Charles Luciano
> in your institution when accompanied by Mr. Polakoff, the
> inmate's attorney. . . . You are authorized to waive the usual
> fingerprint requirements and to grant Mr. Lansky and Mr.
> Polakoff the opportunity of interviewing the inmate privately.[32]

"We went up by train to Albany," Meyer later recalled, "and from
Albany we got a car to take us to the prison."[33]

Charlie Luciano, meanwhile, had no idea what was going on. He
had been told when he was moved south from Dannemora with eight
other inmates that the transfer was for "administrative purposes."[34]
He was not told whom to expect when, late one morning in May
1942, he was led to a special interrogation room beside Warden Morhous's office at Comstock, and was instructed to wait for some
visitors.

"Charlie . . . was very much surprised when he saw us," Lansky
recalled.[35]

In May 1942, Luciano had at least twenty-four years of his sentence still to run, and he would not even be eligible to apply for
parole until April 1956.[36] In the previous six years he had had a few
visits from his brother and sister up in Dannemora, but he had not
set eyes on his friend Meyer since they had been free men together in
New York.

"He stretched out his arms," Meyer recalled, "and shouted, 'What are you doing here?'"[37]

For Meyer Lansky and Charlie Luciano to be embracing each other in Comstock prison under the auspices of the United States Navy was not a reunion that they, or anyone else, could readily have imagined. Hints and half-revelations of the strange process that brought them together became public after the Second World War, and these stimulated all manner of fables, from a description of a lavish reunion banquet served courtesy of the Comstock prison authorities, to the notion that the entire episode could be explained in terms of payoffs to Governor Dewey.

This last, bizarre accusation prompted Thomas Dewey, still governor of New York, to commission an official inquiry in 1954. William B. Herlands — yet another of Dewey's protégés — spent nearly eight months examining official records and correspondence, while also interviewing a total of fifty-seven major witnesses who included District Attorney Hogan, Murray Gurfein, and their staffs; the surviving officers and agents of naval intelligence; and Moses Polakoff, Joe "Socks" Lanza, and Meyer Lansky.

Until Dewey commissioned the Herlands inquiry, naval intelligence had officially denied the existence of "the underworld project,"[38] and, following the inquiry, Dewey agreed to a navy request that Herlands's findings should remain confidential. But when the results of the Herlands inquiry were finally disclosed in 1977, it was established beyond any question that the U.S. Navy actively sought the help of Lucky Luciano during the Second World War — and that the crucial link between the gangster and the navy was Meyer Lansky.

Did Polakoff and Lansky have much trouble persuading Luciano to help the navy? William B. Herlands wanted to know.

"Yes, we did . . . ," Meyer Lansky replied. "He had a deportation warrant attached to his papers."[39]

Charlie Luciano, the man who Americanized the mobs, knew that, thanks to his failure to take out American citizenship, he was due to finish his days where he started them — in Italy.

"He didn't want his cooperation with the United States government to become known," Meyer explained, "because whenever he would be deported and went back to Italy, then he might get lynched. He was fearful of bodily harm."[40]

Lansky and Polakoff assured Luciano they would stress the importance of secrecy to Gurfein and Haffenden. It was in nobody's interest to trumpet the activities of B-3. Luciano suggested that Lansky and Polakoff should come back to Comstock quite soon, bringing Socks Lanza with them. They could work out some names together, and Meyer would then talk to those people on Charlie's behalf.

"Lansky knew Luciano very well, and they trusted each other . . . ," Polakoff explained. "Those people knew that if Lansky said he was acting for Luciano, that statement would not be questioned."[41]

Charlie Luciano had never been the boss of the New York waterfront, but he had enriched many of the people who were. In the 1920s and 1930s Luciano had cut deals with each labor boss who helped fix his smuggling or who had allowed Charlie's lottery and bookmaking runners to do business on their pier — and many of these bosses, like their workers, were Italian Americans.[42]

"The Italians," remarked Moses Polakoff, "appear to have a system where they pay special heed, or homage, to certain individuals."[43]

"I will have word out," Luciano told Socks Lanza when he came up to Comstock on June 4, 1942, in the company of Polakoff and Lansky, "and you won't have no difficulties."[44]

Comstock's warden, Vernon Morhous, was waiting outside when the three visitors emerged. "Dear Commissioner," he wrote to John A. Lyons. "This is to advise you that the visit [sic] which you discussed with me arrived at 10.00 a.m. and left at about 1.30 p.m. The attorney and Lansky who made the first visit were present; also a Mr. Lanza."[45]

In the months that followed, Warden Morhous was to send Lyons eighteen more such communications recording the names of the confidential visitors to inmate Charles Luciano, and Meyer Lansky was listed in more than half of them.[46]

On June 27, 1942, it was announced that, in the course of the previous week, eight German secret agents had been arrested in New York and Chicago. They had been landed by U-boat — four of them in Florida, four on Long Island — and they had brought ashore explosives and more than $170,000 in cash, together with maps and plans for a two-year-long campaign of attacks on defense plants, railroads, waterworks, and bridges, from the eastern seaboard of the United States to the Midwest.

Several U.S. government agencies had been involved in the detection and arrest of the German spies, and it was the FBI which took the public credit. But a crucial role in tracking down the Long Island saboteurs had been played by Commander Haffenden's B-3 agents, using the fishing fleet contacts supplied by Joe Lanza. Haffenden was able to identify precisely where the German agents came ashore, and how and when they traveled to New York City.[47]

It was an early and heartening vindication of B-3's enrolling of the racketeers. Following his trip to Comstock with Lanza, Meyer Lansky was an almost daily visitor of Commander Haffenden's, usually at the Hotel Astor, but also, on one or two occasions, at U.S. Naval Intelligence's headquarters on Church Street. Meyer was introduced to Haffenden's boss, the district intelligence officer, Captain MacFall, and also to MacFall's executive officer and successor, Captain William B. Howe. Meyer was assigned his own code number as a naval intelligence contact.[48]

"At the beginning," said Moses Polakoff, who accompanied Meyer on a number of his visits, "the work was mostly information about the loading and unloading of ships at the piers, the preventing of work stoppage, the bringing of information that might lead to stopping sabotage on the piers."[49]

Meyer spread his net wide on B-3's behalf. He brought in Vincent Alo, Jimmy Blue Eyes, to give Haffenden information on port security,[50] and he enlisted other contacts. Haffenden told Meyer at one of their meetings that he suspected German agents and saboteurs to be using the Great Northern Hotel on West Fifty-seventh Street.

"He wanted waiters that could be trusted," Meyer remembered, "to mix up in the union office and to hear what the different waiters were talking about as to conversations that sailors or military men may have in their different stations. He also thought that we may have to get in waiters and place them in certain restaurants and hotel lounges. One of the places he mentioned was the Pierre Hotel."[51]

In Meyer's opinion, this was a job for one of the Irish waterfront bosses, Johnny "Cockeye" Dunn, a mean and violent character whose power in the waterfront locals extended to other union activities, notably the hotel and restaurant trades. Cockeye Dunn was one of Meyer's carpet-joint clients. Meyer brought Dunn in to meet Haffenden.[52]

"Dunn's job," Meyer later explained, "was to be a watchdog on the piers, to have trusted employees among the loaders to seek out employees, to make friends with the crew, and to stay with them to get reports if there was any bad men around the crowd. . . . Men that may lend themselves to sabotage, or leakage of information. He also got friends along the waterfront in the bar rooms. If any of the crews got drunk, and they would talk something that you would feel is subversive, to report to him."[53]

Dunn had recently been convicted on charges of coercion and intimidating employees on a pier.[54] But he had been released on bail in February 1942, pending sentencing, and he collaborated enthusiastically with the war effort. With the help of his brother-in-law, Eddie McGrath, Cockeye Dunn obtained union cards for B-3's agents, so they could work undercover as longshoremen, waiters, and barmen — wherever Haffenden wanted "ears."

"I cannot give you any specific results . . . ," Lansky later said of Dunn's work. "I don't know how much sabotage this has stopped, but I feel it should have stopped plenty. I feel that it was a great precaution. I knew he took care of it."[55]

Meyer's practice was to bring Haffenden the contact that Meyer reckoned he needed, then leave the men alone together. He got no more involved than he needed to. "I would introduce them," he later explained, "and then they would follow up in their own way."[56]

The visits to Comstock, meanwhile, continued. Meyer would travel up by train with Moses Polakoff the previous evening, eating dinner in the dining car as they swept through the scenery of the Hudson Valley. Next morning, they would drive up from their Albany hotel, getting to Comstock around ten, though on one winter visit, they arrived late when their car skidded off the icy road. Meyer and Polakoff ended up cut and shaken, both having gone through the windshield.[57]

On a more enjoyable visit, in August, Meyer took advantage of the Saratoga races, only forty miles away, to drive over a delegation from the Piping Rock, headed by Frank Costello.

What did Luciano and Costello, two of the great crime czars, talk about when they met?

"I didn't overhear," said Moses Polakoff, "and they were discussing something in Italian. I think the only reason he [Costello] was brought up is that Luciano probably asked that we bring him up. What happened about that, I don't know. He was only there once."[58]

Charlie Luciano was having a marvelous time. The room in which he got together with so many old friends in 1942 and 1943 was designed for the confidential interrogation of prisoners by visiting police and prosecutors. It seems extraordinary that there was no mechanism for bugging the room to record the content of conversations.

Down in New York, however, District Attorney Hogan did take the precaution of initiating wiretaps to check whether Luciano's delegates might not be taking advantage of their "war work" to transact some illicit business on the side. The taps were placed on two phone lines in a hotel frequently used by Joe Lanza, and Hogan discovered that Lanza and his contacts were taking their duties very seriously.[59] Collaborating with B-3 offered a great chance for bad boys to do the right thing. The worst racket that Hogan's wiretaps disclosed was evidence of Joe Socks sending — and of Commander Charles Haffenden gratefully receiving — occasional gifts of fresh crabmeat and lobsters from the Fulton Street Fish Market.

The deliberate obscurity and shorthand of the recorded conversations make clear that racketeers were, by this date, well aware that their telephone conversations might be overheard. Red Haffenden entered into the coded conversations with gusto.

"How about that Brooklyn Bridge thing?" he was recorded as asking Joe Lanza on November 24, 1942.[60] "Brooklyn Bridge" was the telephone code for Harry Bridges, the rabble-rousing president of the predominantly West Coast–based International Longshoremen's and Warehousemen's Union, the more ideological, socialist rival of the International Longshoremen's Association, the ILA. Harry Bridges, a fiery character who was Australian born, was organizing a campaign to woo East Coast longshoremen away from the ILA, which he correctly denounced as a racketeer-dominated organization.

The disruption that this labor rivalry seemed likely to provoke did not please the navy. Concerned to keep the port running smoothly, they were on the side of the racketeers — though Haffenden explained to Moses Polakoff that they must not appear to take sides.

"He said the Navy couldn't butt in," Polakoff later recalled of Haffenden's wish to avoid a strike.[61]

Polakoff contacted Meyer. "I got hold of Mr. Lansky," Polakoff later remembered, "and he got hold of somebody, and I know that in a couple of days later, when I met Mr. Haffenden, he said, 'Gee, you did a swell job. The strike was stopped.'"[62]

By the early months of 1943 cargoes were flowing rapidly and freely through the port of New York, the largest single supply point for the war in Europe. New convoy arrangements out in the Atlantic had significantly cut down the sinkings of merchantmen by the U-

boats, and navy intelligence turned to the underworld for help with
a new mission. With the recent conquest of North Africa, the Allies
were planning an invasion of Italy, and that would almost certainly
involve starting with Italy's southernmost tip — a naval-supported
landing by U.S. forces on the island of Sicily.

The U.S. Navy did not know much about Sicily and its coastline
in the early 1940s. It was not a war theater where there were detailed
plans to fight. So Red Haffenden turned to Meyer Lansky, and Meyer
raised the subject with Charlie on his next visit to Comstock. Meyer
also had a word with his Piping Rock gambling partner, Joe Adonis,
and Adonis proved as keen to help the war effort as every other
gangster that B-3 had contacted.

"He dug up some foreign Italians and we brought them down
together to 90 Church Street," Meyer later remembered.[63] Suddenly
the headquarters of navy intelligence was "black with Sicilians."[64]

Red Haffenden was delighted. He never knew, he later said, "that
there were so many individuals of that type in New York City. Many
of them had handle-bar moustaches, and practically none of them
could, or would, speak English." They were referred to, Haffenden
discovered, as "*padrones.*"[65]

Haffenden set up a special map room in his Church Street office,
installing a huge map of Italy overlaid with a heavy, transparent plastic sheet.

"These Italians were trying to recognize how much knowledge
they had of this map," Meyer remembered, "to relate to the Navy
whether the map was correct. . . . The Navy wanted from the Italians
all the pictures they could possibly get of every port in Sicily, of every
channel; and also to get men that were in Italy more recently, and
had knowledge of water and coast lines — to bring them up to the
Navy so they could talk to them."[66]

Armed with this information, Haffenden's cartographers drew
lines on the plastic overlay of the map, pinpointing particular ports
and beaches, and linking them to code numbers for the different files
in which they stored the data provided by the contacts of Luciano
and Adonis.

The role of the American underworld in the Allied invasion of
Sicily in July 1943 has been a fertile source of legend and exaggeration. Lucky Luciano has been pictured hitting the beaches in person,
waving triumphantly from atop a tank, and there have been dark
tales of planes dropping flags and handkerchiefs bearing the letter *L*

behind enemy lines — signals, supposedly, from Luciano to local Mafia chieftains.

The evidence of the Herlands inquiry provides no support for any of this. Charlie Luciano stayed locked safely inside his cell at Comstock for the duration of the war. But Luciano did play a role through the informants that he, Joe Adonis, and Meyer Lansky sent to navy intelligence in Church Street, for the navy dispatched four of Haffenden's Italian-speaking agents straight from interviewing the *padrones* to land with the invasion forces.

In the small hours of July 10, 1943, Lieutenant Paul Alfieri landed on Licata Beach and made contact with local Sicilians who told him the secret location of Italian Naval Command, hidden in a nearby holiday villa. Inside, Alfieri discovered "the entire disposition of the Italian and German Naval forces in the Mediterranean — together with minefields located in the Mediterranean area — together with overlays of these minefields, prepared by the Germans, showing the safe-conduct routes through the mines."[67]

Had Alfieri's contacts been developed, William Herlands asked the officer eleven years later, through the informants gathered by Lucky Luciano and his friends?

"Yes, mostly."

Did this information stand him in good stead at Licata?

"It certainly did."[68]

On V-E Day, May 8, 1945, Moses Polakoff swore out a petition for a grant of executive clemency on behalf of his client Charles Luciano. Polakoff had made a previous application, in February 1943, requesting commutation of Luciano's jail sentence as a fair return for his help with the war effort, and had been turned down. But the judgment had suggested that "executive clemency may become appropriate at some future date,"[69] and the day when the war ended triumphantly in Europe seemed to Polakoff an appropriate date.

The granting of executive clemency was quite a routine procedure in New York State. Dewey's three predecessors, Governors Al Smith, Franklin Roosevelt, and Herbert Lehman, had, between them, commuted the sentences of seventy-four prisoners, including thirty-two serving long sentences for murder.[70] On receipt of Polakoff's application in the spring of 1945, the New York State Division of Parole began its normal process of investigation. But when its agents approached naval intelligence for corroboration of the lawyer's claims, they ran into a blank wall.

The navy had decided that its involvement with New York's underworld was best forgotten. Charles Haffenden, dashing and cavalier to the end, had managed to escape from his desk to see real action before the war ended, and had been badly shot up at Iwo Jima. In May 1945, Polakoff found the commander recuperating in a hospital, with half his stomach removed, and managed to secure from him a lengthy if somewhat rambling statement of B-3's relationship with the gangster.

When Haffenden's superiors heard of the statement, they ordered the officer to recant. "I was back from the Pacific," Haffenden later said, trying to backtrack. "I wasn't feeling any too hot."[71]

The navy disclaimed responsibility for Haffenden's story. His statement to Polakoff, they suggested, sprang from the wanderings of a valiant but shocked and war-weary mind. In response to the queries of the New York parole board, navy intelligence stated that a review of its files could "not substantiate . . . that information of value to the war effort was supplied by one Charles Luciano. The opinions of Commander Haffenden . . . therefore can be viewed solely as those of an individual which must stand unsupported by official records."[72]

When Joseph Healy, the parole board official checking the facts of Luciano's petition, informed Polakoff of the navy's response, the attorney exploded. Haffenden's superiors, he protested, were "aristocratic snobs," ashamed to acknowledge the allies to whom they had turned in their moment of need.[73]

Meyer Lansky rang Polakoff's office in the middle of the attorney's meeting with Healy, and Meyer readily accepted Polakoff's invitation to come in, there and then, and talk personally to the parole board officer.

With official dossiers getting filled, and newspapers starting to sniff around the story, it might have been prudent of Meyer Lansky not to go on record to a state investigator. But Meyer was proud of his war work, and for all his caution, he was a loyal friend. He gave Healy a statement which, reported the parole board officer, "corroborated the statements made by Commander Haffenden and Polakoff. . . . Lansky stated that his part was to act as intermediary between Luciano and those persons whom Luciano sent instructions to give information to the Naval authorities."[74]

Meyer's testimony was helpful, but in the end it was one of

Dewey's men who provided the key rebuttal of the navy's story. One day in the summer of 1945, Moses Polakoff received a phone call from New York district attorney Frank S. Hogan.

"Moe," said Hogan, "I have several copies in duplicate of an affidavit prepared by Murray Gurfein." The affidavit set out Gurfein's role in connecting B-3 with Luciano. "Murray, for some reason that I don't know," explained Hogan, "insisted that I get Naval clearance before I released the affidavits to you and to the Governor."[75]

This clearance had been denied, but the district attorney had no intention of collaborating in the navy cover-up.

"Moe," he said, "for your personal information and use, and in consideration of the fact that you too may need something like this in the future, I am sending you — off-the-record — a copy of that affidavit."[76]

Off the record, Moses Polakoff made sure that the parole board found out all about Murray Gurfein's affidavit, which, in conjunction with Commissioner Lyons's details of the comings and goings at Comstock prison, made clear that U.S. Naval Intelligence had been involved, through Moses Polakoff and Meyer Lansky, in a complex and lengthy relationship with Charles Luciano. It was enough for the parole board, which made a unanimous recommendation for executive clemency, and it was enough for Governor Dewey.

On January 4, 1946, Warden Morhous, of Great Meadow Prison, Comstock, was officially notified that Charles Luciano, inmate number 15684, was to be released to the custody of the Immigration and Naturalization Service — for the purpose of deportation only.[77]

Meyer Lansky and Moses Polakoff arranged to say their farewells to Charlie Luciano on Ellis Island early in February 1946.

"Is it all right I go along with you?" asked Frank Costello when he heard the news.

"Sure," replied Polakoff.[78]

They met Costello early next morning at the Ellis Island Terminal and went across on the ferry with one of Charlie's closest Italian friends, Mike Lascari, and several heavy bags of Luciano's clothes and personal possessions. They spent about twenty minutes with Luciano.

Meyer Lansky paid his old friend two more visits. On the afternoon of February 5, he went, with Mike Lascari, to pick up about $2,500 in cash from Luciano, and on February 7, Lansky and Lascari were on Ellis Island again, to hand back the money, which they had changed into traveler's checks.[79]

It was the last time that Lansky saw Charlie Luciano in America. Next day Luciano was taken from Ellis Island to the S.S. *Laura Keene,* a converted Liberty Ship that was due to take a cargo of flour across the Atlantic from New York to Genoa.

Frank Costello did visit Luciano on board the *Laura Keene* the night before it sailed. Costello arrived at pier 7, Bush Terminal, on the afternoon of Saturday, February 9, 1946, with a small group of well-dressed men, who all produced cards showing them to be members of the longshoremen's union. Discovering that Charlie's last meal in America was to be some greasy veal cutlets prepared by the ship's cook, they sent ashore to a restaurant in the Fulton Fish Market for lobsters, spaghetti, and some bottles of wine.[80]

The enjoyment of these comfortable supplements to the plain fare of the *Laura Keene*'s mess hall, has grown over the years into the legend of a full-scale bacchanalia, featuring hampers overflowing with cooked turkeys and kosher delicacies, crates of French champagne, and even dancing girls from the Copacabana. The revelers at the party are said to have made up a who's who of gangsterdom in America, from Bugsy Siegel to Owney Madden.[81]

If the well-dressed men flourishing longshoremen's cards had truly included these famous figures, their presence would certainly have been seized on by the crime reporters who were hovering avidly around the waterfront, noting the comings and goings in the days that preceded Luciano's sailing at breakfasttime on Sunday, February 10, 1946. Luciano's pardon and deportation was a major story in the New York tabloids.

But Frank Costello's was the only name mentioned in contemporary news reports, and his was the only name that the immigration officials on board the *Laura Keene* were subsequently able to identify. They told a sober tale of a quiet, warm, and rather subdued farewell, old friends reminiscing fondly together.

Meyer Lansky was not one of the party, and, noting the concentration of newsmen on pier 7, he went to some length to ensure that nobody should think that he was.

"He deliberately left New York," Moses Polakoff remembered.[82]

On the night of Charlie Luciano's farewell supper, Meyer Lansky was more than two hundred miles away, registered in a hotel in Maryland.[83] He had said his own good-byes to Charlie, and he was never one for publicity.

8

---

*"Maybe It Was
My Fault"*

ONE day quite early in her marriage, Anne Lansky answered the
phone to a woman who wanted to speak to Meyer. The woman
called several times more. When Anne asked her husband who the
woman might be, Meyer told her to mind her own business. Anne
went on asking, and Meyer got so angry that he slapped her.[1]

Meyer Lansky was no Don Juan, but neither was he a solidly
faithful husband. It is impossible to discover much about the three
or four casual liaisons which, the evidence suggests, he had at different stages of his life — in Cuba and in Council Bluffs in the early
years, in Israel and in Miami Beach toward the end.[2] None of them
could qualify as a grand affair. In one of the cases, the woman
involved was a waitress. In another, she worked in a hotel where he
happened to be staying. Meyer took his comfort where he found it.

These infidelities were like the rest of Meyer Lansky's life — shadowy, passive, and essentially bloodless. They were scarcely threats to
his family responsibilities as he envisioned them. But Anne was not
the type to laugh off her husband's occasional philandering.

"My mother was a very jealous person," remembered Buddy
Lansky.[3]

Whenever Meyer was away, Anne would telephone him con-
stantly, trying to check on what he was doing and who he was with.

"Who is he registered under?" Buddy would hear his mother asking the hotel telephone operator. "With a wife, or without a wife?"[4]

The marriage of Meyer and Anne Lansky had not worn well. Anne would worry away at her problems, generating strain and stress. She had the tendency to magnify routine difficulties into catastrophes, while Meyer, for his part, had grown intolerant of his wife's anxieties. He dismissed them as hysterical. Meyer was niggardly with his emotions, concealing and denying them. Anne spilled everything out.

It was unpromising chemistry, and Meyer's way of life increased the strains. Anne could not be sure of anything. The basis of her husband's life was dishonest, and that made her life dishonest as well. The Lansky family rented homes in respectable apartment buildings alongside respectable people. But as time went by, and as the neighbors worked out what Mr. Lansky did, they kept their distance. There could be no sharing of intimacies with other wives and mothers in the building, no genuine human contact with outsiders.

It was the sort of thing that Meyer would shrug off — if he noticed. But, left on her own for so long and so often, Anne took it to heart. Nor was she prepared, when Meyer got home, meekly to accept her husband's standard response to all the questions she asked him: that she should mind her own business.[5]

Minding your own business is a basic rule for the wives and families of lawbreakers. It is a matter of security. It is also, in its way, a form of kindness and protection, since the person who does not know anything cannot be punished for it.

The price of such precaution, however, is heavy. The permanent, long-term effects of trying to live with this unsatisfying blend of detachment and deceit are either to deaden genuine feelings to the point of extinction, or else to provoke furious revolt — and this was the response of Anne Lansky. She exploded.

Buddy would hear it through the bedroom wall. In her anger his mother would seize his father bodily and slam him furiously against the door.

"She would throw things at him. . . . There was hollering, screaming. . . . I used to wake up in the middle of the night and hear them fight."[6]

Lying in bed, listening to the sounds of conflict through the wall, Buddy winced at the noise of his parents arguing, and wondered if he was, in some way, to blame. He knew that the reality of his handicap hung permanently in the family atmosphere. The subject was intensely charged for both his parents, and for his mother in particular. She never actually said as much in her son's presence, but Buddy heard from somewhere that his mother would curse his father for their elder son's troubles, saying that little Buddy's crippling was a judgment on Meyer for his way of life.[7]

In 1940, at the age of ten, Buddy Lansky went away to a full-time school for the disabled in Baltimore. Dr. Carruthers in Boston could do no more for him. The Baltimore school was under the supervision of a Dr. Phelps, and although Buddy did not like being sent away from home, he came to enjoy the fellowship of the other crippled children, many of whom were much more badly disabled than he was.

"I would move the chess pieces for them," Buddy remembered. "That's how I learned to play chess."[8]

To keep an eye on Buddy in Baltimore, his father commissioned a local bookmaker, a short, jovial, roly-poly character, Jules Fink, known to his friends as Julie. Meyer had invested some of his gambling capital in a franchise to distribute Wurlitzer jukeboxes in New York and other East Coast cities, and Julie Fink was Meyer's Baltimore agent. Julie would come and visit Buddy at the school, and take him home for the weekend, helping the boy, as the nurses at the school did, with the things that Buddy could not manage on his own — dressing and undressing, and, in particular, putting on his own shoes and socks. At holiday time, Julie Fink would travel with Buddy, packing up his case, and helping him on and off the train.

Julie Fink loved children, and Buddy loved Julie — his own brilliantined, cigar-smelling nanny. At Christmastime, Julie would dress up in a red coat and white beard to give out presents to all the inmates of the little school-clinic, and he gave Buddy a toy that made the boy the envy of every other child — a full-scale, working jukebox, which Julie would replenish each week with the latest big band records.[9]

At the age of ten, Buddy Lansky was used to being indulged. Skilled at playing one parent off against the other, and well practiced at cashing in on adult sympathy for his disability, Buddy was, in many respects, an obnoxious child. At boarding school he became something of a rebel, provoking the principal, Mr. Walpole, after one confrontation, to threaten Buddy with being sent to bed.

"Fine," replied Buddy. "What the hell do I care? I got a jukebox. I got all those records."

It so happened, however, that Anne telephoned the school that day. "Don't tell your mother you're being punished," said Mr. Walpole anxiously, as he took Buddy to the phone. "Mom," Buddy said straightaway. "I'm in the room. I'm being punished."

"Put Mr. Walpole on," his mother replied.

"I'll be down in three hours," Anne Lansky told the principal — and she was, in not much longer than that. She got straight into the car and drove herself the two hundred miles from New York to Baltimore, in order to make sure that her crippled son was not being treated unfairly.[10]

When she was feeling strong, Anne Lansky could take charge of a situation in no uncertain fashion. But her moods varied so. When Buddy got home for Christmas 1940, at the end of his first term in Baltimore, his mother was not there. She had gone away to a special home, his father explained, "to get some rest."[11]

Anne Lansky's "nerves" were getting the better of her. She was seeing doctors. She was acting in ways that were erratic and strange. One evening at a formal dinner which Meyer organized for the agents in his jukebox distributorship, Anne was observed walking up behind her husband with an apple in her hand. Meyer was sitting at a table, talking to his business contacts with considerably more animation and solicitude than he had bestowed upon his wife for some time, when Anne placed the apple on top of her husband's head — then produced her dinner knife and flashed it down through the air to sever the fruit decisively in two.[12]

Meyer later cited this episode as the first indication that his wife might have some sort of mental problem — that she was losing her hold on reality. But seen from another perspective, Anne Lansky's gesture could be judged to have demonstrated a very firm grasp of reality indeed.

It was Paul Lansky, Meyer's younger son, who first put his finger on what was going wrong with the Lansky family.

"It's phony," he said to Buddy in 1944. "It's all phony."[13]

Paul had been sent away to prep school around the age of eight — to the New York Military Academy at Cornwall on Hudson, a few miles away from West Point.[14] Sending Paul to military school was intended to ease the strain on Anne, and also to drum some discipline into Paul himself, who was now becoming as unruly, in his own way, as his elder brother.

Paul Lansky was a special focus of his father's hopes. Buddy was a cripple. Little Sandra was a girl. Paul was the one child that his father saw accomplishing something in the world — and Meyer's expectations were high. When he received Paul's letters from school, Meyer would read through them carefully and would mark their faults of grammar and logic. Then he would send the corrected letters back to the eight-year-old, with the exhortation to do better next time.[15]

Buddy did not see much of his brother for most of the war years. The two boys were away at their respective schools. But in the summer of 1944, at the age of fourteen, Buddy came home for good, his own formal schooling effectively over, while Paul was back in New York, aged eleven and a half, ready to start his studies at Horace Mann, the elite high school at Riverdale, just north of Manhattan.

"I noticed the change in my brother when I came back from Baltimore . . . ," Buddy later remembered. "He was real resentful toward the family."[16]

Paul had not liked being sent away — and, as the disharmony between his parents grew worse, he did not much like coming home, either. He used to dread the train journey back from Cornwall on Hudson, he later recalled, because he would never know the condition in which he might find his mother. The once well-dressed Anne Lansky had been letting herself go. Sometimes Paul got home to find his mother "out of it," wandering vacantly round the family's West Side apartment, smoking a cigarette, and dressed in a fur coat. There was something about the fur coat that upset Paul particularly.[17]

Anne was now seeing psychiatrists regularly, and it was becoming a pattern that she went away to clinics for periods of "rest." But Meyer Lansky did not accept that his wife's depression was a matter of illness, nor that he might bear some responsibility for her unhappiness. If anything, he became rather more intolerant of her failings — more critical and demanding than he had been before.

There was "a general continuance of finding fault," Meyer's brother, Jake, later admitted. "He kept hollering at her and finding fault all the time. . . . I think that would make anybody ill."[18]

Confronted by a husband who did not care for her, Anne Lansky stopped caring for herself. Her "nerves" grew worse. She would cut herself off from everyone else, floating out and away from her life. The onetime client of Wilma's became, little by little, disheveled and unkempt — eccentric, even.

"She got sloppy," Buddy remembered, "shabby-looking."[19]

Paul Lansky, transformed by his four years at Cornwall on Hudson from a problem child into something of a martinet, was bewildered by what he saw happening to his mother. Just entering his teens, he was embarrassed by her strangeness. He did not want to bring friends home when she was around, and he took out his distress on her.[20]

Without anyone's quite realizing it, the Lansky family was getting locked into a circle of division and destruction. Buddy, nearly fifteen, and Paul, a few years younger, were becoming young adults. But their mother was incapable of confiding in them, and their father was disinclined to.

Meyer encouraged the boys to take an interest in politics and world affairs. He liked them to have discussions with him about what was said in the newspapers. But these conversations were like Meyer's playing the grammar teacher with the letters that Paul wrote him. He was schooling his sons in the techniques of communication, while skirting round the heart of the matter — the transmission of feelings.

No one in the Lansky family transmitted their feelings to anyone, in fact, except in the increasingly frequent interludes when feeling erupted in blazing anger — and, in the absence of communication, the hitting began. Anne would hit Meyer. Meyer would hit Anne. Paul would also get violent with her, imitating his father. So then Meyer would discipline the boy, hitting Paul in turn, while telling him that he should not be hitting people.

Meyer Lansky's life inside his family had become a sad reflection of his life outside — a slippery world of hints and indirectness, where nothing was quite straight or clear, and where the only authentic and incontrovertible communication was conveyed in terms of violence.

It was this spiral of disintegration which prompted Paul Lansky to seize on the word "phony." It became his refrain. Neither of the boys yet knew exactly how their father earned his living, but Paul had thought about it enough to realize there was something strange about not knowing.

"Paul would start to tell me how he didn't like the family lifestyle with the phony money," Buddy remembered. "You know, he called it phony."[21]

Meyer threw a party on one occasion, giving Paul the job of organizing the coat closet. His brother was happy to take the tips, Buddy remembered, but Paul worked himself into a fury over all the women's fur coats. He called them "the phony minks."[22]

Anne Lansky was getting worse. She had her rational moments, but she was withdrawing into herself more and more. When her brother, Julie Citron, came round to try to help her, Anne accused him of interfering.[23] She tried different doctors and institutions to help her with what she called her "nervousness." Her doctors started to use the word "schizophrenia."

"She was a Jekyll and Hyde," remembered Buddy. "Good one moment, bad the next."[24]

Anne's appearance grew ever more untidy. She started talking to herself. In the autumn of 1945, she submitted to electric shock treatment.

After that, Buddy recalled, his mother was scared. By 1945 the family had moved to an apartment in the Beresford on Central Park West, a few blocks north of the Majestic, and Anne turned up there one day when she was supposed to be away on one of her "rests." She had composed herself sufficiently to escape from the clinic, and to get safely home — all the way from Riverdale in a nightgown. But once she was home, Anne broke down again.

The nurses were sent for. For the rest of his life, Buddy was to remember the knock on the door from the men in white coats, the protesting cries of his mother, the strange heavy jacket with the strings on the sleeves. The pattern of confrontation with her husband had been turning Anne wild. She had gone for Meyer, on one occasion, with a kitchen knife.[25] So now Meyer kept out of the way.

Anne's father, Grandpa Moses Citron, came round that day to see if he could give his poor daughter some help or comfort, and was totally rejected. Shuffling and shambling, in slippers and a white hospital costume, Anne Lansky had retreated into a world of her own. Buddy could remember his grandfather as the orderlies took her away — the old man bent over, with his head in his hands, sobbing helplessly.

One day soon after the Second World War, Paul Lansky went out with some friends for the evening. Paul was just thirteen years old, and his mother presumed that the boy would only be gone for an hour or two. But as time went by and it grew toward midnight, Anne Lansky began to get worried. Meyer was out as well, and she had no way of contacting him.

Anne was back from Riverdale. She was enjoying one of her better spells. But her life remained lonely. Meyer was still away for weeks at a time, and his eventual return home would be the occasion for disagreements and recriminations, leading to a row — after which

Meyer would quite often walk out of the apartment for nights in a
row without taking Anne with him, or even bothering to tell her
where he was going.[26]

On the autumn evening in 1945 when Paul went out, it was one
o'clock in the morning before Meyer and the boy got home, each
within a few minutes of the other, and by that time Anne was beside
herself with anxiety and fury.

She upbraided her son angrily. It was no hour for a thirteen-year-
old to be out on the streets of New York. But, as usually happened
when his wife criticized the children, Meyer took his son's side, treating his wife's attempts at discipline with disdain. She was being hysterical. Paul's staying out late was not a tragedy. It was the sort of
thing the boy would grow out of. Some day, said Meyer, he would
be a good son.[27]

Anne decided she had had enough. She did indeed suffer from her
weak moments. But there were other moments when Anne Lansky
could see very clearly, and this was one of them. The very next morning, Anne found herself a lawyer and filed for divorce.

"He didn't approve of anything I did, whether right or wrong,"
she testified when the case came to court sixteen months later. "It
was always wrong — it couldn't be right."[28]

"How did he act when he found fault?" inquired her counsel.

"As nasty as he possibly could be," Anne replied, "whether anyone
else was there or not — in front of my friends, or the maid, or the
butler, anybody. Nothing I ever did was right."[29]

Meyer did not contest the case. He was fed up with his wife's
"weak-mindedness." If Anne wanted to end the marriage, that was
fine by him. But since no state in America then permitted divorce by
mutual consent, Anne's grievances had to be presented to a judge,
and corroborated by at least one independent witness. Meyer agreed
that brother Jake should do the job.

"What was the condition of Mrs. Lansky's health when she married Mr. Lansky?" Jake was asked when he was cross-examined on
February 3, 1947.

"Very good."

"Did her health change since her marriage?"

"Very much. She has been a sick girl."

"Nervous and upset?"

"Yes."

"To what do you attribute this change of health on her part?"

"To Mr. Lansky's treatment of her."[30]

Jake Lansky was clearly steering a middle path in his testimony, supplying enough evidence to justify a divorce decree, while doing his best not to make his brother sound an unmitigated bully and tyrant. But his recollections had the ring of truth.

"What would be the occasion for his hollering?" Jake was asked.

"He wouldn't need an occasion. . . . The least little thing would cause him to get excited, and when he got excited, he would yell. . . ."

"When he displayed his temper, was it with regard or without regard to whether other people were in the home or not?"

"It didn't make much difference."

"You say he stayed away from home considerably?"

"Yes."

"How often would he stay away from home?"

"Three or four nights a week."

"Did Mrs. Lansky approve of his remaining away?"

"No sir."

"What occurred when she asked him where he was at these unusual hours?"

"He would tell her to mind her own business."[31]

For Anne herself, after seventeen largely unhappy years of marriage, the divorce hearing was the chance to let it all out: Meyer's undermining of her attempts to impose some discipline on the children, and the nasty, vicious side — the rows and scuffles, the time that Meyer had slapped her and when he pulled and snapped a gold necklace from around her neck.

Meyer had told Anne that he did not love her. He had complained about the bills from the doctors whom she saw for consultations about her nerves. He said that he would not pay her hospital and medical expenses anymore, that he was going to send all the bills to her father and tell him to pay.

Anne was at the end of her tether. She was seeing a doctor at least once a week.[32] It was true that, like her mother, she was highly strung. But whereas her mother had the support system of the Citrons, who did what they could to help Anne as well, Anne found herself treated by her husband as an inconvenience — an enemy, almost. She had had enough. Living with Meyer Lansky had effectively demolished her.

"He's out six nights a week," she testified, "and on the seventh night he's tired. I am just tied up inside. He would think nothing of upbraiding me in the presence of the children. He never approved of anything I would say or do, whether intelligent or unintelligent. I am sick of that kind of stuff. . . ."[33]

Meyer and Anne Lansky were formally granted their divorce decree on February 14, 1947 — St. Valentine's Day. Their separation and support agreement, ratified on the same day, gave Anne custody of the children, while also making clear the hauteur of Meyer's attitude toward his wife. He insisted on a clause which gave him the sole right to select the schools and the summer camps that the children would attend.

The agreement also betrayed a certain minginess. In the event of any of the children not wanting to live with their mother and moving away, Meyer's weekly support payments of $300 would be reduced by $50 per child per week — and when, in the course of time, all the children did grow up and move away, Meyer managed to beat down his ex-wife's long-term monthly alimony payment still further. He paid her just $400 a month — $4,800 a year to cover all her living expenses, including rent.[34]

On his tax return for 1946 Meyer Lansky declared an income of some $86,000 after expenses — over $102,000 before deductions.[35] The $4,800 a year to his ex-wife was nearly double the income of the average American in 1946, but it represented less than an eighteenth of his own, without taking into account the undeclared, untaxed cash which he pocketed from his casinos.

Somehow Anne Lansky, once the toast of Wilma's and the dress emporiums of Fifth Avenue, managed to survive on her $400 a month, through three decades of severe inflation. She moved to a small apartment on Central Park South, beside the St. Moritz, then moved on to a less expensive place on West End Avenue[36] — a little old lady who had once been the beautiful and bubbling young Mrs. Meyer Lansky, wandering ever more vacantly among the drug addicts and derelicts who came to be her neighbors on the Upper West Side.

Anne Lansky refused to be a burden on her children, insisting that she could take care of herself, and sometimes, when they went to see her, she would be the mother that they remembered — the laughing, dark-haired woman who read stories and played games patiently with them when they were sick. But on other occasions, more and more frequently as the years went by, she simply did not recognize them. Anne Lansky was a different person, severed from a world to which she had long since ceased to have much reason to relate.

After one such encounter, Buddy told his father about Anne's sad state, and Meyer was silent for a minute.

"Maybe it was my fault," he said, "not knowing how to handle her."[37]

9

**"Benny Siegel . . . He
Knocked Out
Plenty"**

IN January 1946, America had a lot of fun to catch up on — and
she came looking for it in Florida. The war had given many Americans their first experience of winter sunshine. Stationed for their military training in Miami or Fort Lauderdale, they had drilled on the
beach, and had been billeted in the gaudy holiday hotels as barracks.
In the early winter months of 1946, they came back, liberated and
cash-rich, to enjoy the place properly.

Honeymooners, golfers, jaunty retirees — thousands flocked south
for Florida's winter "season," the new folk rite of America's postwar
consumer high life. You had to book weeks ahead to get a seat on
the train.[1] In the winters of the late 1940s, Miami Beach and its surrounding resorts became America's premier fun complex, a vast,
extended play city that stretched from the Miami River up to Fort
Lauderdale — and right in the center of it lay Meyer Lansky's carpet
joints. There were no fewer than thirty-two illegal gambling establishments of different types, by one estimate, flourishing on the Dade-
Broward line in the years between 1946 and 1950[2] — wire rooms,
horse parlors, small, single crap games, full-blown carpet joints.

If you came up to Hallandale by the coast road, you risked the
waves that sometimes ran over the blacktop, and the shells of the
huge land crabs that were tough enough to puncture your tires. The

first joint you encountered, where the county line hit the beach, was the Club Bohème, a night spot with gambling and a floor show in the Lido tradition, run by Albert "Papa" Bouché, a local impresario with Ben Marden–like aspirations.

If you chose the less adventurous but still unpaved and unlit U.S. 1, you were greeted, to your left, by Greenacres, a packing-shed structure in the raw tradition of Potatoes Kaufman's original Plantation. Greenacres housed a money crap game, New York style, where players would bet against each other, with the house taking a cut. There were no chips — just dollar bills by the thousand.[3]

Meyer Lansky had shares in both these new establishments,[4] and he had kept one or another of his original Hallandale clubs operating in a low-profile fashion through the winters of the Second World War. His brother, Jake, had come to oversee the Broward business as his local general manager. After Jake's first, 1936–37 season in the Plantation turned Farm, the younger brother had decided to make Florida his home, renting a house on one of Hollywood's palm-shaded streets named after presidents — Van Buren one year, Jackson the next.

Jake had married in the 1930s, and had started a family. His wife, Anna, came from a poor family on the Lower East Side. She was a quiet, domestically inclined girl who shared Jake's easygoing tastes. Aged forty-one in 1945, Jake Lansky was a square-faced, burly man, whose nose and eyes gave his features an odd echo of Meyer's. He wore thick pebble glasses. With his dark, curly hair already graying around the edges, Jake looked older than he was — most people assumed that Meyer was the younger brother. Jake Lansky was made to be the stolid front man, and he played the part to perfection.

Jake's working base in Hallandale — and the headquarters for the complicated network of partnerships, cuts, and share-outs that linked Hallandale's various gaming joints — was the baronial, white-painted mansion-clubhouse that Ben Marden had set up in the early 1940s, the Colonial Inn. Grand and porticoed, it sat beside the Gulf-stream Race Track. During the war, the Colonial Inn had served as operations center for an army signal corps unit.[5] There had been cots and showers in the gaming room, a mess hall in front of the stage. Now repainted, refurbished, and twinkling like Tara at the head of its long, curved drive, the Colonial Inn reopened for business in December 1945.

For their first postwar season, the Lanskys brought a member of the thriving Detroit gaming fraternity, Mert Wertheimer, to help operate the Colonial Inn's gaming room, alongside familiar faces like George Sadlo.[6] Wertheimer and his partner, Ruben Mathews, took nearly a third of the Colonial Inn's declared profits. Jimmy Blue Eyes had 7.5 percent. Frank Erickson had 5 percent.[7] With Joe Adonis and Benny Siegel cut in as well, the Colonial Inn represented a partnership of all the talents.

There were a few gaming rooms and a large number of bookies operating in Miami Beach, to the south of Hallandale, but they were vulnerable to the shifting complexities of politics in an urban area. The *Miami Herald* had a crusading young editor, Lee Hills, who had the bright idea of collaborating with northern newspapers to identify and publicize gamblers and undesirables who came down to winter in Miami. He ran a series, "Know Your Neighbor," with photographs and criminal records.[8]

The Miami Beach authorities decided to start their first postwar season "clean." At the end of 1945, the police started a program of raids on the city's private gaming rooms, and they did what they could to make life difficult for the cigar-stand bookmakers in the tourist hotels.[9]

Meyer Lansky and his Hallandale partners could not have been happier.

The authorities in Broward County suffered from no misplaced righteousness. Sheriff Walter Clark had won his position as the county's principal law enforcement officer by popular election in 1933, and he had been reelected regularly and resoundingly in the dozen years since on the basis of what Sheriff Clark liked to call a "liberal" ticket.[10]

Sheriff Clark's definition of "liberal" meant giving the people what they wanted. "I am not going around snooping in private businesses and homes," he later explained.[11]

If pressed, the sheriff would admit that gambling was probably being conducted along the Broward line with Dade County. But it was not his job to interfere, he would explain, so long as none of his constituents made any formal complaints.[12]

Thirty pounds overweight, with a wide, carplike grin and features that were not dissimilar to those of the overfed fish that he liked to hook out of the county's canals and drainage channels, Walter Clark was a gregarious, popular character. He made much in his election campaigns of being a simple, down-home, local boy, and even those who opposed his progambling attitude found it difficult to dislike him personally. He was, he liked to claim, the first white child born in Broward — the county which was carved out from its neighbors, Dade and Palm Beach counties, in 1915, and which had been named after Napoleon Bonaparte Broward, the aptly named governor who, in the years after 1905, initiated Florida's conquest of the Everglades in the cause of farming and real estate.

Law and order was a basic plank of Walter Clark's platform. Under his stewardship, he liked to boast, "Broward has enjoyed the lowest crime-occurrence record of any U.S. resort county for its size"[13] — and the operators of Broward's gambling joints contributed significantly to this record. Prostitution was not the problem in Hallandale that it was in Miami Beach, or, up in New Jersey, in the gambling-connected resort of Atlantic City, because Meyer Lansky and his partners enforced a strict "no B-girl" rule in and around their Florida establishments.

It was his involvement with girls that had got Charlie Luciano into trouble. Girls were complicated and emotional. They were not businesslike, even though they were supposed to be part of a business. Dealing with girls, most of whom came from other states, carried the same risks as dealing in drugs, or not filing your tax return with the IRS. It was a federal offense — and that meant the attentions of the FBI. "Nothing federal" was the motto by which America's wide-open enclaves and carpet joints survived.

In any case, no serious casino operator wanted to encourage girls whose business lay in enticing men and their money away from the tables. It also got the wives upset — and it was one of Meyer Lansky's principles that a good casino should keep the wives happy. A bored, unhappy wife or girlfriend was likely to nag her man and drag him away from the tables early. So, a few hours after the main dinner show, just as the gambling started to gather momentum at the Colonial Inn, the lights would go down in the dining room for an extra midnight spectacle to occupy the ladies' interests while their menfolk kept on gambling.[14]

Meyer Lansky took pride in running a clean operation. For all their illegality, and the sinfulness of gambling, his carpet joints were essentially bourgeois establishments. Claude Litteral, elegant in black tie, and all the more dashing for having his armless sleeve tucked casually into a pocket of his tuxedo, sat at a desk screening the doorway between the dining area and the gambling room, the threshold across which a harmless evening out became, technically, involvement in an illegal act.[15] Locals were politely, and apologetically, turned back toward the bar or showroom. Drunks and suspected hookers were escorted firmly to the door, and men or women in uniform were also banned, since any trouble with them would bring in the military police — another jurisdiction, like the feds, over which Meyer and his partners had no control.

By the winter season of 1946, Hallandale's system of legalized payoffs, via the municipal court, from the casinos and horse parlors directly into the official coffers, had developed from its small beginnings in the early 1940s into a major source of income for the city's government. There were direct handouts to the taxpayers also. Joseph Varon, who was shortly to become Hallandale's city attorney, remembers a system whereby the registered voters, numbered only in the hundreds in the years before 1950, all received a personal cash payment in the course of the season — thirty-five dollars per household, the equivalent of a week's wages.[16]

The local farmers got good prices for their produce from the kitchens of Hallandale's restaurants and dining rooms, and there were jobs as well. The inventory of correspondence of the Colonial Inn, lodged with their accountants, Messrs. Eisen & Eisen, showed twelve letters on Hallandale's official city stationery, all dated December 1947 and introducing twelve individuals anxious "to secure a position with your firm this season." The letters were all signed "H. C. Schwartz, Mayor."[17]

The inventory showed other letters to Jake Lansky — from the North Miami Police Department and from the West Miami Police Association, with thanks for generous donations.[18] Also acknowledged were checks totaling $750, gratefully received by the Florida Sheriff Association, the Justice of Peace & Constables Association, the Police & Sheriff Association, and the Florida Peace Officers Association.[19]

Paid off still more directly were the local Hallandale police, a select corps of three men who had recently graduated from motor bicycles to squad cars, but who were not equipped with radios. When they needed to report an emergency, they would call in from the nearest pay phone — the operator, who recognized their voices, refunded them their nickel at the end of the call.[20] These three local representatives of the law got their cut from the annual invasion of the gamblers by working off-duty stints supervising the parking of cars outside the Colonial Inn and the other gambling joints.

Everyone got in on the act. At the end of the night's business, a call would be made, and a posse of Sheriff Clark's uniformed deputies would arrive to escort the night's take to the bank. The armored truck company, whose vehicle transported the money, was owned by Sheriff Clark's brother, Robert.[21]

We know about these payments because, like all good taxpayers, Meyer Lansky and his partners supplied the IRS with a detailed accounting of their expenses. In 1931, the case of Al Capone had memorably demonstrated that the IRS was not concerned with how a businessman earned his money, so long as he paid his taxes. Meyer's accountants turned this to their advantage.[22]

"Mr. Sadlo's position with the Colonial Inn is a very responsible one," wrote Ben C. Eisen, the Colonial Inn's accountant, in response to an IRS query of George Sadlo's traveling expenses. "It is his job to see that all dealers hired for the casino are honest, trustworthy and of the highest type. . . . In order to be able to hire this type of dealer, Mr. Sadlo travels throughout the country and visits the best casinos." The fact that these casinos were illegal establishments, and that George Sadlo was recruiting dealers for illegal purposes, did not affect the validity of his tax deduction for IRS purposes. "Since the winter season is an off-season throughout the country, except in Florida," explained Ben Eisen to the IRS, "Mr. Sadlo is in a position to get this kind of help, but not before he makes all inquiries. . . . The $2,500 which Sadlo deducted for expenses in the pursuit of business is a very nominal amount."[23]

Like many a good taxpayer, however, Meyer Lansky and his partners did not quite present the whole story in the figures which they submitted to the IRS. At the end of every gambling shift, the "drop" from each table in the casino would be brought into the counting room. There, Meyer and Jake Lansky would personally count the mounds of dollar bills until they reached the "handle" — the amount of money they needed to meet their daily expenses. The handle, with the addition of a moderate sum for cash reserve and profit, would be passed on to be recorded in the credit column of the casino's ledger and, eventually, in the accounts that were presented to the IRS. Anything in excess of this went directly into the pockets of the Lansky brothers and of their partners.[24]

This cash — which might be tallied in the tens of thousands of dollars on a good night — was what came, in later years, to be known as the casino skim. But in the carpet joints of the 1930s and 1940s, it was simply the take, the loot, the boodle — the real return to the partners on their investment — and, as in bootlegging days, it made sense to have a capable, honest partner like Meyer Lansky in charge of the share-out. At the end of every gaming season, Meyer organized the figures that the partners declared to the IRS, and, week by week, he organized the real, cash payments as well.

It was not only the partners who got paid in cash. The top entertainers got money under the table in addition to the fee that their agent negotiated. Joe E. Lewis, the comedian, had a cashbox in the safe of his hotel, into which he would haphazardly stuff hundred-dollar bills each night.[25] Sophie Tucker, a compulsive gambler, would take a proportion of her money in chips, and by the end of a week's engagement, the singer had, quite often, given it all back to the casino again, across the tables.[26]

Frank Sinatra, whose career got started in these years, has become a byword for his associations, real and rumored, with mobsters, and has been much criticized for them. But in the years after World War II, it was the carpet joints which offered America's entertainers their most remunerative live venues. All the stars who played them were paid in illegally earned money, and, unless they were extraordinarily standoffish, they had to hobnob with their paymasters.

Comedians like Jimmy Durante and Joe E. Lewis actually incorporated the nature of their employers, and their fellowship with them, into their act. Lewis became the gangster entertainer to end them all after he was bludgeoned and slashed to within an inch of his life in Chicago in 1927.[27] Scarred for life, Lewis steadfastly declined to identify his assailants, or to give the police any clue as to who they might have been — and he was never out of work again.* From 1946 onward, Joe E. Lewis was a feature of every Hallandale winter season in one or another of Meyer Lansky's clubs, a tipsy, wisecracking whirlwind, drinking, kibbitzing, and playing gin rummy into the small hours with Meyer, Joe Adonis, and the other partners. He kept stuffing his cashbox with money, but he would also hand out large tips — particularly to the down-and-outs who were the special object of his generosity.

"There," he would say, thrusting five or ten dollars into their hands. "This is for you. And don't go spending it on no *food*."[28]

Lewis's brand of low comedy, delivered while he wandered round the audience with a filled tumbler in hand, and relying heavily on his weakness for whiskey, gambling, and three packs of cigarettes a day, struck a chord with his gangster fans. Their own idea of a joke was

*The incident was depicted in the 1957 movie *The Joker Is Wild*, in which Frank Sinatra played the part of Lewis.

the hotfoot — a complicated and stealthy maneuver involving a pack
of matches slipped into the victim's shoe. The folded-back cover of
the packet was slipped inside the side or back of the shoe, exposing
the matches themselves, which were then ignited with a *whoosh*
to the amusement of all around, while the victim jumped up and
down, feverishly endeavoring to prevent his trousers catching fire.[29]

Meyer Lansky tended to stay aloof from this horseplay. The volumes arriving from the Book-of-the-Month Club[30] were the only evidence of recreation on the part of the purposeful accountant, who
juggled the figures and kept the shares straight. But Meyer's partners
admired him the more for his seriousness. He was their resident intellectual, the authority to whom they turned in arguments great and
small, the mediator — the oracle.

Frank Costello was particularly exercised by his own poor reputation, and that of his friends. It irked him that the world regarded
them all as gangsters and hoodlums. Who did gamblers kill? Who
were they hurting, even? It was unfair, he complained. They would
never get respectable.

"Don't worry, don't worry," replied Meyer, the history book
reader. "Look at history. Look at the Astors and the Vanderbilts, all
those big society people. They were the worst thieves — and now
look at them. It's just a matter of time."[31]

Harold Conrad was a young New York sportswriter who started
work at the Colonial Inn at the beginning of 1946. Conrad had been
hired to help with the club's public relations, and he met Meyer Lansky the day after he had submitted his first expense account, for two
round-trip cab fares to Hollywood. Conrad claimed twelve dollars.

Meyer came up to the young man, serious and unsmiling.

"You must be a big tipper or something," he said. "Two round-
trips to Hollywood is eight bucks, and four tips is two dollars. I make
that ten bucks."[32]

Conrad soon discovered that managing public relations for a joint
run by Meyer Lansky could mean, as often as not, keeping the place
out of the newspapers. A few days after he arrived, Lansky told him
that Frank Costello was due from New Orleans the next morning.
"He's got something on his mind," Meyer said. "Maybe you can help.
You wake me up in the morning and we'll go to the airport and pick
him up."[33]

As the two men drove Costello back from the airport — Lansky
at the wheel, Conrad sitting to attention in the backseat — Costello

explained what was on his mind. Walter Winchell was in Miami Beach, and, with Dade County clamping down on its gambling, Costello was worried that the gossip columnist might run an embarrassing story about the wide-open situation that prevailed, by contrast, up in Broward.

"I don't know what to tell you, Frank," said Meyer. "You got any ideas, Harold?"

Harold did have a suggestion. He had been close to Damon Runyon in the writer's final, painful months, when Runyon was dying of cancer. He knew that Winchell had started the Damon Runyon Cancer Fund, and that the fund meant more to Winchell than most things.

"A check for $5,000," suggested Conrad, "would make a big impression."[34]

Next day, Conrad was at the Roney Plaza on Miami Beach, handing over a $5,000 check to a sun-oiled Winchell in a deck chair.

"It's from the boys at the Colonial Inn," Conrad explained. "They really loved Runyon."

Winchell was impressed.

"Why don't you come out to the club?" suggested Conrad.

Winchell went up to Hallandale that evening. He danced three rumba sets, shot craps in the casino, and took a fancy to a show girl in the chorus line who came from Texas. Frank Costello looked at Harold Conrad with new respect.

"You done good, kid," he said.[35]

Harold Conrad's 1946 season at the Colonial Inn was a succession of surprises. When George Raft, the film star, arrived in Hallandale to spend some time with Benny Siegel and his other friends, Conrad assumed that the actor would take advantage of his visit to study the originals on whom his gangster roles were based. But the reverse proved the case. It was the gangsters who spent their time studying Raft, trying to find out the name of his tailor, and who made his elegant, hand-crafted shoes.[36]

Conrad also discovered that, contrary to stereotype, gangsters did not spend their time killing people. It was making money that was on their mind.

In 1946 an off-color, black-market record was making the rounds — "The Farting Range," the vivid depiction of a world championship of flatulence in which contestants gave performances in line with their national characteristics.

When Joe Adonis heard it for the first time, he fell on the floor, laughing. "Wait a minute, wait a minute," he cried. "I've got to get Frank. . . . Frank, you've got to hear this."[37]

Within a minute, Frank Costello was also convulsed with laughter, and Harold Conrad was instantly dispatched to discover where he could get copies of the record made locally. A day or so later, he was back with fifty fresh-pressed records that had cost him four dollars apiece.

"Fifty dollars," said Joe Adonis to the young press agent. "Charge fifty dollars each."

Adonis then turned and addressed himself grandly to the assembled show girls and gamblers. "By special request of Mr. Costello," he declared, "we proudly present a record that has just reached us from England — the latest speech of Winston Churchill."

Conrad then played "The Farting Range," and within thirty seconds pandemonium reigned, everyone doubling up in paroxysms of mirth and pulling out their wallets to hand over their $50. By the end of the day, Harold Conrad had sold out his entire stock of records — a clean and instant profit of more than $2,000.

"You see?" said Joe Adonis. "I'm a Mob guy — I'm a businessman. I want you to know about business."[38]

Carpet joints all over America reaped rich dividends from the nation's new spending patterns in the years following the Second World War. Leisure and pleasure were the peacetime priorities. In 1946, Meyer Lansky and Frank Costello resumed their August partnership in Saratoga, and they also collaborated on the opening of a luxurious new nightclub in Jefferson Parish outside New Orleans, the Beverly Club. Frank gave Meyer a 25 percent cut of the Beverly Club's profits for the first two years in return for his help with the layout and setting up of the casino.[39]

But there were only so many Hallandales and Jefferson Parishes in America, and the fix was never totally reliable. In 1946 Meyer Lansky and Bill Syms had gone back to Iowa to restart their dog racing after the war — and discovered that there had been changes in Council Bluffs. The new mayor was scandalized at the selling of "options" on greyhounds — so that was the end of the Dodge Park Kennel Club.[40]

"Will they open this year?" was the anxious question at the beginning of every season from Saratoga to Broward County.

Since 1931 Nevada had been the only state in the Union where casino gambling was legal, and that was another country. Nevada was eighteen bumpy and unpressurized hours by plane from New York at the end of the 1930s. But the war had made America smaller. In 1941 the Nevada state legislature voted to legalize betting on horse race results coming in by wire, and that caught the eye of Benjamin Siegel, who was then making book in California. The prospect of earning some legal money from his gambling appealed to Benny Siegel, so in 1941 he set off to explore the racing-wire market in Nevada, starting in the first dusty settlement down the road from Los Angeles — the railroad depot town of Las Vegas.

As the crooks and hoodlums of one era have become the heroes of the next, Bugsy Siegel has come, in popular folklore, to be seen as the patron saint and inspirer of modern Las Vegas. There have even been suggestions that the city should raise a statue to him — the founding father who strode out into the empty desert, a modern Mormon of craps and blackjack, to dream of a city of shining palaces, and to lay the foundations which turned that vision into reality. Legend has it that Benny Siegel devised the concept of the modern resort hotel-casino, bought himself a plot of wasteland, and built the first of the great temples of chance, blazing the trail that others were to follow.

In reality, Bugsy Siegel followed a trail pioneered by quite a number of others. When he arrived in Las Vegas in 1941, there was already one luxurious hotel-casino in the desert outside town, El Rancho Vegas, a landscaped and waterfalled resort complex covering sixty-six acres,[41] and in December 1942, El Rancho was joined on Highway 91 — the Strip, as it came to be known — by an even larger and more luxurious development, the Last Frontier.[42] The Last Frontier featured a swimming pool, sun deck, tennis courts and riding stables, a showroom and casino, and 170 individually air-conditioned rooms.[43]

"Each room," reported the *Las Vegas Evening Review-Journal* in awe, "has a private bath, tiled about the tub and on the floor. The color scheme in the bath harmonizes with the theme in the adjoining bedroom. . . . Stream-lined upholstered chairs in harmony with drapes and bedspreads are provided."[44]

War boosted the development of Las Vegas as an American entertainment center.[45] The arrival of the U.S. Army's gunnery school increased the town's population by nearly fifty percent, and in the best carpet-joint tradition, El Rancho and the Last Frontier sent their entertainers to put on shows in the military camps. They also made their showrooms available on quieter weeknights for the celebrations that attended the graduation of each new batch of gunnery officers or airmen, the boys being treated to a slap-up dinner, dancing, and floor show before they were sent off to battle.[46]

The bookmakers of Las Vegas shared in the town's general expansion, and after a couple of years Benny Siegel was doing very well out of his wire-service franchise. But he was not doing nearly so well as the owners of El Rancho and the Last Frontier, the regularly over-booked resorts out on the Strip, and he decided that he wanted to get in on the luxury hotel-casino business. Early in 1943, he got in touch with Tom Hull, the owner of El Rancho Vegas, and made him an offer that Hull found very easy to refuse. The California hotelier knew something of Bugsy's reputation.

"You may say for me," Hull told the *Las Vegas Review-Journal* in March 1943, "that the people of Las Vegas have been too good to me for me to repay them in that way. Mr. Siegel has contacted me several times with an offer to purchase, but I have told him I was not interested — and that goes for all time."[47]

As the war drew to an end, Benny Siegel was by no means alone in seeking to duplicate the spectacular success of El Rancho Vegas and the Last Frontier. "I'm going to build a hotel," was the stock comment of wealthy visitors to Las Vegas in the early months of peace, according to an article in the *Review-Journal* in July 1946.[48]

Mae West was planning a hotel-casino, said the paper. Frank Sinatra was part of a consortium that was trying to develop a resort hotel-casino with its own radio station. Roy Rogers was negotiating to start a dude ranch.[49]

Ben Siegel was in some danger of getting left out when, late in 1945, he heard of the chance to acquire the El Cortez, on Fremont and Sixth Street, a gambling hotel in downtown Las Vegas which had been doing good business for several years. Benny had quite a number of local partners — but he also turned for funds to his old friend Meyer Lansky.

Meyer and Benny had been friends rather than business partners since their Cannon Street garage days — and long-distance friends, most of the time, at that. With the ending of Prohibition, Benny had found a natural place for himself in the film colony of Los Angeles, romancing starlets and earning a nook in the gossip columns as a "sportsman" — the euphemism for someone who made book and organized craps and poker schools. With his dazzling smile and his slicked-down good looks, Benny Siegel became something of a star in his own right.

Meyer Lansky did not share his friend's enthusiasm for Las Vegas. "It was in sorry shape," he said years later, recalling his visits there in the 1940s. "Living conditions were bad. No one wanted to go to Vegas to gamble. Air connections were bad. And the trip by car was bothersome. It was so hot that the wires in the car would melt."[50]

Las Vegas offered Meyer Lansky the second great chance in his life to go legit, but he made no special effort to take it. Several dozen former bootleggers, bookies, and carpet-joint operators flooded into Las Vegas from different corners of America in the late 1940s, seizing the opportunity to sidestep their pasts — and most of Ben Siegel's coinvestors in the El Cortez fell into this category. Gus Greenbaum was an Arizona bookmaker. Willie Alderman and the Berman brothers, Davie and Chickie, had run carpet joints in Minneapolis. Moe Sedway had come out with Benny from Los Angeles to help with the franchising of the wire. All these men invested in the El Cortez in December 1945 while also working there, helping to operate the hotel's casino.

But Meyer's focus remained firmly in Florida. In December 1945, he was busy getting ready for his first postwar season in Hallandale. He was content to be little more than a sleeping partner in the El Cortez project, investing $60,000, a 10 percent stake, and trusting Benny Siegel to handle it.[51]

Benny handled it well. Real estate prices were rising sharply in Las Vegas's postwar expansion, and in July 1946, Benny and his partners in the El Cortez syndicate resold the hotel for a profit of $166,000 — a 27 percent return on their investment in little more than six months.[52] The trouble started when the successful El Cortez syndicate decided to reinvest their money that summer in a new hotel-casino being built out on the Strip — the Flamingo.

The Flamingo Hotel Casino was the brainchild of Billy Wilkerson, the suave, waxed-mustached founder of the *Hollywood Reporter,* who also created the Café Trocadero, Ciro's, and La Rue's, a trio of successful Hollywood nightspots which between them formed the beginning of Sunset Strip.[53]

It was Wilkerson's idea to transport the sophistication of these nightspots to Las Vegas, for though El Rancho and the Last Frontier had their luxury, their atmosphere remained in the "Howdy, pard-ner" dude ranch tradition.[54] Wilkerson envisioned something more glitzy, a refuge from the desert and the sagebrush — a showroom that featured major stars, and a casino ambience that was Beverly Hills, rather than Nevada.

But the impresario's vision outran his budget. Wilkerson had purchased the land for the Flamingo, had drawn up the plans, and had broken ground on construction when he started looking for new investors. Benny Siegel finally had his chance to buy his own hotel-casino[55] — or two-thirds of it, at least. Benny and his other partners, including Meyer, reinvested the $650,000 from their sale of the El Cortez to secure a 66 percent holding in Wilkerson's Flamingo.[56]

As controller of the majority consortium, Benny set himself Christmas 1946 as his deadline for getting the Flamingo finished. But he immediately developed bright new ideas for improving the rooms — not least his own, designated master suite — and he wanted nothing but the best: unique designs, rare woods, the finest marbles. The charming and imperious Ben Siegel totally lacked his friend Meyer's sense of control.

The problem was compounded by his latest girlfriend. Benny's marriage to Esther had fallen victim to his relentless womanizing, and in 1946 his consort was Virginia Hill, a lady whose own varied track record included marriage to a Mexican rumba dancer, and a relationship with Joe Epstein, an elderly Chicago bookmaker who, with touching fidelity, kept sending Virginia checks long after she ceased to be his permanent paramour. Plump and pugnacious, Virginia Hill had a temper to match Benny's, and they made a formidable couple of building inspectors when they drove out to look over the latest elaborations at the Flamingo.

To the surprise of many, Benny Siegel managed to get the Flamingo opened on time — and in some style. "That was the biggest whoop-de-do I ever seen," remembers Benny Binion, who came out of town on December 26, 1946, to cast a professional eye over the new casino on its opening night, and was considerably impressed. "They had Jimmy Durante, Cugat's band and Rosemarie, all in one show."[57]

"You never saw so many black-chip gamblers in your life," says Lou Wiener, Ben Siegel's Las Vegas lawyer.[58]

The problem for Ben Siegel, and for the bankroll of the new Flamingo casino, was that the players who were so energetically putting down their black, $100 chips, were almost all winning back their bets, rewagering, and then winning again.

The Flamingo could have done with Meyer Lansky in the gaming room. Through a combination of poor luck and dealers who had not yet found their rhythm, most of the tables at the Flamingo suffered heavy losses in their first hours of gambling on the night of December 26, 1946. And then, not long after midnight, when some of the biggest winners might reasonably have been expected to go on playing into the small hours, and to lose their gains back to the house, almost everybody cashed in their chips and took their money home.[59]

Benny Siegel had got the casino, showroom, restaurant, and bar of the Flamingo finished by his deadline. But the hotel itself was not complete. There were no bedrooms for the guests. So on the night that the Flamingo opened for business, it was the neighboring El Rancho Vegas and the Last Frontier which made the big money, as the guests from the Flamingo's opening reception came back to their hotels, sent their wives off to bed, and decided to play for an hour or so with the winnings they had brought from the new casino down the road.[60]

The same pattern continued through the entire Christmas week of 1946 and through the New Year's celebrations of 1947. When the holidays ended early in January 1947, the visitors all went home. The whole of Las Vegas suffered a downturn, and farthest out of town, with no captive, residential guests of its own, the Flamingo was hurt hardest of all. Late in January 1947, the new Flamingo Hotel Casino closed its doors, less than a month after it had opened.

Meyer Lansky had originally invested $62,500 of his own money in the Flamingo. This was the sum he had withdrawn in August 1946 from his successful partnership in the El Cortez,[61] and he transferred it to the Nevada Project Corporation, the company formed by Ben Siegel to represent the stake that he and his partners purchased from Wilkerson in the Flamingo. Meyer's $62,500 gave him one hundred shares — a tenth of the total stock in Benny's new syndicate.[62] In all, there were twenty-two partners in the Nevada Project Corporation, including Meyer, Benny Siegel, Gus Greenbaum, Moe Sedway, and the other shareholders in the El Cortez.[63]

On November 29, 1946, the Flamingo consortium had had to borrow more money to keep the project going. Billy Wilkerson signed for a loan of $600,000 from the Valley National Bank of Phoenix, Arizona, which had links to both Gus Greenbaum and Del E. Webb, the Phoenix contractor whose company was building the Flamingo.[64] This brought the money paid out on the Flamingo to some $1.2 million, in addition to the price that Wilkerson had originally paid for the land — and on top of the $1.2 million, Benny Siegel had made quite substantial cash payments in order to secure restricted building materials.

One million dollars, maximum, was the rule-of-thumb construction cost of a decent-sized Las Vegas hotel-casino in the years after the Second World War — to include the price of the land.[65] But by December 1946, the costs of the Flamingo were doubling this, and Benny Siegel was looking for more. He went back to the Valley National Bank for another $300,000,[66] and he was postponing accounts from his builder, Del Webb, which totaled as much again, at least.[67]

With the accountable price tag for the still unprofitable Flamingo at the $3 million level and rising, there was a cash-flow problem which clearly called for the talents of Meyer Lansky. But Meyer did not get involved. Vegas was Benny's territory, and the Flamingo was Benny's baby. There were other partners in the project who were on the spot, and who had stakes of their own to protect. Gus Greenbaum, Davie Berman, Willie Alderman, and Morris Rosen were tough, professional characters. Working in the Flamingo every day, they had as much money invested in the project as Meyer did, and it meant more to them.

Meyer stayed in Hallandale, and it was Benny who made the long trip to Florida. Harold Conrad remembers Benny's reappearance at the Colonial Inn in the early months of 1947 — dashing and elegant as ever, but very much on edge.[68] A customer who did not know the form was so rash as to greet him as "Bugsy," and found himself on the floor a second later, his nose bleeding.

"The name is Ben," said Siegel, looking down at him disdainfully. "B-e-n. Ben Siegel. . . . Don't you ever forget it." And as he walked away, he kicked his victim in the ribs.

"That's very bad manners," said Frank Costello, disapprovingly. "He never should'a kicked him."[69]

Benny's friends were delighted to see him, sweeping him off to the New York cash craps in Greenacres, where Benny made a killing. But once the Bug had gone back to Nevada, Harold Conrad heard the grumbling.

"They had this barroom where they had their own big table at night," he remembers. "Most of them would sit around there. . . . I could tell they were getting fed up, because when Bugsy wasn't there I could hear the discussion — 'That son of a bitch,' and so on. That sort of thing."[70]

Investing in the Nevada desert, they complained, had been Benny's idea. "They were against it from the beginning. 'Why the hell do we need that stupid little sandy town out there?' they said. They thought it was a mistake in the first place. But Costello went along and kept pouring the money in."[71]

Meyer was always Benny's champion, Conrad remembers. "He would say, 'Let's really look into it.'"[72]

Meyer Lansky and Frank Costello gave Siegel the money he needed to get the Flamingo's rooms finished and ready for visitors. But as his palace in the desert reopened for business at the beginning of March 1947, Benny Siegel was under notice. This time the Flamingo would have to work — and it would have to show a profit.

The Flamingo Hotel reopened on March 1, 1947, with its bedrooms finally completed. The reopening show was headed by the Andrews Sisters. Benny Siegel was alive with new ideas. Midweek bingo games were instituted to entice locals out of town on quiet evenings, and Benny was in the hotel every night, sitting in his booth with its own telephone by the door — meeting, greeting, and charming, charming, charming.

People who got to know Benny Siegel personally have countless tales of his warmth and charm. It is difficult, in fact, to find much evidence of his ever doing a mean deed in his life — with the exception of breaking the noses of people who called him Bugsy, and killing the people who really upset him. Benny is said to have confided to Del Webb, the Phoenix builder, that he had killed twelve men in the course of his life[73] — and no one who knew Benny personally would say that was impossible.

Greg Bautzer, Billy Wilkerson's attorney, saw this dark side when he accompanied Wilkerson to a conference to arrange Wilkerson's sale of stock. Ever more strapped for cash, Benny reckoned he could raise the money he needed by buying, splitting, and reselling Wilkerson's 33 percent of the Flamingo — and Wilkerson was not entirely unhappy to get out.

The question was the price, and as the negotiations got tougher, Siegel, who was accompanied to the meeting by Moe Sedway and Gus Greenbaum,[74] resorted to the tactics of a different world.

"You give me the thirty-three and a third and get paid for it," Bautzer recalled his shouting at Wilkerson, "or I don't think any place you live will be healthy for you."[75]

Bautzer told his client to leave the room, and Wilkerson was only too happy to comply.

"It was a frightening experience for him," Bautzer recalled. "He was not used to violence."

The attorney issued Benny a stern warning. "From this moment on," he told Siegel, "you had better put a couple of guys on Wilkerson to be certain he doesn't slip, or get a scratch on his finger, or anything else to hurt him."

Bautzer told Siegel he would be preparing an affidavit that set out the details of the threat he had just heard, and that copies of it would be lodged with the police and with the FBI.

"You can imagine the reaction," Bautzer said later. Benny's fury increased to such a pitch that his own lawyers had to intervene to calm him down.[76]

"He was like a pistol when he got mad," remembers Lou Wiener.[77]

When rage overwhelmed Benny, it would take total possession of him. It was not difficult to imagine Ben Siegel grasping someone by the neck and squeezing the life out of them. His rages were so pure and incandescent, so very much the essence of Benny, that people who knew him did not take offense at them — not until he started to threaten them, at least. Getting violent was just part of the way Benny Siegel was — and the violence claimed him on the night of June 20, 1947.

Benny was down in Los Angeles, staying in the home of Virginia Hill, on North Linden Drive in Beverly Hills. Virginia was not there that night. The couple had had one of their furious rows, and Virginia had flown off in a huff to Paris, via Chicago and New York, where she spent a few nights with Joe Epstein.[78]

Benny was sitting on a chintz-covered sofa, reading the *Los Angeles Times* after dinner, when the first bullet hit him.[79] It was fired from a .30 caliber army carbine, the police later determined, and nine shots were fired into the room. The assassin was found to have rested the carbine on the latticework of a rose-covered pergola just outside the window, close enough to smash in Benny's left eye, crush the bridge of his nose, and shatter a vertebra at the back of his neck. His right eye was blown out completely, and was later found fifteen feet away from his body.

Benny Siegel lolled back dead on the sofa — immortal. Next day his shooting was front-page news across America, invariably accompanied by the photo of his body, incongruously blood stained on

Virginia Hill's demure chintz sofa. The murder of the flamboyant Vegas adventurer roused people's curiosity about the play city on the other side of the country, and if they had to name one hotel that summed the place up, then that hotel was Bugsy's palace in the desert. The Flamingo came to represent the new, wickedly enticing Las Vegas.

Ben Siegel did not invent the luxury resort hotel-casino. He did not found the Las Vegas Strip. He did not buy the land or first conceive the project that became the Flamingo. But by his death he made them all famous.

Lou Wiener heard that Ben Siegel had been shot from a friend whose radio was tuned to a ball game in Los Angeles. Wiener drove straight out to the Flamingo, to discover Gus Greenbaum and Moe Sedway cutting through the general turmoil and confusion with the steely precision of generals mopping up after a coup. Neither man displayed the dismay and shock which characterized almost every other member of the Flamingo's staff, and in the days that followed, it became clear that Greenbaum and Sedway, along with Davie Berman, Morris Rosen, and Willie Alderman, were the new bosses of the Flamingo.

Lou Wiener's conclusion, which he holds to this day, was that it was Benny's Las Vegas partners who got rid of him.[80] Harold Conrad, who was following the story from the East, feels exactly the same. "Benny had spent a lot of their money," he says, "and money was what counted with those guys."[81]

With Benny dead, Greenbaum and Sedway were able to go back to the Valley National Bank in Phoenix and get a loan of $1.4 million[82] — half a million dollars more, in one shot, than the hotel had managed to collect when Benny was in charge. The bank evidently considered that the Flamingo was now a good risk.

Meyer Lansky always denied having any part in the murder of Benny Siegel. "Ben Siegel was my friend until his final day," he told the Israeli journalist Uri Dan when Dan taxed him with being involved with the murder. "I never quarrelled with him."[83]

"If it was in my power to see Benny alive," Meyer said in 1975, "he would live as long as Matusula [sic]."[84]

There is no reason to disbelieve him. But that is not quite the point. Asked in later years if he himself had ever killed anyone, Meyer Lansky firmly replied, "Never. But some of my associates . . . Take Benny Siegel, for example, he knocked out plenty."[85]

Throughout his adult career, Meyer Lansky was careful to distance himself from the "dirty" crimes — drugs, prostitution, and murder. But his closest companions were men who dealt in all three, and as an investor in the Flamingo Hotel, Meyer knowingly put his money behind someone who deployed threats, violence, and murder in the routine pursuit of his business. Meyer knew exactly how Benny Siegel got results — and, after Benny's death, he remained in partnership with the Las Vegas men who, almost certainly, arranged his friend's killing.

The adult Meyer Lansky was not the vicious boy who had wielded a steel pipe on the strike-breaking foreman. Nor was he a Murder, Inc., executive, ordering up hits in the style of Lepke Buchalter. But he was fully at ease with "muscle," and he did not shrink from frightening people when he wished. In other areas, the Lansky moral balance sheet was a gray and elusive compilation, marked by frustratingly little black or white. But when it came to violence, the ruling was unambiguous. Meyer might not have the blood of his best friend Benny on his hands, but he was just as much a gangster as the people who did.

10

"I Don't Sail Under No False Colors"

MEYER LANSKY met Thelma "Teddy" Schwartz in August 1948, eighteen months after he had been granted his divorce decree from his first wife, Anne. Four months later, Meyer and Teddy were married.

It is difficult to imagine two women who were less similar than the first and second Mrs. Meyer Lansky. Teddy was loud where Anne had been quiet, tough and strong-minded where Anne had been vulnerable — and where Anne had been confrontational, questioning Meyer about his life, Teddy was loyally adoring.

Pert and green eyed, with red hair that was veering to blond, Teddy Lansky was even shorter than Meyer — by some three inches — and just over five years younger.[1] Forty-one years old in 1948 when they married, she was the daughter of Jewish immigrants — her father Austrian, her mother from Romania — who had raised Teddy and two other children near the northernmost tip of Lenox Avenue, in the days when Harlem was still white.[2]

Teddy favored clothes in bright, primary colors, preferably red. Her conversation featured knowing, streetwise phrases that could have dropped ready hard-boiled out of *Guys and Dolls*. She looked and sounded like a manicurist, and that was what the newspapers later said that she was. In fact, the young Thelma Scheer had started

160

her career as a secretary working for Louis Gimbel, Jr., one of the partners in the department store, before she met her first husband, Philip Schwartz. Schwartz ran his own small garment-trade business, and when Thelma Scheer agreed to marry him she was just twenty years old.[3]

Starting their married life in 1927 in an apartment on the Upper West Side, Philip and Teddy Schwartz had lived in the same world as Meyer and Anne Lansky, who married two years after them. Eating at Pomerantz and the other local restaurants favored by garment-trade café society,[4] Teddy Schwartz would vaguely hear the names of Lepke Buchalter, Bugsy Siegel, and Meyer Lansky. Teddy used the same dressmaker as Esther Siegel, and she later decided that she must even have met Meyer on one occasion in those early years — in the mid-1930s, on a golf course where he was playing a round with Charlie Luciano.

Teddy had a romantic, almost fanciful side. In her early teens, she changed her name from Thelma, which she hated, when she developed a crush on a boy called Teddy Rosenberg.[5] Part of her was stage-struck. She came to cherish the memory of how the artist Norman Rockwell once walked across in a restaurant and asked her to model for one of his pictures[6] — and it was always her claim that she could have been a chorus girl, a "pony," if she had really wanted. In the early 1940s, the Schwartzes took an unsuccessful stab at running their own nightclub.

In August 1948, Teddy was in need of a little romance. Just starting on the formalities of divorce after more than twenty years of marriage, she was an about-to-be-single mother with one teenage son on her hands. She was staying in a little rented house by the beach in Hollywood, Florida, with a girlfriend, and as the two women walked out to supper one evening, they saw a dapper, good-looking little man walking out of the house next door.

"Hi, Meyer!" called Teddy's girlfriend, whose husband, Teddy later recalled, had some New York connections "in the rackets."[7]

"Where are you ladies going?" asked Meyer, delighted to have company. The threesome went out to eat together.

Four months later, and only a few weeks after Teddy had secured her divorce decree from Philip Schwartz, Meyer and Teddy got married.

Teddy had not been looking for a long-term relationship. "I didn't wanna get married," she later said. "Period." But she loved Meyer's polish. He took her out to classy restaurants, ordering her new dishes that she had not tried before. On their first date he took her up to Lighthouse Point, on the promontory north of Hollywood, with the moonlight shining down on the dark water all around, and introduced her to the delights of stone crab claws.[8] Meyer loved a good meal out, and so did Teddy. He was neat, quiet, and stylish. He also ran some of the East Coast's smartest nightclubs.

Teddy knew that her new husband made his money illegally. Meyer was just getting the Club Bohème ready to open for the winter season. But Teddy saw nothing wrong in gambling — she rather fancied herself a blackjack player — and if there was more to it all than might meet the eye, well, Teddy did not want to know. That was all Meyer's business. Teddy believed in Meyer, and she was happy to leave it at that.

If one thing endeared Teddy Scheer Schwartz to Meyer Lansky, it was that she did not ask questions, and that she trusted him to do as he saw fit. Anne was always putting her husband on the spot, demanding that he justify himself, telling him that he was wrong. Teddy actually believed that Meyer could do no wrong. She was his ally, happily adopting the us-against-them rationale by which lawbreakers come to see themselves as victims, and to feel that it is society which has done wrong to them.

In her innermost heart, Teddy cannot quite have believed in her pose. For nearly four years after she married, she went to the most extreme lengths, breaking stays in Florida to go back to New York, in order to make sure that her old and sick father, who had been quite a gambler himself, should not find out who her new husband was. When Meyer's name — and hers, sometimes, as well — started hitting the newspapers in the late 1940s, Teddy got the attendants at her father's nursing home to intercept them.[9] But whatever doubts she might have had, she kept to herself — and Meyer loved her for it.

"The best part of Meyer's life was the day he married you," Meyer's sister, Esther, said to Teddy one day. "He started to really breathe and live."[10]

The new Mrs. Lansky was strident and abrasive. Her brassiness alienated many of Meyer's family and friends. But his only sister, Esther, saw to the heart of the matter. Teddy's unquestioning support and acceptance of whatever Meyer might do came as a liberation for him.

Anne Lansky had screeched at her husband. Teddy screeched at the world. At his second attempt, Meyer Lansky had found himself the mate that his chosen way of life demanded — a gangster's moll.

In the summer of 1948, Joseph Baum, a Hollywood, Florida, real estate operator, was trying to raise funds for Israel. Following the United Nations vote to partition Palestine, Jews across America had been caught up in the prospect of creating their own homeland in the Middle East. The head of the political department of the Jewish Agency, Goldie Meyerson — the future Golda Meir — had just completed a whirlwind tour of the States in which she raised some $50 million from local synagogues and businessmen.[11]

Baum was working to raise funds for the Haganah, one of the terrorist organizations which had been the cutting edge of Israel's fight for independence, and Baum asked Meyer Lansky if his Haganah committee could organize a charity auction in the Colonial Inn, by far the largest and most luxurious meeting place in the area. Lansky said yes, and gave a donation himself. The Colonial Inn's benefit evening for the Haganah raised $10,000.[12]

The challenge of Israel's battle for survival and acceptance captured Meyer Lansky's imagination. It was, in some ways, a metaphor for his own situation — as he perceived it, at least — and it also enabled him to make his own particular, corner-cutting contribution to the struggle. In New York, the shady and mysterious Hotel Fourteen, above the Copacabana on East Sixtieth Street,[13] became the base for some Israeli agents who were trying, illegally, to purchase American arms for the Haganah. At the same time, they were doing what they could to hamper the supply of American weapons to the Arab countries. When they were introduced to Meyer Lansky, they passed on the name of a Pittsburgh arms dealer who, they had been told, was arranging shipments for the Arabs through the New York–New Jersey waterfront.

"I'm at your service," said Meyer.[14]

It was World War II all over again. Meyer spoke to his waterfront contacts from B-3 days, and part of the Pittsburgh consignment fell overboard. Most of another cargo was, by mistake, redirected and loaded onto ships that happened to be bound for Israel,[15] and in the months that followed, some of the same local contacts who had kept Commander Haffenden so well informed about events on the waterfront gave their assistance to the Israelis in Hotel Fourteen.

Entering the later half of his forties, and embarking, with his second marriage, on a new start in life, Meyer Lansky might well have been expected to offer more commitment to his roots and to his Jewishness. He put the arm on his Hallandale gaming partners to buy Israel bonds — "Hey, these are a great investment!" he would say to Frank Costello and Joe Adonis[16] — and he also made a gesture that was rich in meaning for a man who had declined to send his own two sons to *cheder.*

With the postwar migration to Florida turning Hollywood and Hallandale into settled, year-round communities, the same local Jews who had been active on behalf of Israel decided that the time had come to construct their own place of worship — Temple Sinai, an angular, white synagogue which soon rose, in its own grounds, not far from North Lake, Hollywood. The temple had its own *cheder* attached.

The elders of the new synagogue approached Meyer Lansky for a donation, and he offered to provide the funds that would pay for the Eternal Light, the decorative lantern whose function was to house and shield the candle that burned in the temple, day and night, above the rolled scrolls of the Torah, preserved in the ark of the synagogue — the holy of holies. Lansky paid $1,000 to put his name on the Eternal Light, according to the recollection of Joseph Baum.[17]

Meyer's donation could easily be interpreted as just another payoff, one of the program of handouts that were distributed every winter by the casinos of Hallandale. But it is possible that the gift represented something more personal — the offering of a now middle-aged man who could recall his beloved grandfather walking through the congregation of the wooden synagogue in Grodno to read aloud from the Torah, the memory of the little boy whose name meant Bringer of Light.

Meyer and Teddy flew to Cuba to get married. The ceremony was a private signing in a lawyer's office in Havana. Meyer was leery of newspaper publicity, and he did not want Anne or his children to know that he had remarried. The marriage was on December 16, 1948,[18] and when Meyer and Teddy went back together for the winter season in Hallandale, Meyer was at some pains to conceal that they were now man and wife. His younger children, Paul and Sandra, came down to spend Christmas with their father, and they went back to school in New York quite unaware that they now had a stepmother.[19]

When Buddy came down a week or so later for a longer stay, Meyer decided that he could not continue the pretense. He let Buddy, now nineteen years old, in on the secret. But he swore his elder son to secrecy so far as Anne and the younger children were concerned. When everyone headed back north at the end of the Hallandale season, Buddy returned to New York and moved into the Beresford Apartments on Central Park West and Eighty-first Street with his mother, Paul, and Sandra. Meyer would come to visit them from time to time, treating his ex-wife, Buddy noticed, with more cordiality than for a long time in the past. The divorce, in some way, seemed to have released the poison between Meyer and Anne.[20] But only Buddy knew, when Meyer came to visit their apartment, that his father had come from just across the park, beside the Plaza, at 40 Central Park South, where Meyer was living with his new wife, Teddy, in apartment 14C. When autumn came to the park and the leaves were down, it was almost possible to look out diagonally toward Fifth Avenue and see the one apartment from the other.

Deception was the stuff of life to Meyer Lansky, and his elder son took to it quite naturally. Buddy had lived all his life with the assumption that it was normal not to know the whole story, that the real truths about most situations are not just unspoken, but are deliberately concealed — and now he was invited to be one of the makers of the game. He successfully kept the secret of his father's marriage from his mother, brother, and sister, and he had no doubt that that was the right thing to do. That was how Dad wanted things.

Now on the threshold of his twenties, Buddy Lansky was embarking on adult life. But it was scarcely possible for him to strike out on his own. Meyer got Buddy his first job, working in the Hollywood Ticket Agency on Broadway, right in the heart of Damon Runyon's Manhattan. With his father's love of coffee shop socializing, Buddy frequented nearby Liggett's, the Stage, and the Sixth Avenue Deli. He would teeter in uncertainly, usually on the arm of a friend, to be seated and served promptly — and, most satisfyingly, to be greeted by name. Everyone knew whose son the cheery little cripple was. Buddy spent a lot of time in Dinty Moore's, the preeminent resort of wiseguys in the late 1940s. He knew that he was considered one of the gang when old man Moore casually took his teeth out one day in Buddy's presence and gave them a good wash.[21]

It was a barman at Moore's who arranged Buddy's sexual initiation — with a Puerto Rican hooker who shared an apartment with a large dog on Ninety-ninth Street — and prostitutes became a feature of Buddy's social life. Barmen and waiters helped fix him up with hookers at moderate rates, and George Wood, the William Morris agent who booked the artistes for the Colonial Inn, gave Buddy the key to his apartment on Central Park South, so that he could take the girls there. Buddy hid his habit from his father. He paid for sex because he reckoned he could not get it any other way, but he considered it no shame. He noticed plenty of other people, who were not disabled, doing the same.[22]

In a final attempt to relieve Buddy's disability, his father arranged for rehabilitative therapy at Bellevue Hospital by the East River on FDR Drive. Dr. Howard Rusk, a pioneer in rehabilitative physiotherapy, had established a clinic there which became nationally famous.[23] Rusk had treated the singer Jane Froman after the plane crash which crippled her in 1943,[24] and at his Bellevue clinic could be seen the pair of crutches which, thanks to Rusk's therapy, the singer had been able to discard when she made her comeback some years later.* Buddy's mother, Anne, would often accompany her son to Bellevue, sitting for long hours, watching him intently while he went through his exercises — an echo, nearly twenty years on, of the game little baby on the treatment table having his arms and legs stretched by Dr. Carruthers in Boston.[25]

Vincent Mercurio was a young student training to be a teacher, and he went into Bellevue several afternoons a week as a volunteer to help with the patients in Dr. Rusk's clinic. One afternoon he was assigned to help Buddy with his walking exercises, and the two young men struck up a friendship. Vincent Mercurio became something of a companion to Buddy Lansky, driving Buddy to and from Bellevue in Buddy's car, a two-door Chevrolet which Meyer had bought for his son.

On summer Saturdays, the two young men would almost invariably go to a ball game to see the Yankees or the Giants, who played at home on alternate weekends. Meyer would come with them occasionally, and Vinnie Mercurio remembers being amazed at how, after a few innings, the senior Lansky could instantly compute in his head the percentage points that made up the new overall batting average of any particular player in the game.

---

*Jane Froman was crippled in 1943 when the plane taking her to a concert for troops stationed in Europe crashed. After numerous operations, she returned to Europe to give performances for wounded servicemen. Her comeback was the subject of the 1952 film *With a Song in My Heart*.

Rather than watching sports, Meyer preferred to be doing. In Florida and Saratoga, he enjoyed a brisk round of golf. In New York, he kept himself trim with sessions at George Brown's gym on Fifty-seventh Street, between Seventh and Broadway — he would take Paul there for games of handball.[26] Meyer's more sedentary resort on a wet winter's afternoon, Mercurio remembers, was a session of solid news at one of the Trans-Lux Newsreel Theaters.[27]

The Lanskys made Buddy's friend one of the family, inviting him home for meals. Vinnie preferred the food when they went for dinner with Grandma Lansky and Aunt Esther on Ocean Parkway in Brooklyn. Grandma Lansky — Meyer's mother, Yetta — was an excellent cook. But the Citrons were more fun. Grandma Citron, warm and eccentric, would chatter away to Vinnie in Yiddish.

"Grandma," he would say, "I'm not Jewish. I'm Italian."

"Shut up and eat," she would respond.[28]

Meals out with Meyer were a little more pedagogic, as Meyer played his trick of taking over the menu. "He liked to order for you," remembers Mercurio, "and say 'Now this is good,' 'Try this,' or 'You can't eat that. It's too fattening.'"[29]

Buddy and Vinnie liked going out for meals with Meyer. They always ate in good restaurants, and Meyer always paid the bill. Meyer liked to preside over a table of five or six, and it was on these occasions that Vincent Mercurio got a sense of the authority that his friend's father enjoyed in whatever world it was that he inhabited.

"He was kind of like a king," Mercurio remembers. "He would talk, and they would listen. I watched all that."[30]

Vincent Mercurio felt, at times, that he was entering a different world. He had grown up in quite humble circumstances on Mulberry Street, in the heart of Little Italy, on the Lower East Side. The Beresford, he knew, was one of the finest apartment houses in New York. The tabs that Meyer picked up for dinner must, he calculated, run out around $100, which was what Vinnie had to live on, if he was lucky, for a month.

But there was a control and restraint to it all. Meyer would treat his son's Italian friend to little homilies, explaining why he drove an Oldsmobile when he could easily afford a Cadillac.

"'Winny' — that was the name he used for me — 'Winny,' he would say. 'You must never advertise your wealth.'"[31]

Vincent Mercurio noticed how Meyer Lansky was particularly careful with his clothes. "He would wear good suits, but you would never know the difference. He would wear a nice pair of shoes, or a nice coat. But you could never say, well, that man bought it at a particular store. He just dressed like an average businessman."[32]

An average, and rather successful, businessman was what Vinnie Mercurio assumed his friend's father to be. Meyer's friends and associates were rather like him, quiet and well dressed. Mr. Alo was around quite a lot. He was low key, but in some way very solid. One evening, Buddy introduced Vinnie to a polite and elegant man with an odd, low, whispery voice. He was dressed like a banker, and Buddy called him Uncle Frank.[33]

Buddy himself did not seem too clear on what all these people did, or exactly where the money came from. It was something to do with gambling — and Vincent Mercurio knew enough to know that if that were the case, one did not ask too many questions.

Meyer Lansky, jukebox magnate, had his headquarters on West Forty-third Street, New York. The first time that Buddy went to visit the office, he was impressed to see that his father had his name on the door. There was a secretary who answered the phone and typed letters — and through the back were all the jukeboxes, glass-and-Bakelite beauties like the machine that Julie Fink had installed for Buddy at Dr. Phelps's clinic in Baltimore.[34]

Like all Meyer's businesses, his jukebox distributorship tiptoed in and out of the fringes of respectability. The Emby Distributing Company was a properly constituted corporation which held exclusive licenses to sell Wurlitzers, one of the four principal makes of American jukebox, in New York itself and in specified areas up and down the East Coast — "Just like an automobile agency," as Meyer later explained.[35]

The M in Emby stood for Meyer. The E and the BY stood for his partners, Edward Smith and Bill Bye, former Wurlitzer agents who had gone into business on their own.[36] The legal formalities of the partnership were handled by Moses Polakoff.

Emby sold its Wurlitzers — for $1,080 per machine in 1946 — to the operators of jukebox "routes," who placed them in bars and clubs in the areas they covered. The route operator, who might control several hundred machines in his neighborhood, would then supply the records and a repair service to each of his machines, in return for a cut of 50 to 70 percent of the weekly take — which, in New York in the 1940s, averaged $15 per machine in a good week.[37]

As well as selling Wurlitzers, Emby Distributing also dabbled in the operational side of the business, acquiring run-down routes and beefing them up with fresh outlets. "We would buy a route," Meyer later explained, "then build it up and try to sell it."[38]

It was the techniques used to "build up" a profitable route, bar by bar, club by club, in a tough New York neighborhood that took the jukebox business into the gray area between hard-nosed tactics and illegality. In the mid-1940s, complained Albert Denver, president of a jukebox trade association, Meyer Lansky's Emby Company had tried to hold him and his fellow route operators to ransom, requiring them to buy more jukeboxes than they had outlets for, while also insisting that the operators replace any rival machines that they owned with Wurlitzers. When Denver and his fellow members refused these demands, Denver alleged, Emby Distributing went to work and managed to squeeze him and his fellow operators out of nearly 250 locations in less than three months.[39]

Denver's complaint was partly a matter of Emby's exploiting its monopoly of a hot product — the new postwar Wurlitzer 1015, which set the pace for the entire industry. It was the classic, glowing, neon-tubed jukebox to which jukebox design has done homage ever since. In 1946 and 1947, Wurlitzer shipped 56,246 of the new 1015s at a time when the average manufacturing run for a new jukebox was 10,000.[40] Emby Distributing also had an imaginative financing program by which the company made it possible for bar owners to acquire a new 1015 on attractive, long-term installments — giving the owner the new jukebox that he wanted, while enabling Emby to cut out the middleman and take the full profit on each machine.

It was hardly surprising that a trade association of middlemen — the route operators — should complain. But there was also the question of the official-looking sticker which every Emby Wurlitzer bore, a certificate claiming that the serviceman who stocked the machine with fresh records was a union member. In December 1958, Harold Morris, a serviceman-mechanic along one of Emby's routes in the 1940s, testified to a Senate committee that he had not belonged to a union while he was working for Emby, and that, so far as he knew, none of his fellow servicemen were union members, either.[41] The "union approved" stickers were a fraud.

The Senate committee also discovered that it was an established practice of jukebox operators in search of new outlets to organize their own, bogus union "locals," complete with nominee officials, and "union approved" stickers. Burly and aggressive-looking "members" of these locals would then picket outside bars that refused to take their own particular machines.[42]

Dealing in hard cash and hard-won territories, the coin vending machine business was a murky and sometimes violent world. The jukebox empires of the East Coast engendered border wars whose tactics ranged from intimidation to killings, and it was no coincidence that they were headed by such czars as Joe Adonis,[43] whose routes ran in Brooklyn, Gerry Catena,[44] a New Jersey associate of Longy Zwillman, and Lucky Luciano's boyhood friend Mike Lascari.[45]

Meyer Lansky considered himself a legitimate businessman in his operation of Emby Distributing. His favorite photograph of himself showed him standing to attention in his Emby office in a dark, broad-striped business suit, looking stocky and prosperous, and exuding rather more polish and goodwill than he displayed in his police file photographs. Meyer gave large black-and-white prints of the picture to each of his children — the image, evidently, that he wanted them to have of him. The photograph has since been used in television segments at the moment when the script says something like "If Meyer Lansky had done business in the legitimate world, he could have become the chairman of General Motors."[46]

But the building up of jukebox routes on the urban East Coast of America in the 1940s was not the preserve of legitimate businessmen, and Meyer could hardly have survived if he had not been able to rely on the particular respect that his name inspired. When Wurlitzer woke up to whom the *M* stood for in Emby, its officers asked Meyer to sell out, diplomatically explaining that they themselves were quite satisfied with his integrity but the banks were not.*

"They said that I was a bad risk for them," Meyer later complained.[48]

Neither Wurlitzer nor its bankers produced chapter and verse to justify pushing out Meyer Lansky — but it was significant that Meyer did not ask them to. Ethically and practically, the perceived threat of muscle is the same as muscle itself, and all Meyer's businesses rested ultimately on that threat. People could sense something dark and cold and unsettling in the background, and that feeling provided the special edge that helped Meyer wherever he worked —

---

*This was not a little hypocritical on Wurlitzer's part. In February 1959, Milton Hammergren, who had been the sales manager of Rudolph Wurlitzer, Inc., in the 1940s, conceded that he and his company were well aware that, out on the jukebox routes, violence had often been part of the business. "We didn't like it," he told the Senate Select Committee on Improper Activities in the Labor or Management Field, "but we had to sell jukeboxes."[47]

building up a New York jukebox route, or investing in a casino in Las Vegas.

With the door closed on jukeboxes, Meyer turned to an amusement machine with even more potential. Consolidated Television was a company formed to put TV sets into the same bars and clubs that housed Emby jukeboxes. Ed Smith and Bill Bye were partners once again, and Joe Adonis and Frank Costello bought in as well. Meyer's stake was for roughly 10 percent of Consolidated's $150,000 working capital.[49]

It seemed a clever, forward-looking scheme, to marry the Emby network with the latest entertainment trend. Every bar and club was going to need its own television, and the plan was for Consolidated Television to manufacture functional, large-screen sets to go on a shelf or counter, rather than the monumental, free-standing pieces of furniture — all doors and veneer — which most manufacturers were then producing for the home. Consolidated's seventeen-inch monitors were called Tele Kings.

But Meyer and his partners had failed to think through the theory of their ingenious bid for the future, and there were practical problems as well. Unlike jukeboxes, TV sets did not generate their own cash income. They were a onetime sale. The TV sets in most bars and clubs today are not supplied by vending machine distributors, because they do not need to be serviced or to have coins removed from them. The bar owner buys the TV set he wants, puts it on the wall, and forgets about it.

But the Tele Kings of Consolidated could not, unfortunately, be forgotten about. They were forever breaking down. The Lansky children had one of their father's sets installed in the Beresford, and it drove Buddy crazy.

"We could never get it to work right. I was quite a baseball fan, and in New York baseball was on TV day and night. I'd scream at him, I'd say, 'Get this damn set fixed!' . . . He couldn't understand it."[50]

The engineer from Consolidated became something of a fixture at the Beresford — and at bars and clubs all round the Emby routes, where there was the same, fundamental difficulty. Tele Kings just did not work. They were badly made. Lansky and his partners had done a deal with two engineers who claimed they had discovered a shortcut to making better, cheaper sets than RCA[51] — and, like most shortcuts, it proved expensive.

"These two fellows," commented Consolidated's accountant, George Goldstein, "were not what they should be."[52]

Bars and clubs sent their Tele Kings back to Consolidated in disgust, and in less than two years, the firm went out of business. Smith, Bye, Lansky, Adonis, and Costello lost every dollar they had invested.

In the late 1940s, there were many investors who prospered greatly by staking their money on television. But choosing the right project involved research, application, and a certain staying power. An eye to the main chance and a mastery of figures alone were not enough — and "union approved" labels, padded shoulders, and paid-off sheriffs did not do the trick. There could be no special edge if the product was lousy. The television adventures of Meyer Lansky and his fellow czars of the underworld showed what sort of businessmen they were when the playing field was level.

In the summer of 1949, Meyer Lansky took his new wife on a delayed honeymoon. He had never visited Europe, and he decided he would do so in style. He contacted Thomas Cook and Son, who arranged a luxurious suite for him and Teddy on the liner *Italia* of the Home Lines, docking in Naples. From there Meyer and Teddy could travel up through Italy and Europe to sail home from Brussels. The *Italia* was scheduled to leave New York on June 28, 1949.[53]

The agents of the Bureau of Narcotics kept a close eye on the passenger lists of liners leaving and entering New York, since the steamer trunks of apparently law-abiding passengers were a major means of smuggling drugs into America. This was the route used by drug couriers whom the bureau believed to be working for Lucky Luciano — and as an associate of Luciano, Meyer Lansky featured on the bureau's international list of suspects. Meyer was number 169. It looked highly suspicious to the Bureau of Narcotics that number 169 should be traveling to Naples, Italy, now the base of Charlie Luciano, whose principal business in exile, the bureau believed, was the organization of drug shipments to the United States.

Two years earlier, in February 1947, the Bureau of Narcotics had discovered that Lucky Luciano was in Cuba. After less than a year in Italy, Charlie had traveled discreetly to Havana and had rented an apartment in Miramar, across the Mendarez River to the west of the city. Harry Anslinger, the flamboyant director of the narcotics bureau, assumed that Luciano's intention must be to make Cuba a drug supply beachhead to the United States, and within days of hearing of Luciano's presence in Havana he threatened to cut off the supply of legitimate, medical narcotics from America.[54] The Cuban government rapidly arrested Luciano and sent him back to Italy in March 1947 — on his second and, as it proved, his conclusive trip by cargo ship back across the Atlantic.[55]

It was Anslinger's job to be suspicious when a convicted and well-connected drug peddler showed up so close to the American coast.[56] But the narcotics chief was almost certainly wrong about Luciano's principal intentions. It was much more likely that Charlie was hoping to get into some sort of winter gambling operation in Havana. This would have provided him with a good income — and a very pleasant way to keep in touch with his old friends when they came over for the season. It was also quite possible that Charlie would have gone into partnership in his casino with Meyer Lansky, who was himself trying to reestablish his prewar gaming interests in Cuba. The Cuban police tracked down the record of Luciano's operator calls from his Miramar apartment and passed it on to the FBI, which discovered that several had been made to the Colonial Inn in Hallandale, Florida. One was person-to-person, asking to speak with a "Mr. Lansky."[57]

Harry Anslinger's Bureau of Narcotics, a division of the U.S. Treasury, was the first American law enforcement agency to espouse and publicize the idea that there was an organized, nationwide conspiracy of Italian American criminals called the Mafia, whose roots could be traced to Sicily. For the FBI, a division of the U.S. Justice Department, J. Edgar Hoover disagreed. Hoover saw racketeering and gangsters in localized, American terms — and, as such, a problem for individual states and cities, which lay outside his federal mandate.

But it was in the nature of an agency whose task was to track drug supply routes stretching halfway around the world to be uncovering evidence of international connections — while Anslinger also had to find an explanation for the depressing increase in drug consumption during his years in office. The narcotics director came to believe fervently in crime as a matter of integrated, transnational organization, and Meyer Lansky's trip to Naples fitted perfectly into that picture. On Monday, June 27, 1949, narcotics agents John H. Hanly and Crofton J. Hayes were instructed to make contact with Meyer Lansky and to find out why he was sailing to Italy. Supplied with a photograph of Meyer and his unlisted telephone number, Plaza 3-8176, Agents Hanly and Hayes telephoned Meyer's home that Monday afternoon, to be told by the maid that Mr. Lansky had just gone out. The agents then scouted the streets around 40 Central Park

South, and waited outside the apartment building for nearly seven hours, without success.

They had better luck when they called again early next morning, at 8:30 A.M. Meyer Lansky answered the phone himself and, somewhat to their surprise, he invited them straight up "without quibbling." Three minutes later, the agents were talking to their quarry inside apartment 14C.[58]

Meyer told Hanly and Hayes that he was taking this European holiday with his wife "solely for pleasure," and that, yes, he would probably be seeing Charlie Luciano while he was in Italy. Charlie was an old friend. Meyer had known him for many years. But he denied that he had any current business relations with Luciano, and he strongly deprecated the suggestion that his friend was dealing in narcotics.

"Charlie had a few bucks left over from before he got in trouble," said Meyer, by way of explaining Luciano's current source of income. Meyer freely admitted that he and Luciano had been in the bootlegging business together in Prohibition days, but he insisted that he, Lansky, had "come in with Prohibition and gone out with it."[59]

Invited by the agents to provide a characterization of himself and his current activities, Meyer replied, according to their notes, "Common gambler, I guess. I don't try to fool or impose on nobody. If I just met you casually, I would call myself a restaurant operator. If we warmed up to each other, I would tell you I was a common gambler. I don't sail under no false colors."[60]

For someone talking to two official investigators, Meyer Lansky seemed remarkably forthcoming. He said that the bulk of his income was derived from his gambling interests in Florida, where he was a part owner of the Bohème and Greenacres gambling clubs, both managed by his brother, Jake. Up in New York, they reported him saying, he kept his office "in his hat." He had recently invested in Consolidated Television, though this, he indicated, was "somewhat less than a profitable investment."[61]

Asked to explain the record of phone calls from Havana to Hallandale in February 1947, Meyer said that they must have been made by Chester Simms and Connie Immerman. These were two floor men whom he had taken to help run the Nacional Casino in Marianao in the late 1930s. Simms and Immerman had opted to stay on in Havana to work for the Cuban interests who took over the casino after Lansky left, and they would phone Meyer every so often to check and compare notes on the credit of high rollers. It was possible,

Meyer said, that Charlie came on the line at some point to say hello, but his memory was rather vague on that.

In view of Meyer's old and close ties with Luciano, this was less than convincing — and Meyer seemed rather keener to talk about his family. His son Paul, he told the agents "with some pride," had just graduated from Horace Mann, and was now hoping to get into West Point. As for his crippled son, Buddy, the boy was currently at Bellevue Hospital under the care of the famous Dr. Rusk, who had written a book on his work on rehabilitation. Meyer showed the agents his autographed copy.[62]

In conclusion, Meyer "vehemently asserted that he had never had any part of narcotics trafficking. . . . He claimed that he would not even let the subject be discussed in his presence."[63]

The two narcotics agents said farewell, allowing Meyer and Teddy to go down to the *Italia,* which was sailing later that day. When first phoning Meyer at 8:30 that morning, Agent Hanly had offered a sort of a deal, suggesting that Meyer was better off being interviewed in the privacy of his home than down at the ship, "with the possibility of publicity."[64]

But the agents did not keep their side of the bargain. Down at the ship, a reporter and a photographer from the *New York Sun* were waiting outside the Lanskys' cabin.[65]

"We are not interested in any publicity!" cried Teddy Lansky sharply, when she saw the photographer. "Get out!"

Meyer winced as the flashgun went off. "I don't want any pictures made, please," he said.

"This is just a pleasure trip," he replied to the reporter's questions. "We will be gone about five weeks. No, I don't have any relatives in Italy."

Was he planning to make contact with Lucky Luciano over there?

"By way of answer," reported the *New York Sun* next morning, "the Lanskys slammed the door of their suite, and the lock clicked."[66]

The story was on the front page next day. "Lansky Sails in Luxury for Italy," ran the *Sun*'s headline over the photo of Meyer surprised outside his stateroom. "Expected to Confer with Luciano. Underworld Big Shot and Wife in Regal Suite; Cost $2,600 One Way."

The *Sun*'s reporter had done his homework. He had managed, as he described it, to get "a gander" at the *Italia*'s Regal Suite before the Lanskys arrived, and was able to report that it was the most luxurious on the ship — five rooms at the forward end of the promenade deck, immediately below the captain's cabin.

The Lanskys were traveling, the *Sun* reported, in considerably more luxury than such passengers as the Reverend Walter J. Miller, S.J., director of the Vatican Observatory, or John Coolidge, the son of the late president, and now an art curator at Harvard. Coolidge and his wife and daughter were "in modest cabin class."

For whatever reason — to show his love for Teddy, or perhaps as a reflection of his new wife's flamboyant and assertive style — Meyer Lansky had broken the cardinal rule that he had laid down to Vinnie Mercurio: "You must never advertise your wealth." Visited before their departure by Mike Lascari and his wife, the Lanskys had set sail, reported the *Sun,* "in an atmosphere of champagne and orchids, in the manner befitting Lansky's reputation as a powerful and wealthy underworld figure."[67]

This was the rub. Until June 28, 1949, Meyer Lansky's name had only been mentioned, almost in passing, in occasional articles listing New York's racketeers and gangsters. His name was familiar to rackets investigators and to specialist crime reporters in New York, usually as an associate and, by implication, as something of a sidekick to underworld stars like Luciano and Bugsy Siegel. But with his appearance on the front page of the *New York Sun,* and his first ever newspaper photograph, Meyer Lansky was starting on the path to becoming an underworld star in his own right.

The *Sun*'s reporter, Malcolm Johnson, documented Meyer's record from the clippings. "In 1938," he wrote, Meyer Lansky "was listed by the late Police Commissioner Valentine as one of the nation's public enemies, and was once described in a police investigator's report as 'the brightest boy in the combination,' meaning an underworld syndicate."

The story went on to detail Meyer's associations with Benny Siegel and "the so-called Bug and Meyer gang," and, most recently, with Johnny "Cockeye" Dunn, who, in June 1949, was in the death house at Sing Sing, awaiting execution for one of his waterfront enforcement murders. Dunn had been seen at one of Meyer's Hallandale gaming houses in Florida, it was reported, shortly before the killing.

Meyer Lansky had only a casual acquaintance with Cockeye Dunn. He had made use of him during his wartime intelligence work on behalf of B-3 and also, possibly, when tracking down Arab arms shipments on behalf of the Israeli agents in Hotel Fourteen a year or so later. There was no reason for Meyer to have been involved in Dunn's crude and murderous enforcement activities, and there was no evidence that he was.

But Meyer was not so naive as to be unaware of the basis of Dunn's power on the waterfront. Cockeye was yet another of his violent associates. Meyer was happy to operate in the shadow that they cast, using their menace when it was to his advantage. So he could hardly complain at the sinister inference with which the *New York Sun* concluded its story of the *Italia,* orchids, and champagne.

"Dunn is now scheduled to die in the electric chair on July 7," ran the newspaper's final paragraph. "If he goes to the chair, Lansky will be vacationing in Italy at the time, presumably undisturbed by Dunn's fate."[68]

The *Sun* was the paper that the Lanskys had delivered to the Beresford, and when Buddy Lansky got home on the evening of June 28, 1949, he saw it lying on the floor outside the door. He caught sight of the photograph of his father on the front page, and as he started to read the story, everything fell into place.

"It didn't affect me as far as disliking him, or anything," he remembered. It was more a feeling of the whole picture finally making sense. "I used to say, 'Well, at least he's mentioned with all those other fellows now.'"[69]

Suddenly it became clear to Buddy Lansky, at the age of nineteen and a half, who and what Uncle Ben, Uncle Frank, Mr. Adonis, and all the others really were. Thinking about it, Buddy was just beginning to focus on what it meant for his father to be included in such company, when he realized that the newspaper, in addition to revealing that Meyer Lansky was a gangster, had also revealed that he was married.

Buddy's mother, Anne, would be waiting inside the apartment, Buddy realized, still unaware that her ex-husband had found another woman, let alone that he was, at this moment, taking her across the Atlantic in the flower-laden Regal Suite, to the accompaniment of orchids and champagne.

As Buddy went into the apartment, he made certain that his mother should not catch a glimpse of that evening's *Sun.*[70]

Meyer Lansky always looked quite fit and trim, what with his sessions at the gym and the handball, but his new wife, Teddy, soon discovered that in this, as in other things, appearances were deceptive. One day quite early in their marriage, Meyer started complaining of a sharp pain in his left arm. A doctor diagnosed bursitis and, while examining Meyer generally, he also discovered a hard lump in his back — a tumor. Surgery removed both the bursitis sac and the tumor, which turned out to be nonmalignant. But not long after that, Meyer fell ill again, with agonizing pains in his stomach. He had a duodenal ulcer.[71]

Meyer wanted the best treatment available, and his doctor located it for him — a consultation with Dr. Seymour J. Gray, a professor at Harvard Medical School who had his own practice at Peter Bent Brigham Hospital in Boston, where Gray specialized in the diagnosis and treatment of gastrointestinal disease.* When Meyer Lansky walked into his office, Dr. Gray had only the medical notes to tell him anything about his new patient.

"I really didn't know a thing about him," Dr. Gray remembers. "My secretary just wrote down his name."[72]

To break the ice, Dr. Gray inquired what his new patient's profession might be. "He said, 'Well, you might say I'm a gambler.' Then he leaned back and he said, 'Doc' — I'll never forget it — he said, 'Doc, never gamble. You'll lose.'"

On examining Lansky and confirming the diagnosis of the duodenal ulcer, Seymour Gray was able to offer his new patient some advice of his own. Meyer needed to eat blander, less spicy food — not too much deli-restaurant fare — and no more mini breakfasts on the run. He also needed to get out of himself psychologically, in some way. Seymour Gray had made an extensive study of stress and its chemical effects on the body, and he explained to Meyer that the disease from which he was suffering was stress related.

"I went over that with him — gave him some insight into what he had, and what he should try to do about it."[73]

Lansky was impressed with Dr. Gray's advice. Over the years he returned quite frequently to Boston to consult the Harvard professor about a medical dictionary of complaints that ranged from hernia, osteoarthritis, and bronchitis to a complex of heart disorders.[74] Gray referred Meyer on to other doctors who specialized in these diseases, while he himself continued to treat the Lansky ulcer — which remained a problem. Gray discovered that Meyer did not possess the psychological makeup that lent itself to an easy cure.

"Ulcer people don't show it," Dr. Gray explains. "That's the point. You've got to tell ulcer people to let it out — 'If you feel like screaming, scream! Don't hold it in.' *He* held it in."[75]

Most people put on clean underwear to see their doctor. Meyer

*Seymour J. Gray made his name at the Harvard Biophysics Laboratory, where he isolated and discovered a new radioactive isotope, radioactive chromium, an important tool in the treatment of blood and red blood cell survival.

Lansky's underwear, Dr. Gray noticed, was somehow *exceptionally* clean — freshly laundered, pressed, the very epitome of spotless.

"I have seen a lot of men undress," Gray says, "and I have never seen anyone as scrupulously clean as Meyer Lansky."

Dr. Gray decided that the roots of his patient's disorder lay in Meyer's fastidious and ultra-controlled personality.

"He had difficulty verbalizing," says Gray. "A lot of it had to do, of course, with his stature, being short — and with being an immigrant, his feeling that he came from a low social order. . . . He was an extremely intelligent person. He realized that being an East Side Jew does not put you high on the social scale. He wasn't exactly a Boston Brahmin, and he felt that very keenly."

Meyer used to tell Gray the stories of his youthful gang battles in the streets and alleys of the Lower East Side.

"Being little, he had to fight. He told me, 'I was a good fighter. . . . They used to jump me because I was small, but I was pretty good with my fists.'"

Meyer told his doctor these tales with pride, his message being that he had come a long way from his early days, and that he had successfully put it all behind him. But as his Harvard specialist listened to Meyer's reminiscences, it seemed to the doctor that part of his patient was still fighting those old battles of the Lower East Side.

"He definitely had a feeling of inferiority," says Seymour Gray.[76]

By the end of the 1940s, Meyer Lansky had earned the ranking of a master gangster. He was one of the best in his field, with his Florida gambling joints and his interests in Las Vegas, New Orleans, and Saratoga Springs. Meyer had survived, unlike others — from Rothstein to Luciano to Benny Siegel — because he had no greeds, no overweening appetites. Meyer Lansky was under control.

But Meyer had paid a price for all this. He had turned himself inward — the tension, the deception, the uncertainty of it all. Meyer Lansky had forsaken the tool-and-die shop as a boy because the alternative had seemed so easy and profitable, so much more fun. But his visit to his ulcer specialist gave him notice that nothing ever came free, even in the gangster life.

Part Two

The Chairman
of the
Board

11

"Haven't You Ever Said to Yourself, 'I Hate the Hellish Business'?"

IN December 1947, the city commissioners of Hollywood, Florida, were just concluding a public meeting called to discuss, among other things, the administrative details of the coming winter season, when a local attorney, William L. Flacks, rose defiantly to his feet.

"Mr. Mayor," he asked, "I want to know what you mean to do about the gambling."[1]

The attorney had everyone's attention.

"You all know the situation," Flacks continued, "and you know that the police chief has been given no instruction to stop it. You know that every tavern, pool room, and night spot runs gambling. It has got to come to a stop, and I ask for a motion that will stop it."[2]

It was a crowded, rather noisy meeting, but Flacks's intervention produced an instant hush. In the silence that followed, the mayor of Hollywood, Robert L. Haymaker, could be heard whispering in some agitation to the city attorney.

"Each citizen should proceed on his own account," the mayor finally pronounced, "if there is any objection to gambling. Why don't you swear out a warrant at the police department? This is a legislative body, and not charged with enforcement of the law."

But William Flacks had heard this before. It was the refrain of the Broward County sheriff, Walter Clark — the rationale to which most

183

of south Florida's public officials retreated when they were questioned about the gambling.

"It is not the duty of private individuals to enforce the law," Flacks retorted, "but the duty of officials who know that laws are being violated to see that they are enforced."

The mayor had no answer to that, and it was one of the five elected city commissioners, Lester Boggs, who came to the rescue.

"Let us not pass the buck to the police chief," Boggs said — not coming to the rescue of the mayor, in fact, but lining up alongside the audacious attorney who had dared to speak from the floor.

"Mr. Flacks," said Boggs, "you are the first man in my fourteen years as a city commissioner who has had the guts to get up on this floor and ask that all gambling be closed up tight. You're demanding that we go on record shutting it down, and asking for a motion to that effect. I'm going to make that motion."

Boggs then turned to the city police chief, Phillip A. Thompson.

"That means closing every place in the city," he said pointedly, "hotels, stores, and night spots everywhere, without preference for a chosen few. If you don't, you are going to be held responsible. There's to be no favoritism to anyone."

Still somewhat winded, Mayor Haymaker asked weakly, "Punchboards, too?" — a reference to the rolled-up raffle tickets that were sold for nickels at charity functions.*

"Yes," responded Commissioner Boggs stoutly. "Everything that's illegal — poker games in hotels, and all."

Commissioner Boggs's motion to the meeting that all gambling in the city of Hollywood should, henceforward, be "closed up tight," was seconded by Commissioner Ralph C. Thompson, and was put to a vote. In the still stunned meeting room, not a voice was raised against it.[4]

The December 1947 motion of the Hollywood commissioners was remarkable for several things, not least the sudden conversion to virtue of Commissioner Lester Boggs, who had, until that moment, been

---

*A punchboard was a small, book-sized wooden board, about half an inch thick. It was pierced with several hundred holes, into each of which a rolled-up raffle ticket had been inserted, and players would pay to "punch out" each hole, winning or losing according to the number shown on the ticket that they punched out of the board — a sort of nonmechanical slot machine. Punchboards bore stickers specifying the charity for whose benefit they were supposed to operate, but it was not unknown for these "charities" to be nonexistent. Selling in the late 1940s for around $2 each, the average punchboard would pay out $80 in prize money on a total play of $120.[3]

one of the most prominent citizens fostering gambling in the Hollywood area.

"There was not a bookie joint in town," remembers one Hollywood resident, "from which Boggs did not take his profit."[5]

But Boggs, who monopolized the septic tank business in Hollywood — hence the town's lack of central sewage facilities — was an adroit and nimble politician. He had sensed something significant in attorney Flacks's stubborn question from the floor, and he had jumped firmly with it, to ride it hard.

Next door in Hallandale, a similar wind was blowing. On February 12, 1948, Assistant State Attorney Dwight C. Rogers applied in circuit court for an injunction in restraint of a nuisance — the gambling at the Colonial Inn. Rogers listed ten prominent Fort Lauderdale citizens who were prepared to testify against the establishment, and he got his injunction. When the Colonial Inn opened for business that night, there was dining and dancing — but no casino.

"Everything happens to me," complained that evening's top of the bill, Joe E. Lewis, gesturing across his audience toward the locked doors of the gambling room. "And I was just about to get even."[6]

Philip Weidling, then a journalist with the *Miami News,* remembers being taken into the deserted gaming room of the Colonial Inn a few nights later by Claude Litteral and Meyer Lansky. They had invited the local press to come and finish up the remaining food and liquor before the whole place closed down — it made no sense to operate for any length of time without the profits from the gaming tables — and the two men offered Weidling $5,000 if he would find out and tell them who was the moving force behind the injunction.

"Like a fool," Weidling now remembers, "I refused."[7]

Lansky and Litteral suspected that R. H. Gore, the owner of the local newspaper, had organized the legal campaign. "They wondered if they could maybe fix things with him," Weidling remembers. "Would he be interested in a 'cut'? I told Claude they were dreaming."[8]

Meyer Lansky let Hallandale's vigilantes enjoy their victory. He concentrated his gambling operations in his two surviving, injunction-free clubs, Greenacres and the Bohème, and sold the Colonial Inn to John Minsky, the New York burlesque impresario. Those virtuous citizens who deplored illegal gambling in Hallandale could contemplate whether they thought that legal striptease was better.

In 1949, Greenacres and the Club Bohème opened up again, and this winter there was no trouble from "concerned citizens" in either

Hallandale or Hollywood. But the warning shots had been prophetic. In the late 1940s, there was a general unease in many of the corners of America where gambling had hitherto flourished unchallenged. License that was tolerated in the aftermath of Prohibition and Depression, and in the exuberant liberation from the Second World War, came to seem less acceptable to a society that was heading toward the buttoned-down conformity of the Eisenhower years.

"The clean-up was the result of returning prosperity," says Philip Weidling of the reform movement in Broward County. "The reputation as a lawless county was no asset to growth."[9]

During the 1920s, citizens' crime commissions had sprung up across America in response to the corruption of Prohibition, and the late 1940s saw a revival of the movement. By 1950, crime commissions were active in Chicago, California, Kansas City, Dallas, St. Louis, New York, Miami, and Gary, Indiana — and their immediate focus was "wide open" gambling: illegal bookmaking and carpet-joint casinos of the sort that Meyer Lansky had perfected.

The new postwar crime commissions were headed by campaigning men with a flair for publicity, and they found their natural allies in the local press. Journalists who discovered hints of corruption passed their tips along to the local crime commission, and they were rewarded with exclusives and access to the many half-substantiated allegations which the pressure groups had worked to collect.

It was seldom the sort of proof that a serious district attorney could have brought to court. The evidence against public officials — sheriffs of the Walter Clark variety — was not usually strong enough to withstand the possibility of a libel suit. But the journalists and the crime commissions soon worked out that the corruptors — the Meyer Lanskys who paid off the Walter Clarks — had no good name to defend. It made no sense for Meyer Lansky, for example, to sue the *New York Sun* for its suggestion, in its S.S. *Italia* report of June 1949, that Meyer had been involved in the murder for which Cock-eye Dunn went to the electric chair. Meyer had a criminal record of his own. He was making a small fortune from his illegal gambling establishments in Hallandale and Saratoga Springs. If he launched a libel suit, he would have to answer questions in open court, under oath, on virtually anything in his present or past, stimulating still more publicity and the attentions of the IRS, if not the FBI — while also, almost certainly, incriminating his partners and friends. Silence was his only option.

*   *   *

In the summer of 1943, investigators for the New York district attorney, Frank Hogan, were tapping the telephone of Frank Costello's New York apartment when they were astonished to hear the voice of Thomas Aurelio, a nominee for judge on the state supreme court, come on the line.[10]

"Good morning, Francesco," said Aurelio. "How are you, and thanks for everything."

"Congratulations," replied Costello. "It went over perfect. When I tell you something is in the bag, you can rest assured. . . ."

"Right now," said the grateful judge-to-be, "I want to assure you of my loyalty for all you have done. It's undying."[11]

A grand jury subsequently investigated Thomas Aurelio and discovered that he was guilty of no more than any other judicial nominee who went to a political boss to line up the votes he needed to secure election. Aurelio went on to serve twenty-four years on the New York State Supreme Court, in the course of which he showed himself quite tough on defendants with racketeering connections — and commendably open minded on the subject of secret surveillance. Aurelio was more willing than a number of other New York judges in those years to sign court orders authorizing wiretaps.[12]

The Aurelio episode brought Frank Costello firmly into the limelight. The following year, he accidentally left $27,200, a cash payment from his Louisiana slot machine operation, in a New York taxicab, and made the mistake of sending his lawyer to retrieve the money from the police lost-property office.[13] Fiorello La Guardia, who had started his term of office by attacking Costello's New York slot machine business, promptly labeled the cash "outlaw money," and blocked its return under a New York ordinance withholding lost property that was the proceeds of illegal activity. Costello went to court and proved, to a jury's satisfaction, that he had legal title to the money. But by that time the IRS had filed two tax liens against the cash, and, after court costs, Costello retrieved just $120.[14]

In the course of the case, Costello made some interesting revelations, not all of them forced from him. He admitted to having known Arnold Rothstein. He made no secret of being on friendly terms with Frank Erickson, who was by then the largest bookmaker on the East Coast, if not in all America — and, his vanity betraying him, he also referred to himself as "King of the Slots." To the distress of his lawyer, Frank Costello rather enjoyed testifying in court. He prepared for the occasion with sunlamp sessions, and insisted on appearing in his most elegant, tailored attire.

"Wear a *cheap* suit, for God's sake!" his attorney, George Wolf, would plead.[15]

In vain. The cash-in-the-cab case provided the crime writers with the details they needed. In April 1947, Herbert Asbury, a journalist who had been writing sensational and highly anecdotal accounts of big-city underworlds since the 1920s, published a two-part profile of "America's Number One Mystery Man" in *Collier's* magazine.[16]

"He is the real big-shot of the underworld," asserted Asbury, "where he is known and referred to as the 'Prime Minister.' He has been boss of half a dozen rackets and dominates gambling throughout the country."[17]

Journalists and news agencies rehashed the Asbury story for exposés and series of their own. By the end of 1949, Costello was a national celebrity — "Fast becoming a figure of U.S. legend," in the words of *Time* magazine, which put him on the cover on October 17, 1949. *Newsweek* followed on November 21.

Costello had become the embodiment of all that the citizens' crime commissions felt was wrong with America. Millions considered him, wrote *Time*, "a kind of master criminal, shadowy as a ghost, and cunning as Satan, who ruled a vast, mysterious, and malevolent underworld, and laughed lazily at the law."[18]

The newsmagazines could find little evidence for this popular suspicion. Costello could demonstrate that he made a substantial, legally declared, and tax-paid living from real estate investments and liquor distributorships. These were legacies of his bootlegging activities, but they were as legitimate as many another liquor empire that developed out of Prohibition.

All that could actually be proved about his more recent illegalities was that he had made large sums of money from his partnerships in slot machine companies and carpet joints — on which he had paid some tax, at least — and that he had become a master of the political fix in New York. This political patronage had earned him great prestige in the Italian community, including the respect of street hoodlums and of the gangs and fraternal associations later to be known as crime families.

But there was no evidence that Frank Costello was involved in street activities like loan-sharking, drug dealing, or pimping, and there was no need for him to soil his hands with this. Like Meyer Lansky, he had started on the streets and had a youthful criminal record, and, like Meyer, he had long since moved on to higher, safer, and more lucrative things. Frank Costello's eagerness to prove in court that he had come by his taxicab money legally, and his willingness to give interviews to journalists whom he considered "serious," might possibly have been the deceptions of a cynical and active crime boss. More plausibly, they were the actions of a man who believed he had successfully cast off his street-crime origins.

In January 1949, Costello accepted an invitation to raise funds for the Salvation Army. He threw a dinner at the Copacabana which raised $10,000 in pure profit, since Costello personally met all the expenses. One hundred eminent guests, who included Congressman Arthur Klein, five judges of the New York State Supreme Court, three other judges, and the president of the borough of Manhattan, all accepted Costello's invitation and paid $100 per plate.[19] Costello considered that the fund-raiser proved his community spirit, and also his respectability. The publication of the list of guests, along with the photographs taken as they left the Copacabana, was considered by New York — and by America as a whole — to prove exactly the opposite.

History was recast. Reporters speculated that it must have been Costello who loaned money to Rothstein in the 1920s, rather than vice versa; Costello must have been the guiding genius behind the 1929 Atlantic City gathering when Al Capone came to confer with the bootleggers of the East Coast. In new glosses on the received wisdom about organized crime, it became Costello who had ordered Lepke Buchalter to surrender to the FBI in 1941, who had been behind the labor racketeers who extorted money from Hollywood in the early 1940s — and who had decreed the death sentence on Bugsy Siegel in 1947.[20]

There was no reason for believing that the new story was any more accurate than the old. But by repetition, the speculation became a little more solid and a little more grandiose with every retelling, and the man whose political appetites had earned him the not altogether respectful underworld nickname of "the Prime Minister" now became known as "the Prime Minister of the Underworld."[21]

Frank Costello's attempts to cut his reputation down to size were a total disaster. He aggravated the anxieties represented by the newly formed crime commissions and helped sharpen the demand that something should be done. If America's underworld had its own prime minister and government, it was surely time that the country's legitimate government did something to address the problem.

*   *   *

At the end of 1949, in Washington, D.C., two freshman senators were contemplating the nation's developing anxiety over crime. Joseph R. McCarthy, Republican, was searching for a dramatic issue to boost his reelection chances in 1952. The forty-one-year-old senator from Wisconsin was investigating the involvement of Frank Costello in the liquor business, according to Harold Lavine in *Newsweek* in November 1949.[22] As a member of the Special Investigations Committee, Joseph McCarthy was well placed to launch a crime probe that would attract headlines, and early in 1950, he made an attempt to claim crime investigation as the province of his committee, pointing out that his special investigations staff was "specifically trained for this sort of thing."[23]

Senator Estes Kefauver, Democrat, of Tennessee, however, yielded nothing to Joseph McCarthy when it came to stealing the limelight. The forty-six-year-old Kefauver, a tall, thin, bespectacled lawyer from Chattanooga, campaigned back home in a coonskin cap, thus tempering his absentminded professor looks with a touch of Davy Crockett. He proved an equally adroit maneuverer in Washington, introducing bills in 1949 to ban the interstate shipment of slot machines and gambling information, and starting to badger the Senate leadership, early in January 1950, for his own special committee to investigate crime. In May 1950, he got his way, foiling Joseph McCarthy's bid to cover that territory, and leaving the senator from Wisconsin to go off in search of Communists and fellow travelers.[24]

Estes Kefauver came from a religious background. Every Sunday, as a boy, he sat through the two-hour sermons of his grandfather, a Baptist minister in Madisonville, Tennessee. This austere, rural upbringing had provided the bedrock of his populist style. But Kefauver had developed more worldly tastes by the time he went on from college in Knoxville to law school at Yale. He spent a year in Hot Springs, Arkansas, and by the time he got to Washington, first as a congressman, then as a senator, he was a devotee of horse racing, attending the Laurel and Pimlico tracks near Washington, placing bets, and expecting free passes and courtesy badges from the management.[25]

Kefauver's most vocal ally on his Special Committee to Investigate Organized Crime in Interstate Commerce, pursuant to Senate Resolution 202, came from a similar background but made no apparent compromise with the world. Senator Charles W. Tobey, Republican, of New Hampshire, had, as a child, been forbidden to play cards, to go to the theater, or to read a Sunday newspaper, and he reckoned himself the better for it. Seventy years old in 1950, Tobey believed that the country should turn back to the ideals of the Pilgrim Fathers.

"For many years," he complained, "an unbelievable number in America have been trying to live without God."[26]

As the Kefauver Committee began to move through its witness list of bookmakers, former bootleggers, and carpet-joint operators, Charles Tobey, bald as a turtle, his eyes popping with indignation, became the unashamed voice of the Protestant conscience in America.

"Haven't you ever said to yourself," he once demanded of Frank Erickson, "'I hate the hellish business. . . . This is not worthy of a man, a real American citizen'?"

"I have felt that way," Erickson admitted, dropping his head in apparent contrition.[27]

But in reality, the bookmaker later told Frank Costello, he dropped his head so the senator would not see him laughing.[28]

Meyer and Teddy Lansky took a second foreign holiday in the summer of 1950, and this time Meyer got them away undetected. They sailed off for a month or so in Europe, aboard one of the Cunard Queens.[29]

Meyer and Teddy had moved from Central Park South to an apartment on Thirty-sixth Street, and Buddy had moved in with them. Vincent Mercurio came to stay with his friend while Meyer and Teddy were away, and one day he took delivery of a telegram addressed to Lansky.

"Open it," said Buddy. "It may be from Dad."

It was, in fact, a telegram *to* Dad.

"You are hereby subpoenaed," Vincent Mercurio remembers reading, "to appear in front of the Kefauver Committee on such-and-such a day, in such-and-such a place."[30]

"Which of you opened the telegram?" asked Meyer when he got back.

He thought it was an enormous joke.

"Well, Vinnie — looks like you'd better go and testify."[31]

In the end, it was Patrick Murray, special investigator to the Kefauver Committee, who, just before six on the evening of September 19, 1950, tracked down Meyer Lansky and served him with a subpoena at Dinty Moore's restaurant off Broadway,[32] where "Lansky was seated alone at a table . . . indulging in a drink."[33]

Meyer appeared in front of the Kefauver Committee a few weeks later, on Wednesday, October 11, 1950, in New York.

"May I ask you if this is the subpoena?" he started by asking, holding the document in the air. "I want it known on the record that I was subpoenaed."

"Yes sir," replied Kefauver. "That is the subpoena. May I ask you, did you bring all those books and records we asked for?"

"No," replied Meyer.

"How about it?" inquired Kefauver.

"I decline," replied Meyer, "on the grounds that it may tend to incriminate me."[34]

This opening exchange set the style for what was to follow. Meyer acknowledged knowing a long string of underworld names, starting with Frank Costello, and going on through Joe Adonis, Jimmy Alo, Bugsy Siegel, Longy Zwillman, and Joseph Stacher, to Lucky Luciano. But the moment the committee tried to find out more about his relationship with these characters, Meyer took refuge in the Fifth Amendment.

"On the basis of your refusal to answer," Kefauver said, "there is not much use asking you any further questions."[35]

The committee proposed that Meyer should appear before them the following morning, in the company of his lawyer, in the hope that his attorney might advise him to be more forthcoming about some of the matters on which he was claiming the protection of the Fifth.

Meyer had refused to let Moses Polakoff accompany him to his first appearance. He had heard, he told Polakoff, that the committee was smearing some of the attorneys who accompanied their clients to the hearings as Mob lawyers[36] — and his fears proved well founded.

"I have heard of you," said Kefauver next day, as soon as Polakoff gave his name. "You were in the Luciano case, weren't you?"

"Yes sir," replied Polakoff.

"You were counsel for Luciano?" interjected Senator Tobey suddenly, bristling and incredulous.

"I was," acknowledged Polakoff.

"How did you become counsel for such a dirty rat as that?" demanded Tobey, furiously. "Aren't there some ethics in the legal profession?"

If Tobey thought he could score points off Moses Polakoff, he had picked on the wrong person.

"I don't want to get into any controversy with you about that subject at the present time," replied the lawyer, "but under our Constitution, every person is entitled to his day in court . . . whether he is innocent or not. When the day comes that a person becomes beyond the pale of justice, that means our liberty is gone. Minorities and undesirables and persons with bad reputations are more entitled to the protection of the law than are the so-called honorable people. I don't have to apologize to you —"

"I didn't ask you to," said Senator Tobey.

"— or anyone else for whom I represent."

"I look upon you in amazement," said Tobey in disgust.

"I look upon you in amazement," repeated Polakoff, in equal disgust, "a Senator of the United States, for making such a statement."[37]

The hearing did not progress much beyond that. At Polakoff's prompting, Meyer was prepared to admit that he had been in such places as Saratoga Springs and New Orleans, and that, in 1949, on his trip to Europe, he had gone to the cities of Naples and Rome, where Charlie Luciano was living. Meyer declined to answer any of the committee's questions as to what he was doing there, but, when asked whether he had had any business conferences with anyone while he was in Italy, he went into a huddle with Polakoff, from which he emerged with a very firm denial.

"I didn't have any business conferences with anyone."[38]

The massive and detailed volumes of testimony gathered by the Kefauver Committee in its fifteen months of inquiry between May 1950 and August 1951 add up to the largest single accumulation of data on organized crime in America. But very little of the evidence was unearthed by the committee itself. Its investigative staff was comparatively small. Kefauver's most valuable data came from the citizens' crime commissions, notably in Chicago, Miami, and New Orleans, together with documentation supplied by helpful district attorneys, the most forthcoming of whom was Frank Hogan in New York.

This dictated the structure of the committee's work, which became, in practice, a progress from city to city where a local crime commissioner was available, first to present his own survey of the local situation, and then, in effect, to produce the witnesses who substantiated his particular point of view. Critics of Kefauver were quick to point out that he steered his road show well clear of Tennessee and of any of the other states represented by the senators on the committee, though there were bookmakers, carpet joints, and wide-open enclaves in all of them.*

The focus of inquiry was also selective. Kefauver's self-defined brief was to investigate and then frame new laws to combat any type of organized crime which spilled over state boundaries — a definition which embraced drug trafficking, theft, hijacking, the smuggling of untaxed liquor and cigarettes, kidnapping, extortion, prostitution, pornography, stock manipulation, bond frauds, and a variety of other crimes.

In practice, however, the Kefauver Committee paid only lip service to the investigation of such complicated and multifarious activities — in none of which Costello, Lansky, or the majority of the committee's witnesses were involved — preferring to concentrate, almost exclusively, on the much easier targets of gambling and bookmaking. For the best part of a year, Kefauver traveled round America finding rich pickings in locations like Saratoga Springs and Broward County — where Walter Clark provided an hour of evasive, bumbling, and embarrassed testimony, which totally laid bare his complicity in the gambling there.

But while the committee presented its findings as "revelations," and the newspapers largely reported them as such, Kefauver and his colleagues were, in fact, only describing situations which, as the term "wide open" suggested, had been operating for more than a decade in the clear light of day.

The grandstanding character of the inquiry received an extra dimension in January 1951, when the committee found itself in New Orleans. Cameras from a local television station came to broadcast the proceedings, and the effect was spectacular. There were more crowds for the rest of the committee's hearings in Louisiana than the courthouse could possibly accommodate, and the TV station was flooded with 1,300 letters within three days.[39]

In Detroit, in February, where Kefauver's inquiry did not, for a change, concentrate on gambling, but also covered labor violence and the criminal associations of Harry Bennett, head of the Ford

---

*The full roster of the Special Committee to Investigate Organized Crime in Interstate Commerce was Estes Kefauver, Tennessee, chairman; Charles W. Tobey, New Hampshire; Herbert R. O'Conor, Maryland; Lester C. Hunt, Wyoming; and Alexander Wiley, Wisconsin. Kefauver resigned from the committee after it had completed its original program of investigation in the spring of 1951. Herbert O'Conor took over the chairmanship, and he did hold hearings in his home state of Maryland.

Motor Company's notorious Service Department, two stations canceled their regular programming to televise the hearings, and attracted more viewers, by one account, than the boxing bouts of Joe Louis, the local hero. Later that month, in St. Louis, the television audience exceeded that for the World Series.[40]

By the time Estes Kefauver brought his committee back to New York for its final hearings in March 1951, the senator from Tennessee was a national celebrity. March 12, 1951, saw him on the cover of *Time* magazine. People gathered in fifteen-degree cold to stare at televisions through store windows, and crowded into bars and restaurants which offered a screen they could watch. Housewives converted their afternoon canasta or bridge gatherings into "Kefauver Parties."[41]

Through a pooling agreement with New York's WPIX, an independent station, Kefauver's New York hearings were carried by the three national networks to over twenty cities in the East. Schools released senior students from class to go home and watch American democracy at work. Grocers and butchers reported dramatically increased sales at noon, when the committee recessed for lunch. Senator Hunt observed that New York appeared so fascinated by the hearings of the crime committee that at rush hour there was no rush.[42]

Television had started on its career of magnifying, dramatizing, and oversimplifying the mechanisms of the nation's life. Senator Tobey put on a green visor to shade his eyes from the camera lights — and looked more like a crusading country newspaper editor than ever. Estes Kefauver had stumbled into a new world. The American political process — and America as a whole — could never be quite the same again.

New York was intended to provide a grand climax to the Kefauver Committee's inquiries. The hearings there had been personally researched and prepared by the committee's chief counsel, Rudolph Halley, an intelligent, aggressive lawyer of thirty-seven, who, working full-time, and taking the lead in most of the questioning, deserved as much credit for the popular impact of the committee as Kefauver himself.[43]

The hearings, from March 13 to 21, 1951, did not disappoint expectations. Called to the stand every day for sessions ranging from half an hour to half the day, Frank Costello twisted and turned under the crossfire of Kefauver, Tobey, and Halley,[44] indignant at all the evil being imputed to him, but unable to escape from the undeniable illegality of his income.

Costello's breathy, gravelly voice fitted perfectly into the drama. It was the consequence, Costello later explained, of a skewed operation to singe polyps from his throat in his youth — by mistake the physician had burned some of his vocal cords permanently. Compared by one commentator to "the death rattle of a seagull,"[45] Costello's voice was later said to have provided the model for Marlon Brando's memorable performance in *The Godfather*. When Costello's lawyer, George Wolf, complained about his client's face being televised and the cameras switched to Costello's well-manicured hands wringing and rubbing to the accompaniment of his questioning, America's living rooms were presented with one of the first great images of the television age.

Halley spiced up the proceedings by producing Virginia Hill, now married to an Austrian ski instructor. She looked puffier and more weary than when she had been the consort of Benny Siegel, but she was as pugnacious as ever. Her testimony added nothing to what was known about Siegel's murder, but when, in a mink cape and a striking, wide-brimmed black hat, Miss Hill came out of the committee room to find herself surrounded by journalists, she kicked one reporter on the shins, slapped Marjorie Farnsworth, of the *New York Journal-American,* and shouted that she hoped "the atom bomb" would fall on all of them.[46]

In all this drama, the testimony of Meyer Lansky went largely unremarked. It was Meyer's third appearance in front of Senator Kefauver, and the hearing was held in one of the closed sessions to which the press and TV were not admitted. Five months after he had first testified so inconclusively, however, and after Rudolph Halley and the senators had become practiced in their role of national tribunes, it was interesting how television's demands for a good performance had come to affect both sides.

At their first meeting, Halley had been content stubbornly to present Meyer Lansky with long lists of questions to which Meyer, with equal stubbornness, had responded by pleading the Fifth. By March 1951, however, Halley had learned how to skip adroitly aside when this deadlock threatened.

"I am learning how to play this game with you," he remarked almost playfully at one point in the proceedings.[47]

Meyer, for his part, responded with a sense of equal responsibility to the show. "Through the windshield, too, pardon me!" he interjected at one point, almost facetiously, when Moses Polakoff was describing how, whenever he drove up to Comstock to see Charlie Luciano during the war, Meyer had "always accompanied me."[48]

Halley did his best to avoid the subjects on which he knew his witness would plead the Fifth — gambling, Saratoga, Broward County, or New Orleans, where Meyer had held a share in Costello's Beverly Club. He tried to concentrate on areas where Meyer could talk without fear of incrimination: Emby Distributing, Consolidated Television, and the Gran Casino Nacional in Cuba, where gaming was legal so could safely be discussed. Meyer was also happy to talk about his war work with Charlie Luciano and naval intelligence. Moses Polakoff added his own memories to this part of the testimony, which, when it was later published, became the first accurate firsthand airing of the episode.

Meyer was positively relaxed. "We should have gone into the home-set end," he remarked ruefully of his venture into bars and restaurants with Consolidated Television's Tele Kings, "and maybe I would have been a very rich man today."[49] By March 1951, the national epidemic of Kefauveritis had shut down Broward County, Saratoga Springs, and virtually every other wide-open enclave in America, and he was evidently feeling the financial pinch.

At one point, Halley tried to shift the focus back to the 1920s and Prohibition.

"Were you in the liquor business at that time?" the counsel asked.

"Yes," replied Meyer shortly.

"You were?" persisted Halley.

"Must we go into that, too?" asked Meyer resignedly, and Halley obligingly shifted his questions in another direction.[50]

The hearing concluded amicably, with the committee well satisfied with all the information it had extracted from its witness — though none of it, in truth, shed much light on the nature of Meyer Lansky's illicit gambling. In a private conversation, however, Meyer tried to get Kefauver to address the heart of the matter.

"What's so bad about gambling?" he asked the senator. "You like it yourself. I know you've gambled a lot."

Lansky described this exchange with Kefauver twenty years later, when he was in Israel, and as Meyer recalled it, Kefauver did not attempt to dispute the main point.

"That's quite right," Meyer remembered his replying. "But I don't want *you* people to control it."[51]

By "you people," the senator was almost certainly talking about the underworld — people like Meyer himself and Frank Costello, whom Kefauver considered gangsters beyond redemption. Kefauver's own gambling, so far as is known, was always done legally, through the parimutuel window at racetracks.[52]

But Meyer, suddenly bridling, chose to take the senator's comment as an ethnic slur. "I was convinced that he meant 'you Jews and you Italians,'" he subsequently recounted, "and that infuriated me."

His response to Kefauver was abrupt.

"I'm not one of those Jewish hotel owners in Miami Beach who tell you all sorts of stories just to please you," he flared, referring to the parade of hoteliers who had testified about poolside bookmaking when Kefauver held his hearings in Miami. "I will not allow you to persecute me because I am a Jew."[53]

This retort — often and proudly recounted by Meyer in his subsequent retellings of the confrontation — betrayed Meyer's inability to look at himself with the same clear-eyed scrutiny to which he subjected others. He had broached the very essence of the problem when he invited Kefauver to face up to the senator's own fondness for a flutter, the contradiction inside any human being — and inside any human society — between what it enjoys doing and what it feels that it ought, morally, to restrict and control.

It was a weakness, not to say hypocrisy, on Kefauver's part to fail to acknowledge that gambling was less a vice imposed on unwilling innocents by "you people" than a human pastime of almost universal appeal, springing from appetites and impulses which the senator evidently experienced himself. If Meyer had responded to Kefauver as an unapologetic outlaw, rather than as a defensive Jew, he might possibly have forced the senator to admit, if only in private, that the reality of "crime" was more complex than the simplistic and demagogic terms in which Kefauver was presenting the issue to America.

As it was, Meyer's crippling sensitivity to his own race and background, which Seymour Gray had noted in the psychological assessment of his patient, provoked a display of temper — a rare dislocation of the Lansky calm — which effectively let the senator wriggle off the hook.

"Mr. Lansky, you're very famous," said Estes Kefauver, sidestepping smartly.[54] And that was the end of what might have been a fascinating debate.

Virginia Hill did rather better in confronting the Kefauver Committee with the gap between their moral posturing and real life. In the private session that preceded her public appearance, Senator Tobey pressed the four-times-married Miss Hill on how she survived financially when she was not married, and, in particular, on the large sums of money that she received from other men.

Senator Tobey was particularly intrigued by the pattern of payments from the elderly Chicago bookmaker Joe Epstein, who had exhibited quite remarkable faithfulness in sending Virginia money over the years, through and despite her various marriages and her flagrant liaisons with the likes of Bugsy Siegel. What could possibly induce a man to keep sending a woman money like that, the senator wanted to know, particularly a woman who was young enough to be his daughter?

"Why would he do it?" Tobey kept asking, declining to accept his witness's evasions, until, eventually, she had had enough.

"You really want to know why?" she asked.

"Yes," replied Senator Tobey. "I really want to know why."

"Then I'll tell you why," said Miss Hill, with all the directness that had endeared her to Benny Siegel, Joe Adonis, Joe Epstein, and numerous other gentlemen. "Because I'm the best cocksucker in America."[55]

The Kefauver Committee, like any other congressional or senatorial committee of inquiry, sprang from the exploratory dimension which the fledgling United States inherited from British Common Law. This dimension is seen most frequently, in practice, in the investigative grand jury, which fell into disuse in Britain in the nineteenth century. In America the grand jury has developed into an integral component of the American legal system, and one feature of its workings is the application of the Fifth Amendment, whereby witnesses can be subpoenaed to provide evidence without being compelled to incriminate themselves.[56]

But this can create a surreal situation in which investigators — and, in the case of open committees of inquiry, the general public — feel they are getting right to the heart of a particular criminal situation when they may be miles away. When Meyer Lansky and Frank Costello were asked by Kefauver about their dealings with each other and took the Fifth, the popular imagination concluded they were hiding a vast and interlinked criminal empire — guns and girls and drugs — who knew what? In reality, neither man cared to admit for the record that he was engaged in an illegal gambling operation, and that he was, in all probability, underdeclaring on his taxes.

This confusion tends to magnify the magic of lawbreakers, lending them an aura of invulnerability as they run the gauntlet of reporters and photographers after the questionings that promised so much and said so little. Society is dramatically reminded of both the existence of illegal enterprise and the difficulty of doing anything about it — and the gap between the two is an invitation for the popular imagination to supply the connections which the real world cannot.

In the case of the Kefauver Committee, this helped generate a nationwide hysteria, with overtones of Mob justice which the committee did little to discourage. Using the records which Frank Hogan seized from George Goldstein, accountant to Frank Erickson and to a number of carpet joints in which Meyer Lansky, Frank Costello, and Joe Adonis all held partnerships, the Kefauver investigators were able to piece together a picture of the croupiers, chefs, barmen, maître d's, and waiters who worked in Hallandale or Cuba in the winter, then moved up in the spring to New Jersey, Kentucky, Cleveland, Detroit, or any of the other northern carpet-joint enclaves, with, perhaps, a month's excursion in August to Saratoga.[57]

The research documents of the committee make clear that these men, most of whom did not work at the gaming tables, and who could, thus, only barely be described as lawbreakers, were independent free-lance operators like many another in the catering trade. They paid their income tax and Social Security, and moved, like fruit pickers or any other seasonal workers, on an annual round to where the money was.

But one would not have guessed from the committee's dark talk of conspiracies and complicated nationwide syndicates that the backbone of the casino operation they were describing conformed to quite a logical and routine economic model, and that the "kingpins" of the business like Meyer Lansky operated on the same basis.

Conspiracy was the keynote of the Kefauver investigation. As the sociologist Daniel Bell, in his analysis of the committee's work, remarked, "There is . . . in the American temper a feeling that 'somewhere,' 'somebody' is pulling all the complicated strings to which this jumbled world dances."[58]

Searching — with earnestness and genuine concern, as well as with political opportunism — for some simple explanation of the lawbreaking and corruption which they seemed to encounter wherever they looked, the committee seized gratefully upon the theory of narcotics bureau chief Harry Anslinger: an ethnic conspiracy was at work.

In its second interim report, released in February 1951, the committee published the assertions made to it "that there exists in the United States a crime syndicate known as the Mafia, operating Nation-wide under centralized direction and control." There was "a great deal of testimony" to support this theory, the committee stated, and it promised to continue its investigations.[59]

Three months later it had no doubt.

"There is a sinister criminal organization known as the Mafia operating throughout the country with ties in other nations," announced the third interim report of May 1, 1951, without any reservation. "The Mafia is a direct descendant of a criminal organization of the same name originating in the island of Sicily."[60]

The committee had earlier stated its conviction that there was "a government within a government in this country, and that that second government was the government by the underworld."[61] Now a name could be put to it. The Mafia, announced Estes Kefauver, was "the binder" that tied together two great syndicates dominating crime in America — "the Accardo-Guzik-Fischetti syndicate, whose headquarters are Chicago; and the Costello-Adonis-Lansky syndicate based on [*sic*] New York."[62]

The committee did not explain exactly how these two major criminal syndicates fitted in with the apparently central authority of the Mafia. Nor was it troubled by the fact that two Jews, Jake Guzik and Meyer Lansky, played such a prominent role in what the committee was presenting as an essentially Italian, and even a specifically Sicilian, picture.

Anslinger himself had entered some caveats when he gave his evidence. "It is interlaced and intertwined . . . ," the narcotics director had declared in his testimony of June 1950, "but I would not say that one section of the country controls another."[63]

The committee noted the reservation, but it was not the message of its revelation to the United States. The problems with which Kefauver and his fellow senators were wrestling were of America's own making — the contradictions generated by an unprecedentedly wealthy, still young and confused society which prohibited goods and services with one hand, while paying large sums of money to acquire them with the other. But it was much easier to blame the problem on a small and sinister clique of outsiders who, for reasons which the committee did not choose to go into, were intrinsically evil — and who were also, well, un-American.

"Un-American," of course, was the potent battle cry of Senator Joseph McCarthy, Estes Kefauver's original rival for the chance to mount a national crime investigation, and there were a number of parallels in the national campaigns — and the national panics — that made the two men the dominant populist figures in America in the early 1950s. Both had an unerring instinct for America's capacity, at her moment of greatest world dominance, to feel frightened and, in some way, ashamed of herself. Both men exploited suspicion as a blunt instrument to subdue — and, quite frequently, to substitute for — thought and reason and evidence. And both men (through genuine conviction, it must be repeated, in Kefauver's case, as much as through political opportunism) saw the world in conspiratorial terms. If A knew B, and B knew C, then it must follow that A knew C, and that all three were tied together in a network of conspiracy.

The Kefauver Committee saw connections everywhere.

"The two great enemies within our ranks, the criminals and the Communists, often work hand in hand," declared Senator Tobey in alarm. "Wake up America! Arouse across the country a consciousness of the far-flung empire of crime in all its aspects."[64]

The fact that every Kefauver witness suspected of belonging to the Mafia denied employing the term "Mafia," or even recognizing it, was taken as further evidence of the organization's secretive duplicity.

Suspicion and a nose for conspiracy are the tools of a good investigator. A policeman, detective, or inquirer into any wrongdoing will not get very far if he does not suspect the worst of people. But Estes Kefauver took suspicion so far it overwhelmed his sense of logic, causing him to jumble up cause and effect. Blaming organized crime on the Mafia was like describing southern racism as the offspring of the Ku Klux Klan.

If confronted by a real-life gangster, most people might expect their heart to race a little. Make that several dozen gangsters in succession, in the presence of an audience of millions, and it is not surprising that the thought processes of the Kefauver Committee's members should have grown overheated as they tried to make sense of all the shocking things they heard — most of it for the first time — in their travels around America more than forty years ago.

In the distant and detached calm of retrospect, however, and with all the oversimplification of which Estes Kefauver himself was guilty, it is now possible to see that the legacy of his crime committee has been several fundamental and enduring misconceptions.

The first was inherent in the very structure of his inquiry. As a national, federally constituted body traveling to survey a range of local situations — and not such a wide range, given their preference for the easy, wide-open target — the committee was predisposed to a singular, nationwide explanation for what it saw. In a sense, the Kefauver Committee had no choice but to reach such a conclusion, for if organized crime was not fundamentally a matter of interstate commerce, what business did an arm of the Senate have lavishing so much time and attention on the subject?

When the committee finally got round to asking the director of the FBI his opinion, he told them in no uncertain terms. Gambling — the committee's great preoccupation — was just like any other crime, J. Edgar Hoover told them in March 1951. "It can be controlled." The committee had seen fit to spend nearly a year traveling round the country listening to other people before it consulted the director of the FBI, but that only added to the message that Hoover, an early master of the sound bite, wanted to convey.

"If the laws against gambling presently on the state and local statute books were earnestly and vigorously enforced," testified Hoover, "organized gambling could be eliminated within forty-eight hours in any community in this land."[65]

Hoover had been quite supportive of Kefauver in certain ways. When it looked as if the crime committee was running out of time and money to complete its work before the end of March 1951, he put his prestige behind the securing of an extension of the Senate deadline, in harness with the attorney general, J. Howard McGrath.[66] But Hoover would have no truck with talk of a nationally organized crime conspiracy.

"The basic answer," the director insisted, "[is] an aroused public opinion which will act on a *local* level through *local* enforcement authorities to wipe out the problem" — and each time he said "local" he wagged his finger and stuck out his jaw so he looked more like a bulldog than ever.[67]

Hoover's personal position, that the Mafia did not exist, has proved as erroneous as the Kefauver Committee's belief in a national conspiracy. In the course of the last forty years, countless law enforcement agencies, including the FBI, have shown that America is riddled with local associations of Italian malefactors. Mafia is as good a name for them as any other.

The difficult question — to which no one, including the mafiosi themselves, has the answer — is the nature of the connections which these local associations establish with each other. The Mafia is like Freemasonry — everywhere and nowhere, significant when its individual members are significant, but not significant when they are not. What is certain is that, while local groupings of mafiosi can generate quite active links between each other, they do not constitute, and have never constituted, a centrally, almost corporately structured organization such as the one the Kefauver Committee led America to believe existed in the early 1950s. There was no shadowy General Motors of crime "which could, if not curbed, become the basis for a subversive movement which could wreck the very foundations of this country."[68]

The second Kefauver misconception was the belief that the financial underpinning of this vast and menacing enterprise was illegal gambling.

This was not a theory enunciated in the committee's first two reports, in August 1950 and February 1951. Gambling was pronounced a "basic menace"[69] and "a stench in the public nostrils."[70] But by May 1951, when the third interim report, largely written by Kefauver and Halley, appeared, there had been considerable scorn poured on the committee's fixation with gamblers. Wondering aloud why Senator Kefauver could not find time to take his place at an important meeting of the Senate Foreign Relations and Armed Services Committee, the committee chairman, Tom Connally of Texas, had remarked derisively, "He's out chasing crapshooters somewhere."[71]

In May 1951, Senator Kefauver had an answer to such ribaldry. "Gambling profits," he wrote, "are the principal support of big-time racketeering and gangsterism."[72]

Apologists might excuse gambling as a harmless indulgence but, the senator now revealed, it provided the seed capital for crime in America. The Kefauver Committee estimated that organized, illegal gambling was a business that turned over $20 billion every year[73] — about 7 percent of the gross national product.

Intrigued as to how the Senate committee could arrive at a precise figure for such a diverse, scattered, and secretive array of activities, Daniel Bell asked a committee staffer where the figure came from. If it was rare for one crap game operator to know what the next was making, how did the Senate committee find out?

"We had no real idea," the staffer confessed. "The California Crime Commission said twelve billion. Virgil Peterson of Chicago estimated thirty billion. We picked twenty billion as a balance between the two."[74]

This estimate has set the benchmark for estimates of the illegal economy of the United States to this day, both in terms of figures and as the model for subsequent estimating techniques. Like the rat population of New York, it is a subject on which "experts" can pronounce without much fear of contradiction.[75]

Estes Kefauver had little time for those who questioned his views, which he set out in the best-selling book *Crime in America*.

"A national crime syndicate does exist in the United States of America," he asserted, "despite the protestations of a strangely assorted company of criminals, self-serving politicians, plain blind fools, and others who may be honestly misguided."[76]

The senator's moral self-assurance, however, hindered him from clearly analyzing the mechanisms which prompted his outrage. It was true that the men who were profiting from illegal gambling were lawbreakers. They were that by definition. But there was no reason why someone making tens of thousands of dollars from a casino or profitable horse book would want to reinvest it in prostitution, stolen property, or any other variety of street crime, where the return on capital was comparatively low and the risk of detection and arrest comparatively high.

Insisting on seeing Meyer Lansky, Frank Costello, and even the bookmaker Frank Erickson not as amoral, economic operators, but as "rats" or "scum" — words which he did not hesitate to employ in his official, printed reports — Estes Kefauver failed to understand how a man who had found an easier way of making money might be very happy to forsake his previous street rackets. When Meyer Lansky described himself as a "common gambler," he spoke as a man who had attained a certain status in his world.

Successful criminal businessmen, like successful businessmen of any sort, tend to be specialists. There is no logic — and a great deal of danger — in committing themselves, or their capital, to areas away from their principal expertise. Drugs, smuggling, prostitution, labor extortion in the garment business, arm-twisting by teamsters and truckers, the "protection" of nightclubs and restaurants, rigged construction contracts, bookmaking, the running of illegal crap games and carpet joints — crime in America was a mosaic of specialist rackets in the early 1950s, as it had been for the previous twenty years or more. Some capital inevitably washed from business to business, particularly at the local level. But seeing bookmaking and gambling as the investment bank for the whole system did not reflect how things really worked.

"The rackets," in fact, was a concept that featured comparatively little in the thinking and findings of the Kefauver Committee, and, in the course of the 1950s, the term passed out of popular usage as a means of identifying and understanding organized crime. It was replaced by "the Mafia" and, later, by "the Mob," as singular, conspiratorial explanations of what was going on outside the law. Kefauver's avoidance of the term may possibly have stemmed from its association with the great rackets-buster Thomas Dewey, still a preeminent force in the Republican party. The Kefauver Committee derived no little pleasure from pointing out how the open gaming which the New York Republicans sanctioned at Saratoga Springs every August displayed the double standards of New York's Republican governor, Thomas E. Dewey — which it did.

The Kefauver Committee represented America's largest single effort to catalog, define, and understand the dark side of its national life, compelling a normally secretive substratum of society to go at least partially onto the record. The committee's volumes of testimony, together with its files — ninety linear feet of documents in the National Archives — are a treasure trove for historians of American society and crime.[77]

In terms of politics, the Kefauver Committee provided its once obscure chairman with a spectacular launch into the presidential primaries of early 1952. Estes Kefauver became a leading contender for the Democratic nomination, and he made the ticket as Adlai Stevenson's vice-presidential candidate four years later.

In terms of practical lawmaking, however, the committee was a failure. Its only piece of legislation produced the fifty-dollar "betting tax stamp," a scheme to tax illegal bookmakers which proved unenforceable — while Kefauver's alarmism and oversimplifications bedevil America's understanding of organized crime to this day.

The "Red Scare" generated by Kefauver's contemporary, Joseph McCarthy, proved a comparatively short-term alarm. It was ugly while it lasted, but it did not take America very long to pick apart the package of conspiracy which McCarthy assembled and to realize that awkward and critical left-wing radicals did not pose the same threat to the state as Soviet spies — that there are degrees of dissent.

There are, similarly, degrees of criminality — particularly in a society which chooses to class most varieties of gambling as illegal. On the other side of the Atlantic, the year 1951 saw the report of the Royal Commission on Betting, Lotteries and Gambling, which paved the way for Britain's high-street betting shops and legally regulated casinos.[78] Meyer Lansky's British equivalents headed for their silk hats, morning suits, and the Royal Enclosure. With his naming in the 1951 report of the Kefauver Crime Committee, Lansky found himself heading in a different direction.

12

"Do You Notice Anything Funny About Marvin?"

IN the summer of 1952, Meyer Lansky celebrated his fiftieth birthday. He also contemplated the prospect of his first ever spell in jail. A grand jury had started investigating Saratoga gambling the previous summer, and had focused particularly on the records of the Arrowhead Inn, where, five years earlier, Meyer had shared the running of the casino with James "Piggy" Lynch, a friend and partner of Joe Adonis.[1] On September 10, 1952, Meyer Lansky, Lynch, and five others were indicted on charges of conspiracy, gambling, and forgery.[2]

The forgery charges stemmed from the fact that the Arrowhead's application for its summer liquor license in 1947 had been filed in the name of the local, Saratoga partners, and had made no mention of Lansky or Lynch. It was somewhat overstating the offense to call this forgery, and Moses Polakoff had little difficulty in getting the indictment dismissed before the case came to court.

The lawyer felt confident that he could get Meyer off the gambling charges as well, since the grand jury testimony linked Meyer not to the gaming room, but only to the restaurant of the Arrowhead.[3]

"We could have won the case," remembers Polakoff today, "but he didn't want it. . . . He didn't want to risk a trial."[4]

A trial would have meant publicity, and the chance of testimony that might incriminate others. Meyer pleaded guilty, and on May 2, 1953, he was sentenced — a fine of $2,500 and three months in jail. The judge offered Meyer a few days to put his affairs in order before going into prison, but Meyer declined the offer. He drove the eight miles from Ballston Spa, where the jail sat right behind the county courthouse, into Saratoga Springs to do some last-minute shopping, and returned that afternoon to start his sentence with two books under his arm — an English dictionary and a revised version of the King James Bible.[5]

Meyer's companion in the county jail was Gerard King, a young native of Saratoga Springs. King had been the manager of Newman's, the lake house which stayed open most of the year catering to the local trade. The two men were assigned neighboring cells and, in the absence of any other prisoners, they were given the run of the cell-block, free to visit each other and to walk around the corridors.

King had never met Meyer Lansky before, and he found him to be a fanatic for exercise. Today his memory of Meyer is of a short and muscular man walking briskly up and down the cellblock to keep himself in shape, while urging his new young friend to do the same.

"We used to do calisthenics together," remembers King. "We'd stand side by side and work our arms up and down."[6] It was clear from the way in which Lansky coached his young companion that he had been a regular at a gym.

"I liked him," King says of Meyer Lansky. "He was a gentleman — a man of his word. If he told you anything, you felt you could believe it."[7]

Gerard King, a solid citizen who, his early years of lake house gambling apart, has never broken the law, looks back wryly on his month behind bars as "my time in Ballston College." He remembers a lot of reading, enlivened by occasional games of arithmetic. Meyer would challenge him to write down a block of figures, seven or eight digits across, with as many figures down. Meyer would then start in the top right-hand corner, and would run his finger rapidly up and down the columns as if he were a calculating machine, reeling off the totals in a matter of seconds.

"I think you're wrong, Meyer," King would say occasionally.

"You check it," Meyer would reply.

When King laboriously checked the calculations with pencil and paper, he found, invariably, that Meyer's sums were right.

As a local, Gerard King was on familiar terms with the deputies who supervised the daily round of the two men in the Ballston Spa Jail, and one day — to Meyer's surprise — King had a visit from the district attorney himself, who took time off from a case in the courthouse to come in and see how his old friend Gerard was faring.

"This is Saratoga," Gerard told Meyer afterward. "Things are different here."

King arranged for lunch and dinner to be brought in for the two men, at their own expense, from nearby restaurants, and the mutual discussion and selecting of the bill of fare was one of the high points of the day, Meyer displaying his tendency to take charge of the menu.

"He was a lamb chop man," King remembers.[8]

Two or three times a week, at ten o'clock precisely, Meyer would go to the pay phone in the jail to call his son Buddy in New York and check on the previous night's closing prices on the stock exchange. Buddy would have the *New York Times* financial pages ready. Meyer had some solid stock holdings in quoted companies — Republic Aviation, Eastern Airlines, Barium Steel, IT&T,[9] and U.S. Lines, the shipping company. He also had some stock in his Boston friend Joe Linsey's horse- and dog-racing tracks in New England, Wonderland and Revere.[10]

Meyer's tax return for 1953 listed his stock exchange transactions — eight sales of holdings which dated, for the most part, back to 1935 and 1936. Meyer showed that he had originally paid a total of some $6,800 for the shares, and that he had sold them in 1953 for some $22,100, a capital gain of $15,300.[11]

It was a welcome sum — nearly $100,000 in 1990's money — but it represented a certain cashing-in of Meyer's chips. Though Estes Kefauver had failed to get any meaningful legislation onto the statute book, the furor he generated had shamed several corners of the country into cracking down on their wide-open enclaves.[12] In Hallandale, the Bohème and Greenacres clubs had closed their doors, and in September 1950, Meyer and a group of other local operators, including Jake Lansky and Jimmy Blue Eyes, had been indicted on gambling charges to which they pleaded guilty, paying fines which ranged from $1,000 to $3,000.[13]

Meyer had declared a combined personal income of some $22,000 from Greenacres and the Bohème in their final season of business (1950), but since then he had only been able to report modest receipts to the IRS — some $1,200 in 1951, and $1,500 in 1952, all dividend income from his shares.[14] By 1953 he needed to be able to demonstrate some solid and legitimate income, for almost everyone who had appeared before Kefauver was undergoing IRS scrutiny of their tax returns.

Meyer had always run his life on a cash basis. He had at least five safe-deposit boxes in different banks in New York, Newark, Boston, and Hollywood, Florida,[15] and when he put any money through his bank accounts, it was in simple and unrevealing cash transactions. Records of Meyer's account with the Manufacturers Trust of New York between March 1944 and December 1947 — the postwar boom years when the revenues of the Colonial Inn and his other carpet joints were at their height — showed him depositing a total of $119,000, in parcels ranging from $700 to $16,000 at a time.[16] Over the forty-six months of transactions, this represented an average deposit of just over $2,500 per month.

Meyer Lansky did not seem greatly concerned about the IRS and his tax returns, however, in his conversations with Gerard King in the Ballston Spa Jail. It was the immigration service that worried him.

"He was afraid that he might be sent back to Russia," King remembers.[17]

The Immigration and Naturalization Service (INS) was an agency of the Justice Department, and since it was the contention of J. Edgar Hoover that there was no federal law under which the FBI could meaningfully pursue the Lanskys, Costellos, and Adonises highlighted by the Senate Crime Committee, the INS stepped into the breach. Lansky, Costello, and Adonis had all arrived in America as immigrants, and the INS started probing the pasts of all three men.

Joe Adonis proved an easy target. Though he swore to Kefauver that he was a U.S. citizen, he had never, in fact, taken the trouble to get himself naturalized. Convicted of the perjury, he was deported back to Italy as an undesirable alien in 1954.[18]

Frank Costello and Meyer Lansky had not made that mistake. But neither man had disclosed his criminal record at the time of his naturalization, and the penalty for that was deportation. In the aftermath of Kefauver, INS investigators had been assigned to prepare dossiers on both Costello and Lansky. Benjamin Edelstein, the agent appointed to investigate Meyer, had been particularly diligent.

Edelstein's most substantial witness was the feckless Daniel Ahearn, whom the agent had tracked down to Sing Sing. A jailbird for most of his life, Ahearn had been delighted to scour his memory for recollections of Meyer. He told Edelstein of the lead-pipe attack upon the recalcitrant foreman from Peekskill. He recounted the tale of John Barrett's being pushed from the car and shot at in the night, and also of the subsequent attempt to poison Barrett in the hospital with the "juiced-up" chicken.

Ahearn was not a reliable witness. But Edelstein's further investigations located John Barrett himself, and the policeman, Detective Heinrich, who had first taken Barrett's testimony about the shooting as Barrett lay wounded in the hospital, and had filed attempted murder charges, only to have Barrett mysteriously change his mind and refuse to testify — as a consequence, presumably, of intimidation by Meyer.

Edelstein had located Benny Siegel's widow, Esther, who remembered Meyer's being best man at her wedding, and the agent had even managed to interview the first Mrs. Lansky, who dismissed the idea that she married a tool-and-die machinist — the occupation which Meyer had given at the time of his naturalization, a few months before his marriage in 1929.

This suggested still more concealment of the truth on the part of Meyer in his citizenship application, though Benjamin Edelstein did note that the first Mrs. Lansky might not prove a strong witness in court to that effect. She was "very peculiar," he reported. Anne had insisted on keeping the room in darkness throughout her interview with the man from the INS.[19]

By May and June 1953, the months that Meyer spent in jail in Saratoga County (he got a month off for good behavior), the naturalization service had not filed charges. But Meyer knew that the investigators were on his trail. Edelstein had located Irving "Tabbo" Sandler, and Tabbo had lost no time in contacting his cousin to pass on the details of the interview.[20] Meyer's few weeks in Ballston Spa with the King James Bible would come to seem mild indeed compared to what might follow if the INS managed to make its denaturalization case against him stick.

Gerard King noticed that Meyer would become quite contemplative at times. "He used to tell me about his grandfather, back in Russia, what a wonderful man he was."

Meyer Lansky also expressed an ambition that seemed slightly premature in a man who had only just passed fifty.

"He said that he wanted to be buried like his grandfather was, in Israel — in Jerusalem."[21]

*   *   *

Favorite image — the
photograph Meyer Lansky
gave his children: Lansky in
his office at Emby, his jukebox
distributing company, in
the 1940s.

Sabotage suspected: The liner *Normandie*, burned out and
capsized in New York Harbor, February 1942.

Gangbusters: Special
Prosecutor Thomas E. Dewey
(right) with Murray I. Gurfein,
assistant DA and future rackets
prosecutor, September 1935.

Spymaster: Commander
Charles "Red" Haffenden,
U.S. Naval Intelligence, New
York, who enlisted Lansky's
help in the Allied war effort.

Rackets boss: Joseph "Socks"
Lanza, of the Fulton Street
Fish Market, January 1943.

Cigar-smoking nanny: Jules "Julie" Fink with his charge, Buddy Lansky, Miami Beach, early 1940s.

Anne Lansky with Buddy (left), Sandra, and Paul.

Lansky in Havana with his sons, Paul (left) and Buddy, late 1930s.

Las Vegas pioneer Benjamin "Bugsy" Siegel, August 1940.

Gangsters real and cinematic: Siegel (left) with the actor **George Raft** in 1944.

Virginia Hill, Benny's girlfriend, testifying about his death to the Kefauver Crime Committee in 1951.

Dream in the desert: The
Flamingo Hotel, Las Vegas.

Benny Siegel, dead on Virginia
Hill's sofa, Beverly Hills,
June 20, 1947.

Lansky Sails in Luxury for Italy; Expected to Confer With Luciano

Underworld Big Shot and Wife in Regal Suite; Cost $2600 One Way.

GET MANY FAREWELL GIFTS

Leave in Champagne and Orchid Atmosphere — He Calls It a Pleasure Trip.

By MALCOLM JOHNSON.

Meyer Lansky, underworld big shot and reputed member of a nationwide gambling syndicate which also controls various other criminal enterprises, sailed with his wife for Italy today in the luxurious, flower-laden Regal Suite of the steamship Italia of the Home Lines.

Ostensibly, Lansky, one-time partner of the late Buggsy Siegel, the gangster slain in Hollywood in 1947, is going to Italy for pleasure only, but it is expected that while there he will confer on business with Charles (Lucky) Luciano, the arch criminal who is regarded by the Federal authorities as director of the narcotic traffic for the big crime syndicate.

Questioned by U. S. Agents.

The Federal Bureau of Narcotics in N. Y. York was fully aware of Lansky's sailing and of his destination. It was learned that Federal agents had questioned Lansky in his apartment in Central Park South several hours before he sailed and that Lansky admitted that he might see Luciano while in Italy.

Lansky also admitted that he was a common gambler, it was learned, and said that he owned the Green Acres night club, gambling establishment near Hollywood, Fla., and that he was formerly a part owner of the Colonial Inn, the biggest and swankiest gambling house in the Hollywood area.

It was regarded as a curious coincidence that Lansky should be sailing for Italy at this time, within a matter of two days after the seizure of cocaine valued at $500,000 in Rome, described as part of a shipment bound for this country.

Lansky and his wife, a slender, attractive brunette, whom he married last winter, departed in an atmosphere of champagne and orchids, in the manner befitting Lansky's reputation as a powerful and wealthy underworld figure. The Regal Suite, which they occupied, is the most luxurious that the Italia affords and Lansky's passage for himself and his wife cost him a cool $2,600, one way.

Meyer Lansky aboard the Italia today.

First front-page story: Meyer Lansky caught by the *New York Sun*, June 28, 1949.

Teddy Lansky had stayed in New York for much of the time that her husband was in jail. She had looked after Meyer's daughter, Sandra, who was now fifteen years old.[22]

Meyer's attempt to hide his remarriage from his two younger children had backfired badly. Paul had found out about Meyer's new wife through a friend at school, and had telephoned his father to confront him with it, beside himself with rage.[23]

Sandra's response to the discovery was less direct — but, in the long term, it was to prove more damaging. Only nine years old when the divorce was going on, Sandra had not been aware of all the facts — the comings and goings, her father's long, unexplained absences. All she could be certain of was the deception, and the fact that her father had deceived her in the process of finding himself another woman. She felt as much a victim as her mother did, and it was hardly surprising that she took her anger out on Teddy.

Unlike Paul, Sandra did not do particularly well at school. She made no effort. She became a difficult, rather self-obsessed teenager, unable to value herself in terms of anything much beyond what she wore and what she looked like. At the age of fourteen, she had asked her father for a nose job, and Meyer, who normally denied his daughter few things, had refused.

But Meyer's enforced absence in Ballston Spa offered Teddy a chance to break out from the wicked stepmother syndrome, and she arranged plastic surgery for Sandra, behind Meyer's back.[24]

The extraordinary publicity that attended the Kefauver crime hearings had placed the already frail relationships of the Lansky family under even more strain. Reporters hung around the Beresford from time to time pestering the children for quotes — "the human angle." Vincent Mercurio remembers one particularly persistent journalist from the *New York World Telegram*.[25]

Meyer coached Buddy in what to say if an agent from the police or the FBI tried to ask him questions. "Don't answer them," Meyer said. "Tell them you have to see your lawyer first." More important still, if Buddy was compelled to speak in some way, "Don't lie. . . . Tell one lie, then you gotta tell another lie to compound on the first."[26]

So Buddy went around New York feeling all the more important for the secret he was guarding — though he did not know exactly what that secret was. Staying in his mother's apartment on one occasion, he saw two men in hats lurking watchfully in the street, and panicked. He flushed the telephone list of his girlfriends, all prostitutes, down the lavatory — then discovered that the two men were not policemen, or that if they were, they were not after him.[27]

One good result of the Senate crime hearings, Buddy discovered, was that it was easier than ever to get good seats in restaurants and at shows. In the world of Broadway and Dinty Moore's, Kefauver had immeasurably increased the respect attaching to the name of Lansky. Paul Lansky did not like it, but it induced Paul's elder brother and his sister to walk with that much extra swagger.

This did not make for family harmony, however, and the problem was compounded by Teddy Lansky's own, and only, son, Richard Schwartz. Buddy Lansky had first found out he had a stepbrother when Vinnie Mercurio left the Beresford one day to pick up Buddy's car and had returned to report that it was no longer in the garage.

"The attendant says that Mr. Lansky's son has taken it," Vinnie reported.[28]

This created a mystery, since Paul, the only other son that Buddy knew of, was in the apartment at the time.

"Oh," said Meyer when Buddy asked him what was going on. "I forgot to tell you. Teddy has a son."[29]

It was not the last time that Buddy was to hear of Richard Schwartz passing himself off around New York as "Meyer Lansky's son," and this did not find favor with any of Meyer's own children. Richard Schwartz had been as indulged by his own parents as the Lansky children had. He was short, dark, barrel-chested, and aggressive. Buddy found him loud and pushy, and did not care who knew it — "*Really* Jewish. . . . You could tell who his mother was."[30]

At a time of adversity, when the family might have been expected to stick together, it was starting to drift apart, and Buddy set the lead. Buddy's secret life was his paid sex with prostitutes. Not even his best friend, Vinnie Mercurio, knew why, on some evenings, Buddy did not answer his phone and was nowhere to be found.[31]

Buddy liked to make friends with his girls and take them out to dinner. His father paid him an allowance on top of the wages he received from his job at the ticket agency, and Buddy used the money to buy himself a social life. But this backfired when one of his girlfriends got pregnant by another client and, desperate for money, stole a valuable ring from her pimp. The pimp came after Buddy for the money.[32]

Buddy told some of his drinking cronies, and they warned the pimp off. But Meyer came to hear of the episode, and he was furious.

"For a young fellow who has a disability," he told Buddy, "you can sure get into trouble."[33]

Meyer decided that it would do his crippled son good to be taken away from New York for a while. Buddy's job at the ticket agency had not got the boy anywhere, and appeared to have landed him in bad company. It was always Meyer's hope that his elder son's quick and lively mind might overcome his physical disability. Buddy had the ability, Meyer was sure, to occupy some sort of job in a managerial capacity, to run his own business, even. So he sent him down to Florida for a fresh start.

In 1951, Meyer had transferred what capital he could salvage from his defunct Broward gambling clubs into a motel development sixty miles south of Miami, in the Florida Keys — a small clump of bungalows looking out onto the Gulf of Mexico at Plantation, a stop on the road to Key West.

"If you looked one way, then looked the other," Buddy remembered, "you were through the town."[34]

The motel had a breakwater of concrete debris to provide safe anchorage for small pleasure boats and yachts, and went by the name of the Plantation Harbor. There was no gambling dimension to the enterprise in any way. It was a legitimate, declared investment for Meyer, like his investment in Consolidated Television — with, hopefully, better prospects, since the still undeveloped Keys had considerable resort potential.[35] Meyer sent his elder son down to the Plantation Harbor in order to get him out of trouble — and in the hope that Buddy might, in the process, learn the motel business.

Buddy Lansky did not, in fact, apply himself to the business, but the first hope was quite easily realized. Buddy spent the best part of a year in exile at the Plantation Harbor. There were poisonous snakes in the surrounding mangrove swamps — water moccasins and the occasional rattlesnake — and Buddy preferred not to venture from his bungalow after dark.[36] It made for quiet nightlife.

Buddy's younger brother, Paul, was the only bright spot in this picture of youthful waywardness. In 1950, Paul had accomplished his ambition to gain entrance to West Point, with a view to becoming an air force officer. The New York newspapers — and Senator Kefauver, at one of his private hearings — tried to make something of the fact that Paul's successful application had been made with the help of Arthur G. Klein, a Tammany congressman who had been one of the guests at Frank Costello's notorious Salvation Army dinner.[37]

This was unfair. It was — and is — a requirement of the West Point admissions process that candidates without military connections secure the approval and nomination of a congressman, senator, or the vice president. But that nomination is no guarantee of a place. The nonmilitary, nominated candidates — 75 percent of the total — are pooled and are assessed on their individual merits.[38] Paul Lansky got into West Point on his own ability, and his father was rightly proud of his achievement.

It became one of Meyer's great pleasures to drive up the Hudson Valley to visit his son at the United States Military Academy. He boasted of Paul to his friends. He took the family to West Point for picnics — the other children, his mother, Yetta, his sister, Esther. He would even take his ex-wife, Anne, in sunny good humor, to share his pride and pleasure in their son. One of the consolations of being locked up in Ballston Spa was that it was easy for Paul to come up from West Point on the train to see his father, and Meyer made quite sure, when Paul came, that Gerard King, the sheriff, and everyone around knew where his clever son was studying.[39]

It was a much-needed consolation. The early 1950s were a low point in the life of Meyer Lansky, pilloried as a national pariah, fined in Florida, jailed in Saratoga, with the income from his gambling joints halted, and lacking much prospect of making a legal living in the future. West Point was both a solace and an escape in the midst of all these problems. As Meyer stood proudly to attention among the crowds at West Point, watching his son parade in full dress uniform, the bands playing, and the white caps of the graduates flying into the air, he could tell himself that, in this respect at least, he had made it in America.

In the early 1950s, Jake Lansky — forty-five years old in February 1950 — was living the life of a family man, renting a comfortable white stucco home on Harrison Street, not far from South Lake, in the most pleasant and respectable area of Hollywood, Florida. The streets were broad and clean, and each house stood on its own fenced lot, comfortably shaded by pines and palm trees.

The principal interest of Jake and his wife, Anna, was the raising of their two daughters, Roberta (known as Ricky) and Linda, who both attended Pine Crest, a private school in Fort Lauderdale.[40] The Lanskys were clearly well off, but they were modest and unobtrusive, and they tried to ignore the sudden notoriety which the Kefauver Committee brought to their name.

It was difficult. Jake had not been subpoenaed to appear before the committee. But his name featured quite frequently in the testimony as Meyer's partner, manager, and front man, running the Colonial Inn and representing the Lansky stake in ventures like Frank Costello's slot machine business. When Meyer was indicted for his Florida gambling in September 1950, Jake had been indicted too, and had been fined $2,000.[41]

Jeannie Henry, a friend of Jake Lansky's younger daughter, Linda, eleven years old in 1951, remembers the change. Hollywood was a small community, and a number of parents told their children to stop being so friendly with the Lansky girls. Jeannie's father, Robert, a modestly successful builder and developer who had made his own way in the world, thought that was ridiculous. He did not know Linda's parents, but the girl seemed a nice, bright, well-behaved friend for Jeannie.

Anna Lansky came round one night to thank Robert Henry for not keeping his daughter away from Linda when all the reports had started in the newspapers. "Think nothing of it," said Robert Henry. "Jeannie is not a fair-weather friend."[42]

Just entering seventh grade, Jeannie herself did not think much about it at the time. Linda was her best friend, enjoying a home life that seemed to Jeannie just about the model of what a home life should be. After school and on weekends, Jeannie Henry would run the few yards down the rear service alley that connected their homes. She rather preferred being at Linda's house to her own, and when the two girls had sleep-overs, it was usually at Linda's.

"Elegance" is the word that Dr. Jean Henry would today use to characterize the Jake Lansky household. Dinner was always served at a long table with a white tablecloth. There was fine china, crystal, silver — and not a ketchup bottle in sight. The Lanskys had two black maids, Ruth and Louise, and when Mrs. Lansky rang the little bell that she kept beside her place, the maids would come in to clear the table and bring the next course.

But there was nothing pretentious or standoffish about the Lansky home on Harrison Street. What Jeannie Henry liked was the warmth and the structure, and the way in which people worked things out by talking together, and with a certain discipline. Linda Lansky was taking piano lessons, and it was understood that if she wanted to go with Jeannie to the Saturday-morning movies, then she would just have to get her practice done before she went.

Jake was affectionate and kind to his wife. If the couple had hard words, they had them in private. Jean Henry remembers Jake as a genial and well-tempered man who enjoyed his role as paterfamilias at the head of the table at home, or at one of the neighborhood restaurants, like Joe Sonken's Gold Coast, on the weekly excursion when Jake took the whole family — and Linda's friend, Jeannie — out for dinner. Jake was unflustered and considerate. Ruth and Louise risked being picked up by the police if they were found on the streets of the white section after dark, so if the maids had to stay late, Jake would ferry them home.

Meyer Lansky was "Uncle Meyer," and he came round quite frequently — usually without Teddy, whom everyone found rather a strain. Cousin Sandra, about the same age as Ricky Lansky, was also difficult, and Paul was the absent family hero, away at West Point. Buddy was a more frequent visitor, and everyone was pleased to see him, tottering in whenever he was in town, cheery and full of conversation.

It is only with hindsight that Jean Henry can piece together the other side. Mr. Adonis would come round some evenings in the early days. Mr. Alo lived around the corner, in his own detached white house at the end of Monroe, looking out over South Lake, where it was still possible to spot occasional groups of Florida's odd, seal-like marine mammal, the manatee. Mr. Alo had a young niece, Carol, who used to play with Jeannie and Linda sometimes.

One evening, Jeannie got an excited call from Linda and went round to 1146 Harrison to find her friend upstairs in the bedroom of her parents, who were out. Linda had been looking through their closet and had discovered some wooden cigar boxes filled with dollar bills, and a big black gun. But next time the girls looked in the closet, the money — and the gun — were gone.

Jake was quite often away from home "on business" — usually in Las Vegas. He would fly out to keep an eye on Meyer's piece of the Flamingo, now under the profitable supervision of Gus Greenbaum, Davie Berman, and their Las Vegas partners, and Jake would also collect the dividend on the $190,000 cash which the brothers had put into a more recent hotel-casino, the Thunderbird.[43] Marion Hicks, the principal owner of the Thunderbird, had been short of bankroll when the casino opened, so Jake had made up the difference, "lending" the money to the Texas gambler, George Sadlo, who had passed it on, in turn, to Hicks.[44] The cash which Linda Lansky and Jeannie Henry discovered in Jake's closet was probably the proceeds of a Flamingo or Thunderbird skim, since, thanks to Estes

Kefauver, the Lanskys had no other gaming ventures in the early 1950s.

Jean Henry disputes the picture of Jake Lansky as the stupid, younger brother. Solid and loyal, yes. Stupid, no. "I've sometimes wondered," she says today, "if Jake wasn't the backbone behind his elder brother — like Bobby Kennedy and JFK."[45]

She has only good memories of simple, sunny years beneath the palm trees and the stands of pine in Hollywood, Florida, in the early 1950s, feeding bread to the mermaidlike manatees, floating melon-shell boats in the storm drains in the summer rains, and running down the service road to spend her evenings in the elegant white house where people said there were gangsters living, but which Jean Henry gratefully remembers as the model for what a considerate and civilized family life should be.

"I knew them," she says of Jake and Anna Lansky, "as gentle, kind, loving people, who were really good to their family, and who were good to me, a strange little girl from down the street."[46]

One day in the autumn of 1953, after Meyer was out of jail, and after Buddy had returned quietened, but not entirely subdued, from his year of exile in the Florida Keys, Sandra Lansky confided in her elder brother. She had met a handsome young man at the New York Horse Show — Marvin Rappaport, the brother of Raymond Rappaport, Buddy's friend who ran Rappaport's restaurant — and she wanted to marry him.

"Sandra," Buddy replied, astonished. "You're going on sixteen. Sandra, you're too young."

"What have I got?" replied his sister. "A broken home? A stepmother I can't get along with?"

"I really had no answers for her," Buddy remembered.[47]

Virtually unsupervised from the age of ten onward, indulged with a generous weekly cash allowance from her father, and sallying forth from the Beresford, Sandra Lansky had grown into a wayward and headstrong young woman. She was frequently at loggerheads with her father. The pedant in Meyer was infuriated by his daughter's poor progress in school. He was certain to oppose her wish to get married at fifteen for many reasons, not least because it would say good-bye to any chance of Sandra's graduating from high school or going on to college.

The best advice Buddy could give his sister was that she should talk to the doctor who looked after the family when they were down in Florida, Dr. Harris, an old and wise general practitioner in whom everyone confided.

Sandra spoke to Dr. Harris, who spoke in turn to Meyer — and early in 1954, after Sandra's sixteenth birthday, Meyer duly swallowed his anger and sat down for a serious talk with his daughter.

"We've got it all straightened out," he told Buddy afterward. "She's going to get engaged in June, finish her high school the following year, and then get married."[48]

"Dad says I can get married this summer!" Sandra reported excitedly to Buddy, as she described the same conversation.

Teddy Lansky tried to sort out the confusion.

"You tell one thing, and she tells another," Teddy said to her husband. "Now you go up to New York and meet Marvin's family."[49]

In the end, it was the Rappaport family who managed to make some sense of the crossed wires inside the Meyer Lansky clan, where everyone talked to everyone, except to the person most directly concerned in what they were talking about. It was agreed that there was no point in waiting. Both families were finding their respective offspring difficult to handle, in different ways, and the best hope seemed to be to give the young couple their head, and to hope that they would sort each other out.

Buddy met his future brother-in-law for the first time on the morning of the wedding. He worked out immediately why the Rappaports were so anxious to get their son married.

"The guy was a queer up and down," he remembers. "A three-dollar queer. And all his brothers knew it, too. Nice fellow, but a queer."[50]

Marvin was taking his bride-to-be off to the hairdresser for a special session of prewedding hair styling and beautification, so Buddy went off to his own New York barber, at the Paramount.

"Come back home, stick my head in the door — and see a white-haired lady. 'Who the hell is this?' Paul says to me, 'Keep your mouth shut.'"

"Sandra," said Buddy, declining the hint. "I'm gonna tell you before your father does. You look like a damn fool."

Buddy was correct in his forecast of Meyer's reaction to his starkly bleached daughter.

"For two cents," Meyer said, "I'd call off this wedding."

It took the emollient efforts of Aunt Esther to calm everybody down. "Leave them alone," Esther told her brother sternly. "It's not your wedding. Leave them alone."[51]

Two years later, after Sandra's marriage to Marvin Rappaport had collapsed, leaving Sandra, now eighteen years old, with a baby son to look after, Meyer Lansky was returning with Buddy from a visit to his daughter and his first grandchild. Something had evidently got Meyer thinking, for he fell silent for a while.

"Do you notice anything funny about Marvin?" he asked Buddy finally and cautiously.

"It took you this long to figure it out?"

"Well," replied Meyer, "you could have told me."[52]

In marriage, as in higher education, it was Paul Lansky who did something to redeem Meyer's hopes for his children. A little more than a year out of West Point, and stationed as a pilot at McChord Air Base,[53] overlooking the waters of Puget Sound near Tacoma, Washington, Lieutenant Lansky met and fell in love with Edna Shook, a purposeful and handsome blonde who had been married once before and was six years his senior. It was late in the autumn of 1955, and the couple decided to get married at the end of the following year.

Edna Shook Lansky was impressed with her new father-in-law when he arrived in Tacoma a few days before the wedding. He carried himself with such dignity. Not speaking much, and then only on high and weighty subjects, like politics, Mr. Lansky had the stamp of authority about him. He also seemed to be quite rich, taking rooms in the Winthrop Hotel, Tacoma's best.

Paul had been evasive about what his father did, so Edna came to the conclusion that, like his son, Mr. Lansky must be doing government work one did not talk about. She liked her father-in-law, she decided, and the sentiment seemed to be reciprocated.[54] After all the troubles with Buddy and Sandra, Meyer seemed happy that one of the children, at least, had found a good, strong, and sensible mate.

The wedding was to be a small military ceremony in the chapel at nearby Fort Lewis, with the Lanskys represented by just Meyer, Teddy, and Sandra. It had been decided that Buddy's disability made it too complicated for him to fly so far.

Sandra had recently been separated from Marvin Rappaport, and the moment that she arrived in Tacoma, she started telephoning back to New York to issue instructions to the maid whom she had left in charge of her baby, Gary. Edna was very impressed that someone could spend quite so many minutes on long distance talking about the importance of *fresh* orange juice.[55]

Then, suddenly, on the day of the wedding, the Lansky representation was down from three to two. Sandra had had to fly back to New York for a more pressing engagement — a last-minute New Year's date, Edna later discovered, which the nineteen-year-old had decided to take up, despite her father's telling her she should stay in Tacoma for one more day and do her family duty.[56]

"It's the most amazing thing," Buddy Lansky later remarked. "Here's a man that could control men — but he couldn't control his kids."[57]

13

Dance of the Millions

IN March 1952, at the age of fifty-one, Fulgencio Batista made himself president of Cuba for the second time. He had held the position once previously, from 1940 to 1944, when he took Cuba into the war on the side of America. After a year or so of exile in Daytona Beach, Florida, he had returned to Havana, swearing allegiance to the democratic process. But now, in the small hours of March 10, 1952, Fulgencio Batista repeated the tactics that first brought him to prominence as a sergeant-stenographer nearly twenty years earlier. He rounded up a group of ambitious young supporters in Camp Columbia, the army headquarters outside Havana, and organized a coup d'état.[1]

No one seriously resisted. Cuban government was corrupt and autocratic, whether its leaders were selected through the ballot box or not, and people looked back with nostalgia to Batista's prewar regime, when sugar was up, when the tourists had flocked in from America, and when the whole island had enjoyed one of the bursts of prosperity in its fabled playground tradition — the Dance of the Millions.

Cuba was not doing that badly, in fact, when Batista seized power in the spring of 1952. Havana had a claim to being the world's premier play city — the Paris of the New World, swaying to the rhythms of its rumbas and sambas and mambos, which it exported to Europe and America via a dozen white-tuxedoed orchestras, the hottest dance bands anywhere on earth. Internationally, only Beirut could compare with Havana for sophistication and civilized seaminess. Cuba had the most accommodating girls, the finest cigars, the strongest daiquiris, Errol Flynn most winters, and Ernest Hemingway all year round.

The one problem was the gambling. The incident that brought matters to a head occurred within a few weeks of Batista's seizing power. One evening in April 1952, Dana C. Smith, a California attorney who was a friend of California's junior senator, Richard M. Nixon, was gambling in the Sans Souci, one of the lavish, open-air, under-the-stars nightclubs in the garden suburbs of Havana. Smith was playing cubolo, an eight-dice casino version of Cubilete, a local game.[2]

"You can't lose if you keep doubling" was the come-on line, so Dana C. Smith kept on doubling — and lost $4,200. Smith wrote out a check for his loss. But later he decided that he had been lured into the game, which he had never played before, and that it had been rigged. He canceled his check. The contract for running the gaming that season at the Sans Souci, which was owned by Cubans, was held by Norman Rothman, the operator of a Miami Beach nightclub, and Rothman decided to sue Smith for his $4,200 — more than $26,000 in 1990's terms.

Smith was not just any friend to Richard Nixon. He was a political adviser and fund-raiser — the organizer, in fact, of Nixon's controversial senatorial expense fund, which was to lead to the famous "Checkers" speech — and by the time Smith's troubles at the Sans Souci got into lawyers' hands, Richard Nixon was well on his way to becoming Dwight Eisenhower's vice president. So when Nixon's office wrote to the State Department at the end of August 1952 requesting its assistance, Dana C. Smith was given rather more help than the average visitor who welshed on his gambling debts.[3]

On September 19, 1952, the U.S. embassy in Havana informed the State Department that there could well be some merit to the case of Senator Nixon's friend. "During the past winter season," reported an operations memorandum to Washington, "the Embassy received several complaints from American tourists with regard to the conduct of this particular game at the Sans Souci nightclub."[4]

Writing under cover of Senator Nixon's letter, Dana C. Smith had asked the State Department several questions about the legality of cubolo under Cuban law, and the embassy commissioned answers from a local attorney.

Armed with this material, Smith went into court in Los Angeles in January 1953 to fight the suit brought against him by Norman Rothman, via a California collection agency, for his $4,200 — and won.[5] The newspaper coverage of the case provoked a miniature epidemic of American tourists complaining of cheating in Cuba's clubs and casinos, and the U.S. embassy in Havana confirmed its opinion that the visitors were justified in their complaints.[6]

Havana's gaming was a free-for-all — no more regulated than a fairground whose operator subcontracted the individual sideshows and stalls. The Cuban owners of the city's nightclubs were leasing out their gaming rooms — and sometimes even individual games and tables — to just about anyone who claimed to have a bankroll to risk. Some were serious, professional operators. But others had less experience — and less bankroll.

The come-on games like cubolo were the result of this. They offered quick returns on minimal investments. Stories proliferated of gullible American tourists being cheated by smiling and plausible dealers — some Cuban, but many American — who brought the cards and dice to their table, and who took their money off them as they ate. One young honeymoon couple, it was reported, had lost their apartment-furnishing savings in this fashion. A mother of four had lost her husband's salary for a month.[7]

To start with, Fulgencio Batista had left the problem in the hands of his tourist commission. But following the Smith case, the matter was discussed at cabinet level.

"The President of the Republic," announced the *Havana Herald* on February 10, 1953, "has given definitive instructions to the various police forces to intensify measures of protection for foreign tourists."[8]

It was "unprecedented," said the newspaper, for the president to express himself personally on this subject, and he had dispatched the minister of the interior on a tour of Havana's gaming rooms to look out for fraudulent multidice games like cubolo and razzle-dazzle, a variant on the theme. The Cuban Tourist Commission even had a form printed which authorized visitors who believed that they had been cheated to stop payment on their checks.[9]

These measures had scarcely had a chance to work, however,

when, at the end of March 1953, the *Saturday Evening Post* ran an exposé headlined on its cover, "Suckers in Paradise: How Americans Lose Their Shirts in Caribbean Gambling Joints."

"Sophisticated players who can 'rumble a gaff' (detect cheating) have long given Havana casinos a wide berth," reported the story, which went on to compare Cuban gambling with the official government casinos recently opened in Puerto Rico — to the considerable disadvantage of Cuba.[10]

The author of the article, Lester Velie, had been on a thorough tour of Havana's nightspots. All, he reported, had succumbed to the operators of razzle-dazzle, cubolo, and the come-on games, and must now be considered "bust out" joints — or fraudulent. Nor were the traditional casino games above suspicion. Most dealers in Havana were dealing blackjack from a hand-held pack, which was open to manipulation, rather than from a box, which had long been the standard practice in America.[11]

In the length and breadth of Havana the reporter could discover only two locations where the gambling was honest. One was the so-called "louse ring" underneath the grandstand at the Oriental Park horse track, where Cubans gambled with Cubans for modest stakes. The other was at the very opposite end of the scale — the Montmartre Club, a luxurious, plush-and-gilt, third-floor establishment a few blocks away from the Nacional Hotel in downtown Havana. The operation of the Montmartre's gaming tables had recently been taken over by Meyer Lansky, whom Velie described as a "mobster" — the reporter giving full credit to Meyer's past involvement with Benny Siegel, the "Bug and Meyer" mob, and to Meyer's role as "arbitrator for the big Eastern syndicates."[12]

But for all this, reported the magazine, "little Meyer has a following among the big-time professional players who frequent his craps tables."[13] The serious high rollers knew cheating when they saw it, and there was no suggestion of sleight-of-hand or come-on games in the Montmartre Club. To the contrary. Thanks to Meyer Lansky, honestly conducted high-stakes gambling was still alive and well in one corner of Havana, at least.

Rather against the odds, Fulgencio Batista's comeback in Havana had meant a comeback for Meyer Lansky as well. In the years after World War II, Meyer had made several attempts to regenerate his gaming interests in Cuba, without success. But within months of

Batista regaining power, Meyer was back on the island,[14] working out a partnership with the Cuban operators of the Montmartre Club.

The furor over Havana's crooked gambling rackets landed Meyer a still more surprising role. For the winter season of 1953–54 — and for an annual retainer, according to Meyer's lawyer, Joseph Varon, in the region of $25,000[15] — President Batista invited Meyer Lansky to become his adviser on gambling reform, and to carry out, on a larger scale, a cleanup job like the one he had performed so effectively at the racetrack and at the Gran Casino Nacional in the late 1930s. Meyer might be an outlaw in America, but in Cuba he was welcomed as the man who knew how to put things straight.

Fulgencio Batista saw the enhancement of revenues from foreign visitors, and from Americans in particular, as a major source of future income for Cuba — and for himself. With the development of hotel chains and airline travel in the early 1950s, tourism was just starting to be seen as an industry in its own right, and the new president enthusiastically endorsed it as a priority of his new regime. One of his first actions was to reorganize the old National Tourism Corporation — "to assist and stimulate private enterprise," as Batista later wrote.[16]

Cuba's climate and beaches, its proximity to New York and Miami, "the striking beauty of our women," and "the traditional hospitality of our people" were all assets that were sadly undeveloped, in the opinion of the new president.[17] He simplified entry regulations so that Americans could spend up to a month in Cuba without needing a visa and could also bring their private cars and boats with them. At Barlovento, to the west of Havana, canals were planned for a marina–housing development, with a view to luring the investment of Floridian boaters who lived in similar developments in Miami and Fort Lauderdale. And, when it came to gambling, it was Batista's ambition, with the help of Meyer Lansky, to turn Havana into the Monte Carlo of the Caribbean.

The first priority was to flush out the crooked gambling subcontractors. The only casino operator in Havana for whom Meyer had any respect was Santo Trafficante, Jr., son of the numbers boss of Tampa, Florida. Trafficante, ten years younger than Meyer, had been operating in Cuba since 1946. Quiet of manner, with a crew cut and spectacles that gave him the air of a college professor, Trafficante went about his business conservatively.

Meyer also knew, and had less respect for, Norman Rothman, the

Sans Souci gaming room operator, whose suing of Dana C. Smith had started the unfavorable publicity. Meyer warned Rothman, in so many words, "You run clean, otherwise, you can't operate,"[18] and the Sans Souci stopped its program of come-on games.

But other dishonest croupiers, many of them Americans, continued to operate on a free-lance basis. They had been approaching victims away from the gaming tables — in restrooms, even — with their card shuffles and dice games that a sucker "just could not lose." On March 30, 1953 — two days after the *Saturday Evening Post* exposé — Cuban military intelligence arrested thirteen such card-sharps, all Americans, and immediately deported eleven of them.[19]

Cuban gambling opened up for the winter season of 1954–55 in its reformed state. Blackjack everywhere was dealt from a box, not from the hand. Floor men became "ladder men," hoisted up to sit in little jockey seats, atop stepladders, from which they could more effectively spot sharp practice at the tables — and where they could very obviously be seen to be making that inspection.[20] Most important, the nightclubs offered no house room to the operators of razzle-dazzle, cubolo, or any other come-on games.

The fairground had been policed. There were no more newspaper stories about tourists being swindled in Havana, and the American embassy was able to close its file on the subject. The last complaint about dishonest Cuban gambling practices dated from the spring of the previous year, at the same time as the *Saturday Evening Post* article, and referred to an incident that had happened the previous New Year's Eve.[21]

Meyer Lansky's Montmartre Club remained the premier destination for high rollers. The Montmartre did not have floor shows or ambience to match the under-the-stars nightclubs of the garden suburbs. But it did have Meyer's table crews, and that attracted the best players. It was serious gambling for serious gamblers, like the high-cash games at the Greenacres Club in Hallandale. The Montmartre was also only a few minutes' stroll from the Nacional, the grandest hotel in Cuba — or in the entire Caribbean.

Meyer had long nursed a plan to install a casino in the Nacional Hotel itself.[22] The hotel stood imposingly on a rocky bluff looking out across the bay toward the Morro, the ancient and picturesque fortress guarding the entrance to Havana harbor. Ten stories high and of classic design, the Nacional bore a striking resemblance to the Breakers Hotel in Palm Beach, whose architect it shared,[23] and Meyer's scheme was to take over a wing of the Nacional and refurbish it with luxury suites for high-stakes players, a deluxe Caribbean version of the formula which Las Vegas had been developing so successfully since the death of Benny Siegel.

This idea did not accord with the habits of Havana's American colony, who used the rambling gardens and corridors of the Nacional as something of an expatriate club. A few yards along the Malecón, the sea wall, from the U.S. embassy, the Nacional was a cozy and noncommercial setting for tea and bridge parties, tennis tournaments, and gatherings on the Fourth of July. But Fulgencio Batista liked Meyer's casino idea, and since the Cuban government owned the Nacional, he seized on the project as a chance to show off his dynamic new tourist development policy.

In 1955, the Nacional was placed under new management. International (later Intercontinental) Hotels, Inc., a subsidiary of Pan Am, the principal air carrier to Havana, took over the management of the hotel and embarked upon an extensive program of refurbishing. They did not designate a particular wing of bedrooms for gamblers, but at the northern end of the long entrance hall, inside the curved loggias looking out over the Malecón, an elaborate and luxurious new complex of public rooms was created — a bar, a restaurant, a showroom, and a casino. This complex was sublet by the hotel for a substantial rent to a casino operator,[24] and that operator was Meyer Lansky.

Eartha Kitt was the star of the floor show with which the new Nacional Hotel casino opened for business in the winter season of 1955–56.[25] It proved an immediate success. Meyer put Jake in charge of the casino floor, and night after night Jake surveyed the proceedings from atop his giant ladder.

Jake's younger daughter, Linda, flew across to the Nacional for a week's holiday, and she brought her classmate Jeannie Henry. The two schoolgirls, now in their teens, were met at the airport by a big black car and were given a suite to themselves. Before they left, Linda's mother, Anna, had helped them pack, and had explained how they should hang their clothes where the steam from the shower could smooth out the creases. The girls were not old enough to gamble in the casino, but they looked as if they were. So Jake gave them $100 worth of chips to play with.

"We cashed them in," remembers Jean Henry, "and spent the money on clothes."[26]

Jake Lansky was in charge of credit at the Nacional Hotel casino, and he earned the awed respect of the Cuban employees for the resoluteness with which he was willing to refuse credit to the Cuban officials — including police and army officers — who strutted into the Nacional in expectation of a free ride.[27] The Cubans nicknamed Jake El Cejudo — the Bushy-Eyebrowed One.[28]

The Lansky brothers were operating in partnership with a regime which was corrupt. But they did not allow that corruption to touch the purity of what made them real money — serious, professional gambling. Their partner, Fulgencio Batista, shared their professionalism. Flamboyant and high profile in many respects, the Cuban president was not, himself, a gambling man. He also realized, as clearly as the Lanskys did, that tableaux of Cuban officials gathered round roulette tables in their caps, epaulettes, and Ruritanian trimmings would not be good for anyone's business.

Batista seldom visited Meyer Lansky's casinos — in the winter season of 1955–56 Meyer was operating at both the Nacional and the Montmartre, and had a piece of another, more modest club, the Monseigneur[29] — and the two men were almost never seen together in public. Nor did they socialize privately. Their relationship was strictly business. In the half-dozen years that Meyer operated in Cuba in the 1950s, his wife, Teddy, never once met Fulgencio Batista.[30]

But Meyer did take his Hollywood lawyer, Joe Varon, on one occasion, to the formal opening of a hotel casino at which Batista was present, and Varon was struck by how familiar and almost instinctive the two men were together.

"They were very, very close," Varon remembers, "like brothers."[31]

Varon was impressed by how well Batista spoke English, and by the president's evident warmth toward Meyer. Batista kept hugging and embracing his little American friend in a most Latin fashion.

Meyer seemed distinctly uncomfortable with this aspect of the relationship, wriggling unhappily in the bear hug of the nation's strongman. Such public fraternization was not the Lansky way — as Varon discovered a few minutes later, when one of the several beautiful women in Batista's party started talking to the attorney, asking him about the rules of craps and where he thought that she should place her bets.

Varon was with his wife, Helen, and he felt sure that he was responding to the president's attractive friend with no more than normal courtesy. But suddenly, across the table, he caught "the look" from his client.

"So I went over and said, 'What's wrong?' And he said, 'Stay away!'"[32]

Meyer Lansky and Fulgencio Batista were, to all intents and purposes, partners in the commercial development of Cuban gambling, but there was nothing so crass as a direct transfer of funds from one to the other. It made more sense for both sides to operate through middlemen, and though the payoff might sometimes take the form of cash, it more often involved jobs, supply contracts, and a whole network of patronage.

In 1955,[33] the system reached its culmination in the promulgation of Hotel Law 2074, by which the Cuban government granted tax exemptions to "all new hotels, motels, and similar establishments providing tourist accommodations."[34] Any hotel with more than $1 million of new investment, and any new nightclub valued at $200,000, was entitled to apply for a casino license.[35] The government even announced itself ready, in certain circumstances, to provide "direct financial assistance" for the construction of tourist projects it considered particularly valuable.[36]

Fulgencio Batista was later to cite this law as the reason why, in a matter of years, the number of hotel rooms in Havana nearly doubled — from some 3,000 in 1952 to nearly 5,500 in 1958.[37] All these new rooms were modern, luxurious, and air conditioned, and Batista was entitled to take credit for his achievement. By 1958 Cuba was experiencing the booming tourist economy that did not come to other corners of the Caribbean for ten years or more.

But Hotel Law 2074 was also the channel by which the president could dispense government money to associates like Meyer Lansky, who then made sure that it was friends and relatives of the president who profited privately from the construction and operation of the new hotel-casinos that they built. No customs duties were levied on the gaming tables and equipment that came in to fill the new casinos, and Cuba's strict labor quota laws were relaxed to allow foreign croupiers and casino staff into the country on special two-year visas as "technicians."

In the spring of 1956, less than three years after he had been in jail in Saratoga, Meyer Lansky started work, under the terms of Hotel Law 2074, on the construction of his own hotel, the Riviera, a twenty-one story, 440-room skyscraper, towering above the Malecón in Havana. When it opened, the Riviera would be the largest purpose-built casino-hotel in Cuba — or anywhere in the world, outside Las Vegas. Fulgencio Batista had surprised many people when he resurrected his power in March 1952. But his accomplishment was more than matched by the resurrection of his friend Meyer Lansky.

In 1956, Enrique Rousseau, a young Cuban businessman and playboy, was living in the Nacional Hotel — "between divorces," as he now puts it.[38] A gregarious and dashing character, Rousseau spent many of his evenings in the Nacional's casino, playing baccarat and blackjack, while a good number of his days were spent lying out beside the Nacional's swimming pool, where the show girls from the casino room's chorus line liked to sun themselves.

By 1956, Havana had attracted many of America's professional gamblers from the wide-open era, including a number who had become prominent in Las Vegas. It was not Meyer's style to exploit his special relationship with Batista, but there was not much point in a casino operator's coming to Havana in the 1950s if Meyer Lansky did not like him. Meyer, Jake, and their friends would gather for sandwiches at lunchtime beside the Nacional's pool, where they all had cabanas. The memories they shared went back more than twenty years.

Moe Dalitz, Sam Tucker, and Morris Kleinman, Meyer's partners in Molaska Corporation, were there. So was their Cleveland partner, Thomas "Black Jack" McGinty, along with Wilbur Clark, who fronted the Desert Inn, not far down the Vegas Strip from the Flamingo.[39] Dalitz and his partners had bought into the Nacional casino, and they were due to take it over entirely when Meyer's Riviera Hotel got started properly. Eddie Levinson, the brother of the famous gambler from Covington, Kentucky, "Sleep Out" Louis Levinson, was working with Meyer, along with a number of other names from the Broward and Saratoga days — not least among them, Jimmy Blue Eyes.

Benny Binion, the Texas gambler, was one of the few friends of Meyer's who did not come over to check out the prospects for business in Havana. He later explained: "I don't like operating anywhere that I don't speak the language."[40]

Younger than Meyer and his generation, but respected for the position he had carved out for himself in Cuba, Santo Trafficante, Jr., was admitted to the inner circle. The cream of American gamblers liked to spend their afternoons beside the Nacional Hotel pool, playing poker or gin rummy on the slatted seats of their sun chairs. Enrique Rousseau was drawn into their games. Rousseau took the precaution of discovering beforehand the size of the stakes for which he was playing — unlike Joe Varon, who once got involved in a poker game with Meyer Lansky, to find bids of "Raise you twenty-five" flying round his head. As Meyer calculated the final tally, Varon steeled himself to pay out hundreds of dollars, to learn that the bids of "twenty-five" had been in cents. He owed just $1.98.[41]

Sitting beside the pool of the Nacional Hotel, Enrique Rousseau discovered, with some pleasure, that he could more than hold his own with his uniquely experienced fellow players. He fared very well at gin rummy, and when he lost, the financial penalty was scarcely painful. But one day Meyer took his new Cuban friend aside to discuss the rather heavier gambling in which he indulged during the evenings.

"Enrique," he said, "I see you every night losing money at twenty-one, and I don't like it. Let me give you some advice. At fourteen, you always ask for a card. At fifteen, you ask. And at sixteen, you *stick*."[42]

It was not every day that Meyer Lansky imparted the secret of casino success, so that evening Enrique Rousseau went eagerly to the blackjack tables. He applied the Lansky system conscientiously that night, and for many nights to come. But he found that he still lost.

Meyer Lansky set his sights high when it came to the construction of his own hotel-casino in Havana. He had had pieces of hotels before — most notably in Benny Siegel's Flamingo. In Florida he had the Plantation Harbor down in the Keys, and he had a stake, in Buddy's name, in a motel development, the Tuscany, which brother Jake was developing in Hollywood, near the site of the old Bohème.

But the Havana Riviera was Meyer's own baby. Thanks to Kefauver, it was impossible for Meyer Lansky to hope that he could ever get a Nevada gaming license or operate openly in Las Vegas. But now, just over the horizon from Miami, and in an open, legal setting that was more agreeable in many ways than the dusty and remote Nevada desert, he could build a luxury, resort hotel-casino which showed how it should be done. People in the know declared that Meyer Lansky was the dean of American gambling.[43] The Riviera in Havana would prove it.

To construct the Riviera, Lansky selected Irving Feldman, a builder who had a dozen hotels and prestigious apartment blocks to his credit on Miami Beach. Short, swashbuckling, and dynamic, Feldman was a Napoleonic figure who had the reputation for bringing high-quality jobs in on time. In his private life, Feldman was an unashamed gambler and ladies' man. But when it came to construction, he was all business.[44] He broke ground on the Riviera in January 1957, and eleven months later it was finished.

Meyer's brief for his hotel was that it should contain nothing but the best. The Riviera was the first major building in Havana to have central air conditioning, in contrast to the new Capri Hotel, completed a few months earlier not far from the Nacional, which had individual box units, rattling and dripping from every window. Cold hissed smoothly and silently into the Riviera's luxurious rooms from ceiling vents, and every window had its own view of the sea. Seen from the air, the two broad curves of the Riviera swept back from the Malecón in the shape of a tremendous Y, with cantilevered balconies at every end.

In terms of style and decor, the Riviera was angular and futuristic. Echoing and reflecting the waters of the Florida straits, the hotel was clad in turquoise mosaic, while the casino itself, a curved and windowless pleasure dome covered in gold mosaic, nestled on the ground beside it like an enormous, gilded ostrich egg. The furnishings were by Albert Parvin of Parvin-Dohrman, which was supplying the latest luxury hotels in Las Vegas. Modernistic chandeliers glittered from the ceilings of the casino, restaurant, and public rooms, like so many convoys of winking flying saucers. The overall effect did not, perhaps, win prizes for taste, but it was undeniably exciting.

Everyone in Havana knew that the Riviera was Meyer Lansky's project. He sent excited progress reports and photographs of the construction back to his son Paul, in Tacoma, as the steel skeleton of the main tower rose in the sky.[45] But, as ever, Meyer hid his own participation behind the names of his partners and associates. The casino license, for which the hotel paid the Cuban government $25,000 a year, was held by Eddie Levinson. The casino manager was an associate of Levinson's, Eddie Torres — and the Riviera Hotel Corporation itself was headed by the Smith brothers, Ben and Harry, two Toronto hoteliers with whom Meyer had negotiated the management contract. The only place in which Meyer's name appeared on the paperwork was as director of the hotel's kitchens.

This comparative obscurity was in the established tradition of Meyer Lansky's personal modesty — and in his equally established tradition of cheating on his taxes. Like all the other Americans involved in the Riviera, Meyer Lansky made annual declarations of his income to the IRS, and he paid comparatively little tax on the salary he declared as an employee of the Riviera Hotel Corp., Havana, Cuba — $9,000 for 1956, when the hotel was in the planning stage, $36,000 in 1957, during construction, and $36,500 once it was open in 1958.[46]

But Meyer took his position as kitchen director very seriously. Since his Saratoga days he had stuck by the lake house principle — good casinos serve good food. When he went out west to Paul's wedding at the end of 1956, his new daughter-in-law, Edna, had been surprised how, within hours of his arrival at the Winthrop Hotel in Tacoma, Meyer had found his way into the kitchens, where he got the chef to give him a tour of the facilities. In Miami Beach, Meyer went down to Collins Avenue for earnest seminars with Wolfie Cohen, discussing the advantages of one piece of stainless steel equipment over the next. And after the Riviera had opened, it was the kitchens that Meyer first took his guests of honor to inspect.[47] Everyone knew that Meyer Lansky could set up and run a good casino. But a good kitchen . . . .

The Riviera Hotel opened with a fanfare on the evening of December 10, 1957. Its Copa Room floor show, which was carried in part on American network television, was headed by Ginger Rogers.[48] Expecting nothing less than brilliance, Meyer was critical of his star.

"She can wiggle her ass," he complained. "But she can't sing a goddamn note."[49]

No one else minded. The Riviera was universally judged an immense success. Its casino started making money from the first night. Its 440 double rooms were booked solid through the winter and spring season of 1958, and beyond. It took the deployment of several large-denomination bills to secure a decent seat in the Copa Room, where the performers that winter included Vic Damone, Abbott and Costello, and the Mexican comedian Cantinflas. Most satisfying of all, it was even harder to secure a table to eat in the Riviera Room, the hotel's gourmet restaurant, which offered, by general consent, the city's finest fine dining, and steaks of a particularly high quality.[50]

Havana in the winter of 1957–58 offered the visitor many rare and extravagant experiences. For courtesans of legendary youth and freshness, you went to the Casa Marina by the airport, strategically situated as the first and last stop on the Cook's tour of the libidinous. For spectacle, you went to the glittering treetop review at the Tropicana in the gardens of Marianao — and for spectacle of another sort you gawked at Superman, who measured his prodigious masculinity with twelve silver dollars lined up side by side. An evening which sampled the license of Batista's Havana — with the menacing edge provided by the odd nighttime blast of gunfire from his touchy police — was not complete without dinner and gambling at the sea-side pleasure palace raised by the man whom Kefauver had named one of the leaders of the U.S. East Coast Crime Syndicate.

But the memories of visitors to the Riviera Hotel in its heyday are of an ambience that was anything but gangsterish. The gaming in the egg-shaped casino was hushed and reverent, as befitted the serious-ness of the stakes. A strict dress code was enforced. Many men wore tuxedos. The women wore serious jewels. The marbled halls of Meyer Lansky's Riviera were an asylum of quiet and gentility, com-pared to the raucous carnival to be found outside.

Segundo Curti Messina, a minister in the government ousted in 1952 by Batista, read stories in exile of the gangsters who had moved into Havana, and felt sure that his worst fears had come true. But his relatives back home reported that it really was not quite like that. The new hotels and casinos were very strictly and respectably run. Curti Messina heard of a friend turned away by the Riviera because he had been drinking too much.[51]

An American visitor asked the U.S. ambassador, Earl Smith, why all the gangsters were tolerated.

"It's strange," the envoy agreed, perplexed. "But it seems to be the only way to get honest casinos."[52]

Frank Atlass, a young man just getting his start in the Chicago broadcasting business, visited the Riviera soon after it opened. He was a friend of "Colonel" Charles Barron, an old-time Chicago gam-bler who was the manager of the hotel.

"I'm going to take you to meet someone very important," said Barron to Atlass one day, and led him over to the elevators in the Riviera lobby.

Atlass was struck by the sudden reverence of his friend. They trav-eled up side by side to the top floor of the Riviera, then walked down the corridor to one of the penthouses with a balcony overlooking the sea. There were no guns or viziers or bodyguards, but Frank Atlass got the impression that he was treading on hallowed ground.

Sitting on one of the sofas was a short, trim, middle-aged man, healthily suntanned, with quite a big nose, deep lines and wrinkles, and neat, dark, graying hair. He was wearing a sport jacket with an open shirt, no tie. Atlass noticed, as Meyer Lansky rose to shake his hand, that the skin crinkled deep around his eyes as he smiled.

Frank Atlass cannot recall the particular pleasantries of his brief conversation with Meyer Lansky at the summit of the Riviera Hotel. But the general atmosphere of awe is still vivid in his mind — the hush, the respect, the feeling of a certain majesty.

"It was," he says, "as if I was being taken to meet the king."[53]

14

"I Crapped Out"

AT 10:12 on the morning of October 25, 1957, Detectives William
Graff and Edward O'Connor of the New York City Police Department were tidying their desks at the Eighteenth Detective Squad
office on Fifty-fourth Street. They had just completed a successful,
year-long investigation of racketeering on the waterfront, and they
were filing away the loose papers when the telephone rang. It was
the switchboard sergeant who handled emergency calls.

"You have a shooting in the barbershop at the Park Sheraton
Hotel," he said.[1]

The two detectives drove at top speed the few blocks from their
office to the Park Sheraton on Fifty-fifth Street, and while O'Connor
parked the car, Graff strode in through the lobby. As he walked
through the double glass doors, he saw a small handgun lying on the
ground. He knew at once that he was dealing with a professional hit.

The professional hit man discards his weapon as he leaves the
scene of the crime so that, if he is stopped, there is nothing incriminating about him. It is his less-exposed partner, following watchfully
behind, who retains a weapon, so that he can, if necessary, shoot the
two men out of trouble — and, indeed, an hour or two after Graff
had spotted the first weapon, a second revolver was discovered,

thrust into a trash can in the subway through which the killers had escaped.

The body was lying blood stained on the floor of the Park Sheraton barber's shop. It was riddled with bullets, and when William Graff heard the name of the victim — Umberto, or Albert, Anastasia — his first thought was of a possible connection with the waterfront inquiry that he and O'Connor had just completed. The dead man's brother, Tony, was a power in the longshoremen's union, and it was not long before Tony — who spelled his surname Anastasio — was at the Sheraton, kneeling distraught on the floor, weeping and kissing and hugging the inert form.

Albert Anastasia's grisly and dramatic demise in the Midtown Manhattan barbershop was to lift him immediately into American gangsterdom's hall of fame. Erratic and psychopathic, Anastasia was a Bugsy Siegel without the charm. He had hurt and threatened so many people that, once it had happened, his violent end could be seen to have had a certain inevitability — even a certain justice — about it. By odd coincidence, the Park Sheraton, where Anastasia died, had previously been the Park Central Hotel, where Arnold Rothstein had been shot dead twenty-nine years earlier.

Feverishly searching for fingerprints, organizing photographs, and trying to marshal and protect their evidence, Detectives Graff and O'Connor were occupied with more immediate concerns.

"At least we've got eyewitnesses," said Graff to O'Connor, as they looked around the shop at the seven Italian barbers, who were still transfixed by the carnage that had occurred in their midst.

"Don Umberto! Don Umberto!" the chief barber was moaning.[2]

The barbers, in fact, swore that they had seen nothing — nothing of any practical use, at least. They gave the police no help at all in identifying the killers. But as the young detectives searched and cataloged the contents of Albert Anastasia's pockets, they found an unmarked hotel key.[3] In the course of the next twenty-four hours, they discovered that the key came from the nearby Warwick Hotel, room 1009, which Anastasia kept permanently as a Midtown base of operations — and that staying recently in the Warwick, and meeting with Anastasia, had been a group of four Cubans, headed by Roberto "Chiri" Mendoza, a well-connected contractor who was building Havana's new Hilton Hotel, an edifice even larger than Meyer Lansky's Riviera, with 630 rooms to the Riviera's 440.[4]

Anastasia, the detectives discovered, had been talking to Chiri

Mendoza about getting a piece of the syndicate that would operate the casino in the soon-to-be-opened Hilton — and Santo Trafficante, who had given his address as the Sans Souci nightclub in Havana, had been staying in the Warwick at the same time. Trafficante had checked out of the hotel and had taken a taxi to the airport in some haste, according to the Warwick doorman, on the very morning of the killing.[5]

Graff and O'Connor had read of the other gangsters who were prominent in Havana — and of Meyer Lansky, in particular. The money to be made in Cuban gambling suggested an obvious motive. If Albert Anastasia had been trying to muscle in on the territory of Lansky, or of someone else in Cuba, via Chiri Mendoza and the Hilton Hotel casino, could it be that Lansky, or someone close to him, had ordered Anastasia's elimination?

Three weeks later, there was still more to think about. Some two hundred miles to the northwest of Manhattan, in the small, upstate hamlet of Apalachin, New York, a watchful state trooper, Sergeant Edgar D. Croswell,[6] was struck by the large number of cars and black limousines congregating at the fifty-eight-acre estate of Joseph Barbara, a local beer and soft drink distributor.

Joseph Barbara was a shadowy character. He had, in his youth, been arrested and released in the course of various murder investigations which had connections with both narcotics and bootlegging rackets.[7]

The guests at Joseph Barbara's Apalachin mansion proved more shadowy still. When the inquisitive Sergeant Croswell set up a roadblock and detained 58 of the men leaving the house, it turned out that 50 had arrest records, 35 had convictions, and 23 had served prison sentences. All were Italian Americans, hailing, for the most part, from cities in the northeastern United States. They included such figures as Carlo Gambino, Vito Genovese, and Joseph Profaci, some of the leading mafiosi of New York.[8] They averred, to a man, that they had all come to visit Joseph Barbara on that day because they had heard he was sick, and throughout their subsequent investigation, indictment, and conviction — overturned in 1960 by the U.S. court of appeals* — none of Barbara's guests could ever be persuaded to provide a better explanation.

---

*Though lacking solid evidence as to what the Apalachin participants were discussing, the Justice Department brought conspiracy charges, and secured lengthy jail sentences against twenty of them in January 1960. But on November 28, 1960, the U.S. Court of Appeals, Second Circuit, overturned the convictions. "Bad as many of these alleged con-

The most plausible interpretation of the Apalachin gathering was that it had been provoked by the grisly and highly publicized slaying of Albert Anastasia. Five months earlier, a gunman had taken a shot at Frank Costello as he returned home one night to his apartment in the Majestic on Central Park West, wounding him slightly. New York's newspapers were linking the two incidents as evidence of turmoil in the underworld. The solicitous visitors to Joseph Barbara's sickbed made up a who's who of the Italian gangsters and racketeers active in and around New York. One of the half-dozen guests who were not from the area was Santo Trafficante, Jr., who gave the police the name he often went by in Cuba, Louis Santos.

Havana gambling again. In the weeks following the killing in the barbershop, the New York City Police Department had mounted a major effort to track down the murderers of Albert Anastasia. The young detectives, Graff and O'Connor, were put on the team, working to the orders of more senior officers. The most promising line of inquiry seemed to be the one uncovered by the key to room 1009 at the Warwick Hotel — some connection between the booming Cuban casino business and the warring ganglords of New York. In February 1958, the Anastasia murder team received news that the man whom their sources had identified as the American kingpin of Cuban gambling was about to arrive in New York. The word went out:

"Bring in Meyer Lansky!"

Meyer Lansky found himself in jail within hours of his arrival at Idlewild Airport on the evening of February 11, 1958. It was a cold and snowy night. Detectives followed Meyer's taxi into the city, and when he got out at the junction of Fifty-third Street and Broadway, they moved in and arrested him.[10] They questioned him for three hours in the West Fifty-fourth Street police station and, getting nowhere, finally booked him on a charge of vagrancy. It was next morning before Moses Polakoff could get to the precinct house with a bond of $1,000 to get his client out on bail.[11]

The police brought the charge of vagrancy because their question-

---

spirators may be," read the unanimous judgment, "their conviction for a crime which the Government could not prove . . . and on evidence which a jury could not properly assess, cannot be permitted to stand." Justice J. Edward Lumbard amplified the thinking behind this. "Even an otherwise law abiding citizen who is stopped and interrogated by police," he wrote, "and who is given no reason for his detention and questioning, may feel it his right to give as little information as possible, and even perhaps to respond evasively if he believes he might thereby be earlier rid of police inquiry."[9]

ing had yielded nothing. What, they had asked Meyer, did he do for a living?

"Business," he replied.

"What kind of business?" came the question.

"My business," came his answer, and Lansky absolutely declined to elaborate further.[12]

Bringing a charge of some sort allowed the police to conduct a search of their suspect. But their investigation of Meyer's pockets and luggage uncovered no more than their questioning had done — and the newspapermen waiting outside the precinct house hardly fared better.

What did Meyer know, called out one reporter, about the murder in the barbershop?

"As much as an Eskimo in Alaska," Meyer replied[13] — and he drove off with Moses Polakoff to the Hotel Navarro on Central Park South.*

In the days that followed, William Graff and Edward O'Connor were among the dozen or so detectives assigned to shadow Meyer Lansky as he moved around New York, and while their surveillance told them nothing about who killed Albert Anastasia, it did give them some insight into the tastes and habits of their quarry. Lansky liked visiting bookshops — he was in and out of both Brentano's and Barnes & Noble, according to the police surveillance report sheets. He went to see his doctor and lawyer. He spent a lot of time in restaurants of the middling sort — Dinty Moore's, the Forum, the Italian Pavilion, Billy Gwon's, Old Timers, and Longchamps. An expedition to the Hoffritz Cutlery shop indicated his interest in kitchen equipment.[14]

One chilly Sunday, William Graff got the Lansky surveillance detail inside the lobby of the Hotel Navarro. There was snow and slush on the sidewalks outside, and Graff was just thawing out, relaxing on a sofa against the wall, his wet shoes dripping onto the carpet, when he saw his quarry come into the lobby and go up to the reception desk. Meyer Lansky was leaning forward, talking earnestly, and a little conspiratorially, with the clerk. There were glances being thrown in Graff's direction — and then, to his horror, the young

---

*In 1980, the Hotel Navarro, at 112 Central Park South, was renovated and reopened as the Ritz-Carlton Hotel, New York.

detective saw Lansky turn and walk quite deliberately across the lobby toward him, to come and sit down on the sofa at his side.

Graff did not know what to say. The police academy had not prepared him for the chief suspect's making a move like this. But Lansky did not say much, either. He sat beside Graff, rubbing his stomach, and making little oohs and ouches of discomfort, as if inviting sympathy. His ulcers were playing him up, he informed his companion on the sofa, dispensing with introductions.

"He was lonely, I think," says Graff today.

Meyer was wearing a jacket with an open-collared shirt, and every so often he glanced across the lobby toward the hotel's glass doors, through which could be seen the whirling snowstorm outside. No one would want to go out into that unless they had to, and Graff had to admit that Meyer Lansky looked as sick as he claimed to be.

"I've got something on my mind," Lansky said suddenly, after a few minutes of silence.

Detective Graff jerked himself instantly alert. Was this it? Was the chief suspect about to confess? Graff made a noise that he hoped was encouraging.

"It's the chickens," said Meyer.

William Graff could not believe what his ears were telling him.

"The chickens," repeated Meyer Lansky. "You can't get good chickens in Havana."

Detective Graff sat stunned as Meyer Lansky — suspect in New York's most spectacular gangster killing in decades — gave him a lecture on the difficulty of finding fresh chickens in Havana. Beef was no problem. The Riviera had good steaks. Nor was it hard to get seafood or lamb. But chickens . . . You just could not find them fresh and meaty in any quantity from the Cuban farmers. So that was why he had come to New York, Meyer explained, to arrange for a supply of decent chickens by air — and to get his ulcers treated as well, of course.

William Graff sat beside Meyer Lansky for the best part of half an hour, listening to the problems of the Riviera kitchens and wondering how he might contrive to turn the conversation in a more fruitful direction.

"He was playing with me," says William Graff today.[15]

The young detective did not log the details of his encounter with Meyer Lansky, or even the fact of it. He had learned nothing to help advance the police assumption that Lansky was connected with the murder of Albert Anastasia, and it would have been laughable to submit a report about ulcers and fresh chickens.

In the months that followed, however, it came to seem likely that Meyer Lansky had visited New York in February 1958 for no more sinister purpose. Anxious to avoid any suggestion that they were leasing their Havana casino to gangsters, Hilton Hotels threw open their files to the police, and the politics of Cuban gambling became much clearer to William Graff and his colleagues.

Thirteen different syndicates, almost all of them separate from the gamblers already established in Havana, had applied to sublease the new hotel's casino which, it was calculated, should produce about $3 million profit per year. Hilton wanted $1 million annual rental, paid in advance, and Roberto "Chiri" Mendoza was the candidate that the company favored. Mendoza had Batista's personal blessing, and he was also the candidate favored by the Cuban Hotel and Restaurant Workers Union, which was the owner of the new hotel. The union was financing the project as a source of employment for its current workers and as an investment for their pension fund, leasing out the management and international marketing to Hilton.

William Graff himself developed several Cuban contacts who told him of the veto that Meyer Lansky was generally believed to possess over who could operate as a gambler in Cuba. But it seemed agreed on all sides that Lansky had nothing to do with who got the Hilton. His own casino at the Riviera was going full swing. There were Americans running the gaming in the Nacional Hotel, the Sans Souci nightclub, and in the recently opened Capri Hotel — where George Raft, the movie star, was acting as front man and meeter and greeter for a syndicate headed by Santo Trafficante.[16] Americans had more than their fair share of gambling in Havana, and when it came to the new Hilton casino, Batista had given the word that this one was for the Cubans.

Chiri Mendoza was a business partner of Batista in several ventures. He came from an old and respected Cuban family who owned Havana's leading baseball team, and he had been taken with the notion that the great Yankee center fielder Joe DiMaggio might become the meeter and greeter at the new Hilton casino. The idea had been put to Mendoza by Joe Rivers, an American crap game operator, who invited the Cuban to New York to meet DiMaggio — which was how Mendoza had come to be registered at the Warwick Hotel in October 1957.[17]

The meeting had not proved very productive so far as the Hilton casino was concerned. The baseball hero explained at the outset that he could not endorse liquor or gambling because of the adverse effect that would have "upon the youth of the nation."[18] But a most enjoyable baseball discussion had ensued, and as Joe Rivers ushered DiMaggio out, he ushered in the real object of the exercise — his dear friend Albert Anastasia, who proposed himself as an appropriate associate with the union-owned Havana Hilton on account of his U.S. labor connections. As part of their waterfront empire, Anastasia and his brother, Tony, a union vice president and head of Longshoremen's Local 1814, held considerable influence in New York's hotel, restaurant, and bar workers' locals.

"Can the boss fire you?" Anastasia had asked the headwaiter in Chandler's, the New York restaurant where he entertained Chiri Mendoza and his friends for lunch in October 1957.

"No," the headwaiter had replied, "because of the union." Anastasia gave the waiter ten dollars.[19]

As the New York police pieced together the curious chain of events that had brought Albert Anastasia and Chiri Mendoza together in the Warwick Hotel, they could discern no role for Meyer Lansky in the barbershop murder. Cuban gambling, they decided, was not the issue after all — and their New York inquiries were revealing an abundance of evidence as to the trouble which Albert Anastasia had been stirring up closer to home. Gangland territories, floating crap games,[20] jukebox routes, who controlled what in the expanding sprawl of Long Island — there were any number of local areas in which Don Umberto had been giving his fellow mafiosi reason to kill him. The Anastasia murder squad shifted its focus from Cuba to Queens, Brooklyn, and the Bronx — and finally gathered the evidence to develop charges against five New York suspects.*

Meyer himself shook loose on February 27, 1958, when he appeared in front of Magistrate Reuben Levy in the Manhattan Arrest Court. Moses Polakoff represented Meyer, and he was in fighting form, pointing out that his client had arrived in New York with a paid airline ticket, that he had luggage, a checkbook, a hotel reservation — and $1,085 in cash in his pocket. Had the police bothered

---

*These suspects were never named publicly, and the charges were never brought, since after reviewing the evidence, the New York district attorney's office felt it did not have a case that was strong enough to take to a judge and jury. So the murder of Albert Anastasia in 1957, like that of Bugsy Siegel in 1947, remains officially unsolved.[21]

to check the details he gave them, they would have discovered he had decent residences in Florida and Cuba, and $35,000 in the bank.[22]

"Everyone knows," said Polakoff, "that this man is not a vagrant."[23]

The magistrate agreed.

"Under our form of government," the judge declared, "possible social undesirability is not the equivalent of lawlessness, and the police have failed to establish the crime of vagrancy. The basic elements — the lack of funds, lack of job, and lack of home — are not proven. Dismissed."[24]

Havana had something of fairyland about it in the winter season of January, February, and March, 1958. There were more visitors than ever before. The operators of the newly opened casino-hotels could hardly believe their good fortune. At the Capri, J. "Skip" Shepard, a Miami hotelier who had a twenty-year contract to operate the hotel, remembers that the flow of money — sheer, naked profit — was "just unbelievable."[25]

Thanks to Meyer Lansky's reputation and connections, it was the Riviera that attracted the most serious, high-stakes players — men who thought nothing of writing a check for $20,000 or $30,000 at the end of an evening's gaming. The checks were gathered up before dawn, and packed into the briefcase of Dan "Dusty" Peters, a tall, dapper character, typical of the slick and affable figures who hang around casinos with nothing very obvious to do. In the 1940s, Peters had been a host at the Colonial Inn and at Meyer's other Florida gambling joints.

From the Riviera, Peters would take the first morning flight to Miami, and by lunchtime he had had all the checks express-cleared by banks in Miami, or on Miami Beach. By evening, he was back at the Riviera again, and if any of his checks had not cleared, then the name of the player in question had been phoned round Havana.

Norberto Peña, a discreet and well-spoken young Cuban, had the job of collecting the money.[26] Meyer had set up a croupier school to train Cubans to work in the Riviera casino, under the tuition of Dino Cellini, a courtly young Italian much given to kissing ladies' hands.[27] Students knew they had graduated when Cellini sent them to get their dinner jackets fitted. But Peña was never sent to the tailor. Cellini told him that he had been singled out for higher things.[28]

Peña could not see debt collection in that light, but the job proved surprisingly easy. The worst thing that can happen to a serious, high-stakes gambler is to be cut off from his gambling. So it was a rare evening that the check bouncer was not down within minutes, responding to Peña's call from the lobby. It was surprising, Peña discovered, how many high rollers actually had the cash on them to cover their debt, and in all his months working for the Riviera, Peña never encountered a debt that he was not able to collect.

Meticulous credit control, Peña discovered, was one of the secrets of Meyer Lansky's success. If one of the Riviera's cashiers or floor men let a player sign a marker for $10,000 or $15,000, it was because someone knew that the man was good for the money — and that someone was usually one of the affable, well-dressed men hanging around the gaming room with nothing very obvious to do. It was only part of a casino host's job to attract and amuse high rollers, keeping them happy with "comped" (free) rooms and meals and friendly conversation. The bottom line was to make very sure that his players could pay what they had wagered.

A well-run casino, Norberto Peña discovered, was a complex thing. Right around the curved, oval wall of the Riviera's chandeliered temple of chance ran a ledge on which sat the slot machines. They added a jangling, down-market note to the serious action in the center of the room, and Peña noticed how the casino's own work force never touched them. The one-armed bandits were serviced, repaired, and milked of their cash by a totally separate cadre of workers, reporting to a separate cashier.[29] This cashier reported in turn, via various intermediaries, to a relative of the president.[30]

Meyer Lansky plugged himself very comfortably into the corruption of Batista's Cuba. Bribes, payoffs, favors — they were meat and drink to him. He had always been adept at cutting corners, and in Cuba in the mid-1950s that sort of corner cutting was raised to a fine art. The waitresses in the coffee shop were slow and stupid? Pay the union to send better ones. Diego Gonzalez, a local columnist, was giving the Riviera bad reviews? Pay him a monthly "consultancy" fee.[31] It was never Meyer's way to be mean or greedy. There was money enough to keep everyone happy.

Yet money for its own sake corroded other values. Many of the applicants to Dino Cellini's croupier school were university graduates — teachers, vets, and doctors whose skills were sorely needed in Cuba's underdeveloped rural areas. The Riviera did not let prostitutes parade in its casino, restaurant, or bars, but part of Havana's casino-stimulated money culture was the Casa Marina, near the airport, where, for the right price, American tourists could buy the right to deflower thirteen-year-old girls.

Meyer Lansky, the expert on history, politics, and current affairs, was blind to the political and social rot to which he was contributing — and, morality aside, he was blinder still to the way in which this ethical laissez-faire threatened the position of the man on whom Meyer's own position in Cuba ultimately depended.

Fulgencio Batista had first come to power through the fall of a tyrant, but by 1958, for all his charm and his genuine ambition for his country, the sergeant turned stenographer had turned into a tyrant himself. His not-so-secret police, the SIM, used assassination and torture as routine procedures. The bodies had been left hanging, American diplomats reported, from trees and beside roadways.[32] Political dissidents who got arrested were lucky if they escaped with a beating.

Cuba's middle and upper classes were profiting handsomely, on the whole, from the tourist-led economic boom which Batista had helped stimulate. But there was a vast underclass who benefited scarcely at all. Guests at the Riviera could look out from the luxury of their rooms to a street at the rear, where poverty-stricken Cubans camped out on the sidewalk and sheltered in derelict cars.[33]

Batista's opponents had resorted to violence of their own, and Meyer had had firsthand experience of the results. One evening in October 1956, Colonel Antonio Blanco Rico, chief of the SIM, had dropped into the Montmartre Club for an evening's gambling, and had been shot to death by assassins who made good their escape.[34] The rebels were up in the hills. Fidel Castro landed his little expeditionary force in Oriente Province in December 1956 — a matter of weeks before ground was broken on the new Riviera Hotel. The reputation and following of the young radical had been growing ever since.

To undercut the appeal of the bearded rebels in the Sierra Maestra, the church and some concerned liberal Cubans had made efforts to persuade Batista to modify his most authoritarian excesses, and to hold out the promise of some steps, at least, toward democracy and reform. But Batista was inflexible.

Meyer Lansky, for his part, was not too concerned. His focus was firmly fixed on making back the investment that he had sunk in his new hotel, and when people asked him about local politics, he would just shrug his shoulders. If someone new came along, he said, he had no doubt that he could pay them off as well.[35]

Early in December 1958, Fulgencio Batista sent his children's passports to the American embassy to be stamped with U.S. visas. On December 9, President Eisenhower dispatched a personal emissary to Batista promising unhindered access to, and asylum in, the dictator's Daytona Beach home, providing that Batista was willing to leave Cuba rapidly and quietly. Just over a week later, on December 17, 1958, Ambassador Earl E. T. Smith repeated the message more officially.[36] For those who were in the know, there was ample warning that Fulgencio Batista's days of power were numbered.

Meyer Lansky was not in the know. He had flown to Florida late in December 1958, and he flew back into Havana on New Year's Eve for the big party that the Riviera was organizing that night.[37]

Meyer felt ill, however. He had been hospitalized twice in recent months on account of his ulcers,[38] and he was currently suffering from a swelling of the knee which meant that he could scarcely walk. So on the night of December 31, 1958, he stayed up in his room while Teddy danced in the new year with the hotel's Cuban attorney, Eduardo Suarez Rivas, in the Copa Room[39] — which was the scene of a curiously forlorn and empty celebration. Reservations for the Copa Room's New Year's Eve party had been brisk and busy in the previous days, but on the day itself, in the hours leading up to the fiesta, the Riviera was puzzled to receive some two hundred cancellations.[40]

The news reached the central Havana hotels soon after one o'clock in the morning. An hour or so earlier, President Batista had driven secretly to Camp Columbia, where he had commandeered three planes at the neighboring air force base, filled them with his wife, family, closest aides, and baggage — and fled the country.[41]

Fidel Castro and his followers were still in Oriente Province, nearly 500 miles from the capital, while the Cuban army, larger than it had ever been, remained generally loyal to Batista. But afraid for his life, and concerned to make sure of his money, the sergeant-stenographer with the engaging smile had chosen to pick up his winnings and to leave the table while he could.

Francis Ford Coppola's *Godfather II,* filmed partially in the Dominican Republic in 1974, memorably captured the menace and frightened confusion in Havana the night that everything came to an end. Repeating popular legend, the movie showed Hyman Roth, the Meyer Lansky figure, warned in advance by Batista, organizing private planes to get himself and his fellow gangsters out of the country.

In reality, very few in Batista's circle were given any notice of what was happening. Chiri Mendoza rocked perceptibly with shock when he heard the news — along with everyone else — in the newly opened Hilton casino in the small hours of January 1.[42] Over at the Riviera, Teddy's escort, attorney Suarez Rivas, had been no better warned. American consular officers, rousted from their beds, struggled with their New Year's Day hangovers as they went round the hotels, telling American citizens to stay indoors, while compiling lists of visitors' names in case an evacuation became necessary.[43]

As dawn rose on the suddenly Batista-less Havana, there was dancing in the streets. The workers at the Riviera deserted their jobs to go out and celebrate, and Meyer, limping on his swollen knee, worked personally in the kitchens to give out food, free of charge, to the bewildered and apprehensive guests. Entering into the make-do spirit, Teddy Lansky poured some vinegar into a bucket of water, took a mop, and started wiping up the Riviera's marble floors.[44]

In the egalitarian atmosphere of the new Havana, Teddy's washerwoman role was both appropriate and necessary. In the early weeks of January 1959, peasants who had only dared to look wistfully at the outside of the chrome-and-glass towers housing the visiting Americanos now strolled with impunity into the lobbies — and brought their pigs with them.

"Pigs, for Christ's sake!" Teddy told the newspaperman Paul Sann twenty-five years later. "You wouldn't believe it, in this gorgeous, gorgeous hotel. I was mopping up floors in the restaurant."[45]

It was several days before life in Havana returned to some sort of normality, and as Meyer Lansky struggled to look after the Riviera's guests, collaborating actively with the American embassy to arrange the departure of those who wished to go home, he was infuriated to receive a phone call from Miami Beach checking on the truth of a story which had appeared in the *New York Daily News* of January 3, 1959. According to the *Daily News,* Meyer Lansky, Santo Trafficante, and the "elite" of Havana's casinos had left Cuba on the afternoon of New Year's Day.

"The gamblers took their cue," reported the paper, "from their benefactor and protector, President Fulgencio Batista, and fled the country in three charter planes."[46]

The *New York Herald Tribune* was running a story to similar effect — "City, State and Federal Agencies Alert for Any Influx of Gangsters."[47]

Meyer got straight on the phone to the U.S. embassy in Havana, which logged his call on January 4, 1959. He wanted the embassy to know that he had not run away from Cuba. He was at the Riviera Hotel, "taking care of the personnel there, even though he was very sick and should be in the hospital."[48]

Meyer Lansky had a practical reason for making sure that his presence in Havana was recorded by the U.S. embassy — and in particular by the FBI agent who was stationed in the embassy as the "legal attaché." Meyer was under subpoena to appear in Washington before Senator John McClellan's Select Committee on Improper Activities in the Labor or Management Field. He had been careful to keep the embassy fully informed of his whereabouts, and he was worried, he told the FBI man, that newspaper tales of secret charter flights might be interpreted as his showing contempt for the committee's writ.[49]

When Meyer Lansky did fly into Miami three days later — on January 7, 1959, on a scheduled Pan Am flight — he was more forthcoming than he normally might have been to the reporters waiting at the airport. Yes, he told Milt Sosin of the *Miami News,* he had read the stories about his fleeing Cuba by chartered plane on the day of the revolution, and he was "much amused" by them.[50]

"I called up the FBI office in Havana, and asked them if I was wanted," he said. "They told me, 'No.'"[51]

Meyer was carrying a small, cloth overnight bag. That was the full extent of his luggage. He had just come to Florida for a few days to see his doctor, he explained. Then he was planning to go back to Cuba.[52]

By the end of January 1959, Meyer Lansky was in Havana again, working, like all the other casino operators who were supposed to have fled with him, on some sort of accommodation with the new realities of Cuban politics and life. In all the disorder and relatively bloodless chaos of the Cuban revolution, the gangsters of Havana had kept their heads low and had not acted like gangsters at all — with one exception.

As the crowds of jubilant Cubans had spilled out onto the streets on the morning of January 1, 1959, they had headed for the most visible and hated targets of the corruption that had characterized the

old regime — the parking meters, whose revenues were supposed to
support soup kitchens for the poor but were believed to end up in
the pocket of a Batista relative. With no one to protect them, the
meters were beheaded quicker than the victims of the guillotine, and
the mob turned from the streets to the city's other mechanical extortion, the slot machines in the American casinos.

The crowds' first stop was the Salón Rojo — the Red Room —
the casino of the Capri Hotel, and the cheering revolutionaries
stormed confidently up the steps. But as they reached the top, they
were stopped dead in their tracks by the sight of George Raft, the
film-star host of the establishment, who had a small share of his own
in the Salón Rojo, and who was standing defiantly outside the doors.

"Yer not comin' in my casino," growled Raft, summoning up his
best gangster snarl — and, by the account of Wayne S. Smith, one of
the U.S. consular officers doing the rounds of the beleaguered tourist
hotels that New Year's morning, the crowd meekly turned on its heels
and went to look for trouble elsewhere.[53]

So at least the movie gangster knew how to act the part.

One of the first decisions of the new revolutionary government of
Cuba in January 1959 was to shut down the national lottery and the
casinos. Both were inappropriate to the ethic of the new, reformed
Cuba. If the country's tourist business depended on gambling,
announced the new prime minister, Miró Cardona, then the tourist
business would just have to suffer.[54]

Fidel Castro had already proclaimed from the mountains his intention of sluicing away the Yankee gangsters who ran the casinos of
Havana.

"We are not only disposed to deport the gangsters, but to shoot
them," declared the rebel commander.[55]

The gangsters were symptoms, in Castro's eyes, of all that was
wrong with Batista's Cuba, a country that had become both an
accomplice and a victim of U.S. imperialism. The shadowy figures
who ran Havana's casinos were the ultimate, crooked metaphor of
the American free-enterprise system.[56]

The realities of government, however, soon caused Castro and his
ministers to think again. At the end of January 1959, several thousand waiters, croupiers, dealers, and barmen who had been thrown
out of work by the closing of the casinos paraded in protest through
the streets of Havana.[57]

Castro had delegated responsibility for the casinos and the national lottery to Pastora Núñez, one of the woman guerrillas who had fought in the Sierra Maestra, and at the end of February 1959, Señorita Núñez summoned the major casino owners to her office.[58]

"I highly disapprove of the way you make a living," she lectured, "but we are reconsidering our earlier decision."[59]

Money proved the final persuader. The casino owners agreed to give their employees seven weeks' back pay for the time that they had been out of work, and with that assurance, the government rescinded its earlier decree.

CASINOS REOPEN IN HAVANA, proclaimed the banner trailing behind a plane which flew up and down Miami Beach in the last week of February 1959.[60] There were about six weeks left until Easter, and, with luck, the Riviera and the other hotels could recoup enough of their losses to break even for the season. Cautious optimism filled the gaming rooms at the prospect of coexistence with a regime that seemed both clean and pragmatic.

"Me, I'm glad those greedy Batista crooks got bounced," declared one unnamed gambler to *Time* magazine.[61]

There was similar optimism in New York, where Fidel Castro arrived in April 1959 to a hero's welcome. The Batista regime had received negative and critical press coverage in its final months, and the young guerrilla leader, charismatic in his beard and fatigues, was hailed as a liberator in the finest South American tradition — another Bolívar.[62]

Meyer Lansky was not so sure. It was true that Fidel Castro had proved flexible enough to let Havana's casinos reopen, for the time being, at least. But there were the show trials — three hundred or so executions by March 1959[63] — and the influence in the new government of Marxist hard-liners like Ernesto "Che" Guevara and Castro's brother, Raul. The unions with whom the Riviera had to deal, day to day, were proving suddenly combative and ideological, with hot talk of ousting the Yankees and instituting workers' control.

Meyer's greasing of the palm did not work with these radicals as he had predicted it would — and on May 6, 1959, his brother, Jake, was taken from the Riviera by Cuban immigration officials and detained in Triscornia, the immigration prison, pending expulsion. Dino Cellini was arrested and imprisoned with Jake.[64]

Meyer read the *New York Times* every day.[65] Its sympathetic dispatches from Herbert L. Matthews, who had traveled with the rebels in the Sierra Maestra, were doing much to influence American opinion. But the friendly and reasonable regime about which Meyer was reading did not correspond to the Fidel Castro whose officials were locking up his brother without trial. Still sick in the spring of 1959, Meyer was shuttling between Havana and Florida seeing doctors, and he came to feel that American opinion was dangerously out of touch with the way things were really moving in Cuba.

"Someone should tell the government what's actually going on over there," he said to Joe Varon one day in May 1959.

"Meyer," replied his lawyer, "that someone has to be you."[66]

On May 22, 1959, Meyer Lansky met in Varon's office at 2432 Hollywood Boulevard with Dennis O'Shea, the assistant senior resident agent of the FBI's Fort Lauderdale office.[67] O'Shea had accepted Varon's invitation to meet Meyer Lansky, and he brought with him an agent from Miami who was an expert on the Cuban situation.

Meyer had prepared for the meeting with some care. He prefaced his remarks with a general historical overview, based on his reading, of how popular revolutions in many countries had become repressive and retrograde as the hard-liners consolidated their power.

"He held himself out as a historian," Dennis O'Shea remembers, "as a buff."[68]

Meyer clearly relished the chance to play professor to the two FBI men, and he made the most of it. "He did a song and dance," recalls O'Shea, "which I thought was rather impressive with regard to what he knew of those situations in the past. . . . And he led on from this to say that he could see the same thing coming in Cuba. . . . As far as I was concerned, it was very insightful."[69]

"Throughout conversation," noted the FBI's official, slightly shorthand report of the meeting, "Lansky showed an excellent grasp of political science, current and past, and the ability to express himself."[70]

Before the encounter, the two agents had discussed the self-serving reasons that might have inspired Meyer to volunteer the briefing, via his attorney — and Meyer put his motives on the table at the outset. He admitted that American gambling interests had been "hamstrung" by the policies of the Castro regime, and that he and his fellow gamblers stood to lose heavily if the situation did not change.

"He could not deny," the agents reported, "that the possibility of this loss contributed to his decision to discuss the Cuban situation.

Nevertheless, he felt that the United States government should be well aware of the changing political situation in Cuba before it developed into a threat."[71]

Meyer saw himself as a patriot, and he wanted the FBI men to know that he felt very strongly about national security.

"It was his feeling," recalls O'Shea, "that whether people held him up to be a criminal or professional gambler or what have you, America was still his country."[72]

Meyer then spoke for the best part of an hour on Cuban politics as he had observed it, the burden of his argument being that anti-American influences held far more power inside the Cuban government and the unions than outsiders realized.

"The time [is] ripe," he said, "for communist factions to entrench themselves." There were already Communists in high places inside the Cuban government, "and the entire government will soon be communistic."[73]

Meyer felt that the American newspapers were particularly naive in their depiction of Castro as a benign and liberal "savior."[74]

"Castro at the time was being held out as the white knight coming in," remembers O'Shea. "He ran past us the names of the people that he felt might be involved in the Communist or Red group trying to take over."[75]

Meyer's attitude struck the agents as decidedly friendly, but he did not seem to them to be a healthy man.

"Lansky appeared pale and drawn," they reported. "He moved very slowly and seemed to be in pain."[76]

The prospect of losing all that he had put into the Riviera was clearly not doing Meyer's ulcers any good. His doctor had told him, he said, that he should not remain on his feet more than three or four hours a day, and he was not planning to go back to Cuba soon. It was quite likely, however, that his sources would provide him with more information about Communist infiltration, and he offered to pass this along to the FBI.[77]

The offer was not taken up. Dennis O'Shea made copious notes on the meeting and sent his report to Washington, where it was placed in the FBI's fattening file on Meyer Lansky. But the FBI took no action on it, and there is no evidence that the report was even passed on to the State Department, or to the Office of the Legal Attaché in Havana.[78] It was like Detective Graff's decision not to file a report on Meyer's remarks in the Hotel Navarro the previous spring. Lansky's reputation was such that anyone who accepted what he said at face value risked being labeled tainted or naive.

Subsequent events in Cuba suggested that the FBI might have paid more attention to what Meyer Lansky said. Jake Lansky and Dino Cellini were let out of jail after a matter of days. But six months later, a trade delegation from Moscow was given the red-carpet treatment in Havana. Then, in the spring of 1960, the Cuban leader embraced Khrushchev's lieutenant Anastas Mikoyan, and announced that the Cuban revolution was indeed committed to socialism. On May 7, 1960, Cuba opened diplomatic relations with Moscow.[79]

For thirty years there has been a debate among the students of Cuban-American relations as to the nature of Fidel Castro's seventeen-month progression from radical but ostensibly nonaligned reformer to committed Russian surrogate and ally. Was Castro telling the truth when he dramatically announced to the world in 1961 that he was a Marxist-Leninist, as if he had always been one? Did U.S. policies heedlessly accelerate Cuba's drift into the Russian camp, and could America, with better intelligence, have done anything to prevent it?

The debate remains open. But the records of the FBI's meeting in Joseph Varon's Hollywood office on May 22, 1959, show, with rare clarity, that Meyer Lansky predicted almost exactly what was going to happen in Cuba the best part of a year before it did.

Meyer Lansky's ability to foresee the political evolvement of Fidel Castro in the spring of 1959 was some small consolation for the fact that, in terms of his own personal career and investment, Meyer had got the future of American involvement in Cuba absolutely and catastrophically wrong.

In April 1958, nine months before Batista's departure, when the recently opened hotel-casinos of Havana were going full swing, the Nevada Gaming Board had banned the holders of Nevada gaming licenses from operating in Cuba. The spectacular success of the Havana Riviera, Capri, Nacional, and Hilton hotel-casinos was hurting business in Las Vegas, where the most recently opened hotels were all in financial difficulties.

Five Nevada gamblers had acted immediately to safeguard their positions in Las Vegas. In the autumn of 1958, Moe Dalitz, Wilbur Clark, Sam Tucker, Morris Kleinman, and Thomas "Black Jack" McGinty all sold out the interests they had developed in Havana. On New Year's Day 1959, they looked very clever indeed. They had got themselves clear of Cuban gambling, and they even had a profit to show for it.

Meyer Lansky did not look so clever. The Riviera Hotel had cost $14 million to build and equip, by the reckoning of the Batista government[80] — $18 million by the estimate that Meyer himself later gave to friends in Israel.[81] Six million dollars of that investment was provided by the Batista government under the provisions of Hotel Law 2074.[82]

No paperwork survives to provide exact figures, but $8 million to $12 million seems a fair estimate of what Meyer and his associates personally invested in the Riviera's bricks and mortar, chandeliers, roulette tables, and mosaic tile. The mosaic tile, Meyer used to grumble, almost in pain, was *very* expensive.[83]

At the time of Batista's departure, the Riviera Hotel had been open for a few weeks longer than a year, and by the estimate of the Hilton's analysts, who studied the Riviera's success in order to predict how much revenue their own casino might be expected to generate, gaming at the Riviera showed a clear annual profit of some $3 million.[84]

But after little more than a year of operating profits, that still left $5 million to $9 million of investment paid out and buried in the hotel — with the deficit getting larger, since the Riviera did not register a single month of clear profit in the period that it operated under the unwilling and unhelpful aegis of Fidel Castro.

Meyer Lansky never disclosed his personal investment in the Havana Riviera. He shrouded it in the mystery with which he camouflaged all his financial dealings. Willing as ever to share in his good fortune, he had cut some of his friends in on what seemed to everyone to be a profitable deal with enormous potential, and this meant that his friends bore a share of the losses.[85]

But less cautious in this instance than he normally was, Meyer had also staked his personal bankroll solidly on the success of the Riviera — to the exclusion of almost anything else. His spectacular hotel-casino was to be the culmination — and ultimate vindication — of his career. Meyer Lansky might never be able to operate openly in Las Vegas, or anywhere else in America. But here, standing tall, and glinting magnificently over the straits of Florida, was his Xanadu, grand, profitable, and legal. It was the Colonial Inn reborn, Meyer's own Flamingo.

"That hotel," says Joseph Varon, "was his crowning glory."[86]

Meyer Lansky invested much more than his money in the Havana

Riviera. He invested himself. He gambled everything — and, as he later put it, "I crapped out."[87]

On October 24, 1960, the *Gaceta Oficial de la República de Cuba* announced the confiscation and nationalization of the Havana Riviera Hotel. The gazette announced the same fate for 165 other American enterprises, including the Cuban subsidiaries and franchises of Kodak, Woolworth, Canada Dry, Westinghouse, and Goodyear. Meyer Lansky was in distinguished company.

The massive confiscation was one of the final steps in the poisonous and depressing tit-for-tat between the United States and Cuba that was to culminate the following spring at the Bay of Pigs. It came as no surprise to Meyer Lansky. He and Jake had both been harassed by the ever more aggressive Cuban authorities, as the two brothers struggled to keep the Riviera afloat. With the hotel and casino both losing money, Meyer had had to borrow and beg, and to dig ever deeper into his own pocket in order to keep open, operating on the slender hope that something might change. It was almost a relief when Castro's confiscation brought the ordeal to an end.

The strain and impossibility of it all affected Meyer badly. Dennis O'Shea and his fellow FBI agent had noted his obviously poor health in the spring of 1959. Eighteen months later, Meyer was sicker still. His ulcers continued to flare, and he was brought low with spasms of sharp pain around his heart. His doctors diagnosed pericarditis — inflammation of the tissues surrounding the heart wall. It was not a heart attack per se, but with Meyer approaching the age of sixty, it was a severe and worrying condition.

The ending of the dream of the Riviera seemed to finish Meyer Lansky as well. He often became breathless, and he could only move slowly, like a very old man.[88] The pains in his chest grew worse, and eighteen months after he had had to write off the Cuban hotel, Meyer collapsed. This time it was a heart attack.

He was hospitalized twice — in New York, and down in Florida, at the Hollywood Doctors' Hospital. Meyer spent nearly a month in an oxygen tent, struggling for breath, while the specialists wondered whether he would make it. Things got so bad at one stage that the rabbi was called, and the family was summoned together. Paul flew in from Tacoma.[89]

One day when Meyer was particularly ill, Buddy Lansky was talking with his brother and sister about what might happen if their father died. How would they survive without Dad? Uncle Jack walked in at that moment, and he caught the drift of their conversation.

"Don't expect a lot of money," Jake said to his nephews and niece. "If your father died today, he's broke."[90]

15

"This Little Man — What Could He Do to You?"

IN August 1962, a month after his sixtieth birthday, Meyer Lansky visited Israel for the first time in his life.[1] It was part of a general tour of Europe marking Meyer's recuperation from his heart attack earlier in the year,[2] and his two weeks in Israel proved a particular tonic.

"He was never Jewish minded when we were growing up," remembered Buddy Lansky. "The Christmas trees, the bacon — no Bar Mitzvah. . . . We didn't know what Jewish was."[3]

Then Meyer Lansky visited Israel, and he seemed to discover a new dimension. He started talking and reading about Israeli politics. He would get angry about the Arabs, and about American policies that seemed to favor them. He also started reminiscing more about his youth in Grodno, and about his fondness for Grandfather Benjamin.

"I never heard that before," said Buddy Lansky.[4]

Meyer Lansky's commitment to Israel went back nearly twenty years, to the help that he gave to the Haganah, both in Florida and on the New Jersey waterfront in the late 1940s. A decade before that, he had been organizing the toughs who broke up the meetings of the German-American Bund. But from the early 1960s, Meyer Lansky was "Jewish minded" in a new and more consuming fashion.

260

Meyer had celebrated his sixtieth birthday on July 4, 1962, short of breath, half immobile, with doctors trying to stave off the collapse of organs in every corner of his body. Anyone reaching the age of sixty in that condition might be expected to look back to his roots and to wonder a little about his place in eternity, and Meyer had found himself at a particularly intense personal watershed. The demolition of American interests in Cuba, which took so many people by surprise, had demolished most of his personal fortune. It had also effectively ended the possibility that Meyer Lansky could ever do again what Meyer Lansky was noted for among his peers — run a high-class, high-stakes casino.

The money was not the worst problem. There were several ways by which Meyer could restore his fortunes and put his life back together in a material sense. It was putting himself back together that was more difficult, and as he set out on that path, he found comfort in the separate, serving tradition that is the Jewish way. At the suggestion of his Boston friend Joe Linsey, he made some donations to the sports center that Linsey was building for Brandeis University,[5] a New England college founded in 1948, when quotas still excluded many Jewish students from the Ivy League and other schools.

Meyer also made a point of visiting his Hollywood synagogue with cash donations every holiday.

"There's no need for you to come here personally, Mr. Lansky," said one of the fund-raisers on one occasion, worried by Meyer's evident ill health. "We can send someone to pick up the money."

"Thank you," said Meyer, "but I like to feel part of the community."[6]

When Israel embarked on the Six-Day War in 1967, sweeping into the West Bank and occupying all of Jerusalem, Meyer hastened to phone his rabbi and to pledge his support. He was by no means the biggest giver. Meyer Lansky's donation to Hollywood's Emergency Fund for Israel was in the region of his gifts to Brandeis University — less than $1,500, remembers his rabbi.[7] But Meyer lobbied his friends to contribute,[8] and he was one of the first to come forward.

"A few times he came to my office," remembers Rabbi David Shapiro. "We sat and talked. He always impressed me as being quiet, intelligent — a thoughtful human being. . . . He loved to discuss the world and Israel and so on — which I did."[9]

In the fortunes of Israel, Meyer Lansky had found something that he could really care about, an issue to bring out and to transport his angers, hopes, and anxieties — all the emotions that he routinely attempted to suppress or to ignore. Other men might cheer for their sports teams, or for the fortunes of their children. But Meyer Lansky had never been a sports fanatic — and his children did not give him much to cheer about.

Buddy Lansky met his wife, Annette, at the Rascal House, the northern extension of Wolfie Cohen's salt beef and bagel empire, set amidst the motels of North Miami Beach. Annette was a Rascal House hostess, seating the customers as they came off the long lines waiting for a table, and she always gave Buddy a good seat.

Buddy would bypass the queues, wobbling to the head of the line on the arm of a friend, and when he first introduced himself to Annette, he claimed priority of another sort.

"Hi, I'm Buddy Lansky," he said. "I'm Meyer Lansky's son."[10]

Annette knew who Meyer Lansky was. She was impressed — and, as she looks back on it today, her entire relationship with Buddy came to be conducted in the shadow of his father.

Buddy courted Annette with flowers and perfume and phone calls, and with lavish meals out. She liked him. He was funny and good natured, and she felt sorry for him. When, quite soon after they met, Buddy proposed marriage, it seemed the perfect arrangement. Twenty-six years old in 1955, Annette had been married twice before, and she had a young son. She would look after Buddy, helping him to wash and dress, giving him friendship, warmth, intimacy. She would make him a good home, and he would provide her with security in return. He might even prove a good father to her son.

"I figured, I'll be good to him," she says, "and he'll be good to me."[11]

Meyer Lansky was not so sure. He had ample reason to mistrust his elder son's judgment, and he thought that Buddy was rushing things. Sandra's quick marriage had not served her well. Meyer told Buddy that he would have to wait two years.

"They were the roughest two years I ever went through," remembered Buddy Lansky. "Because Annette didn't want to wait. But I told her, that's the way it had to be. My father came first."[12]

Even after two years, however, Meyer remained suspicious. "Why would any woman want to marry Buddy?" he asked.[13]

Annette was a tall and handsome girl, with Ava Gardner looks — striking high cheekbones and flowing dark hair. She was self-assured and stylish, and she had a taste for elegant clothes. Meyer suspected that she was a gold digger. In the spring of 1957, when it was finally agreed that Buddy and Annette could wed, the skeleton of the Riviera was rising high above the Malecón. Under Jake Lansky's supervision, the Nacional Hotel's casino was pulling in as much money as any gaming room in Las Vegas. The Lanskys were rich, and they seemed set to be much richer. In ten or twenty years' time, Buddy could be the inheritor of millions.

One day Joe Varon, the lawyer, got a phone call from Buddy. "Dad thinks Annette should sign an agreement," he said.[14]

Varon phoned Meyer, to discover that Meyer did indeed have his doubts. "Frankly," recalls Varon, "he was not in favor of that marriage."

"Let me talk to her," the lawyer suggested, and he phoned Annette, inviting her to come to his office for "a plain, informal little talk."[15]

The crux of the meeting, as Annette recalls it, was the question of what would happen if the marriage went wrong. Was Annette willing to waive any claim against Buddy's property in the event of a divorce?

"Of course," she replied. "I'm not looking to divorce the guy. I'm looking to live with him."[16]

There was no further talk of agreements.

"I saw it as a test," remembers Annette Lansky today. "It didn't trouble me. I knew that I was playing it straight."[17]

After all the doubts and delays, the wedding was a surprisingly happy occasion — held, by Annette's choice, at the House of Prime Ribs, a Chinese restaurant overlooking the water.[18] Buddy had not shown himself to have his father's sense of business, and he had no great application. But it seemed that he had found himself a strong and practical Jewish girl who was willing to take care of him — and who was decorative into the bargain.

Paul flew over from Tacoma. His wife, Edna, could not come, because they were expecting their first child. Sandra managed to forgo the enticements of New York long enough to be present for at least one of her brothers' weddings. Grandma Yetta, old, shrinking, and mumbling happily in Yiddish, nibbled appreciatively on the spareribs.

"They're lamb chops, Grandma," Buddy told her.[19]

Jake and Meyer had brought their mother down from Brooklyn several years previously, and now Yetta was installed in her own little apartment near the ocean in Hallandale.[20]

Meyer's wedding gift to the couple was to be a house. But when he came to work out the details, he wondered if his first estimate of his new daughter-in-law had really been so wide of the mark. Jake had recently bought a home in Hollywood for his elder daughter, Ricky, who had just got married. It was a modern, but modest, free-standing house which had cost $22,000, and Meyer offered Annette and Buddy the same.

Annette said no thank you. "It was fine," she remembers, "but I didn't like the thing. It was cracker box. So I looked at a home that was thirty-two thousand. I said, 'That's what I like.' "[21]

Meyer Lansky was not amused by what he saw as extravagance in his daughter-in-law. "I'll buy you that one, or nothing," he said, indicating the less expensive choice. "If it's good enough for Ricky, it's good enough for you."[22]

Annette would not compromise, so she and Buddy had to go without a house. Her relationship with her father-in-law never quite recovered.

"He was a cold man," she remembers, "as cold as ice. He had a look. He could look right through you. He was intimidating. You didn't know why. This little man — what could he do to you? But you felt afraid."[23]

When Annette Lansky was with her father-in-law, she felt at times as if she were a defendant being questioned by a hostile attorney.

"He'd pick your brain," she remembers. "If you said, 'It's Tuesday,' he'd say, 'Why is it Tuesday? How do you know it is Tuesday?' Or you might say, 'That's a nice glass plate.' And he would say, 'How do you know it's glass, and not plastic?' If you think it's glass, you'd better know why. You couldn't make a statement without backing it up. That shirt is blue? Or is it turquoise? Turquoise is a mixture. What is it a mixture of? He was something else."[24]

Annette found it much easier to get on with Uncle Jack, whom the couple saw rather more frequently than Meyer, since it was Jake Lansky who organized the $100 a week allowance that Buddy received on top of his $100 weekly wage for working on the switchboard of the Tuscany Motel, on the border of Hollywood and Hallandale.

"Jake always had a smile on his face," Annette remembers. "You didn't feel that he was looking through your brain."[25]

Annette also felt sympathy with Buddy's mother, Anne, whom she visited in New York.

"She was a real lady," she remembers. "She had been a very elegant woman. You could see that. She had a touch of class."[26]

But Annette could also see that her mother-in-law was by no means the woman that she once had been. "There were cockroaches all around the apartment," Annette remembers. " 'Don't kill that cock-a-roach!' she would say. 'That's a person!' And for her, she was quite right. Those 'cock-a-roaches' were her friends."[27]

Annette did not take long to decide that she did not like Buddy's stepmother, Teddy. "This houserobe is wonderful . . . I'll buy it for you," Annette recalls Teddy insisting when the two women went shopping together. "It's sixty dollars reduced to ten."

"She never bought me what I wanted," Annette remembers. "It was always what she thought was a bargain."[28]

On Meyer's instructions, Teddy Lansky paid cash for everything that she bought. Credit cards and charge accounts left evidence. But she and Meyer had a post office box in Hallandale, and she gave this as her address to department store assistants, so that they could send her notification of special offers and private sale days.

"Lane," she would say, "Lane. Address it to Mrs. Lane."[29]

Annette Lansky found that she had entered a world where nothing was quite straight, where everything seemed to have a twist or hidden angle. It was seldom wise to rely on the most immediate meaning of what was said to you. Annette shared a bank account with Buddy, and the statements showed quite large sums of money shifting about.

"One day we'd have fifty thousand dollars. Next day it's down to twenty thousand. So I'd say, 'What's happening here?' And Buddy would say, 'Dad told me to write out a check.' Well, you never questioned what *Dad* did."[30]

But one day Uncle Jack came to see Annette, his normally genial composure very obviously fractured.

"Did you know," he said, "that your account is overdrawn? Buddy's been gambling. He's been passing bad checks."[31]

Buddy had lied to his wife. His check writing had been for his own expenses, not his father's — and it was still worse than that. Meyer and Jake Lansky had invested in the Tuscany Motel on Ocean Drive in the early 1950s, after their gambling joints had shut down. The motel had not done that well, and after a year or so, it needed a fresh injection of funds.

"Sell your insurance," Meyer had told Buddy, "and put it in the Tuscany."[32]

Buddy had an endowment policy with the Equitable Life that was worth $25,000. His father had taken it out for him as a child, and had paid all the premiums, so Buddy saw no problem with his father telling him, at the age of twenty-seven, what to do with money that was legally his.

"His word was the ultimate, whether I agreed or didn't agree," he said. "He was older than me. He knew better than I did. I just felt that that man couldn't make a mistake."[33]

The Tuscany did not prove a good investment for Buddy. The motel continued to go downhill, and in the late 1950s its operation passed to a group of investors headed by a Miami businessman, Milton Hoff. It was Hoff's idea to upgrade the place and turn it into a health resort — the Carlsbad Spa — and Meyer agreed to let Hoff's group have the Tuscany for the investment of their conversion costs, plus installments. They could convert and operate the motel in its new health spa name and style, paying off the purchase price from their income, month by month.[34] As one of the stockholders in the old Tuscany, Buddy received a portion of these payments.

Annette knew that her husband gambled, but she imagined that it was on the scale of $10 or $20 a time. She had no idea that, operating a credit account with one local bookmaker, Buddy had got himself in debt to the tune of $12,000.

He went for help to Joe Sonken, the operator of the Gold Coast Restaurant in Hollywood, and Sonken put him in touch with a loan shark — a shylock — who lent Buddy the $12,000.[35]

To this point, Buddy's situation had been both helped and exacerbated by the fact that he was Meyer Lansky's son. The bookmaker and the jai alai fronton at Dania, near Fort Lauderdale, where Buddy also gambled, had been happy to advance him credit and to accept his checks on the assumption that they would certainly be paid.

The shylock was not so trusting. He insisted that Buddy should surrender the stock certificate that he held in the Tuscany — and it was this that really led Buddy into trouble. When his father found out about the shylock, he paid the man off, and gave Buddy a dressing-down which he never forgot.

"You've hung around all these guys," said Meyer, scarcely believing that his own son could have become a sucker. "You know what it is."[36]

"I would rather have faced a judge," Buddy remembered, "and done five years."[37]

Twelve months after that, Buddy received a letter from the IRS. "I got a notice. Someone wants to check my records. . . . Fine. Go ahead. And I said, 'What's this all about?'"[38]

It was all about the $12,000 — which Buddy had deposited in his account relating to the Tuscany. Buddy had got himself into debt by cashing the payments from Milton Hoff's group and using them to finance his gambling. So it seemed logical to Buddy to make up his Tuscany account deficit with the cash that he borrowed from the shylock.[39]

An IRS investigation. Gambling debts. A loan shark. The transfer of business funds for illegal purposes. Financial manipulation in the name of Lansky. It was all Meyer needed in 1962 — sick, sixty, and under ever closer FBI and IRS examination. After decades of skillfully juggling his own financial affairs, hiding behind fronts, concealing cash, and successfully fighting off almost annual IRS inquiries and audits, Meyer Lansky was suddenly betrayed by his crippled son's stupidity.

"He didn't curse me out," remembered Buddy Lansky. "But he looked at me, you know. . . . I was always in awe of my father. He was the patriarch. He didn't terrify me as far as threatening to beat me or anything. It was just the way he looked at you. Cold eyes. . . ."[40]

Overwhelmed by Meyer's anger, Buddy swallowed a bottle of sleeping pills one night. "I cannot stand my father's contempt," he wrote in a suicide note which he left for Annette.[41]

His wife rushed him to the hospital, and in the months that followed helped Buddy put his life back on some sort of footing. The IRS investigators proved surprisingly forgiving once they felt sure they had got to the bottom of the $12,000 deposit and all it entailed. But the older generation of Lanskys blamed the whole mess on Annette. She had not accomplished what they had hoped of her. She had not pulled Buddy into shape. And Buddy made it worse by telling his father that he had gambled so heavily because he wanted to buy nice things for Annette.

Annette was furious when she heard it. "What nice things?" she inquired. "A nice house? A nice car? Some nice diamonds? We've had some nice meals out — and you have eaten half of them."[42]

Buddy smiled weakly. "Well," he said, "Dad thinks we should get divorced."[43]

"Buddy had got in over his head," says Annette today. "And it just compounded. I can't really blame him. He lived in his father's shadow." Buddy, Annette says, "was a kid his whole life long."[44]

One of the saddest things about Annette Lansky's short-lived marriage to Buddy, as she now looks back on it, was that Buddy never once tried to play the father to her own six-year-old son.

"There was nothing parental there," she says. "It just was not in him. Buddy had never been taught what a father should be."[45]

Meyer Lansky had scarcely provided his elder son with much of a role model — and in Annette Lansky's eyes, he was not much of a father-in-law, either. After Annette agreed to the divorce which Buddy said that his father wished, she remained true to the spirit of her unsigned prenuptial agreement and did not request any alimony or financial compensation. So Meyer sent Annette's mother some money — $1,000, in cash.[46]

"I know that she's got expenses," Meyer said.[47]

Sandra Lansky Rappaport lived a life of some luxury in Manhattan. Late in 1960, Paul and his wife, Edna, stayed in Sandra's apartment during a trip to New York, and it was then that Edna, who came from a modest southern family, realized for the first time that the Lanskys were rich.

"It was beautiful — really luxurious — with a maid who met us at the door and took the baby," she remembers. "I opened the closet one day to get something warm to put on, and I counted twenty-four fur coats."

Paul and Edna were not so impressed, however, with Sandra's lifestyle.

"Asleep all day, and out all night," remembers Edna. "'Bring me my breakfast, and don't disturb me.'"

Paul was furious.

"He was very annoyed with his sister," remembers Edna. "He was angry. She turned her son, Gary, over to the maid for hours on end. Paul said, 'The kid hasn't got the proper food.'"[48]

Paul went out and bought a crate of oranges.

Sandra moved with the fast set. One of her dates was Charles Revson, the playboy cosmetics king, famous for flooding the apartments of his girlfriends with red roses.[49] Though now separated from Marvin Rappaport, Sandra stayed on good terms with him. Marvin's homosexuality was no longer concealed. He presided over the smart, brittle crowd who met at his restaurant, Spindletop, and Sandra was quite a frequent visitor there.[50]

One of Sandra's New York friends was Ed Hartnet. Sandra had met Hartnet at West Point, where he was a contemporary and acquaintance of her brother Paul. Hartnet was handsome and out-going, and after graduating from West Point and serving out his time in the army, he decided on a change of career. Ed Hartnet became an agent with the FBI.[51]

It is difficult today to discover exactly what transpired between the FBI man and Meyer Lansky's only daughter. Hartnet is dead. Sandra will not talk. The FBI's strict rules protecting the identity of sources preclude the release of any documents. But Ed Hartnet's colleagues in the FBI remember the excitement.

The FBI had opened a file on Meyer Lansky following the allegations of the Kefauver Committee. The murder of Albert Anastasia, the Apalachin meeting, and the Cuban casino connection had intensified their interest. For most of the 1950s, the thrust of the Justice Department's investigation had been through the Immigration and Naturalization Service, whose agent, Benjamin Edelstein, had been building the dossier with which the INS hoped to bring about the deportation of Meyer Lansky. But now the FBI had a source of its own — and that source was Lansky's daughter.

Sandra Lansky Rappaport did not prove a reluctant witness. "She told us everything she could find out about him," remembered one of Hartnet's colleagues. "If we asked if he was planning a specific trip, where he was going. . . . She listened to the phone calls-and all that. . . . She tried like hell to help us to put him down."[52]

The agents were members of the FBI's Criminal Intelligence Squad, New York, and they assigned Sandra her own code number.

"Every time I called her, or I met her, or we met," remembers one of the agents, "— and I never met her alone, except in a crowded room — I dictated the memorandum for the file. The Lansky file."[53]

Sandra was probably not aware that every remark she made was noted straight afterward, so carefully. But she was under no illusion as to whom she was talking: "She knew who Eddie was. She knew who we all were. She had a real thing for her Dad — a hard-on for it. I think that's the way you'd put it. . . . She thought that he had had her mother committed so that he could marry his second wife."[54]

In the absence of her own explanation, the best rationale that can be advanced for Sandra Lansky's apparent betrayal of her father is emotional confusion and distress. She had nothing incriminating she could tell the FBI. The agents ranked her only as a "source." Eager rather than well informed, Sandra never qualified for the more formal status of "informant" — and the FBI men wondered at times about her mental stability. "Who wouldn't be wacky in that atmosphere," said one of them, "when your father puts your mother in the bin so he can marry a younger girl?"[55]

Teddy Lansky was, in fact, four years older than her predecessor, Anne. Teddy did not meet Meyer until eighteen months after he had been divorced — and this was several years after Anne had been sent away for her first spell of enforced "rest." So it was quite untrue to say that Meyer had had Anne committed in order to marry Teddy.

But Sandra Lansky, nine years old at the time of the divorce, did not know this for sure. Her experience was of uncertainty and deception — of her father bringing her down to Florida for Christmas 1948, for example, and pretending to be single, when he had, as she later discovered, married Teddy a few days earlier. Angry and rebellious, Sandra had looked for certainty in her own early marriage, to encounter another man who turned out to be other than he appeared. It was scarcely surprising that she should feel mixed up.

"She was schizo," remembers Annette Lansky of her sister-in-law in these years. "I thought she was going the way of her mother."[56]

"She was strung out," remembered Buddy. "I tried to talk to her, and couldn't. She ran around all these places. . . . She was in every bar in New York City. Every lounge. And she was on pills. Prescription pills. Diet pills. Doctors' prescriptions."[57]

"I have to get her out of New York," Meyer said to his daughter-in-law Edna one day. "The drugs are killing her."[58]

Meyer Lansky never knew that his daughter had become a source for the FBI. Nor did anyone else in the family. But Meyer did get the word about her increasingly frenetic social life.

"The owners of the lounges told Dad what was going on," remembered Buddy. "And all he could do was say 'Watch her for me.' . . . He figured there'd be trouble down the line. And sure enough, it came to trouble."[59]

One day in the early 1960s Buddy got a phone call from his sister in New York. She was feeling terrible, she said. She had got to get some treatment. She was going into the hospital.

"If Dad calls," she said, "tell him I went away for a few days."

"Sandra," replied Buddy, "I can't do that. You've already told me you're going in the hospital. . . . Who's at your house?"

"A maid."

"Can she hear you?"

"Yes."

"What do you think Dad would tell me," asked Buddy, "if he calls and asks for you, and the maid says, 'She went to the hospital and your son knows' — and I don't tell him?"

"All right," replied Sandra. "You call him and tell him."[60]

When Meyer heard that Sandra was ill enough to be hospitalized, he flew up to New York to visit her.

"They had her in a maternity ward," Meyer told Buddy, slightly puzzled, when he got back. "They said that the reason they put her there, they had no room anywhere else."[61]

Edna, Paul's wife, remembers how worried the family was when Sandra got out of the hospital.

"The poor thing looked awful . . . like something the cat had brought in. She had had the flu, and we must nurse her back to health. . . . The whole family was gathered around."[62]

Then a month or so later, Meyer got a phone call from a doctor at the hospital. There was a big bill to pay, and the doctor also wanted to know what Mr. Lansky was planning to do about the baby.

Sandra had been put in the maternity ward because she was pregnant, and she had given birth to a child. It was a boy, whom Sandra had left in the hospital, unnamed. Baby Lansky. And there was worse. Born prematurely, the child was crippled. It suffered from birth defects — cerebral palsy, or something similar.

The family rallied round. The baby was not Marvin's, and Sandra never said who the father was. But Marvin gave the child his own name — David Jay Rappaport.[63]

More help came from a most surprising quarter. Not so out of touch as she might sometimes seem, Meyer's ex-wife, Anne, made a remarkable comeback. She tied up her hair, exchanged her slippers for shoes, and clicked dramatically into action. The baby was brought out of the hospital, and Anne Lansky came over to Sandra's apartment every day to help take care of him.[64]

This was one good thing to come out of the whole mess, everyone agreed. For Anne, it was like nursing Buddy again, and she flourished for a season, suddenly useful and wanted.

But her little grandson did not make much progress. David Jay Rappaport turned out to be far more severely damaged than Buddy had been, both in mind and in body. After coping valiantly for months, Anne Lansky had to give up the unequal struggle, and in the absence of anyone else to look after him, the little boy was put in a home — "a vegetable," according to his uncle Buddy.[65] David Jay

Rappaport, now approaching his thirties, remains institutionalized to this day.

The normally calm and dispassionate Meyer Lansky was transported with rage when he found out what his daughter had done — and had failed to do. Was it the drugs that Sandra had been taking which harmed the baby? Or the fact that she had laced herself up tight to hide the evidence of her pregnancy?

Edna Lansky was some distance from the phone when Paul took the call in which his father passed on the news, and she could hear the shouting clear across the room. Paul turned white with shock.[66]

"I'm never going to visit her again," stormed Meyer to Buddy.

"What about Gary?" asked Buddy, who knew how fond his father was of Sandra's elder son.

"Well, poor Gary will have to suffer."[67]

A short time afterward, Meyer was in the hospital himself. He had come up to Peter Bent Brigham in Boston for another session with Seymour Gray, hoping to calm his ulcers, and Edna Lansky went to visit her father-in-law. Paul had been stationed in New England for a brief tour of duty.[68]

Edna usually felt on edge and somewhat apprehensive of "Grandpa," as she had taken to calling him since the birth of her own son. Meyer would cross-question her in the same fashion that he interrogated his other daughter-in-law, Annette. He was always on his mettle, in some way, with these women who married his sons, anxious to demonstrate his own mental superiority.

But on this occasion Grandpa was different. He was sick and depressed — vulnerable. He seemed almost pitiful to Edna, as he sat on the edge of the hard hospital bed in his pajamas, his short legs swinging clear of the floor. Meyer Lansky wanted to talk.

"Why is she like this?" he kept puzzling. "Why is she like this? Why couldn't she *do* something with her life?"

At this point a candy-striper, a young volunteer nurse in her white-and-red uniform, came into the room.

"Look at these little girls," he said. "They didn't go to college, but look at them! I'd be so glad if she did something like that. Why is she this way? I don't understand. She had all the money. She could have gone to school. I'd give her anything. I've always given that girl everything she could want. . . ."[69]

The home and family that Paul Lansky created with his wife, Edna, were in striking contrast to the debacles in which Buddy and Sandra played starring roles. The army sent Paul to the University of Michigan, at Ann Arbor, for two years to study for a master's degree in engineering, which he acquired with honors. The energetic Edna got her real estate license, made some useful income on the side, and bore two healthy, well-mannered children, a boy and a girl.

Paul's achievements were a reproach to his brother and sister, and he took some pride in that. "I don't ever want to be like my brother, and mooch off my old man," Paul said to his own son in later years. "You make your own way in this world."[70]

This pride could be stiff-necked at times.

"Hey, son," said Meyer, as Paul and Edna were driving him proudly around Ann Arbor at the time of Paul's graduation. "Drive down to the nearest car dealership, and I'll buy you a new car as a graduation present."

"No thank you," said Paul, suddenly rigid. "No thank you, sir."[71]

Edna Lansky thought that her husband took his independence to unnecessary extremes. All through 1957 and 1958, Meyer had sent them reports on the progress of the Riviera Hotel, with fervent invitations to come out for a holiday to Havana, all expenses paid. But Paul had refused.

"He rejected it totally," Edna remembers. "He didn't want to have a thing to do with it."[72]

Paul's prickly independence seemed to come from an anger that, like his sister's, went back far into his childhood.

"He told me once," remembers Edna, "that he had cried when he had to go away to military school as a little boy, and that he promised himself that he would never cry again."[73]

Paul's feelings echoed the protest he had articulated, as a child, at the "phony" lifestyle and income that went with his father's way of life. But beneath Paul's rejection lay an equally defiant loyalty and respect. Meyer Lansky's son had not had an easy time at West Point, trying to prove himself good, solid officer material at the same time that his father was being denounced by a U.S. Senate committee as a national menace. There was anti-Semitism among his fellow students, and even the suggestion, on the part of certain instructors, that Officer Cadet Lansky might be advised to change his name.[74]

Paul gave his answer when Edna bore their first child, on August 4, 1957 — a son. Edna had been thinking in terms of "Philip." But Paul had a better idea, which he had not mentioned until after the birth. They would call their son Meyer Lansky II.

Meyer's delight at having another grandson quite vanished when he heard the news.

"Dad got mad," Buddy remembered. "He thought it was not fair on the kid that he should have to live with that."[75]

"I told your father never to name you that," said Meyer to his grandson Meyer II, many years later, with feeling.[76]

Meyer's original objection was based on the notoriety that his name carried. But his Jewish friends who were more versed in the traditions than either Meyer or Paul gave him another reason. Jews, they explained, do not name children after the living.[77]

Edna was not very keen on the name, but her husband seemed so happy. Caught up in the pleasure and excitement of being a mother for the first time, Edna thought no more about it — until the spring of the following year, when *Life* magazine, for March 10, 1958, carried an article "Mobsters Move In on Troubled Havana." The article told the story of Batista and the Cuban casino boom. It featured the Riviera, the Capri, George Raft, and Santo Trafficante. There were a number of photographs, and there, on the very first page, in pride of place, named as "No. 1 gambler and organizer of the Havana boom," was the man that Edna knew as Grandpa.[78]

Edna was astonished.

"Here, Paul," she cried. "Look at this! Here is a picture of your father!"

Edna already knew that her husband did not like discussing his family background, but she was not prepared for the fierceness of his reaction. "He slammed the book," she remembers. "He said, 'Don't buy those things!' And he threw the book away. 'I don't want to talk about it.'"[79]

A family mystery! From that moment, Edna Lansky became more intrigued than ever with her father-in-law. Paul had proved slightly disappointing as a husband, less dashing and glamorous than his West Point background and pilot's uniform had promised. He was careful with money — oddly like his stepmother, Teddy, whom he disliked so much. He had few friends. He did not like going out, and he spent long hours closeted alone in a room which he had set up as a study.

Grandpa, by contrast, was generous. When he noticed, one day, that his daughter-in-law did not have a wristwatch, he gave her one the next time they met — solid gold and delicate, clearly expensive.[80] No one could call Meyer Lansky ostentatious or extravagant, but there were some things on which he knew that money had to be laid out, and when he had to spend, he spent properly. The high points in the life of the Paul Lanskys out in Tacoma, Washington, were the two or three occasions each year when Grandpa came out to visit.

"He would step off the plane so dignified and erect," remembers Edna. "It seemed to me he was cut of steel."[81]

Meyer did not stay at the home of his son and daughter-in-law. He would take a suite in the penthouse of Tacoma's finest hotel, the Winthrop, with a circular bed and a fine view over the waters and islands of Puget Sound.

He would drive down to the house in the afternoon to play with little Meyer. Then early in the evening came the high spot of the day — dinner out with Grandpa in the Winthrop's grand dining room, or in some other smart restaurant in Tacoma or Seattle.

Paul considered eating out an extravagance, "but when Grandpa came," remembers Edna, "we went fancy."[82]

"I used to think he knew everybody," says Meyer II today, still impressed by the way in which maître d's and waiters would bustle round his grandfather, making sure that he was comfortable, and that he had everything he needed.

"He would walk right into the kitchen — and people would let him, as if he owned the place."

Meyer II remembers his grandfather as favoring navy bean soup, and as always being picky about his food. "It had to be just right. Always plain. No mayonnaise. No butter. Just a few spices. The interesting thing would be to watch the waiter get it wrong, then to see how quickly it would go back to the kitchen.

"'Waiter,' he would say in his deep voice, 'I said *no* onions.'"[83]

The visits were warm family occasions, still remembered by Edna Lansky and her children as treasured, halcyon days. After one miscarriage, Edna had a second child in May 1965, a daughter. This time, it was Edna's turn to give the baby a name, and she chose her own mother's name, Myra, which complemented little Meyer's name while also doing additional, incidental homage to Grandpa.[84]

The arrival of Myra made the family gatherings — usually in Tacoma, more rarely in Florida — even more warm and enjoyable. But there was a distance separating Paul and his father, Edna came to notice. It was less a coldness or hostility than an emptiness — as if the two men had nothing much to share. Father and son were like strangers together. They never seemed close, and they never talked of anything personal.

"Gandhi, Golda Meir, the government," remembers Edna. "It was all very important, what they talked about. But they never hugged or kissed."[85]

Edna noticed how, at airport greetings and farewells, her father-in-law almost flinched, maneuvering his body around the geography of the occasion in order to avoid physical contact.

Paul's elder brother was warmer and more tactile. When Buddy came to stay, Meyer and Myra loved to play with their uncle, teasing and tickling him as he lay helplessly in bed. Buddy would chuckle and cry out in mock panic as the two children spun him around in the wheelchair in which he now had to sit quite a lot of the time.

But Paul remained unmoved. He went on with his life as if the family did not have a houseguest — let alone his own brother — staying with them. Paul would come home dourly from work and go straight up to his study as usual. When the two brothers did sit together, they were strained and uncomfortable, talking about politics, or sports teams, or the weather.

"They were like two businessmen sitting there," says Myra Lansky, remembering her father and uncle sitting woodenly, side by side, in their armchairs.[86]

Edna wondered if the trouble stemmed from the traumas of the divorce of their parents, about which Paul would only speak rarely and grudgingly — or, more worryingly, if it reflected some mental weakness inherited from their mother. The first time Paul had taken Edna to visit his mother in New York, Anne Lansky had shut the door in their faces, not recognizing him.

"I'm busy now," she said.[87]

At the second try, she recognized Paul but seemed confused about the time frame. "How's school, son?" she asked.

Anne was in her nightgown and slippers, with long, straight hair that was turning gray and hanging down her back in a thick, uncut, uncombed strand. She chain-smoked, talking to Edna, then breaking off every few minutes, for no apparent reason, to whistle.

"She had a habit of going to the bathroom and flushing the toilet every three or four minutes," remembers Edna. "She would flush the toilet for no reason, then come back and smoke and whistle."

After some time, Edna asked if she could use the bathroom herself.

"She said, 'Yes, it's right in here.' So we passed through her bedroom." There, set out casually on shelves and cupboards, were several years of Christmas and birthday presents sent to Anne, none of which she had bothered to unwrap — while in the bed, which had been carefully made that day, were some of Anne's "friends": a dead canary and two dead cockroaches.

"She had them laying on the pillow with the cover turned back. 'Shh!' she said, 'they're sleeping!'"[88]

Anne Lansky was, in fact, looking after herself rather better than her eccentricities might suggest. She was living comfortably within the limits of her alimony payments from Meyer, and she seemed able to pull herself together if she felt that the situation really required it, as when she rallied to help care for Sandra's spastic baby. Invited to visit Paul, Edna, and little Meyer when they were stationed in Boston in the early 1960s, Anne organized herself onto the plane and got herself safely there and back again without any special assistance.

The evidence that Anne Lansky could have been leading a reasonably normal and fulfilled life, if only she had had some basic care and company, intensified Paul Lansky's animus toward the woman who had taken his mother's place. Meyer never brought Teddy with him when he came out to Tacoma.

"It was just an unspoken thing that Teddy was not welcome," Edna recalls, "and Dad accepted that."[89]

Hostility to their stepmother was one of the few things that Meyer Lansky's three different, and increasingly separate, adult children had in common. "Everyone agreed Teddy was crude and loud and flashy," remembers Edna. "Even his friends would complain that she would go into bargain basements and those sorts of places to buy her clothes."[90]

The trouble was that Paul Lansky could scarcely complain at that particular characteristic in his stepmother. As the years went by, his own commendable insistence on being nondependent had progressed to something which his wife considered close to miserliness.

"He would check through what I brought home from the supermarket, and get angry if I'd bought Heinz ketchup," she remembers. "'Buy generic!' he would say. 'Heinz costs three cents extra.'"[91]

"It became sort of obsessive," remembers his daughter, Myra. "He started telling Mom to wear a uniform in the house instead of a new dress each day, to save laundry costs."[92]

Paul refused to buy himself a new car, insisting on driving around in a battered old Ford Falcon, whose venerability embarrassed both his wife and his children. When Edna bought herself a four-year-old Cadillac with the money that she made out of her own real estate dealings, Paul was furious. The car was a '59 Eldorado, a riot of yellow and chrome fins.

"There's your Cadillac," said Paul grimly to Edna one day, when a similar model drove by occupied by a family of blacks.[93]

Paul and Edna Lansky were growing apart, and among the several reasons for their disenchantment was the fact that Edna had persuaded Paul to give up his career in the military. Edna was tired of moving her family around. In the early 1960s, she had had to shuttle her home and baby from Ann Arbor, Michigan, to Boston, down to Florida for a few months, back to Washington — seven moves in eight years. It was in the course of all this traveling that she had had her miscarriage.[94]

In 1962, Paul went to Vietnam for a year, leaving his wife and son at home. He was one of the first of the American "advisers" sent to Saigon by the Kennedy administration, and when his tour was over, Paul bowed to Edna's wish not to sign on for another term. He came back to civilian life in Washington State, working first for a timber company and then for Boeing, as one of the engineers hired for the Apollo space program.

Paul's specialty was cost control. At the timber company, he worked out a more efficient and uniform process for packing waste sawdust into artificial fireplace logs. At Boeing, where he had one of the highest security clearances, Paul worked on the design and pricing of components used in the lunar program.[95]

Edna thought that her husband brought too much of his cost control home with him — and too much of his work as well. Paul would spend whole weekends shut away from the family in his study with the door firmly locked, indifferent to the entreaties of Edna, and even of his seven-year-old son.

"You're not coming in, so you might as well give up," Meyer Lansky II remembers his father shouting through the door, as Meyer II knocked and pleaded with his father to come out and play with him.[96]

It could not be said that Paul acquired this cold and distant version of parenting from his father. Meyer Lansky did play with his own children from time to time.

"He believed in families," remembered Buddy Lansky.[97]

There were the family summers on the Jersey shore. Every Christmas in New York, Meyer had taken the children to see the skaters in Rockefeller Plaza, then on to Radio City Music Hall.[98] Meyer Lansky might not have been a demonstrative, hugging parent by the standards of Dr. Benjamin Spock, but he enjoyed family life, and he made some effort to give it texture and ritual.

On the other hand, there was a great deal of Meyer in the secret and separate life which Paul Lansky created for himself in Tacoma, Washington. Paul seemed to derive a sense of security — of power, even — from his secrecy. The big silence had been the rule in his family as a child. You did not talk about the really important, central things.

Paul clearly had his grievances and differences with his wife, Edna, resentments and angers that seethed away inside him. But he dealt with them as he had seen his father deal with his disagreements with Anne. Meyer would stalk out into the night without saying a word. Paul Lansky would go into his study and lock the door.

Over the years, a daybed went into the study, Paul's clothes, and a television as well. Paul would pat his desk affectionately, and call it "my friend."[99] But there was no longer much pretense that the study existed for the purpose of his work. It had become, in many ways, the principal focus of the ex-USAF captain's solitary and detached life.

One of the few pleasures that Paul Lansky took with his family was the playing of recordings of West Point marches at full volume on the phonograph. Paul would stand in the center of the room, recapturing the pleasures of his cadet days in the early fifties, when his father would come up proudly to see him parade. Delighted to have a game that she could play with her daddy, little Myra, two or three years old, would march in circles around her father, saluting him, and raising her knees high in the air.[100]

"I would march for hours," Myra remembers, "until Mom told me that I had to stop."[101]

From Edna Lansky's point of view, all of this was strange, but none of it was absolutely intolerable. She had her real estate sales and investment businesses, in one of which she was a partner with Paul — Lancer Investments, a name derived from Paul's call sign when he was a pilot. The children were at good schools, and Edna had managed to buy a solid family house in the quiet and scenic streets of the North End, Tacoma's smartest neighborhood. Grandpa would shake his head in admiration every time he came to stay. What a gorgeous home! Edna had really made a fine life for his son and his grandchildren, he would tell his daughter-in-law with gratitude.

Then Edna started noticing the withdrawals from the bank account.

"Fifty dollars, fifty dollars, fifty dollars. Cash, cash, cash . . . ," remembers Edna Lansky. "Two and three times a week, fifty dollars."[102]

"I have to have lunch," said Paul defensively.

"For fifty dollars?" queried Edna. When had Paul last spent fifty dollars on a meal out for her or the children?

Some evenings, Edna started noticing, Paul was getting home two or three hours late.

"There was a competition on at the mall," he explained on one occasion. "I went all around putting our name in."[103]

One day in 1965 when Edna had been resting in her room, pregnant with Myra, she walked out into the hall, startling Paul, who had not realized that his wife was in the house.

"Oh! Hiya, Peaches!" said Paul, taken by surprise.

"Peaches?" asked Edna, suddenly suspicious. "Who's Peaches?"

Paul reddened and stuttered, and went to his room.

Paul Lansky, his wife discovered, had a secret life which extended some way beyond his hours at home, locked away in his study. One day when the couple were out shopping together, Paul grew suddenly excited, and took Edna to look inside one of the new Japanese massage and bathhouses that were springing up in the Tacoma area, particularly in the neighborhood of the McChord and Fort Lewis military bases.

"Look at all these little rooms," he said, apparently quite familiar with the way, leading his wife through to the back, where the girls bowed and giggled submissively.

Suddenly, Edna guessed what had been going on for years — since her husband came back from Vietnam, by her reckoning — and when she confronted Paul with it, he confessed.

"Grandpa," cried Edna, calling Meyer long distance in Florida. "I've got a very bad problem. . . . I want you to come out here right away. I don't want to talk about it on the phone."

Meyer was out in Tacoma within hours. Paul and Edna went to talk to him at the Winthrop, away from the children.

"What's the problem?" asked Meyer.

"Well, Dad," said Edna, and she broke off, starting to cry.

"Wait a minute, honey, I'll tell him," said Paul — and he did.

Edna could not believe the look that came over the face of her father-in-law. "His mouth actually fell open and it was like he froze for a moment. . . . He could not have been whiter, I swear, if he had been in his coffin. I felt so sorry for him. I thought, 'Oh, my God!

Why did we do this to him?'. . . . It was like pulling the pins right out from under him."

Then Meyer Lansky got angry.

"He was a soft-spoken man. He never raised his voice. But he came unglued. If looks could have killed . . . . And Paul was shaken. He was shaking so hard and standing in front of his father like a little tin soldier — 'Sir! Sir! Yes, sir! Yes, sir!' Well, he just lectured him. He read him off real good."

Meyer Lansky stayed at the Winthrop for a couple more days, until everyone had calmed down a little. Edna and Paul came to see him off at the airport, and as Meyer walked down toward his plane, he turned and fixed his son with his basilisk gaze.

"You shape up!" he said. "You get in line with your family!"[104]

"Every one of us hurt our father," said Buddy Lansky. "Every one of us. There is no exception to the rule. Nobody can say, 'I was perfect,' 'cause God knows, I wasn't. Sandra, that's another story. And Paul was another . . ."[105]

"When I knew him," says Annette Lansky, talking of Meyer, "he actually worked quite hard to be a father. In my opinion, he really tried. . . . Trouble was, I don't think any of them had any idea how a family ought to work."[106]

16

"Bigger Than U.S. Steel"

IN May 1962, Meyer Lansky was recovering from his latest bout of heart trouble. He had just been released from the Trafalgar Hospital in New York and was staying nearby in the Volney Hotel, where he spent most of his time in his room, chatting idly with Teddy and with friends who came to visit.

The FBI was listening to every word he said.[1]

J. Edgar Hoover had changed his views on organized crime since the uncovering of the Apalachin meeting five years earlier. Apalachin had shown, beyond reasonable contradiction, that the big-city criminal syndicates had contacts with each other that extended across state lines. They might not constitute the integrated and centralized "secret government" pictured by Estes Kefauver, but they were groups of men who systematically broke the law and who corrupted public officials in more than one state. That put them squarely in the FBI's bailiwick, and Hoover set out to pursue them with his customary thoroughness.

"Meyer Lansky [is] one of the very most important individuals in the national crime picture," minuted the FBI director to his offices in Miami and New York. "You should not overlook the possibility of employing extraordinary investigative techniques."[2]

282

The "extraordinary investigative techniques" which the FBI belatedly turned upon organized criminals and gamblers at the end of the 1950s had been developed by the Bureau in its cold war campaigns against Russian spies and Communist infiltrators. For a whole generation of FBI agents, it was quite routine to break into homes and offices, to steal or copy documents, to tap telephones, and to install hidden microphones — without any form of warrant or court order. The agents knew, in fact, that if they were caught and exposed in the course of their illicit activities, they would be disowned by the very superiors, including Hoover, who had given them their orders.[3]

In New York, the FBI had developed a more subtle method of surveillance. Agents worked out arrangements with some of the principal hotels, whereby certain rooms and suites should contain hidden wires and microphones, with the hotel's knowledge, on a virtually permanent basis. The hotel would then allocate these "sound studios" to suspects on whom the Bureau wanted to eavesdrop.[4]

There was no such arrangement at the Volney on East Seventy-fourth Street, a small and rather remote hotel which the Lanskys had selected on account of its proximity to the Trafalgar Hospital. But the managers of the hotel were willing to cooperate with the FBI, and it was with their knowledge that Meyer's conversation was monitored in the spring of 1962.[5]

The lengthy FBI transcripts of the goings-on in room 8E of the Volney Hotel in the late spring of 1962 were heavy on personal detail, but none of it proved very criminal. According to one transcript, Meyer was currently reading a history book, a grammar book, and a book of French quotations — all at the same time.

"He stated these are the things you need with no education, because you can get mixed up."[6]

His dietary tastes were noted to include matzos, sardines, Jell-O, Irish lamb stew, and ham.[7]

Meyer philosophized from time to time. "Some people never learn to be good," he remarked. "One quarter of us is good. Three quarters is bad. That's a tough fight, three against one. . . ."[8]

The conversation got around to wiretapping, and the bill to regulate it that was currently before Congress.[9] Wiretapping was "okay against the Communists," declared Teddy Lansky, but otherwise it was "most sickening." In her opinion, President Kennedy and his brother Robert, the attorney general, who had stepped up the fight against organized crime since 1960, were acting "sincerely and in their best beliefs."

Meyer disagreed.

He was brought up "on the wrong side of the fence," Teddy reminded him.

Better say the "unhypocritical" side, Meyer replied.[10]

Meyer Lansky spent a lot of time discussing his own ailments, and those of his friends and acquaintances. Toothaches, crutches, rheumatism, heart trouble — nobody seemed to be in very good shape, and Meyer felt particularly sorry for himself. Making a living, he complained, was "taking a lot out of [me]." How lucky people were that "just fall into it."[11]

Then, on the evening of Sunday, May 27, 1962, David Susskind came on the television, presenting his program "Open End." It took the form of a documentary report on organized crime, followed by a discussion among a studio panel of experts who included Gus Tyler, the editor of a recent book of readings on the subject, and the Washington attorney Edward Bennett Williams. Meyer sat in silence through the discussion, according to the FBI report, until one of the panelists "referred to organized crime as only being second in size to the government itself. Lansky remarked to his wife that organized crime was bigger than US Steel."[12]

This comment does not survive on tape. It was standard FBI procedure for the agents who were running a Misur, or microphone surveillance, to listen to a tape, take notes, and then put the tape back onto the machine, recording and rerecording over it many times, since the bug was intended to gather intelligence, not evidence.

Nor was Meyer's comment written into the Misur report of May 27, 1962, as a direct quotation. Agents would exercise their own judgment as to whether they transcribed a tape word for word or chose to paraphrase it. In the case of Meyer Lansky's remark to his wife, the written transcript shows that the agent chose to paraphrase.

Somehow, however, by the time that Lansky's comment became public five years later, leaked from the original report via channels that cannot be determined, the paraphrase had turned into a direct quotation — and it had also been subtly altered:

"We're bigger than U.S. Steel."[13]

Life magazine attributed this remark to Meyer Lansky in September 1967.[14] Two years later, *Time* repeated the "boast" in a seven-page feature that it ran on "The Conglomerate of Crime," in August 1969.[15] Five years after that, cinema audiences around the world saw

Hyman Roth, the Meyer Lansky character in *The Godfather II*, narrow his eyes and whisper, "Michael! We're bigger than U.S. Steel!"

Meyer Lansky tried to disown the words which, after their first publication, came to be attributed to him so often that they became his popular trademark.

"When am I supposed to have said that?" he would ask, aggrieved.[16]

Meyer Lansky fancied himself a student of history. As he received his Book-of-the-Month Club biographies, he would dive into them eagerly, reading with his dictionary open beside him so that he could check on new words, filling his mind with fresh knowledge. Meyer had little time for novels. He was scornful of mere fiction. History was the truth, he would say to his son Buddy, the telling of real facts.[17]

But as Meyer Lansky became part of history himself, he discovered that the facts could be rearranged — and even improved upon somewhat — in the telling.

In the spring of 1960, Meyer Lansky located life in an ancient investment. He reported fresh income from his old Las Vegas venture with Ben Siegel — the Flamingo Hotel Casino.

Meyer had never been actively involved with the management of the Flamingo. He visited Las Vegas infrequently, making his last visit ever in 1956.[18] In the late 1950s, Meyer's tax returns had showed some minor interest payments from his long-standing holdings in the Nevada Project Corporation, and in 1958 he wrote off his original investment as a capital loss.[19] Since the Flamingo had made a handsome operating profit every year since Ben's death in 1947, it must be presumed that Meyer received his real share of the profit in some form of skim, delivered to him in cash.

The partners who owned, or in some cases fronted, investments in the Flamingo, had changed over the years. In 1960, they included Albert Parvin — whose company, Parvin-Dohrman, had supplied most of the furnishings for the Havana Riviera — the actor and Havana hero George Raft, and the singer Tony Martin. These were among the owners listed as selling the Flamingo, in May 1960, for a purchase price of $10.6 million, to three Miami Beach hoteliers — Sam Cohen, Morris Lansburgh, and Daniel Lifter.[20]

Meyer Lansky's name was not mentioned in the sale documents, though he had, in fact, brought buyer and seller together. Albert Parvin had told Meyer of his wish to unload the Flamingo, and Meyer knew that the Miami hoteliers — Morris Lansburgh in particular — were anxious to get a foothold in Las Vegas.[21] So Meyer had acted as go-between, and in return he claimed a 2 percent finder's fee — $200,000.

It was normal in Las Vegas casino transactions for this sort of cut to be handled as cash under the table. Nevada did not consider itself part of America when it came to paying its share to the IRS. But in the sale of the Flamingo — a legal transaction, openly conducted — Meyer saw the chance to secure himself some "show money."[22] The $36,000 which he declared as his annual "salary" as "restaurant and cabaret manager" of the Havana Riviera had come to an end with the hotel's confiscation and loss. His Flamingo finder's fee — divided into thirty-two quarterly installments of $6,250, to be paid over eight years — provided the ideal replacement. So Meyer declared the first four installments of his finder's fee — a total of $25,000 — on his tax return for 1961.[23] In the early 1960s, Meyer Lansky needed to show $35,000 or so every year to demonstrate how he lived.

Since 1951, when Estes Kefauver had exhorted government agencies to focus more closely on the malefactors that his Senate committee had identified, the IRS had been subjecting Meyer Lansky's tax returns to special scrutiny. The intelligence division had been executing complicated calculations based on what it could find out about Meyer's home, his cars, his family commitments, and so on. The aim was to arrive at a "net worth analysis" — an estimate of what Meyer's real income and expenditure might be. The hope was to compare this figure to his declared income and to identify a difference that might prove Meyer Lansky guilty of underdeclaration, and hence tax evasion.

In 1953, the IRS had filed a "jeopardy assessment" against Meyer for nearly a quarter of a million dollars, claiming taxes that he had not paid, by its calculation, in the years 1944–47. Meyer fought back with more detailed figures, and an affidavit to the effect that he had, in his gambling activities in the eleven years up to January 1, 1944, built up cash in hand of $150,000.[24] With the help of Moses Polakoff, Meyer had got the assessment withdrawn in 1956 with a payment of $9,000[25] — but he was more careful with the tax returns that he submitted thereafter.

Every year the IRS special agents went to work on the figures that Meyer provided in his tax return, and every year they were disappointed. Meyer Lansky had genuinely sober tastes. He did eat out quite a lot of the time, and he was partial to quality clothes. But

Meyer indulged none of the extravagance which characterized many of the suspects that the official documents referred to as "hoodlums." In Hallandale, Meyer and Teddy drove unpretentious Chevrolets, leased at moderate, long-term rates from a local car rental agency.[26] The house that they bought for themselves was modesty itself.

The Lanskys' low, compact bungalow at 612 Hibiscus Drive, Hallandale, lay in Golden Isles, a residential development close to the Broward-Dade county line. The house was slightly grander than those that Annette Lansky called "cracker box," but only marginally so. It was like tens of thousands of other concrete-block ranch homes backing onto brown canals between Miami Beach and Fort Lauderdale. When Meyer and Teddy bought the house in 1959, new from the builder, it cost them $49,000, with a mortgage of $34,000.[27]

Finding a bolt-hole — the first home that Meyer Lansky had ever owned — had been both a precaution and a consolation in the dismaying months in which Meyer had watched his Cuban investment disappear. Until the advent of Castro, Havana had been the Lanskys' main base. Meyer had his suite in the Riviera, and Teddy had furnished an apartment nearby with new furniture shipped in from the States.[28] When they came back on trips to Florida, they had stayed in the Tuscany on South Ocean Drive in Hollywood, which was the closest they had to an American address.

Teddy loved her new little home in the Golden Isles development, and she threw herself into decorating it in her own particular style. Beige, blue, and lavender were the keynotes of her color scheme, as Annette Lansky remembers it. "Nothing at retail, of course," recalls Teddy's former daughter-in-law. "Everything on sale, or forget it."[29]

The FBI agents who drove down Hibiscus Drive to plot their surveillance patterns could not understand it. The Lanskys' house was in a dead-end street. Number 612 had no back alley or means of escape to the rear, except by water. It was one of the first homes built in the development, so it stood, for the moment, almost alone on its long, thin, man-made island.[30] This would make it difficult for an agent to watch the house without being conspicuous — until a few other homes were built, at least.

On the other hand, there was only one road leading to and from the house, with only one entrance to the entire area. The "Golden Isles" were like so many branches off the central trunk of a Christmas tree. Unless Meyer Lansky was planning to come and go by boat, a single surveillance car parked on the central, feeder road could monitor his every coming and going — and his every visitor as well. If this man was a national crime boss, he could not sensibly be planning on holding any operational meetings at his own home.

There were those in the Miami office of the FBI who wondered whether Meyer was much of a crime boss at all. Washington had designated Lansky a target for priority investigation,[31] but a strand of south Florida thinking continued to doubt the easy linking of gambling and organized crime. It seemed a poor use of Bureau resources to be trailing Meyer Lansky as he limped in and out of heart clinics.

"There are more important and active top hoodlums in the Miami area," Miami minuted to headquarters in February 1961.[32]

Lansky was clearly ill. He seemed to be inactive. Investigation to date had "never established concrete evidence that Meyer Lansky has ever directly violated a federal statute under the FBI's primary investigative jurisdiction."[33]

J. Edgar Hoover had no time for objections. "Lansky has been designated for quote crash unquote investigation," he insisted in one of his peppery, all-capital-letter teletypes. "The importance of this case cannot be overemphasized. . . . The Bureau expects this investigation to be vigorous and detailed." It was his specific recommendation, Hoover minuted, that Miami should consider deploying a "highly confidential source" — the FBI code for a bug.[34]

Miami did not argue again. Its engineers went to work. Whenever they were sure that Meyer and Teddy were out of town, FBI men secretly entered and explored the interior of 612 Hibiscus Drive, charting the location of the phone, Meyer's desk, and where he might be expected to entertain his guests.

"Attempts to establish HCS [highly confidential source] continuing," reported Miami to Washington on May 25, 1962, "but technical problems are formidable."[35]

It was not until June 12, 1962, that the agents struggling with their technical problems were able to report success — only hours before Meyer and Teddy landed at Miami airport after their stay at the Volney in New York.

"Microphone surveillance established in study of subject's residence, 612 Hibiscus Drive, Golden Isles, Hallandale, Florida, at 1:00 P.M., this date," they reported in triumph.[36] A month later they were able to report that a second "confidential source" had been deployed in the subject's residence.[37]

The reports do not make clear how the FBI men were able to break into the Lanskys' home at least twice in order to set up the mechanics of their eavesdropping, but Meyer had certainly not installed elaborate security arrangements. In March of the following year, he called the local police to report the theft from his home of a TV set, some jewelry, and a fur coat of Teddy's, together with $250 in cash. The thief had, apparently, forced open a sliding glass patio door while Meyer and Teddy were out enjoying a late Sunday supper.[38]

To all appearances, Meyer Lansky was leading the life of any other Florida retiree in his early sixties, taking things slowly and spending quite a lot of his time playing with his grandchildren, among whom were now included the children of Teddy's son, Richard Schwartz. The watching FBI agents noted long hours of fishing, as Meyer sat on his back porch.[39] Indoors, their listening devices monitored nothing much more exciting than domestic bickering:

"12/22/62: Later in the evening Meyer and Teddy have another argument . . ."[40]

"I don't care if the whole house falls down," Meyer was recorded as shouting at Teddy in the course of one row. "I want you to take care of me first!"[41]

Meyer usually started his day in the coffee shop of the Tuscany or at the nearby Diplomat Hotel, eating breakfast with his brother, Jake, and with friends like Jimmy Alo. In the afternoon the company might gravitate to Gulfstream, to follow the horses, or risk a dollar or so on the dogs at Bill Syms's Hollywood Kennel Club.

One of Meyer's frequent companions at the track was Benjamin Sigelbaum, a short and scrappy wheeler-dealer who had made his money in the electrical supply business, and from dabbling in local real estate — he sold Wolfie Cohen the land for the Rascal House.[42] Sigelbaum had hung around the Broward gambling joints in the 1940s. He had a brain for figures and odds,[43] and he had got close to Meyer in Havana at the Riviera — in which, some said, Sigelbaum had had a stake. Rotund and self-important, with a penchant for wearing gold medallions and one-piece jumpsuits which did not flatter his figure, Ben Sigelbaum added a garish note to the group.

As Meyer recovered from his heart problems, he started to take moderate exercise, venturing out on leisurely rounds of golf at the Hollywood Country Club, a municipal course which was no longer a club, and where membership was not required. One morning the FBI man assigned to that day's surveillance tracked him down at the driving range, working quite seriously on his swing.[44]

Teddy would fly off the handle whenever she got a chance to confront the men whose almost daily presence — down the street, or in the car behind theirs — became, in these years, a new and uninvited fixture in the life of the Lanskys.

It was "a shame," she complained to one agent who came to her door, asking for Meyer. The way that the FBI was pestering his friends, snooping around and asking questions, was "a source of embarrassment." Her husband had "a clean record and nothing to hide."

"Mrs. Lansky went into a tirade," reported the agent, "about the 'harassing tactics of the FBI.'"[45]

Meyer was more politic, declining to discuss his own business when questioned, but giving quite full and frank answers if the question did not concern him directly. To save themselves the journey, and long hours of waiting, agents would sometimes telephone him at home with what their reports described as "pretext calls" to check on his whereabouts. Meyer would always take the calls, and the reports described his responses to them as "friendly" and "helpful."[46]

If Meyer was due to go away, he often phoned, or had his lawyer phone, the Miami FBI office, to let them know his travel plans — and he would treat it as a joke, in a grim sort of way, when he spotted new "shadows" waiting for him at the Seattle-Tacoma airport on a visit to Paul and his family, or up in Boston when he checked into Peter Bent Brigham Hospital.

It was the FBI who would first warn Seymour Gray when his notorious patient was due for a checkup.

"They'd phone and say, 'Meyer's back in town,'" Dr. Gray remembers. "So I'd check with Eileen, my secretary, and sure enough she'd say 'Yes. He's due, such-and-such a date.'"

"How is it that they know so much about you?" Gray asked Meyer on one occasion.

"Doc," Meyer replied, "they know everything."[47]

The answer feigned lightheartedness. But as Meyer's ulcer specialist, Seymour Gray detected more bitterness in his patient's tone than he was entirely happy with.

Vincent Alo was like his friend and neighbor Meyer Lansky. He liked to view himself as semiretired. Living a mile or so to the north of Meyer, on a somewhat grander and more open stretch of water in Hollywood, Jimmy Blue Eyes took things easy, happy to be operating at a certain remove from the street crime and violence with which his career had started. Jimmy had spent several years in Sing Sing in the

1920s, convicted of armed robbery, and he never tried to suggest that this was undeserved. To friends, in fact, Jimmy Alo would confess that he had carried off several quite successful bank robberies in his youth.[48]

Two years younger than Meyer, Jimmy Alo was a couple of inches taller. He had a lean, almost ascetic face. His cheeks were sunken. The central, projecting bone of his nose appeared very sharp, and his eyes were, indeed, a blue of the most compelling clarity and strength. In *The Godfather, Part II*, Jimmy Alo was represented, the vowels cleverly shuffled, by a character named Johnny Ola. But Johnny Ola, the silent and sinister Italian bodyguard of Hyman Roth, bore little resemblance to the real-life Jimmy Alo — as Jimmy's friends knew him, at least.

Alo's manner was contemplative, and his tastes were bookish and almost intellectual, like Meyer's.

"A well self-educated man," remembered Buddy Lansky. "Well read. Could tell you anything. Discuss world politics — and one of the nicest people you'll ever want to meet."[49]

Though still wreathed, like Meyer, with an aura of toughness, Jimmy Blue Eyes had come, in his senior years, to exude wisdom and even a certain kindliness, so that people felt drawn to him for advice. There was something pastoral, almost monkish, about him. When John Huston, the film director, met Jimmy Alo in Rome in the mid-1960s, he was captivated by the man, spending long hours in his company. Huston was filming the Dino de Laurentiis epic *The Bible*, in which Alo and some of his partners had a financial stake, and Huston was not entirely joking when he lobbied for Alo to play the role of God.[50]

Meyer and Jimmy agreed that their friendship went way back — so far back, in fact, that they had different stories of how it started. They had become working partners in the 1930s, when Potatoes Kaufman consented to cut Jimmy and his associates in on the gambling in Broward County, and they had stuck together all the way through, Jimmy pleading guilty and paying his gambling fine along with Meyer and Jake when the end came in 1950.

Representing himself and some of his New York associates, Jimmy Alo had invested with Meyer in the Riviera in Havana, and earlier in the Flamingo in Las Vegas. He was the last of Meyer's Italian partners, significantly more low key than Luciano, Adonis, or Costello, and outlasting them all for that reason — as Meyer did. Jimmy Blue Eyes was the link between Meyer's gambling expertise and the cash generated by the lucrative street, labor, and construction rackets of New York and New Jersey. In the early 1960s, the two men came to work more closely together — almost as a team.

As the study of organized crime — part science, part gossip, part theology — developed in the years after Apalachin, its experts tried to codify Jimmy Blue Eyes and his relationship with Meyer Lansky. Vincent Alo, they said, was a *capo regime* — a captain — in the Vito Genovese crime family.[51] As for Meyer, well, he was Jewish, and as such, he clearly did not qualify for membership in the Mafia, or La Cosa Nostra — which, following the confessions of Joseph Valachi, was the label of choice of the FBI. So Meyer was accorded the rank of "LCN Associate."[52]

Joseph Valachi, testifying before the Senate Permanent Subcommittee on Investigations in September and October 1963, made the point which Estes Kefauver had refused to believe a dozen years earlier, that no one who was involved in what outsiders called the Mafia ever actually used the word.

"We say, 'Cosa Nostra,'" Valachi explained to John McClellan, the committee's chairman.[53]

Cosa Nostra could be literally translated as Our Thing, and the term helpfully conveyed the impression of organized crime as a way of life, rather than as a corporate structure.

But Joseph Valachi was only a comparatively minor figure in one subgroup of New York Italian criminals. The strength of his testimony was that he had had firsthand experience of life in this group. His weakness was that he knew little, at first hand, about crime elsewhere — in Chicago, for example, where Capone's successors talked neither of Cosa Nostra or Mafia, but of The Outfit.

"I'm only a two-dollar bum," Jimmy Blue Eyes was reported as saying, "and Valachi is dirt under *my* feet."[54]

Valachi's credentials as a small-time hood were impeccable, but like any self-respecting wiseguy offered a credulous audience that was in no position to contradict him, he could not resist the temptation to tell tall stories.[55] His memoirs, *The Valachi Papers,* written by Peter Maas in 1968, repeated as gospel the story of how, in 1931, Lucky Luciano organized the purge of "some forty Cosa Nostra leaders . . . slain across the country" — all in a single day.[56]

Valachi's pooh-poohing of "the Mafia" provided J. Edgar Hoover with welcome ammunition in his long-standing dispute with Harry Anslinger, the drug enforcement chief, as to whether there really was an organization with that name. Hoover hastened to proclaim the existence of La Cosa Nostra as a nationwide menace. But "La Cosa Nostra" was a title of the FBI's own adaptation and devising. "Cosa Nostra" had been Valachi's term, without the definite article. So after all the arguments, the FBI dedicated itself to the pursuit of an entity which did not literally exist.

The FBI and other law enforcement agencies compounded this by setting out their criminal intelligence data on huge organization charts, complete with photographs. These charts had the virtue of demonstrating, in graphic and human terms, the pool of criminal activity in any major city. But they reflected the bureaucratic and semimilitary cast of thought prevailing in the average police office. Everybody had a rank, and they did little justice to the confused, fluid, and essentially entrepreneurial character of most criminal activity.

"You don't get any salary, Senator," said Joseph Valachi, trying to explain to Senator Karl Mundt of South Dakota that being in a crime family was more like belonging to a trade association than having a job.

"Well," persisted Mundt, "you get a cut then."

"You get nothing," repeated Valachi. "Only what you earn yourself. Do you understand?"[57]

Jimmy Alo and Meyer Lansky had this much in common with Valachi. They were entrepreneurs, not components in a corporate structure. They had their ties, and links, and loyalties — partners they had worked with before, friends who wanted some spare capital invested. They seized their opportunities where they found them, and as legalized gambling expanded in Nevada, Jimmy had found many of his opportunities in Las Vegas. He supervised the New York interests in a number of Vegas casinos, among them the Sands, built in 1952[58] on the Strip, a quarter of a mile into town from the Flamingo.

The Sands hotel-casino was headed by Jack Entratter, the one-time doorman-bouncer at the Stork Club who had risen to be maître d' at the Copacabana before coming out to Las Vegas. But one day in the early 1960s, an acquaintance of Entratter's who had business at the Sands discovered that the hotel's power structure was not quite what it seemed.

Jimmy Alo had flown into town to inspect his investment, and Entratter made the mistake of welcoming him in the new suite that he had just had built for himself at the cost of over $1 million. Entratter was puffing on a fat cigar, and as he showed Alo around the suite, gloatingly detailing its cost, he was accompanied by a bevy of his fellow Sands directors — looking for all the world like a parade of penguins as they waddled behind him, nodding contentedly in their shiny, tailored suits.

Jimmy Alo said nothing to start with. But as he grew more and more silent and rigid, it became obvious that his temperature was rising. Suddenly, he exploded.

"I should have left you a headwaiter," he said. "You come over here and spend millions of dollars. You smoke your big cigars. You dress in your two-thousand-dollar suits. And you're nothing more than lackeys. . . . I should send you all back where you belong."[59]

At that moment, it became very easy to believe that Jimmy Alo had once robbed banks for a living — and to see who it was who really decided what happened at the Sands Hotel.

Jack Entratter had a 12 percent holding in the Sands — twelve points, in the casino argot of the times. But only two of these points were his own.[60] Entratter held the remaining ten points for other investors who preferred to remain anonymous. Some, like Alo himself, had a criminal record or reputation that might endanger the casino's gaming license — Doc Stacher was a power behind the scenes at the Sands until 1964. But many hidden partners were guilty of nothing much more sinister than tax evasion. It was Entratter's job to ensure that the points holders for whom he fronted got their share.

Skimming was the name of the game in Las Vegas in the early 1960s. The simplest form of skim — taking cash out of the counting room every night — had been perfected in the carpet joints as their take was split among their seasonal, short-term partners. But this had proved quite complicated to operate in the year-round, semicorporate casinos. As a rule, Las Vegas cash skims in the early 1960s paid out a couple of thousand dollars per point per month, with one much larger payment in February or March after the accounting of the year-end figures — and of the casino's official, declared profit. With envelopes and briefcases of bank notes being ferried by couriers to different corners of the country, the cash skim was cumbersome and vulnerable.[61]

It was more usual for the hidden points holder to visit Las Vegas in person, and this was the system preferred by most investors. They would stay in their own hotel — "comped," caviared, and champagned like pashas — and would gamble on credit which they did not have to pay for, up to the amount of their share. Some would cash in their chips so they could pocket every penny, but most would stay around to have some fun with their money. They were gambling men, for the most part, unlike Meyer.

Points holders who chose not to come to Vegas might be given the debt of one particular high roller to collect.* Others might organize junkets of gamblers who flew to the casino in a group to gamble on credit, and who would then pay their debts directly to the junketeer. An entertainer who held points might get his share from extra bookings in that hotel. In order to secure a really big-name entertainer, it was often necessary for a casino to offer extra cash or free gambling credit, which made the task of computing the casino's profit, declared and undeclared, that much more complicated.

Still greater complications arose when a points holder died — a not infrequent eventuality, given the prevailing age, tastes, and physical condition of the breed. It was the rule in illegal casino syndicates — as always in the underworld — that shares died and were redistributed among the surviving partners when the shareholder died. There was never any legacy for the heirs of a dead partner, unless that heir had been active in the syndicate before the partner's death. The last thing that these invariably male conspiracies wanted was a widow, innocent or knowing — or, perhaps, some clever son or daughter — becoming privy to their affairs.

On the other hand, there was an understanding that the good widow of a good partner should be provided for. It was a matter of honor. So the discussions in the cigar smoke grew long and complicated, on occasions, as to how $20,000 might be passed to a widow without her knowing where it came from. Would it make her ask for more? Would she report it to the IRS? Was there a way, perhaps, if the partners were feeling crafty, that the money might be paid out so it could also be claimed as a tax-deductible expense?

Couriers. Satchels. Money in shoe boxes. Junketeers coming and going. Croupiers wanting their cut. The IRS getting curious. How to skim the growing banks of coin machines. Did the points really add up to one hundred? The challenge of carving an honest and accurate accounting out of the complicated casino syndicates of Las Vegas in the early 1960s was a daunting and almost impossible task, and to the mind of Jimmy Alo, who had several casino syndicates to take

---

*This debt would probably be for more than the points holder's share, and he would be entitled to pocket the difference for his trouble — if he could collect it. Though Las Vegas casinos do not care to publicize the fact, it is quite routine for regular high rollers to negotiate and to settle their gaming debts at a discount, usually in the region of seventy to eighty cents on the dollar.

care of, and several dozen investors, managers, and front men to juggle, there was one obvious man for the job.

Meyer Lansky really did not want to be involved. From 1958, when he was arrested and interrogated about the killing of Albert Anastasia, his life had presented a fairly unrelieved vista of trauma and stress. He was confronted almost daily by the evidence of the FBI's intense interest in his activities, and there was the IRS as well. Meyer could be under no illusion as to what would happen to him if he were caught breaking the law — and the masterminding of casino skimming (conspiracy and tax evasion) was certainly that. When Lansky told people that, with the ending of the game in Cuba, he was really "retired" from the business, he was telling the truth about his mental state, at least.

On the other hand, the business was his life — and however modest Meyer's personal tastes, he still needed to make a living. Meyer Lansky had an unerring ability, as he ruefully remarked more than once to Jimmy Blue Eyes, to lose money whenever he went legit.[62] His Florida hotel investments in the Tuscany and in the Plantation Harbor had fared no better than Consolidated Television or Emby Distributing. What alternative to Las Vegas did he have?

By 1961, the FBI's bugs in Nevada provided the evidence.

"Meyer wants a breakdown," demanded the imperious Ben Sigelbaum, as he hustled into the office of Eddie Levinson, the original manager of the Havana Riviera casino, who was now running the Fremont Hotel in Las Vegas.[63]

As the FBI men pricked up their ears, Sigelbaum and Levinson proceeded to go through a list of names, nicknames, and initials which appeared to set out the secret points holders of a casino skimming syndicate. At the top of the list was Meyer's own name. Second came the initials J.B. The listening agents postulated that J.B. might stand for "Joe Batters," the nickname of Anthony Accardo, a Chicago crime boss. But J.B. could also have been a code for Vincent Alo, Jimmy Blue Eyes, whose name did not feature anywhere else on the list. Ben Sigelbaum's own share was noted, as was that of Gerry Catena, principal inheritor of the New Jersey empire of Joe Adonis and Longy Zwillman.[64]

The FBI had managed to plant one of its highly confidential sources in the working headquarters of a full-scale casino skim — and as the agents listened to the comings and goings in Eddie

Levinson's Fremont office in the months that followed, they were fascinated to hear how loud money can sound when it is counted in large quantities.[65]

On the other side of the country, in New Jersey, an FBI bug eavesdropping on Angelo "Gyp" DeCarlo, a thuggish henchman of Catena's — picked up more details. Catena was receiving $150,000 a month from his investments in Las Vegas, boasted DeCarlo, but he was not getting as much as Meyer Lansky. "Lansky," reported DeCarlo, "has a 'piece' of virtually every casino in Las Vegas."[66]

This grandiose claim did not mesh with the FBI's intelligence in Las Vegas. Lansky had nothing to do with the casinos that were the preserve of the Chicago Outfit. Moe Dalitz and his Cleveland partners took care of their own concerns. But it seemed clear from the conversations in Levinson's office that Meyer's skimming syndicate extended beyond the Fremont. Cash was also coming in, from the sound of it, from the Sands, the Flamingo, and Benny Binion's Horseshoe. Carried to the Fremont, the money was counted, divided, and then dispatched to points holders in different corners of the country.[67]

As the bug picked up names, the FBI used physical surveillance to tail its suspects. Ben Sigelbaum was the most obvious courier, shuttling with his briefcase between Miami and Las Vegas two or three times a month for more than two years.

A more leisurely traveler was Ida Devine, the wife of Irving "Niggy" Devine, who owned a company that supplied meat to the Fremont, and who appeared to have points in the place as well. Ida Devine did not like flying. She made her journeys by train, stopping off in Chicago and Hot Springs, Arkansas, on her regular journeys from Las Vegas to Miami, carrying over $100,000 a time. Muffled in furs on the northern sector of her circuit, Ida came to be known to her secret FBI admirers as "the lady in mink."[68]

Meyer Lansky seemed to be the ultimate authority in the picture that the agents pieced together. They listened in on one lengthy session as $168,000 cash was counted and recounted and compared to the records. Meyer had asked for an accounting, so the figures had to be straight.[69]

As the Bureau's listeners tallied their own interpretation of what they heard, they estimated that Meyer Lansky controlled no less than forty-two hidden points in the skims going through the Fremont, and that each point brought in $2,000 per month. This monthly average appeared to have been set by Meyer himself, as was the price for which one point could be purchased — $52,500. On this reckoning, Meyer Lansky was the conduit for Las Vegas casino investments worth $2.2 million, yielding just over $1 million income in cash, per year.[70]

This was a massive position for one semiretired and ailing man living in a ranch house in the suburbs north of Miami. Was every one of his forty-two points to Meyer's own, personal account? Or was he, to some degree, the custodian, not the owner, of this enormous trust? In the original list which Sigelbaum and Levinson analyzed together, Lansky's name was linked to two separate shareholdings — suggesting that Meyer held some of his points as a front man himself.

The picture was growing more complex when, one day toward the end of April 1963, the FBI agents listening to a conversation coming live from Eddie Levinson's office in the Fremont were amazed to hear Levinson reading out to Niggy Devine the contents of a confidential Justice Department memorandum which the agents themselves had only just received. Written in Washington the previous week, the memo summarized the findings of the Fremont bug and the surveillances that accompanied it, including details of the cross-country train journeys of "the lady in mink."

"My God, Niggy," exclaimed Levinson. "They know about Ida!"[71]

Levinson's consternation was hardly greater than that of the listening FBI agents as, following Levinson's progress, word for word, through a copy of the document that they themselves held in front of them, they participated in the only known read-along in the thinly documented history of secret surveillance.

Four days later, the FBI's bug in the Fremont office went dead, and the FBI was to find itself the object of attack in a court action for illegal entry, invasion of privacy, and violation of constitutional rights. The suit against the FBI was framed and filed by Levinson's formidable Washington lawyer, Edward Bennett Williams.[72]

The ramifications of the case proved many and complex, finally ending in a trade-off in March 1968. The government accepted Levinson's plea of no contest to a minor skimming charge developed from nonbugged evidence. Levinson was lightly fined and he agreed, in return, to drop his suit.[73] Drawing attention to the FBI's untrammeled use of illegal entry, wires, and bugs, the episode was a preliminary step in the process which led, after much controversy and an official ban for a period, to the controlled license of such techniques under the so-called Title III rules of 1968.[74] As to who leaked the crucial document, the FBI never discovered — or, if it did, it is not telling.[75]

For Meyer Lansky, the discovery of the FBI's intrusion into the executive office of the Fremont in April 1963 proved a blessing in disguise. It brought an abrupt halt to his skimming arrangements there. But by perverse good fortune, it also provided a guarantee preventing prosecution of Meyer himself, Ben Sigelbaum, Ida Devine, and every other name that was picked up in the course of the unlicensed surveillance.

Illegally obtained evidence was not admissible in court in 1963.* The FBI bugged and wiretapped in these years in order to secure intelligence — leads to other evidence which it could then present as part of a legally watertight indictment. When the bug in the Fremont was uncovered, the Bureau was in the process of gathering such evidence from the physical tails that followed Ben Sigelbaum and Ida Devine around the country — and these inquiries might, or might not, have eventually led to an indictment involving Meyer Lansky. As it was, the uncovering of the bug stopped the investigation dead in its tracks. Whatever was legally discovered had been fatally tainted by its illegal origin.

Meyer Lansky's apparent invincibility to prosecution became one of the principal ingredients in the reputation that gathered around him in the course of the 1960s. It was part of his mystery and cleverness — his secret and almost magical power that could only be guessed at. But in 1963 the talisman that protected Meyer Lansky against prosecution in the Fremont skimming case was less his own cleverness than government illegality and incompetence.

In 1951, Estes Kefauver's naming of Meyer as one of the three leaders of the "eastern crime syndicate" had made Lansky a priority target for the Justice Department, without supplying the evidence of any crime — bar his gambling — for which he could be indicted. Throughout the 1950s, the thrust of the department's effort against Meyer had been through the Immigration and Naturalization Service, with its attempts to prove that Meyer had lied about his criminal record when he applied for his U.S. citizenship in 1928. This

---

*The latest U.S. Supreme Court decisions now permit illegally obtained evidence in certain circumstances — if, for example, the law enforcement officer concerned can be said to have acted "in good faith."

effort had been abandoned in 1958 when it became clear that the confused memories of immigration clerks, plus the self-serving testimony of the jailbird Daniel Ahearn — the teller of the tale of the poisoned chicken — would not stand up in court thirty years after the event.[76] The FBI's tails and bugs in Miami and Las Vegas had taken over from the denaturalization campaign, and, taken together, the two investigations — the first by the INS, the second by the FBI — added up to more than a decade of wasted government effort.

Meyer Lansky was plain lucky to escape scot-free from the Fremont skimming case, though he did not prove unintelligent in the lesson that he drew from his narrow escape. The exposure of his skimming activities led to a change of direction for him — and for Jimmy Alo — which proved as dramatic as the ending of his business in Cuba.

The FBI's interest in the casinos of Las Vegas and their hidden eastern points holders had started in 1957 with the discovery of a scrap of paper in the pocket of Frank Costello, following the shooting attempt against him in the lobby of the Majestic on Central Park West. The paper in Costello's pocket had listed "casino wins" which precisely matched the April 3–26 take at the recently opened Tropicana in Las Vegas.[77] Six years later, the bug discovered in the Fremont dramatically betrayed how far the government had got — and the lengths to which it was prepared to go — in order to uncover the practice of skimming for secret casino points holders.

Skimming was to remain the way things worked in Las Vegas for many years after 1963, but Meyer Lansky and Jimmy Alo could read the writing on the wall.

"We're getting too old," Jimmy used to say. "We can't do this forever."[78]

How much had the government heard in Eddie Levinson's office? How many other bugs had it installed in executive offices and counting rooms in Las Vegas? This particular inquiry might have failed, but it could only stimulate investigations which might prove less fallible.

Jimmy Blue Eyes already had some experience at yielding territory gracefully. "If the blacks want the numbers, let them have it,"[79] he had said in Harlem a few years earlier, and he had walked away from the policy empire that he built up in the 1930s with Charlie Luciano.

When it came to Nevada, it was clear to both Meyer and Jimmy that the glory days were over. The two decades of expansion that Las Vegas had enjoyed since World War II had been a period of transition in which illegally acquired expertise — and illegally acquired capital — had constituted the main engine of development. Nevada was the biggest enclave of them all. It could hardly have been built without the outlaws of the carpet-joint fraternity, and Las Vegas's network of hidden points holders was a reflection of that. From the viewpoint of law enforcement, casino skimming was an outrage to be eliminated. In terms of economics and history, it was an evolutionary stage in the mutation from illegal to legal — and it would have no function once that process was complete.

"Let's take the money," said Jimmy, "and have a quiet life."[80]

It took a little time, but in 1967 the Sands became the second Las Vegas hotel to be owned by an outside company, when Jack Entratter and the other owners of record sold it to Howard Hughes for $14.6 million. The first sale had been of Moe Dalitz's Desert Inn, also to Hughes, a few months earlier — the beginning of the transformation by which Las Vegas has become the preserve of conglomerates and publicly quoted corporations, wooing the mass market, Disneyland style, with mechanical volcanoes, medieval jousts, and video poker. In this new Harvard- and Wharton-inspired world, the computer and the CPA are kings, while the poor, hard-pressed skimmer — not to mention the arm-around-the-shoulder host, and even the old-fashioned high roller — are species facing imminent extinction.

In 1967, according to one insider, Meyer Lansky collected just over $1 million as his share of the Sands's sale, reflecting his personal ownership of roughly half the points he had controlled.[81] Clear of tax, it was not a bad payoff from an enterprise that had nearly landed him in jail. Jimmy and Meyer congratulated themselves, as did the other old-time points holders who sold out in these years, on the prices which they induced legitimate corporations to pay.

But the new purchasers had picked themselves a bargain. In the course of the next decade, Las Vegas casinos multiplied many times in value and came to change hands for hundreds of millions of dollars. It was like the legal state lotteries which proliferated in the 1970s and 1980s, instantly dwarfing the numbers games they mimicked. The corporate inheritors of Las Vegas have proved that the legitimate world can run a racket better than any crook.

17

Three Hundred Million Dollars

WHEN Dick Jaffe joined the Miami office of the IRS, one of his first jobs was to cover the administration of the new fifty-dollar gaming tax stamp, the confused and solitary piece of legislation that came out of the deliberations of the Kefauver Committee. This new law required all bookmakers to purchase fifty-dollar "bookie tax" stamps in settlement of the federal tax due on their illegal activities. But it soon ran into hopeless theoretical and constitutional difficulties, since the purchase of the tax stamp appeared to license the book-maker while simultaneously requiring him to incriminate himself.*

Dick Jaffe faced more practical problems. As he investigated local bookmaking and loan-sharking rackets, he began to suspect that the profits from these enterprises were not staying in Miami. Jaffe kept stumbling upon connections with the British colony of the Bahamas, the scattering of islands which lay little more than a hundred miles, and a forty-minute plane ride, to the east of Miami. So in December 1962, the IRS man decided to pay the islands a visit.[1]

The Bahamas had long had a reputation as a leisurely tax haven, convenient for playboy heirs and covetous moguls in retirement who

---

*The gaming tax stamp law was declared unconstitutional by the U.S. Supreme Court in 1968 on the grounds of self-incrimination and infringement of the Fifth Amendment.

302

could not bear to loose a penny from their grasp. The islands had served as a staging post for bootleg liquor in Prohibition days, and now it seemed that they might be connected with racy commerce of another type.

Dick Jaffe found what he was looking for on the very first afternoon that he started going through the company files in Government House in Nassau. The list of stockholders of the grand-sounding Bank of World Commerce, chartered in Nassau on June 9, 1961, made up a roll call of names whom Jaffe knew to be prominent in layoff betting and casino gambling in America — among them Irving "Niggy" Devine and Edward Levinson of the Fremont Hotel Casino in Las Vegas.[2]

The 1962 visit of IRS Agent Jaffe to the Bahamas, and the reports that Jaffe wrote following this and subsequent visits to Nassau, marked the beginnings of serious awareness in U.S. law enforcement circles of international hot money and the unregulated world of offshore finance. It was a new dimension to domestic crime. One of the first things that the excited young IRS agent did when he got home, just before Christmas, was to phone the local FBI office.

"You ought to take a look in the Bahamas," he told his FBI contacts. "There are some *very* interesting names out there."[3]

The subsequent inquiries of Jaffe and other IRS agents shed further light on how the system operated. It had to be presumed that hot money reached the Bank of World Commerce in the old fashioned way, in bank notes and cashier's checks brought physically to Nassau. But in Miami some years later, Jaffe discovered that couriers from Las Vegas were unloading their satchels on the mainland, without having to risk any customs or immigration inspections.

The Bank of Perrine, a small, local South Miami bank, had come to a correspondent arrangement with the Castle Bank of Nassau whereby depositors could do business in Florida as if they were in Nassau. You could walk into the Bank of Perrine with $100 cash — or $100,000 cash — for deposit in your Castle Bank account, and that money would be credited to you in the Bahamas, without your name being mentioned in the Bank of Perrine's records. IRS inquiries determined that Morris Kleinman was a Castle Bank depositor who had made use of this convenient arrangement, and that Moe Dalitz and Sam Tucker also held Castle Bank accounts.[4]

There was no American paperwork. It was like having your own little rocket that magically transported your cash out of reach of the IRS and up into the stratosphere of unregulated, offshore money movement. Your options were endless. You could dispatch your money onward to Panama, Hong Kong, Monaco, Liechtenstein, Switzerland — or you could bring it back home via the shell companies, dummy loans, and other cleaning processes that came to be known as money laundering.

As "money laundering" became a modish term in the early 1970s,* the legend grew that Meyer Lansky was the magician who had devised the trick — and, in particular, that he was the man who taught the Mob how to launder its money.

This belief could not be supported from the researches of Dick Jaffe, nor from the inquiries of any other of the IRS, FBI, and Securities and Exchange Commission agents who went hunting for American tax dodgers in the paperwork of Government House, Nassau — and later, with a great deal more difficulty, in Switzerland. Undeniable evidence came to light in the course of the 1960s that Meyer Lansky was sending money out of the country — possibly via the Bahamas, and certainly to Switzerland. But there was nothing to suggest that he brought any money back.

Money laundering means more than simple tax evasion. It means bringing your hot money back so you can use it openly and legitimately. Sneaking it back into America in a briefcase is not laundering. By definition, your dirty income must show up clean and legally declared on your tax return, or on the return of some entity you control. Journalistic accounts of the practice in the 1970s suggested that this could be done by borrowing your own money in Switzerland, and then claiming the interest paid, effectively to yourself, as an American tax deduction — thus generating an extra set of profits from the wash cycle.

There may have been clever Wall Street operators who brought their money full circle in this fashion in the 1960s and early 1970s, but in no case prior to the drug-profit laundering trials of the 1980s did the government establish evidence of anyone actually pulling off this ingenious trick.[5] *United States v. Payner,* for example, the case growing out of Dick Jaffe's Castle Bank inquiries, proved tax evasion, money going out of the country, and an undeclared foreign bank account. It did not show laundered money coming back.

None of the tax returns of Meyer Lansky showed foreign interest

---

*The term entered the language in connection with the Watergate inquiry, according to the first published usage that the *Oxford English Dictionary* can locate. On April 19, 1973, the *Guardian* newspaper wrote of $200,000 of Republican party campaign funds being "laundered" in Mexico.

payments, or any transactions that might be interpreted as money laundering. Nor did he hide behind the "miscellaneous income" headings to which lawbreakers often resort. With the ending of his Cuban income in 1960, Meyer listed simple, American sources of revenue on his tax returns — the Flamingo finder's fee, dividends from some oil and gas investments that he started making in the early sixties. All were thoroughly investigated and confirmed by the IRS. The returns of enterprises connected to Meyer — brother Jake's hotel and motel holdings, for example — were equally straightforward.[6]

Meyer Lansky cheated on his taxes. From some date quite early in the 1960s, he started sending money abroad, and it ended up in Switzerland in a classic numbered account. But his money did not return "laundered" to America. Meyer seems to have treated his new Swiss bank account as an elaborate version of cash under the bed.

John Pullman had been a bootlegger in the 1920s, and he and Meyer used to agree, without too much conviction on Meyer's part, that they had known each other in those good old days.[7] Born in eastern Europe in the same year as Meyer, Pullman had anglicized his name, and had spent much of his career in Canada, taking advantage of Canada's comparatively trusting securities and exchange regulations to build up a small fortune with stock-boosting schemes. In the 1950s, he had taken up residence in Switzerland.

Pullman had got to know Meyer properly in Cuba, in 1959, in the aftermath of Castro's takeover. He had used his non-U.S. credentials to get surprisingly close to Castro himself, appearing on a podium with the great man on one occasion, and earning general admiration for his ability to sit through one of the leader's famous three-hour speeches, in Spanish, with an expression of rapt attention on his face.

Pullman felt confident he could work out a deal whereby Meyer, using his association with the Canadian Smith brothers, could get his money out of Cuba. The scheme came to nothing, but in the process, John Pullman introduced Meyer Lansky to the possibilities of using offshore banks as channels and repositories for the cash being generated by Meyer's Las Vegas skims. Offshore money was the latest thing. Pullman had given up his Canadian stock schemes in the late 1950s. In June 1961, Pullman founded the Bank of World Commerce in Nassau, and became its first president.

A confirmed optimist in his personal life, as in his business affairs, John Pullman had married and remarried no fewer than eight times. ·For one of his divorces Ben Sigelbaum's lawyer, Gerson Blatt, sent

Pullman out to Las Vegas,[8] where Pullman met Eddie Levinson and
Niggy Devine and preached to them the offshore gospel. This was
how Levinson and Devine came to be involved in the Nassau bank,
and it was not long before Pullman was handling the offshore banking arrangements for most of the skimming fraternity — Moe Dalitz,
Morris Kleinman, Doc Stacher, Jimmy Blue Eyes, and Meyer Lansky
himself.[9]

Popular descriptions of the numbered Swiss bank account and its
use by American criminals and gamblers have set the connection as
far back as the 1930s. The evidence for this is uncertain.[10] It is not
obvious why anyone should have wanted to transport his cash halfway round the world by steamer and railway at a time when it was
much easier to use a little tin box, or to hide almost any amount in
the unregulated and uncomputerized records of a cooperative local
bank.

The 1960s was the decade when offshore hot money became big
business, under the pressure of more demanding, expensive governments, and more efficient tax collection. It was also facilitated by
developments like accelerated interbank transfers and the advent of
the commercial passenger jet.[11]

The overwhelming majority of customers in the rush for offshore
tax schemes and numbered Swiss accounts were otherwise law-abiding citizens — tycoons, brokers, entertainers. Meyer Lansky, Eddie
Levinson, and Ben Sigelbaum were new to the game like everyone
else, and those who dealt personally with Meyer in these years agree
that his guru was the loquacious and likable John Pullman, who had
a clever new way to do everything, and who had never met a problem
that he could not fix.

Events in 1965 offered a glimpse into the mechanics of the process. In March of that year, Sylvain Ferdmann, a young Swiss courier
who helped Pullman collect and transport the funds from his clients,
accidentally dropped a piece of paper in the parking lot at Miami
airport:

> This is to acknowledge this 28th day of December, 1964, the
> receipt of Three Hundred and Fifty Thousand ($350,000)
> Dollars, in American bank notes for deposit to the account of
> Maral 2812, with the International Credit Bank, Geneva, the
> said sum being turned over to me in the presence of the name
> signed below.

The name of the witness was John Pullman, and below his own signature, the cautious Ferdmann had added a postscript:

> The above is subject to the notes being genuine American bank notes.[12]

By this date, the FBI was already on the trail of the roly-poly and far from inconspicuous Pullman. Its agents trailed him on his visits to Miami, and when he went north of the U.S. border, they worked in collaboration with the Royal Canadian Mounted Police. In September 1966, Pullman was staying in the Royal York Hotel in Toronto, and the Mounties managed to plant a bug inside his suite.

"Now listen," Pullman was recorded saying to an unknown caller. "I must talk to the little guy. I hear he is sick."

"Yeah," replied the caller, "he's in the hospital with an ulcer."[13]

A few days later, Pullman was getting worried.

"He's in the hospital, very bad, you know," the Canadians heard him telling his wife, Yvonne, on September 20. "Oh, terrible, and I have to see him again. If I could see Meyer, I would have right now 20,000 francs to deposit in the bank. If Meyer dies, it goes to his estate. . . . The problem is that Meyer is the only one that they can rely on. With Meyer, it will always come."[14]

As Pullman admitted to his wife, his anxiety for Meyer's health was by no means disinterested. His mention of 20,000 francs referred to money he was due to pick up from his friend. The International Credit Bank in Geneva paid Pullman 1 percent of all the funds that he collected and delivered for deposit there.[15]

In the summer of 1965, Meyer and Teddy had gone on another of their European holidays. John Pullman met them at Geneva airport and acted as their guide and host in Switzerland, taking them round Lake Geneva to Lausanne, where he lived. Pullman also introduced Meyer to his boss, Tibor Rosenbaum, the man who owned and ran the International Credit Bank, Pullman's Swiss base of operations. Pullman was the prophet and salesman who had brought the gospel of the numbered account across the Atlantic to Meyer and his friends, but he got most of his ideas from Rosenbaum. At the International Credit Bank, Pullman was only Tibor Rosenbaum's agent.

Tibor Rosenbaum was a picaresque character who had trained as a rabbi, and who claimed to have been an agent in Operation Hazalah, the World War II operation in which Hungarian Jews went so far as to impersonate SS officers to secure the escape of their fellow Jews to Switzerland and Palestine. Having cheated death at least once, Tibor Rosenbaum lived life by his own set of rules.

In 1948, Rosenbaum had arranged Czechoslovak arms shipments to help the fledgling Israeli state in its war with its Arab neighbors. By the time Meyer Lansky met him in 1965, the banker-salesman was acknowledged as the principal conduit for the Israeli government's foreign commercial dealings, covert as well as official. Rosenbaum had his own personal hotline to Israel's finance minister, Pinkhas Sapir,[16] spending millions, on occasion, on the authority of a single telephone call.[17]

Meyer Lansky was impressed to meet someone so actively and intimately involved in Israel's destiny — a Jew using his Jewish talents so unashamedly for the sake of the cause. The swashbuckling Rosenbaum, cutting corners, getting the job done, struck a chord with Meyer's Israel-centered interests of recent years. Us against them. No holds barred. Meyer admired Rosenbaum's style.

Lansky was not a trusting character. He was wary and suspicious on instinct. But when he gave his trust, he gave it completely, and just as he had decided that he trusted John Pullman, so he came to place his confidence with equal unreservedness in Tibor Rosenbaum.

Rosenbaum was a hard worker. The lights burned in his office until late at night. He was also a pious and observant Orthodox Jew. His friend Bernie Cornfeld remembers the difficulty of finding a kosher restaurant where he could lunch with Tibor. So the two men drove out of Geneva until they saw an old pear tree beside the road. They sat down beneath it and talked business, lunching on the fruit that they plucked from the tree.[18]

Pious and industrious though he was, however, Tibor Rosenbaum was not a conventional or prudent banker. The International Credit Bank was not a big institution. It held only $60 million in deposits at its peak, with reserves of $6.5 million.[19] But in the late 1960s Rosenbaum committed half his bank's funds — some $30 million — to the development of a stretch of woodland in Italy between Rome and the sea, an estate which had once been the property of the Italian royal family. Rosenbaum had been given to understand that money in the right hands could secure zoning permission to build resort hotels and luxury homes and apartments there.[20]

"It was beautiful," remembers Bernie Cornfeld. "It could have been a spectacular development."[21]

"The Chairman of the Board."
Meyer Lansky, New York,
1958.

TIME

TIME

THE WEEKLY NEWSMAGAZINE

Crime crusader: Senator Estes Kefauver, riding high, March 24, 1952.

On the spot: Sheriff Walter Clark, of Broward County, Florida, testifies to the Kefauver Crime Committee in Miami, June 1950.

PRESIDENTIAL CANDIDATE KEFAUVER
Was Truman treed on a TV aerial?

Different angle: Cameras focused on Frank Costello's hands after he refused to have his face televised during the Kefauver hearings in New York, March 1951.

On trial: Attorney Moses Polakoff (left) escorts Lansky to court at Saratoga Springs, September 1952, to face gambling indictments which led to Lansky's only spell behind bars.

His own hotel, his own casino: Meyer Lansky at the Riviera Hotel, Havana, 1958.

The Havana Riviera today.

Action in the Riviera casino, November 1958.

Signs of trouble: President Fulgencio Batista of Cuba inspects captured rebel arms, August 1955.

Cuban gamblers — two of
the losers. *Above:* Vincent Alo,
"Jimmy Blue Eyes," in 1966.
Alo was one of Lansky's
partners in the Riviera Hotel.
Right: Santo Trafficante, Jr.,
"Louis Santos," in 1958.

Cuban gamblers — two who
got out in time: Morris Barney
"Moe" Dalitz (left) and Sam
Tucker, in 1951.

Murder victim: Albert
Anastasia on the floor of the
Park Sheraton Hotel barber-
shop, October 25, 1957.

Murder suspect: Lansky
booked for vagrancy by New
York City police detectives,
February 11, 1958.

Family gathering, for the marriage of Buddy and Annette Lansky, May 19, 1957. *Right:* Meyer and his brother, Jake. *Below:* Back row (left to right), Sandra, Meyer, Teddy (Meyer's second wife), and Paul Lansky; front row, Annette, Buddy, and Grandma Yetta.

But Tibor Rosenbaum paid off the wrong politicians, and the Rome city council declared the area a national park, banning all development there.[22]

Rosenbaum's security in this adventure was cut-price Liberian government bonds that he had obtained through President William V. S. Tubman of Liberia — one of his several unusual friends in high places. Rosenbaum had recorded these Liberian bonds in the accounts of his bank at their inflated face value, however, so when worried depositors started asking for their money, he had to confess that he did not actually have the funds to back his deposits.

Tibor Rosenbaum's International Credit Bank closed for the High Holy Days in 1974 and never reopened. The bank declared bankruptcy in October of that year, wiping out the reserves of all its depositors, among them Meyer Lansky. Rosenbaum devoted the rest of his life to trying to repay his depositors, the sincerity of his efforts providing some vindication of the trust that Meyer had placed in him. But the episode scarcely suggested that Meyer Lansky could be considered an infallible guide when it came to the dangers and complexities of international high finance.

In 1964, Meyer Lansky finally laid hands on a legitimate investment that made some money. He bought himself an oil well. In the early 1950s Meyer had acquired three oil and gas leases in Nevada which had come to nothing.[23] But a dozen years later he tried again, buying a seven-sixteenths working interest in State Summerfield A, an oil and natural gas concession in Clare County, Michigan. Meyer had been drawn to this unlikely corner of the Midwest by an old friend, Sam Garfield.

Born Samuel Garfinkle in Russia in 1899, Garfield had gone to grade school in Detroit with Moe Dalitz.[24] He had grown up a friend of Dalitz, and he had got on good terms with Eddie Levinson and the other members of the Midwest's bootlegging and gambling fraternity. Garfield had connections for a time with a basketball betting business. He was one of the major investors in the Havana Riviera.[25] In the early 1960s he was tripped up in some stock manipulations, but he proved more successful than most of his friends at maintaining a respectable front. In Ohio he built up a successful magazine distributorship.[26]

By the late 1950s, Sam Garfield was living in Clare, Michigan, a small town in the center of the state, where he had applied himself

to the local business of oil and natural gas production. He formed
his own company, Mammoth Producing, and once he was established, he invited Meyer to risk some money with him. In 1964, the
year in which Meyer bought his stake in State Summerfield A,
Michigan crude commanded $2.81 per barrel at the wellhead. The
next year it went down to $2.79. But the year after that the price
rose, and it continued to rise every year thereafter — $3.07 in 1969,
$3.20 in 1972, and $8.59 in 1974 with the Arab oil embargo and
the advent of the mid-seventies energy crisis.[27]

Under the tutelage of Garfield, Meyer expanded his oil and gas
holdings. The two men bought more Michigan leases together, and
they extended into Ohio. Eddie Levinson was their partner on some
deals. Meyer sank about $250,000 into his energy investments in the
course of five or six years.[28] He was scarcely an oil tycoon — and
never an oil millionaire. But, thanks to Sam Garfield, he was
successful. His energy concessions brought him revenues in the
$25,000–$30,000-a-year range, and that kept his show money nicely
topped up, while also confirming the impression that he sought to
convey, of a retired businessman, living on his investments.

Clare County had one added attraction. It provided a useful refuge
whenever Meyer found the pressure of surveillance in Miami too
much. From time to time he would give his minders the slip and fly
up to Detroit to talk business with Sam Garfield. It was a little time
before the FBI thought to look for Meyer Lansky in the middle of
Michigan.

The "Know Your Neighbor" article was a tradition at the *Miami
Herald* which went back to the crusading days of Lee Hills. In the
late 1940s, Hills had run exposés of the northern gamblers and crime
bosses who wintered in the Miami area, and in the 1960s Hills's successors on the *Herald* kept up the tradition.

"They bask in the sun," wrote the *Herald* staff writer Clarence
Jones in an October 1965 article, which colorfully traced the criminal career of such winter visitors as Angelo Bruno of Philadelphia
and "Black Bill" Tocco of Detroit — so many alligators as they lay
beside the pools of their North Miami homes.

On December 12, 1965, it was Meyer Lansky's turn. "Lansky
Rules Crime Cartel from Florida," proclaimed an article by *Herald*
special writer Hank Messick. The first of a three-part series, the article was run across the top of the front page of the *Herald*'s Sunday
edition.

A stocky and bespectacled man, quite diffident and kindly in his personal life, Hank Messick was an aggressive investigative reporter who had been working for some years on crime and gambling in Kentucky and Ohio. His ground-breaking researches there, which were to be published in 1967 as a book, *The Silent Syndicate,* laid bare the early bootlegging and gambling activities of Moe Dalitz, Sam Tucker, Morris Kleinman, and their associates in the Cleveland area. The *Herald* hired Messick as a consultant to initiate similar exposés in Miami.

Messick's interest in Meyer Lansky had been piqued by the story of the Molaska Corporation and its links with illegal distilleries in the 1930s. Molaska was Messick's own discovery, a good example of his ability to secure and analyze previously hidden law enforcement materials, and it provided a solid part of his December 1965 series on Meyer Lansky, which opened with a startling claim:

> The Boss of the Eastern Syndicate, and probably the biggest man in organized crime today, lives at 612 Hibiscus Drive, Hallandale. His real name is Maier Suchowljansky, but it is under the name Meyer Lansky he won his wealth.
>
> Lansky's wealth is reliably estimated at $300 million.[29]

Hank Messick today stands back a little from this colossal estimate of Meyer Lansky's fortune.

"Whenever people have contacted me to confirm this," he says, "I have always told them it was not my figure. It came from an expert who was supposed to know what he was talking about."[30]

It is difficult to imagine who this expert could have been.

"Hank didn't get it from me," says Dick Jaffe, the IRS expert on Miami's hidden fortunes in the mid-1960s.[31]

It did not come from the FBI's experts on Meyer's Las Vegas skim, either. Based on what they could hear via their bug in Eddie Levinson's office, the FBI set the value of the Lansky-designated income from the Fremont casino syndicate at a little over $1 million cash a year. Meyer had been involved with this syndicate for three or four years, at the most. So in 1965 the most that Meyer could have accumulated from this, his most lucrative source of income, was $5 million — and that was on the assumption that all the points attributed to him were his, and his alone.[32]

"Holy Christ!" the Mounties heard John Pullman exclaim, via their bug, in September 1966, as the courier-banker heard mention of Messick's $300 million, and evidently calculated the value of his own 1 percent. "Where in the fuck is that money? I haven't seen a nickel of it yet!"[33]

Three hundred million dollars in 1965 is over $1 billion in 1990's money,[34] and it is impossible to square the figure with anything that is known, or can reasonably be imagined, about the finances of Meyer Lansky — the man whose success and longevity stemmed from his lack of appetites and from his scrupulousness in never taking too much for himself from a share-out.

Meyer's personal holding in the Havana Riviera may have extended to $4 million — and he had lost that. His share of the Sands Hotel when it was sold in the late 1960s came to about $1 million. In 1965, Meyer's oil and gas holdings in Michigan were not yet worth more than $100,000. His house was worth $50,000 — and he had fifteen years to go on his mortgage.

If Meyer Lansky had been compelled to present his net worth, legal and illegal, to a hypothetical bank manager in December 1965, when Hank Messick published his article, Meyer would have had a hard job listing realizable assets and cash resources that stretched as far as $3 million. This reflected wealth on a higher scale than the $40,000 or so that Meyer declared to the IRS every year — but $300 million was sheer fantasy.

Fantasy, however, is an integral element of how organized crime is experienced, perceived, and reported. Many of the criminals themselves are fantasists. It is the character flaw that first drew them to that world. Law enforcement officers, often for the best of reasons, tend to exaggerate the problem they are up against — and what reporter, or reader, can resist a good story?

In December 1965, $300 million became the price tag attached to Meyer Lansky, and it was to be relentlessly applied to him for the rest of his life. It usually featured in the first paragraph of the story, followed soon afterward by the quotation "We're bigger than U.S. Steel." In the succeeding paragraphs, Bugsy Siegel, the poisoned chicken, Cuban casinos, and the murder of Anastasia in the barbershop would mingle with domestic details like Paul's appointment to West Point — proof of the mysterious influence that the boy's father must be able to exercise in high places.

Meyer's miraculous immunity from serious indictment was invariably cited as evidence of his cleverness, with hints at even more mysterious influence in high places. In later years Gyp DeCarlo's claim that Lansky had a piece of every casino in Vegas was included, and the whole account would be liberally sprinkled with words like "mastermind," "genius," and "controller" of organized crime. Since the man was worth $300 million, it was difficult to claim any less a role for him.

Starting with *Doctor No* in 1962, the 1960s saw the success in America of the James Bond movie which, in addition to fast cars, gadgets, and showers à deux, featured solitary, sinister villains, who masterminded organizations with acronyms like Spectre or Smersh. Unprepossessing little men for the most part, they terrorized with the power of their minds. Their Caribbean island headquarters might get pulverized, but they would slip away magically to resume their evil somewhere else, and to judge from their names, they could never be mistaken for Wasps — Blofeld, Stromberg, Dr. Julius, Drax.[35]

Often hinted at, if seldom explicitly stated, Meyer Lansky's Jewishness was an important part of his mystique. Meyer was the Arnold Rothstein of his day — damned if he fixed the World Series, and damned if he did not. The myth of his omnipotence provided people with a satisfyingly clear and simple explanation of evil — and since he was omnipotent, it was only natural that no one could come up with chapter and verse to sustain the case against him. He knew how to hide the evidence.

Belief and knowledge had always been confused in the American understanding of organized crime, and this was reflected in the literature on the subject, where fact and fiction came together in a misleading brew, heavily laced with conspiracy theories and melodrama. The tradition went back to the "police gazettes" of the nineteenth century, which took real-life cases and turned them into blood-curdling, eyewitness thrillers, complete with fanciful dialogue, the villain's chuckles, and the victim's last gasp. "True" detective magazines continued the genre* — and the popular excitement generated by the Kefauver Committee saw the technique extended to organized crime.

Murder, Inc., a book published in 1951, set the style. Ostensibly a work of reportage, it told the story of the 1940–41 organized crime prosecution which could claim to be the most successful ever, in that the boss who ordered the hits, Lepke Buchalter, and some of his most

---

* *Carrying a Gun for Al Capone* by Jack Bilbo (Putnam, 1932) was a best-seller on both sides of the Atlantic, going through several editions and remaining in print as late as 1948. Subtitled *The Intimate Experiences of a Gangster in the Bodyguard of Al Capone*, it contained many rich details of the Chicago gangster's life — all flowing from the imagination of the book's real author, Hugo C. K. Baruch, an eccentric English artist and litterateur who never met Capone in his life.[36]

important accomplices actually went to the electric chair.[37] *Murder, Inc.*, the book, however, did not stop with the facts. It mixed solid, court-proven evidence with speculative dramatization, without distinguishing the two. It interspersed real testimony with invented dialogue, again without distinction — and at crucial points in the story, the reader was treated to the "thoughts," literally rendered, that were going through the protagonists' minds.

Coauthored by Burton Turkus, the assistant DA who tried the cases, and Sid Feder, a New York crime reporter, *Murder, Inc.* was a runaway success, its exaggerations perfectly suiting the tenor of the Kefauver years.[38] The book went through three printings in three months, and its mixture of fact and imagination came to be widely imitated by a series of organized crime books in a hybrid formula that was half documentary and half soap opera. They could only be described as pulp nonfiction.

The books which Hank Messick started to publish in the late 1960s built on this confusing tradition. They incorporated the fruits of Messick's solid newspaper researches, but they also featured crisp and dramatic dialogues which purported to be the actual words used by Meyer Lansky, Bugsy Siegel, and Lucky Luciano. These dialogues were "best recollections," Messick explained, reconstructed from tape recordings, firsthand witnesses, or from the memory of people who had got it from witnesses. But on at least one occasion, one of his witnesses got it wrong.

Syndicate Abroad, which Messick published in 1969, opened in Havana with Fulgencio Batista making phone calls on New Year's Eve, 1958. "The message to crook and crony was the same. Only those who had proven their value in the past received the warning." A few paragraphs later, Meyer Lansky was on his own charter plane heading for Florida, and the author was providing a detailed picture of Meyer's innermost thought processes as he flew to safety through the night.

"As the lights of the Gold Coast began to glitter below the plane," wrote Messick, "the Chairman of the Board reached a decision. Regardless of what Castro might do, the Syndicate International would concentrate upon the Bahamas."[39]

It is possible today, under the Freedom of Information Act, to read the files that the FBI gathered on Meyer Lansky — more than three linear feet of documents. They constitute more than two filing cabinet drawers full of telegrams, internal memoranda, and surveillance reports — as well as the newspaper articles, which have been carefully clipped out to be remounted neatly, column by column, on purpose-designed "information sheets."[40]

Some original documents have been censored. The names of agents and informants have been deleted, as have whole sections where confidential agency protocol is concerned. But what survives conveys a reasonable impression of the picture that the law enforcement arm of the U.S. Justice Department came to form of Meyer Lansky in the course of the 1960s, and the evidence upon which that picture was based.

Some of the evidence is hard to locate. It takes a lot of digging, for example, to sift through the documents and track down the surveillance reports of Meyer and Teddy's conversations in room 8E in the Volney Hotel, and to discover the transcripts of what Meyer was actually overheard saying about organized crime and U.S. Steel.

By contrast, the dramatically amended version of his remark as subsequently reported by *Life* and *Time* magazines jumps right out in several, repeated copies of those articles, set out on their information sheets with no cross-referencing or any suggestion that the quotation might be incorrect.

Also set out on the information sheets at regular intervals — without, again, any attempt to assess if they are right or wrong — are the photocopied articles by Hank Messick, "Lansky Rules Crime Cartel from Florida," clipped from the *Miami Herald* in December 1965, and setting Meyer Lansky's worth at $300 million.

Sometimes Meyer treated it all as quite a joke.

"I don't want to spoil the 'drammer' of your stories," he said when cornered by reporters after one grand jury appearance. "So I don't think I'll say anything."[41]

He even dealt face to face with Hank Messick on one occasion.

"I think," he told the sleuth, "that you ought to pay me half the money that you've made writing about me."[42]

Rabbi Shapiro got a sneaking suspicion that Lansky rather enjoyed the fact that all that cleverness and power were being attributed to him[43] — and Meyer's elder son agreed.

"They always made him out like the financial wizard," remembered Buddy. "And I really think he believed it."[44]

The FBI men tailed Meyer more closely than ever, and to their company was added the occasional news reporter. "Lansky," reported the *Miami Herald* on March 17, 1967, "[is] the most publicized organized crime figure in the world these days."

By this date, Meyer had acquired the mascot which came to give his newspaper pursuers the greatest delight of all — his little dog. Anne Lansky had bought dogs for the children in the 1930s, a bulldog and a fox terrier which Meyer had hated. He proved no more receptive when, in 1966, Teddy bought herself a Shih Tzu, a blond little creature which she named Tiger.

"At first," remembered Buddy, "he'd look at the dog and want to know what it was doing here." But then Tiger died. Teddy was brokenhearted, and to console her, Meyer bought her another dog, a second Shih Tzu, which Meyer named Bruzzer — and to which, he found, he could relate.

"He really took a liking to this dog," Buddy remembered. "In fact, he took it away from her."

When Bruzzer needed walking, it was Meyer who did the honors. "It was his excuse," said Buddy maliciously, "to get away from Teddy when he wanted to."[45]

Bruzzer proved useful to the FBI as well. His canine schedule provided a predictable timetable around which the watching agents could work. Every morning and evening without fail, Meyer Lansky could be seen walking briskly up and down Hibiscus Drive, with Bruzzer straining at the leash.

The Chairman of the Board had his final accessory.

In March 1967, two reporters of the *Detroit Free Press* stumbled on Meyer Lansky on one of his trips to Michigan, staying in an eighteen-dollar-a-night Howard Johnson's just outside Detroit. Teddy was with him, and the couple seemed to the newsmen to be positively relaxed. Meyer treated the reporters with good humor, and he did not seem disconcerted by their questions — which focused on the recently opened Bahamas casinos that the British government was about to investigate, suspecting further expansion of the Lansky empire.

"I certainly don't get any money out of there," Meyer said.[46]

The suspicion that Meyer Lansky was the secret owner of the new Lucayan Beach Casino at Freeport, Grand Bahama, and also of a London gambling establishment, the Colony Club on Berkeley Square, provided a happy hunting ground for both serious reporters and cranks in the years around 1966. It fitted with the picture of Lansky as the worldwide master of crime.

The suspicion was prompted by the extraordinary number of Meyer's associates involved in the two operations. Dino Cellini was active in both Freeport and London, where he had set up a Mayfair version of his Havana Riviera croupier school. Familiar figures in Freeport included George Sadlo, Dusty Peters, and half a dozen bookmakers and gamblers who had worked with Meyer at different times, particularly in Cuba.

One of the American partners in the Colony Club remembers Meyer's dropping in on the Berkeley Square club in 1965 just before it opened. Meyer was on the European trip that took him to Switzerland. Casting his eye over the proposed layout of the gaming room, Meyer ventured some suggestions.[47] But no one jumped to implement them, or reacted as if the boss had spoken, for Meyer only had a small stake in the Colony Club — five or six points, at the most. The American partners in the operation had been gathered together by Jimmy Alo, and it was he who called the shots.[48]

In the Bahamas, the Lucayan Beach Casino on Grand Bahama was a tissue of skimming, junkets, and hidden points — all the tricks of the trade — and here it seems likely that Meyer also had some involvement. He was a friend of Lou Chesler, one of the prime movers in the project, and he certainly gave advice when the casino was in the design and planning stage. He made no secret of his wish to have a declared participation. Lunching with Jimmy Alo one day in May 1963, he surprised an FBI agent who had followed him into the restaurant and put his grievance to the man directly.

"By painting him as a hoodlum," the agent reported Meyer complaining, "the FBI was successful in keeping him from participating in any Bahama venture."[49]

Meyer almost certainly found himself some sort of income from the Lucayan Beach — a rake-off, perhaps, from the junkets which Dusty Peters ran to the casino. But the evidence scarcely justified the wilder tales that were given credence by newspapers, and which even formed the subject matter for full-length books. Meyer Lansky's infiltration of the Bahamas went back, it was said, to the Second World War, when the Duke of Windsor was governor of the islands. Meyer's name was suggested as the key to the great mystery and scandal of those wartime years, the murder of Sir Harry Oakes. Meyer had the baronet killed, it was alleged, because Oakes opposed Meyer's plans for Bahamas gambling.[50] When, in 1971, the reclusive English architect Seymour Harris started building himself a high-walled estate outside Freeport, local rumor instantly made it the headquarters of Meyer Lansky, and tourist buses brought visitors to see the "machine gun slits" — the artistic embrasures designed in the walls by Harris.[51]

"At one stage we began to wonder," reported the Royal Commission of Inquiry into the Bahamas Casinos in 1967, "whether the name of Meyer Lansky was not some vast journalistic piece of fiction, so ghostly and mythical a figure did he appear."[52]

Such was the magic of the Lansky name that Lansky and the underworld had become virtually synonymous. Like the word "Mafia" itself, "Meyer Lansky" had become shorthand for a particular sort of evil. If an operation was cunning and financially complicated, it had to have been devised by Meyer Lansky. To write "Lansky," indeed, was a substitute for analyzing the complications, and when reporters found that the facts could not support the concept of the hidden Lansky command structure that had become an article of investigative faith, they resorted to expressions like the "Lansky Group" or "Lansky Associates."

In February 1967, the British home secretary prohibited the entry to Britain of Dino Cellini and George Raft, who had been playing his Havana role as host at the Colony Club on Berkeley Square.[53] Meyer's stake in the club had been comparatively minor, but when the Home Office gave background briefings to journalists, its spokesmen made frequent reference to his name. It explained things more easily than talking about the comparatively unknown Vincent Alo.

The U.S. Justice Department had a similar mindset. In 1966, a new strategy had been proposed against organized crime — the big-city Strike Force, which would coordinate all the law enforcement efforts in any particular place. The local offices of the FBI and the IRS, the city police department, and, if applicable, certain state agencies would all be brought together under the direction of a Justice Department attorney who would direct both investigation and prosecution. The Miami Strike Force was organized at the end of 1968,[54] and its first chief was Dougald D. McMillan, a tough young attorney who had grown up and trained in Florida, and who went for his targets asking no quarter and giving none.

"I knew that Meyer Lansky was a murderous, villainous bastard," says Dougald McMillan today, as blunt and aggressive as he was in Miami in the late 1960s. "He did refine his act, of course, after Prohibition. But he still remained a crook."[55]

Dougald McMillan had been told that Meyer Lansky was "the number one Mob figure in the country," by Henry E. Petersen, chief of the organized crime and racketeering section of the Justice Department, and McMillan had no reason to disbelieve his boss. It squared with surveillances like the DeCarlo tapes, in which the name of Lansky had surfaced occasionally and had always been mentioned with admiration.

"I have learned," says McMillan today, "that one way to assess the significance of an organized crime figure is what other organized crime figures think of him."[56]

This was not, in fact, a reliable way to assess the significance of Meyer Lansky. Bugs and telephone taps can provide invaluable evidence of lawbreaking in which criminals are personally involved. When it comes to their views of the wider picture — Gyp DeCarlo's New Jersey assessment of Meyer Lansky's Las Vegas holdings, for example — they may well be repeating rumor or what they have picked up from movies, television, or the newspapers.

Gangsters revel in the folklore that popular culture has constructed around them. It provides a glamour and importance all too often lacking in their personal lives. Operating clandestinely and in comparative isolation, they look to the media for information on their peers, on new developments in their profession — and even on their so-called traditions. Professor William Howard Moore has noted how the terminology used by Joseph Valachi started to proliferate in criminal surveillance reports after Valachi's testimony publicized them[57] — though this might also, in part, have reflected the preconceptions of the hidden listeners who paraphrased the conversations. It is a paradox of law enforcement that its agents serve as curators and altar boys to the gangster cult whose raw material they preserve and propagate.

Dougald McMillan saw himself as anything but an altar boy, and the establishing of his Miami Strike Force in 1968 introduced a new, abrasive note into the law enforcement efforts against Meyer Lansky. The FBI's pursuit of Meyer had always been marked by a certain perplexed tolerance on both sides, an uncertainty as to whether the whole process was real life or just a game. Meyer liked to get on first-name terms with the agents who followed him, while the agents, for their part, struck up friendly conversations in the hope of gleaning useful information.

On May 6, 1969, the subject for discussion was Cuba. "He [Lansky] noted," reported FBI Agent Jerris Armstrong, "that he would be sympathetic towards any group that would overthrow Castro or any communist country."[58]

Meyer reminded Armstrong that he had given the U.S. government ample warning that Castro was a Communist and would present a problem, and that nothing had been done about it. The government probably thought, Armstrong reported Meyer's saying, that "he was just being greedy in as much as he would lose his gambling interests in Cuba."[59]

By the autumn of 1969, however, the rapport between the agent and his quarry had soured. On October 28, 1969, Armstrong followed Meyer into the steam room of the Doral Beach Spa on Collins Avenue, where he found Meyer sitting with his friends Hymie Siegel and Harry Stromberg. Armstrong served all three men, as they sat in the steam, with subpoenas to appear before a forthcoming federal grand jury. Dougald McMillan was anxious to investigate newspaper allegations that Meyer, through his network of "Lansky Associates," secretly controlled some of the principal hotels on Miami Beach.

Meyer was sarcastic.

"If he gave Special Agent Armstrong one of his hotels," Armstrong reported Meyer as saying, "maybe all his troubles would cease."[60]

Next day, even the sarcasm was gone. Meyer had just set off on a trip down Collins Avenue, driving Teddy, when he realized that Jerry Armstrong was following him. He immediately made a U-turn and drove back to his starting point. Getting out of his car, Meyer strode angrily over to where Armstrong had parked.

"Jerry, get off my back," he said as he leaned into Armstrong's car. "A word to the wise is sufficient."

Meyer's hands were shaking, Armstrong noticed, and his voice was quivering.

Was that a threat? the FBI agent wanted to know.

Meyer said nothing, standing back and glaring furiously at Armstrong, beside himself, until Teddy came over and took him by the arm.

"As Lansky walked away," noted Armstrong's report, "he turned and stated, 'Jerry, you should read Kipling's poem, *If.*'"[61]

> *If you can keep your head when all about you*
> *Are losing theirs, and blaming it on you . . .*

It was one of Meyer Lansky's strengths to display grace under pressure. His calm was legendary among his friends. His loss of composure at the end of October 1969 reflected the fact that he really did have something to be worried about.

In August 1969, IRS agents had raided the New York office from which Morris Lansburgh had been organizing junkets of eastern gamblers to the Flamingo in Las Vegas. The junkets were part of the skimming mechanisms which Meyer had helped Lansburgh and his partner Sam Cohen establish after the hoteliers purchased the Flamingo from Albert Parvin in 1960 — the deal in which Meyer had acted as "finder" and go-between.

The FBI bug in Eddie Levinson's office had picked up references to cash being brought from the Flamingo counting room to the Fremont, but the way in which the Flamingo's gambling debts were collected from Lansburgh's junkets was a different, and separate, skim. If the IRS developed the evidence from its New York raid into an indictment, Lansburgh, Cohen, and Lansky could not hope to use the illegality of the Fremont bug as a defense.

Meyer's involvement in the Flamingo's junkets was slight. He had provided his advice at the beginning of the exercise — and had, most crucially, suggested the men who could be trusted to run the casino and to operate the skim effectively on the spot. In the case of the Flamingo, this was Chester Simms, a veteran of both Broward County and Havana.[62] Meyer had had no part himself in the essence of the tax evasion — the arrangements whereby the customers of Lansburgh's junkets settled their debts directly when they got back from Las Vegas, without the money's being recorded in the official books of the Flamingo.

On the other hand, Meyer had been part of the conspiracy which set up the whole arrangement. His finder's fee linked him inescapably, on the record, with the owners of the Flamingo, and he could have no doubt as to the energy with which the Justice Department would seek to establish some sort of connection and make him answer for it in court.

In March 1970, Meyer and Teddy flew to Acapulco for a holiday. The FBI followed them there, suspicious that Meyer might have business to discuss with another group of guests at the resort, some Canadian gamblers.[63] The surveillance revealed nothing.

But when the Lanskys arrived back in Miami, on March 4, 1970, they were searched at the airport by customs agents, and the search disclosed a vial of Donnatal tablets, the mild antispasmodic that Meyer took for his stomach. Meyer explained to the customs agents that he had suffered from ulcers for a number of years, though he could not produce his prescription for the pills.

Three weeks later, there was a knock on the Lanskys' door. The Florida Department of Law Enforcement had uncovered two prescriptions for Donnatal filled for Meyer at Breedings, his local drugstore. But they had not found any authority for the plastic vial of tablets that had been found on Meyer at the airport. The vial had, in fact, been sold to Meyer by the pharmacist, who knew him well, without a prescription.[64]

"Lansky Is Jailed on Drug Counts," announced the *Miami Herald* next day,[65] and the headline was echoed all over the country. The Chairman of the Board was finally being brought to justice — and on drugs charges at that.

Surrounded by reporters and cameramen, Meyer was taken to the Miami Strike Force offices to be fingerprinted, and was charged with two indictments, one a felony, one a misdemeanor, for possession of barbiturates and unlabeled drugs without a prescription. The felony charge carried a two-year prison sentence and a fine of up to $1,000, the misdemeanor, six months in jail and $500.

It was not a federal prosecution. The investigation and the drug indictments were all in the hands of the Florida Department of Law Enforcement, and the case was argued in court by a prosecutor of the state attorney's office. But, as chief of the Miami Strike Force, Dougald McMillan gave the drugs charges his blessing.

"I held his feet to the fire, absolutely," he says of his general approach to Meyer Lansky in the five years that he was to tangle with him in Miami. "Why should I cut Lansky any slack? I didn't think he deserved any."[66]

Florida criminal court judge Carling Steadman was not impressed. He wasted little time in dismissing the charges, accepting Joseph Varon's argument that the state had no jurisdiction over the U.S. customs enclosure at Miami airport where the pills had been seized, which was federal property.[67]

"If the Defendant were John Smith instead of Meyer Lansky," said Varon after the case, "there would never have been a prosecution."[68]

Meyer Lansky was acquitted of drug possession on June 19, 1970. But he did not find it a consoling triumph. Three weeks earlier, Morris Lansburgh had been summoned in front of a Miami grand jury that was investigating the skimming at the Flamingo Hotel. The May 1970 edition of *Reader's Digest* had published a profile of Meyer, "The Shocking Success Story of 'Public Enemy No. 1,'" and a few weeks after that, *Atlantic Monthly* carried an article by Nicholas Gage, "The Little Big Man Who Laughs at the Law."[69]

Meyer Lansky, wrote Gage, "is as much of a visionary and innovator as Andrew Carnegie, Henry Ford, and John D. Rockefeller. . . . Lansky is the main architect of the giant conglomerate that is organized crime in the United States."[70]

A year before, it would have been funny. In the aftermath of the drugs case — which Meyer could see in no other terms than victimization and harassment — it was all too much to take. Earlier in the year, the twelve-year-old Meyer II, on his way to school in Tacoma, had been accosted by two strange men who knew his name, and from whom the boy had run away in terror. Were they FBI agents? Nosy neighbors? Kidnappers?

"Lansky has been extremely irritable," reported a digest of Meyer's phone conversations in the first half of May 1970. "[He] is deeply concerned either for his freedom or for the safety of his family."[71]

"When I walk the streets," Meyer told the FBI agent who brought him the news of Meyer II's adventure in Tacoma, "I never know when I may get it."[72]

There were too many "nuts" running around — and, Meyer noted, "he no longer has friends he can trust among the Italians."[73]

The man who had made a science of intimidation was afraid. Lansky had been consulting E. David Rosen, a Miami criminal attorney who worked in the federal courts, and he got Rosen to convene a meeting with Jerris Armstrong, the FBI man. Did Armstrong know of any charges or subpoenas that were pending? inquired Meyer. Did the FBI have any legal grounds to prevent Meyer from going abroad for a time?

The answer to both questions was no.[74]

In 1964, Meyer's old friend Doc Stacher had avoided the worst consequences of a conviction for tax evasion by consenting to deportation and going to Israel to live. In July 1970, Meyer Lansky decided not to wait for the conviction — or anything else. He booked flights for himself, Teddy, and Bruzzer to Tel Aviv.

18

Sanctuary in Zion

MEYER LANSKY landed in Israel on July 27, 1970, for the second time. In 1962 he and Teddy had been on holiday. But now Meyer's intention stretched beyond visiting. He wanted to stay in Israel — and he wanted to live there not as a visitor, but as an Israeli citizen.

The Lanskys had booked into the Dan Hotel on the seafront in Tel Aviv, one of a forest of high-rise hotels and apartment buildings which give that stretch of Mediterranean coastline something of the flavor of Miami Beach. When the Dan Hotel had first received the Lanskys' reservation, the management had wondered if the booking could really be for Meyer Lansky, the gangster. They had telephoned the local branch of the Ministry of the Interior, who could tell them nothing. The local officials checked with their superiors in Jerusalem, who could, for the time being, see no reason why the Lanskys should not be registered like any other guests.[1]

At the end of the first week Meyer went down to the front desk to settle his bill. He and his wife really liked the place, he told the cashier, and intended to stay there quite a while. Could they please have a discount?

Discounts, he was told, started after four weeks.[2]

Meyer Lansky decided that he felt at home in Israel. He soon had his own daily routine worked out. He would get up early — before seven — and walk Bruzzer for half an hour or so beside the sea. Then he would come back to the hotel for a leisurely breakfast.

To start with, he ate mainly in his room. But as he developed a local circle of acquaintances, he found his own favorite corner in the lounge, where he liked to sit with a pot of coffee on the table, Wolfie's-style. Many of his new friends were introduced to him by Doc Stacher, who had developed, in the six years he had lived in Tel Aviv, a lifestyle that was not much different from the way he had lived in Las Vegas and New Jersey.[3]

Lansky enjoyed talking to his new friends about what had brought them to Israel. Many of the staff of the hotel had an east European background, and he discovered that one of them, Mira Sukenik, a housekeeper, came from Poland, not far from Grodno.

"How is it that you're alive?" he wanted to know.

She explained that her parents had fled eastward into Russia when the Nazis came. Everyone left behind was killed.

"I am from Poland, too," Meyer told her, and he asked her to speak some Polish or Russian to him, to see if the words could pry out something extra from his past.[4]

Every Israeli of Mira Sukenik's generation had a story to tell, and Meyer Lansky was moved by them. It started him reminiscing about his boyhood in Grodno, and about his grandparents coming to Israel.

During his first visit to Israel eight years earlier, Meyer had not been able to discover where Benjamin and Basha Suchowljansky were buried. In 1962 Jordan controlled the Jewish graveyards on the Mount of Olives. But Israel's occupation of East Jerusalem in 1967 had restored Jewish access to the mount, so a few months after his arrival in 1970, Meyer Lansky went to Jerusalem in search of his roots.[5]

The Chevra Kadisha, the organization which keeps records of where Jews are buried, supplies guides to take people out into the maze of crumbling headstones that cover the hillside, and it was one of these guides who led Meyer Lansky to a simple pair of stones across the valley from the Wailing Wall and the Mosque of Omar. Lying in the dust, the monuments were no different from the thousands of others scattered weather-beaten in the sun. But the fading Hebrew characters told how Benjamin Suchowljansky, from Grodno, had died in Jerusalem on September 10, 1910, and how his wife, Basha, had died just one month after him.[6]

Meyer Lansky had traveled through his own life with no particular sense of destination, moving from circumstance to opportunity like many another. But here, in the historic rubble of the Mount of Olives, was something that offered some sort of shape to his life, a sense of things coming full circle. Looking at these headstones, Meyer could contemplate and share in a little of the homecoming for which his grandfather had traveled so far.

Lansky found himself caught up in more than he had expected when he decided to flee to Tel Aviv. The conversation in the lobby of the Dan Hotel was less of points and deals, than of the West Bank, the growth of the religious parties, the buildup of Egyptian troops along the Suez Canal.[7] It was ennobling to be brushed by the currents of history and destiny, which are difficult to escape in Israel.

The question was how to stay there. As American citizens, Meyer and Teddy had needed no special papers to land in Tel Aviv. Their passports had been stamped with twelve-week tourist visas at the airport as a matter of routine. In normal circumstances, it would not be difficult to get these visas extended every three months — indefinitely, in theory.

In practice, however, such an arrangement would offer little defense against any serious legal attempt to force Lansky back to America. The tourist was beholden every three months to the goodwill of the Interior Ministry — and if the U.S. government were to revoke or cancel his passport, then Meyer Lansky would find himself with no standing whatsoever. He could only feel secure once he had become an Israeli citizen, and that meant satisfying the requirements of the Law of Return.

Israel's Law of Return was — and is — an immigration law unlike any other in the world. Dating back in concept to the birth of the Zionist movement, it was less an entry regulation than part of the country's identity — a practical embodiment of the right of any Jew to be granted Israeli citizenship, to find sanctuary in Zion.

"This right is inherent in every Jew by virtue of his being a Jew, if it but be his will to take part in settling the land," David Ben-Gurion declared when this cornerstone of Israel's original Declaration of Independence was enacted into law.[8]

The original Law of Return defined a Jew quite simply as the child of a Jewish mother, and since this described Meyer Lansky, he was clearly embraced by the Law of Return's intent and principle. But within a few years of the law's framing, the practicalities of statehood had modified the openness of the law's first invitation; one 1954 provision denied citizenship to a Jew "with a criminal past, likely to endanger the public welfare."[9]

It was this last provision, Section 2(b)(3) of the Law of Return, that posed the main obstacle to Meyer Lansky's ambition to make a new, permanent home for himself in Israel. He undeniably had a criminal past, and it could also be argued that his presence in Israel represented an endangerment of the "public welfare."

Set in its own very particular context of Israeli law, however, this issue would not be decided as a criminal matter. Lansky needed a constitutional expert rather than a criminal attorney to help him acquire Israeli citizenship — and his choice fell upon Yoram Alroy, a bright young lecturer in constitutional law at Tel Aviv University, who was just beginning to make a name for himself in private practice.

The name Meyer Lansky did not mean anything to Yoram Alroy in the late summer of 1970, when the young lawyer shook hands in his office with a short, quiet, rather unprepossessing Jewish American who explained that he wanted to settle in Israel, but that he had had "certain troubles with the FBI."

"Before you represent me," said Meyer as he left Alroy's office, "you should see what they write about me." And he pulled from his pocket a copy of the May 1970 issue of *Reader's Digest* — "The Shocking Success Story of 'Public Enemy No. 1.'"[10]

By the time Alroy had read the article carefully several times, he knew that this was a case he wanted to take. The *Reader's Digest* article painted the picture of a monster. But it did not seem possible to the young lawyer that the journalist who wrote the piece, or any of the experts who were quoted, could actually have met and have taken the measure of the man who had just been in his office. They were talking about an idea, not an actual human being.

It was not a matter of an old man's weary charm, or the truthfulness of anything that Meyer had claimed on his own behalf. That, Alroy realized, could all be quite false. It was a question of personality and intelligence. Meyer Lansky struck Alroy as being reasonably sharp and quick-witted, but there was nothing about the man to suggest the vision and command — the sheer mental horsepower — to engineer the awesome accomplishment that the magazine claimed for him.

More relevant to the matter in hand, it seemed to Alroy that the basic message of the article, the thesis that Meyer Lansky currently reigned over and had shaped the nature of American organized crime for the best part of half a century, was derived from supposition, not from proven courtroom evidence. It was a hypothesis based upon uncertain facts — and that, Alroy felt quite sure, was not enough in itself to deny a Jew his fundamental right of Israeli citizenship.

Alroy had set this very problem to his constitutional law students the previous year. What should the judgment be under the Law of Return when there are suspicions and allegations of a criminal past, but little solid evidence? The Law of Return, he had taught his students, was intended to guarantee Jews from everywhere a home in Israel — a unique and very precious civil right, which could only be abrogated for the most solid and irrefutable of reasons. Suspicion and supposition alone were not sufficient barriers.

He would take the case, Alroy told Lansky the next time they met. A bad reputation of itself was not an obstacle under the Law of Return — and if the *Reader's Digest* article represented the most solid evidence that could be brought against Meyer Lansky's bid for Israeli citizenship, then his new Israeli lawyer had little doubt that he would win.[11]

On Monday, September 14, 1970, Meyer Lansky's federal attorney, E. David Rosen, flew to Washington for a private meeting, "lawyer to lawyer," with William S. Lynch, chief of the Justice Department's organized crime and racketeering section.[12]

Rosen had a proposition for the Justice Department. His client was currently in Israel, where he was planning an application for Israeli citizenship — and the success of that application could very well turn upon the attitude that Lynch and his department chose to adopt. The Israeli authorities would almost certainly seek the views of the U.S. Justice Department, and if they were supplied with nothing more than Meyer's existing criminal record, "together with a factual statement that he is not a fugitive and has no legal process outstanding against him," there was a very good chance that they would grant him citizenship.

If, on the other hand, Justice's response was less neutral and took the form, say, of an endorsement of the charges in the recent *Reader's Digest* article, with the addition, possibly, of similar material and allegations, then Meyer's chances were not so good.

Rosen was fishing, trying to discover whether the Justice Department had gathered enough from its investigation of the Flamingo skimming case to lodge charges against his client — and, though he was careful not to say it in so many words, he was also, effectively, offering the department a convenient way to close its file on Meyer Lansky.

His client, Rosen pointed out, was "67 years of age [with] a cardiac condition and stomach ulcers." In a "lawyer to lawyer" context, this was less a bid for sympathy than a practical reminder that mounting a complicated and awkward prosecution against a man of Meyer Lansky's age and condition could well consume thousands of taxpayers' dollars — and years of legal time — only to be cut off with nothing to show for it.

"Basically," Lynch wrote in his report of the meeting, "Rosen wanted to know whether or not we wanted to 'get rid of Mr. Lansky' by going along with his residence in Israel."[13]

E. David Rosen got his answer before the winter was through. On February 19, 1971, Dougald McMillan issued a subpoena for Meyer Lansky to appear in Miami before the grand jury that was investigating the Flamingo skimming. When Meyer, through Rosen, pleaded illness from Israel, the court offered him a second date. But when Meyer failed to make this second deadline, there was no indulgence.

On March 24, 1971, Lansky was charged with contempt of court for failing to appear before the grand jury in Miami. On March 25, he was charged with being part of the conspiracy to skim from the Flamingo Hotel — and on March 26, John Mitchell, President Nixon's attorney general, made a national statement citing these two charges and their associated arrest warrants as tokens of the Justice Department's determination, at the highest level, to bring Meyer Lansky to justice.

Two months later, the U.S. embassy in Israel contacted Meyer through his Tel Aviv lawyer, informing him that his passport had been revoked by the State Department. He should surrender the passport to the embassy, which had all the facilities to arrange for his direct and immediate return to the United States.[14]

For most of the 1950s, the U.S. government had devoted itself to getting Meyer Lansky deported. Now that Meyer had left America of his own accord, the government was devoting its best efforts toward getting him back.

By March 1971, when Dougald McMillan filed the subpoena and indictments against him in Miami, Meyer Lansky had already taken his first steps for self-protection. He had written to Israel's minister of the interior on December 7, 1970, requesting permanent citizenship under the Law of Return, and had followed that up a week later with a personal affidavit:

"My association with Israel stands for many years back. . . . I was born a Jew, have all my life lived as a Jew and have never changed my faith."[15]

Meyer presented a matter-of-fact account of himself which, on the face of it, confronted the difficult issues head-on. He admitted his convictions from gambling — his fine in Florida in 1950, and his 1953 jail sentence in Saratoga — but he pointed out that, though technically illegal, his casinos had been patronized by "high ranking politicians and business men. . . . It was only as a result of public inquiries," he wrote, "that some of the people who had interest in the Casino were prosecuted for gambling contrary to the law, and frequently these were Jews as opposed to Christians."[16]

This self-serving inference was inaccurate. Of the ten men fined in 1950 for their Broward gambling activities, only three, including Meyer, were Jews,[17] while the only other gambler jailed with Meyer in Saratoga had been Gerard King, a local resident who was a Catholic.

So far as his current activities were concerned, Meyer claimed to have retired from active business in 1959, and to be living exclusively on the dividends of real estate and oil investments — Sam Garfield's projects — in Ohio and Michigan.[18] His annual income, he said, was "roughly $60,000 (before taxes)."[19]

> I am a member of the Temple Sinai congregation in Hollywood Florida and I would like to spend the rest of my days in Israel. . . . I have no criminal past which is likely to cause a breach of the peace and I am not now likely to endanger the peace in any country.[20]

In the months that followed, E. David Rosen secured nearly a dozen testimonials from prominent Jews in the Hollywood and Hallandale area in support of Meyer's citizenship application.

"During the first few days of the Six Day War," wrote Rabbi David Shapiro of Temple Sinai, "he came of his own inclination to my home, and gave me a substantial sum of money for the Israel Emergency Fund."[21]

"It has always been known to me that Mr. Lansky was a generous contributor to all Jewish charities," wrote Harry Permesly, the doctor who had looked after Yetta Lansky in her final Florida years.[22]

Dr. Yosef Burg (pronounced Borg) was an Orthodox rabbi who served as Israel's interior minister from 1970 to 1984. Burg represented the National Religious Party, a conservative grouping whose price of support to a succession of Israeli coalition governments was effective control of the Interior Ministry, and of the particular power which that ministry had in deciding questions of Jewishness. A heavyset man who had lost his mother and grandmother in the Holocaust, Yosef Burg regarded the civil right enshrined in the Law of Return as one of the most precious items under his stewardship.

"In a world full of countries where a Jew could enter in spite of the fact that he is a Jew," he says, "here is a country where he can enter *because* he is a Jew."[23]

It was Yosef Burg who had decided, when the first query about Meyer Lansky's status in Israel reached his desk from the Dan Hotel, via the ministry's officials in Tel Aviv, that there was no reason why the Lanskys should not receive visas like any other tourists. When Meyer lodged his application for citizenship a few months later, Burg let Yoram Alroy know that, pending his decision on the larger matter of citizenship, he would be happy to keep renewing Meyer's tourist visa without question.[24]

The omens looked favorable, and tiring of hotel life, the Lanskys started looking around for a home they might rent, or even buy, somewhere in Tel Aviv. They bought themselves a car — a sporty BMW — and Teddy went back to Florida to pack up their things. She filled six trunks with the clothes and household knickknacks they would need now that they were putting down roots in Israel.[25]

It was the newspapers that spoiled it. The Israeli press had been slow to latch onto the presence of Meyer Lansky in Tel Aviv. Even when the *Miami Herald* caught up with their favorite local gangster and reported Meyer's presence in Israel in November 1970, Israeli journalists did not appear to appreciate that the alleged boss of the U.S. underworld was walking his dog around the streets of Tel Aviv every morning.

Hank Messick put them straight. Since his 1965 series in the *Miami Herald*, Messick had been doing further research and had reworked his material into a book of his own. *Lansky*, by Hank Messick, was published in the first weeks of 1971 — "an astonishing exposé of American crime and the astonishing man who runs it — Meyer Lansky, Chairman of the Board of the National Crime Syndicate."[26]

The book did not actually define this syndicate, any more than it explained precisely who was on the board, or how it operated. But Meyer's flight to Israel, even as Messick was putting the finishing touches to his manuscript, provided telling corroboration of the author's claim that what he called "the Lansky Group" represented a worldwide menace.

"That Lansky could continue to direct his international empire from Israel, no one doubted," he wrote in an epilogue added as his volume went to press.[27]

Messick's book was widely reviewed in Israel, and suddenly Meyer Lansky was news. Photographers began stalking Meyer and Bruzzer on their morning excursions around the streets. Meyer was photographed having coffee and going to the shops. He was even snapped strolling unsuspecting beside the hotel pool in his swimming trunks — looking considerably more agile and healthy than E. David Rosen had claimed two months earlier, when explaining why his client was too sick to travel to Miami to help the grand jury.

Hoping to shake off his pursuers, Meyer checked out of the Dan Tel Aviv, and moved to the Dan Accadia, a more secluded hotel set in its own grounds in Herzliyya, a seaside suburb to the north of Tel Aviv. But Meyer's vanishing act and subsequent reappearance among the exclusive villas of Herzliyya became a story in itself.

The problem was less the photographs than the written material that accompanied them. Some of Israel's numerous tabloid newspapers and magazines took the trouble to send a reporter over to Miami. Most were content to lift and embellish previous articles, making much of Daniel Ahearn's tale of John Barrett and the arsenic-laced chicken, which became, in the retelling, a strychnine-laced turkey.[28] The daily *Ha'aretz* confidently reported that the reason Meyer was staying in Dan hotels was because he was a secret investor and controller of the Dan Hotel Group.[29] The daily *Yediot Aharanot* approached Meyer through Yoram Alroy, offering "sympathetic" treatment of his client in return for an exclusive interview[30] — only to publish the most scathing articles of all when the proposal was rejected.

In the first days of June 1971, the coverage reached a climax when Benny Sigelbaum, who had been traveling in Europe and was on his way to visit Meyer in Israel, was stopped by the immigration police at Tel Aviv airport. Sigelbaum was interrogated, placed in a waiting room for an hour or so, then put on a plane leaving the country.[31]

"We do not want the State of Israel to become a meeting place for undesirables," said a spokesman for the Israeli Justice Ministry.[32]

Sigelbaum flew home deeply incensed, insisting to anyone who cared to listen that his journey had had no more sinister purpose than to pick up some cash in Switzerland and to deliver it to his old friend Meyer.[33] Previously a generous contributor to Zionist causes, Benny Sigelbaum never gave a dollar to Israel again.

If Sigelbaum's coming to visit Meyer in Israel was judged undesirable, however, what did that say about Meyer's permanent presence in the country? Yoram Alroy's first advice to Meyer Lansky in 1970 had been to apply for his citizenship immediately, and then to exploit various rights of appeal that were open to him through the supreme court. This should make it possible, thought Alroy, to force the interior minister into a rapid decision. But E. David Rosen, who had come to Israel following his meeting with the U.S. Justice Department, had argued for a less aggressive approach, letting the minister come to a decision in his own time. Meyer had accepted the advice of his Miami lawyer.

Events seemed to be proving that Alroy's strategy had been the wiser. "Had he applied on the spot for Israeli citizenship," said Y. S. Shapiro, the Israeli justice minister, commenting late in June 1971 on Meyer's arrival the previous year, "he would certainly have got it."[34]

Twelve months previously, little had been known about Meyer. But now things were very different. Thanks to the storm of press coverage, Meyer's presence in Israel had become a matter of public controversy, with politicians beginning to take sides on the emotive issues that his citizenship raised.

Meyer Lansky and Yoram Alroy had a public relations problem on their hands, and they decided to go on the offensive. For the first — and only — time in his life, Meyer Lansky sued a newspaper for libel, challenging the *Yediot Aharanot* to substantiate the critical articles it had published about him. And he also granted his first ever interview — a lengthy conversation with the journalist Uri Dan, published in three parts by *Ma'ariv,* a respected daily newspaper which agreed, in return for the scoop, that the three articles should be basically pro-Lansky, and could constitute Meyer's plea to his fellow Jews.[35]

"I don't care what they wrote and write about me in America," Meyer declared at the beginning of the first article. "I care what they think of me in Israel."[36]

As in his affidavit to the interior minister, Meyer played heavily on his Jewish credentials — his fund-raising for Israel and his breaking up of the meetings of Nazi sympathizers in the 1930s. But he offered no explanation as to how he had been able to command the muscle to break heads and throw people out of windows at that stage of his career; and when he boasted how, in 1948, he had "dealt with" shipments of Arab arms being smuggled through the New York waterfront, he appeared oblivious to the dark connotations that an expression like "dealt with" raised.[37]

Meyer's willingness to speak out in his own defense, and the threat embodied in his libel action against *Yediot Aharanot,* went some way to calm the extremer aspects of the controversy. At the end of July 1971, *Ha'aretz,* which had been sued by the Dan Group, apologized, and withdrew its allegation that Meyer was a secret owner of the hotels.[38] In the same week, Dr. Yosef Burg told the Knesset that he was granting a further extension to Meyer's tourist visa, which had been due to expire before the end of the month.[39]

But it was now clear to Dr. Burg that the status of Meyer Lansky in Israel was a public issue that would involve the whole government, and for guidance he went to speak to his prime minister. Yosef Burg knew better than to raise the matter with Golda Meir in full cabinet. So he waited until after a meeting of ministers, then took Mrs. Meir aside and explained the main outlines of the Lansky problem — the articles in the papers, the questions that were starting in the Knesset.

In the summer of 1971, Golda Meir was much occupied with the buildup of Egyptian forces along the Suez Canal, and she did not seem familiar with the details of the Lansky case. She listened a little distractedly as Burg outlined Meyer's eastern European origins, his Jewish background, his criminal record — until Burg uttered the word "Mafia." Then, suddenly, he had his prime minister's full attention.

"'Dr. Burg? Mafia?'" Yosef Burg recalls Golda Meir saying. The prime minister was horrified. "She opened her big, green eyes. 'Dr. Burg, Mafia? No Mafia in Israel.'"[40]

At the time that Golda Meir opened her big, green eyes and pronounced what turned out to be the decisive political word on Meyer Lansky's future in Israel, she was lobbying the Nixon administration in Washington to supply Israel with more Phantom F-4 jet fighter-bombers. Israel needed these, she maintained, to counter the arrival of new Soviet weaponry on the Suez Canal, and the theory subsequently arose that Mrs. Meir's "no Mafia" decision amounted to a trade-off — Meyer Lansky for Phantom jets.

This theory overrates Meyer Lansky's importance to either the U.S. or the Israeli government. Israel was, in fact, just taking delivery in July 1971 of the last of seventy-four promised Phantoms,[41] and the American reluctance to supply more was based on such factors as Israel's intransigence over its occupied West Bank territories, and the goodwill which Washington wished to maintain with Anwar Sadat in Cairo.

Of all Israeli politicians, however, Golda Meir was sensitive to American public opinion, and to how Israel's giving shelter to an alleged crime boss might play in the suburban synagogues when Bonds for Israel time came round. She was, in many senses, American herself, having grown up and lived in the U.S., so "Mafia" held layers of menace for her that were lost on Rabbi Burg.

Meyer Lansky had expressed the hope to his friends that the woman who made her political reputation with her spectacular fund-raising trips around America in 1948 might have special sympathy for someone who had provided help in his own way at that crucial time. But it was precisely because of all Mrs. Meir absorbed while she was in America in 1948 that, twenty-three years later, she decided against him.

In August 1971, Buddy and Sandra Lansky came to visit their father. Buddy could still walk with difficulty for short distances, but he was becoming more and more dependent on a wheelchair.

Meyer enjoyed showing Israel to his children. He had been in the country for more than a year now, and he felt something of a native. He took the family to Jerusalem, and had his photograph taken with Sandra beside the Wailing Wall. The cobblestones were too rough for Buddy to make it all the way in his wheelchair. Meyer booked some extra rooms at the Dan Accadia, then at the height of its summer season. Sitting beside the crowded pool, and eating together at their own table in the dining room, the Lanskys were one big family party among many — enjoying, some thirty years on, an echo of their family summers on the Jersey shore.

Meyer introduced his family to the new friends he had made in Israel, among them a young acquaintance he had made quite recently, a law student, Yoram Sheftel, who had organized a petition that summer in support of Meyer's right to Israeli citizenship. Sheftel had been engrossed by the public controversy over Meyer Lansky and the Law of Return, and he had no doubt where his sympathies lay. Jewish gangsters like Lansky, Bugsy Siegel, Waxey Gordon, Doc Stacher — even Lepke Buchalter, a convicted murderer — might have broken the law. But that law, in Sheftel's eyes, was the law of "white, Christian countries . . . based on Christianity, which is the most anti-Semitic phenomenon in human history."[42]

"I don't see anything wrong," says Sheftel, "with a Jewish person breaking the law of countries which were persecuting, murdering, torturing, and discriminating against Jews for the past two thousand years."[43]

Such fierce opinions were not uncommon among young Israelis in the early 1970s, emboldened by their country's recent success in the Six-Day War. Their feelings about the Law of Return had been greatly influenced by the case of Robert Soblen, which had convulsed Israel a few years before the war.[44]

In 1963, Dr. Robert Soblen, a convicted spy awaiting sentencing on bail, fled from the United States to Israel to claim asylum under the Law of Return. Turned away from Israel under provision 2(b)(3), and heading back by plane under police escort, Soblen had managed to secrete a knife from his lunch tray and slash his wrists under cover of a blanket, losing large amounts of blood before his wounds were discovered. When the plane reached London, Soblen was rushed to a hospital but died a few days later.

Sheftel had no sympathy with Soblen — "He was a Jewish Communist, an anti-Zionist, who remembered Israel only when he faced life imprisonment"[45] — but Soblen was entitled to refuge in Israel, for all that.

"In my opinion," says Sheftel today, "the state of Israel should exist to provide Jews with shelter from the goyim [the Gentiles], never mind the reason why a Jew is seeking shelter."[46]

Sheftel saw Meyer Lansky as a potential martyr like Soblen, a victim of American interference in Israel's internal affairs — and for this reason alone, Sheftel knew he would have no difficulty getting signatures from his fellow students on Lansky's behalf. But before he organized his petition, it struck Yoram Sheftel that he should first obtain the permission of Meyer Lansky himself. So having read that Meyer had moved to the Dan Accadia in Herzliyya, the young law student went, one weekend, to the hotel, where he found Meyer sitting in the lobby, taking coffee with Teddy, Doc Stacher, and a few other friends.

No shrinking violet, Yoram Sheftel went straight up to Meyer Lansky to introduce himself and ask if he could have a few minutes of Meyer's time.

"He answered me very politely, very nicely," Sheftel remembers. "He said he was very sorry, but he was in a very delicate and peculiar position. He could not allow himself to speak to a person of whom he knew nothing, so he asked me to write him a letter and explain exactly what is the purpose of the meeting. . . . I went back home and I wrote the letter that same day."[47]

Sheftel made it clear in his letter that he and his fellow students did not seek any financial assistance from Meyer. On the contrary, they insisted that they themselves should meet any expenses that the organizing of the petition might incur.

It was one of the nicest letters that he could ever recall receiving, Meyer told Sheftel when they met.[48] He was more than happy for the young student's petition to go ahead, and in the next few weeks, Sheftel was able to gather several thousand signatures among the students and faculty of Hebrew University.

It was the beginning of a fast friendship between Sheftel and Meyer Lansky. Sheftel took Meyer home to meet his parents on Friday nights for *Shabbes* supper, and they spent long hours discussing religion and politics. Meyer was delighted to find a young, self-confident Jew whose opinions both echoed and gave a new cutting edge to his own. The Kefauver Committee, for example, when discussed by Lansky and Sheftel, became a conspiracy by the goy establishment to spoil and steal the profitable business of gambling in America from enterprising ethnic minorities.

"The Wasps couldn't have it," Meyer told Sheftel, "that a bunch of Jewish and Italian street boys could make so much money in Vegas and other places. They wanted to drive us out — and finally they succeeded."[49]

As Sheftel got to know Lansky better, he tried to initiate his new friend into some of the subtleties of the Israeli political process. Petitions, newspaper articles, and legal action were all very well, he explained, but should not Meyer offer some behind-the-scenes help? He might usefully consider making some financial contributions to the various institutes and charities that were associated with the National Religious Party — the party of the interior minister, Dr. Burg.

Meyer Lansky shook his head.

"Not through the window," he said to Sheftel, "I want to get in through the door."[50]

In Israel, at the age of seventy, Meyer Lansky had finally found something too valuable to buy.

At the end of September 1971, Dr. Yosef Burg arrived at his decision. After a careful study of the evidence, the interior minister announced, he had come to the conclusion that Meyer Lansky was a person with a criminal past, likely to endanger the public welfare. Meyer's application for Israeli citizenship was, accordingly, denied, and he would get no further extensions on his tourist visa.

Yoram Alroy had only one weapon left, a hearing before the Israeli Supreme Court. The lawyer had never had much doubt that it would, eventually, come to this. Nor did he doubt that, when subjected to the laws of evidence in the high court, the case against his client would appear considerably less damning than it did when set out in books and newspaper articles.

But the young attorney had questions he wanted to ask Meyer Lansky. Alroy had discovered nothing over the months to shake his original impression that this less-than-supercharged individual could not possibly be the organizing genius of American crime. But neither had he discovered much evidence to suggest that Meyer Lansky was any kind of saint. The attorney was concerned that his client had not told him the full story about his past — and Alroy's suspicions were well founded.

Meyer had claimed to his lawyer that he had lost some $18 million when Fidel Castro confiscated the Riviera Hotel in 1960, that he had then withdrawn from all involvement in casinos and gambling, and that he had put most of his surviving funds into Sam Garfield's Ohio and Michigan oil ventures. Throughout the 1960s, therefore, he had, for all practical purposes, been "retired."[51] This tale was not totally false, but, like so much to do with Meyer Lansky, it was far from being totally true either. It quite left out of account Meyer's skimming activities in Las Vegas.

Not knowing the full story about all their clients' activities is, in fact, the situation that experienced criminal attorneys prefer. They need to rely absolutely on the facts necessary to win a case, but they are generally happier to remain in ignorance about every dark detail in their clients' lives.

"It is usually preferable," explains E. David Rosen, choosing his words carefully, "to operate on a need-to-know basis."[52]

Being in the dark, however, troubled Yoram Alroy. The case that he was fighting revolved around the content of a whole life — the life of a Jew who desired to come to live in Israel — and Alroy wanted no surprises when he made his first appearance in Israel's ultimate legal forum. So before formally starting the application that would lead to the supreme court, the young lecturer in constitutional law extracted a promise from Meyer Lansky that Lansky would give a truthful answer to whatever question Alroy might privately ask him, and that if Alroy were to catch his client lying just once, on any subject, then the lawyer could immediately give up the case.

In the months that followed, Alroy availed himself fully of this agreement. He asked Lansky everything he could think of, and by the time the Israeli Supreme Court was ready to try the case in the late spring of 1972, he felt he could make a fair assessment of his client's criminality.

Drugs and prostitution, he came to feel certain, had never been numbered among Lansky's adult rackets. There was a fastidiousness to the man which made his denials on those scores quite believable to Alroy. Nor did the lawyer consider that personal violence was part of Lansky's mature style — though Alroy decided that Lansky could well have been rough and violent in his youth. Meyer Lansky was also quite capable, the Israeli thought, of shutting his eyes to violence if it were deployed by others.

Yes, Alroy could see Meyer Lansky being turned to by other crime figures as an arbitrator when disputes arose — "He was not intelligent, but he was wise"[53] — and, yes, it was easy to see how any business partnership would trust him with their money. On the other hand, Yoram Alroy did not really feel he could say, when he came to look at the total picture, that his client's record of personal achievement justified the claim that Meyer Lansky had lived his life as a positive member of society. By his own admission, Lansky had facilitated the business activities of some most violent and disreputable characters.

As the two men prepared themselves for the moment of confrontation in the high court, often working and talking together late into the night, Yoram Alroy saw Meyer Lansky under pressure, his defenses down. The old man was too anxious and tired to pretend, and Alroy was surprised to discover a certain vulnerability in the apparently more hardened and experienced character.

"In many ways," says Alroy, "he still saw himself as a poor little Jewish boy from the Lower East Side."[54]

There were some sources of self-esteem. When Lansky looked back on his career, he took inordinate pride in the casinos and hotels that he had helped create, describing their functioning in practical and strangely mundane detail — particularly the Riviera and how its kitchens worked. Alroy was struck by the relatively banal satisfaction that Meyer Lansky derived from such pleasures as a good steak in a well-run restaurant, a hedonism which provided some leavening to a lean, almost puritanical way of life.

Yoram Alroy decided, on balance, that he liked the man. Meyer Lansky took a genuine interest in the people that he met and in their problems. Lansky was also quite sincere, in Alroy's judgment, in his anxiety that his gifts to good causes in Israel should not be taken as bribes.

Yoram Alroy could not help asking his client the big question — How much money was Meyer Lansky really worth? — and he received quite a detailed answer which he considered accurate, and which he declines today to discuss.

"He was not poor," he says. "But if I were to tell you the reality, it is so far below the fantasy that you would not believe me."

Hank Messick's $300 million? The more conservative $100 million proposed by *Reader's Digest?* Both, says Yoram Alroy, "absolutely ridiculous."[55]

As the two men worked together through the winter of 1971–72 — and became quite firm friends — Lansky became more expansive. He told Alroy of slight contacts he had had with John F. Kennedy in the 1950s when the young senator from Massachusetts came to Havana. Everyone in the business knew that Kennedy had a voracious sexual appetite, Lansky confided disapprovingly. The senator pursued women with a recklessness which was extraordinary in someone entrusted with a public office.

JFK happened to be one of Yoram Alroy's heroes, and the lawyer was dismayed by this revelation. He felt sure that this was one subject on which Meyer Lansky must be well wide of the truth. But it was not reason enough, he decided, to invoke their agreement and stop handling the case.[56]

On March 22, 1972, the Israeli Supreme Court, sitting as the High Court of Justice, convened in Jerusalem to hear the suit of *Meyer Lansky v. the State of Israel.* The normal quorum of judges to hear an appeal was three, but considering the important issues involved, Israel's chief justice, Shimon Agranat, decided that the panel to hear the Lansky case should be increased to five — and that he would preside over it personally.

Yoram Alroy had brought the case under a procedure that went back to the British Mandate, an order nisi requiring the high court to invalidate the minister of the interior's decision "unless" the minister could show the court just cause for depriving Meyer Lansky of his civil rights. So, technically, the case was not an appeal. After a lifetime on the receiving end of the legal process, Meyer Lansky found himself the plaintiff — effectively seated at the prosecutor's table — with the state of Israel answering his complaints in the defendant's seat.

The state of Israel was represented by its state attorney, Gavriel Bach, a bright-eyed, birdlike man who had served his legal apprenticeship in England, and who had made his name as one of the prosecutors of Adolf Eichmann in the famous trial of 1961. As state attorney, Bach was responsible for all litigation involving the state — a sort of solicitor general, in Anglo-American terms — and his role in the defense of the Interior Ministry against Meyer Lansky was part of a strategy devised with Yosef Burg. Anticipating that the decision over Lansky's Israeli citizenship would be subject to legal challenge whichever way it went, and that the state attorney would then have the job of defending it in court, Burg and Bach thought it made sense that the person who would eventually defend the evidence should be the person who originally gathered and analyzed it. So, with the concurrence of the justice minister, Gavriel Bach had been sent to Washington in the summer of 1971.[57]

Bach had been made very welcome in the United States, being received personally, and spending several hours with Richard Nixon's attorney general, John Mitchell. Mitchell told Bach how pleased he was that Israel had taken this initiative of its own accord. The U.S. government wished to avoid the impression of interference in another country's internal affairs, he said, so it had deliberately held back from any diplomatic contacts or pressure over the Lansky affair. Now that Bach had come to Washington of his own accord, however, the attorney general was happy to tell him that the Justice Department considered Meyer Lansky a major figure in U.S. organized crime and that it wanted him back in America under arrest.*

Gavriel Bach spent the next two weeks in the Justice Department, in Washington, granted free access, on John Mitchell's orders, to any file he needed to assemble the best available case. Bach was given all the material gathered by the Immigration and Naturalization Service in its attempt to denaturalize Meyer Lansky in the 1950s, together with the illegal wiretaps of the early 1960s. Such evidence was inadmissible in an Israeli court, as it was in the United States, but Bach decided that it would be part of the interior minister's administrative duty to consider it.

*The charges brought against Lansky in Miami in March 1971 were not covered by the extradition agreements between Israel and the United States.

Bach collected the transcripts of Meyer Lansky's appearances before the Kefauver Committee, and a minilibrary of popular paperbacks on organized crime. The books and documents Bach brought home with him in 1971 filled two suitcases, but, looking back today, the state attorney, who has since become a justice of the Israeli Supreme Court himself, considers that the most persuasive evidence he hit upon in Washington was nothing written on paper.

There had been one document, not especially important in itself, which Bach would have liked to take back to Israel, if it had not been so poorly photocopied. It was a New York court judgment, so Bach had made the obvious suggestion that the New York police department might be contacted with a request for a better copy.

The response to this suggestion amazed him. Such a request, he was told, was against Justice Department practice. The department's basic attitude toward local police departments — and, indeed, toward the offices of all local district attorneys — was that local officials were tied up in, and were thus compromised by, the local electoral process. Whatever their personal skills and integrity, they had to be considered fundamentally untrustworthy.

"We never rely on local police if we can help it," he was told, "nor on district attorneys."

Bach was horrified, reflecting on how such a situation would affect his own work as state attorney at home.

"We, in Israel," he says, "may have a corrupt policeman somewhere, or some attorney who comes under suspicion. But the very idea that, as state attorney, I would be afraid to apply to a district attorney, or to the police, is something that just would not occur to me."

Gavriel Bach looked again at the evidence of Walter Clark and the sheriff's department cars which had escorted Meyer Lansky's illegal casino earnings to the bank in Broward County in the 1940s. It was a situation which stood on its head every principle on which Bach's legal training and career was based.

"They more or less appointed the policemen and district attorneys who were supposed to investigate them," he says.

Bach had traveled to Washington very conscious of the guiding principle of the Law of Return — "The state of Israel," he says, "was created not for the benefit of the six hundred thousand Jews who happened to be here in 1948, but as a home for Jews from everywhere." But the possibility that one branch of law enforcement could

not trust another seemed to Bach to threaten civil rights and processes in a still more serious dimension, and he returned from
Washington seeing Meyer Lansky in a new and sinister light —
as a dangerous example of poison that perverted the legal processes
of a great democracy.

"I felt very strongly," he says, "that we had not set up this state to
become a haven for people like this."

When the issues surrounding Meyer Lansky came to be debated
in Israel's High Court of Justice, State Attorney Bach was to be criticized for the passion with which he argued the case against Lansky.
It seemed to some reporters that he was fighting a personal crusade.
But Gavriel Bach today makes no apology.

"I must admit," he says, "that the idea that this sort of thing might
come to this country was what prompted me to act rather forcibly in
this matter."

The case of Meyer Lansky versus the state of Israel was played out
in the historic surroundings of the former Ottoman Palace of Justice
in the old Russian quarter of Jerusalem. Tall cypress trees and
greened copper domes surrounded the dusty piazza where Meyer
Lansky, tidy and respectful in a dark suit and tie, arrived with his
lawyers at eight-thirty each morning.

Inside the building, the worn flagstones, whitewashed walls, and
dark wood benches once occupied by British colonial administrators
imposed a certain detachment on the proceedings. To the disappointment of the press corps in attendance, the legal protocol of the order
nisi did not call for personal testimony. Neither Meyer Lansky nor
the interior minister took the stand. The battle was fought out by
their lawyers. But the passion that Gavriel Bach had come to feel
about the case, and the fervor with which Yoram Alroy argued for
his client's civil rights, provided drama enough.

Bach had come prepared for what he anticipated would be one of
Alroy's key arguments — the slight and comparatively trivial nature
of Meyer Lansky's criminal record. This was no indication of
Lansky's innocence, argued the state attorney. On the contrary, it
confirmed his guilt, since it was in the nature of U.S. organized crime
that those who were the masterminds of criminal activity should
insulate themselves from its practical execution. This meant that they
were seldom caught, and, when brought to justice, tended to escape
conviction. It followed, therefore, that those who were the most

culpable usually had the fewest convictions — so the very lack of
solid evidence against Meyer Lansky must, in fact, be considered the
strongest possible evidence against him.

Yoram Alroy had little difficulty dealing with this ploy — which
was, essentially, the rationale of Hank Messick and the various journalists who had made the absence of solid data about Meyer Lansky
the proof of his cleverness. The state attorney's argument, responded
Alroy, was no different from that of the naive archaeology student
excavating Masada, who claimed that the city's ancient inhabitants
must have used wireless.

"What is your proof?" his professor had asked him.

"We have discovered no wires," said the student with pride.[58]

The justices of the Israeli high court enjoyed that little joke. But
Alroy did not fare so well when he argued against the heavy reliance
that Gavriel Bach placed upon Lansky's use of the Fifth Amendment
in his testimony to the Kefauver Committee. Lansky had acknowledged in 1950 and 1951, in response to questioning by Kefauver and
Rudolph Halley, that he knew such men as Lucky Luciano and Frank
Costello. But then, said Bach, when Meyer Lansky was invited to
detail his dealings with these notorious characters, he had responded
that any answer he gave might be incriminating. This answer, argued
Bach, could reasonably be taken as an admission of complicity on
Lansky's part.

Shimon Agranat, the chief justice, broke in. Lansky, he pointed
out, had been exercising the constitutional right of any American
citizen.

Bach responded by agreeing that this argument was legally correct
in a courtroom situation, when it came to deciding what evidence
might properly be considered by a judge or jury. But the minister of
the interior was not a judge. He was a bureaucrat trying to assess the
criminality of a difficult and elusive man, and faced with such a challenge, argued the state attorney, the minister was entitled to take
account of all the circumstances. Meyer Lansky had been given the
chance by the Kefauver Committee to clear his name in a public and
official forum, and had declined the offer on the grounds that any
answer he gave might tend to incriminate him. The Israeli minister
of the interior was entitled to draw the same conclusion from that as
any reasonable man in the street.

Lansky listened intently to the legal sparring, sitting beside E.
David Rosen, who had flown in from America for the hearing. The
two men hunched attentively, looking over the shoulder of a bearded

interpreter who was translating the proceedings in longhand onto a legal pad.

Sitting just behind the two Americans was David Landau, a young reporter for the *Jerusalem Post*, who was engrossed by the drama of the old Jew fighting for sanctuary in the Promised Land.

Landau was impressed with Lansky. Halfway through each morning's hearing the court would adjourn, and the lawyers and reporters would stretch their legs and gossip in the shade of the cypress trees outside. Meyer Lansky would light up a cigarette. He seemed extraordinarily calm, thought Landau, for a man who was really in quite desperate straits. The reporter was particularly struck by the low, firm tone of Lansky's voice, and by the fact that he never raised it.

"You felt," remembers Landau, "that he had lived a whole life of people obeying him, and people listening to him, and being very quiet in order to hear what he had to say."[59]

Lansky would chat quite freely and informally with Landau and the other reporters, including a young UPI man who made a dashing arrival each morning in an open sports car.

Lansky admired the car. "With your youth and my money," he said, "we could go a long way."[60]

"Gallows humor," thought David Landau — though when he reflected on all he had been listening to in the courtroom, it seemed to him that Meyer Lansky stood a good chance of cheating the noose.[61] The five high court justices, serious and well-respected legal heavyweights, represented the different sides of the Israeli political spectrum, and there was quite a possibility that their different prejudices might strangely gel in Lansky's favor, the conservatives standing behind his rights as a Jew, the liberals skeptical of the hearsay evidence produced against him. None of the judges wanted the proudly independent Israeli legal system to be seen as biddable by the state — let alone by the American government, which was patently eager to get its hands on Meyer Lansky.

After five days of arguments, the court adjourned for the judges to consider their verdict. It would take several months for the judgment to be agreed and written, and, in the meantime, the state attorney, Gavriel Bach, did some reflecting of his own about the man whose life he had examined in such detail, and whom he had now had the chance to study in the flesh.

For more than two years in the early 1960s Bach had looked across the courtroom with similar curiosity at Adolf Eichmann,

another man held by the world to represent the very epitome of deg-
radation and evil. Now Bach had to admit that he did not see the
wickedness written into Lansky's features any more than he had seen
it in Eichmann's: "If you had asked me, if you had seen him on a
bus, I would not have thought these things likely."[62]

But appearances had been deceptive in Eichmann's case, and the
courteous demeanor of the seventy-year-old Meyer Lansky in the
Israeli High Court of Justice did not, in Bach's eyes, disprove the
violence of a young hoodlum on the streets of the Lower East Side
in the 1920s, nor the cunning of Lucky Luciano's onetime partner
and best friend. Wickedness was imagined by the world to be dramatic and exciting and fairly easy to identify. But when confronted
in real life, the face of evil could be quite drab — and rather difficult
to fathom.

By the summer of 1972, Meyer Lansky and his wife had spent two
full years in Israel. They were no longer tourists, and they had put
the hotel life behind them. Their Tel Aviv address was 4 Rehov
Beeri — Beeri Street — a long residential street notable for containing the home of the American ambassador, and also for being
named, according to a plaque below the street sign, in honor of Berl
Kaznelson (1887–1944), founder of the Hebrew trades union newspaper, Davar, and "spiritual leader of the working movement in
Israel."[63]

There was a smart end of Beeri Street — where the American
ambassador lived — and a scruffy end, where the Lanskys rented
their apartment in a run-down concrete box on stilts that was similar
to thousands of others in the suburbs of Tel Aviv. The building contained eight tenants, who parked their cars between the stilts, and
who learned to be nimble as they covered the distance between the
small, doorless Schindler lift and their individual apartment doors.
The hall light switches operated on a very brief time release.[64]

The occupants of 4 Beeri Street kept themselves to themselves.
Their doors had spyholes and security chains to rival those of
a New York apartment. But the door frames also sported mezuzahs,
the little metal cylinders holding fragments of the Torah, the sign
in Tel Aviv, as in Grodno, that here was the threshold of a Jewish
home.

Meyer Lansky walked Bruzzer, morning and evening, up and
down Beeri Street. He met regularly with Israeli friends, as well as
with Doc Stacher, who had an even more modest apartment in the

neighborhood. And he had regular assignations with an attractive young woman whom he had first met at the Dan Hotel, where she was working.

Meyer Lansky presumably thought that he was being discreet in this, and the lady herself, today, declines to comment. But to the staff of the Dan Hotel where she worked the affair was no secret. To Ykutiel Federman, owner and founder of the Dan Hotel Group — still exercised, twenty years later, by the 1971 allegation that Lansky was, in some way, a secret investor in his company — Meyer's affair with one of his staff was one more routine detail in a routine stay by a routine guest.

"I met him once. He was very modest, very quiet. He was not a genius. But maybe this was his life, to appear what he was not."[65]

Teddy Lansky, meanwhile, was less than enchanted with the faintly depressing atmosphere of Beeri Street. She had fallen ill during the hearings in the supreme court. At the hotel there had at least been the bustle of other people's lives going on around her. In the apartment there was little to do in the evenings except read and go early to bed.[66]

Teddy developed more enthusiasm about a little apartment in Ramat Gan, a development to the northeast of Tel Aviv.[67] Meyer put some money down on a place there, and Teddy busied herself working out the details of the drapes and furnishings. But her heart was not really in it. People who met Teddy Lansky in Israel could not escape the impression that she would rather have been in Miami Beach.

On September 11, 1972, the journalists, lawyers, and plaintiff who had spent so much time together during the spring hearings nearly six months earlier reassembled in the high-ceilinged courtroom of the old Palace of Justice in Jerusalem to hear the outcome of *Meyer Lansky v. the State of Israel.*

Chief Justice Agranat delivered the judgment himself. Quite unusually, all five justices were agreed on their verdict and, even more unusual, they were also agreed on the eighty-three pages of legal arguments that were set out in the final judgment, which took Agranat nearly three hours to deliver. He had written the judgment himself.[68]

The chief justice started with a lengthy chronology of the events that had followed from Meyer Lansky's arrival in Israel on July 27, 1970, going into particular detail about the correspondence and meetings between the ministry on the one hand, and Meyer and his lawyer on the other. This process of consultation was important, said Agranat, because the right of every Jew to immigrate to Israel was a fundamental right which should only be denied after the most meticulous investigation and observance of the law.

Agranat then reviewed Meyer Lansky's criminal record, essentially agreeing with Yoram Alroy's contention that the offenses, as set out, did not in themselves constitute a criminal record likely to endanger the state of Israel — and at the end of his judgment the chief justice singled Alroy out for particular praise for the cogency with which he had marshaled and presented every possible argument on his client's behalf.

However — and here Agranat acknowledged how much he and his fellow justices had been swayed by Gavriel Bach's arguments — convictions on paper were not the whole story. The five Israeli judges decided that they attached quite considerable credence to the findings of the Kefauver Committee. They accepted these, and other official American inquiries into the nature of organized crime, as honest attempts to define a major problem. They found Kefauver's conclusions about Meyer Lansky quite credible, and, while agreeing that such evidence might not be technically admissible in a court of law, they held that Dr. Yosef Burg had done nothing improper in relying on these and a number of other secondary sources in arriving at his decision to deny Meyer Lansky citizenship under the Law of Return.

"There is no reason," declared Justice Agranat, "why the Minister should not take into account facts and evidence not directly concerned with that person's criminal past but which could indicate, in addition to that criminal past, the likelihood of his being a danger to the public welfare."[69]

This was the crucial factor in the judgment. Yoram Alroy and Meyer's many Israeli supporters, from Sheftel, the law student, to Landau, the journalist, had argued that the speculative and unproven evidence against Meyer was not sufficient to deny him his civil rights as a Jew. David Landau was particularly scornful of the way in which State Attorney Bach, at one stage of his arguments, had rested his hand dramatically on his pile of American crime paperbacks.

But the high court held that Section 2(b)(3) of the Law of Return called on the minister of the interior to cast his net wider than the narrow legal record. The minister was not a judge, and the ministry was not a court of law. It would, indeed, be quite improper, said the high court, for a minister to attempt to exercise such legal functions.

He had to operate according to the looser rules of natural justice — which were that the plaintiff should be given a fair hearing, and that the final decision be "based on evidence which responsible and reasonable persons would regard as having probative value."[70]

By these two criteria, declared the chief justice, the minister of the interior had acted quite properly, and had more than satisfied the requirements of the law. The record of correspondence and meetings between the ministry's officials and Meyer Lansky's lawyer, often involving Meyer himself, had given the would-be citizen several chances to state his case. Some people might disagree with the minister's conclusion that "the petitioner [Meyer Lansky] had operated within the framework of organized crime in the United States and had been closely associated with it." But in the judges' eyes this conclusion had been arrived at "in good faith" and after a thorough evaluation of the evidence. "It could not be said to be unreasonable."[71]

The judges came to a similar finding on the question of whether, whatever the facts about his criminal past, Meyer Lansky could currently be considered a threat to the public welfare of Israel. The Law of Return charged the minister with a responsibility to the whole community, and Dr. Burg had interpreted this strictly, deciding not to take any risks that "the ugly phenomenon of organized crime, as it exists in America," might be transplanted to Israel.[72]

The minister's decision was, again, open to debate. But the judges could not say that the minister's prudence was unreasonable, taking account of circumstances which included Benny Sigelbaum's visit in the previous year. There was, in summary, no cause for the high court to interfere with an administrative decision which had been thoroughly researched and conscientiously arrived at. The minister had observed the law.

Chief Justice Agranat's opinion of September 11, 1972, was less a judgment against Meyer Lansky than one in favor of Dr. Yosef Burg. Looking at Meyer's legal challenge to Dr. Burg, as posed by the order nisi, it was difficult to see how the five Israeli justices could have come to any other conclusion — and it was suddenly clear that the terrain of this final battlefield had been badly chosen from Lansky's point of view. Had these same high court justices been invited to pass judgment, say, on the issues raised by the libel action which Meyer Lansky had brought in the previous year against the newspaper *Yediot Aharanot*, they would probably have found in Meyer's favor, since they were agreed that the hearsay evidence against him was not technically admissible. Gavriel Bach's pile of paperbacks would have been laughed out of court — and *if* Meyer Lansky had been able to clear his name through a libel case heard in an Israeli court, then the interior minister would have had a solid reason for finding that the Law of Return's criminal prohibition did not apply.

This line of tactics had, in fact, been considered in discussions between Meyer, Alroy, and E. David Rosen the previous year, and had been rejected. Meyer and Rosen were unhappy about fighting the libel action, so the suit against *Yediot Aharanot* had been dropped. But by opting for a process which required the high court to pass judgment on Dr. Burg's conduct rather than on Meyer Lansky's, a situation was created in which Dr. Burg's victory could only mean Meyer Lansky's final and total defeat.

After the verdict, Lansky and Alroy ruefully discussed the might-have-beens. Should Lansky have applied for citizenship at the moment of his arrival? Should they have pursued the libel action harder? Had the order nisi not, perhaps, been a mistake?

"Well," said Meyer Lansky. "Now we know."[73]

19

"A Jew Has a Slim Chance in the World"

As Meyer Lansky walked out into the sunlit courtyard of the Supreme Court Building in Jerusalem on September 11, 1972, he slipped into the easy self-pity of the little boy from the Lower East Side.

"A Jew has a slim chance in the world," he said,[1] apparently dismissing the considered judgment of five very eminent and committed Jews as anti-Semitism. In response to the reporters crowding round, he tried to be a little more profound.

"That's life," he said. "At my age it's too late to worry. What will be, will be. Look what happened last week in Munich" — referring to the kidnapping and murder of eleven Israeli athletes at the Munich Olympics a few days earlier. "Young branches cut down. I'm an old man."[2]

Behind this stoic exterior, however, there was dismay. Meyer's canceled U.S. passport, which he had declined physically to surrender to the American embassy, could only take him to a U.S. destination, where the FBI would certainly be waiting. In the aftermath of the high court decision, Dr. Burg had announced that his ministry would now issue Meyer Lansky with an Israeli laissez-passer, a document which would authorize him to travel to any state that was willing to admit him. But what country in the world was likely to welcome Meyer Lansky after the publicity of the previous months?

Suddenly Lansky's strategies for survival went down a notch or two in high-mindedness. The once upright applicant for Israeli citizenship was now prepared to entertain suggestions as to how, even at this final hour, he might be able to bribe his way into the country.

One day soon after the high court verdict, Meyer came to Yoram Alroy with a scheme to make some payments which would, someone had assured him, persuade Dr. Burg to reverse himself. Meyer did not seem discouraged when his lawyer said that he would have nothing to do with the scheme, and it was only when Yoram Alroy pointed out that the proposal could possibly be a device to entrap Meyer and to discredit him totally, that the older and supposedly more worldly-wise man thought better of it.[3] When Lansky had told Sheftel, the law student, that he wanted to enter Israel through the door and not the window, he had evidently been counting on the door's swinging open to quite a gentle push.

It was a time for desperate measures. Throughout his life, Meyer Lansky had declined to trade on the achievement of his younger son, Paul, the West Point graduate and air force pilot. Meyer had kept in touch with his younger son, briefing him on Israeli politics and the current situation, in the tradition of the father and son discussing anything together but personal matters. Meyer sent Paul subscriptions to *Israel* magazine, and to the weekly overseas edition of the *Jerusalem Post*.[4]

In his hours locked away from his family in his study, Paul Lansky had been reading books on Israel — a biography of David Ben-Gurion, studies of Golda Meir — and had come to feel he could be of real help to his father. The arguments in the high court had not seriously addressed the question of the monies which Meyer Lansky had contributed in the past to Israeli causes, and it was Paul Lansky's belief that a proper appreciation of these past contributions could sway things in his father's favor, even after the adverse verdict of the high court. On October 9, 1972, Paul typed an angry, rambling, three-page open letter to Dr. Yosef Burg, which he sent to his father to get published in Israel.

David Landau, of the *Jerusalem Post*, had already noted the element of collective hypocrisy in Israel's exclusion of Meyer — "the denial of the shadowy past that is part of the American Jewish experience, but which we, in Israel, like to feel that we are above and beyond."[5]

Paul Lansky took this same perspective, but presented the debate in essentially materialistic terms:

> Simply put, Dr. Burg, Israel was in dire need. You asked for help. You got the help — and some of it came from people like my Dad. . . . I wish that you would tell me where you would be today if that support had been denied to you.[6]

Dr. Burg's comments on the Lansky case had been published in the weekly *Jerusalem Post* of September 20, 1972, and Paul Lansky went through the minister's arguments, responding to them one by one.

> Did Israel not accept assistance from people like my Dad about whom unfavorable comments had been made? When did they not accept such assistance? . . . Why didn't you selectively research all these people about whom things have been written before you accepted assistance?[7]

The problem with the letter was its rough and sarcastic tone — "My Dad and many people with backgrounds similar to his have been assisting their ancestors (which happens to be you people) since the time the latest problems started" — and also the repetition of its basic argument.[8] Meyer Lansky's younger son appeared to be reducing everything to terms of money.

It was a brave gesture on Paul's part, the only time in his life that he went public on behalf of his father, and in a spirited and supportive fashion. Suddenly he was prepared to be part of the family. But Paul may have felt in special need of family ties in October 1972, for two weeks earlier, his wife had left him, and had taken their children with her.

In the summer of 1972, young Meyer Lansky II had been playing in the loft over the garage at North Twenty-seventh Street, Tacoma, when the boy had discovered spools of what he thought were movies. It turned out that the spools contained audio tape — recordings of telephone conversations, most of them between Edna and her mother.

Paul explained, as Edna now remembers it, that he had sent away for a surveillance tape recorder which he had connected into the telephone system, and that, for the last six years, since shortly after the incident which had brought his father out from Florida, he had been systematically bugging his own family. Paul would put a new tape into the machine when he left the house every morning at six A.M., he told his wife, and would listen to the old tape on his way in to work in the car.[9]

It was bizarre that Paul should have been doing this at a time when, Edna and Paul were agreed, their phone, and possibly their house itself, was being bugged by the FBI. But what Edna found most disquieting, when she thought about it, was the way in which Paul would come home every night, greet her, and inquire brightly what was for supper, after he had been listening to her talking to her mother about him in terms which, she knew, were bitter, heartbroken, and interspersed with tears. Did the man's emotions function normally at all?

Edna Lansky decided that she could not live with him any longer, and her rejection went further than moving out. She did not want to be a Lansky anymore. The name had become a source of embarrassment and pain — and the strange accosting of Meyer II on the way to school in 1970 suggested that the name might be dangerous as well. Edna had come to feel contaminated by it.

She liked the name of her church, Mason Methodist. So she adopted Mason as her surname, taking the opportunity to jettison Edna, which she had never liked particularly, in favor of something more musical. Malana Mason became Edna Lansky's new identity — and her children became Masons as well. Myra kept her first name, but her elder brother changed his, by official deed poll, to Bryan Mason. Meyer Lansky II was no more.[10]

The breakup of Paul Lansky's family shattered one of his father's principal sources of pride. Meyer's weeks in Tacoma as a grandfather had given him uncomplicated times of pleasure and satisfaction in a life where pressure and intricacy were increasingly the rule. No matter what strain and mess prevailed in other areas, here, it had seemed, was one area of achievement and pride.

Meyer had come to feel the same about his involvement in Israel — his new Israeli friends, the chance to develop something new and positive from his Jewishness. But now, in the month of September 1972, both of these hopes had failed.

By the middle of October 1972, Meyer Lansky had to accept that Israel was played out for him. If he did not wish to go back and face arrest in the United States, he would have to seek refuge somewhere else, and for a man just branded as a dangerous international criminal, Lansky displayed some curious gaps of knowledge as he grappled with where in the world he might go. An Israeli friend of his, Joseph "Yoskeh" Sheiner, who hatched a scheme to fly Meyer secretly out of Israel to a nearby country in a small private plane, was astonished by Meyer's unfamiliarity with false travel documents, or with the channels through which concealment — and even a new identity — could be acquired in some of the less regulated corners of the globe.[11]

Yoskeh Sheiner had been director of security to the Israeli prime minister in the days of David Ben-Gurion, and had gone on to a career of secret government work.[12] Recently retired from the world's most obviously accomplished intelligence community — which had slid Nazi-hunters in and out of Latin America, and was even capable of slipping a miniarmy into Entebbe, Uganda — he had the background to give Meyer sound advice on the only course now open to him.*

Yoskeh felt great sympathy for Meyer's plight. There was much common ground between two men who had spent their lives working so hard to conceal the truth about themselves — for it was no easy job, Sheiner knew, to remain true to yourself and to deal honestly with those who mattered to you, while also generating the lies necessary to deceive the world.

"He never told me a lie, I am sure of that," remembered Sheiner of Meyer. "If he didn't want to tell me something, he would go silent. He would not answer. But if he did tell me something, then I knew that it was true."[13]

On the basis of this Jesuitical protocol, Yoskeh became one of Meyer's regular kaffeeklatsch companions. He would breakfast with Meyer and Doc Stacher, and he came to act informally as vizier and charity adviser for his American friend, screening the various local suitors for Meyer's attention and money. Yoskeh organized the payment of $2,000 every three months to a local group working with deaf children, drawing the money from an account Meyer had opened with the Bank Leumi in Tel Aviv. On one occasion Yoskeh arranged for the presentation of twenty television sets — their cost shared by Meyer and Doc Stacher — to a military hospital.

Meyer was insistent that these donations should be made anonymously. With a new twist to his original wish not to be seen as buying

---

*Joseph "Yoskeh" Sheiner was the subject of obituary articles in the Israeli press following his death in November 1990. Government censors deleted those paragraphs which described his official career.

his way into Israel, he told Yoskeh that he had nothing against bribery, but that he refused to give "one cent" to purchase something that
was due him for nothing. Israeli citizenship, he said, was his right as
a Jew.[14]

His principles having become more flexible following his defeat in
the high court, Meyer Lansky conferred with Yoskeh Sheiner in September 1972, literally scanning the map of the world in search of a
safe harbor. Meyer was not enthralled with Sheiner's plans for a
flight by private plane to one of the countries in the Middle East.
Doc Stacher had a friend called Mushki — Moshe Idelson — who
had another idea. Mushki knew an Israeli who was the honorary
consul for Paraguay in Tel Aviv. As such, he had authority to issue a
limited number of visas every year to agricultural workers. For
$50,000, the honorary consul told Mushki, he was prepared to issue
such a visa, and to get Meyer and his family on the list of approved
agricultural immigrants to Paraguay.[15]

Yoskeh argued against the scheme. His own project was inexpensive. It would cost no more than $5,000. Nor did Yoskeh think it
appropriate for his friend Meyer to be seeking asylum in a country
that was notorious as a refuge for Nazi war criminals.

"I told him, 'It is not the place for you.'"[16]

Meyer seemed unconcerned, operating almost in a daze.

"He didn't know about Nazis living there. He didn't know
Paraguay. He didn't know nothing. He asked me where it was, and I
said, 'In South America. Look on the map.'"

When Meyer told Sheiner, a few days later, that he had decided to
opt definitely for Paraguay, and that Mushki had already fixed things
with the consul, Yoskeh assumed that Meyer knew something he was
not telling him.[17] Meyer must, he assumed, be relying on something
in addition to an agricultural laborer's visa arranged via Doc Stacher's feckless coffee shop friend: "Meyer Lansky . . . the world connection . . . the Mafia . . . I didn't want to ask."[18]

After nearly two months of indecision, reluctant to accept the reality that he could no longer stay in Israel, Meyer Lansky suddenly
wanted to move fast. Two days later, Yoskeh Sheiner was in Zurich,
arranging to get his friend Meyer across the world to Paraguay.

The plan was that Meyer would leave Teddy in Tel Aviv with Bruzzer,
to tie up loose ends and pack up their things. Teddy would stay on
in Israel for a little, then take the BMW to Europe on a touring holiday, waiting for word from Meyer. She had no idea, she later said,

where he would be heading, but she was planning to join him, after six months or so, wherever in the world he might be.[19]

Meyer packed two suitcases with his own clothes, which he gave to Yoskeh. Meyer himself would be traveling with just a carry-on bag. Yoskeh took the suitcases with him to Zurich, where he checked into a hotel and purchased two first-class tickets from Switzerland to Paraguay, via Rio de Janeiro and Buenos Aires, in the name of himself and his friend Mr. Meyer.[20]

Although the Israeli Ministry of the Interior had promised that Meyer could leave the country without hindrance, Meyer and Yoskeh felt certain that the FBI would be watching the airport.[21] Once the Americans knew that Meyer was on the move, they would then be able to track his intentions through flight reservations and their network of "legal attachés" at U.S. embassies all over the world. But if Meyer were suddenly to fly, without warning, to a major international airport, like Zurich's, then switch rapidly to the tickets and flight plan that Yoskeh had arranged for him, it might just be possible to elude the pursuit.

On the night of Sunday, November 5, 1972, Yoskeh Sheiner was waiting in the international transit area of Zurich airport for the arrival of the El Al flight from Tel Aviv. He had already checked in the bags and had secured the boarding cards for himself and Mr. Meyer. The weather was bad that night, and there was an announcement that the El Al flight was being diverted to Geneva.

But the weather cleared. The plane was able to land in Zurich, after all. Meyer Lansky walked into the terminal with the other passengers arriving from Tel Aviv. As soon as Yoskeh saw his friend, he pulled him aside, shepherding him quickly into the waiting area for Swissair's flight to Rio, with a connection, by Pan Am, to Buenos Aires. The flight was due to take off in two hours' time, and if the police who were checking the arriving passengers from Tel Aviv did not think quickly, there was a good chance that Yoskeh and Meyer could be away before anyone worked out what had happened.[22]

Meyer told Yoskeh that he had been detained for half an hour by the Israelis before he left Tel Aviv. Surprised and confused by his unheralded appearance at the airport, the passport police had asked him some questions and made some phone calls, and had then let him go on his way. Meyer had no idea whether they, or anyone who might have been watching the airport in Tel Aviv, had sent word of his departure on to Zurich.

With less than an hour to go before they boarded their plane to South America, the two men found out. Swiss police appeared in the waiting area, going up to each passenger and asking for identity documents.

"Mr. Lansky?"

Meyer made no attempt to pretend, and, once they were satisfied that he was not intent on getting into Switzerland, the Swiss were happy for him and Yoskeh to board their flight for Rio. But the travelers' hopes of a clear run to Paraguay were now dashed. From this point onward, it was quite clear, somebody — the FBI, perhaps, or Interpol — would be on their trail.

When Yoskeh and Meyer touched down in Rio early next morning, however, there was no sign that the Brazilian authorities had received any communication from Switzerland. The two travelers transferred quietly to their Pan Am flight to Argentina, and when, several hours after that, they landed in Buenos Aires, with only one more leg of their journey to accomplish, they were able to pick up their bags and saunter out of the airport with temporary transit visas. It looked as if Yoskeh's plan might have succeeded after all. Meyer saw a barbershop and decided to have a shave to celebrate.[23]

There had, in fact, been a communications breakdown. Six months earlier, when the Israeli supreme court started hearing the arguments in Meyer's case, Henry E. Petersen, the Justice Department attorney in charge of organized crime, had sent a memorandum warning the FBI to be on the alert for Meyer leaving Israel at short notice. Petersen suggested close coordination between the FBI's "overseas representatives" — the Bureau's legal attachés — and the border authorities in any country with an international airport that could be reached from Israel. It was important, wrote Petersen, to try to keep Meyer in the international section of any airport.[24] If he were allowed to slip into a national jurisdiction, it might be difficult to lay hands on him again.

From Tel Aviv to Zurich, the FBI had kept ahead of Meyer. But the overnight flight, with the change of time zone, had defeated them on the next stage of his journey. Yoskeh and Meyer were able to land first in Rio, and then in Buenos Aires, before anyone had taken proper account of the news of their flight plans telexed from Zurich. If, on the morning of Monday, November 6, 1972, the two travelers had chosen to take a taxi with their luggage into the crowds of Buenos Aires, they could have got clean away. Meyer Lansky might have found himself a new identity somewhere on the pampas.

Meyer and Yoskeh realized the opportunity they had missed as soon as they walked back into the airport to check in for their flight to Asunción, Paraguay. The previously quiet building was now swarming with police.[25]

"They were running here, running there," remembered Yoskeh. "Something is wrong here!"

The news from Zurich had finally arrived, and the two men were seized, searched, and put behind bars in one of the airport's immigration cells.

"You cannot go out from the cell," they were told. Meyer and Yoskeh held no authority to enter Argentina, so they would not be allowed to leave the international transit area.

It was some consolation for Yoskeh to be able to tell the Argentinians — there were no Americans to be seen — that he and Meyer had already been out of the airport, and that they were quite happy to stay in international transit. But things did not look promising as the two men were escorted onto the plane to Paraguay. In return for his $50,000, Mushki's friend the honorary consul had agreed to fly ahead to Paraguay to be on hand in case anything went wrong, and when their aircraft touched down in Paraguay — Braniff flight 974 was a DC-8 — Meyer and Yoskeh looked out across the tarmac and saw the man waiting for them.

"Okay," Yoskeh told Meyer. "Okay, he's there."

But then Yoskeh saw two other men, Germanic looking, with short-cut hair, walking out across the tarmac toward the plane in an official fashion. The two men came into the first-class cabin.

"You cannot come out," they told Meyer. "You stay on the plane."

When Yoskeh asked for some sort of reason, the Paraguayans cited Meyer's drug prosecution in Miami just before he went to Israel — and they were quite unmoved by the fact that Meyer had been acquitted. Their minister of the interior, they explained, had wide discretion in deciding who could be admitted to their country. It was not the first time that Meyer Lansky had heard that.

An American who had come onto the plane with the two officials tried to be helpful. He told Meyer and Yoskeh that they could go outside, if they wished, for a walk.

"Who's he?" Yoskeh asked one of the Paraguayans, and, as one secret policeman to another, the Paraguayan told him: "He's from the embassy."

"What are you doing here? What do you want?" Yoskeh asked the

American, going on the offensive. "I can understand if Paraguay doesn't want him. But what do *you* want?"

The American did not answer. He would not be drawn, and Yoskeh could not immediately work out why this embassy official — presumably the local FBI man — was not making more fuss. He was being quite conciliatory, in fact. There was no talk of arrest warrants or custody. The American seemed perfectly happy for Lansky to stay on the plane.

Then, suddenly, Meyer and Yoskeh Sheiner understood what was happening. Braniff flight 974 was due to continue its way northward across South America, with stops in Bolivia, Peru, and Panama, after which it would fly on to its final destination — Miami. All the FBI had to do in order to catch its man was to keep him on the plane.

Subsequent newspaper accounts of Meyer Lansky's odyssey across South America — a thirty-six-hour journey, including the time spent traveling from Israel via Zurich and Rio — gave the impression of the wandering Jew getting out at every stop and beating helplessly on the doors of various banana republics for asylum. In point of fact, says Yoskeh Sheiner, who was at Meyer's side until just before the end, the fugitive never once left the plane after he boarded it in Buenos Aires. Meyer Lansky realized in Asunción that the game was up, and as Braniff 974 came down successively in La Paz, Lima, and Panama City, he stayed in his seat — depressed, defeated, and physically quite sick.

Yoskeh had noticed his friend slip a nitroglycerin pill under his tongue when the trouble started — in the detention cell in Buenos Aires, where the prospect of freedom had first wavered — and, as the two men sat silently with their thoughts in the plane leaving Paraguay and heading northward, it seemed to Yoskeh that Meyer was looking very ill indeed. His friend had gone white, and was breathing badly. Meyer looked as if he had had some sort of heart attack. He slipped another pill beneath his tongue.

After the plane landed in Lima, the captain — an American — came out to talk to Yoskeh. He had received instructions from the FBI over the radio. The U.S. Justice Department had issued a warrant assuming responsibility for Meyer's fare to Miami. But the captain wanted to know the status of this other man, who had only paid to travel as far as Asunción. Yoskeh must pay for the extra miles he was traveling, said the captain, or he must get off the plane.

Yoskeh protested. His friend was ill and needed his help, he said.

In the end, Yoskeh agreed that he would get off in Panama City, the next-to-last stop, on condition that the captain call ahead to the States and arrange for a doctor to be standing by, ready for Meyer when he got off the plane.

As the plane flew from Lima to Panama, the two friends said their farewells. They had nearly pulled it off — and, as after the defeat in the Israeli supreme court, Meyer Lansky's narrow failure raised countless what-ifs and might-have-beens. Meyer might have reproached his friend for booking him onto an American plane which was heading for Miami. But it was not a moment for recrimination.

As the plane flew northward over the Andes, it seemed to Yoskeh that Meyer was almost relieved to be going home. There would be no more uncertainties. At least he knew what to expect. Yoskeh's principal anxiety was whether Meyer would actually make it back to Miami alive. Meyer himself, breathing with increasing difficulty, his voice getting quieter, seemed at one moment to fear the same.

He whispered into Yoskeh's ear the name of the bank that he should contact in Switzerland in the event of his death, and the name of the man he should talk to there. Meyer had already given Yoskeh power of attorney to help clear up various loose ends in Israel, and now, to make quite sure that Teddy and Buddy were not short-changed, he told Yoskeh Sheiner roughly how much money he should expect to find when he emptied the account for them.

When he heard the amount, Yoskeh was astonished.

"It never passed the million," he later remembered. "Never. I knew the bank. I had all the details. It was in francs, Swiss francs."[26]

Yoskeh had heard the tale of the $300 million. It was a staple of Israeli reporting on his friend the famous gangster. Like the lawyer Alroy, Sheiner had been struck by the gap between these fabled millions and the relatively routine resources that Meyer appeared to have at his disposal, but he had never felt it polite to probe. Now Meyer had volunteered actual figures.

Looking back on the revelation in later years, Yoskeh had to wonder if his friend told him the whole story. But if Meyer Lansky was lying about his wealth in the small hours of November 7, 1972, he chose a strange time to do it. Fearing that he might not make it to Miami, and wanting to make sure that his family was provided for, Meyer told Yoskeh, unprompted, of a bank account whose balance was enviable by any normal standard — "I said to myself," remembered Yoskeh, "that that would be a lot of money for me"[27] — but which, the Israeli recalled with great certainty, did not exceed one million dollars.

Yoskeh said good-bye to his friend in Panama City. Meyer insisted that Yoskeh should take back to Israel the $2,000 cash they had brought with them for the journey,[28] and Braniff flight 974 flew on across the Gulf of Mexico, touching down in Miami at dawn.

It was a few minutes after six A.M. on Tuesday, November 7, 1972, when FBI agents Ralph Hill and Ken Whittaker walked into the first-class cabin of the DC-8. Slumped in his seat, half dozing, Meyer Lansky nodded wearily when the agents told him he was under arrest. It was two years, three months, and thirteen days since he had left Miami for Israel. His thirty-six-hour journey from Tel Aviv through Switzerland and South America had covered 13,407 miles.[29] The wandering Jew had come home.

Meyer Lansky's homecoming from Israel was depicted in a chilling episode near the end of *The Godfather, Part II* — one of the score-settling sequence of deaths which make up the climax to the film. As Hyman Roth emerges, tired and rumpled, from his fruitless journey across Latin America into a melee of police officers and cameramen at Miami airport, a neatly dressed man steps forward from the crowd, puts his hand inside his jacket, and, almost inviting the press photographers to record his act, draws a gun, Jack Ruby–style, and shoots his victim at point-blank range — a powerful evocation of one of America's darkest memories and nightmares.

Reality was less dramatic. As Miami came to life on the morning of November 7, 1972, the melee of photographers followed Meyer Lansky in their cars through the morning traffic from the airport to FBI headquarters in the middle of town, where he was formally charged with the indictments that had been issued while he was in Israel. The doctor who had been promised to Yoskeh Sheiner was not waiting for the plane's arrival. So it was E. David Rosen, the lawyer, who went out to a sandwich shop in search of something to settle his client's stomach — a piece of bread and a glass of milk.[30]

Newspaper reports had described Meyer Lansky as offering as much as a million dollars to any country that would take him, so the FBI eagerly searched the laden red carry-on bag which the fugitive was carrying with him. There was no money, only cartons of duty-free cigarettes.[31]

Later that day, bail was set at $250,000, paid on Lansky's behalf by a professional bail bondsman.[32] Then Meyer went straight from the courthouse to Mount Sinai Hospital overlooking Biscayne Bay on the Forty-first Street Causeway, where doctors started monitoring his heart.

It was the arrival in Miami of Teddy Lansky, three days later, which provoked the theatrics. By mutual agreement, Teddy had said good-bye to Meyer in Tel Aviv with no real idea of where he was going. Her ignorance would make it that much easier for her to deal with the authorities if Meyer did succeed in getting away. He would phone her, he promised, when the moment was right.

As things turned out, however, Teddy Lansky discovered the details of her husband's odyssey in the same fashion that the world did. Meyer's confinement in Buenos Aires and his rejection in Paraguay were broadcast as headline news in Israel. When Teddy heard of Meyer's going into Mount Sinai Hospital, she booked herself on the first flight she could find to Miami. It went via New York.

As her plane from New York headed toward Florida, Teddy Lansky discovered that the flight was scheduled to make a preliminary landing in Fort Lauderdale, not much more than twenty miles north of Miami, and it occurred to her that she might quietly step off the aircraft there, then travel by taxi for the half hour or so it would take her to reach Miami Beach. In New York, Teddy had been shielded by airline officials from the crowd of reporters and photographers who had been waiting for her, but she could not be sure she would get the same protection when she arrived in Miami.

The problem was little Bruzzer, separated from his mistress down in the cargo hold. Teddy had not been allowed to take the dog into the cabin of the aircraft with her, and she could not bear the thought of the animal crying for her, alone and unclaimed, in the baggage area of Miami airport. So, for the sake of Bruzzer, Mrs. Meyer Lansky stayed in her seat and flew on for the last brief leg of the journey, steeling herself for whatever ordeal awaited her in Miami.[33]

On the afternoon of Friday, November 10, 1972, there were even more cameras and reporters waiting for Teddy Lansky than there had been for her husband three days earlier. They crowded round her, holding flashguns and microphones in the air. Teddy's son, Richard Schwartz, met her at the gate and did his best to run interference, pushing the questioners from his mother's path. But Teddy Lansky, in fire-engine-red lipstick and nail polish, was in a combative mood.

"Get out of here! Get out of here, I said. . . . What did I ever do that you do this to me? . . . Why are you harassing me?"[34]

Teddy got caught in a dialogue with Bernice Norton, a reporter for WCKT-TV.

"Mrs. Lansky," cried Miss Norton, "you're supposed to be 70 and sharp. You don't look 70 and sharp."

"You," replied Mrs. Lansky, "look terrible. You look 90."

"Godmother!" cried Bernice Norton.

Teddy Lansky spat in her face.[35]

After Teddy had reclaimed Bruzzer and her luggage, she went straight to Mount Sinai Hospital, where she found Meyer weak and ailing. Her husband had been on oxygen for two days.[36] Cardiac tests showed that he had had some sort of heart attack on the plane journey. He did relatively well in the hospital, but on November 29, after he had been discharged — at the very moment, in fact, that he was paying his Mount Sinai bill — Meyer was overcome with sweating and dizziness. He felt a sharp, squeezing pain in his chest which three nitroglycerins could not relieve, and he was readmitted to the hospital for another two weeks.[37]

As he lay in bed recuperating, Lansky had ample time to reflect on what had gone wrong with his convoluted bid for freedom. He wondered how his friend Yoskeh had fared on his own return to Israel, and he started a correspondence which, with regular phone calls and occasional trips by the Sheiners to America, became the basis of a long-distance friendship of real solidity.[38]

November 7 every year, the anniversary of what Meyer took to calling "our historic flight," became a particular occasion for calls and reminiscences, and Meyer made a point of passing on his best wishes to Doc's friend, Mushki, whose scheme to slip Meyer into Paraguay as an agricultural worker had proved so ill-starred.

"Wish him the best of everything," he told Yoskeh on one occasion. "I still think he has a good warm heart."[39]

Such fond afterthoughts were scarcely those of a ruthless syndicate boss betrayed by the botching of an underling. But every detail in Meyer Lansky's bizarre chapter of misadventures from Tel Aviv to Miami belied the popular legend. A criminal genius with $300 million at his disposal could surely have come up with a more effective means of escape than long, prebooked journeys on scheduled airlines. As disguises went, "Mr. Meyer" was scarcely the product of particular ingenuity. The adventure revealed no evidence of the worldwide network of contacts which Meyer Lansky was supposed to have at his disposal — Hank Messick's "Syndicate International."[40] On the contrary.

Pondering the entire episode, FBI officials in Miami had to confess themselves "puzzled." Their number-one target had, effectively, delivered himself into their hands.[41]

20

"The Biggest Damn Crook in the Whole Wide World"

E. DAVID ROSEN'S journey to Washington in the autumn of 1970 achieved the very opposite of what the attorney had intended. When invited to consider whether they wished to close their file on Meyer Lansky, the prosecutors of the Justice Department decided most emphatically that they did not.[1]

After June 17, 1972, Richard Nixon's Justice Department was to become best known for its embroilment in the scandal of Watergate. Prior to the Watergate break-in, however, the department was generally judged to be doing an efficient job in the pursuit of organized crime. In less than two years, the attorney general, John Mitchell, more than doubled the number of big-city organized crime Strike Forces.[2]

"Mitchell was right behind us on everything," remembers Will R. Wilson, Mitchell's assistant attorney general in charge of the Criminal Division. "There was not a single request for funding or manpower that he refused us."[3]

Wilson was a slight, intense man, with a strong background in law enforcement — he was a former district attorney of Dallas and attorney general of Texas, and had served six years on the Texas supreme court. Wilson had studied the Justice Department files, and all the articles about Meyer Lansky, and he confessed himself "fascinated" by the picture of widespread financial manipulation which they conveyed.[4]

"I spent a lot of time," Wilson remembers, "trying to analyze and get the whole scope. . . . From what I was reading, Lansky was into all kinds of things."[5]

Lansky had to be considered a major target, in Wilson's opinion. From Wilson's discussions with his deputy, Henry Petersen, and with Bill Lynch, the chief of the organized crime and racketeering section, came the idea that Meyer Lansky should be made the focus of a special investigation, "Project Financier." In January 1971, this investigation was handed to a driving young attorney from the tax division, R. J. Campbell, and Campbell proposed it should be upgraded further.[6] There were seventeen Strike Forces operating at the start of 1971, each focusing on a particular city. In February 1971, Strike Force 18 became the first to be aimed at a single person.

"It was kind of like Bobby Kennedy's Hoffa squad," remembers Campbell. "Doug McMillan had all sorts of things to chase down in Miami. The idea was that we should just concentrate on Lansky. . . . The thinking was that if we could not get the man whom everyone said was number one, then the organized crime program as a whole did not have much credibility."[7]

Campbell got a major break when Gavriel Bach, the Israeli state attorney, arrived in Washington.

"The word came down," Campbell remembers. "'Do whatever this guy wants,' they said."[8]

Campbell and Bach spent ten days together combing the FBI files on Lansky. It was a particularly satisfying job, Campbell remembers, because Bach could fill his dossier with evidence that would not normally be admissible in an American court — the testimony of Daniel Ahearn in the past and some of the more recent wiretaps. Amassing the data that denied Meyer Lansky his Israeli citizenship and forced him back to America was the first great success of Strike Force 18.

The more difficult task was building a case that would actually prove Lansky guilty of all the things that the books and articles said he was doing. Campbell remembers getting a phone call from Wilson at the very outset of his research. The assistant attorney general had just read Hank Messick's book.

"It's all in here," Wilson told the young lawyer excitedly.[9]

Campbell looked at the book, but all he could find was melodrama and unsubstantiated speculation.[10] To make a case, he needed hard evidence and firsthand testimony. The IRS was already pursuing

Meyer's involvement in the skimming at the Flamingo. Dougald McMillan was in charge of the contempt of court indictment which had grown out of that, when Meyer refused to travel back from Israel in March 1971 to appear in front of the grand jury investigating the Flamingo. Campbell had to develop a case of his own — and he stumbled on it at home one evening in the summer of 1971 when he happened to switch on the news. An overweight wiseguy turned informer from New England, Vincent "Fat Vinnie" Teresa, was on the screen talking about his dealings with Meyer Lansky.[11]

Teresa's court testimony had secured the conviction of twenty significant hoodlums in the Boston area. But it was Fat Vinnie's claim to have done business with Meyer Lansky that got him on television. Teresa had helped organize "junket" groups of gamblers traveling to George Raft's Colony Club in London in the mid-1960s, and he said that he had paid a proportion of his profits to Meyer Lansky.[12]

Teresa repeated his story to R. J. Campbell, describing how, at the conclusion of two successful junkets, he had traveled down to Miami and had personally handed Lansky the best part of $100,000. Campbell had no evidence of the small stake that Lansky had held in Jimmy Alo's Colony Club syndicate. But the attorney had studied Meyer's meticulous tax returns closely enough to recite them by heart,[13] and he knew that none of them declared payments like those that Teresa was describing. So now Strike Force 18 had its own case against its target — tax evasion.

Contempt of court, the Flamingo skim, and failing to declare his income from Vinnie Teresa's junkets — these were the three sets of indictments facing Meyer Lansky on his return to America in November 1972. On the contempt charge, Meyer could be fined, or sentenced to an indeterminate time in jail. The "hidden interest" indictment that the IRS was developing from its Flamingo investigations could put him away for three years, and he could go down for five more years if convicted of tax evasion. As he recuperated in Mount Sinai at the age of seventy, Meyer Lansky could contemplate the prospect of spending the rest of his life behind bars.

Meyer Lansky's return to Miami had provoked a media feeding frenzy. When Meyer came out of the hospital, when he moved into a temporary, rented apartment on Collins Avenue, when he went to visit the doctor, when he went back to court for the brief hearings postponing his cases until his health had improved — Meyer Lansky found himself dogged by cameramen and reporters at every turn.

Meyer was the top of the news. His every appearance in public provoked at least thirty seconds of footage on the local evening bulletins, and whenever the press of microphones and cameras grew too thick around him, U.S. marshals would be summoned to help him make his way through the crowd.[14] The resulting pictures of burly officials towering on either side of the little man made the newsreels that much more dramatic.

For the past ten months, movie-goers across America had been flocking to see *The Godfather*,[15] Mario Puzo's brilliant and unforgettable film fiction that did for the Mafia what *Jaws* did for sharks.

"I never met a real honest-to-god gangster," declared novelist Puzo proudly at the time of the movie's release, emphasizing that his story was only intended to bear a loose connection to reality.[16]

But *The Godfather* struck America as very real. The movie played to a general feeling, in the shadow of Vietnam and of the unfolding Watergate drama, that there was something rotten in the state of the nation. If America had felt insecure in the comparative serenity of the early 1950s — the years of Kefauver and of Joseph McCarthy — she had been in trauma since the incomprehensible tragedy in Dallas.

In the 1950s, it was the reds that were to blame. Now the pendulum swung the other way. Ex-generals, right-wingers, and the forces of reaction were suspected of the dark plotting — though the majority of the conspiracy theories that flowered in the America of the late 1960s and early 1970s were not so much explanations as symptoms of the uncertainty and pessimism that had come to afflict the national will.

Consummately acted and directed, *The Godfather* (1972) and *The Godfather, Part II* (1974) snared the imagination with their uncanny blend of human warmth and viciousness. Red-blooded and chilling, glorious and melancholic, the two movies were compelling dramas that proved to be landmarks in popular culture. With the brooding image of the godfather (a crime title of Puzo's own imagining), the gangster definitively replaced the cowboy as the necessary myth for a neurotic society — the man who raised his arm when it all got too much for him, and — BOOM! — just blew everything away. What was intimidating in real life became the dream of escape when experienced in the weightless universe of make-believe.

It was the fables that stuck in the mind, in the final analysis — the severed horse's head bleeding onto the sheets of a Hollywood bed, the wrists slit in the bath after the Kefauver-style Senate hearings. What people most enjoyed and took away from the two movies were the bits that were not true, and these alluring twists of cinematic fiction came to subvert reality in the public imagining. So Meyer Lansky was Hyman Roth? Was Marlon Brando Frank Costello? The confusion was compounded when quite serious newspapers started incorporating *Godfather* comparisons into their reporting on organized crime.

As the media pursued Meyer ever more fiercely, the Associated Press showed a certain awareness of the confusion, describing him as a "reputed underworld financial genius" (January 5, 1973), and a "reputed underworld financial wizard" (January 19, 1973). But all the newspaper and TV reports talked of Meyer Lansky as if he held some position in an underworld that was corporately organized — and the *Miami Herald* had no doubts: on February 25, 1973, with no particular evidence, the newspaper awarded Meyer the unqualified rank of "Gangland Finance Chairman."

It proved difficult to impanel a jury of twelve people who had not heard or read of Meyer Lansky when the U.S. District Court convened in Miami at the end of February 1973. On the docket was the first of the cases against Meyer — the contempt indictment for failing to return from Israel to answer the questions of the grand jury two years earlier. Prospective juror Edward J. Hall, of Fort Lauderdale, had to confess that he had certainly heard of Meyer Lansky somewhere. Was he not the mayor of Miami?[17]

Seated rather gloomily, until this moment, beside David Rosen, and wearing horn-rimmed spectacles which gave him a severe look, Meyer Lansky thought that that was a huge joke. He burst into laughter along with the courtroom spectators.

Meyer's basic defense in the hearings that followed was that he would willingly have returned to the United States to testify in the spring of 1971 if his Israeli doctor — a Tel Aviv general practitioner, Dr. Dov Peled — had permitted him to travel. Meyer even claimed that he had been planning a trip home to sort out his U.S. tax return at the end of February 1971, just prior to the arrival of the grand jury subpoena, only to be forbidden to make the journey by Dr. Peled, who was concerned at the state of his ulcers and of his heart.

Dougald McMillan, the Miami Strike Force chief, who had traveled to Tel Aviv the previous year to interview Dr. Peled, was derisive of this claim. "Mr. Lansky told Dr. Peled what was wrong with him," he asserted to the jury, "Dr. Peled wrote a letter [to that effect], and

Mr. Lansky relied on it. . . . Does that sound like an honest doctor?"[18]

McMillan, as aggressive a character inside the courtroom as out, could not produce the evidence to prove collusion between Lansky and his Israeli physician. But his arguments and questioning in the course of two and a half days of testimony[19] were strong enough to win the day. The jury took four hours to find Meyer Lansky guilty.

Delivering sentence three months later, federal judge James Lawrence King declared that, in view of Lansky's medical history, he would recommend that Lansky should serve his time in the Medical Center for Federal Prisoners at Springfield, Missouri.

Respectfully dressed for sentencing in white shirt, dark tie, sport coat, and dark trousers, Meyer offered an apology of a sort. "I never meant no contempt of this court," he said.[20]

But Judge King was unmoved. He sentenced Meyer Lansky to one year and one day.

It was a disheartening defeat. David Rosen immediately announced his intention of appealing the contempt conviction. But it was a setback nonetheless. Within a few months of coming home, Meyer Lansky had lost the first of the three cases against him, and the Justice Department, elated by its victory, was pressing to get the two remaining prosecutions onto the calendar at the earliest possible moment.

"It is really disgusting," Teddy complained to Yoskeh in March 1973. "Just more newspaper material."[21]

Meyer was not feeling well. He was running short of breath, and he could not walk more than a block before his heart started to squeeze.[22] He had gone back into Mount Sinai for more tests, and the results were not promising. The valves in his heart were weakening. His specialist recommended a bypass. But before he would perform the operation, the doctor insisted that his patient should stop smoking. The surgery would be of little benefit if Meyer did not give up his three to five packs of Parliaments a day.

Buddy Lansky remembered that his father gave up the Parliaments there and then, cold turkey. "That's my last pack," he said — and it was. Soon afterward, to his elder son's mild annoyance, Meyer Lansky took to preaching against cigarettes — the smell, the mess, the general menace to one's health.[23]

"What's the way to kick a five-pack-a-day habit?" he liked to ask. "Have a triple bypass."[24]

Meyer had gone into St. Francis Hospital, Miami Beach, in the middle of March 1973 and had spent three hours under anesthetic. One artery, the surgeons discovered, was totally blocked, and the second was 85 percent obstructed. But they were able to bypass the third with a vein they had taken from his thigh.[25] The healing process, they told him, would take up to a year.

It was Meyer's hope that he would not have to face another trial until his recuperation was completed. David Rosen went to court on several occasions to request postponements of the next scheduled case — Strike Force 18's indictment for tax evasion, based on the informer Vinnie Teresa's allegation that he had paid Meyer Lansky a percentage of his takings from junkets to the Colony Club in London.

But R. J. Campbell was opposed to any delay. The Justice Department was keeping Vinnie Teresa in hiding in Virginia under the Federal Witness Protection Program, supporting him and his family financially, and providing them with round-the-clock protection. It was Campbell's suspicion that Meyer's hospitalization was no more than a ruse to delay, or even to invalidate, his prosecution.

But the St. Francis surgeons had taken the precaution of retaining, and of sending to the laboratory for analysis, a small portion of withered heart tissue which they would routinely have discarded. It could hardly be doubted that the operation had been quite genuine, and Judge Joseph Eaton took a strong line with the prosecution's attempt to rush Meyer Lansky into court. He had heard of many devices to avoid court appearance, said the judge. But enduring the major trauma and risk of open-heart surgery was not one of them.[26]

The government's own medical witnesses spoke in similar terms. Dr. Edward St. Mary, the court-appointed specialist who had declared Meyer fit enough to face trial on his contempt charge in February, now testified that, were Meyer Lansky his patient, he would advise against him being subjected to the rigors of a trial.

Meyer had complained of dizzy spells. "I don't balance myself well," he testified. "My memory has become quite lapse."[27]

It seemed to Dr. St. Mary that the patient he was now examining was a distinctly older man than the Meyer Lansky he had examined just a few months earlier.

"He looked more fragile," remembers Dr. St. Mary today. "He had a way of forgetting things. There were lapses."[28]

These lapses were quite genuine, decided the doctor, who was the chief of cardiology at Miami's Mercy Hospital. Small blood vessel blockages and memory dislocations were not unusual in someone recovering from the surgical ordeal that Meyer Lansky had just been through. The first time Lansky had been sent to Dr. St. Mary, Meyer had actually told the doctor, when directly asked, that he felt fit enough to stand trial. Now Meyer was saying that he felt sick, and Dr. St. Mary was sure his temporary patient was behaving with an equal lack of pretense.[29]

"The government has a right to try this man," declared Judge Eaton, listening to the medical evidence and seeking to bridge the arguments of the two sides. "But we don't want to kill him."[30]

The judge's compromise was that Meyer Lansky should go to trial at the end of July 1973, just over three months after his operation, but that each day's hearing should last for no more than three to four hours — less than half a normal court session. Meyer should also have the right to request a recess whenever he felt tired or ill. A room near the courtroom would be set up for him as a private hospital ward, complete with bed, oxygen equipment, and a permanent nurse in attendance.[31]

On this basis, jury selection began on July 18, 1973 — and having pondered his defeat in the previous case, E. David Rosen decided to try a new tactic. As he asked each potential juror whether he or she had heard of the defendant, Rosen rejected all who said they had not. Any inhabitant of south Florida who said he had not heard of Meyer Lansky after the events of the previous months, Rosen had come to feel, was either lying or lacking in his faculties to a significant degree.[32]

The responses of the prospective jurors provided an illuminating review of how the American public had come to view Meyer Lansky.

"To be perfectly candid," declared Frederick E. Hafner, "I connect Mr. Lansky's name with the Syndicate."[33]

"Meyer Lansky?" responded Hezekiah McGowian, a Miami shoe-shine boy, rolling his eyes heavenward. "I done heard he's the biggest damn crook in the whole wide world!"[34]

Hafner and McGowian were both approved by David Rosen for selection (McGowian as an alternate), along with a Broward County judge's wife, a Miami banker, and a retired Hollywood, Florida, military officer, all of whom attested to their belief that Meyer Lansky was "connected with the rackets."[35]

"I know he has a heart problem," declared one lady who was not selected. "But I've been so busy reading about Watergate, I haven't had time for Lansky."[36]

The jury was treated to a good show. Fat Vinnie Teresa was a grossly overweight character of forty-two, with cascading double chins that were only sketchily camouflaged by a false beard and mustache. This disguise, whose intense blackness bore little relation to his graying hair and sideburns, was intended to provide Teresa with protection from Mob assassins, who, he claimed, were attempting to silence him.[37] Special marshals were stationed around the courthouse and acted as personal bodyguards to Teresa, heightening the drama.

Vincent "Fat Vinnie" Teresa was an informer in the tradition of Joseph Valachi, a small-time crook who enjoyed far greater success in his career testifying to law enforcement officials and to awestruck committees of politicians than he did as a working criminal. Like Valachi, Teresa decided to turn state's evidence when the alternative was a significant period of imprisonment, and, like Valachi, he succeeded in getting a ghostwritten book fashioned from his sensational version of his life. According to Teresa, he kept two piranhas in a fishbowl, to stimulate the cash flow of his loan shark business.[38] Slow payers would be threatened with having their hands plunged into the bowl.*

Fat Vinnie's principal criminal connections were in the New England area, where he had, among other things, helped round up parties of gamblers to go to London's Colony Club in the mid-1960s. Depositions taken in London confirmed that Teresa had indeed visited the Colony Club on a couple of occasions, but as a fairly lowly escort, not as the junket organizer he claimed to be. Fat Vinnie's description of the Colony Club revealed a penchant for exaggeration: "You'd see royalty there every night."[40]

Teresa's claim was that he collected the gambling debts, or markers, of his junketeers when the gamblers got back to America. He then deducted his own commission of 15 percent,[41] and passed on the balance directly to Meyer Lansky, thus evading both British and American income tax.†

---

*Another of Teresa's stories was that the murder and robbery for which the anarchists Sacco and Vanzetti were executed in 1927 was the work of a pair of New England hoodlums, Joseph and Butsey Morelli. Teresa claimed that Butsey Morelli had confessed to him privately before he died. This was not a new theory, however. It was first advanced, in substantial detail, in the *Boston Globe* in the 1950s.[39]

†Meyer Lansky declared his income to the IRS as $71,411.27 in 1967, and $42,563.23 in 1968.[42]

Teresa was quite specific about two occasions when, he said, he traveled down to Miami and made a couple of payments — of $42,000 and $52,000 — to Meyer Lansky in person.[43]

A few years later, Teresa was to confess that he never expected he would actually have to testify against Meyer Lansky in open court. Meyer had had no connection with the case that originally brought Teresa to justice. It was only after signing up as a federal informer in New England that Fat Vinnie had started talking grandly of having had dealings with Meyer Lansky — at the time when Meyer was in Israel, and when it looked to Teresa as if he was going to stay there.

"I didn't think I had anything to worry about," he told his ghost-writer, Thomas C. Renner, in 1975, sharing with Renner his theory as to what federal prosecutors really wanted to hear from their witnesses: "I think all these guys get their rocks off hearing that word: MAFIA! They go to sleep at night dreaming of ways to get that word into testimony."[44]

R. J. Campbell did not carry out the original government examination of Teresa. It was another federal Strike Force prosecutor, Al Friedman, who had persuaded Vinnie to describe his dealings with Lansky to a Miami grand jury.

"He [Friedman] said then that I'd never have to testify in a trial," Teresa claimed later. "Lansky was in Israel at the time. I believed Friedman. He was a man of his word. He didn't believe they'd ever get Lansky back to the States."[45]

Dependent solely on his stipend as an informer, Teresa agreed to be flown down to Miami.

"Right away, they give me a curve ball," he remembered. "They spring Cellini, Lansky's partner, on me. He was holed up somewhere in Yugoslavia at the time. I didn't really know that much about Cellini. Okay. I went the route. What the hell else could I do in the jury room?"[46]

Having testified under oath, however, that he had met both Lansky and Cellini, and had handed money to them, Teresa now faced two alternatives in the event either man was brought back to trial in America: "If I don't testify, I get hit with contempt from some Federal judge. If I do testify, they [the Justice Department] keep paying my family subsistence for at least another year."[47]

Dino Cellini never came home. He stayed in Europe and later died there. But at the end of July 1973, Vincent Teresa did find himself in Miami again, staring across a courtroom at the man who, he had been assured, would never come to trial — and also contemplating what he had discovered to be one of the basic facts of life for a federal informer: "If you don't go to bat for the prosecutor, the money stops."[48]

As he started his examination, R. J. Campbell lost no time in establishing Teresa's record as an expert in bogus checks, false credit cards, "loan sharking, hijacking, bank robbery, bookmaking, a little bank fraud, and quite a few other things."[49] This career record, argued Campbell, gave Teresa the ideal credentials to reveal the truth about Meyer Lansky from the inside.

On Lansky's behalf, David Rosen predicted, "You'll not only find Mr. Teresa is a thief and a fraud. . . . He is also what a thief and a fraud must be — a consummate liar."[50]

Watching the proceedings from behind his whiskery disguise, Vinnie Teresa was struck by the contrast in styles between the opposing attorneys. He thought that Campbell seemed like a college professor, setting up his display board, complete with maps and charts, and lecturing the jury.[51]

Rosen, however, was crisp and affable — he had "a nice friendly smile and a soft voice that could hypnotize any jury. He got up there and talked real smooth and then, when he knew he'd practically put them to sleep listening to him, he'd narrow his eyes like a snake and hit them with some piece of important information. He got it done, that Rosen."[52]

E. David Rosen certainly got it done with Vincent Teresa. Rosen totally ignored the details presented by Campbell of how Teresa claimed to have organized his London junkets, since that could have involved anyone, or no one. The proof of Meyer Lansky's involvement depended on the two occasions when Teresa said he had actually met Lansky and had handed him money. Rosen concentrated on one particular meeting, sometime "on or about May 17, 1968," according to the indictment, getting Teresa to describe in detail how he had come down to Miami and handed cash to Lansky in an office in the Dupont Plaza Hotel beside the Miami River.

Modishly dressed, with more hair than the average lawyer, Rosen had a flair for the theatrical. He clearly enjoyed toying with Vinnie Teresa, getting Teresa to admit that he had lied when testifying in his own defense, and had later sworn to a different version of the same story, after "I made a deal with the government."[53]

Rosen then inquired why, in his previous trials and testimony, Teresa had never once mentioned his dealings with Meyer Lansky.

"Nobody asked me," replied Vinnie.[54]

When Teddy Lansky walked to the stand, dressed in turquoise and white and sporting her favorite fire-engine-red lipstick, her husband blew her a kiss. Meyer had been feeling some discomfort with his chest. So he kept his hand tucked inside his jacket, striking a pose that seemed almost Napoleonic as he listened to his wife's testimony.

Teddy had the copy of a hotel bill from the Sheraton Plaza, Boston, from May 7 to May 28, 1968. This showed that Mr. and Mrs. Lansky had occupied a double room in the hotel between those dates, except for the period from May 8 to May 19, when Mr. Lansky had been away. Between these dates, the frugal Mrs. Lansky had asked for, and had received, a reduction on her room rate, to reflect the fact that, for these twelve days, she was occupying the room alone.

Rosen then called Dr. Seymour J. Gray, the Harvard medical professor, who testified that Meyer had left the hotel between May 8 and May 19 in order to undergo surgery for a double hernia at the nearby Peter Bent Brigham Hospital on May 10, 1968, and that he, Dr. Gray, had been in the operating room, and had witnessed the operation, which had left Meyer weak and scarcely able to walk. Dr. Gray subsequently saw Meyer on May 24 and May 27, in order to carry out X rays and examinations, and he noted how his patient was walking very slowly "with a shuffling gait, dragging his feet."[55]

Teddy Lansky had testified that on or about May 17, 1968, when Vinnie Teresa said he was handing money to Meyer in Miami, her husband was fit enough to feed himself, but that she had had to help him get dressed. Meyer could walk only with great difficulty. Teddy also described how, when the Lanskys checked out of the hotel, on May 29, 1968, she had had to help her husband lie down in the back of their rental car, and that she had to drive him down to New York, because he was still too ill to travel by plane. Bruzzer, the dog, she added, was also sick at the time, so she had had two invalids to nurse.

It was not possible to doubt the fact of Meyer's double hernia operation in Boston on May 10, 1968. The only conceivable way of reconciling this with Teresa's claim of a meeting on or around May 17 was that Meyer had slipped away from his sickbed — with or without his wife's knowledge — had flown secretly down to Miami, and had then flown, equally secretly, back.

Invited by David Rosen to explain the discrepancy between his account of a meeting in Miami and the very solid evidence of Meyer Lansky's being hospitalized in Boston, Fat Vinnie Teresa could only suggest lamely that Meyer must have had a double.[56]

The prosecutor was rocked back on his heels. R. J. Campbell had become increasingly mistrustful of Teresa as he prepared the case. He found the man personally distasteful, and he had had difficulty getting corroboration of a number of things to which Teresa had sworn before the grand jury. There was a gap of a month in the FBI's surveillance of Lansky around the crucial date.[57] Campbell knew that the informer's tendency to exaggerate was the weak point of the government's case — and now it was clear that, so far as the Miami meeting in May 1968 was concerned, Vinnie Teresa had been lying.

The jury split 6-6 to start with, but took little time in finding for Meyer. Interviewed afterward, one of the jurors, Mrs. Dorothy Varney, explained that they simply had not believed Vincent Teresa, and without his evidence the government's case amounted to nothing.[58]

"It was a great victory for me," Meyer exulted to Yoskeh. "Whatever else happens does not matter."[59]

There was a flurry of jubilant phone-calling.

"The year [and a day contempt sentence] doesn't annoy me at all. I just wanted to win this frame-up."[60]

Meyer Lansky did not even have to serve his year and a day. Sitting in New Orleans, on June 28, 1974, the Fifth Circuit Court of Appeals reviewed the contempt case arising from Meyer's failure to return from Israel in March 1971. The court had a reputation for independence and logic — the fifth circuit was the source of some of the landmark civil rights judgments of the 1960s — and it focused on the extraordinarily brief amount of time which the government had given Meyer to comply with its subpoena in the spring of 1971.

The original case and the arguments over Meyer's fitness to travel from Israel had taken place in Miami late on the afternoon of Tuesday, March 9, 1971, while Meyer was in Tel Aviv. The grand jury had then been available to hear Meyer in Miami two days later, on Thursday, March 11, or some two weeks later, on March 24.

The judge in Miami had given the government prosecutor, Michael DeFeo, the choice as to when his witness should be required to appear — in two days or in two weeks — and DeFeo, known to his colleagues in the Justice Department as Iron Mike, had opted for the earlier, tougher option. Meyer Lansky must be back in Miami by March 11, he requested — inside forty-eight hours.

At that time, it had been nearly midnight in Israel. The court's decision could not possibly reach Meyer's lawyer, Alroy, or the U.S. authorities in Tel Aviv before the following morning, Wednesday, March 10, when there would be just two or three hours to track the witness down and book him on a flight, if one was available, in order to deliver him back in Miami ready to appear in court the following day. It would have been a difficult accomplishment for anyone in good health, let alone someone whose claims of sickness had already been the subject of discussion and delay.

"When the government requested that the court fix March 11 as the return date of the subpoena," declared the three appeals judges of the fifth circuit, "it made compliance by the defendant virtually impossible."[61]

The government's insistence that Meyer hurry back by March 11, rather than take his time and return by March 24, smacked of Dougald McMillan's wish to hold Meyer Lansky's feet to the fire. But if that was the case, the aggression had backfired.

The third and final case against Meyer Lansky was the big one, the investigation that had originally driven him to Israel. It involved the network of skimming and tax evasion that had surrounded the Flamingo Hotel in the early 1960s, and by the time Lansky was ready, late in 1973, to face the particular indictments with which he was charged, his fellow defendants had all had their day in court. All had pleaded guilty.[62]

This, on the face of it, did not augur well for Meyer Lansky. His friends and business associates — Sam Cohen and Morris Lansburgh, in particular — had all admitted to having been part of a systematic and long-standing conspiracy to skim and distribute more than $10 million of untaxed income amongst themselves. Most had received jail sentences — twelve months each in the case of Cohen and Lansburgh[63] — and Meyer was tied to them by the signed contract for his finder's fee.

The problem for the Justice Department was that Meyer's finder's fee had turned out to be the government's only solid evidence linking him to this Flamingo skim.

"Our skimming and tax evasion case on the other defendants was so strong," admitted a Justice Department memorandum, "that we anticipated that they would plead and furnish evidence that would bolster the case against Lansky. It was a hope that did not materialize."[64]

In pleading guilty, Cohen, Lansburgh, and the other defendants had admitted skimming. But they had said absolutely nothing that could implicate Meyer Lansky, the master of the skim, in their wrongdoing. So the government was left with only the finder's fee contract, which Meyer Lansky had executed openly and legally, in triplicate. Meyer had, furthermore, made a full declaration in his tax returns of the income that the finder's fee generated.[65]

The way in which the prosecution turned this law-abiding declaration into an indictment was to make use of the Nevada gambling statutes and regulations, which prohibited the holding of a "hidden interest" in a casino. Meyer's finder's fee contract provided for his $200,000 to be paid out in installments over a period of time. This made it possible to argue that he was being paid out of the income of the hotel. Meyer could thus be said to be enjoying a dividend from the hotel's gambling activities — which made him the beneficiary of a hidden interest.

This ingenious argument was good enough to get Meyer Lansky included in a group prosecution from which further evidence of conspiracy might be expected to emerge. But in the absence of further evidence, the government lawyers knew they were going into battle with only a threadbare protection from the sarcasm they could expect from E. David Rosen, or from any decent lawyer whose client faced a charge that was a technicality at the best.

Rosen had petitioned that the case be transferred from Florida to Nevada, since the bulk of the evidence involved Las Vegas rather than Miami. The government happily consented to this. It eased the strain on its budget and manpower. Lansburgh, Cohen, and the other defendants flew to Las Vegas for the hearings, at which they pleaded guilty, later returning to receive their fines and sentences.

Meyer Lansky, however, pleaded sickness. He could not travel. And then it was appreciated that there is no provision in U.S. federal law, once a case has been transferred out of one court, for it to be transferred back to that same court again.

Doctors who examined Meyer in Miami on the government's behalf came to the same conclusion as his own physicians. Not only was Lansky unfit to travel, it was doubtful whether, ailing and in his seventies, he could reliably remember details and episodes that had occurred the best part of twenty years earlier.

So *United States v. Meyer Lansky* became a series of brief and fruitless hearings in Nevada, without the defendant, in which defense and prosecution listened to the latest update on Lansky's medical record — which incidentally revealed no history of venereal disease, an allergy to tetracycline, and the fact that, in Israel, Meyer had started taking Valium. A 5 milligram dose made him too sleepy, so his American doctor had scaled it down to 2 milligrams.[66]

Roger Foley, the Nevada judge in charge of the case, grew increasingly exasperated. The repeated hearings consumed his valuable court time and, with no evidence that Meyer's health was likely to improve, the judge was faced with the prospect of *United States v. Meyer Lansky* sitting on his calendar indefinitely — in practice, until Lansky died.

This was a prospect not unpleasing to a number of FBI agents and Justice Department officials. If Lansky could not be brought to justice in his lifetime, ran the thinking of men who had devoted years to tracking him down, then at least he should die under indictment — his feet to the fire to the end.[67]

Judge Foley, however, saw it as no function of the judicial process to facilitate punishment without trial, and on August 22, 1974, he attempted to bring matters to a head. It was the sixth time that *United States v. Lansky* had come before him, and the judge felt the time had come, in the words of another lawyer involved in the case, for someone "to pee or get off the pot."[68]

That someone, however, could not be the judge. Short of dismissing the case, Foley had no discretion to do anything but postpone the stalemate. The defendant's lawyers had no duty to force their sick client to trial. So that left the government. Judge Foley addressed an appeal to the prosecuting attorneys.

"From the medical evidence in the record of this case," declared the judge, "the court finds that it is almost a certainty that this elderly and seriously ill defendant will never be well enough to undergo the rigors of the trial of this complex case. . . . His memory is impaired now, and probably will worsen."[69]

This inconvenient but inescapable reality was based on the evidence of the government's own physicians. It was, said the judge, both "arbitrary" and "unrealistic" of the Justice Department to refuse to dismiss the charges in these circumstances.

Unmoved, government prosecutors kept the case on Judge Foley's calendar for two more years — until, on September 30, 1976, Judge Foley had had enough. "Why are we continually having hearings on it?" the judge demanded, having listened to still more government-supplied evidence on Meyer's deteriorating health. "The man's getting worse. . . . And yet the Government won't dismiss.

"They're being arbitrary. So I'm going to be arbitrary and I'm going to dismiss the indictment. . . . I don't know what the Court of Appeals is going to do, but I'm closing the case in my court."[70]

On November 3, 1976, the Justice Department announced that it would not be appealing Judge Foley's decision.[71] Meyer Lansky was free of the last charge against him.

Says one FBI man: "He was able to go to his grave laughing that he whipped us all."[72]

"Government counsel," Judge Foley had said in 1974, "lack the courage to dismiss this case because of the reputed association of Meyer Lansky with organized crime."[73]

The judge discovered that government counsel might have been justified in its lack of courage when he finally decided to take matters into his own hands, and to dismiss the case against Lansky in September 1976. Making no mention of the dozen stalemated hearings, newspaper accounts managed to make the judge sound like Lansky's dupe or paid lackey — and today the dark opinion persists in certain law enforcement circles that someone, somehow, "got to" Judge Foley in 1976, and that his final decision to end the Lansky case after more than four years of deadlock represented not exasperation, or justice, or a bureaucratic wish to clear his court calendar, but a good old-fashioned fix.

Judge Roger Foley is not known in Nevada as an easy, even-tempered, or consistently reasonable man. But his sternest critics would not accuse him of being susceptible to influence. His general reputation at the Nevada bar is one of brusque, and rather detached, impartiality.[74] There was no need, in any case, for Meyer Lansky to try to fix a case which, if he had gone to court, he stood quite a reasonable chance of winning.

It was not "the fix" that did in the government's three cases against Meyer Lansky in the early 1970s, but the thinness of the evidence that its investigators managed to gather, and the mistakes of its lawyers when they got that evidence into court.

Michael DeFeo, still employed by the Justice Department, today declines any comment on his decision in March 1971 to give Lansky less than two days to get back from Israel to Miami — the "virtually impossible" deadline which lost the government its contempt case on appeal.[75]

R. J. Campbell, now in private practice in Kansas City, remains convinced that his tax evasion case was basically valid. But he admits the unreliability of the witness on which the entire prosecution rested,* and that the trial effectively proved Teresa to be a liar.[77]

---

*Following his testimony against Meyer Lansky, Vinnie Teresa went into the Federal Witness Protection Program under the name Charles Cantino. He supplemented his official

In the Flamingo skimming case, the government's attorneys are today willing to admit that, even if they had got Meyer Lansky into court, they had no solid evidence to link him into the skimming to which the other defendants pleaded guilty.[78]

The most telling verdict on the Justice Department's attempts to convict Meyer Lansky comes from within the department itself. After Meyer's year-and-a-day contempt sentence was overturned in the Fifth Circuit Court of Appeals in June 1974, a determined group of prosecutors inside the department lobbied to keep the case alive. This required filing a petition for a rehearing en banc — a request that the decision of the three appeals judges be reviewed by the full bench of judges of that circuit.[79]

To file this petition, the prosecutors needed the consent of their boss, Robert H. Bork, the solicitor general, and on July 24, 1974, Bork gave permission for a rehearing en banc petition to be filed. "This is an important defendant," noted Bork in his thick, black handwriting on the foot of a memorandum summarizing the case, "and our position appears legally sound."[80]

The fifth circuit court, however, declined to agree to a rehearing en banc. The court saw no reason why Meyer Lansky's conviction and sentence should not remain overturned, leaving the Justice Department prosecutors with their final option — an appeal to the U.S. Supreme Court.

Such an appeal, however, involved much weightier considerations than inviting a local U.S. circuit court to reconsider its verdict. Appeal to the Supreme Court required filing a petition for a writ of certiorari, setting out the legal issues that were important enough to be reviewed by the ultimate legal authority in the land. In long and detailed memoranda, those Justice Department prosecutors who wished to keep the heat on Lansky presented their arguments for continuing the fight with a writ of certiorari.[81]

Now Solicitor General Bork looked at the case of *United States v. Meyer Lansky* in a different light. Bork would have to put his own personal credibility, and the credibility of the Justice Department, behind the legal arguments to be set out in the writ. The desire to put Meyer Lansky behind bars for something was not good enough. There had to be solid legal reasons for inviting the Supreme Court to

---

income as an informer with the smuggling of endangered birds into America, together with some cocaine dealing, for which he was jailed in Seattle, under the name Cantino, for five years in 1982. He was sentenced to another ten years, at about the same time, on charges of mail fraud. Vinnie Teresa died in February 1990.[76]

consider the case, and when Robert Bork looked for them, he could find none. From the point of view of a disinterested outsider, it was impossible to escape the conclusion that by giving Meyer Lansky the stringent deadline of only two days, Iron Mike DeFeo had, effectively, shot the government's case in the foot.

In four terse, handwritten paragraphs, the solicitor general summarized his prosecutors' arguments and found them wanting. "Nor do I think Lansky's importance is any justification for a petition [for a writ of certiorari]," Bork concluded. "On the contrary, the filing of such a virtually frivolous petition would be an open act of intellectual dishonesty."[82]

"No certiorari," wrote the solicitor general on a record sheet dated November 21, 1974 — and that closed the file on *United States v. Meyer Lansky*.[83] The Justice Department had admitted defeat.

21

Shalom, Meyer . . .

ON November 3, 1976, Meyer Lansky received the news that the Justice Department would not be challenging Judge Foley's dismissal of his Flamingo skimming case. The fighting was finally over — and it gave Meyer great pleasure to reflect that, after the many dramas and surprises of the past four years, it was not Meyer Lansky, but the U.S. attorney general, John Mitchell, who had ended up in jail.[1]

Meyer was looking forward to his seventy-fifth birthday. He had recovered from his bypass operation and was the fitter for it. Life was easier in many ways. Teddy had found the couple a cozy apartment on the second floor of the Imperial House on Collins Avenue.

The children were settling down at last. Through Yiddy Bloom, an old friend from bootlegging days, Meyer had got Buddy a place in the Hawaiian Isle Motel on Collins, just across from the Rascal House. Wheelchair-bound, but by no means totally incapacitated, Buddy worked on the motel switchboard, and had a little room of his own. Sandra also seemed happier and quieter — remarried, with a home in North Miami and an interest in breeding dogs. There were many ways in which Meyer could look forward to his final years in the Florida sunshine, surrounded by family and friends.

But Meyer Lansky had been defeated by his very success. If he had been found guilty and convicted in the two principal cases against

him — the Colony Club tax evasion and the skimming at the Flamingo — it might have become easier to see Meyer Lansky for what
he really was: a professional gambler who had been caught dodging
his taxes. A crook, yes — *the* crook, no. The most that the court
evidence, or any solid evidence, suggested was that Lansky had been
a master of the casino skim share-out in its final years. High finance,
major corporate manipulation, and sophisticated money laundering
all lay beyond his horizons and talents.

This undramatic diagnosis, however, did not accord with America's belief in a corporate Mob — and it sadly disappointed the
nation's sweet tooth for fantasy. Meyer Lansky had withstood the
best that the government could throw against him — batteries of
lawyers, a high-profile informant, Strike Force 18* — and his escape
from it all came to be seen as the final proof of his cleverness. No
one could lay a finger on the Chairman of the Board.

With the elevated status accorded Meyer Lansky since his return
from Israel, it had become the habit of prosecutors far beyond Miami
to subpoena him to appear in front of their grand juries.[2] If you were
investigating something nefarious and financial almost anywhere in
America in the mid-1970s, the assumption was that Meyer Lansky
had something to say or to hide on the subject.

"I think it is a fair criticism of our whole drive in those days," says
Will R. Wilson, the former assistant attorney general, "that we
focused on individuals who caught the attention of the press. We
were head-hunting. . . . There was this whole floating public image
that Meyer Lansky was behind it all."[3]

Meyer Lansky knew people who knew people, wrote the *Village
Voice*, who were involved with Bebe Rebozo — and hence with Richard Nixon — in real estate dealings on Key Biscayne.[4] *Rolling Stone*
revealed a Howard Hughes–Nixon–Lansky nexus with connections
to the CIA.[5] Meyer was mentioned most frequently of all in that
happiest of hunting grounds for conspiracy theorists, the assassination of President John F. Kennedy.[6] Each fresh set of allegations
brought the camera crews round to the Imperial House — and it
wore Meyer down.

"Always subpoenas and publicity," he complained to Yoskeh.
"The same old bullshit."[7]

---

*Following its failure in the Vinnie Teresa case, Strike Force 18 switched its focus away
from Meyer Lansky and achieved some significant successes investigating and prosecuting
cases that centered on the finances of organized crime.

Meyer's courtroom victories had proved to be battles in a larger campaign that he did not know how to win. The unremitting pressure confused and embittered him. He had come to feel an outsider in his own country — though since 1970, America was no longer the only country that Meyer Lansky thought of as his own.

On May 18, 1977, David Landau was sitting in his office at the *Jerusalem Post* in Jerusalem, digesting the results of the Israeli general election that had been held the previous day — a political earthquake.[8] The onetime terrorist Menachem Begin and his hard-line Likud party had unexpectedly ended the reign of the Israeli Labor party, the party of David Ben-Gurion and Golda Meir, which had dominated Israeli governments for thirty years.

Now a political correspondent for the newspaper, Landau was summoning his thoughts on what it would mean for Israel to have a governing party that was proud to trace its lineage back to the Jewish state's violent origins, when his telephone rang. It was Meyer Lansky, calling from Miami Beach.

"What do you think, David?" he asked. "Do you think I can come back now?"[9]

It was the small hours of the morning in America. Meyer Lansky had been following the Israeli election results on television, and he was anxious for Landau's opinion on this new power in Israel. Menachem Begin, after all, was the man whose guerrillas had actually made use of the rifles which Meyer was so proud of having helped to smuggle through the piers of New Jersey.

"I am sure Begin would appreciate what I did for them in 1948," he said to Landau.[10]

Meyer Lansky was anticipating a clean sweep of the Israeli government — a brand-new, 100 percent pro-Begin cabinet — and David Landau had to explain to him how the Israeli electoral system did not deliver clear majorities. Begin would be prime minister, but he would have to govern through coalition. If one thing was certain, it was that the price of support from Dr. Burg's National Religious Party would be that the Interior Ministry should stay in the hands of Dr. Burg, who would remain a most substantial political figure.

Meyer was surprised and cast down.

"It was rather a sad conversation," Landau remembers.[11]

Landau had last seen Lansky in the courtyard of the Russian compound in September 1972, standing disconsolately among the parked cars after the high court's adverse judgment on his order nisi. Since then, the journalist had been surprised to receive greeting cards every Passover and Hanukkah signed "Shalom, Meyer," a number of the cards featuring views of Old Jerusalem.

David Landau had taken these greetings to be tokens of memory, fond backward glances from the melee of Meyer's legal battles in the States. But now suddenly, and rather poignantly, it was clear that when Meyer Lansky thought about Israel, it was the future he was dreaming of.

It was four and a half years since Meyer Lansky had left Israel, but part of him was still there. In his twenty-seven months as a resident of Tel Aviv, Meyer had enjoyed the closest thing to normal life he had known for more than twenty years — and in terms of being liberated from the tensions and deceits of his adult life in North America, it was the most relaxed and natural existence he could remember since his Grodno days with Grandfather Benjamin. It had felt very good again to be a proper Jew.

When Yoskeh Sheiner's son, Oded, reached the age of Bar Mitzvah, Meyer gave the boy some advice he recalled from *The Merchant of Venice:*

> Dear Oded:
> . . . On May 4, you will be declared a man. I'm enclosing $100.00 to start your Bank Account. Always in life carry this motto with you:
> When you lose your money, you lose nothing.
> When you lose your health, you lose something.
> When you lose your character, you lose everything.
> Again, I say all the best from Teddy and I.[12]

Meyer Lansky was able to proffer such advice without embarrassment because his view of himself was very different from the view held by most of the world. But, even at his most self-approving, Meyer could scarcely accord his own life great success or honor. His belated embracing of his Judaism offered him meaning and purpose — a way to gloss over the less satisfactory aspects of his past. From Miami Beach, and with the help of his friend Yoskeh, he continued his modest program of donations to Israeli charities.[13]

The Yom Kippur War of October 1973 brought his loyalties to a boiling point. When Lansky discovered that his young friend and champion, the law student Yoram Sheftel, had been drafted, he tele-

phoned Sheftel's mother every day.[14] Anxious that Yoram Alroy, half
a dozen years older than Sheftel, might also have been called up, he
telephoned the lawyer — full of fury, Alroy remembers, at the American government's willingness, at this moment of danger, to take
some account of the Arab point of view.

"Those bastard Americans!" he said. "What are they doing to
Israel?"[15]

In the heat of war, Meyer had actually become an Israeli.

If Meyer Lansky had not forgotten Israel, there were people in Israel
who had not forgotten him. Yaacov Aloni, an artist and intellectual
whose work for the Jewish Agency involved the immigration and
settlement of foreign Jews,* had not met Meyer in 1970–72. But he
had avidly followed the high court arguments over Meyer's attempt
to secure Israeli citizenship, since they revolved around what Aloni
had come to feel was a dangerous aspect of the Law of Return — the
sweeping power which the law bestowed upon the minister of
the interior. Aloni wanted to curtail the minister's powers, and in the
spring of 1977, he came to Miami Beach to ask Meyer Lansky for
help.[16]

Aloni had discovered an obscure procedure whereby someone
who felt that a particular Israeli law contravened his personal civil
rights could appeal to the supreme court for a judicial review. Such
a suit, however, could only be brought by a person who could claim
to have suffered personally from the current working of the law.
Aloni had to persuade Meyer Lansky to let him put Meyer's name to
the suit which he wished to bring. So the Israeli decided to travel to
America, securing himself a guest fellowship at Temple Beth Shalom
in Miami Beach, in the late spring of 1977.

Aloni had an old friend on Miami Beach, David Russin, who happened to be Benny Sigelbaum's doctor, and through Russin and Sigelbaum, Aloni secured an invitation to breakfast with Meyer Lansky
in the coffee shop of the apartment building into which Meyer and
Teddy had moved on their return from Israel — the Imperial House,
at 5255 Collins Avenue.

The Imperial House was a tall, aging condominium tower like
scores of others to the north of the Fontainebleau Hotel on Miami
Beach. Its prestressed concrete curves were painted blue to enliven its

---

*Aloni was then director of the Institute for Leadership and Development, an arm of
the Jewish Agency.

white facade in an almost nautical fashion. The uniformed doormen gave Meyer Lansky the same protection they afforded the other occupants, checking all visitors to make sure they were welcome before letting them through the lobby.

Yaacov Aloni was dispatched along the curved corridor toward the glass doors of the building's little coffee shop, where he found Meyer Lansky with Benny Sigelbaum and half a dozen other friends sitting round a table, making short work of several pots of coffee.

"Shalom," said Meyer, and shook his hand, introducing Aloni to his friends around the table.

"Meyer Lansky was rather a short person," Aloni remembers. "Skinny. He was a healthy-looking person, a nice color to his face, and a nice shake with his hand — a dry hand, kind of square hands, a little larger than the normal palm. . . . The man had a strong look, strong will power in his eyes. You felt that the person was a leader in whatever capacity and whatever business he is doing. The way he spoke and his look gave him a tremendous charisma."

After breakfast Meyer invited his Israeli visitor upstairs to meet Teddy in their small, one-bedroom apartment, whose modesty surprised Aloni. "Simply decorated. Not especially guarded. I didn't see any television, or any other gadgets or systems."

Bruzzer had not yet had his morning walk, so the two men took the dog out for some exercise.

"He held my hand like this, arm-in-arm, and he asked me about myself and about Israel. He asked me if I knew this person and that person. 'I would like you very much to give this person or that person my regards,' he would say. He mentioned all kinds of names. And I told him exactly what I wanted from him, and why. He said, 'Yes, let's do it.'"

Later that morning, Meyer took his Israeli visitor down to see his synagogue on South Beach. "This is my beloved place," he said. "This is the place that I really love, and I want you to spend some time here with me."

Meyer introduced Aloni to his rabbi. Then the two men went outside and sat on a bench in the sun. They talked some more about Israel.

"It was kind of a hazy day," remembers Aloni. "We were sitting there and he was holding my arm, and I could tell that he really enjoyed the situation very much. 'I want to meet your wife,' he said. 'Can we go and meet her?'"

At his hotel, Aloni introduced Meyer Lansky to his wife and daughter, who was then a baby less than one year old: "He took the baby in his arms and you could see that the man was hungry to be a grandfather, to touch the hands and legs of the little baby. He could not let her go. He had to hold her and hug her. He enjoyed every minute of it for a very long time — and then he told me about his grandchildren, and about his son Paul, who had married a Gentile woman, and who was divorced, and how she was now blocking his grandchildren from seeing their own grandfather."[17]

"That shiksa bitch!" Meyer spat out, his eyes narrowing as he spoke to Aloni of Edna, his Gentile daughter-in-law.

The Israeli was struck by the bitterness of Meyer Lansky's language — and also by its sudden coarseness. The old man's whole manner changed. The doting grandfather, clucking and squeezing the chubbiness of a little baby's limbs, was replaced by a fierce, intimidating presence, in which Aloni finally felt manifest all the menace of the Lower East Side hoodlum, Bugsy Siegel's old partner, the gangster boss — the Meyer Lansky, in fact, that he had expected to meet.

Meyer Lansky was incorrect in saying that his daughter-in-law, Edna, was blocking his access to his grandchildren Meyer II and Myra. The 1974 divorce settlement between Paul and Edna Lansky had given Paul full visitation rights, with no mention of the children's not being able to see any of their grandparents.[18] In 1975, in fact, the young Meyer Lansky II, now a teenager, had spent a couple of weeks in Florida visiting his grandfather and the rest of the family, and the summer visits of Meyer II were to become an annual ritual.

Old Meyer would be waiting for his grandson at the airport — always in the background, behind the crowd. Meyer II had changed his name, following his mother's example, some time before his first visit, and he was worried that his grandfather would be angry with him. But Grandpa Meyer seemed rather in favor of the move.

"I always told your father he shouldn't call you that," he said. He cheerfully insisted on addressing the new Bryan Mason as "Bryant."[19]

From the airport, grandfather and grandson would drive to the Hawaiian Isle Motel, where Meyer II would stay on a spare bed in Buddy's room for the duration of his visit.

"Here's some pocket for you," Grandpa would say as he left young Meyer II at the hotel with Buddy, snapping a red rubber band from a wad of notes in his pocket and peeling off $300. Meyer II noticed that his grandfather always kept his money in his pocket "raw" — never in a wallet.

When Meyer came to collect his grandson from the Hawaiian Isle next morning, he would go straight into the closet to check that the boy had hung his clothes up correctly. Meyer II used to flap his pants casually over the bar of a hanger, but that was not good enough for Grandpa.

"He would show me how to wrap the pants legs," Meyer II remembers, "so that they would not break the crease. He was very meticulous. . . . He wanted to make sure I knew the correct way to do everything."[20]

Meyer II did not see much of Teddy on his visits to Miami Beach. Sensitive to the animosity between Paul and Teddy, Meyer never took his grandson home to the Imperial House. They ate out instead.

"Well, Bryant," Grandpa would say. "Where do you want to go for lunch?"

Wolfie's, the Rascal House, the coffee shop in the Singapore — grandfather and grandson went to them all. Afterward they would cruise around Miami Beach in an old car driven by one of Buddy's friends, or by Hymie Krumholz, a member of the Wolfie's set who was as much a crony to Meyer as a chauffeur. To Meyer II's horrified fascination, the two men would argue with each other nonstop, trading insults.

"Hymie," Meyer would say. "You must be the dumbest Jew in the world."[21]

Every so often the car would stop by a pay phone and Meyer would jump out, rummaging in his pockets for change.

As they drove down Collins Avenue, Meyer would brief his grandson on the state of the world, talking to him about Israel, in particular, and passing judgment on those issues of the day about which he felt strongly. Then he would start cross-questioning his grandson.

"He would question me on every little thing, running me down on detail, what I knew, what I knew about, how I was doing at school, what was going on in the world, who was the senator of my state."

Meyer never stopped quizzing his grandson. There were times when Meyer II felt he was in the care of a marine sergeant. The boy found it more relaxing, in many ways, to be with Uncle Jack — "a lot easier to approach than Grandfather. . . . Just glad to see you, like a jolly old uncle."[22]

One day on South Beach, Meyer caught sight of a long-haired and distinctly grubby-looking hitchhiker.

"Grandpa rolled down the window," Meyer II remembers. " 'Get a haircut and take a bath,' he yelled, 'and I might give you a ride next time.' "[23]

It was the great ambition of young Meyer II to be a bartender and, perhaps, to own his own bar one day. He had attended bartender's school in Seattle. But though this ambition was directly in his grandfather's line of business, Meyer II was shy about admitting it. When his grandfather asked him what he was planning for a career, Meyer II panicked and talked in terms of becoming a builder or carpenter.

"There's nothing wrong with that," his grandfather told him. "There's nothing wrong with a trade. If you do a service for somebody, do a good service, and don't cheat people."[24]

Plucking up his courage on one of his later visits, Meyer II tried to get closer to the truth by telling his grandfather that what he really hoped for, one day, was to be "big time" like him.

Meyer gave his grandson a long, slow, sardonic look — "As if to say," Meyer II remembers, " 'It's not as great as you think.' "

Grandpa was grinning slightly.[25]

"Bryant," he said finally. "Read a few good books. Write a few letters. What more do you want out of life?"[26]

On the evening of June 30, 1977, Teddy's son, Richard Schwartz, treated himself to a few stiff drinks to celebrate a good day's business. For several years Schwartz had been running a little restaurant, in Bal Harbor, not far from the Singapore Hotel, and after he had closed the place up on June 30, he went on to continue his drinking at the Forge, a bar-restaurant in Miami Beach. There he got in an argument with Craig Teriaca, a twenty-nine-year-old golf professional who had also had too much to drink. Meyer Lansky's stepson pulled out a pistol and shot Teriaca twice in the chest.[27]

Richard Schwartz and Craig Teriaca lived a few doors away from each other in Bay Harbor Islands, to the north of Miami Beach. But the police could discover no better motive for the shooting than a drunken argument over a ten-dollar bill left on the bar. The two men had started tussling when Teriaca put the bill into his pocket. Schwartz flared up, pulled out his gun, wrestled off a bartender who tried to restrain him, and then shot Teriaca. Charged initially with aggravated battery and possession of a firearm, Richard Schwartz, forty-eight, found himself facing a murder charge after Craig Teriaca died the following day in Mount Sinai Hospital.[28]

It was two days before Meyer's seventy-fifth birthday, and Paul had flown in for the celebrations. Since the breakup of his marriage, Meyer's younger son had left Boeing and was working in logistical support at a U.S. military base in Korea. Meyer's sister, Esther, came down from New York with her son. Sandra had invited everyone to her canalside house in Keystone Point. But Meyer called the birthday party off.

"I didn't think it would be proper," he explained to Yoskeh, "for us to rejoice while one family was mourning. You would think *I* killed a man. On television, radio, newspaper, they show my picture most of the time about him — my stepson."[29]

Craig Teriaca was the son of Vincent Teriaca, a bookmaker reputed to be part of several illegal gambling syndicates in the Miami area. Press and TV cameramen who tried to cover Craig Teriaca's funeral found their way blocked by laconic, heavyset men who surrounded the funeral party and kept reporters at bay.[30] Meyer Lansky had never had any dealings with the dead man's father. But he had a good idea of what would happen next.

"Trouble," recalled Buddy Lansky, going solemn.[31]

Richard Schwartz had broken the rules. He was scarcely in the same league as Bugsy Siegel or Albert Anastasia, but his offense was of the same kind. There was a chain of consequences that had to flow from such an act of arrogance and stupidity, and there was little that Meyer or anyone else could do to prevent it.

From the time of his mother's marriage to Meyer Lansky, Richard Schwartz had traded on the reputation of his stepfather. He had got jobs through Meyer. His business ventures had been in fields where it did no harm at all for people to whisper respectfully about his family connection.

In reality, Meyer Lansky had never co-opted his stepson as a partner, or even a helper, of any significance. Meyer had a low opinion of Richard Schwartz. His references to his stepson when talking to people outside the family displayed little suggestion of affection or respect. It was Teddy who was the caring parent, cooking chocolate cheesecake for Richard to sell in his restaurant, and boasting that he sold half a dozen large cakes a week.[32]

The tragedy of Richard Schwartz was that, uniquely placed though he was to assess the practical limitations and banalities in the life of Meyer Lansky — to know the truth about his stepfather — he was happier with the fantasies that others cultivated. It did wonders for the self-importance of Richard Schwartz, failed restaurant owner, to be associated with the legend of the hidden empire. But it also fostered a grandiosity in him — an illusion of invincibility — that turned out to be disastrous.

Teddy wanted Meyer to help raise bail for her son, but he refused.

"Dad warned Teddy not to let him out of jail," remembered Buddy. " 'Don't post bond,' he said. . . . He was afraid something would happen."[33]

Yaacov Aloni was still in Florida when the shooting happened, and he remembers how Meyer looked.

"He was gray," he remembers. "He was like holding a storm in his chest. He was angry with the boy. He told me that it was the beginning of a very bad thing."[34]

At the end of August 1977, Meyer Lansky's stepson was set free on his own recognizance, having pledged what he said was his entire bank account — $84,000.[35]

He would have been safer behind bars. On October 12, 1977, Richard Schwartz drove up to the service entrance at the rear of his restaurant shortly after nine o'clock in the morning. He switched off the ignition, but he never got out of the car. He was killed by a single shotgun blast, at close range, through the chest.

The murder occurred in broad daylight in the palm-lined street behind Kane Concourse, Bal Harbor. The killer shot Schwartz through the front window of his Cadillac, blasting an ugly hole through the glass, and in the body of his victim. But the police could discover no witnesses to the shooting. None of the neighboring shopkeepers would admit to having seen or heard anything untoward in the service street that morning, and the murder of Richard Schwartz remains, to this day, an unsolved killing.[36]

Meyer Lansky sat in the front row of mourners at the memorial service for his stepson on Friday, October 14, 1977. He comforted his sorrowing wife, the rabbi reported afterward. He was "serious, sad, and humanly depressed."[37]

"But," remembered Buddy, "he had expected it."[38]

In August 1977, Meyer Lansky decided he could no longer wait. He was seventy-five years old. There would not be a better time for him to try to visit Israel. He filled out a visa application to join a B'nai B'rith tour group that was going to Tel Aviv later that year.

Within a month, Meyer's application was denied. There was no reason, said a spokesman for the Israeli Interior Ministry, to alter the decision taken by the minister in 1971 and confirmed by the high court. An unnamed "top legal source" — almost certainly the state attorney, Gavriel Bach — went further. Meyer Lansky, he stated, "is one of the most dangerous men in the world."[39]

Emboldened by his success in his three American court cases, and by his recent contacts with Yaacov Aloni, Lansky allowed himself a sort of public response through his rabbi, Dr. Shmariyah Swirsky.

"We have forgiven Nazi criminals," Rabbi Swirsky quoted Meyer as saying. "So why can't the State of Israel forgive a Jew who may have made an error?" The high holidays were coming up, the rabbi pointed out, the traditional Jewish season of forgiveness. "Why can't one Jew," he asked, "forgive another Jew?"[40]

When the rabbi's plea went unanswered, Meyer decided to take matters into his own hands. He had nothing to lose. On November 28, 1977, he addressed a personal letter to Menachem Begin, a handwritten appeal that was certainly the letter to convince the Israeli prime minister that Meyer Lansky was no suave mogul of criminal enterprise.

> Prime Minister
> Menachem Begin
> Jerusalem, Israel
>
> Dear Sir:
>   I won't go into too many overtures, and will state my case as briefly as possible.
>   Mr. Begin, I have a very keen desire to live in Israel, but unfortunately I am verboten. To begin with, when I spent time in Israel, I fell more in love with the country than I was before. My one wish is to be able to spend the rest of my life — which, I presume, can't be too long, as I am 75 yrs. old.
>   I have, unfortunately, become a product of the media. Much of this has been exaggerated, as only the press can do. They, as you must know, can make or break. On the other hand, I do not profess to being a Saint, but I have never been 90% of the way I was built up. As you may know, charges in the U.S. were built up against me, but the courts threw all that out. So how much *harm* can an elderly, sick man do to Israel, as has been used in pretext against me?
>   It may please you to know I carry a pretty good reputation

among many important Jews. I can enter, as I have, any other country without criticism, except the place of my heritage.

I would appreciate if you would consider my case and help me enter the one country I truly desire to be in.

Thanking you, and hoping, after you review this case, I may hear favorable news.

Yours Respectfully,
Meyer Lansky[41]

Meyer Lansky had not had much experience putting his propositions in writing. He had always done his business face to face, or on the phone — nothing on paper — and his letter to the prime minister of Israel showed it. Casually presented, and considerably more difficult to grasp in its original, scrappy, handwritten form than when repunctuated and set out in print, it read as if Meyer had imagined himself sitting beside Begin in Wolfie's, sketching the outlines of a deal.

Presentation and persuasion, the key tools of the legitimate businessman, were foreign to Meyer Lansky, and in his letter to Menachem Begin — moving and genuine, but also pathetic and naive — could be seen the reason Meyer Lansky had shrunk from ever testing himself against the standards of the real world. His avid reading of books and his tutoring in math were not tokens of his strengths. They were admissions of what he knew to be his weaknesses. The great reader did not know how to write. He could not articulate what he felt, while the master of mental arithmetic could not grasp what added up to a genuine, two-way deal.

Meyer sealed his letter and put it in the post — to be received and sorted by the Israeli prime minister's staff as part of their daily ration of handwritten outpourings from cranks and busybodies. Begin never acknowledged seeing the letter. It was passed on by his office, without comment, to the Interior Ministry, where, on January 4, 1978, a spokesman reaffirmed the rejection of the previous September.[42]

A few weeks after his appeal to Menachem Begin was rejected, Meyer Lansky received a letter from Yoram Sheftel, the young law student and petition-organizer, who had qualified as a lawyer and who had now set up in business on his own account.[43] Sheftel had been following the reports of Meyer's attempts to come back to Israel, and he thought that he could help. He would work to secure an entry visa on Meyer's behalf free of charge, he offered, provided that he could have a free hand and sole control of the case. If Sheftel could succeed where others had failed, he would have accomplished Meyer's dearest remaining ambition — and he would have made a name for himself as well.

Meyer Lansky had his reservations about Yoram Sheftel. The young man could be abrasive. He had a fondness for publicity which worried Meyer's Israeli friends. Yoskeh Sheiner was particularly wary of Sheftel's flamboyant style.[44] But, after two attempts, and two rejections, Lansky had little to lose, and he gave Sheftel the go-ahead.

In Israel, Yoram Sheftel directed his attack on the Interior Ministry, phoning the office of Dr. Burg, and of his assistant director general, Judith Huebbner, on an almost daily basis. For nearly four months, it was the first thing Sheftel did when he got into his office each morning.[45]

"I really drove everyone there crazy," remembers Sheftel. "And finally, they kind of hinted that if he can provide a doctor's prescription that he is ill and needs rest, it will help them to issue that visa."[46]

Sheftel got the medical papers to the ministry within days, and he went on phoning. A tireless lobbyist who, say his friends, has never known the meaning of the word embarrassment, Sheftel managed one day to corner Dr. Burg himself in the lobby of the Dan Hotel, Tel Aviv. The worried minister urged the lawyer to refer to Lansky as "L" in case their conversation was overheard, but he agreed that he could not, in principle, oppose an ailing Jew's wish to visit Israel again before he died. Dr. Burg said that he would need some assurance or guarantee that Meyer would not make use of a tourist visa in order to get into the country and then launch a citizenship application, as he had done in 1970.

Late on the afternoon of June 10, 1980, Sheftel was told that Dr. Burg had made it official. Meyer Lansky could come to Israel, so long as he undertook to go quietly when his time was up. At eight o'clock the following morning, the lawyer was at the ministry asking to have the decision in writing. He stayed at the ministry all day, until he could go home, triumphant, with the paperwork.[47]

A few days later, Sheftel was astonished to hear on the radio that Dr. Burg had had second thoughts. There had been questions asked in the Knesset. "Public criticism," said an Interior Ministry spokesman, had prompted indefinite deferral of the tourist visa.[48]

Sheftel had his documentation, however, and he used it as the basis of Meyer Lansky's second filing with the Israeli High Court of Justice of an order nisi — nearly nine years after his first, 1971 challenge to Dr. Burg's denial of his citizenship.

Meyer Lansky's high court suit of August 1980 met with more success. The justices of the high court decided that the interior minister should be required to explain and justify his reasons for going back on the commitment contained in the papers which Sheftel had extracted from the ministry. Rather than do this, Dr. Burg capitulated. Following the decision of the court, the Interior Ministry told Sheftel that Meyer Lansky could have his tourist visa after all — provided that he stay no more than thirty days in the country, and that he give satisfactory guarantees.

Sheftel had negotiated these guarantees with the ministry in the course of his incessant phone calls and meetings. His client, he had agreed, would sign a sworn undertaking to spend no more than a month in Israel. He would notify the ministry of "the hotels and other places in which I shall stay during my visit" — and he would also deposit with the ministry a bank guarantee in the sum of $100,000.

"Should I not leave Israel one month after entry, for any reason whatsoever," ran the clause in the letter of undertaking which the ministry required Meyer to sign, "the abovementioned sum of $100,000 will be forfeited to the Treasury of Israel without any notification to me and without my having any further claim or right to the said sum."[49]

Yoram Sheftel had not mentioned this $100,000 to Meyer in his regular phone calls to Miami Beach. Nor did he mention it when he phoned Meyer, early in September 1980, with the glad news of Dr. Burg's final surrender. The monetary bond and the letter of undertaking seemed minor details to Sheftel in the overall context of the triumph. The celebration of Rosh Hashanah, the Jewish New Year, was just coming up.

"He said it was a wonderful present for the Jewish high holidays," Sheftel recalls.[50]

But when, after the holidays, Sheftel rang Meyer to work out the details of the letter of undertaking and the $100,000 bond, he encountered a blank refusal on his client's part. Meyer was horrified that he should have to pay.

"He said, 'Out of the question.' It was a matter of principle. He would never do it, he said. He would never pay this money."[51]

By the autumn of 1980, Meyer Lansky had made no fewer than six attempts to enter Israel, either as an immigrant or as a tourist.[52] The last four initiatives had been made after he had got free of the charges facing him in America, so there could be no question, from that point onward, of his needing to seek refuge from justice.

In the autumn of 1980, Meyer Lansky was seventy-eight years old. His health was failing. He wanted to visit Israel one more time before he died, and he was offended to the very depths of his being that, having made all these efforts, he should still be required to post a bond for his good behavior like some juvenile delinquent.

"I will not visit Israel under conditions," he declared in fury.[53]

For Israel to set a price on his honor was the ultimate rejection. Meyer Lansky never tried to enter the country again, and he abandoned the plans he had to get his body buried there.

"Fuck Burg," he wrote, "and his restrictions."[54]

22

A Legend in His Lifetime

WHEN Meyer Lansky refused to deposit $100,000 with the Israeli Ministry of the Interior in order to secure a tourist visa in September 1980, he was moved by a combination of pride, principle, and sheer exasperation. But even if he had been willing to pledge the money, it is by no means certain that he had that much money to pledge.

Meyer first started complaining of his financial problems in 1974, when he was embroiled in his legal battles — and their expenses. For half a dozen years he had retained the services of E. David Rosen, one of Miami's most respected and highly priced lawyers, on an almost continuous basis, and the bill for Rosen's intensive — and ultimately most successful — efforts cannot have been less than $30,000 a year. The bail bond charges on the first of the huge sureties that Meyer had to stand came to $35,000 alone.[1]

When Yoskeh Sheiner wrote to Meyer, mentioning some legal bills that Doc Stacher had run up in Israel, Meyer sent Doc his sympathy. "When the lawyers get through with me," he said, "I will be looking for a ham sandwich too."[2]

While Meyer Lansky was living in Israel, Yoskeh had acted as his friend's adviser on philanthropy. He had shielded Meyer from scroungers, while also scouting good causes on Meyer's behalf — a

401

private charity for blind children, some direct assistance to a friend or neighbor whose child had a Buddy-like disability.

Yoskeh had continued to fulfill this function by letter from time to time, but when he wrote to Meyer late in 1974 with news of one recently discovered good cause, he received an unexpected response.

"Yushki, you know how I feel about someone sick or in need, especially a young person," Meyer replied in December, explaining how he would like to help. But on this occasion, he had to say that he could not. "My personal financial position is real bad," he told Yoskeh. "The way I live and have lived — nothing coming in for six years, and plenty went out. It leaves you to thinking. . . . If I can interest someone to help, I will contact the people. I'm sorry that I personally can't be of help."[3]

Until this date, Meyer's correspondence and phone calls with Yoskeh involved regular discussions of financial contributions — made on Meyer's own initiative or on Yoskeh's advice — to causes as diverse as the welfare of Israeli soldiers or Doc Stacher's gambling debts. The sums were always quite modest, the largest amount being 5,000 Israeli pounds (some $2,500) sent to soldiers wounded in the Yom Kippur War. But at the end of 1974 the charity stopped entirely.

Meyer's statement to Yoskeh, in December 1974, that he had had "nothing coming in for six years," accurately described what we know about Meyer's Las Vegas casino skimming, which ended in 1968 with his $1 million share from the sale of the Sands. Deposited in Tibor Rosenbaum's bank, this nest egg had financed Meyer's two and a quarter years living in Israel, and his return.

But throughout his time in Tel Aviv, and even more after his return to America, it was impossible for Meyer Lansky to do any serious business. His every movement and meeting was monitored, by the media as much as by the law enforcement authorities. With his indictments, his heart bypass, and his other health problems, Meyer had more than enough to occupy his mind. Then, in October 1974, Tibor Rosenbaum's bank closed its doors, swallowing the money of its depositors. It was six weeks after this that Meyer told Yoskeh he no longer had spare cash for worthy causes.

Some friends who were talking about organizing a partnership to invest in one of the Florida racetracks in these years were surprised at the eagerness with which Meyer tried to get himself cut in. It was almost undignified.[4] In easier times he had stood back from such ventures, declining to take a piece of Bill Syms's Hollywood dog track on the grounds that his notoriety would harm a friend.[5] But now, when Meyer Lansky was more notorious than ever — when even his doctor got investigated by the IRS — he seemed suddenly anxious to participate. Could it be that Meyer really needed the money?[6]

His family noticed the squeeze. Working on the switchboard of the Hawaiian Isle Motel, Buddy Lansky was starting to have difficulty with the buttons. When the old cord board had switched to a new computer system, he had handled the transition so well that the phone company wanted to use him as a demonstrator. But now Buddy's fingers were seizing up. He was finding it more and more difficult to operate the little lever with which he had been able to get himself around in his electric-powered wheelchair.[7]

As he approached the age of fifty, Buddy Lansky was facing the prospect of almost total paralysis. His legs were quite frozen already. He had difficulty feeding himself properly. Friends would push his wheelchair, or give him lifts in their cars. When they went out to restaurants, they would give Buddy help with his fork and spoon.

But Buddy still had to get himself up every morning, shave, and cope with his toilet needs, and put himself to bed at night. He paid a young black porter at the Hawaiian Isle to help him with all this, on a casual basis. As he grew more incapacitated, he had to pay the porter more, and his other expenses also increased. When he went out for meals with friends, Buddy felt that he had to pick up the tab, because the others had done him a favor, transporting him and helping to feed him.

He started borrowing money to make ends meet, cashing the medical insurance checks that he was supposed to send on to his doctors. When his father found out, and had to pay the best part of $5,000 to settle his son's debts, he was furious.[8] Meyer assumed that Buddy had been gambling again, and he only reluctantly accepted that his son's problems stemmed from his medical condition.

Buddy tried to suggest that the realistic solution was a full-time medical aide.

"Do you want me to see what an aide will cost?" he asked.[9]

Meyer was not very receptive to the idea.

"Disgustedly, he says to me," Buddy remembered, " 'Go ahead and look.' "

So Buddy did some research. Jack Tweddle, one of the partners in the Hawaiian Isle, had a sick mother who required full-time, live-in assistance. Tweddle paid the aide $50 a day, and that was the sum which Buddy reported back to his father.

Meyer Lansky was horrified. "Where am I going to get that sort of money from?" he asked. "Does money grow on trees?"[10]

By the late 1970s, Buddy was quite unable to work. He continued to live at the Hawaiian Isle free of charge, but it was no longer possible to justify the wage of $300 or so a month that the motel had been paying him.

Meyer agreed to make up for Buddy's loss of income by increasing his monthly allowance, but he insisted that Buddy would have to find the money for his nursing help out of this. The $50 a day which Buddy had discovered that a full-time medical aide would cost amounted to a monthly expense of some $1,500. Meyer Lansky told his crippled son that he could not afford to pay him more than $800.[11]

"Three hundred million dollars?" Teddy Lansky would ask derisively, almost taunting her husband, who would tell her to shut up. "Three hundred million dollars? I'd be happy with just one."[12]

After Meyer Lansky told Yoskeh Sheiner about his cash flow problems in December 1974, his friend made no further mention of Israeli good causes until the beginning of 1981, when Yoskeh himself got into financial difficulties. Staking his savings and his pension, Yoskeh had tried to set up in business in a sports shop which did not do as well as he hoped. He had heavy debts and, for the first time in the ten years that he had known Meyer Lansky, he asked his friend for some personal help.[13]

"I'm sorry to hear of your distressed financial predicament," Meyer replied on February 10, 1981. "I wish I could help you personally. . . . This I can't. My money days are over."[14]

If Meyer had concluded the discussion at this point, or if he had changed the subject, one might have interpreted his refusal as prudence or meanness, a disinclination to throw good money after bad. But Meyer continued: "Yoshke, I do want to help you. If you can be patient, I will help you to the extent of $1,000.00 after April 15."[15]

This offer to Yoskeh of what amounted to a pittance in more than two months' time — when, presumably, some small deposit matured, or some payment became due to Meyer — could have been a cynical, and rather complicated, effort to play the miser. The more likely explanation is that, nearly twelve expensive years after the money stopped coming in, Meyer Lansky was running close to empty, but that he still wanted to give as much as he could to help an old friend. On April 16, 1981, Meyer sent Yoskeh his $1,000.[16]

Accountant, retired: Meyer Lansky and Bruzzer, Miami
Beach, 1970s.

Grandfather: Meyer with
Meyer Lansky II, summer
1958.

Edna Shook in 1955, the year
before her marriage to Paul
Lansky.

The only granddaughter,
Myra Lansky, in 1983.

Meyer Lansky II in Mount
Nebo cemetery, Miami, 1990.

"HIS NAME IS MEYER LANSKY AND HE SAYS HE'LL MAKE US AN OFFER WE CAN'T REFUSE"

Cartoon by Don Wright, *Miami News*,
September 19, 1972.

"Battle Around Meyer Lansky": Israeli tabloid
coverage, 1971.

After the verdict: Lansky and Yoram Alroy
outside the Israeli supreme court, Jerusalem,
September 11, 1972.

Would-be citizens: Meyer
Lansky and Bruzzer, Tel Aviv,
1971.

Personal appeal: A portion of
Lansky's letter to Menachem
Begin.

Nov. 28, 1977.

Prime Minister
Menachem Begin
Jerusalem, Israel.

Dear Sir:
I wont go into too many overtures and will state my case as briefly as possible.
Mr Begin I have a very keen desire to live in Israel but unfortunately I am verboten. To begin with, when I spent time in Israel I fell more in love with the Country than I was before. My one wish is to be able to spend the rest of my life which I presume cant be too long, as I am 75 yrs. old.
I have unfortunately become a product of the media. Much of this has been exaggerated as only the press can do. They as you must know can make or break. On the other hand I do not profess to being a saint, but I have never been 90% of the way I was built up.

Meyer Lansky arrested on drugs charges, March 27, 1970.

"You guys are sure good at walking backwards." Lansky goes to court with attorney E. David Rosen and cameraman, June 14, 1973.

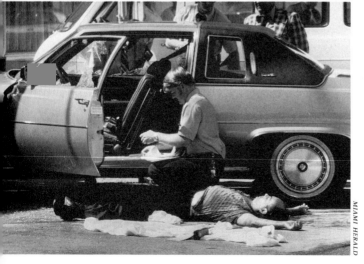

Richard Schwartz, Meyer's stepson, murdered October 12, 1977.

Informer Vincent "Fat Vinnie" Teresa, 1971.

Teddy spits. Mrs. Meyer Lansky (dark glasses) returns to Miami, November 10, 1972.

Buddy Lansky after his "halo" operation, 1982.

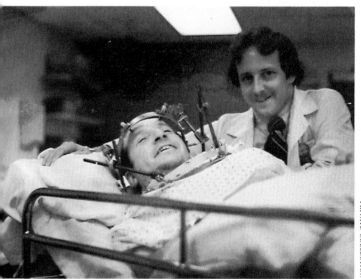

Left: Teddy and Meyer, January 15, 1980. *Below:* Meyer Lansky's funeral, January 16, 1983. From left to right: Jake Lansky, Teddy Lansky, and Esther Chess, Meyer's sister.

Meyer Lansky's fabled millions were the cornerstone of his legend. It was with Hank Messick's valuation of $300 million in 1965 that all the other grand suppositions had taken flight, for if that was the sort of fortune Meyer Lansky commanded, he had to have done something to amass all the money.

It was Messick himself, however, who first pointed out Meyer's lack of appetites — the fact that Meyer Lansky survived as long as he did because he was not a greedy man. Meyer never took more than his fair share, and in his later years, he appears to have been willing to give people a helping hand without taking much of a cut for himself.

The fantasies that depicted Meyer Lansky as the "Accountant of the Mob" misrepresented organized crime as a corporate entity, and they also failed to take note of how much money the accountant in any deal tends to finish up with in real life — if he is an honest accountant, at least. Accountants are not entrepreneurs. The owner or chief executive of a corporation may become a millionaire. The chief financial officer remains on a salary.

The greatest mistake was failing to understand how little of any illegal enterprise sticks in one partner's hands, after all the payoffs and share-outs have been made. American popular culture derives a curious comfort from exaggerating the glamour, power, and money of the gangster. But in reality, Dutch Schultz, Benny Siegel, Joe Adonis, Frank Costello, and Lucky Luciano all died without much money to their names. The multimillionaires of their generation were Moe Dalitz, Morris Kleinman, and the other moguls of Las Vegas — the truly clever ones who went straight.

Charlie Luciano seemed to realize this before the end. Tracked down in Italy before his death in 1962, he was asked by a reporter whether, if he had the chance, he would do the same things over again.

"I'd do it legal," he replied. "I learned too late that you need just as good a brain to make a crooked million as an honest million. These days, you apply for a license to steal from the public. If I had my time again, I'd make sure I got that license first."[17]

Yoram Sheftel had been downcast by his client's refusal to pledge $100,000 to visit Israel in the autumn of 1980. It would have been a coup for the young lawyer to bring Meyer Lansky to Tel Aviv in triumph. Sheftel had been talking to "Panorama," the BBC television newsmagazine, about an interview with Meyer Lansky, and at the producers' suggestion, Sheftel flew to Miami early in 1981 to see what he could arrange.[18]

Meyer was delighted to hear that the young lawyer was coming, though he told him very firmly that he would have nothing to do with any television interviews.

"I want you very much to come by 12 February," Meyer told Sheftel. "I will wait for you at the airport."[19]

When Sheftel arrived in Miami late on the afternoon of Thursday, February 12, 1981, his host was waiting for him in the crowd with his daughter, Sandra. Meyer had got Sheftel a hotel room, he told the Israeli, but first there was a surprise — a rather special dinner at the house of a friend. They drove there directly from the airport.

As they entered the house — quite a luxurious mansion, in its own grounds, on one of the countless waterways that crisscross Miami Beach — Yoram Sheftel was struck by the row of hats hanging side by side in the hall. They were "Mafia hats," according to his memory, ten or twelve of them, all hanging on hooks just inside the door.[20]

It is remarkable how people who met Meyer Lansky in the later years of his life describe the experience as if they were walking into a movie — and, in the case of Yoram Sheftel, on February 12, 1981, this turned out, in a way, to be true. The young Israeli found himself in a room with twenty or so neatly dressed people who were all clearly friends — "Half women, half men. Half Jewish, half Italian." Most of the men seemed, at first glance, to be in their late seventies. They were generally short, suntanned, and well upholstered. Sheftel remembers being introduced to Meyer's brother, Jake, to Benny Sigelbaum, and to Vincent Alo, whom everyone called Jimmy.

They sat down for an elegant dinner — Italian food served by domestic staff — and then doors were thrown open, and the whole party moved through to the sitting room, where chairs had been arranged around the television.

Until this point, Sheftel, weary and somewhat jet-lagged after his flight across the Atlantic, had been under the impression that the entire gathering was for his benefit. Meyer had been introducing him proudly to everyone as the young David who had done battle with the Goliath of the Israeli Interior Ministry. But then, on the huge television set, started appearing some title credits: *The Gangster Chronicles*. Meyer Lansky had asked Yoram Sheftel to get to Miami by February 12, 1981, because this was the first night of the NBC-TV miniseries based on the lives of Lucky Luciano, Bugsy Siegel, and Meyer Lansky.

There were squeals of amusement and delight as the names of the principal characters were displayed on the screen — Charles "Lucky" Luciano, Benjamin "Bugsy" Siegel, and Michael Lasker, the name given to the Lansky character by the film's producers for legal reasons, since unlike Lucky and Bugsy, Meyer was not yet dead.

"Hey, Meyer," cried brother Jake, jumping up from his seat, "since when you changed your name?"

This became the pattern for the whole film, the audience interjecting jokes and running commentary into the melodramatic adventures on the screen.

"I never knew you were so *frum*," laughed Jake at the candles and yarmulkes in the scenes of the young Meyer Lansky's wedding and early married life — *frum* being the Yiddish word for pious and religiously observant Jews.

Vincent Alo was scornful of the scenes showing Bugsy Siegel driving a convoy of bootleg liquor down from Canada, toting a machine gun. "When a Yiddisher boy goes into that sort of business," said Jimmy Blue Eyes, "he is not going to work as the truck driver."

The women enjoyed the handsome young actor playing Lucky Luciano. "Charlie," they cried. "Charlie, the great swinger!"

Everyone had something to say. Benny Sigelbaum took exception to the depiction of Bugsy Siegel as a violent and unthinking desperado. The television company should be sued, he said.

"What are you going to sue them for?" Meyer asked, laughing. "In real life, he was even worse."

It was a rare occasion when the legend of Meyer Lansky could provide its hero-victim with some fun.

"Hey! Look at Meyer," called out Hymie Siegel to everyone at one point. "He's really enjoying himself!"

"And why not?" retorted Meyer, with a happy grin.

The following Thursday, and the Thursday after that, Sheftel joined Meyer and most of the original party to watch the second and third installments of *The Gangster Chronicles*. The group derived ever greater enjoyment, as the weeks went by, from the way in which television, when it focuses on something that you really know about, always seems to get it wrong.

Meyer Lansky told Sheftel that the actor who played Michael Lasker in the TV series had tried hard to get in touch with him in preparation for the part — and that Meyer had ignored his overtures. But it was clear from the three evenings that Yoram Sheftel spent watching television with Meyer Lansky during his 1981 holiday on

Miami Beach that the shy man who said that the world had mis-
judged him derived not a little pleasure from the legends that everyone had come to nurse about him.

When Seymour Gray was talking to David Rosen after giving evidence in the July 1973 trial arising from the allegations of Vinnie
Teresa, he had remarked that someone on the inside should really try
to write a book about Meyer Lansky. It would be fascinating, he said,
to contrast the truth with the legend — and the doctor proposed
himself as the man to do it.[21]

David Rosen declined the offer politely, and just a little conde-
scendingly, thought the doctor. The lawyer said that he and Meyer
already had someone in mind for such a project — a professional, he
explained, who had previous experience in such matters.

It was true that in 1973 Dr. Seymour J. Gray had only medical
articles to his credit. But it was, perhaps, a pity that E. David Rosen
did not take the doctor's offer more seriously. A few years later, Dr.
Gray was appointed medical director of the state-of-the-art King
Faisal Hospital and Medical Center in Riyadh, Saudi Arabia, where
he kept a diary, and wrote a vivid account of his experiences, *Beyond
the Veil* (1983), a wise, humorous, and eminently readable memoir,
which became a best-seller.

The "professional" whom David Rosen and Meyer Lansky had in
mind to tell Meyer's story was the comedian Jackie Mason.[22] As a
young entertainer, Mason had risen rapidly through the ranks of the
Borscht Belt comedians who played the Catskills in summer and
Miami Beach in winter, only to find himself back where he started
after he waved his fingers at Ed Sullivan in what was generally taken
to be an obscene gesture on prime-time television.

Meyer sympathized with Mason in his misfortune. He enjoyed the
unabashed directness of Mason's routine, the sharpness with which
the comedian played on his audience's pride and discomfort in being
Jewish. Lansky and his friends liked to take a table when Mason did
the Collins Avenue show lounges — the Deauville, the Newport, or
the Konover. It was almost like the old days at the Colonial Inn,
sitting round to laugh and listen to Joe E. Lewis, especially when the
comedian came over afterward for a drink. Mason and Meyer struck
up a sort of friendship, and one day Mason, down but not out, proposed a project that could mark his comeback — a movie, *The Life
of Meyer Lansky*, with Jackie Mason in the title role.

Lansky had been pondering the idea of getting his personal feelings to the world in book form. "I'm sure no one will want to publish it," he mused to a friend at the end of 1974. "The establishment will not like what I have to say about them."[23]

Meyer was both wrong and right. Any American publisher would gladly have signed up Meyer Lansky to tell his story in the mid-1970s. But the story they wanted was different from the story he had to tell, and Meyer did not even want to tell that. When he talked of a book to Yoskeh, he seems to have been thinking in terms of some sort of testament — the musings of an outcast — rather than a biography in any conventional sense.

Meyer Lansky had become a legend in his own lifetime, and when he talked in terms of the establishment, he was trying to explain how that had come about. He was seeking some explanation of the process in which he had been swept up, the reason his admitted misdeeds and illegalities had been given such significance that he had come to head the pantheon of the nation's demonology.

His wish to provide a testament, some sort of extended editorial analysis, rather than a simple biographical account of his life and doings, was, in part, the instinct of a man with a secret. Meyer Lansky knew he had something to hide. He had broken the law. He had consorted with killers, and he had ridden on the fear that their violence generated — knowingly, willingly, and to his own personal profit.

But Meyer's quest for meaning also revealed a mind with genuine aspirations to insight. Meyer Lansky could sense, in some way, that he was part of a larger and more complex picture, and it seemed to him that a Borscht Belt comedian with a knack for almost anthropological observation might be the interpreter he needed.

Jackie Mason disappointed him. The draft film script that the comedian submitted for Meyer's comments in 1975 was little more than a rehash of the yarns spun by the pulp nonfiction writers of the 1960s, spiced up with jokes about chicken soup. This was hardly surprising, since Meyer did not spend any time talking with Mason or his screenwriter. Confronted with the specifics of how Hollywood would translate him into celluloid, Lansky did make some effort to correct the script,[24] but, three-legged from the outset, the project never had much chance of success.

By the summer of 1975, in any case, Meyer Lansky was already pursuing other avenues. Carl Erbe was a short, loquacious PR man who made his reputation planting plugs for Ben Marden and the Riviera nightclub into the New York gossip columns of the 1940s. As an acknowledged expert in the field of image-making — Erbe had clients as diverse as the United Mine Workers and Charles Revson of Revlon[25] — he ventured to give Meyer some advice on the sort of writer who could do his life story justice.

The man Erbe nominated was Paul Sann, a swashbuckling New York newspaperman, who had been executive editor of the *New York Post* since 1949. Sann had a lifelong interest in gangsters and New York's demimonde. He had written a biography of Dutch Schultz, and had a nose for the milieu of Damon Runyon. He was the ideal man, in Erbe's view, to set the life of Meyer Lansky in perspective — and, though Lansky did not know Sann, he liked what he knew about him. In the early 1950s, Sann's *Post* had been one of the few newspapers to stand up to Joseph McCarthy.

Carl Erbe was not a totally disinterested godfather to the project, first developed in April 1975, that Paul Sann should write an authorized life of Meyer Lansky. An old friend of Sann's, Erbe had got Sann to agree to a fifty-fifty split of any monies Sann might make. The PR man then got Lansky to agree to a fifty-fifty split with Sann.[26] So Carl Erbe stood to make 25 percent of the revenues from the project.

Money had played a big part in Meyer's own readiness to do the book, according to Sann's notes of Erbe's negotiations in Miami. "$ $ $" was how the newspaperman recorded the principal reason for Meyer's willingness to get involved. Lansky kept pushing Erbe for figures: How much might a book about himself be worth? he wanted to know. It was Paul Sann's professional opinion that a book in which Meyer Lansky talked openly about his life could command at least $1 million, and for that price — or at least for his 50 percent share of it — Lansky was willing to talk about talking.

On July 25, 1975, Paul Sann flew down to Miami to meet his proposed subject for the first time. The two men liked each other, and started a series of phone calls — Meyer calling long distance from pay phones, Sann discovered, when, on occasion, his caller ran out of quarters.

On the basis of these conversations, Paul Sann started compiling a list of questions for Meyer, trying to wrap his specific queries inside the broader generalities with which, he knew, Meyer felt more at ease. The idea was that Meyer would provide answers to these questions as a preliminary to detailed interviews and meetings.

Sann had been worried that his subject would shy away from direct questions about his criminal past, and the newsman was right. Lansky was evasive when it came to the specifics of his lawbreaking. But he proved able to look at himself with surprising bluntness — and even a little humor. Questioned about a tale of Hank Messick's that Lansky's first arrest was the result of an incident in which he battered the young Lucky Luciano over the head with a crowbar, Lansky replied: "At that time, I never heard the name of Lucky Luciano. But I wouldn't mind hearing of that Hank Messick being hit on the head."[27]

Meyer expressed eagerness to go into certain topics in greater depth. "I can go on, on this subject, for many pages," he reacted in response to a point of Sann's about the way the overworld makes use of the underworld — buying liquor during Prohibition, for example, or recruiting street muscle into labor disputes.[28]

"What is organized crime?" he replied to one question. "Your answer will be 'When people sit down to talk of committing an illegal act.' But what about the acts that should be illegal? . . . Licenses . . . banks . . . tax shelters. I could go on and on. If the rich didn't try to use the poor for their selfish interest, organized crime could never exist. . . . They chased the skimmer, but what was picked up in its place? The legalized tax gimmicks exempt from criminal prosecution called depreciation."[29]

Meyer Lansky had steered close, throughout his life, to the fine line between right and wrong, and society had judged him to have strayed far on the wrong side. But there were many respectable citizens, as Meyer saw it, of whom the same could be said.

"What have I done that's worse than all those fixers on Wall Street?" he complained once to Seymour Gray. "But I'm the one that gets all the blame."[30]

In January 1976, Paul Sann started making plans to come down to Miami for two months of solid interviewing and writing. He and Erbe put their fifty-fifty agreement into a signed document, and they also drafted the letter which, they proposed, should serve as the agreement between Meyer and themselves. Carl Erbe rented an apartment which would serve as their writing headquarters until the beginning of April.

Then, on January 24, 1976, when his bags were packed, ready for Florida, Paul Sann got a phone call from Meyer Lansky.

"What's the problem?" Sann asked.

"The problem is," replied Meyer, "we're not gonna do it."[31]

Sann had already heard from Erbe, the contact man down in Miami, that Meyer was having second thoughts. But when Sann rang Moses Polakoff, who had lent his own support to the project from New York, the lawyer could not suggest why Meyer had changed his mind.[32]

"Meyer said he needed the money," said Polakoff, according to Sann's notes on the conversation. The attorney sounded surprised by Sann's news.[33]

For nearly a year Meyer Lansky had flirted with the practicalities of publishing the authorized story of his life. He had involved E. David Rosen, his Miami lawyer, as well as Moses Polakoff. He had held lengthy conversations with both Sann and Erbe, and had started to answer Sann's questions, after a fashion. But in the final analysis, his old shyness and secrecy were too much for him. What Meyer Lansky had to hide, apparently, was worth more than half a million dollars.

"I have given one interview against my wishes and inner judgment," he told Yoskeh in December 1974, referring to the interviews that he granted in Israel to the *Ma'ariv* journalist Uri Dan.[34]

One interview was enough.

When Carl Erbe and Paul Sann had flown down for their first meeting with Meyer Lansky in the summer of 1975, they booked into a hotel which Meyer had suggested. He knew the owner, he told them. They would get a good rate.

This fitted with what Sann had read about Meyer Lansky in the clippings — the stories of how Lansky associates controlled the hotels of Miami Beach. Sann and Erbe were rather surprised, therefore, to be charged the full rate for their rooms, and when Erbe mentioned this to Lansky, Meyer was outraged. He picked up the phone, there and then, to talk to his friend, only to put it down, after a brief conversation, looking rather sheepish.

"I guess that's the rate," he said.[35]

By the mid-1970s, Meyer Lansky's money days were over, and so were his days of power. He was retired. As a pensioner, he collected his Social Security check regularly. A member of the American Association of Retired Persons, he received his monthly copy of *Modern Maturity*,[36] an anthology of helpful bran recipes, advertisements for large-print books, and cheap deals at Holiday Inns. As an AARP member, he was a paid-up, card-carrying Senior Citizen — though unlike the average American senior citizen, he had not pursued a career which entitled him to an occupational pension.

In this respect, however, Lansky was like most of his friends, and it was with his friends — Benny Sigelbaum, Hymie Siegel, Harry Stromberg, Yiddy Bloom, Jimmy Blue Eyes, Jack Cooper, and brother Jake — that he spent his retirement days.

Singly or collectively they were his companions over breakfast. They told jokes, argued and tested each other's memory, reminisced about the old days, and grew morose when the subject got round to their own ailments, or those of their wives.

Almost all Meyer's friends lived better than he did. Hymie Siegel had an apartment in the Crystal House that was three times the size of the Lanskys'. Jack Cooper lived in a grand mansion on the water with a tennis court, where the group often gathered on Sunday mornings. Meyer said he was no longer fit enough to go out on the court. But he liked to bring foil carryout dishes of deli snacks on Sundays to sustain spectators and players.[37]

His own sport remained gin rummy, which he played for hours with Hymie Siegel and Harry Stromberg. They liked to sit outside at the back of the Eden Roc, where a fresh wind whipped off the ocean, the neatly lined cards in their winning tricks held down by rubber bands snapped round the corners of the table.

Lunch was soup of the day and perhaps a tongue sandwich on rye — middle slice. Milt Sosin, the *Miami News* reporter, shared this with Lansky one day in 1978, when Meyer consented to the only interview he ever gave to a member of the American press. There was a proposition on the Florida ballot that year which would have made it possible for a city like Miami Beach to license casino gambling, and Sosin phoned E. David Rosen, an old friend, to see if his notorious client would grant an interview on the subject.[38]

Two hours later, Sosin was out at the Imperial House jotting down Meyer Lansky's views on Miami Beach casinos: "There are always people who will gamble, and there are a lot of people here who gamble. They go to Vegas. They go to Puerto Rico and the Bahamas. Why not let them gamble here and benefit this area?"[39]

The terms of the interview restricted Sosin to discussing the ballot proposition. But he did manage to find out what Meyer Lansky was reading — the works of Spinoza, the Jew who got himself disowned by both the Jews and the Gentiles. Sosin also got an answer, though not the one he wanted, to where retiree Lansky's money came from.

"I'm not telling. But it's all in my income tax returns. I can tell you one thing: When I die, they're not going to find any millions."[40]

After lunch, Lansky liked a nap. Then it was time for a late-afternoon stroll with Bruzzer, and possibly with Teddy as well, if she was home. Her days were largely centered on her late son's family — her daughter-in-law, Susan, and her granddaughters.

The law and the media still bothered him occasionally. One Sunday morning outside the Imperial House, Meyer found his way blocked by a couple of former FBI men, Ralph Hill and Bill Roemer, now working in private practice and trying to gather evidence on behalf of Bob Guccione, the publisher of *Penthouse,* in the defense of a libel suit that Moe Dalitz had brought against the magazine.

Meyer gave the two men his look.

"Listen," he said. "I'd rather be counted a pal of Moe Dalitz than that fucking Guccione who peddles slime and pornography to the youth of the country." Meyer then launched into a diatribe against *Penthouse, Playboy,* men's magazines, magazines, and the media in general. Bob Guccione could whistle for his testimony.

As Meyer walked on his way, Roemer and Hill, both good Catholics, looked at each other, nonplussed.

"Well," said Roemer. "I don't reckon we need to go to Mass today. We've just had our sermon from Meyer Lansky."[41]

Meyer and his friends spent many a happy hour playing their quiz game with the trivia of their mutual past. One day in the late 1970s, Lynn Russin, the wife of David Russin, Benny Sigelbaum's doctor, arrived at the Executive House to pick up Benny. She was due to drive him to a clinic for some medical tests. Finding him engaged in conversation with Meyer Lansky and a third, younger man, who was soberly suited and carrying an attaché case, Mrs. Russin waited discreetly in the background — though she did notice, as the meeting concluded, that Sigelbaum handed the third, courierlike character a check, which the young man accepted with a certain ceremony, locking the little piece of paper into his attaché case before leaving briskly.[42]

The Russins had come to be on quite close terms with Benny Sigelbaum. Lynn Russin was accompanying the old man to his medical tests that afternoon more as a friend than as his doctor's wife, and she could not restrain her curiosity.

"Benny," she said, after they had been driving some minutes together in the car. "You don't have to tell me this if you don't want to. But who was that man with you and Meyer? And what did you give him that he put in his briefcase?"

"It was the monthly payment," Benny explained. "We're getting too old to go down to the library every time we have an argument and need to find out the answer. So we got together to buy a set of *Encyclopaedia Britannica*. The young man was the salesman."[43]

Sometime around his eightieth birthday, Meyer Lansky received his first credit card. It was a Visa card that came, unsolicited, from his bank. Unwilling, or unable, to break a lifetime's habit, Meyer did not use the card. But he was rather proud of the little piece of plastic embossed with his name. He would tell his friends about the card, then take it out of his wallet to show it off to them.[44]

Meyer's Visa card became something of a joke in his circle, particularly as the months went by and he did not use it — until one day Hymie Krumholz warned him, "Meyer, use the card or they are going to take it away from you. They don't want an inactive card."[45]

Meyer liked the kosher chickens that came from Espanola Way, just south of Fifteenth Street, off Washington. They were the best kosher chickens on Miami Beach, and Teddy had a particular way with them. So next time Meyer went to pick up a chicken, he handed over his credit card.

The chicken man said nothing, and processed the card. But he was a friend of Jack Cooper's, and Meyer never heard the end of it. "I guess America just went broke," the chicken man told Cooper. "Meyer Lansky bought a four-dollar chicken — and he had to put it on his credit card."[46]

With the coming of his eighties, Lansky also regained the right to vote — an eightieth birthday present from Joseph Varon. Meyer's civil rights had been suspended since 1950. His Hallandale gambling conviction was classified as a felony.

But Joe Varon had some useful contacts in Tallahassee. There was no need for it to get into the newspapers, the lawyer told his friends in the governor's office. The conviction had been essentially a technicality, a guilty plea, thirty years back, to an offense — illegal gambling — that reflected the values of a different age. And besides all that, his client had cancer.[47]

Life had been tough on both of the Lanskys, in terms of their health, since they got back from Israel. Meyer had had his bypass operation in 1973. Then, in 1974, Teddy went down with breast cancer.

Surgery caught the disease and halted it, but it left Teddy feeling depressed. Meyer had not been a good nurse to his first wife, Anne, and he did not put up a much better performance with his second, even though the physical basis of her mental distress was easier to understand. Nearly two years after her operation, Teddy Lansky was still suffering from bouts of depression, and nearly two years after that, in 1978, her health remained poor.[48]

By this date the greater problem was Buddy Lansky's paralysis, which had grown almost total. Buddy had to be fed by someone else, like a baby, and his father found this embarrassing. When there were family gatherings — Meyer's own July Fourth birthday, Buddy's fiftieth birthday in 1980, or a rare visit from Paul — Meyer told his crippled son to arrive early so that his feeding could be dealt with before the other guests arrived. Meyer never actually said that he was distressed by the sight of his son being spoon-fed, but Buddy knew his father well enough to tell.[49]

In an attempt to correct his physical decline, Buddy underwent an operation in the early 1980s to realign his neck and the top of his spinal cord. A metal ring was fixed, halolike, around his skull, and the halo was then attached to a back brace, temporarily immobilizing his head. The halo itself was secured to Buddy's skull by metal screws that were wound tightly into his flesh. When Meyer went to visit his son in the hospital, he just could not look at the device. As he talked to Buddy, his eyes wandered around the room — looking at the television, out the window, at any spot where he did not have to contemplate the metal contraption fixed so painfully around his son's head. It reminded Buddy of his father's discomfort nearly fifty years earlier when Meyer used to come and visit him in the hospital in Baltimore.[50]

There was general concern in the family when, sometime before Buddy went into the hospital, his brother, Paul, met a California woman whom he decided to make his second wife, and who turned out, when she came to Florida, to be a heavy drinker.

It was Sandra who first discovered this when the couple came to stay at her house, and she tried to raise the subject with her father. But Meyer sidestepped the issue. "If you would throw that goddamn liquor away," he told his daughter, "maybe she wouldn't drink."[51]

Paul had decided to get remarried in Florida, and Sandra offered her home for the wedding party, inviting a number of her father's friends.

"Paul was cheated on his first wedding," Sandra explained to Buddy — meaning that Paul's small and distant celebration in Tacoma in 1956 had deprived him of expensive wedding presents. So Sandra sent out invitations to Yiddy Bloom, Ben Gaines, Benny Sigelbaum, and even to Sigelbaum's lawyer, Gerson Blatt, who was prosperous and benevolent, but scarcely a friend of the family.

Meyer thought that his daughter was being greedy on her brother's behalf, and he complained to Buddy.

"Why don't you say something?" he asked.

"Dad," replied Buddy, "she's your daughter, and it's her house. I'm lucky she invited me."[52]

With so many of the family gathered together, Uncle Julie Citron went round canvassing what would happen to Buddy after his father's death. He had spoken to Meyer and was shocked to discover that there might not be the money to pay for the care and medical attention that Buddy would surely need. Paul had been the most provident of the children, so Julie spoke to him. Since Meyer did not enjoy the fortune that the world imagined, Julie inquired, could Paul perhaps do something to help his brother?

"No," replied Paul flatly, well aware that he had been the provident one. "They've never saved. I have. Why should I be the one to pay out for Buddy?"[53]

The incident marked the end of whatever relationship remained between Meyer Lansky's two sons. They never spoke again.

In public, Meyer Lansky maintained the smiling persona of his later years. "You guys are sure good at walking backwards," he liked to joke as the cameramen and reporters retreated in front of him.[54]

In private, however, he was less jaunty. The deaths of old friends hit him particularly hard. Joseph "Doc" Stacher went in March 1977.

Buddy started to notice small signs of deterioration in his father — a tendency to fall asleep, a certain forgetfulness. Meyer had had the habit of giving his children money for Christmas — $100 each. But sometime in the mid-1970s the Christmas money stopped, and Meyer started to forget his children's birthdays as well.[55]

In time-honored Lansky fashion, Sandra went sideways about the matter, going to Buddy to get him to confront their father with the problem that was worrying her.

"Who am I to complain?" he replied. It was fifteen years since

Buddy had put up his Tuscany stock as security to a loan shark, and he still recalled the incident with shame. "I have no right to complain," he said.[56]

Meyer's ulcers gave him less trouble as he grew older. Teddy kept a firm eye on his diet — no corned beef, no salami, not too many spices with the chicken. She nursed Meyer better than he had nursed her. It was the packs of Parliaments that finally caught up with him, half a dozen years after he had given up smoking. By the late 1970s, when he was seventy-seven, Meyer Lansky started finding himself short of breath after quite gentle bouts of exercise. He would huff and puff, and would have to sit down to rest.

In February 1980, at a meal out to celebrate his brother Jake's birthday, Meyer announced to the family that he had been coughing up blood, and that he was going into Mount Sinai to see what the doctors could do about it. It was a small gathering at Joe Sonken's Gold Coast. Buddy and Sandra were there.

"Blood did not sound good to me," remembered Buddy Lansky. "I know enough about illnesses. . . ."[57]

The surgeons cut out half a lung, hoping to stop the spread of the cancer. Yaacov Aloni, back in Miami Beach to see his old friends, was horrified when he met Meyer, weak and frail after the operation.

"He was gray. He was a different person. He had lost his spring, his vital being. I asked him about his dog, and I don't remember his reply. Then I asked him about his synagogue. And he said, yes, he was still going there, and he was still talking with the rabbi. And then he fell asleep, just like that, in the middle of the conversation."[58]

The following year found Meyer and Teddy driving across to Miami, out to the western, Spanish-speaking suburbs. It was not a neighborhood that either of the Lanskys would normally have visited, but it was the site of Miami's pet cemetery, Pet Heaven, and they had come to attend the funeral of little Bruzzer, the Shih Tzu, who had died a few days earlier, at the age of thirteen.

The dog lay in an open casket while Teddy wept.[59] Bruzzer had been Meyer's companion, morning and evening, in the toughest years of surveillance in Miami Beach in the late sixties. The dog had been with Meyer in Tel Aviv, in Beeri Street, and then back again on Collins Avenue — much traveled, much followed, much photographed, like his master.

Bruzzer (1968–1981) was laid beside Tiger (1966–1968) beneath a flat bronze plaque that was set in granite: "Too Well Loved To Ever Be Forgotten. The Lanskys."

In the weeks following Bruzzer's death, Meyer wondered about getting another dog. But he decided that he just did not feel well enough.[60]

In the summer of 1982, the Lanskys decided to take a holiday, a cruise off Alaska. But Meyer was feeling weak again, and when he went back to Mount Sinai, the doctors had to confess that their earlier optimism was unfounded. The cancer was back.

Meyer flew to the Mayo Clinic in Rochester, Minnesota, for a second opinion, which confirmed the diagnosis. Howard Grumer, the Lanskys' doctor, told Teddy that her husband only had from three to six months to live. The cancer had spread down from the lung into the diaphragm, and into various almost inaccessible spots close to the kidney and the spine. Radiation treatment might slow the cancer somewhat, but the doctor could not hold out much hope.[61]

Teddy could not take the bad news in. She heard what the doctor said, but she refused to let it register. She did not discuss it with Meyer, even when one of the hospital doctors asked him if he had got his affairs in order.[62]

Meyer did not press Teddy about what the doctors said. But he had few illusions. He told his gin rummy partner Harry Stromberg that he reckoned he only had a month or so to go.[63] Their third partner, Hymie Siegel, had died himself, quite recently — a loss which both Meyer and Stromberg took very hard. Toward the end of October 1982, Meyer quietly went in to David Rosen's office in Miami to make his will.[64]

In the final months of the year, Harold Conrad, entrepreneur of the farting record and PR man for the Colonial Inn, came down to Miami Beach. Still a journalist of ambition and wit, Conrad was hoping for the great Meyer Lansky interview before the end, and he got Carl Erbe to arrange a meeting with his former employer in the lobby of the Imperial House.

Meyer came downstairs looking haggard. He had been through more than twenty radiation treatments, and he wasted little time with formalities.

"I got absolutely nothing to say, nothing. What do I need interviews for? What do I need it for? Nobody's gonna write anything good about me."[65]

Conrad protested that he was not going to do a hatchet job, but Meyer waved him aside. His voice was so low that Conrad had to move his chair closer to catch what he was saying.

"If you quote me or say I gave you an interview, the day after it's printed there'll be twenty reporters chasing me up the street." Meyer fell silent. Then he ventured a sort of smile. "That Colonial Inn was a hell of a joint. . . . A real gold mine, and a lot of laughs."[66]

As he got to his feet, wheezing badly, Meyer told Conrad to call again if he was in Miami the following Monday. But when Conrad rang, he was told that the patient had been hospitalized again, and that things did not look too good.

Teddy Lansky took her husband into the hospital for the last time on December 31, 1982 — New Year's Eve. She could not look after him anymore. He complained that the radiation was burning him, that it hurt his throat. He could scarcely speak, and he did not want to eat much, either.

Teddy tried to sit him up in a chair to feed him like a baby — like Buddy, in fact. But Meyer was not biddable. He would shut his mouth and move his head away from the food. He was losing weight, and he was becoming dehydrated as well.

Then he started falling. His legs would give way under him, and Teddy had to rush to catch him, or to push a chair in the way to break his fall. She was terrified that he was going to hit his head on the floor.[67]

In Mount Sinai, they gave him an injection to make him comfortable. There was not much more they could do. Esther and Paul flew in, and there was a family gathering around the hospital bed, a sort of farewell.

"When I go," Meyer said to Sandra, talking about Buddy, "make sure you take care of your brother."

"Yes," replied Sandra. "Yes, Daddy, I will."[68]

Meyer Lansky lay in bed, with medical tubes going in and coming out of his body, and in considerable distress. Though he was sedated with regular injections, he would pick away at the tubes, and on the morning of Friday, January 14, 1983, he managed to pull out the tube that ran down his throat. Teddy was there as the doctor and nurses struggled to force the tube back down again. Meyer Lansky fought them off, screaming as Teddy had never heard him scream before. Later that evening he suffered a nosebleed which the nurses could not stem. In the end, they could do no more than pack the nostril, and leave him lying there, exhausted but conscious enough to recognize his wife.

"Let me go!" he cried out to Teddy. "Let me go!"[69]

Heavily sedated, Meyer Lansky fell into a slumber from which he never awoke. He died in Mount Sinai Hospital in the small hours of the following morning, Saturday, January 15, 1983.

"Let me go!" were the last coherent words that he spoke.

23

"If There's a Life After Death . . ."

MEYER LANSKY was buried the morning after he died, on Sunday, January 16, 1983, in Mount Nebo cemetery in West Miami. Quick burials are in the Jewish tradition, and the hope was that a fast funeral might outflank a few of the camera crews. There were no far-flung relatives to wait for. Esther was already in Miami. Paul had said his good-byes and had headed back to the Far East.

Teddy led the mourners with Jake and Esther, the three of them sitting side by side, in front of the coffin. With Meyer's brother to one side of her and his sister to the other, Teddy broke down, burying her head in her hands. Esther wept with her. Wearing a black bow tie and black skullcap, Jake sat stolidly with his memories, staring out across the top of the open grave.

Alone among the few dozen gathered in Mount Nebo in the pale January sunlight, Jake Lansky had been with Meyer from the beginning. He had lived through it all as an insider, the loyal brother from start to finish — from Russia to Brooklyn, from the Lower East Side to the gilded casino of the Havana Riviera. Better than anyone else, Jake Lansky knew the inside story, the twists and turns that had carried one little boy from the muddy streets of Grodno to end up here, in warm, southern ground.

To the disappointment of the cameramen nimble enough to get to the cemetery on the morning of Sunday, January 16, it was not a gangland funeral — there were no limousines, exotic wreaths, or broad-shouldered ushers. The casket was not even particularly grand. By the standard of Florida farewells, Meyer Lansky's was a low-budget send-off.[1]

Detective John Sampson, of the Metro-Dade Police Department, remembers the ceremony as being lengthy and cold. He was parked outside the cemetery in a surveillance van. More reticent than the press, the police decided not to intrude on the mourners at the graveside. So far as the detective could see, in any case, there were only family and the surviving friends from Wolfie's to photograph — though Sampson did get a new picture of Vincent Alo.[2]

Mount Nebo cemetery — named after the mountain where Moses died in Canaan — is one of Miami's leading Jewish gardens of rest. Schiff, Bloom, Wexler, and Applestein are the names on the memorials around the little plot of ground in which Meyer Lansky was buried, in the northwest corner of the grounds. But the names and signposts outside the cemetery have a different flavor — Havana Plaza, Varadero Market, Pueblo Café Cubano. In the years since 1959, this dusty quarter of Miami has become the heart of the exiled Cuban community in Florida, and the neon signs, bars, and restaurants of Little Havana create a fair facsimile of the hustle and bustle that swirled around the Nacional and the Riviera in the days before Castro.

People around the world who read the obituaries that morning would not easily have made a connection between the unpretentious ending in Mount Nebo cemetery and the passing of the "Godfather of the Godfathers,"[3] whose ingenious and all-powerful career was being memorialized — eulogized, almost — in newspapers from Miami to London.

> "He would have been chairman of the board of General Motors if he'd gone into legitimate business," an agent of the Federal Bureau of Investigation once said of Meyer Lansky with grudging admiration. And in a moment of triumph, Mr. Lansky once boasted to an underworld associate, "We're bigger than U.S. Steel."[4]

This opening paragraph of the full-page tribute published by the *New York Times* was typical of most. In none of the stories was there much trace of an old man on Valium trailing round Miami Beach looking for pay phones and running out of quarters.

Trying to enhance the report with a local angle, the *Detroit News* linked Meyer's name, in a front-page story, with Jimmy Hoffa and the Teamsters,[5] who had provided a number of loans to Moe Dalitz and his associates, but none, in fact, to Meyer Lansky. Equally erroneously, the *Chicago Tribune* described Lansky as a "frequent adviser to the Chicago mob."[6] With more factual basis, the *Omaha World-Herald* proudly recalled Meyer's time in the early 1940s running the Dodge Park Kennel Club in Council Bluffs.[7]

Meyer was variously described as "the Mob's treasurer," as "the Mafia's banker," and as "the most influential Godfather in the history of American organized crime."[8] In wire service feeds syndicated around the country, the story of an impressive and purposeful criminal career was woven from references to Murder, Inc., money laundering, "financial wizardry," and to an undocumented process by which crime in America was said to have graduated, under Lansky's direction, "from back alleys to executive boardrooms"[9] — though no names were given to indicate where the boardrooms controlled by Meyer Lansky might be.

This crowning fancy, that the underworld had grown so powerful that it had seized control of legitimate business, was the ultimate expression of America's film script view of itself. Meyer had come to personify the dark side — an easy and singular explanation of many complex and worrying things. In the early 1980s, America was losing its certainty about good, coming to acknowledge that there might be many ways to heaven. But she still sought the consolation of explaining evil in simple and conspiratorial terms. Meyer Lansky was given the credit for an entire facet of the country's life and modern history. It was as if the man who had passed away was comparable in stature to the president — or to the chairman of the Federal Reserve, at least.*

In all the hyperbole on a poor weekend for news, only the *Miami Herald,* whose stories had seeded so many of the misconceptions twenty years earlier, pointed out that Lansky's reputation was a matter of "popular belief, never proved legally," and that Lansky's links to mob killing were "more by speculation than proof."

"How much of the legend is true," wrote *Herald* staff writer

---

*In fact, Lansky's death happened to be listed in *Time* magazine's Milestones column beside that of Nikolai Podgorny, the president of the USSR.

Arnold Markowitz, "and whether it truly disturbed Lansky, seem unlikely ever to be known publicly."[10]

The 2,200-word story, which ran on the front page of the *Miami Herald* on the day of Lansky's funeral, was unusual in its reluctance to depart too far from proven facts and probabilities. It was also unique among the several dozen versions of Meyer Lansky's life and career published on January 16, 1983, in failing once to mention the sum of $300 million.

Meyer Lansky II learned of his grandfather's death through the newspapers, and he got on the first plane he could to Miami. He arrived too late for the funeral, but next day Uncle Jake took him to the Imperial House apartment for sitting shivah — the seven days of Jewish mourning comparable to the Christian wake. On the table, like a shrine, with candles lit in front of it, sat a photograph of Meyer wearing a yarmulke. Through the front door shuttled a succession of neighbors and friends, murmuring their comfort and grief.[11]

"So," said someone that Meyer II did not recognize, "our little giant is gone."

It was the first time that Meyer II had ever seen the apartment where his grandfather spent the final ten years of his life, and he was struck by how spartan it was — very small, with no view to speak of, and just one bedroom, in which two single beds were set against the walls on either side of the room.

There was no sign of Sandra. She had had a row with Teddy and the two women were not speaking.[12] Buddy had gone back to the hospital. But Jimmy and Flo Alo were there, and Flo told Meyer II how she remembered Paul and Edna bringing him proudly, as a little baby back in the late 1950s, to their apartment in New York.[13]

In the small sitting room the television was on, and every so often news bulletins flashed photographs of Meyer, with Lucky Luciano and Bugsy Siegel — who was pictured in his memorable final pose on Virginia Hill's chintz sofa.

"The king is dead," announced one newsreader.[14]

Teddy cried out angrily when she heard that, hurling a towel against the screen and making as if to spit. She was up and down from one moment to the next, veering from her habitual jauntiness to tearful confusion.

"What shall I do with all his clothes?" she asked. "I feel as if I'm throwing him out."

Meyer II remembers looking around the apartment and trying to work out what was going to happen next. Was it really all over? he wondered.

But what Meyer Lansky II remembers most is discovering quite accidentally, in the course of conversation with Uncle Jake, that his father, Paul, had found himself a new wife, that Paul had remarried, and that he had been living with her for the last couple of years. Paul Lansky had neglected to tell his children that.[15]

On February 7, 1983, the last will and testament of Meyer Lansky was lodged in the Dade County Courthouse, in downtown Miami.[16] So many people were curious to see what clues the will might yield to the disposition of the Lansky millions that Circuit Judge Francis Christie, to whom the will was assigned for probate,[17] ordered that it should be locked in the safe in his office. The judge had no right, strictly speaking, to limit access to what was a public document. But the will scarcely revealed any secrets.

After the customary clauses revoking all previous wills and codicils, the bulk of the document was concerned with the creation of a trust whose terms effectively concealed what Meyer Lansky's assets were at the time of his death. Teddy Lansky was entitled to 35 percent of the trust's net income — that income being unspecified — and the remainder was assigned, to be paid out at the trustee's discretion, to "the medical care, comfortable maintenance, and welfare" of Bernard I. Lansky.

If Meyer Lansky's fortune had indeed stood at $300 million when he died, and if it had been conservatively invested to produce a return of, say, 8 percent, then the income arising from this trust would have amounted to some $24 million a year — up to $15.6 million annually for Buddy, when divided according to the 65-35 split laid down by the will, with $8.4 million going to Teddy.

But Teddy Lansky soon discovered, if she ever had any doubt, that the difference between the fortune that legend attributed to her husband and the money that he actually left her was so vast as to constitute rather a cruel joke.

"*Big* problem!" she said to Paul Sann, referring to the will and the trust a few months after Meyer died.[18]

Teddy had invited Sann to Miami to try to revive the book project which Meyer had developed with Sann and Carl Erbe eight years earlier — with Teddy supplying the memories instead of Meyer. In the months before his death, Meyer had dwelt more than once on how much money might be made by a book telling the inside story of his life. It would be "Teddy's pension," he said.[19]

After a few days of conversation with Teddy, however, Sann decided that the widow's perspective scarcely added up to a book. Teddy Lansky would not — and, Paul Sann suspected, she could not — reveal the inside story of anything to do with Meyer's business activities. She had also come, in her bereavement, to cherish a Queen Victoria–like view of her dear departed.

"I never knew Meyer to hate," she told Sann. "Really. . . . There was something in this man that was imperial. He reminded me of somebody, like, out of the Bible."[20]

Paul Sann talked to his literary agent, then withdrew from the venture, though he did get the impression that Teddy was seriously short of cash.[21]

Buddy Lansky was even worse off. Since May of the previous year, he had been effectively confined to Jackson Memorial Hospital, close to the Miami River, completing the spinal correction which, the doctors promised, would check his physical decline. This was the painful and lengthy treatment involving the "halo" that connected his head to his spine, and when the device was finally removed, it did seem that the decline had been arrested. His condition had been stabilized. Buddy Lansky was able to talk and eat and smile — and to think — as cleanly and clearly as he had ever done.

But there had been little improvement in Buddy's underlying physical state. He now had to be categorized, officially and permanently, as a quadriplegic, and he was clearly destined to stay that way for the rest of his life. His mechanisms were paralyzed in every significant respect from the neck downward. He was unable to shave, scratch his nose, or write his name. He could not even lift his little finger. His bodily functions were now totally dependent on bags and catheters. During the day Buddy needed someone who could push his wheelchair. After he had gone to sleep, he had to be awakened and shifted three times through the night to prevent bedsores developing beneath the pressure of his dead weight. The moment had arrived that Buddy Lansky had feared for so long. He now needed medical care on a twenty-four-hour basis.

After Meyer's rejection of his son's fifty-dollar-a-day nurse proposal, Buddy had not liked to push his father on the subject of getting the full-time assistance that he needed. Spending most of 1982 in Jackson Memorial Hospital, he had hoped that the pain and tedium of the long rehabilitation might be rewarded, by some miracle, with a positive reverse in his condition. By the time it became clear that any improvement was out of the question, his father had only weeks to live.

Still, there was the promise that Meyer had extracted from Sandra, on his deathbed, that she would look after Buddy. And Buddy also remembered what his father had said on numerous occasions: "If you've got a problem, go to Uncle Jack."[22]

"Your father's left me in charge of you," Jake Lansky had confided to Buddy at the time of Meyer's heart operation in the early seventies.[23]

So Buddy was not surprised, in February 1983, about a month after his father's death, when Uncle Jack came to visit him, in the company of Jimmy Alo. Buddy had been moved out of Jackson Memorial into Arch Creek Convalescent Home, a low-budget private nursing home in the suburbs of North Miami, quite close to where Sandra lived.

Buddy had assumed that his stay in Arch Creek was just a temporary arrangement — until, perhaps, he could go back to his old room and to his friends at the Hawaiian Isle, which had been his home for nearly twenty years. But Jimmy Alo, who did all the talking, told Buddy that Arch Creek must now be his permanent home. Buddy could not go back to the motel. There was no way to look after him properly there. He needed full-time medical attention.

Jimmy said that he had been talking to his father's friends — Mike Wassell, Ben Gaines, Yiddy Bloom. They all wanted to help. It would take some time for the details of the will and the trust to be worked out. But in the meantime, Buddy should not worry about money. One way or another, the expense of Buddy's living in Arch Creek — some $400 a week — would get paid.

Jimmy Alo wanted to make it clear, however, that Buddy would have to take care of his own spending money. As a permanent invalid, he had a government disability pension of $498 a month, and that, in the opinion of Jimmy and the friends, was enough for all of Buddy's personal expenses — clothes, drinks, meals out. If Buddy blew his pension before the month was over, Jimmy emphasized, in an allusion to the trouble Buddy had got himself into with his gambling debts, then that was his tough luck.[24]

Jack Lansky sat silent, saying nothing at all as Jimmy Alo set out the details of Buddy's life in the future — and this seemed strange to Buddy. His uncle seemed oddly passive. As Jimmy Blue Eyes explained to Buddy how things would now be, Jake sat beside him nodding vacantly, his broad, heavy version of Meyer's features looking dead, his eyes blurred and empty.

Jake Lansky's eyes were not in good shape. He suffered from glaucoma, and he had other problems with his vision. He had undergone surgery, but this had not enabled him to see very much better. With his thick, pebble-lens glasses, Jake already moved in something of a daze. He shuffled like a man far older than his years — and now, numbed and disoriented by the disappearance of his best friend, his older brother, he showed a mental fogginess as well. Soon after Meyer died, Jake suffered a stroke.[25]

By the summer of 1983, six months after his brother's death, Jake Lansky's mind was half gone, his faculties visibly disintegrating. He could not remember names and faces, and he did not seem to care.[26] Without Meyer's concerns to take care of, Jake stopped taking care of himself. He was inconsolable in his mourning, the structure of his life gone. With whom should he now have breakfast every day?

"He missed Dad terribly," Buddy remembered.[27]

There was nothing much left for Jake Lansky to live for. He died in September 1983, aged seventy-nine. Two years the junior, Jake had outlived Meyer by only eight months, his poignant decline and death providing its own memorial to one of the more successful dimensions of Meyer's life. He had been a good brother.

Jake Lansky's will, probated on September 21, 1983, was very similar in form to that of Meyer.[28] It pooled all Jake's assets into a trust fund for the benefit of his widow, Anna, with the trust income being divided equally, after Anna's death, for the benefit of the couple's two daughters, Ricky and Linda. The size of the trust was not a matter of public record, but when the accountants and lawyers had finished doing their sums, it turned out that whereas Meyer Lansky had left practically nothing in his will, Jake Lansky had left quite a lot.[29]

This was, in fact, to be expected. It was the logical outcome of the arrangement that had existed between the brothers during their lifetimes, that Meyer should hold as little as possible in his own name, and that Jake should be the paper owner of the brothers' legal, recorded assets — the shares in the Singapore, for example, and in the Hawaiian Isle Motel.

This arrangement had seemed convenient and ingenious when Meyer and Jake were both alive. But after their deaths, it meant that the widow and children of the junior, second-ranking brother got almost all the legally saved and invested "show money," while the heirs of the clever brother, the one who had called the shots, ended up with next to nothing.[30]

After Jake died, and the disparity between the two brothers' legacies became clear, Yiddy Bloom went to Jake's widow, Anna, on Buddy's behalf, asking her to contribute something toward Buddy's medical expenses. But Aunt Anna did not want to know.

"I wish Jake had stayed a furrier," she kept on saying.[31]

Yiddy tried to explain to Anna how much of her husband's money had really been Meyer's, and how poor, crippled Buddy was in great need of help. But Anna went on talking about Jake's days in the fur business — her mind, on this matter, at least, apparently afflicted by the same fogginess from which her husband had come to suffer.[32]

How close to nothing Meyer Lansky legally bequeathed to his heirs became clear as his will was executed, and as trust income was organized from the assets and investments he had left. The Collins Avenue apartment had been acquired in the names of both Meyer and Teddy, so Teddy now owned that and could continue to live there for the rest of her life. Meyer had made the bulk of his legal investments, however, in oil and natural gas — his Michigan and Ohio ventures with Sam Garfield in the 1960s — and these had proved to be of fluctuating value.

With the lights in Times Square switched off and America standing in line at gas stations in the mid-1970s, Meyer Lansky could have realized a handsome capital profit if he had chosen to sell off his oil and natural gas investments in the years after he returned from Israel, and his leases held their value for some time after that. In the early eighties, however, the price of oil started to soften.

In his better moments Meyer managed to laugh at his atrocious sense of timing as a businessman[33] — Molaska, Consolidated Television, the millions lost in Cuba, his inability to take legal advantage of Las Vegas, the Bahamas, Atlantic City, or anywhere else that his own game of casino gambling became legal in his later years.

Meyer fumbled his oil and gas investments just as badly. Getting old, feeling ill, fighting cancer, coping with Buddy — Meyer Lansky did not focus in the early eighties on what was happening to energy investments, and the direction in which their price was starting to head.

It was Teddy and Buddy who found out. In 1981, two years before Meyer's death, Michigan oil had fetched over thirty-five dollars per barrel at the wellhead. By 1986, three years after his death, the price had fallen below fifteen dollars.[34]

David Rosen had passed on the task of administering Meyer's will to a Miami colleague, Stanley Kaplan, and as Kaplan started to pull together the components of the Lansky estate, he discovered that the essence of the portfolio, the energy investments, was losing its value at a spectacular rate. Not only were oil and gas prices falling, but Meyer's wells had been suffering for some time from technical problems — brine flooding and "souring" from hydrogen sulfide buildup. In 1987 State Summerfield A, the first and most profitable of all the concessions that Meyer bought with Sam Garfield, went out of production for these reasons, and by the end of the year all the other Lansky-Garfield ventures through Mammoth Producing had been shut down and plugged — their income yield at zero and their asset value scarcely more than that.[35]

Five years after Meyer Lansky's death, the Meyer Lansky Testimentary Trust was worth virtually nothing.

It took a time for Buddy, or anyone else, to realize this. The oil and gas revenues held up reasonably well through 1983, 1984, and 1985,[36] and in the period immediately following Meyer's death, his old friends took care of Buddy's bills at Arch Creek. Jimmy Alo also organized a roundup on behalf of Teddy, Buddy, and Sandra, coming down to Miami to call in the cash that had been owing to Meyer Lansky at the time of his death.

This help for the widow and children was in the tradition of the more honorable secret syndicates. Jimmy Blue Eyes managed to collect the best part of $300,000, which divided very neatly into $100,000 each for Teddy, Buddy, and Sandra. It was felt that there was no need to subsidize Paul Lansky, who was independent and living comfortably with his second wife on his government salary.

Buddy found out about Jimmy Blue Eyes's financial roundup from Teddy. It was in the spring of 1985, when income from the trust fund was starting to slow down.

"Did I know that Dad left cash for me?" Buddy remembered his stepmother asking him. "I said, 'No.' She said, 'Well, don't say I told you so.'"[37]

Buddy spoke to Ben Gaines and Mike Wassell, who confirmed the story. Buddy's $100,000 had been placed in Sandra's care, they said.

Buddy remembered Sandra's promise to their father on his deathbed. He needed his sister's help now, if he ever did. He called Sandra, and she agreed to pay $5,000 to the nursing home. Later that year, when Buddy still had not received any money from the trust fund, she paid Arch Creek a further $5,000.[38]

Just before Yom Kippur, September 1985, Buddy Lansky received some good news. "Teddy calls me, says, 'Buddy, you're going to get a check, probably after the holidays.'"[39]

Teddy had just received her own trust fund check, which meant that Buddy's share must be on the way. But when, after a week, the check did not appear, Buddy put in a call to Stanley Kaplan, the lawyer administering the trust.

Making a telephone call, for Buddy Lansky, meant asking one of the Arch Creek nurses to wheel him to the pay phone in the hall outside his room. The nurse would dial the number at Buddy's direction — Buddy kept several dozen phone numbers in his head — and would then press the receiver against his ear. So Buddy was sitting in the corridor at Arch Creek in this fashion, when he got the bad news.

"I had to pay Sandra back," said the lawyer. Buddy's sister, explained Kaplan, had billed the trust for the two $5,000 payments that she had made to Arch Creek. She had made the payments as loans, not gifts, so Kaplan had repaid her out of the latest monies due to Buddy. Buddy had not actually raised the question of the $100,000 when he spoke to Sandra earlier in the year. He had just asked for help.[40]

"But that's *your* money!" exclaimed Teddy, when Buddy told her what had happened.

"Well," replied Buddy, "Stanley doesn't know that."[41]

Given the origin of the money, it was hardly a problem that could be handled by lawyers, so Teddy went to talk to Mike Wassell and Yiddy Bloom, who put in a call to Jimmy Blue Eyes.

"They brought Jimmy down from New York," Buddy recalled, "and he went over to Sandra — it's all I heard, I don't know how true it is — to find out where the money was. And she said, 'I blew it.'"

Jimmy Alo might be forgiven for wondering why, more than three years after his partner's death, he was still having to sort out the personal problems of the Lansky family.

"If I had a gun," Jimmy said to Sandra and her husband, according to Buddy, "I would shoot both of you."[42]

The relationships between the various members of the Lansky family had never been especially convivial, but the row over

Buddy's money shattered them completely. Teddy and the surviving Schwartzes — her daughter-in-law and her four grandchildren — took Buddy's side. If the $300,000 gathered by Jimmy Alo was all they were going to see of the fabled Lansky fortune, then Sandra had managed to get her hands on two-thirds of it.

Yiddy Bloom also took Buddy's side, as did the dwindling members of the Wolfie's set — Benny Sigelbaum had died in 1984. Sandra was almost totally ostracized. Jake's daughters lined up with Buddy, which was fortunate for him, since they came into their father's money after their mother died in 1987, and felt a deeper obligation than she had. Ricky Szyperski and her sister, Linda Baker, agreed to make monthly contributions to their crippled cousin's living expenses. Even Aunt Esther, the peacemaker, was incensed by Sandra's conduct toward her crippled brother. Like everyone except Paul, Aunt Esther stopped speaking to Sandra.

Living on the other side of America, Meyer Lansky II and his sister, Myra, the children of Paul, were relatively detached from this bleak and angry battleground. But they had problems of their own. For eight years they had no idea where their father was, and they knew virtually nothing about him until the Imperial House shivah, when Meyer II heard the news of Paul's remarriage.

Edna, now Malana Mason, received her alimony check from Paul every month with confusingly varying postmarks, and never a return address. There was no extra money for the children on their birthdays, and seldom a birthday card.

"It was as if," says Myra Lansky, "he had wiped us right out of his life."[43]

When Myra reached the age of eighteen, she decided that the nonsense had to stop. She wanted to see her father again. Her phone calls to the family in Miami Beach were rebuffed. Aunt Sandra was especially unhelpful, telling her niece not to be a nuisance and to stop trying to harass her father. He was entitled to his privacy.

But from her aunt, Myra did gather that Paul was working in Washington, D.C. That must mean the Defense Department, she reasoned. So she rang the Pentagon, and after several hours of phoning, she eventually got through to the chief of her father's department, with a story about being desperately ill.

"I didn't know he had a daughter," said the chief. But he eventually agreed to put her in touch with Paul.

Myra had got herself a job in advertising in New York, and her father agreed to come up and see her. He had business there, and he could spare her half an hour. They could breakfast together.

"Didn't you think about me at all in those eight years?" Myra asked him when they met.

"Honestly, no," Paul Lansky told his daughter. "I never ever thought of you. Or your brother."

Myra asked her father if he would like to come and see the little room where she was living in a women's residence.

"That's not necessary," Paul replied. He had to get back to Virginia.

Myra complained to her father about the way in which Aunt Sandra had refused to give her Paul's phone number or address, but Paul seemed surprised by his daughter's grievance.

"She was only trying to protect me," he said.[44]

One son crippled physically, the other emotionally incapacitated. Meyer Lansky left a human legacy that was scarcely more satisfactory than his threadbare will. After their strained and brief meeting in New York, Myra Lansky started sending letters to her father. Paul responded with brief replies — and with his notes he would enclose his daughter's last letter to him, its faults of grammar and reasoning marked and corrected.

Paul Lansky retired from government service in the late 1980s, and went to live in Gardnerville, near Carson City, Nevada. He had chosen it, he told his children, after careful research. It was the least expensive place in America to retire.[45]

A few years later, in search of some form of reunion, Meyer Lansky II went to live in Gardnerville with his father, and his time in Nevada reawakened his dream of operating his own bar — in Las Vegas.

Thirty-three years old in 1990 — lean, rather handsome, and surprisingly tall — the former Bryan Mason decided to resume his original identity and to move down to Las Vegas as Meyer Lansky II. When he went to hotels and casinos looking for work, his name aroused great interest, and he would, occasionally, find himself passed on to senior executives or managers who said they knew his grandfather. The manager would shake Meyer II warmly by the hand, would tell him what a fine man his grandfather was, and would promise to call the moment he could find the right job. But the calls never came.[46]

*   *   *

The last occasion on which any number of the Lansky family gathered together in relative harmony was in 1985, for the unveiling of the gravestone of the first Mrs. Meyer Lansky, who had died in the previous year. Somehow Anne, the mother of Buddy, Paul, and Sandra, had survived to the age of seventy-four, alone in her West End Avenue apartment with her fur coats, dead birds, and cockroaches. The furs holed and shabby, her hair straggling and unkempt, Anne Lansky had so lost contact with the world that she would leave the door of her efficiency unlocked, to be raided and vandalized by the drug addicts of the seedy neighborhood in which she spent her declining years.[47]

But Anne Lansky had not lost touch with reality in one respect. After she died, it was discovered that she had left no less than $120,000 in cash in a safety-deposit box for her children. Given the scale of her alimony — $4,800 a year for thirty-seven years — Anne had made a significantly greater effort to provide for her offspring than her husband had.

The children did not get any of it, as events turned out. Sometime before she died, while her ex-husband was still alive, Anne Lansky had fallen and broken her hip, spending months in Roosevelt Hospital and then in a convalescent home. All the money she left went to pay the bills incurred during her final years of illness.[48] Sandra paid to have her mother's body brought down to Miami and buried in Mount Nebo.

"Anne Lansky, 1910–1984, Forever In Our Hearts," reads the modest little stone which lies in a different plot, round the corner and about 150 yards away from the grave of her husband, Meyer.

Sandra has said that she wants to be buried beside her mother. She has put up a freestanding "Lansky" headstone to mark the area. It was agreed before Meyer's death that Buddy should be buried beside his father. Teddy, who has a strong dislike of bugs and creepy-crawlies, says she does not want to be buried in the ground. She has made arrangements to lie in the Sigelbaum mausoleum, a high, filing-cabinet-like structure of marble on the other side of the Malaleuca trees, a hundred yards from Meyer's grave in the opposite direction from Anne. Divided in life, the Lansky family has made careful arrangements to stay that way in perpetuity.

Meyer Lansky's most material memorial still stands today in Havana, rising turquoise-tiled and twenty-one stories high above the salt spray and sputtering Fiats of the Malecón. Thirty years on, the

Riviera Hotel remains the best hotel in the peeling, subdued city that is Castro's Havana, and, though the distinction scarcely means what it used to, the Riviera still boasts Cuba's finest hotel dining room. In the absence of anything so frivolous and luxurious — or anything at all — being built in Cuba in the last thirty years, the marbled lobby and chandeliers of the Riviera Hotel have provided uniquely plush hospitality for the modern guests of honor in Dr. Castro's Socialist Republic — the engineers from Moscow, Kiev, and Leningrad.

Have they heard the history, these technicians, of this mosaic pleasure palace, and of the curiously elaborate, egg-shaped "convention hall" in which they hold their seminars? It would amuse them, perhaps, to learn that it was all conceived and built by one of their fellow countrymen — the little bringer of light from Grodno, born a subject of Czar Nicholas II.

And what of the memorials that really matter, all those potent currents of the mind to which Meyer Lansky's career gave such life — the imagined cleverness of great malefactors, their wealth beyond dreams, their presumed ability to defeat circumstance and to accomplish anything, no matter what? We derive more satisfaction from the fantasized exploits of one Meyer Lansky than from the efforts of twenty honest men because, somewhere inside us, we yearn to break the rules as he did. We cherish the illusion that vice commands a cunning which virtue cannot rival.

The life of Meyer Lansky says that we are wrong. Far from being cunning, vice, for him, proved both banal and self-defeating. Meyer Lansky and his family discovered that there is a price to be paid for a life based upon deceit, and that somehow, somewhere, that price is exacted in the end.

At the age of fifty-nine, Bernard "Buddy" Lansky bore a striking resemblance to his father. He was short and neat, with the same nose and bright eyes — intelligent with a streak of mischief. He thoroughly lived up to the cheerfulness of his nickname. Small and genial, Buddy Lansky had an impishness about him as he surveyed the world, alertly turning his head — the only part of his body which he was able to turn or move in any way.

But the world that Buddy Lansky came to be surveying in March 1989 was not one that would make many people feel impish. No longer a resident of Arch Creek Convalescent Home, Buddy was living in a low, one-story building in which the predominant atmosphere was of unemptied bedpans. The inmates who lined the corridors had dead, incurious stares. Two women were moaning to themselves inconsolably. A white-whiskered old gentleman wrestled halfheartedly with his straitjacket. Six years and a few weeks after his father's death, Buddy Lansky had been moved to the poorhouse. He was now destitute. The eldest child of Meyer Lansky was living on charity.

Buddy did not feel that he was to blame. He had stuck to his own part of the deal that Jimmy Alo laid down when he came to Arch Creek with Uncle Jack in February 1983. Buddy had kept his personal spending money strictly within the budget of his $500-a-month disability pension. No more betting or loan sharks.

"No more girls either," he would remark rather wistfully.[49]

It was the income from the trust fund that ran out. Well number 6754 in Clare County, Michigan, was shut down in the summer of 1987, and Stanley Kaplan sold it in June of that year on behalf of the fund, on the grounds that a small amount of capital was better than no income at all.[50]

Hearing of the problems with the trust fund, Yiddy Bloom organized some money to keep Buddy going. Buddy's cousins, Jake's daughters, also provided some help. In the absence of money from the trust, Buddy managed to soldier on for nearly two years, until early in 1989 when, after laying out nearly $50,000, Yiddy Bloom said he could not manage any more.[51] He had sick dependents of his own to support.

With no one to pay his bills, and with only his disability pension, Buddy Lansky was evicted from Arch Creek. His belongings — one battered suitcase, a few plastic bags of clothing, and an old television set — were packed up, and he was transported to a broken-down corner of North Miami that was noted for its tattoo parlors and for the thick wire mesh on storefront windows.

Technically, Buddy had been moved to an alternative nursing center, a minimum-provision convalescent home. But this new home was Bedlam, a way station to nowhere — a hostel for the down and out. Almost all the other occupants, indigents like Buddy, were living on the charity of Dade County. But unlike the other occupants, Buddy Lansky did have all his wits about him.

"The basic trouble," he said, looking calmly at his grubby and depressing surroundings, "is that I have lived too long. People expected me to die before now."[52]

Imprisoned helplessly in this grisly asylum — able only to shout protests when other inmates went into his locker to rummage boldly

and gleefully, in front of his eyes, through his plastic bags of possessions — Buddy Lansky grew very angry.

He could hardly complain at his father's friends or at Uncle Jack's
daughters for declining to support him forever, particularly when it
was possible for the government to meet his bills. It was the attitude
of his closer family that angered Buddy — the indifference of Paul
and Sandra, and the way in which Teddy would plead poverty whenever Buddy started talking about money. Buddy simply could not
believe that his stepmother was that poor. She had admitted receiving
Jimmy Alo's $100,000, and somehow she still found the money to
go shopping at Bal Harbor.

Buddy Lansky felt humiliated. As a young man, he had had
Manhattan as his oyster. He had had his own apartment on the park,
the friendship of men like George Wood and Frank Costello. He
could walk into the Copa, Dinty Moore's, Spindletop, and be greeted
by name. He would be shown to a good table. He was Meyer
Lansky's son — and he had come down to this, waiting in a North
Miami refuge for the help of the Medicare man.

"If there's a life after death," he said in April 1989, "I don't want
to come back."[53]

Soon after his father died, Buddy had met a young journalist on
the *Miami Herald,* Kathy McCarthy, and had given her a brief interview, describing his life in the old days — the story of the little boy
who grew up in the Majestic and had his own jukebox. Now he
called Kathy McCarthy with a different sort of story.

"You can pick your friends," he told her. "But you can't pick your
relatives."[54]

Ms. McCarthy chose this remark to conclude the piece she wrote
for the *Miami Herald* on April 9, 1989.

"A sister, Sandra, who lives in North Miami," she reported baldly,
"and a brother, Paul, who lives in Nevada, have no contact with
him."

The article described how Teddy Lansky did bring her stepson
chicken soup, from time to time, in mayonnaise jars — and how
Teddy would ask the nurses to save the jars for her so she could have
them back again later.

Buddy Lansky had been abandoned by his family, to his shame,
and he wanted to spread some of his pain to those whom he felt
deserved it. The article ended whatever relationship he had had with
his stepmother, and he never saw or spoke to his sister again.

He did continue to receive Christmas cards from his brother, Paul, but, a long-standing practice of Paul's, there was never a return address on the card, nor on its envelope.[55] So Buddy could not reply to his brother, even had he wanted to.

In the summer of 1989, Buddy Lansky was approved for Medicare payments. With his basic living and medical expenses underwritten, he was able to move back into a shared room in Arch Creek. But late in December, he fell sick. His sixtieth birthday would be on January 15, 1990, which would also be the seventh anniversary of his father's death. Buddy had had plans to go to the cemetery — a few days before the fifteenth, he reckoned, since there was the chance that he might find Teddy at the grave if he went on the anniversary itself.[56]

Buddy had been complaining for some time of sharp pains in his chest.[57] He had recently been back to Jackson Memorial for an operation to cut out painful scar tissue where the weight of his body pressed on the support struts of his wheelchair. Prior to that operation, he had signed a living will, a declaration which refused emergency resuscitation or life support in the event of his becoming critically ill.[58]

"I'd like to get it over with," he would say. "What have I got to live for? . . . I pray every night that He'll take me out of here."[59]

If he had only realized, Buddy used to say, how close to dying his father had been in 1982, he would never have consented to the lengthy "halo" operation and therapy that had arrested his own decline.

"I would have gone with him — laid next to him."[60]

One morning just after Christmas 1989, Buddy Lansky suddenly refused to eat his breakfast. He wanted to stay in bed, he said. He did not want to be dressed or to be put in his wheelchair. He refused his lunch. He refused his dinner — and he refused to drink water all day. When the night shift came to change his position in bed, he refused to be moved. He wanted to stay lying where he was, he muttered, his face set toward the wall.

One of the nurses who knew him well came round and knelt down to talk to him. "Buddy," she said, "I can tell. You're giving up."[61]

Buddy looked at her hard with his bright, intelligent eyes, and then nodded his head.

Two days later, continuing to refuse food and water, Buddy Lansky died, his face still turned toward the wall.[62]

Author's Note and
Acknowledgments

It was in December 1987, on the first of two research trips to Israel, that I began to wonder whether the evil genius whom I had been pursuing for the previous ten months really existed. There, for the first time, I met people who had actually got to know Meyer Lansky personally, and who had taken his measure. I also discovered in the office of the prime minister, in Jerusalem, still tied neatly in their legal ribbons, the five bundles of documents which had lain in front of the five justices of the Israeli Supreme Court as they sat in judgment on Lansky's attempt to become an Israeli citizen in 1972.

Many of these documents were in Hebrew. There were also lengthy extracts from the books on organized crime which I had been reading myself since the previous February. But interleaved with these, and bearing the handwritten notes of the Israeli justices, were "raw" uncensored American government reports and papers that had originated with the FBI, the U.S. Department of Justice, and a number of other government departments in Washington. These, I later discovered, were the documents which the Israeli state attorney Gavriel Bach had collected in 1971, following the Israeli government's request to Washington for information about Meyer Lansky.

The excitement of this discovery can, perhaps, only be fully appreciated by the author or researcher who, having waited up to three years for the processing of his application to view U.S. government documents under the

Freedom of Information Act, finally receives his package, and tears it open — to discover page after page, and every interesting name, blacked out in heavy felt-tip marker.

Unique and wonderful though the Freedom of Information Act is — particularly for a British writer accustomed to the Official Secrets Act and the Thirty-Year Rule — it still leaves an inquirer with the uneasy suspicion that there is something extra in the black stuff, that the real story remains hidden in all the deletions and omissions. Here, however, by the serendipitous process which brought these documents from various corners of America to Washington, and then on to the supreme court in Jerusalem, was the U.S. government's best shot — every detail, undiluted and undeleted, of the strongest case that the FBI and the Justice Department could marshal after twenty years of investigating Meyer Lansky, the supposed mastermind of American organized crime.

The documents left no doubt that the man was a crook, that he had made his living on the wrong side of the law, that he knowingly consorted with men of violence — that he was a gangster. But here was no Satan. Meyer Lansky had not dealt in drugs — or prostitution or loan-sharking or stolen property. He had not been a director of Murder, Inc., killing or ordering hits to contract. He was not the head of a shadowy underworld corporation, laundering money and infiltrating legitimate business. It was remarkable, in fact, looking at the evidence, what Meyer Lansky had *not* done. There was nothing here to sustain the notion of Lansky as king of all evil, the brains, the secret mover, the inspirer and controller of American organized crime — the man whom I had set out to write a book about.

Looking back, I can see this quite clearly as the turning point. At the time, my feelings were less defined: disbelief, confusion, and irritation that here was yet another story where the truth could not be black and white, but would involve the sorting of different shades of gray, as it usually does.

So my first thanks must be to those who helped me in Israel, and who gave me my first taste of the extraordinary openness and energy that characterize so many activities in that country: the former interior minister, Dr. Yosef Burg; his assistant director general, Judith Huebbner; the former state attorney, now supreme court justice, Gavriel Bach; Ehud Olmert, who introduced me to Yaacov Aloni; Yoram Alroy, whose own thoughts started so many of my own running; David Landau; Dan Raviv; Robert Rockaway; Bill Seamens; Yoram Sheftel; and, at the Dan Hotels, Yehuda Barash, Menachem Tamari, and Ykutiel Federman.

The Intifadah was in its violent early days when I visited Israel in December 1987 and January 1988. I am grateful to Joseph Levy, who drove me and picked out the routes to keep me safe on our expeditions in and around Jerusalem. My greatest debt is to Evelyn Chen, who translated and organized so many things, and who arranged, through Zev Chafets and Eliahu

Ben Elissar, my meeting with the late Joseph "Yoskeh" Sheiner — another of the memorable moments in the shaping of this book.

We met in Tiberias, beside the Sea of Galilee, looking across at the Golan Heights. Yoskeh strode into the hotel, short-sleeved and energetic, bearing a large Samsonite briefcase. It was his private archive of ten years of friendship — notes, letters, cards, and other memorabilia of Meyer Lansky. We explored it for hours together as he relived his journey with Meyer halfway around the world in November 1972 — another adventure whose reality, when described at first hand, proved rather different from the version shaped by legend and the media. I am grateful for the help, since Yoskeh's death last November, of his son Oded.

In February 1988, I moved with my family to south Florida, where I met the first of what can only be described as my "Deep Throats." Such was the notoriety of Meyer Lansky by the mid-1970s that almost anyone who knew him socially, or who knew or did business with people who knew him, risked being described as a Lansky front, associate, or, if young enough, his heir apparent. This involved IRS audits, dark finger-pointing in the newspapers, and even law enforcement investigations.

My sources were not without sin themselves. Some were involved in illegal gambling and bookmaking. Others profited from nimble-footed arrangements with offshore banks and corporate entities. They preferred — and prefer — to remain anonymous. But they saw no shame in their links, such as they were, with Lansky. The only hurtful thing, as one of them put it to me, was "the idea that Meyer made my money for me."

Through mutual friends, I met Teddy, Mrs. Meyer Lansky, who spent a gracious afternoon with my wife and me beside the pool of the Imperial House. She told me she was working on her memoirs, with a collaborator. I also met Sandra Lansky, who told me that she wished to reserve her memories of her father for a project of her own. Through Sandra I contacted her brother Paul, who also declined to be interviewed.

It was not until March 1989, more than two years into my research, that I first met Buddy Lansky. He had just been evicted from his nursing home and was living on charity in the unhappy circumstances described in the final chapter of the book. Sandra told me that Buddy was not a reliable witness. I did not find this to be the case. Buddy was honest in his memories — painfully so at times, and not always to his own credit. He was usually generous in his judgments of other people, and he was always perceptive. What he said checked out precisely against the memories of others, and against such documentary sources as were applicable. I got into the habit of spending the best part of one day a week with Buddy, taking him to lunch, helping him with his phone calls, running errands to the bank, taking him to visit his parents' graves in Mount Nebo cemetery.

Between March and December 1989, we became friends. It was our plan to travel together, once the book was completed, on a cruise to Alaska — the same trip his father made before he died. There will be no cruise now, but I hope that this book stands as some sort of memorial to a brave and vital life. It would not have been much of a book without him.

It was through Buddy that I made contact with his niece and nephew Myra and Meyer Lansky II, with their mother, Malana Mason, formerly Mrs. Edna Lansky, and later with Buddy's ex-wife, Annette. They were forthright, as Buddy had been, with the same freshness of spirit in the face of misunderstanding. Meyer II told me he has friends who really believe that his modest way of life is a clever front to conceal the millions that he must have inherited from his grandfather. If this book helps to dispel such fantasies, it may slightly repay the debt I owe these Lanskys for their help and candor.

Americans cherish their gangsters, I have discovered. They delight in the myths of cleverness, power, and wealth which they wreath around these defective outlaws and in the specter of the dark, countrywide corporation which is popularly identified as the source of so much wickedness. Belief in "the Mob" explains things so simply, making it possible to shrug off responsibility for the violence, profiteering, and disregard for the law which are such enduring features of the American way. The gangster fascinates America as the twisted fulfillment of some of her most cherished dreams, and this has made writing about Meyer Lansky — the imagined Chairman of the imaginary Board — a venture into systems of almost biblical belief. There are the fervent disciples of the Mafia and its FBI refinement, the "LCN." There are those who assert with equal ardor that the Mafia does not exist.

Meyer Lansky himself came to be the focus of such a belief system, and if my research goes some way toward demolishing that, it should not be taken as a comment on the others. After four and a half years talking to law enforcement officials, interviewing some lawbreakers, and eating in a certain sort of restaurant, I find it impossible to deny the existence of characters who can only be described as mafiosi. But I remain unconvinced of the organizational abilities attributed to them, and I would not quarrel with those who argue that many of the hallmarks of the average mafioso, and much of his self-esteem, stem from the stereotypes that have been created by the media. Criminals are seldom innovators, as far as I can see. Their lives are pale copies of the vigor and creativity of the straight world — and the clever ones like Meyer Lansky learn to copy its honesty as well.

Firsthand, contemporary witness has been my touchstone, and reliance on contemporary documents has been part of that. As explained in the note on sources that follows, the New York City Municipal Archives provide a particularly solid resource against which subsequent folklore can be checked, and I must record my special thanks to its director Kenneth Cobb for his quiet help and tireless missions to the warehouse in search of yet another dusty volume of magistrates' judgments.

I would also like to thank those who helped me make a significant addition to those archives. Jenna Weissman Joselit, the author of *Our Gang,* a clear-eyed study of Jewish crime in New York in the years 1900–40, told me of an old filing cabinet she had seen in the offices of the New York district attorney. Long ignored, it contained the dossiers of investigation into the murder of Albert Anastasia in the barbershop in 1957 — interviews, surveillance reports, and even items of evidence. It brings research to life when you open a manila envelope and a used bullet drops into your hand.

With the help of Judge Joseph Stone, a sage and solid ally at several stages of my research, these files were transferred to the municipal archives, where they now await any researcher interested in making a document-based analysis of a major organized crime investigation.

There is a dire need for objectively analyzed data on organized crime, an area which academics have too readily surrendered to the custody of popular entertainment. Almost every authentic, core American business, from advertising to carmaking, is executed more skillfully these days by foreigners. Entertainment is the one exception. You can beat Americans at almost any game in the 1990s, it seems, but not at the fabrication of escapism and dreams, and this has had a corrosive impact on the country's appetite for confronting the irregular, untidy reality of things. Television news programs "re-create" events with the help of actors. Journalists invent polished sentences that are what they feel their subjects "meant" to say. Running up the national overdraft, refusing to let politicians talk about taxes, idolizing the theatrics of professional wrestlers and bogus TV preachers — America seems to suffer from an increasing preference for fantasy over reality, and to be losing the ability to tell which is which.

The myths surrounding organized crime and the cult of the gangster are part of the confusion.

Israel, Florida, and New York were the principal research locations for this book. Research also took me to Cuba, the Bahamas, Haiti, Morocco, London, Boston, Saratoga Springs, Cleveland, Detroit, New Orleans, Tacoma, and Las Vegas. My acknowledgments to the people who helped me in each of these places can be found in the source notes to the particular chapters with which they assisted.

I have had most generous help from law enforcement professionals: from the former attorneys of the Justice Department R. J. Campbell, Bill Hundley, Dougald McMillan, Marvin R. Loewy, and Will Wilson; from former FBI agents Jack Danahy, Bill Kane, Welton Merry, Bill Roemer, Dennis O'Shea, and particularly Joe Yablonsky; from members of the Broward County Organized Crime Center, David Green, John Sampson, and Don Veliky. William Graff has been the source of many insights, Ralph Salerno a most open-hearted and informed guide. On IRS matters, my thanks to the tenacious Richard Jaffe and to Mike MacDonald.

Among librarians, I would like to thank: Luis Bueno of the *Miami Herald*; Joe Wright of the *Miami News*; Chris Kucharski of the *Detroit Free Press*; Raymond Teichman of the Franklin D. Roosevelt Library; Karl Kavelac, Department of Rare Books and Special Collections, University of Rochester; Kathy Nicastro and Sally Marks at the Civil Branch of the National Archives and Records Administration, Washington, D.C.; the staffs at the London Library and the New York Public Library; Barbara Staubly, and the staff of the West County Branch Palm Beach Public Library — and the countless librarians who supplied volumes through the wonderful interlibrary loan system. For help with the locating of hard-to-find books, my thanks to Patterson Smith and to Howard Schwartz of the Gambler's Book Club.

I am most grateful for the expert guidance and help I received early in my researches from Phillip Manuel in Washington, and also from the staff of the Permanent Subcommittee on Investigations of the Senate Committee on Governmental Affairs.

My thanks to all the hard-worked administrators of the Freedom of Information Act who helped process my applications, including, at the U.S. Department of Justice, Emil P. Moschella; Bonnie L. Gay and Margaret A. Smith, Executive Office for U.S. Attorneys; Caroline D. Poindexter, Office of Legal Policy; L. Jeffrey Ross, Office of Enforcement Operations, Criminal Division; Alice M. Neary, Immigration and Naturalization Service; Helen Ann Near, FOIA Reading Room, FBI Headquarters. Also: Carol A. Garrett, National Security Agency; Paul E. Wilson and Quintin L. Villanueva, Jr., U.S. Customs Service, Pacific Region; Joan Woodin, Department of the Interior, Bureau of Land Management, Reno, Nevada; Sheila J. Jackson and Sara Downes, Department of State; C. R. Clauson, chief postal inspector; Paul J. Knapp, Selective Service System; Joyce A. Thomas, Bureau of Alcohol, Tobacco, and Firearms. My special thanks to Irma Jackson of the Immigration and Naturalization Service.

There may be nothing like the Freedom of Information Act in London, but D. J. Blackwood in the Home Office was painstaking in his replies to my queries. My thanks to him.

Four and a half years' research builds up obligations for many kindnesses. My warm thanks to Susan Albert; Steve Allen; the nurses and staff of Arch Creek Convalescent Home; Eric Arens; Jane Barton; Stephen Birmingham; Gerson Blatt; John Blundell; Carl Brandt; Janet Brooks; Warren de Brueys; Vincent Bruno; Davis Chant; Joseph Cohen; Renata Coleman; Craig Colwart; Bernie Cornfeld; David Crippen; Harry Dann; Douglas Day, Q.C.; Larry Deitch; Helen Dickinson; Rodney Dillon; Anne and Dwight Doskey.

Adrian and Ghislaine Foley; Paul Frances; David Frankel; Dr. Bill Fredrix; Lee Gaffney; Georgie Anne Geyer; Mildred Gilbert; Paul Greenberg; Bill Griswold at the Byte Shop; Ed Gudeon; Dr. Ian Hassin; Danni Hay; Sir

Jack Hayward; Dr. Jean Henry; Craig Herron; C. David Heymann; Julian and Patricia Hipwood; Milton and Irma Hoff; David Jamison; Robert and Phyllis Jordan.

Kitty Kelley; George Kennedy; Tessa Kennedy; Ronald Kessler; Gerard King; Rick Kohen; Bob Lappin; Jennifer Lee; Harry and Charlene Leopold; Victor Lowndes; Peter Maas; Mike McClaney; Lionel Martin; Jackie Mason; Mario de Mendoza III; James Mercurio and Vincent Mercurio; Richard Meyer and Denise Apter; Dr. Ernest Mitler; W. C. Moffit, Jr.; Christopher Moorsom; Bryan and Greta Morrison; Leonard Newman; Jim Nicholson; Columbus O'Donnell; Jim Orowitz.

Dominick Palermo and John Podracky of the New York Police Academy Museum; Andrew and Davina Palmer and the staff of the British embassy in Havana; Andrew Paneycko; John Parsons; Edward and Anna Lee Porter; Marianne Pressman; Michael Pye; Bruno Redman; Carol Renno; Dean Richards and Michael Richards; Ronit Richman; Dr. Douglas Rossdale; Dr. David Russin.

Barry Salz; Howard Sann; Sam Seitlin; J. "Skip" Shepard; Martin Short; John Simpson of the *Oxford English Dictionary*; Doug Soifer; Jacques von Spiro; Anna Strasberg; Bob Talbert; David Thomas; Lila and Coleman Ullner; Jeanne Vanderbilt; Sir Ronald Waterhouse; Irving Weiss and Phillip Weiss; Mike Wheeler; Mr. and Mrs. John Wilds; Gregory Wolfe; Frank Wright.

My thanks to Daniel Bell, Lowell Bergman, Lee Hills, Howard Kleinberg, William Howard Moore, Jim Savage, Ira Silverman, and Milt Sosin, fellow toilers on their different slopes of the vineyard. I must pay particular tribute to Hank Messick, now disabled from writing by illness. He knew that I questioned many of his findings — $300 million and all that — and that I had the considerable advantage of him in terms of time, hindsight, and documentation. He nevertheless saw his task as helping me toward further truth, displaying a largeness of spirit I can only salute and envy.

My debt to Joseph Varon, Meyer Lansky's Florida lawyer, is apparent from the text. My thanks, too, to Moses Polakoff in New York; to E. David Rosen, courteous and canny, in Miami; to Saul Radler, Lansky's accountant at the Plantation Harbor; and to Rabbi David Shapiro.

I am grateful to my friend Gabe Gutman, who first encouraged me to write about Lansky. Thank you to Dave Critchley and Tommy Prior for their help with many aspects of my research. My researcher par excellence has been Jacqueline Williams, tirelessly checking and breaking open crucial new routes of inquiry. My thanks to Marvin Gelfand for sharing his unparalleled knowledge of New York and its streets.

Publishers are supposed to do it anyway, but I have to express my admiration for the energy, expertise, and support that Little, Brown has brought to the publishing of this book from the very beginning of its lengthy gestation. Thank you to Peggy Leith Anderson, Karen Dane, Kevin Dolan,

Megan Gray, Judith Kennedy, Colleen Mohyde, John Taylor Williams, and, most of all, to my editor, Bill Phillips, who kept the faith through the dark and wandering days, and who helped point the way home. At Random Century in London, my thanks to Mark Booth, David Crane, and Louise Weir, all new friends, and most invigorating. Mort Janklow, my new agent in New York, has proved full service, all he promised — that service including the additional help and counsel of his associate Anne Sibbald. In London, Michael Shaw at Curtis Brown has remained so solid.

My thanks to Christine Marshall, who has worn out a transcription machine in the transcribing and typing of the interviews on which this book is based. My debt is still greater to Alison Glass Mahoney, who transcribed and indexed all the Buddy interviews, typed and helped shape the whole book, and developed several important lines of research.

My greatest debt of all is to my wife, Sandi, who read every version of every chapter, and told me it was good — then showed me how it really might be. Gangsters were not an easy stint, after Detroit and Saudi Arabia, but they proved no match for her. Her love, support, and creative disagreement have been the making of the book — and of me, as ever.

Dedicating a book is always a good feeling, and this book especially so. It is for my three children, Sasha, Scarlett, and Bruno. In the last four years, each of you, in your own right and in your own different ways, has given me more pride and pleasure than I could possibly say.

ROBERT LACEY   *June 18, 1991*

Source Notes

Research for this book began in February 1987 and was completed with the writing, in June 1991. Details of the interviews, documents, books, articles, and other sources are set out under the chapter headings that start on page 452, and in the Bibliography starting on page 515.

Documentary Sources

The eagerness of the U.S. Department of Justice to bring Meyer Lansky back from Israel in 1971 has meant that the most complete and uncensored collection of law enforcement documents on Lansky's life is located in Jerusalem. Some may be consulted in the archive room of the Office of the Prime Minister, where they are to be found in the bundles of judges' papers, catalogued as Supreme Court, *Meyer Lansky v. the State of Israel, 442/71.* A number of others, including tax return details and normally confidential IRS documents, are not in the judges' papers. They leaked in some way to Israeli journalists at the time. I was able to locate a number of these, and there may well be other documents that are still in private files in Tel Aviv and Jerusalem. All may be identified by notarized Department of Justice cover sheets dated August and September 1971; in the chapter notes, STRIKE FORCE 18 PAPERS is the designation given this entire collection.

By curious coincidence, the files of Rabbi Judah Magnes's New York Kehillah, with its detailed reports on criminality around Lansky's home on

Grand Street and throughout the Jewish community of the Lower East Side in the first decades of the century, have also ended up in Jerusalem, only a few hundred yards away from the prime minister's office, in the library of Hebrew University. They are catalogued as the Magnes Papers in the Central Archives for the History of the Jewish People.

Of the various sets of U.S. government documents on Lansky that are available under the Freedom of Information Act, the largest is that gathered by the FBI. This contains a surprising amount of quite detailed surveillance material. The papers can be consulted, by prior appointment, in the FOIA Reading Room, FBI Headquarters, Washington.

The New York City Municipal Archives house the records of the district attorneys of New York and of Kings County (Brooklyn). These therefore include the files on Thomas E. Dewey's prosecution of Lucky Luciano, as well as the Murder, Inc., papers (which include the examination of Charles Workman, one of the killers of Dutch Schultz), the dockets of the magistrates' courts detailing Lansky's early convictions, and the investigative files on the murder of Albert Anastasia. New York District Attorney Frank S. Hogan's interest in the bookmaker Frank Erickson means that these archives also contain Eisen and Eisen's inventory of tax documents relating to the Colonial Inn, Hallandale, and the Lansky brothers' other gambling enterprises in Florida.

The National Archives in Washington now house the research files of the Kefauver Committee, and also, in the State Department Papers, the correspondence of the American Embassy in Havana relating to gambling in Cuba, President Batista, and Meyer Lansky.

The records and report of the Herlands inquiry into the World War II collaboration between U.S. Naval Intelligence and Lucky Luciano, via Moses Polakoff and Meyer Lansky, are in the University of Rochester Library, Department of Rare Books and Special Collections, Rochester, New York.

The archives of the Fort Lauderdale Historical Society; the Douglas County Historical Society in Omaha, Nebraska; and the Office of the City Historian in Saratoga Springs, New York, contain small but useful collections of contemporary materials, usually in the form of local newspaper clippings, on gambling in the carpet-joint era. Similar material can be found in the Louisiana Room of the New Orleans Public Library, which has well-organized newspaper files. The most complete archives on the underdocumented history of gambling in America are to be found in the libraries of the University of Nevada in Reno and Las Vegas. See the notes to chapter 9 and the Oral Histories section of the Bibliography, below, for more details.

Paul Sann, the author and journalist, compiled a Lansky library of his own in the course of his preparations for writing Lansky's biography in the mid-1970s. In addition to thirty-five years of newspaper clippings and uncensored U.S. government documents which Sann obtained through his own confidential sources, the primary materials include extensive notes of his interviews, conversations, and meetings with Meyer and Teddy Lansky in Miami Beach in 1975, and with other contemporaries including E. David Rosen and Moses Polakoff. Paul Sann died in September 1986. Howard Sann, Paul's son, has written his own, as yet unpublished account of his father's association with Lansky — *Getting the Man to Talk*. It is the intention of Howard Sann eventually to add his father's Lansky research materials to the existing collection of his father's papers in the Special Collections section of the Mugar Memorial Library at Boston University.

Secondary Sources

The ambition of gangsters, their ghostwriters, and of crime writers in general to make their books sound like movie scripts, means that the vast corpus of secondary literature on organized crime is shot through with inaccuracy and exaggeration. The challenge is to separate the truth from the tissue of hearsay and folklore woven around it, and often this is quite impossible. For this reason, the purported memoirs of Lucky Luciano, the so-called last testament published in 1974, have not been relied on in the writing of this book. My own research has more than confirmed the doubts cast on their veracity by critics.

Of the two existing biographies of Lansky, Hank Messick's (*Lansky,* 1971) contains valuable material on the Molaska episode and provides a useful corrective, like all of Messick's work, to the Valachi-dominated view of American organized crime as an exclusively Italian matter. *Meyer Lansky: Mogul of the Mob* by Eisenberg, Dan, and Landau (1979) amplifies the fascinating personal recollections of Lansky to Uri Dan which were first published in the three-part series "Meyer Lansky Breaks His Silence" in *Ma'ariv* in July 1971.

Readers interested in the relatively small number of works which have attempted to measure the available data on organized crime against recognized academic and historical standards should consult the books and articles listed in the Bibliography under Albini, Bell, Block, Chubb, Haller, Hawkins, Ianni, Kwitny, Lupsha, Moore, Morris, Nelli, Powers, Reuter, and Dwight C. Smith. None of these authors has written about Lansky per se, but what they have to say about the meaning and nature of organized crime in their own fields of study makes a lot of sense to me, and I am happy to acknowledge the intellectual debt I owe them.

Abbreviations Used in the Notes

FBI   Documents obtained from the Federal Bureau of
                Investigation under the Freedom of Information Act

INS   Documents obtained from the Immigration and
                Naturalization Service under the Freedom of
                Information Act.

JUSTICE   Documents obtained from the Department of Justice
                under the Freedom of Information Act

KEFAUVER   Hearings and reports of the Kefauver Committee,
                issued by the U.S. Senate as *Organized Crime in
                Interstate Commerce* (see Bibliography)

PASSPORT OFFICE Documents obtained from the U.S. Passport Office
                under the Freedom of Information Act

Sann Interviews Notes of and materials gathered by Paul Sann (see
                introductory section Documentary Sources, above)

STATE   Documents obtained from the Department of State
                under the Freedom of Information Act

STRIKE FORCE 18 Documents sent to the Israeli government by the U.S.
PAPERS   Justice Department in 1971 (see introductory section
                Documentary Sources, above)

For details of the books and articles cited, see the Bibliography.

Godfather, Retired

I am grateful to Robert Bialos, librarian, for describing Meyer Lansky's visits to the Miami Beach Public Library, and to Milt Sosin for first telling me of Lansky's patronage of the library. Lieutenant David Green, now of the Broward County Organized Crime Unit, was helpful in many ways, not least in showing me the surveillance video which he made of Meyer Lansky and his friends gathering at Wolfie's.

Lowell Bergman, a generous guide through the mysteries of organized crime, first drew my attention to the FBI's finding the photographs of Al Capone and Meyer Lansky in the Hole in the Wall luncheonette, Newark. Judge Harold Ackerman kindly confirmed to me that evidence of the two pictures was presented in the trial over which he presided.

1. Robert Bialos, interview, May 18, 1989.
2. Milt Sosin, interview, September 28, 1988.
3. Joseph Varon, interview, January 31, 1991.
4. Harold Conrad, interview, July 18, 1988. Conrad recalls these remarks from the conversations of Siegel and Lansky at the Colonial Inn, Hallandale, Florida, in 1946. See p. 147.

5. Harold Conrad, interview, July 18, 1988. Book-of-the-Month Club membership confirmed, March 23, 1989, by Buddy Lansky, who was also a member. Book-of-the-Month Club today does not have accessible records of membership in the 1940s.

6. Director to Legat, Havana, June 23, 1952. FBI.

7. Gerry Coyle, interview, March 21, 1990.

8. Buddy Lansky, interview, April 10, 1989.

9. Surveillance video, Lieutenant David Green, Broward County Organized Crime Unit.

10. Dr. David Russin, interview, September 25, 1989. (Answers: Twenty-first Amendment; Estes *was* the middle name of Carey Estes Kefauver.)

11. *Miami News*, December 18, 1975.

12. FBI Criminal Investigative Division, "Chronological History of La Cosa Nostra," p. 300.

13. *Wall Street Journal*, November 19, 1969.

14. Lowell Bergman, interview, March 6, 1989.

15. Judge Harold Ackerman, interview, September 16, 1989.

16. Shepard Broad, interview, June 1, 1989.

17. Author's conversation with Gary Rappaport, January 30, 1989.

18. John Sampson, interview, May 22, 1991.

19. KEFAUVER, Third Interim Report, May 1, 1951, p. 1.

20. Lieutenant David Green, interview, February 16, 1989.

21. Ibid.

22. Strasberg, p. 7.

23. Anna Strasberg, interview, October 30, 1988.

24. Ibid.

25. "The Gangster as Tragic Hero," February 1948, in Warshow, p. 127.

1. *"Little Child, Close Your Eyes"*

Grodno became part of Poland after the First World War. The town was occupied by Nazi Germany from 1941 to 1944. It has been part of Soviet Russia ever since, and there are today, by all accounts, few traces of the Jewish community that once dominated the town. Those Jews who did not emigrate before 1941 were wiped out during the Nazi occupation. The Jews of Grodno now living in Israel have formed an association to preserve the memory of Jewish life in the town, and this chapter draws upon interviews with members of the Grodno Association. I am grateful to Evelyn Chen for conducting these interviews and for translating them into English.

The best printed source on Jewish life in Grodno is volume 9 of the *Encyclopaedia of the Jewish Diaspora* (Tel Aviv: Memorial Books, 1973), edited by D. Rabin. I am grateful to Ronit Richman for translating this.

Meyer Lansky often spoke to his friends, associates, and family about his life as a boy in Grodno. He gave at least one interview on the subject to the Israeli journalist Uri Dan, who incorporated it into the biography of Lansky he wrote with Dennis Eisenberg and Eli Landau. Lansky also remembered those years in conversations with the writer Harold Conrad.

Miriam Weiner generously shared her unique knowledge of Jewish genealogy in eastern Europe, and helped me track down the Lanskys' Ellis Island records.

Dr. Benjamin Borkaw attended PS 165 at the same time as Meyer Lansky, and I am grateful to his wife, who attended the school shortly afterward, for her memories of life in Brownsville.

Hugh N. Griffith, the headmaster of PS 165 in Brownsville, and his deputy, Jay M. Eskin, kindly supplied me with the Brooklyn pupil record cards of the Lansky brothers and showed me round the school — still a vibrant and inspiring center of learning in the midst of daunting problems.

1. I am grateful to Dr. Yosef Burg for bringing these historic and symbolic connotations to my attention.

2. File F396, Grodno. Museum of the Jewish Diaspora, Tel Aviv. The precise figure was 68.7 percent.

3. Ibid.

4. Abraham Broide, Grodno Association, interview at Kibbutz Kfar Menachem, May 12, 1988.

5. Ibid.

6. Zborowski and Hertzog, p. 38.

7. Eisenberg et al., pp. 22, 23.

8. Deuteronomy, 6:9.

9. Eisenberg et al., p. 23.

10. Vishniac, p. 10.

11. Ibid., p. 11.

12. Aleichem, p. xiv.

13. Eisenberg et al., p. 25.

14. Harold Conrad, interview, April 2, 1990.

15. Rabin, "Grodno," p. 130.

16. Ibid.

17. Ibid., p. 115.

18. Howe, *World of Our Fathers*, p. 2.

19. Eisenberg et al., p. 17.

20. Ibid., p. 29.

21. Office of the Chevra Kadisha, Mount of Olives, Jerusalem, December 16, 1987.

22. Eisenberg et al., p. 17.

23. Ibid., p. 31.

24. Ibid.

25. Ibid.

26. Digest of INS and Other Inquiries into Meyer Lansky (pages 3–24 of

untitled document datelined Miami, Florida, June 22, 1959; C-2 517 814; Top Priority, Racketeer). STRIKE FORCE 18 PAPERS. Libau today is known as Liepaja. It also appears in some records as Libava.

27. Eugene Smith, p. 138. The S.S. *Kursk,* 7,890 tons, was commissioned in 1910 from the Glasgow shipyard of Barclay, Curle.

28. Eisenberg et al., p. 31.

29. Meyer Lansky's Certificate of Arrival, Ellis Island, June 26, 1926, numbered 74174 and 209559, in his naturalization papers (INS), shows Lansky as having arrived in the United States on April 4, 1911. This must be a clerical error, however, since the original register from which the 1926 certificate can only have been transcribed was the List or Manifest of Alien Passengers for the United States Immigration Officer at Port of Arrival. This handwritten ledger containing twenty-nine items of information about each new arrival can be consulted in the National Archives in Washington, D.C. This clearly shows the Suchowljanskys as sailing on the S.S. *Kursk* from Libau on March 21, 1911, and arriving at New York on April 8, 1911.

30. Howe, *World,* pp. 47, 48.

31. Status Report, July 26, 1961, Meyer Lansky, MM 92-102, b7c, p. 3. FBI.

32. Eisenberg et al., p. 32.

33. Meyer Lansky's Brooklyn school record cards from 1911 to 1914 gave his birthday as August 28, 1902. The dockets of his early arrests, which started in 1918, recorded only his age (FBI). July 4, 1902, was first recorded as his birthday in his Declaration of Intention of August 1921, the initial step in his naturalization process. This was a document whose details were, essentially, supplied by Lansky himself (FBI). Other Russian Jewish immigrants who adopted July 4 as their birthday included the Hollywood mogul Louis B. Mayer.

34. Information gathered by Paul Sann, known henceforward as Sann Interviews (see pp. 450–451).

35. Cited in Howe, *World,* p. 138.

36. Mrs. Benjamin Borkaw, interview, November 10, 1988.

37. Rosten, pp. 327, 328.

38. Dr. Alexander Dushkin's study is quoted in Landesman, p. 96.

39. Mrs. Benjamin Borkaw, interview, November 10, 1988.

40. Sann Interviews.

41. The record cards of Meyer Lansky and Jacob Lansky are in the archives of PS 165 in Brooklyn. Transcripts of these record cards can be found in the files of the FBI and the INS. But these transcripts contain certain inaccuracies.

42. Landesman, p. 161.

43. Sann Interviews.

44. Ibid.

45. Golden, p. 21.

46. Lavine, "Intellect."

47. This change of address is shown on Meyer Lansky's school record card at PS 165 and was probably the reason for the move from PS 84, which was close to Chester Street, to PS 165, a few blocks down from 894 Rockaway Avenue.

48. Mrs. Benjamin Borkaw, interview, November 10, 1988.

49. Sann Interviews.

50. Mrs. Benjamin Borkaw, interview, November 10, 1988.

51. Buddy Lansky, interview, June 20, 1989. Both girls were buried in Mount Carmel Cemetery, Queens, New York, beside their father, Max (buried April 11, 1939). Lena Lansky was buried, aged nine months, on March 28, 1915, Rose Lansky on April 29, 1928, aged sixteen. Meyer Lansky, Anti-Racketeering, September 25, 1958, p. 6. FBI.

52. Sann Interviews.

53. Ibid.

54. Eisenberg et al., p. 34.

2. *Growing Up on Grand Street*

I am grateful to Ralph Salerno, who first drove me, on a wet spring night, around the tenements of the Lower East Side, and to the other guides who later shared with me their special knowledge of the area — Hope Cook, Justin Ferate, and Marvin Gelfand, in particular.

It was Arthur Goren, in Jerusalem, who guided me toward the Kehillah's reports on Lower East Side crime in the Judah Magnes archives at the Hebrew University, and also toward the work of Jenna Weissman Joselit, whose book *Our Gang* is the outstanding study of Jewish crime in this area and in this period.

Jacqueline Williams navigated me on many a weary expedition in pursuit of the addresses revealed by the Kehillah reports and court records. From the New York City Municipal Archives, she uncovered the contemporary street maps which made it possible to reconstruct the patterns of residence in areas that are now redeveloped. I owe special thanks to Kenneth R. Cobb, director of the New York City Municipal Archives, for his help in unearthing the ledger books of the magistrates' courts in which the details of Lansky's first offenses are recorded.

Ruth J. Abram, president of the Lower East Side Tenement Museum, tracked down information about 546 Grand Street, and showed me the vivid reenactment of immigrant life, Jewish and otherwise, which the Tenement Museum is recreating at 97 Orchard Street. Daniel Bell and his wife, Pearl, very kindly guided me toward accurate and vivid sources describing Lower East Side life.

I have Saul Radler, Meyer Lansky's accountant for a period in the 1950s, to thank for such insight as I now possess into the mysteries and logic of craps. David Shapiro, Lansky's rabbi in Florida, helped with many things, not least with his own memories of the *cholent*.

1. Sann Interviews.

2. Archives of the Lower East Side Tenement Museum.

3. Sann Interviews.

4. Marvin Gelfand, interview, September 26, 1989.

5. Seward Park Library, New York, photo archive.

6. Sann Interviews.

7. The Educational Alliance was founded in 1889. Its building on East Broadway was opened in 1891.

8. Marvin Gelfand, interview, September 26, 1989.

9. Belle Lindner Israels, "The Way of the Girl," *Survey,* vol. 22 (July 3, 1909), p. 494, cited in Fried, p. 16.

10. Gold, p. 15.

11. Cited in Howe, *World of Our Fathers,* p. 99.

12. Newberger to Judah Magnes, April 7, 1916, p. 6, cited in Joselit, *Our Gang,* p. 46.

13. Joselit, *Our Gang,* p. 14.

14. Ibid., p. 37.

15. *New York Evening Post,* September 18, 1908, p. 4.

16. Cited in Tyler, p. 44.

17. Judah Magnes was born in California in 1877 and ordained as a Reform rabbi in 1900. Criticized for his pacifism in World War I, he emigrated to Palestine in 1922, where he worked for the creation of a binational Arab-Jewish state. He helped found the Hebrew University, whose chancellor and first president he became. His papers — including the Kehillah's reports on Jewish crime and vice in the Lower East Side — are today in the archives of the Hebrew University in Jerusalem.

18. List of joints called to the attention of the police commissioner between June 1, 1914, and December 1, 1914. Magnes Papers, P3/1768.

19. Ibid.

20. Schoenfeld to Magnes, January 5, 1915. Magnes Papers. The Magnes archives contain a four-sheet list of criminal slang, dated November 19, with no year given.

21. Rabbi David Shapiro, interview, December 5, 1988.

22. Marvin Gelfand, interview, September 5, 1989.

23. Eisenberg et al., p. 35.

24. Ibid., p. 37.

25. Ibid.

26. Meyer Lansky's school record card at PS 34 is today at PS 134, Manhattan.

27. Sann Interviews.

28. The plaque on Benjamin Siegel's crypt in Beth Olam Cemetery, Los Angeles, gives his dates of birth and death as February 28, 1906, and June 20, 1947, according to Jennings, p. 22.

29. Eisenberg et al., p. 55.

30. Ibid.

31. Buddy Lansky, interview, June 12, 1989.

32. Memorandum to File, 1957. Re: *U.S. v. Meyer Lansky* (INS Denaturalization). Benjamin B. Edelstein. Interview with John Barrett, January 1957. STRIKE FORCE 18 PAPERS.

33. "He [Irving Sandler] stated he had known the subject [Meyer Lansky] since the day the subject arrived in the United States; that he and subject are first cousins, his mother and subject's father being brother and sister." Digest of INS and Other Inquiries into Meyer Lansky (pages 3–24 of untitled document datelined Miami, Florida, June 22, 1959; C-2 517 814; Top Priority, Racketeer), p. 11. STRIKE FORCE 18 PAPERS.

34. When Doc Stacher met up with Lansky in Israel in the years 1970–72, both men talked of knowing each other in the old days on the Lower East Side. Meyer told his friend Yoskeh Sheiner that he had known Stacher "from 1910 in New York . . . from '15, '18, I don't know." Joseph Sheiner, interview, January 26, 1988.

35. Sann Interviews.

36. Eisenberg et al., p. 52.

37. Ibid.

38. Ibid., p. 53.

39. Dan, "Meyer Lansky Breaks His Silence," July 2, 1971.

40. Eisenberg et al., p. 46.

41. Rockaway, "Scoundrel Time," p. 13.

42. Yoram Alroy, interview, December 16, 1987.

43. Digest of INS and Other Inquiries, p. 14.

44. Grand Street Boys Association, Program, Third Annual Dinner, January 15, 1921, Hotel Commodore, New York.

45. Eisenberg et al., p. 59.

46. Digest of INS and Other Inquiries, p. 14. Extract from Selective Service Questionnaire dated July 6, 1942: "Occupation: Machinist. Kind of work done: Worked on lathe, shaper and bench. Years worked: 1917 to 1921." INS.

47. Sann Interviews.

48. Ibid.

49. Joseph Sheiner, interview, January 26, 1988.

50. Marvin Gelfand, interview, May 11, 1990.

51. Ibid.

52. Eisenberg et al., p. 59.

53. Digest of INS and Other Inquiries, p. 18. Barrett said that the tool-and-die shop was owned by Lansky's uncle.

54. Deposition of Daniel Francis Ahearn, March 15, 1957, New York. STRIKE FORCE 18 PAPERS.

55. Ibid.

56. Ibid.

57. Ahearn's recollection, in the 1950s, was that he and Lansky were paid $500. This seems unlikely. Five hundred dollars in the years around 1918 is the equivalent of $10,000 in 1990's money.

58. Digest of INS and Other Inquiries, p. 16.

59. Ibid.

60. Notes from the testimony of Daniel Francis Ahearn, deposition made March 4, 1957. Investigative File, Meyer Lansky. INS.

61. Moses Polakoff, telephone conversation, March 9, 1989.

62. Ledger of the Magistrates' Court, First District Manhattan, September 9, 1918 to April 7, 1919 (vol. 40). NYC Municipal Archives.

63. Ibid.

64. Digest of INS and Other Inquiries, p. 14.

65. Buddy Lansky, interview, May 1, 1989. Speaking of his father's first — and only — job, Buddy said, "He never let me forget it. . . . Any of us. . . . He'd keep bringing it up."

66. Ibid.

3. *"A Gray Rat, Waiting for His Cheese"*

I am grateful to Judge Joseph Stone for his invaluable guidance through the original magistrates' courts dockets and the court archives, which are the only surviving original evidence of Meyer Lansky's criminal activities in these years, and to Kenneth R. Cobb, of the New York City Municipal Archives, who made the material so rapidly available — and is a skilled pathfinder himself. Judge Stone also unearthed material on the Grand Street Boys Association, which completed at least one important connection.

1. Eisenberg et al., p. 38.

2. Magnes Papers, P27/123, Hebrew University, Jerusalem.

3. Reports of Abraham Shoenfeld on 267 Grand Street, December 16, 1913, and May 16, July 3, July 6, July 22, and August 27, 1914. Magnes Papers, P3/1788.

4. Ibid.

5. When Meyer Lansky was invited by Lou Smith to organize the gambling section of his racetrack concession in Cuba at the Oriental Park track in Havana in 1937, he took "another Jew who was twenty years older than himself and a brand name in gambling — Al Levy." It was with Al Levy's help, said Lansky, that he organized the Gran Casino Nacional and the casino at the track. Dan, "Meyer Lansky Breaks His Silence," July 4, 1971.

6. *Oxford English Dictionary*; "Varieties," *Columbus Evening Dis-*

patch, April 10, 1896. See also "Riots at Chicago Polls," *New York Times,* April 8, 1896.

7. For a good account of Tammany's early years, see Werner, chapter 1.

8. Peterson, *The Mob,* p. 89.

9. *New York Times,* March 9, 1900.

10. Supreme Court, Appellate Division, First Judicial Department, *In the Matter of the Investigation of the Magistrates' Courts . . . , Final Report of Samuel Seabury, Referee,* New York, March 28, 1932. NYC Municipal Archives.

11. Runyon, *On Broadway,* pp. 328, 329.

12. Fitzgerald, p. 46.

13. Cited in Joselit, *Our Gang,* p. 142.

14. For the most factual available summary of the "Black Sox" scandal, see Katcher, pp. 138–148. The genesis of the affair was the ill feeling between the members of the team and their parsimonious owner, Charles Comisky. Eddie Cicotte, the team's best pitcher, organized a group of players willing to throw the Series for $10,000 a head, and he contacted a couple of professional gamblers, asking for $100,000, payable in advance. These men, in turn, put the scheme to Rothstein, who turned it down, not for moral reasons, but because he did not see how the fraud could possibly succeed without becoming public. Events were to prove him correct. A grand jury whose impartiality has never been questioned heard detailed testimony with regard to Rothstein's involvement in the scam, and brought no charges against him. Once Rothstein had heard of the plan to throw the Series, he had no need to get involved, in any case. He could bet against the White Sox like anyone else, and pocket his winnings — which he did.

15. Eisenberg et al., p. 79.

16. Ibid., p. 81.

17. Katcher, p. 246.

18. Mitgang, p. 166.

19. Statement of Estelle (Esta) Siegel, February 12, 1959. Digest of INS and Other Inquiries into Meyer Lansky (pages 3–24 of untitled document datelined Miami, Florida, June 22, 1959; C-2 517 814; Top Priority; Racketeer). STRIKE FORCE 18 PAPERS.

20. "Re Moe Sedway." Kings County DA's Papers, Box 7. NYC Municipal Archives.

21. "Supreme City: New York in the 1920's," *American Heritage,* November 1988, p. 62.

22. Eisenberg et al., p. 87.

23. "Re Moe Sedway."

24. *U.S. v. Meyer Lansky.* Interview with John Barrett, January 1957, p. 2. STRIKE FORCE 18 PAPERS.

25. Luciano's headquarters were in offices of a trucking company owned by Al Marinelli, whose political career in Tammany Luciano later assisted.

The office was at the corner of Mulberry and Kenmare Streets, near the liquor curb exchange. Ralph Salerno, letter to author, April 18, 1991.

26. Ibid. See also Thompson, p. 368.

27. *U.S. v. Meyer Lansky*. Interview with John Barrett, January 1957, pp. 2, 3. Like Cannon Street, Goerck Street vanished in New York's urban redevelopment after World War II.

28. Author interview with associate of Jake and Meyer Lansky.

29. Buddy Lansky, interviews, March 27, April 10, and July 25, 1989. Ratner's was a dairy restaurant, serving no meat, in accordance with kosher practice. So Lansky must have eaten his beef and tongue elsewhere.

30. Statement of Jake Harmatz, June 30, 1954. Digest of INS and Other Inquiries, pp. 14, 15.

31. Lieutenant David Green, interview, April 26, 1989.

32. Sann Interviews.

33. Ibid.

34. Eisenberg et al., p. 107.

35. Ibid., p. 108.

36. Ibid.

37. The best material on Ohio's "silent syndicate" was gathered by Hank Messick in his book of that title.

38. Birmingham, *The Rest of Us,* p. 153. Stephen Birmingham was told of the relationship between Samuel Bronfman and Meyer Lansky in an interview with Lansky's second wife, Teddy. According to Teddy Lansky, Bronfman treated Lansky to lavish dinners, while Lansky got Bronfman tickets to the Jack Dempsey–Luis Angel Firpo fight in 1923. Stephen Birmingham, interview, June 6, 1988.

39. Eisenberg et al., p. 122.

40. Ibid., p. 56.

41. Deposition of Daniel Francis Ahearn, March 15, 1957. Digest of INS and Other Inquiries.

42. Ibid.

43. Long Island City Magistrates' Court Ledger, volume commencing November 7, 1927, Ledger nos. 1708, 1709, 1710, March 6, 1928. NYC Municipal Archives.

44. Re: *U.S. v. Meyer Lansky*. Memorandum for File, File no. 2271–74174, January 29, 1953. STRIKE FORCE 18 PAPERS.

45. Ibid. "He said that he refused to identify Lansky or Siegel to the police because he feared for the safety of his two brothers."

46. Dan, "Meyer Lansky Breaks His Silence," July 2, 1971.

47. Ibid. Also Moses Polakoff, interview, August 11, 1988.

48. There are at least two versions of Meyer Lansky's criminal record; they do not tally exactly, but do not contradict each other, either. The Immigration and Naturalization Service prepared one such list in 1951. The FBI prepared another list in the 1960s, which was among the documents gath-

ered by Strike Force 18, and sent to Israel in 1971. With the exception of the 1925 traffic violation and the 1931 Volstead Act offense, the charges and details of each list can be confirmed by reference to the original dockets of the magistrates' courts, as given in the source notes to this and the preceding chapter.

49. Kenneth C. Shelver to Olaf W. Osnes, January 12, 1959. Meyer Lansky, C-2 517 814: Possible Institution of Denaturalization Proceedings, p. 3. INS.

50. Ibid. See also *New York World Telegram,* October 1, 1927, p. 1, and Magistrates' Court, Homicide, Manhattan, March 9, 1928, Docket 101.

51. FBI, NY 92-660. December 26, 1957. Meyer Lansky, Anti-Racketeering, p. 7. FBI. "The records of the Bureau of Criminal Identification, and the Bureau of Special Services of the New York City Police Department were reviewed, and it was learned that all records prior to June of 1936 had been destroyed by that Department for records other than fingerprint cards and the bare records of the arrest."

52. Katcher, pp. 2, 3.

53. *New York World Telegram,* November 5 and 6, 1928.

54. Ibid., November 5, 1928.

55. Katcher, chapter 24.

56. Charles Luciano, Box 13, Folder 2. Lucania, Cross-examination by Mr. Dewey, 6006-6016. NYC Municipal Archives.

57. Anslinger and Oursler, p. 102.

58. Bonanno, pp. 17, 22.

59. Ibid., p. 76. See the *New York Herald Tribune,* September 12, 1931, for references to Maranzano's illegal immigrant smuggling.

60. Bonanno, p. 150.

61. Eisenberg et al., p. 119.

62. Bonanno, p. 117.

63. Ibid., p. 122.

64. Ibid., p. 121.

65. The conventionally related version of this killing is that Lucky Luciano went to the restaurant with Joe the Boss and that, after the shooting, he waited until the police arrived, cheekily informing them that he had been in the men's room at the time of the murder. See Maas, p. 103, for an example of the tale. This does not sound likely. It seems probable that Luciano did arrange the lunch (in the Nuova Villa Tammaro Restaurant, also known as Scarpato's). He could also have accompanied Masseria to the restaurant. But there is no mention in the police record, nor in contemporary newspaper reports, of Luciano, or of any other material witness, being found at the scene of the crime.

Luciano was relatively notorious by 1931, a known gang figure, mentioned in newspaper reports as a protagonist in what were described as the "gang liquor wars." It seems unlikely that his presence at the scene of the murder would have gone unremarked by the police or by the several report-ers present. Flamboyant in many respects, Luciano was prudent when it came to his lawbreaking. It made no sense for him to wait in the restaurant to test out such a thin alibi when everyone else had escaped.

66. Maas, p. 104.

67. *New York Herald Tribune,* September 12, 1931.

68. Bonanno, p. 125.

69. Ibid., p. 126.

70. Bonanno, p. 139. "Luciano told me he was forced to strike against Maranzano after learning that Maranzano had hired Vincent Coll to kill Luciano. Vincent 'Mad Dog' Coll was an American hoodlum, a hired gun."

71. Davis, "Things," August 5, 1939, p. 44.

72. Maas, p. 113.

73. It has been suggested that Luciano and Lansky were in Chicago in preparation for the Democratic Convention which nominated Roosevelt in June 1932. Thomas Dewey later alleged that Luciano attended the conven-tion in the company of the Tammany figure Albert Marinelli, staying in the Drake Hotel. This cannot be confirmed from Drake Hotel records. All we know for sure from surviving documentation is that Lansky and Luciano were detained in Chicago on April 19, 1932, by a Lieutenant Kelly.

74. Bonanno, p. 127.

75. Moses Polakoff, interview, August 11, 1988.

76. Eisenberg et al., p. 143.

77. See Chandler, p. 160, for one version of this oft-recounted myth.

78. Davis, "Things," August 5, 1939, p. 44.

79. Maas, p. 111.

80. FBI Criminal Investigative Division, "Chronological History of La Cosa Nostra," p. 301.

81. Block, *East Side, West Side,* pp. 3–9.

82. FBI Criminal Investigative Division, "Chronological History of La Cosa Nostra," p. 300.

83. For details of still more Jewish hoodlums in the 1930s, see Fried, chapter 3.

84. See Roemer, *Man Against the Mob,* for more details of Capone's suc-cessors in Chicago.

85. Bonanno, p. 140.

86. For details of these changes, see FBI Criminal Investigative Division, "Chronological History of La Cosa Nostra," pp. 296–305.

87. Davis, "Things," August 5, 1939, p. 44.

4. *"There Was Never Anything We Wanted"*

1. Anne Lansky, interview. Digest of INS and Other Inquiries into Meyer Lansky (pages 3–24 of untitled document datelined Miami, Florida,

June 22, 1959; C-2 517 814; Top Priority, Racketeer). STRIKE FORCE 18 PAPERS.

2. Ibid.

3. Digest of INS and Other Inquiries. Also, Buddy Lansky, interview, June 20, 1989.

4. Memorandum, July 25, 1958. "Facts and Discussion," p. 2. INS.

5. Harold P. Shapiro to Kenneth C. Shelver, Re Possible Denaturalization Proceedings Against Meyer Lansky, April 28, 1951, p. 3. INS.

6. *U.S. v. Lansky,* Civ. 81-205, U.S. District Court, Southern District of New York, February 19, 1953.

7. Dan, "Meyer Lansky Breaks His Silence," July 5, 1971.

8. Ibid.

9. Buddy Lansky, interview, March 23, 1989.

10. Moses Polakoff, interview, August 11, 1988.

11. Buddy Lansky, interview, March 23, 1989.

12. Ibid., April 17, 1989.

13. Ibid., March 23, March 29, and June 12, 1989.

14. Ibid., June 12, 1989.

15. Ibid., March 23, 1989.

16. Ibid.

17. Ibid.

18. Ibid.

19. Ibid., June 12 and June 20, 1989.

20. Ibid.

21. Ibid., July 3, 1989.

22. Ibid., June 5 and June 12, 1989.

23. Ibid., March 23, 1989.

24. Ibid.

25. Malana Mason, interview, July 24, 1990.

26. Buddy Lansky, interview, April 3, 1989.

27. Ibid., October 4, 1989.

28. Both these teams have since migrated, the Braves via Milwaukee to Atlanta, the Giants to San Francisco.

29. Buddy Lansky, interview, March 23, 1989.

30. Ibid., June 5, 1989.

31. Divorce Papers, *Anne Lansky v. Meyer Lansky,* Eleventh Judicial Court Circuit, Dade County, Florida, no. 106443-F, January 30, 1947.

32. Buddy Lansky, interview, March 23, 1989.

33. Ibid., March 29, 1989.

34. Isabelle Schlossman Lerner, letter to author, November 29, 1988.

35. Ibid.

36. Ibid.

37. Ibid., November 29, 1988, and March 21, 1989.

38. Ibid., November 29, 1988.
39. Ibid.
40. Author interview with one of the doctors who attended Mrs. Lansky at the request of Meyer and Jake Lansky.
41. Buddy Lansky, interview, November 27, 1989.
42. Ibid.
43. Ibid., March 23, 1989.
44. Ibid., August 28, 1989.
45. Ibid., June 5, 1989.
46. Katcher, p. 20.
47. Buddy Lansky, interview, March 23, 1989.

5. *"Gambling Pulls at the Core of a Man"*

The fascinating history of the Saratoga lake houses has, regrettably, never been the subject of a thorough investigation, book, or even a respectable monograph. I am most grateful to Judge Michael Sweeney and Mrs. Sweeney for their help. Judge Sweeney was a law partner of Jim Leary, the Republican boss of Saratoga County. Beatrice Sweeney was the city historian of Saratoga Springs for many years. Dr. Martha Stonequist, the present city historian, presides with great cheer over the archives, which contain some very useful, but not always dated, contemporary newspaper clippings.

I have also relied on the help of a number of people — croupiers, managers, and operators — who were actually involved in the operation of the lake houses, but who still, today, prefer not to be named.

Jim Kilby, Boyd Professor of Gambling at the University of Nevada, Las Vegas, guided me through the statistics and other practicalities of casino operation and casino games.

The paragraphs on the FBI and the automobile bandits are based on the thoughtful and illuminating works of Richard Gid Powers. The paragraphs on racketeers owe much to a contemporary scholarly thesis unearthed by Jacqueline Williams, "Hands in Your Pockets," by Edward R. Finch, Jr., as well as to the entry on racketeering by Murray Gurfein in the *Encyclopaedia of the Social Sciences* (reprinted in Tyler, pp. 181–189).

The notes taken in court and prior to Thomas Dewey's prosecution of Lucky Luciano are in the New York City Municipal Archives.

1. Messick, *Silent Syndicate,* p. 93.
2. Ibid., p. 119.
3. Eisenberg et al., p. 81.
4. See Haller, "Bootleggers as Businessmen," for a good account of Bronfman, Rosensteil, and other bootleggers who went straight.

5. IRS Criminal Reference Report, p. 3. STRIKE FORCE 18 PAPERS.

6. The bankruptcy petition was filed on March 2, 1935. Messick, *Silent Syndicate*, p. 126.

7. Aaron Sapiro became nationally famous in 1924, when Henry Ford, the carmaker, published a series of articles attacking the produce cooperatives which Sapiro had organized among farmers in thirty-two states. Ford denounced the "Sapiro Plan" as "Jewish exploitation of farmers," suggesting that Sapiro — who did well, personally, out of the cooperatives — was a cheat and a racketeer. Sapiro sued Ford in 1927, compelling the carmaker to retract his accusation, and also to publish a lengthy apology for all he had said about the Jews in general.

The papers of the Molaska Corporation, however, showed that Aaron Sapiro was, initially, the attorney of record, organizing the mechanisms whereby Meyer Lansky, Moe Dalitz, Sam Tucker, and their fellow bootleggers concealed their investment behind legitimate fronts. In 1934, Sapiro was indicted in Chicago with a number of defendants, who included Al Capone, for having conspired to damage plants of cleaners and dyers. Sapiro and Capone were acquitted after a key prosecution witness committed suicide. So perhaps Henry Ford was not entirely wrong about Aaron Sapiro.

8. Testimony of Anne Lansky, p. 8. Divorce papers, *Anne Lansky v. Meyer Lansky*, Eleventh Judicial Court Circuit, Dade County, Florida, no. 106443-F, January 30, 1947.

9. Buddy Lansky, interview, August 28, 1989.

10. Gaby, "What Would It Cost Today?" p. 24.

11. Dan, "Meyer Lansky Breaks His Silence," July 4, 1971.

12. Buddy Lansky, interviews, April 3 and April 24, 1989.

13. Ibid.

14. Judge Michael and Beatrice Sweeney, interview, August 9, 1988.

15. Ibid., May 25, 1991.

16. Judge Michael Sweeney, interview, July 10, 1990.

17. Dan, "Meyer Lansky Breaks His Silence," July 2, 1971.

18. Buddy Lansky, interview, April 3, 1989.

19. For a good analysis of casino odds, see *Scarne's Complete Guide to Gambling*, chapter 3.

20. Jim Kilby, interview, July 19, 1990. See *Scarne's Complete Guide to Gambling*, chapters 12 and 13, for strategies to beat the casino odds at blackjack without "counting."

21. Dan, "Meyer Lansky Breaks His Silence," July 2, 1971.

22. Ibid.

23. Ibid.

24. *New York Times,* September 13, 1944.

25. "Saratoga Venture," p. 2. Inventory of Records Obtained from Eisen

and Eisen, Accountants. New York DA's Files, Box 410. NYC Municipal Archives.

26. Author interview with a dealer in the illegal casinos of the 1930s and 1940s.

27. O'Connor to Hogan, March 31, 1948, 95–97. New York DA's Files, Box 410.

28. "August at Saratoga," p. 64.

29. *Daily Express*, September 14, 1928.

30. The *Oxford English Dictionary* cites an 1812 reference for "racket" meaning fraud or robbery.

31. Joselit, *Our Gang*, p. 107.

32. Luciano's earliest arrests were for narcotics dealing. Harry Anslinger, director of the Bureau of Narcotics, insisted that Luciano was a drug dealer all his life. Anslinger's evidence for this was not solid, but heroin was certainly part of the prostitution scene in which Luciano was involved in the 1930s. It seems unlikely that Luciano would have passed up the chance to profit from the narcotics traffic through the New York waterfront in these years.

33. Sann Interviews. This claim received some official confirmation in a Bureau of Narcotics Report on Lansky to the FBI, July 29, 1958: "No information was ever developed by that Bureau to the effect that the subject was a narcotics user or addict." SAC Miami, to Director, August 8, 1958. FBI.

34. Landesman, p. 331.

35. Sann Interviews.

36. Ralph Salerno, letter to author, April 17, 1991.

37. Sann Interviews.

38. Ibid.

39. Lippmann, "The Underworld," p. 67.

40. For the story of Valentine's life, see *Honest Cop*, by Lowell M. Limpus.

41. *New York Times*, October 14, 1934.

42. Dewey, p. 68.

43. See Richard Norton Smith, pp. 159–160, for a longer description of Dewey's radio address of July 30, 1935.

44. Ibid.

45. Ibid., pp. 154, 155, 160.

46. For the full transcript of Schultz's final words, see Sann, pp. 55–64.

47. Charles "The Bug" Workman was convicted and served a long jail term. Emmanuel "Mendy" Weiss was never tried because he went to the electric chair for another killing. Both men were close associates of Lepke Buchalter, and the shooting of Dutch Schultz is usually classed as a Murder, Inc., hit. The particular reason for the killing, however, remains a mystery. See Sann for the best account.

48. *New York Times,* October 26, 1935, p. 1.
49. Richard Norton Smith, p. 197.
50. Ibid., p. 198.
51. Ibid., p. 200.
52. Eisenberg et al., p. 164.

6. *The Carpet Joints*

Little has been written about the carpet joints. The best account is in *Scarne's Complete Guide to Gambling,* and that is brief. Off-the-record interviews with former dealers and professional gamblers provide the source for much of this chapter. Benny Binion, the Texas gambler who moved on to Las Vegas, kindly granted the author a lengthy and revealing interview in November 1989, shortly before his death. Philip Weidling, the Fort Lauderdale journalist and local historian, worked for Claude Litteral in the Plantation as a young man, and was generous with his memories.

I am grateful to Bob Flood and to Wally Provost in Omaha, Nebraska, for their detective work investigating Meyer Lansky's interlude in Council Bluffs, Iowa. In Havana, Miss Margaret Reid, MBE, first told me of Lou Smith and of his work cleaning up the Oriental Park racetrack. Miss Reid, later a British vice-consul in Cuba, worked in the pressroom at the track in the late 1930s.

June Depp, city clerk of Hallandale, kindly granted me access to the court ledger for 1927–41. Most of all, I must express my debt to Joseph Varon, lawyer to both Meyer and Jake Lansky, as well as to Vincent Alo. Mr. Varon is preparing his own book on the Florida gambling years through which he lived.

1. Harold Conrad, interview, September 12, 1988.
2. For a firsthand description of the Barn, see Scarne, *Complete Guide,* pp. 207–208. In the opinion of Scarne, a professional gambling consultant to Hilton Hotels for a period, the Barn was the "biggest moneymaker in [the] history of all illegal gambling casinos." He reckoned the annual profit the Barn made from its high-stakes, cash crap games at $10 million.
3. Inventory of Records Obtained from Eisen and Eisen, Accountants. New York DA's Files, Box 410. NYC Municipal Archives.
4. W. C. Moffitt, Jr., interview, March 22, 1988.
5. Gordon and Gordon, pp. 109, 194.
6. Excerpts from the New York State Joint Legislative Committee on Crime, 1970, filed August 24, 1971. JUSTICE.
7. Joseph Varon, interview, June 9, 1989.

8. Author interview with an associate of Vincent Alo. In accounts of this episode to friends, Jimmy Blue Eyes has described himself as knowing Kaufman for a number of years before they went into partnership in Hallandale. He gave Kaufman shelter in New York, he said, after Potatoes got into some trouble in Chicago.

9. Joseph Varon, interview, June 9, 1989.

10. See Inventory . . . from Eisen and Eisen, pp. 33, 34, 35, 36, for local charities and organizations receiving contributions from Jake Lansky.

11. Author interview with a dealer who worked for Ben Marden in New Jersey and Florida.

12. Inventory . . . from Eisen and Eisen, p. 3.

13. "Re Moe Sedway." Kings County DA's Papers, Box 7. NYC Municipal Archives.

14. Benny Binion, interview, November 18, 1989; also, Cliff Jones, interview, November 21, 1989

15. Hallandale Municipal Court Docket, Case 499, p. 250.

16. Hallandale Court Ledger, 1927–41.

17. Ibid., Case 744, p. 373; Case 751, p. 377; Case 773, p. 388; and Case 781, p. 392.

18. Joseph Varon, interview, December 2, 1988. Hallandale court archives from this period have been destroyed.

19. Ibid.

20. Federal Bureau of Investigation, Omaha, April 10, 1958. Meyer Lansky, Anti-Racketeering, OM 92-112, p. 11. FBI.

21. Wally Provost column, *Omaha World Herald,* June 6, 1974.

22. Wally Provost, letter to author, June 28, 1988.

23. On his 1949 application for a U.S. passport, Meyer Lansky stated that he had lived in Cuba from December 1938 until March 1939 and from December 1939 to March 1940. U.S. Passport Office, file on Meyer Lansky, WFO 92-138. PASSPORT OFFICE.

24. FBI Criminal Investigative Division, "Chronological History of La Cosa Nostra," p. 303.

25. Dan, "Meyer Lansky Breaks His Silence," July 4, 1971.

26. Margaret Reid, interview, May 18, 1988.

27. Dan, "Meyer Lansky Breaks His Silence," July 4, 1971.

28. Ibid.

29. Ibid.

30. Buddy Lansky, interview, June 26, 1989. Also October 4, 1989.

31. Ibid., April 24, 1989.

32. Ibid.

33. Ibid., May 15, 1989.

34. Ibid.

35. Ibid.

7. "I'll Help You. It's Patriotism"

The voluminous and definitive source on the collaboration between U.S. Naval Intelligence and Lucky Luciano, Meyer Lansky, and the New York underworld is the report of William B. Herlands, of September 17, 1954. This was never printed, and remained secret until 1977, for the reasons explained in the chapter. The report, together with the testimony and evidence upon which it is based, is located today in the Thomas E. Dewey Papers, at the University of Rochester, New York.

I am grateful to Moses Polakoff for sharing and confirming his memories of his own considerable role in the adventure.

The findings of William Herlands were most ably summarized and extended, with additional research, by Rodney Campbell, in his book *The Luciano Project*. Alan Block's article "A Modern Marriage of Convenience: A Collaboration Between Organized Crime and U.S. Intelligence" provides a radical critique of the Herlands material, pointing out the anti-Communist assumptions of Haffenden in his dealings with the waterfront.

1. Jennings, p. 69, is the source of this oft-repeated story. It seems clear from Jennings's biography of Siegel, *We Only Kill Each Other,* that George Raft, who was certainly a friend of Siegel's, gave Jennings considerable help with the book.

2. Dan, "Meyer Lansky Breaks His Silence," July 2, 1971.

3. Judge Joseph Stone, interview, July 7, 1990. For details of Perlman's career, see *New York Times,* June 30, 1952.

4. Dan, "Meyer Lansky Breaks His Silence," July 2, 1971.

5. Sann Interviews.

6. Eisenberg et al., p. 185.

7. Dan, "Meyer Lansky Breaks His Silence," July 2, 1971 — the first published version of the episode.

8. Ibid.

9. Campbell, p. 25.

10. Maxtone-Grahame, p. 361.

11. See Maxtone-Grahame, pp. 361–392, for an excellent and detached account of the fire, which deals with all the conspiracy theories. I am grateful to John Maxtone-Grahame for his additional help, and his information about his correspondence with J. Edgar Hoover on the subject of sabotage.

12. Campbell, p. 13.

13. Herlands Report, p. 88. Dewey Papers, Series 13, Box 13.

14. Block, *East Side, West Side,* p. 43.

15. *New York Daily News,* January 9, 1941.

16. Campbell, p. 67.

17. Herlands Report, p. 39.

18. Witness: Moses Polakoff, June 21, 1954, p. 8. Dewey Papers, Series 13, Box 13.

19. Ibid.

20. Herlands Report, pp. 42, 45.

21. Witness: Moses Polakoff, p. 9.

22. Selective Service Questionnaire, order no. 10902, July 6, 1942, Local Board 27, Hotel Belleclaire, Room 103, 250 W. Seventy-seventh Street, New York. INS.

23. Buddy Lansky, interviews, May 15 and July 25, 1989.

24. Cliff Jones, interview, November 21, 1989.

25. For an interesting account of Dave Berman's life, see his daughter's lucid and moving memoir, *Easy Street*.

26. Moses Polakoff, interview, August 11, 1988.

27. Witness: Moses Polakoff, p. 9.

28. Witness: Meyer Lansky, p. 8. Dewey Papers, Series 13, Box 13.

29. Twelve years later, Meyer Lansky did not recall this first meeting with Haffenden as taking place immediately following his meeting with Gurfein and Polakoff. But the recollections of Polakoff and Gurfein contradict him.

30. Witness: Meyer Lansky, p. 16.

31. Ibid., Luciano's prison movements. Memo of conference, Morhous and Herlands, March 23, 1954.

32. Statement of Vernon A. Morhous, p. 2. Dewey Papers, Series 13, Box 13.

33. Witness: Meyer Lansky, p. 11.

34. Herlands Report, p. 93.

35. Witness: Meyer Lansky, p. 12.

36. Campbell, p. 81.

37. Witness: Meyer Lansky, p. 12. Polakoff's memory was that Luciano cried, "What the hell are you fellows doing here?"

38. Herlands Report, p. 91.

39. Witness: Meyer Lansky, pp. 13, 14.

40. Ibid.

41. Witness: Moses Polakoff, p. 14.

42. "One thing is very observable, and that is the predominance today of Italians and Italian-Americans." Swanstrom, p. 9.

43. Witness: Moses Polakoff, p. 45.

44. Campbell, p. 99.

45. Ibid., p. 101.

46. Herlands Report, p. 60. The notes of Warden Morhous specified the dates of eleven visits by Meyer Lansky, but other testimony to the Herlands inquiry suggested that Lansky visited on other occasions, when his name was not noted.

47. For details, see Campbell, pp. 111, 112, 113.

48. Herlands Report, p. 63.

49. Witness: Moses Polakoff, p. 29.

50. Herlands Report, p. 87.

51. Witness: Meyer Lansky, p. 19.

52. Herlands Report, p. 63.

53. Witness: Meyer Lansky, p. 21.

54. *New York Times,* January 3, 1942.

55. Witness: Meyer Lansky, p. 22.

56. Ibid.

57. Testimony of Meyer Lansky, March 1951. KEFAUVER, Part 7, p. 607.

58. Witness: Moses Polakoff, pp. 59, 60.

59. Herlands Report, pp. 71–77.

60. Ibid., p. 73.

61. Witness: Moses Polakoff, p. 26.

62. Ibid., p. 27.

63. Witness: Meyer Lansky, p. 30.

64. Dan, "Meyer Lansky Breaks His Silence," July 4, 1971.

65. Testimony of Jeffrey J. Robertson, cited in Campbell, p. 204.

66. Witness: Meyer Lansky, pp. 25, 26.

67. Campbell, pp. 177, 178.

68. Ibid., p. 176.

69. *New York World Telegram,* May 22, 1945.

70. Campbell, p. 246.

71. Testimony of Charles R. Haffenden, March 1951. KEFAUVER, Part 7, p. 1193.

72. Letter of Captain Wallace B. Phillips to Parole Board Supervisor Jeffrey Robinson, cited in Campbell, p. 225.

73. Testimony of Joseph Healy, cited in Campbell, p. 228.

74. Campbell, p. 230.

75. Witness: Moses Polakoff, p. 34.

76. Ibid.

77. Campbell, p. 247.

78. Ibid.

79. Ibid., p. 252.

80. Ibid., p. 255.

81. See Eisenberg et al., pp. 223–226, for an example of the legend.

82. Witness: Moses Polakoff, p. 59.

83. Ibid.

8. *"Maybe It Was My Fault"*

This chapter is based on family interviews and on the testimony in the case *Anne Lansky v. Meyer Lansky,* Eleventh Judicial Court Circuit, Dade

County, Florida, no. 106443-F of January 30 and February 3, 1947, referred to below as Divorce Papers.

1. Testimony of Anne Lansky, p. 13. Divorce Papers. Anne Lansky gave 1934 as the date of this incident, but she may have been confused about the time or the place. In her divorce evidence, she described the incident as happening in the Nacional Hotel in Cuba, where the Lanskys did not live, according to Buddy, until the late 1930s.

2. The evidence with regard to the woman who kept phoning, asking for Meyer, is contained in the Lansky Divorce Papers.

So far as Lansky's liaison in Council Bluffs is concerned, this was described by one of his gambling colleagues, "The Baron," talking to Wally Provost, the columnist with the *Omaha World Herald,* June 6, 1974: "He lived at the Paxton Hotel, and his favorite hangout was the coffee shop in the basement. The same waitress waited on him all three meals a day." Provost's informant went on to tell him that Lansky "saw to it" that the lady had "a fancy apartment, a diamond ring, sharp clothes, etc." Wally Provost, letter to author, June 28, 1988.

For details of Lansky's liaison in Israel, see chapter 18, p. 347.

The evidence with regard to a liaison in Miami Beach in his final years is the least reliable. Several informants told the author that they heard that Meyer Lansky had a mistress. But no name or evidence was produced, and this could easily have been just another of the rumors that came to be attached to Lansky by the end of his life.

3. Buddy Lansky, interview, June 5, 1989.
4. Ibid.
5. Testimony of Anne Lansky, p. 13.
6. Buddy Lansky, interview, June 5, 1989.
7. Ibid., March 23, 1989.
8. Ibid., October 4, 1989.
9. Ibid., March 23, 1989.
10. Ibid., March 27, 1989.
11. Ibid., May 8, 1989.
12. Meyer Lansky II, interview, September 10, 1990.
13. Buddy Lansky, interview, March 23, 1989.
14. Ibid., December 4, 1989.
15. Myra Lansky, interview, January 16, 1990.
16. Buddy Lansky, interview, March 23, 1989.
17. Ibid., April 17, 1989.
18. Testimony of Jake Lansky, pp. 4, 6. Divorce Papers.
19. Buddy Lansky, interview, March 23, 1989.
20. Malana Mason, interview, January 17, 1990.
21. Buddy Lansky, interview, March 23, 1989.
22. Ibid., April 17, 1989.

23. Ibid., March 29, 1989.
24. Ibid., April 17, 1989.
25. Ibid., May 8, 1989.
26. Testimony of Anne Lansky, pp. 6ff.
27. Ibid., p. 14.
28. Ibid.
29. Ibid.
30. Testimony of Jake Lansky, pp. 2, 3.
31. Ibid., pp. 4, 5.
32. Testimony of Anne Lansky, pp. 6–15.
33. Ibid., p. 15.
34. Buddy Lansky, interviews, April 24 and May 8, 1989.
35. IRS Criminal Reference Report, pp. 25, 26. STRIKE FORCE 18 PAPERS.
36. Buddy Lansky, interview, October 16, 1989.
37. Ibid., March 29, 1989.

9. *"Benny Siegel . . . He Knocked Out Plenty"*

The description of Hallandale in the late 1940s is based largely on interviews and correspondence with people who lived through and participated in Broward County's extraordinary half-dozen years of consumer high life after the Second World War: Joseph Baum, Jesse Martin, W. C. "Bill" Moffitt, Jr., Rabbi David Shapiro, Joseph Varon, Philip Weidling, and a number of off-the-record sources. I am grateful to Cooper Kirk, Stuart McIver, and Mike Phillips for sharing their own research and contacts.

The Kefauver Committee focused closely on this era, subpoenaing accounts and records, in addition to evidence produced at their hearings. The archives of the Fort Lauderdale Historical Society and the Broward County Historical Commission contain limited amounts of material on Broward's great age of gambling — still a touchy subject, about which some people today remain reluctant to speak with total candor.

Modern Las Vegas is scarcely less coy about its past, but Benny Binion, Arturo Gilbert, Dennis Gomes, Oscar Goodman, Cliff Jones, Mort Saiger, William S. Weinberger, and Lou Wiener did go out of their way to help me. The University of Nevada, with campuses at Reno and Las Vegas, is a rich source of oral histories and of newspaper archives which provide some correction to the gambling industry's PR men. I am grateful to Professors Jim Kilby and Bill Thompson, and to Susan Jarvis and David Robrock in the James R. Dickinson Library, Special Collections, Las Vegas. In California, George Kennedy recalled his experiences working with Billy Wilkerson, and also with Bugsy Siegel.

The Arizona Project was a remarkable exercise in collective journalism prompted by the murder of Don Bolles, a reporter for the *Arizona Republic,* in 1976. Investigative reporters from all over America converged on Arizona to continue Bolles's work, and to prove that killing could not halt the process of journalistic inquiry. The resulting report shed interesting light not only on Arizona, but also on the early history of Las Vegas. The report, titled *The Arizona Project,* is available from the University of Missouri, Columbia, School of Journalism, 100 Neff Hall, Columbia, Missouri, 65211.

This chapter owes a particular debt to Harold Conrad for his memories and insights in the course of a number of lengthy interviews. He has written about his experiences at the Colonial Inn in his memoirs, *Dear Muffo: 35 Years in the Fast Lane.* Readers anxious to read more about George Wood, Joe Adonis, and Lucky Luciano — as well as Al Capp, Muhammad Ali, the Brooklyn Dodgers, the Duke of Windsor, and just about anyone who was anybody between 1947 and 1982 — are warmly recommended to this sharp and unfailingly amusing book.

1. Joe Russell, interview, August 22, 1990.

2. Carlton Montayne, "County-Wide Blackout Closes Gambling Rooms in Broward," *Miami News,* February 13, 1948. The count was made, in fact, when all thirty-two happened to have suspended their gambling operations temporarily following the injunction which Dwight C. Rogers brought against the Colonial Inn in February 1948 (see p. 185).

3. Joe Russell, interview, August 22, 1990.

4. Inventory of Records Obtained from Eisen and Eisen, Accountants. New York DA's Files, Box 410. NYC Municipal Archives.

5. TenEick, p. 253.

6. Inventory . . . from Eisen and Eisen, p. 10.

7. Ibid.

8. For details of Lee Hills's long campaign against organized crime in Miami, for which the *Miami Herald* was awarded the Pulitzer Prize, see Smiley, chapter 22.

9. Joseph Varon, interview, June 9, 1989.

10. "Born in Broward — Bettered Broward — Best for Broward!" Walter Clark election flyer. Fort Lauderdale Historical Society.

11. Testimony of Walter Clark, May 1950. KEFAUVER, Part 1, p. 452.

12. Philip Weidling, letter to author, April 16, 1988.

13. "Born in Broward" election flyer.

14. Harold Conrad, interview, September 12, 1988.

15. Philip Weidling, letter to author, April 9, 1988.

16. Joseph Varon, interview, June 9, 1989.

17. Inventory . . . from Eisen and Eisen, pp. 33, 34.

18. Ibid., pp. 33, 34, 35, 36.

19. Canceled checks for the account of Greenacres Restaurant at the First National Bank of Hollywood, November 1946–March 1949. New York DA's Files, Box 410. NYC Municipal Archives.

20. Cuddy, p. 142.

21. Testimony of Walter Clark, May 1950. KEFAUVER, Part 1, p. 466.

22. Ben C. Eisen, for George Sadlo, to the IRS agent in charge, P.O. Box 4760, Jacksonville, Fla., Attention: D.A. Highgate, July 20, 1948. Inventory . . . from Eisen and Eisen.

23. Ibid.

24. Author interviews with a number of dealers who have described the process of skimming.

25. Harold Conrad, interview, April 2, 1990.

26. Author interviews with dealers who worked in the carpet joints where Sophie Tucker played.

27. *New York Times,* June 5, 1971.

28. Harold Conrad, interview, April 2, 1990.

29. Ibid., July 18, 1988.

30. Ibid.

31. Ibid., September 26, 1989.

32. Conrad, "Meyer Lansky," p. 60.

33. Conrad, *Dear Muffo,* p. 9.

34. Ibid., p. 10.

35. Ibid., p. 11.

36. Ibid., p. 8.

37. Harold Conrad, interview, July 18, 1988.

38. Ibid.

39. Sann Interviews.

40. Wally Provost column, *Omaha World Herald,* June 6, 1974.

41. Paher, p. 156.

42. William J. Moore, "Pioneer Developer on the Las Vegas Strip," August 29, 1981. Oral History Program, University of Nevada.

43. Kaufman, "The Best City of Them All," p. 171.

44. *Las Vegas Review-Journal,* October 28, 1942.

45. See Wright, *World War II and the Emergence of Modern Las Vegas,* for an excellent summary.

46. Kaufman, "The Best City of Them All," pp. 49, 55, 56, 59.

47. *Las Vegas Review-Journal,* March 4, 1943.

48. Ibid., July 31, 1946.

49. Ibid.

50. Dan, "Meyer Lansky Breaks His Silence," July 4, 1971.

51. IRS Criminal Reference Report, p. 5, states that El Cortez was purchased for $613,649.85 by Lansky, Siegel, and their partners in December

1945, and sold for $780,000.00 in July 1946, Meyer's stake in the venture being $70,432.32 STRIKE FORCE 18 PAPERS.

52. IRS Criminal Reference Report, p. 5.

53. Wilkerson, p. 5.

54. Stamos, *Las Vegas Sun*, April 1, 1979.

55. George Kennedy, interview, September 4, 1990.

56. This figure is an estimate. IRS Criminal Reference Report, p. 5, states that El Cortez was purchased for $613,649.85 by Lansky, Siegel, and their partners in December 1945, and sold for $780,000.00 in July, 1946. Nevada Project Corporation documents inspected by the researchers of the Arizona Project, but not by this author, who was unable to locate them in current Nevada records, showed that 1,000 shares were issued in the Nevada Project Corporation, and that Meyer Lansky was allocated 100 of these (*Arizona Project,* p. 15). The IRS Criminal Reference Report, p. 5, states Lansky's involvement in the Nevada Project Corporation as $62,500.00. If this represented 10 percent of the stock, it follows that the corporation's total worth was $625,000.00. According to Billy Wilkerson's attorney, Greg Bautzer, interviewed by researchers of the Arizona Project before his death, Siegel and his partners came to a two-thirds/one-third arrangement when they went into the Flamingo with Wilkerson (*Arizona Project,* p. 17).

57. Lester Ben "Benny" Binion, "Some Recollections of a Texas and Las Vegas Gaming Operator," p. 21. Oral History Program, University of Nevada.

58. Lou Wiener, interview, November 21, 1989.

59. Ibid.

60. Ibid.

61. IRS Criminal Reference Report, p. 5. According to this report, the sum that Lansky withdrew from El Cortez in August 1946 was, in fact, $62,330.92. He had previously withdrawn $8,253.90 in April 1946.

62. *Arizona Project,* p. 15.

63. IRS Criminal Reference Report, p. 5. See also *Arizona Project,* p. 15.

64. *Arizona Project,* p. 6.

65. Cliff Jones, interview, November 21, 1989.

66. *Arizona Project,* p. 15. Siegel signed the papers on this $300,000 loan on February 6, 1947.

67. *Arizona Project,* p. 15. In March 1947, Del Webb filed a $1,000,000 lien on the Flamingo.

68. Harold Conrad, interview, April 2, 1990.

69. Conrad, *Dear Muffo,* pp. 13, 14.

70. Harold Conrad, interview, April 2, 1990.

71. Ibid.

72. Ibid.

73. Reid and Demaris, p. 27.

74. *Arizona Project,* p. 17.

75. Ibid.

76. Ibid.

77. Lou Wiener, interview, November 21, 1989.

78. Jennings, p. 166.

79. Ibid., p. 177.

80. Lou Wiener, interview, November 21, 1989.

81. Harold Conrad, interview, April 2, 1990.

82. *Arizona Project,* p. 15.

83. Dan, "Meyer Lansky Breaks His Silence," July 2, 1971. The last time he saw Benny Siegel, Lansky told Uri Dan, was in the spring of 1947 in New York, three or four months before the shooting in Los Angeles.

84. Sann Interviews.

85. Dr. Seymour J. Gray, interview, March 1, 1990.

10. *"I Don't Sail Under No False Colors"*

1. Teddy Lansky told Paul Sann that her date of birth was November 18, 1910. But in her June 1949 application for a passport, which she signed and had notarized, she gave her date of birth as November 18, 1907. PASS-PORT OFFICE.

2. Sann Interviews.

3. Ibid.

4. Ibid. Pomerantz is at 2532 Broadway.

5. Sann Interviews.

6. Author meeting with Mrs. Meyer Lansky, July 26, 1988.

7. Sann Interviews.

8. Ibid. It is possible that Teddy mixed up the occasion on which Meyer ordered her stone crab claws. She recalls first going out with him in August 1948. But stone crabs are out of season in August, and are not usually served in south Florida until October.

9. Ibid.

10. Ibid.

11. Meir, p. 206.

12. Joseph Baum, interview, December 5, 1988. See also Baum to Yoram Alroy, July 14, 1971, a letter which Baum sent in support of Meyer Lansky's attempt to settle in Israel. Israel, Supreme Court Papers. Office of the Prime Minister, Jerusalem.

13. Howard Shapiro, interview, April 1, 1991.

14. Dan, "Meyer Lansky Breaks His Silence," July 2, 1971.

15. Eisenberg et al., p. 295.

16. Harold Conrad, interview, September 26, 1988.

17. Joseph Baum, interview, December 5, 1988.

18. U.S. passport application of Meyer and Thelma Lansky, June 15, 1949. PASSPORT OFFICE.

19. Buddy Lansky, interview, March 23, 1989.

20. Ibid., March 23 and March 29, 1989.

21. Ibid., April 17 and April 24, 1989.

22. Ibid., March 23, 1989.

23. Vincent Mercurio, interview, October 10, 1990.

24. *New York Times,* April 24, 1980.

25. Vincent Mercurio, interview, October 10, 1990.

26. Buddy Lansky, interviews, April 24 and July 25, 1989.

27. Vincent Mercurio, interview, October 10, 1990. In the late 1940s there were Trans-Lux Newsreel Theaters at Broadway and Forty-ninth and at Madison and Sixtieth.

28. Ibid., November 13, 1988.

29. Ibid.

30. Ibid., October 10, 1990.

31. Ibid.

32. Ibid., November 13, 1988.

33. Ibid., October 10, 1990.

34. Buddy Lansky, interview, March 27, 1989.

35. Testimony of Meyer Lansky, October 1950. KEFAUVER, Part 7, p. 603.

36. Testimony of Moses Polakoff, with Meyer Lansky, October 1950. KEFAUVER, Part 7, pp. 602, 603.

37. "Figure your repairs come to about $15 a month. Costs $12 a week servicing, records, needles, kids going around picking up the nickels, and repair the machine. So if you can run your machine for less than $20 a month you are going good. . . . Any spot where you can get $15 a week in nickels it is a very good spot." Statement of John Kennedy before Bernard Yarrow, ADA, on September 24, 1941. Miscellaneous — Rackets, p. 1. New York DA's Files, Box 304. NYC Municipal Archives.

38. Testimony of Meyer Lansky, October 1950. KEFAUVER, Part 7, p. 603.

39. Testimony of Albert Denver, December 1958, U.S. Senate, *Final Report of the Select Committee on Improper Activities in the Labor or Management Field,* Part 45, p. 16759.

40. Bill Barol, "The Wurlitzer 1015," *American Heritage,* September/October 1989, p. 28.

41. Testimony of Harold Morris, December 1958. U.S. Senate, *Final Report . . . on Improper Activities in the Labor or Management Field,* Part 45, p. 16768.

42. Statement of John Kennedy before Bernard Yarrow, ADA, on September 24, 1941. Miscellaneous — Rackets, pp. 1–6.

43. Ibid., p. 3.

44. *New York Times,* February 11, 1959.

45. Campbell, p. 277.

46. Meyer Lansky II, interview, September 6, 1990.

47. *New York Times,* February 11, 1959.

48. Testimony of Meyer Lansky, October 1950. KEFAUVER, Part 7, p. 606.

49. Ibid., p. 605.

50. Buddy Lansky, interview, April 17, 1989.

51. Testimony of George Goldstein, August 1950. KEFAUVER, Part 7, p. 145.

52. Ibid.

53. Bureau of Narcotics, Report of Agent John H. Hanly, June 28, 1949. STRIKE FORCE 18 PAPERS.

54. See, for example, on the lifting of the embargo, outgoing telegram, Department of State, Marshall to American Embassy, Habana, February 24, 1947. State Department Papers, National Archives.

55. Luciano left Cuba on March 20, 1947, aboard the Turkish vessel S.S. *Bakir,* which arrived in Genoa on April 12, 1947. Letter from American Consulate, Genoa, April 15, 1947, to Secretary of State, Washington. Box 4088, State Department Papers.

56. Anslinger's letter of February 21, 1947, from the Treasury Department, to the Secretary of State, Washington, filed February 25, 1947, made clear that he had no current evidence of Luciano smuggling drugs, and that he was acting on suspicion. State Department Papers.

57. Bureau of Narcotics, Report of Agent John H. Hanly, June 28, 1949, p. 3.

58. Ibid., p. 1.

59. Ibid., p. 2.

60. Ibid.

61. Ibid.

62. Ibid., p. 3.

63. Ibid., p. 3.

64. Ibid., p. 1.

65. *New York Sun,* June 28, 1949.

66. Ibid.

67. Ibid.

68. Ibid.

69. Buddy Lansky, interview, March 23, 1989.

70. Ibid.

71. Sann Interviews.

72. Dr. Seymour J. Gray, interview, March 1, 1990.

73. Ibid.

74. Report of Edward W. St. Mary, January 5, 1973.
75. Dr. Seymour J. Gray, interview, March 1, 1990.
76. Ibid.

11. *"Haven't You Ever Said, . . . 'I Hate the Hellish Business'?"*

Kefauver's successive reports and the large volumes of testimony to his committee stand as evidence in their own right. Daniel Bell was the first to subject the work of the Senate Crime Committee to detached critical analysis. William Howard Moore's *The Kefauver Committee and the Politics of Crime, 1950–1952* provides the latest and most comprehensive overview, and has been the principal secondary source relied on in this chapter.

1. TenEick, p. 401.
2. Ibid.
3. KEFAUVER, Third Interim Report, pp. 59, 60.
4. TenEick, p. 402.
5. Author interview. Boggs later became mayor of Hollywood.
6. Carlton Montayne, "County-Wide Blackout Closes Gambling Rooms in Broward," *Miami News,* February 13, 1948. Montayne reported the closing, out of prudence, of almost all the gambling establishments in Broward County for a period after February 12, 1948, but that injunctions had only been filed against the Colonial Inn and against the Lopez Restaurant. This was a small place to the north on Federal Highway which ran its own gambling and had no special connection with Meyer Lansky.
7. Philip Weidling, letter to author, April 16, 1988.
8. Ibid.
9. Ibid.
10. *Time,* November 28, 1949, p. 27.
11. Ibid.
12. Ralph Salerno, letter to author. April 17, 1991. Aurelio retired from the state supreme court on December 31, 1967, and died on January 5, 1973. *New York Times,* January 6, 1973.
13. George Wolf, Costello's attorney who went to retrieve the money, told the story in his book, *Frank Costello: Prime Minister of the Underworld,* pp. 148–152.
14. $121.65, to be precise. Wolf and DiMona, p. 152.
15. Ibid., p. 3.
16. *Collier's,* April 12, 1947, pp. 16–17, 26–33, and April 19, 1947, pp. 33–44.
17. Ibid., April 12, 1947, p. 16.
18. *Time,* October 17, 1949, p. 27.

19. Costello's lawyer, George Wolf, told the story in chapter 22 of his biography of Costello. Wolf and DiMona, pp. 182–184.

20. See Moore, p. 32, for all these examples.

21. This was the title of the biography of Costello written by his attorney, George Wolf.

22. Cited in Moore, p. 44.

23. Ibid., p. 49.

24. Ibid.

25. Fox, pp. 304, 305.

26. Tobey, p. 88.

27. This exchange occurred on April 28, 1950, in a meeting of the McFarland Committee examining "A Bill to Prohibit Transmission of Certain Gambling Information in Interstate and Foreign Commerce by Communications Facilities." U.S. Senate, *Transmission of Gambling Information*, p. 480.

28. Wolf and DiMona, p. 29.

29. Vincent Mercurio, interview, October 10, 1990.

30. Ibid.

31. Ibid.

32. Dinty Moore's was at 216 West Forty-sixth Street, New York.

33. Tail Report on Meyer Lansky, September 20, 1950. New York DA's Files, Box 409, Subpoenas. NYC Municipal Archives.

34. Testimony of Meyer Lansky, October 1950. KEFAUVER, Part 7, p. 148.

35. Ibid., p. 156.

36. Moses Polakoff, interview, August 11, 1988.

37. Testimony of Meyer Lansky, October 1950. KEFAUVER, Part 7, pp. 157, 158.

38. Ibid., p. 160.

39. Moore, p. 168.

40. Ibid., p. 169.

41. These examples are among those described in the excellent account of the televising of the Kefauver hearings in Moore, pp. 184, 185.

42. Ibid.

43. Rudolph Halley died in 1956, aged only forty-three. Obituary, *New York Times*, November 20, 1956.

44. Some sessions went into the evening. Costello testified on March 13, 14, 15, 16, 19, 20, and 21, 1951; most of his testimony took place on the first two days.

45. Moore, p. 190.

46. Ibid., p. 192.

47. Testimony of Meyer Lansky, March 1951. KEFAUVER, Part 7, p. 605.

48. Ibid., p. 607.

49. Ibid., p. 603.

50. Ibid., p. 604.

51. Eisenberg et al., p. 306.

52. William Howard Moore, interview, November 2, 1990.

53. Eisenberg et al., p. 306.

54. Ibid.

55. Conrad, *Dear Muffo,* pp. 236, 237.

56. For a recent discussion of the Fifth Amendment and the latest judgments affecting it, see Johnny H. Killian, ed., *The Constitution of the United States of America: Analysis and Interpretation (Annotations of Cases Decided by the Supreme Court of the United States to July 2, 1982).* Washington: Library of Congress, 1987.

57. Copies of these documents are to be found in the files of the New York District Attorney, in one file marked Kefauver. New York DA's Files, Box 410. NYC Municipal Archives.

58. Bell, pp. 140–141.

59. KEFAUVER, Second Interim Report, p. 11.

60. Ibid., Third Interim Report, p. 2.

61. Ibid., Second Interim Report, p. 4.

62. Ibid., Third Interim Report, p. 1.

63. Testimony of Harry Anslinger, June 1950. In ibid., Part 2, p. 89.

64. Tobey, pp. 89, 91.

65. Transcribed by author from Hoover's testimony on Universal Newsreel, March 27, 1951, Universal Newsreel Library, National Archives, vol. 24, no. 442.

66. Moore, p. 207.

67. Transcribed by author from Hoover's testimony on Universal Newsreel, March 27, 1951.

68. KEFAUVER, Second Interim Report, p. 4.

69. Ibid., First Interim Report, p. 4.

70. Ibid., Second Interim Report, p. 3.

71. *New York Times,* February 17, 1951.

72. KEFAUVER, Third Interim Report, p. 2.

73. Ibid., Second Interim Report, p. 13.

74. Bell, p. 132.

75. Martin Plissner's article "Take the Numbers with a Grain of Salt" provides an illuminating analysis of how inexact the statistics of organized crime can be.

76. Kefauver, p. 23.

77. Professor William Howard Moore gives the history of these documents, and others, in his bibliographical essay, Moore, pp. 243–259. The Kefauver files were transferred to the National Archives and are now open to researchers.

78. See Mitler, "Legal and Administrative Problems," pp. 266ff., for an interesting account of the Royal Commission and the development of British gambling in the years since 1951.

12. *"Do You Notice Anything Funny About Marvin?"*

1. Scarne, *Mafia Conspiracy*, p. 35.

2. FBI, NY 92-660, Meyer Lansky, Criminal Record — State Police, Troy, New York. FBI.

3. "Indictment Links Lansky, 6 Others to Arrowhead," by Reginald F. Torrey, September 10, 1952. Unidentified clipping, Gambling File, Office of the City Historian, Saratoga Springs. Also "Indictment Voted Against Arrowhead, 7 Defendants," by Reginald F. Torrey, September 11, 1952.

4. Moses Polakoff, interview, August 11, 1988.

5. "Lansky Selects Holy Bible for Jail Reading," unidentified, undated clipping, Gambling File, Office of the City Historian, Saratoga Springs.

6. Gerard King, interview, May 25, 1991.

7. Ibid., August 9, 1988.

8. Ibid.

9. IRS Criminal Reference Report, p. 39. STRIKE FORCE 18 PAPERS.

10. Buddy Lansky, interview, July 10, 1989.

11. IRS Criminal Reference Report, p. 40. The precise figures, as given in the tax return, were: sale price, $22,136.18; purchase price, $6,796.75; capital gain, $15,339.43.

12. Some, but not all. The gambling clubs and bookie joints in Covington and Newport, Kentucky, across the Ohio River from Cincinnati, operated "wide open" throughout the 1950s, and were only closed following the controversial election of an antigambling sheriff, George Ratterman, in 1961.

13. There were ten accused: Meyer Lansky, Jake Lansky, Vincent Alo (Jimmy Blue Eyes), George Sadlo, William Bischoff (Lefty Clark), Claude Litteral, Samuel Bratt, and Frank Shireman, together with Louis Oliver and Paul Alexander, who were named as the operators of the "It" Club near Fort Lauderdale. All ten men pleaded guilty. *Miami Herald*, September 17, 1950.

14. IRS Criminal Reference Report, pp. 36, 39.

15. In an affidavit of December 15, 1955, to the IRS, Appellate Division, New York City, Meyer Lansky declared that he maintained safe-deposit boxes at the Corn Exchange Bank and the Manufacturers Trust Company, New York City; the Union National Bank of Newark, New Jersey; the Shawmut Bank of Boston, Massachusetts; and the First National Bank of Hollywood, Florida. Meyer shared this Hollywood safety-deposit box with his brother, Jake. IRS Criminal Reference Report, p. 9.

16. IRS Criminal Reference Report, p. 8.

17. Gerard King, interview, August 9, 1988.

18. *New York Times,* January 4, 1956.

19. Digest of INS and Other Inquiries into Meyer Lansky (pages 3–24 of untitled document datelined Miami, Florida, June 22, 1959; C-2 517 814; Top Priority, Racketeer), p. 24. STRIKE FORCE 18 PAPERS.

20. Ibid., p. 11.

21. Gerard King, interview, August 9, 1988.

22. Sann Interviews.

23. Buddy Lansky, interview, March 23, 1989.

24. Sann Interviews.

25. Vincent Mercurio, interview, October 10, 1990.

26. Buddy Lansky, interview, April 3, 1989.

27. Ibid.

28. Ibid., May 1, 1989.

29. Ibid.

30. Ibid.

31. Vincent Mercurio, interview, October 10, 1990.

32. Buddy Lansky, interview, March 23, 1989.

33. Ibid.

34. Ibid., October 4, 1989.

35. Meyer Lansky made his investment in the Plantation Harbor in the name of his lawyer, Joseph Varon, and his holding in the motel was, thus, concealed in the corporate sense. But he declared his investment in his tax returns. IRS Criminal Reference Report.

36. Buddy Lansky, interview, June 5, 1989.

37. Arthur Klein first won election to Congress, representing the Nineteenth District, in 1941. An unashamed machine politician, he became a New York State Supreme Court justice in 1956. His most famous judgment (upheld by the U.S. Supreme Court) was his rejection of a state ban on the novel *Fanny Hill,* and his opinion, which began: "While the saga of Fanny Hill will undoubtedly never replace 'Little Red Riding Hood' as a popular bedtime story. . . ." *New York Times,* February 22, 1968.

38. *Avenues of Admission to West Point.* Public Affairs Office, United States Military Academy, West Point, March 1986.

39. Judge Michael Sweeney, interview, August 9, 1988.

40. Dr. Jean Henry, interview, March 18, 1988.

41. *Miami Herald,* September 17, 1950.

42. Dr. Jean Henry, interview, March 18, 1988.

43. The details of the Lansky brothers' investment, through George Sadlo, in the Thunderbird remain confused. Clifford Jones, the former attorney general of Nevada, who was Hicks's minority partner in the Thunderbird, says he had no idea that Hicks had accepted money from George Sadlo. Clifford Jones, interview, November 19, 1989.

44. See Turner, pp. 127–130, for a lucid summary of the case which arose from the Lansky brothers' loan to the Thunderbird through George Sadlo.

The memoirs of Robbins E. Cahill, one of the oral histories in the James R. Dickinson Library, Special Collections, at the University of Nevada, Las Vegas, contain new and illuminating material on the incident. (Chapter 13, "The Thunderbird Case.")

45. Dr. Jean Henry, interview, March 18, 1988.
46. Ibid.
47. Buddy Lansky, interview, March 27, 1989.
48. Ibid.
49. Ibid.
50. Ibid.
51. Ibid.
52. Ibid.
53. The Department of the Air Force was created in 1947, but air force officers continued to be trained at West Point until the opening of the Air Force Academy in 1955.
54. Malana Mason, interview, January 16, 1990.
55. Ibid.
56. Ibid.
57. Buddy Lansky, interview, March 27, 1989.

13. Dance of the Millions

This chapter draws heavily on the memories of the refugees — Cuban and American — who lived in Havana in the years before Castro. Chief among these was the late Johnny Parker, whose essays, *Yankee, You Can't Go Home Again,* memorably preserve the texture of that era of trolley cars and crumpled linen suits. Two of Johnny's friends, Clarence Moore, editor of the *Times of the Americas,* and Martin Guillermo de Salazar, a pillar of Johnny's beloved American Club in both Havana and Miami, were also valuable resources.

In Havana itself, some of the original documentation of the Riviera Hotel survives and is in the care of the public relations office of the hotel. Mrs. Hilda Watson was a gracious hostess and kindly shared her memories of working at the Nacional Hotel in the mid-1950s. I am grateful for the recollections of Segundo Curti Messina, briefly prime minister of Cuba in 1949 and 1952, and for help in Havana from Gabriel Molina of *Granma* and from Rafael Padilla Ceballos. My special gratitude to my friend and lawyer in Florida, Mario de Mendoza III.

Among the casino fraternity itself, discretion remains the rule. But Enrique Rousseau, Mike McLaney, and Frank Atlass were willing to put their names to their memories. My thanks to them — and to those who were not.

1. *Time,* April 21, 1952.

2. Amembassy, Habana, to Department of State, September 19, 1952. Operations Memorandum, State Department Papers, National Archives.

3. Richard Nixon's letter is not, today, in the State Department documents relating to the incident, but the documents make clear that he sent such a letter. An operations memorandum, dated September 19, 1952, to the Department of State, from the U.S. embassy, Havana, re "Inquiry from Mr. Dana C. Smith Concerning Certain Gambling Practices in Cuba" begins:

> The Embassy received on September 3, 1952, a letter from Mr. Dana C. Smith, under cover of a transmitting letter from Senator Richard Nixon. Senator Nixon informed the Embassy that Mr. Smith is a highly respected member of his community, and that the Senator would appreciate anything that the Embassy might be able to do to assist him in his problem.

According to *Look* magazine for February 24, 1953, "Nixon's correspondence files show that the letter to the Embassy was written by a secretary and signed by her in his name on the instruction of a superior. Nixon did not know the letter had been written, or anything about the facts of the case."

Look went on to say that the *St. Louis Post-Dispatch,* a pro-Stevenson paper, claimed, on October 30, 1952, just before the presidential election, that Nixon had accompanied Smith on his gambling trip in April 1952. This charge was repeated a few days later by Drew Pearson, in his weekly radio broadcast.

According to *Look,*

> The statement that Nixon was with Smith at Havana is branded by Nixon as a lie. The records of his office account for his whereabouts from the middle of March through April. In fact, every day from March 14, through April, is accounted for with adequate corroboration for his whereabouts, including a 10-day visit to Honolulu to participate in territorial political festivities. He was neither in Miami nor in Havana in April, according to these records.

4. Amembassy, Habana, to Department of State, September 19, 1952.

5. *New York Times,* January 30, 1953.

6. Amembassy, Habana, to Department of State, February 2, 1953. Operations Memorandum, State Department Papers.

7. Velie, "Suckers in Paradise," p. 181.

8. *Havana Herald,* February 10, 1953. Clipping attached to Foreign

Service Dispatch from Amembassy, Habana, February 13, 1953. From David S. Green, Commercial Attaché. State Department Papers.

9. Velie, "Suckers in Paradise," p. 181.

10. Ibid.

11. Ibid.

12. Ibid.

13. Ibid.

14. On June 23, 1952, three months after Batista's coup, J. Edgar Hoover asked his legal attaché in Havana to investigate reports that Meyer Lansky had recently been observed in Cuba. Confidential Air Pouch to Legal Attaché, Havana, Cuba. From John Edgar Hoover, June 23, 1952. FBI.

15. Joseph Varon, interview, June 9, 1989.

16. Batista, p. 193.

17. Ibid., pp. 193, 194.

18. Joseph Varon, interview, June 9, 1989.

19. McLoud to Senator Tobey, June 9, 1953. 837.45/5-2753. State Department Papers.

The thirteen professional gamblers arrested were: Charles Glick, Vernon Windham, Joseph Henry Tamburro, Regina Marsch (alias Georgina Marsh, alias Diana Reynolds), James Davis (alias Jackie Davis), Patrick Smith, Charles White, Robert Edward Ayoub, Sid Jacobs, Alfred Howard, Thomas Joseph Craven, Michael Bliss, and Morris Weinberg.

20. W. E. Graff, to Commanding Officer, New York County District Attorney's Office Squad. "Resumé of Cuban Gambling Situation," September 30, 1966. NYC Municipal Archives, uncatalogued.

21. Hirsch to U.S. Ambassador, Cuba, April 22, 1953. 837.45/4-2253. State Department Papers.

22. See, for example, his interview with the Federal narcotics agents prior to his departure on the S.S. *Italia*. Bureau of Narcotics, Report of Agent John H. Hanly, June 28, 1949. STRIKE FORCE 18 PAPERS.

23. Enrique Rousseau, interview, January 24, 1989.

24. Jim Potter, interview, February 22, 1989.

25. Phillips, p. 283.

26. Dr. Jean Henry, interview, March 18, 1988.

27. "Lansky, 'El Cejudo' no hace caso," *Granma*, August 29, 1988, p. 3. I am grateful to Margarita Newcomer for her help with the translating of this article.

28. Ibid.

29. IRS Criminal Reference Report, pp. 40, 41, 42. STRIKE FORCE 18 PAPERS.

30. Sann Interviews.

31. Joseph Varon, interview, June 9, 1989.

32. Ibid.

33. *Life* magazine, March 10, 1958.

34. Batista, p. 194.

35. Phillips, p. 283.

36. Batista, p. 194.

37. Ibid.

38. Enrique Rousseau, interview, January 24, 1989.

39. *Miami Herald*, October 28, 1958.

40. Benny Binion, interview, November 18, 1989.

41. Joseph Varon, interview, June 9, 1989.

42. Enrique Rousseau, interview, January 29, 1989.

43. Bahamas Islands, *Report of the Commission of Inquiry into the Operation of the Business of Casinos in Freeport and in Nassau,* para. 254, p. 86.

44. Author interview with a construction executive who lived in Havana in 1957 and 1958, in frequent contact with Irving Feldman and Meyer Lansky.

45. Malana Mason, interview, November 7, 1990.

46. IRS Criminal Reference Report, pp. 42, 43, 44. Lansky listed his principal source of income for 1956, under the heading of "wages, etc. from employers," as $25,000 paid by Irving Feldman, of Miami Beach. Feldman agreed to let Meyer list himself as an employee/consultant of Feldman's in the construction of the Riviera — and found that his own tax returns and business books were subjected to IRS audit and scrutiny for the next three years.

47. Sonny Harris, interview, January 24, 1989.

48. Carmen Casal Sanchez, interview, May 17, 1988. Ms. Sanchez is the public relations director of the Riviera Hotel today. Her office holds several files on the early history of the hotel. For advertisements of the opening show, see *Diario de la Marina*, December 11, 1957.

49. Author interview as in note 44, above.

50. Ibid.

51. Segundo Curti Messina, interview, May 14, 1988.

52. Alexandra Landau, April 19, 1989.

53. Frank Atlass, interviews, September 14, 1988 and May 23, 1991.

14. "I Crapped Out"

The debt that this chapter owes to the recollections of Detective William Graff is obvious. His memories are confirmed by the papers of the Albert Anastasia murder investigation, which were unearthed, thanks to Jenna Weissman Joselit, in the course of the research for this book and are now located, thanks to a number of people, in the New York City Municipal Archives (see p. 445).

Wayne Smith's memories of the Cuban revolution, and of the equally troubled years since, are gracefully set out in his memoir, *The Closest of Enemies*. My thanks to him and to the others named below who shared their firsthand memories. Also to Frank Sturgis, who, long before he became famous as a Watergate burglar, was Fidel Castro's liaison officer with Cuba's American casinos.

1. William Graff, interview, November 7, 1990.
2. Ibid.
3. Ibid.
4. Batista, p. 194.
5. William Graff, interview, November 7, 1990.
6. Sergeant Croswell, who retired as a captain and later joined the New York State Organized Crime Force, died on Saturday, November 17, 1990, at the age of seventy-seven, according to his obituary in the *New York Times* of Wednesday, November 21, 1990. Most histories of organized crime spell his name Crosswell.
7. *New York Times*, November 17, 1957.
8. For a list of the fifty-eight men detained by Sergeant Edgar Croswell, with their ages, addresses, and occupations as given to the police, see *New York Times*, November 16, 1957.

Joseph Bonanno, age fifty-two, of 1726 DeKalb Avenue, Brooklyn, retired, was included on the list, but he was not there, by his own account in his autobiography, *A Man of Honor*, p. 216. The details came from his driver's license, which he had given to his brother-in-law to be renewed, and which was in the possession of Gaspar DiGregorio, a lieutenant of Bonanno's, who was at the meeting. According to his book, Bonanno had been invited to Joseph Barbara's house, however, and *A Man of Honor* provides the only published insider's account of how and why the Apalachin participants came together.

For a detailed analysis of the criminal records and business backgrounds of the Apalachin participants, see U.S. Senate, *Final Report of the Select Committee on Improper Activities in the Labor or Management Field*, No. 1139, Part 3, March 28, 1960, pp. 487ff.

9. *New York Times*, November 29, 1960.
10. Ibid., February 12, 1958.
11. Sann Interviews.
12. *New York Herald Telegram*, February 28, 1958.
13. *New York Daily News*, February 13, 1958.
14. Supplementary Complaint Reports. People Re: Umberto Anastasia, Deceased. NYC Municipal Archives, uncatalogued.
15. William Graff, interview, November 7, 1990.

16. Cuban Gambling Report. People Re: Umberto Anastasia, Deceased.

17. Ibid.

18. Memorandum, February 10, 1958. Scotti to Fay, Re: Albert Anastasia (Homicide), p. 2. People Re: Umberto Anastasia, Deceased.

19. To Mr. Scotti, from Investigator Whiteside, January 23, 1958, Memorandum of meeting with Roberto Mendoza and others on January 18, 1958. NYC Municipal Archives, uncatalogued.

20. Albert Anastasia, deceased, report of March 11, 1958. Interview by Detective Nicholas Looram, shield 1314. NYC Municipal Archives, uncatalogued.

21. People Re: Umberto Anastasia, Deceased.

22. *New York Daily News,* February 12, 13, and 28, 1958. *New York Times,* February 28, 1958. *New York Herald Tribune,* February 28, 1958. Also Sann Interviews.

23. *New York Herald Tribune,* February 28, 1958.

24. Ibid.

25. J. "Skip" Shepard, interview, June 26, 1988.

26. Norberto Peña, interview, May 19, 1988.

27. Christopher Moorsom, interview, November 5, 1987.

28. Norberto Peña, interview, May 19, 1988.

29. Ibid.

30. *Life,* March 10, 1958, p. 36.

31. Gonzalez was known as Tendedera, and was paid a retainer by the Riviera of sixty dollars per month. Norberto Peña, interview, May 19, 1988.

32. Wayne Smith, p. 16.

33. Tessa Kennedy, interview, December 15, 1989.

34. Phillips, p. 283.

35. Joseph Varon, interview, June 9, 1989.

36. Wayne Smith, p. 34.

37. Sann Interviews.

38. "During late August or early September, subject was hospitalized, Boston, Massachusetts, for ulcers. . . . The 'New York World Telegram,' night edition, issue of September 23, 1958, in an article called 'Day by Day' by Frank Farrell mentioned the subject and stated 'Meyer Lansky, former czar of gambling in Miami Beach, is now seriously ailing with ulcers in a Florida hospital.'" FBI, New York, November 25, 1958, Meyer Lansky, NY 92-660. FBI.

39. Sann Interviews.

40. Phillips, pp. 394, 395.

41. Ibid. See also Thomas, pp. 1025–1027, for the details of Batista's final hours in Cuba.

42. Lysandro Otero, interview, May 17, 1988.

43. Wayne Smith, p. 38.

44. Sann Interviews.

45. Ibid.

46. William Federici and Loren Craft, "Cops Await Mugs from Cuba," *New York Daily News,* January 3, 1959.

47. Milton Lewis, "Facing Trouble in U.S.: City, State and Federal Agencies Alert for Any Influx of Gangsters," *New York Herald Tribune,* January 3, 1959.

48. To Director, from Legat, Havana, Subject Meyer Lansky, February 27, 1959. FBI.

49. Ibid.

50. *Miami News,* January 7, 1959. Also, Milt Sosin, interview, July 28, 1988.

51. *Miami News,* January 7, 1959.

52. Ibid.

53. Wayne Smith, p. 40.

54. Dispatch 1037, Amembassy, Habana, to Department of State, March 19, 1959. State Department Papers, National Archives.

55. Ibid.

56. Ibid.

57. Ibid.

58. "Cuba: The Mob Is Back," *Time,* March 2, 1959.

59. Ibid.

60. Ibid.

61. Ibid.

62. "City Gives Castro a Noisy Greeting," *New York Times,* April 25, 1959.

63. *Newsweek,* March 2, 1959.

64. *Miami Herald,* May 8 and May 29, 1959.

65. Lavine, "Intellect."

66. Joseph Varon, interview, April 18, 1990.

67. "Cuban Political Situation," Field Office File MM 92-102, Bureau File 92-2831, Miami, December 3, 1959, Meyer Lansky. FBI.

68. Dennis O'Shea, interview, April 26, 1990.

69. Ibid.

70. "Cuban Political Situation," Field Office File MM 92-102.

71. Ibid.

72. Dennis O'Shea, interview, April 26, 1990. Also November 21, 1990.

73. "Cuban Political Situation," Field Office File MM 92-102.

74. Dennis O'Shea, interview, April 26, 1990.

75. Ibid.

76. "Cuban Political Situation," Field Office File MM 92-102.

77. Ibid.

78. The State Department documents relating to the American embassy in Havana in the late 1950s are notable for the attention that they pay to

Meyer Lansky. So it is surprising that they contain no mention of his meeting with O'Shea on May 22, 1959.

79. Wayne Smith, pp. 52, 53.

80. Fuentes, "Mafia in Cuba," p. 61.

81. Joseph Sheiner, interview, January 26, 1988.

82. Riviera Hotel, Havana, Corporate Archives. These papers show a declared investment by the hotel's owners of $5.4 million.

83. Joseph Varon, interview, June 9, 1989.

84. For various contemporary estimates of the money involved in Cuban gambling in the final year of Batista's rule, see Memorandum to File, from Mr. Fay, Albert Anastasia and Gambling Casinos, January 13, 1958, and related correspondence in People Re: Umberto Anastasia, Deceased. Also see Scarne, *Mafia Conspiracy*, pp. 94–104.

85. Joseph Varon, interview, June 9, 1989.

86. Ibid.

87. Ibid.

88. Buddy Lansky, interview, March 29, 1989.

89. Ibid., July 25 and December 4, 1989.

90. Ibid., March 27, 1989.

15. *"This Little Man — What Could He Do to You?"*

1. *Jerusalem Post*, August 24, 1962.

2. The heart attack had occurred in April 1962. *Jerusalem Post*, August 24, 1962.

3. Buddy Lansky, interview, August 28, 1989.

4. Ibid., March 23, 1989.

5. "Boston's Mr. Linsey," *Wall Street Journal*, January 18, 1968.

6. Author interview with a fund-raiser in the south Florida Jewish community.

7. Rabbi David Shapiro, interview, December 5, 1988.

8. Dan, "Meyer Lansky Breaks His Silence," July 2, 1971.

9. Rabbi David Shapiro, interview, December 5, 1988.

10. Annette Lansky, interview, September 27, 1990.

11. Ibid.

12. Buddy Lansky, interview, March 27, 1989.

13. Malana Mason, interview, January 17, 1990.

14. Joseph Varon, interview, December 7, 1990.

15. Ibid.

16. Annette Lansky, interview, September 27, 1990.

17. Ibid.

18. Ibid.

19. Buddy Lansky, interview, March 27, 1989.

20. Dr. Jean Henry, interview, March 18, 1988.

21. Annette Lansky, interview, September 27, 1990.

22. Ibid.

23. Ibid., March 19, 1990.

24. Ibid., September 27, 1990.

25. Ibid.

26. Ibid., March 19, 1990.

27. Ibid., September 27, 1990.

28. Ibid.

29. Ibid., March 19, 1990.

30. Ibid., September 27, 1990.

31. Ibid.

32. Buddy Lansky, interview, November 3, 1989.

33. Ibid., April 3 and November 3, 1989.

34. Milton Hoff, interview, May 25, 1989.

35. Buddy Lansky, interview, April 10, 1989.

36. Ibid., June 12, 1989.

37. Ibid., April 10, 1989.

38. Ibid., July 31, 1989.

39. Ibid., July 25, 1989.

40. Ibid., July 31, 1989.

41. Annette Lansky, interview, May 23, 1991.

42. Ibid., March 19, 1990.

43. Ibid., September 27, 1990.

44. Ibid., March 19 and September 27, 1990.

45. Ibid., March 19, 1990.

46. Buddy's memory was that the payment was $100. Annette remembers $1,000, and that her mother paid the money over to her.

47. Annette Lansky, March 19, 1990.

48. Malana Mason, interview, January 16, 1990.

49. Lacey, p. 107.

50. Rennold Wacht, interview, April 10, 1988.

51. Author interviews with three agents of the Criminal Intelligence Squad, FBI, New York, two of whom met Sandra Lansky and developed her as a source.

52. Ibid.

53. Ibid.

54. Ibid.

55. Ibid.

56. Annette Lansky, interview, September 27, 1990.

57. Buddy Lansky, interview, March 27, 1989.

58. Malana Mason, interview, February 5, 1990.

59. Buddy Lansky, interview, March 27, 1989.

60. Ibid.

61. Ibid.

62. Malana Mason, interview, January 16, 1990.
63. Ibid.
64. Ibid.
65. Buddy Lansky, interview, March 27, 1989.
66. Malana Mason, interview, January 16, 1990.
67. Buddy Lansky, interview, March 27, 1989.
68. Malana Mason, interview, January 16, 1990.
69. Ibid.
70. Meyer Lansky II, interview, September 6, 1990.
71. Malana Mason, interview, January 16, 1990.
72. Ibid.
73. Ibid.
74. Ibid.
75. Buddy Lansky, interview, October 16, 1989.
76. Meyer Lansky II, interview, September 7, 1990.
77. Buddy Lansky, interview, October 16, 1989.
78. Havemann, "Mobsters Move In on Troubled Havana," p. 32.
79. Malana Mason, interview, January 16, 1990.
80. Ibid.
81. Ibid.
82. Ibid.
83. Meyer Lansky II, interview, November 24, 1990.
84. Malana Mason, interview, January 17, 1990.
85. Ibid.
86. Myra Lansky, interview, January 16, 1990.
87. Malana Mason, interview, January 17, 1990.
88. Ibid.
89. Ibid.
90. Ibid., January 16, 1990.
91. Ibid.
92. Myra Lansky, interview, January 16, 1990.
93. Malana Mason, interview, January 16, 1990.
94. Ibid.
95. Ibid., January 17, 1990.
96. Meyer Lansky II, interview, September 7, 1990.
97. Buddy Lansky, interview, April 10, 1989.
98. Ibid., October 4, 1989.
99. Malana Mason, interview, January 16, 1990.
100. Meyer Lansky II, interview, September 7, 1990; Myra Lansky, interview, January 17, 1990.
101. Myra Lansky, interview, January 16, 1990.
102. Malana Mason, interview, January 16, 1990.
103. Ibid., January 17, 1990.
104. Ibid., January 16 and February 7, 1990.

105. Buddy Lansky, interview, July 25, 1989.
106. Annette Lansky, interview, March 16, 1990.

16. *"Bigger Than U.S. Steel"*

The FBI notes on the bugging of Meyer Lansky's room in the Volney Hotel, and the surveillance reports on his activities in Florida were obtained by the author under the Freedom of Information Act. The surveillance details from the bug in the Fremont Hotel were obtained from someone who noted extracts from the material prior to their being sealed by court order in 1968. My thanks to Fred Mark Palmer for his interview with Sheriff Clay White, who, as an FBI agent in the early 1960s, participated in the surveillance of Ida Devine, "the lady in mink," when she visited Hot Springs, Arkansas.

1. Plain Text, Airtel, June 1, 1962. To Director, from SAC New York, Meyer Lansky. FBI.
2. To SAC Miami, from Director, March 23, 1960. FBI.
3. For an excellent firsthand account of FBI work in the late 1950s and 1960s — and especially microphone surveillance — see the memoir of William F. Roemer, Jr., *Man Against the Mob.*
4. Author interviews with two former FBI agents and also a New York police detective, who all described the practice of the "sound studio."
5. Memorandum to Mr. Belmont, from C. A. Evans, Meyer Lansky, Anti-Racketeering, May 22, 1962. FBI.
6. Teletype, Urgent, to Director and SAC Miami, from SAC New York, May 30, 1962, p. 2. FBI.
7. Ibid., pp. 1, 2.
8. Plain Text, Airtel, June 11, 1962. To Director, from SAC New York, Meyer Lansky, p. 7. FBI.
9. *New York Times,* February 2 and March 30, 1962.
10. Plain Text, Airtel, June 5, 1962. To Director, from SAC New York, Meyer Lansky, p. 3. FBI.
11. Ibid.
12. Plain Text, Airtel, June 1, 1962. To Director, from SAC New York, Meyer Lansky, p. 6. FBI.
13. Sandy Smith, "Mobsters in the Market Place," p. 98.
14. Ibid.
15. *Time,* August 22, 1969, p. 18.
16. Joseph Varon, interview, May 2, 1991.
17. Buddy Lansky, interview, March 23, 1989.
18. Sann Interviews.
19. The interest payments which Meyer received were for $1,700 a year in 1955 and 1956, and $850 in 1958. The capital loss declared in 1958 was

$25,000. IRS Criminal Reference Report, pp. 41, 42, 44. STRIKE FORCE 18 PAPERS.

20. *Miami Herald,* October 23, 1969.

21. Author interview with a friend and associate of Morris Lansburgh during his years operating the Flamingo.

22. Ibid.

23. IRS Criminal Reference Report, pp. 43, 44.

24. IRS Criminal Reference Report, pp. 22ff. For some details of the original lien, see *Miami Herald,* September 9, 1953.

25. $8,858.10, to be exact, paid to the IRS on December 30, 1955. The lien was dismissed on February 28, 1956. FBI, New York, September 25, 1958. "Meyer Lansky. Anti-Racketeering," p. 18. FBI.

26. Springer Motor Company. Teletype, to Director, from SAC Miami, September 9, 1961. FBI.

27. Broward County, Real Estate Title and Property Records, Book 1592, pp. 512, 513.

28. Sann Interviews.

29. Annette Lansky, interview, September 27, 1990.

30. To Director, from SAC Miami. Recommendation for Installation of Technical or Microphone Surveillance, March 1, 1961. FBI.

31. To SAC Miami, from Director, March 23, 1960. FBI.

32. To Director, from SAC Miami, Meyer Lansky, February 20, 1961. FBI.

33. Ibid.

34. To SAC Miami, from Director, September 14, 1961. FBI.

35. Ibid., May 25, 1962.

36. Ibid., June 12, 1962.

37. Ibid., July 13, 1962.

38. Ibid., March 19, 1963. This break-in might, of course, have been staged by the FBI in order to cover further surveillance installation — or, possibly, to remove the Misur installed in June of the previous year. The break-in occurred only weeks before the preparation of the Justice Department memorandum described later in the chapter. There is no reference, however, to any such operation in the FBI documents that are currently available, under the Freedom of Information Act, for the period in and around March 1963.

39. To Director, from SAC Miami. Daily Summary, July 25, 1963. FBI.

40. Ibid., MISUR, December 22, 1962. FBI.

41. To Director, from SAC Miami, July 30, 1962. FBI.

42. Dr. David Russin, interview, September 25, 1989.

43. Ibid.

44. To Director, from SAC Miami, September 1, 1964. FBI.

45. Ibid., re Miami Airtel, May 3 and May 21, 1961. FBI.

46. Ibid. See, for example, October 3, 1963. FBI.

47. Dr. Seymour J. Gray, interview, March 1, 1990.

48. Author interview with a close friend and associate of Vincent Alo in the 1960s.

49. Buddy Lansky, interview, May 8, 1989.

50. Author interview with a friend of Vincent Alo who traveled to Rome with him.

51. See, for example, Gomes, "Investigation," p. 20.

52. See, for example, U.S. documents cited in the statement of Dr. Yosef Burg, interior minister, p. 25, in Israel, Supreme Court Papers. Office of the Prime Minister, Jerusalem.

53. U.S. Senate, *Organized Crime and Illicit Traffic in Narcotics,* Part I, p. 80.

54. Hank Messick, "Gold Coaster Filled Shoes of Frank Costello," *Miami Herald,* December 20, 1966.

55. "Valachi gave an interpretation to My Tradition that made it look cheap and totally criminal in operation," complained Joseph Bonanno in his autobiography, *A Man of Honor* (p. 164). "Because he never rose very high himself, Valachi mainly came in contact with the dregs of our society, our lowlife. . . . Often he described historical events in which he never participated, but nonetheless inserted himself to make himself seem important to his gullible audience."

56. Maas, p. 111.

57. U.S. Senate, *Organized Crime and Illicit Traffic in Narcotics,* Part I, p. 109.

58. Roemer, p. 128.

59. Author interview with a participant in the meeting.

60. Information from a participant in the sale of the Sands Hotel to Howard Hughes.

61. This paragraph, and other details of skimming and tax evasion practices, are based on author interviews with a participant in several skims and with a number of Las Vegas dealers.

62. Author interview with a friend and business associate of Vincent Alo in the 1960s.

63. The FBI transcripts of this and all other conversations illegally transmitted from the office of Eddie Levinson in the Fremont Hotel casino in the years up to April 1963 were sealed by court order, following the court case in which Levinson pleaded no contest to a skimming indictment and was fined $5,000 in March 1988. The account given here is based on author interviews, and also on the series of articles on Las Vegas skimming by the investigative reporter Sandy Smith, published in the *Chicago Sun-Times,* on July 10–13, 1966. Smith, later a member of the *Life* investigative unit, wrote a number of articles in these years that were remarkable for their familiarity with confidential material gathered by the FBI and other law

enforcement agencies, but he declines today to discuss the sources for his 1966 articles about the Fremont bug. See also *New York Times,* January 18 and March 29, 1968.

64. Author interview. Also *Chicago Sun-Times,* July 11, 1966.

65. Author interviews with former FBI agents.

66. To Director, FBI, from SAC Newark, May 1, 1963. STRIKE FORCE 18 PAPERS.

67. *Chicago Sun-Times,* July 11, 1966.

68. Interview by Fred Mark Palmer with Sheriff Clay White, March 7, 1991.

69. *Chicago Sun-Times,* July 12, 1966.

70. Ibid., July 13, 1966.

71. Author interviews with FBI agents.

72. *New York Times,* January 18, 1968.

73. Ibid., March 29, 1968.

74. See Mollenhoff, chapter 7, for some insights into this process.

75. The FBI had disclosed some of its Fremont skim information to the Justice Department. J. Edgar Hoover was said to have suspected Justice of having passed the material on to Treasury to build a tax case, and that the leak came from Treasury.

76. The files of the INS contain a number of legal opinions pointing out the weakness of the denaturalization case against Meyer Lansky. See, for example, Harold P. Shapiro to Regional Commissioner, Southeast, 38-51-3702, in reply to Zimmerman's Memorandum of October 20, 1959; Weixel to Shelver of January 9, 1963; and Shapiro to Winings of February 8, 1963: "It is doubtful the Government could meet the heavy burden required of it in denaturalization cases with the above evidence. . . . This Division will take no further action in this case." INS.

77. *New York Times,* June 12, 1957.

78. Author interview with a confidant of Vincent Alo in the late 1960s and early 1970s.

79. Ibid.

80. Ibid.

81. Author interview with a participant in the sale of the Sands Hotel to Howard Hughes.

17. Three Hundred Million Dollars

1. Richard Jaffe, interview, April 13, 1989.

2. For a full list of the directors and stockholders of the Bank of World Commerce, see Gomes, "Investigation," p. 6.

3. Richard Jaffe, interview, December 13, 1990.

4. Ibid., December 6, 1990. Kleinman was also a major stockholder in Castle Bank. The Bank of Perrine issued Castle Bank depositors with a

receipt, and notified Castle of the depositor's identity. In its own records, however, the Bank of Perrine only showed a deposit for the credit of Castle Bank, the depositor unnamed.

5. Money laundering did not become an offense per se in America until the passing of the Money Laundering Control Act of 1986. Prior to that, prosecutors brought cases under a variety of taxation statutes relating to the defrauding of the government, and under the Bank Secrecy Act, which required the reporting of foreign bank accounts and of other transactions. See Plombeck, "Confidentiality," p. 71.

6. R. J. Campbell, interviews, April 26, 1990, and June 20, 1991.

7. The paragraphs on John Pullman that follow are based on author interviews with people who had close business and personal associations with Pullman in these years.

8. Gerson Blatt, interview, March 13, 1990.

9. Author interview with a friend and professional associate of John Pullman.

10. See Eisenberg et al., pp. 156–157 and 250–251, for the full extent of this evidence — remarks attributed to Joseph "Doc" Stacher in Israel before his death.

11. Pan Am started daily jet service out of New York on October 26, 1958, flying to Paris.

12. Cited in Sandy Smith, "Mobsters in the Marketplace," p. 100.

13. Gomes, "Investigation," p. 10.

14. Ibid.

15. Author interview with client of John Pullman.

16. Faith, pp. 216, 217.

17. Bernie Cornfeld, interview, May 24, 1989.

18. Ibid.

19. *New York Times,* October 3, 1974.

20. Bernie Cornfeld, interview, May 24, 1989.

21. Ibid.

22. Faith, p. 284.

23. Oil and gas leases, Nevada 03443, 03444, and 03445, July 20, 1950. Department of the Interior, Bureau of Land Management.

24. Turner, p. 66.

25. Author interview with investor in the Riviera Hotel, Havana.

26. Author interview with a business associate of Sam Garfield.

27. "U.S. Average Wellhead Value per Barrel of Crude Oil by State," *Basic Petroleum Data Book: Petroleum Industry Statistics,* vol. IX, no. 3, September 1989.

28. See oil and gas lease records of Stark County, Ohio, and the Department of Natural Resources, State of Michigan, Lansing: Lansky, Levinson, Garfield.

29. *Miami Herald,* December 12, 1965.

30. Hank Messick, interviews, June 7, 1989, and May 27, 1991.

31. Dick Jaffe, interview, October 5, 1989.

32. *Chicago Sun-Times,* July 13, 1966.

33. Gomes, "Investigation," p. 11.

34. Gaby, "What Would It Cost Today?" p. 24.

35. See *Variety,* May 13, 1987, p. 62, for a full list of James Bond villains.

36. I am grateful to Patterson Smith for drawing Bilbo/Baruch's book to my attention.

37. Buchalter was electrocuted in March 1944 with two of his accomplices, Louis Capone and Mendy Weiss.

38. The voluminous but sober files of the original Murder, Inc., investigation in the New York City Municipal Archives show the raw material from which Turkus and his co-writer departed.

39. Messick, *Syndicate Abroad,* p. 7.

40. These information sheets were circulated to other FBI offices.

41. See Milt Sosin, *New York Post,* April 9, 1969, and Nicholas Gage, *Wall Street Journal,* November 19, 1969, for two reported versions of this remark.

42. Hank Messick, interview, July 1, 1991.

43. Rabbi David Shapiro, interview, December 5, 1988.

44. Buddy Lansky, interview, July 3, 1989.

45. Ibid., March 27, 1989.

46. *Miami Herald,* March 17, 1967.

47. Author interview with a partner who held four official shares in the Colony Club, plus two hidden points in the skim.

48. Author interview with another American partner, who held only hidden shares. He recalls the Colony Club as a highly profitable, illicit venture for the hidden partners. His clear recollection is that Vincent Alo was the organizer and controller of the syndicate.

49. Surveillance Report, May 28, 1963 (File 92-2831, Section 10, Serials 652–790). FBI. Lansky always denied the claim of Sir Stafford Sands that Lansky offered him $2 million in 1960 or 1961 if Sands could secure him a Bahamas gambling license. Sands volunteered this information to the Royal Commission of Inquiry in 1967, in questioning by his own attorney. It made the $515,900 which the Royal Commission had discovered Sands charged the Lou Chesler consortium for a license sound quite modest.

50. See Houts, *King's X,* for the original version of this myth. See Pye, *The King over the Water,* p. 219, for a refutation.

51. Sir Jack Hayward, interview, March 8, 1990.

52. Bahamas Islands, *Report of the Commission of Inquiry into the Operation of the Business of Casinos in Freeport and in Nassau,* para. 253, p. 86.

53. *Evening News,* London, February 23, 1967. See also Hansard, February 28, 1967.

54. Dougald McMillan, interview, July 3, 1991.

55. Ibid., November 30, 1989.

56. Ibid.

57. Moore, pp. 252, 253.

58. *Miami Herald*, March 2, 1973.

59. Ibid.

60. Ibid.

61. Ibid.

62. Author interview with an associate of Morris Lansburgh. See also *U.S. v. Meyer Lansky and Others*, U.S. District Court, Nevada, Criminal No. 2408, March 25, 1971.

63. Lowell Bergman, interview, June 22, 1989. See also *Miami Beach Sun*, April 2, 1970.

64. Author interview with a friend who was close to Meyer Lansky at the time of his drugs arrest.

65. *Miami Herald*, March 28, 1970.

66. Dougald McMillan, interview, February 26, 1990.

67. *Miami Herald*, June 19, 1970.

68. Ibid.

69. *Atlantic Monthly*, July 1970.

70. Ibid., pp. 62–63.

71. Surveillance Summary, May 14, 1970. FBI.

72. Ibid.

73. Ibid.

74. Yoram Alroy, interview, December 16, 1987.

18. Sanctuary in Zion

I owe a particular debt to Evelyn Chen for helping to organize and check the interviews and documentation on which this chapter is based.

1. Dr. Yosef Burg, interview, December 18, 1987; Ykutiel Federman, interview, January 25, 1988.

2. Ibid.

3. Doc Stacher had settled in Israel in 1964.

4. Mira Sukenik, interview, January 24, 1988.

5. The opening chapter of Uri Dan's book with Dennis Eisenberg and Eli Landau, *Meyer Lansky*, describes Lansky's visit to his grandparents' grave with Uri Dan, in May 1971, and seems to suggest that, thanks to Dan's help, this was the first time that Lansky had managed to see the graves. However, in his Affidavit of December 15, 1970, Lansky declared that he had "recently" visited his grandparents' grave on the Mount of

Olives "and found it intact." Israel, Supreme Court Papers. Office of the Prime Minister, Jerusalem.

6. Author's visit to grave, December 18, 1987.

7. Joseph Sheiner, interview, January 26, 1988.

8. *Encyclopaedia Judaica,* Jerusalem, 1972. Law of Return, col. 1486.

9. Klein, "The Lansky Case," p. 287.

10. Yoram Alroy, interview, December 16, 1987.

11. Ibid.

12. William S. Lynch to Will Wilson, Assistant Attorney General, Criminal Division, September 15, 1970. JUSTICE.

13. Ibid.

14. Chester J. Pavloski, to Mr. Meyer Lansky, express registered letter, dated May 18, 1971. STATE.

15. Affidavit of Meyer Lansky, December 15, 1970, clauses 9 and 10. Israel, Supreme Court Papers.

16. Ibid.

17. See chapter 12, source note 13, for the ten men fined. The Lansky brothers and Samuel Bratt were the only Jews. Joseph Varon, interview, May 2, 1991.

18. Affidavit of Meyer Lansky, clause 2. Lansky states in this clause that he "retired from active business since 1969," but this date appears to be a mistyping for 1959. Elsewhere in the document, in clause 50, and in the interviews which Lansky later gave in Israel, he set 1959, the date of his departure from Cuba, and of his heart trouble, as the year of his retirement.

19. Ibid., clause 3.

20. Ibid., clauses 11 and 13.

21. Letter of Rabbi David Shapiro, April 20, 1971. Filed with Affidavit of Meyer Lansky.

22. Letter of Harry M. Permesly, M.D., July 7, 1971. Filed with Affidavit of Meyer Lansky.

23. Dr. Yosef Burg, interview, December 8, 1987.

24. Yoram Alroy, interview, December 16, 1987; Dr. Yosef Burg, interview, December 18, 1987.

25. *New York Times,* June 10, 1971.

26. Messick, *Lansky,* dust jacket.

27. Ibid., p. 277.

28. *Jerusalem Post,* July 6, 1971.

29. As reported in ibid., May 16, 1971. Also *Miami Herald,* May 17, 1971.

30. Yoram Alroy, interview, December 16, 1987.

31. Gavriel Bach, interview, December 16, 1987.

32. *New York Times,* July 6, 1971.

33. Dr. David Russin, interview, September 25, 1989.

34. *Jerusalem Post,* June 24, 1971.

35. Yoram Alroy, interview, December 16, 1987.

36. Dan, "Meyer Lansky Breaks His Silence," July 2, 1971.

37. Ibid.

38. *Jerusalem Post*, July 23, 1971.

39. Ibid., July 22, 1971.

40. Dr. Yosef Burg, interview, December 18, 1987.

41. *New York Times*, September 21, 1970, and October 16, 1971.

42. Yoram Sheftel, interview, December 15, 1987.

43. Ibid.

44. For details of the Soblen case, see Klein, "The Lansky Case."

45. Yoram Sheftel, interview, December 15, 1987.

46. Ibid.

47. Ibid.

48. Ibid.

49. Ibid.

50. Ibid.

51. *Guardian*, September 12, 1972.

52. Author meeting with E. David Rosen, July 8, 1988.

53. Yoram Alroy, interview, December 16, 1987.

54. Ibid.

55. Ibid., and May 26, 1991.

56. Ibid.

57. The account in these paragraphs of Bach's trip to the United States is based on Gavriel Bach, interview, December 15, 1987.

58. Yoram Alroy, interview, December 16, 1987.

59. David Landau, interview, December 16, 1987.

60. Ibid.

61. Ibid.

62. Gavriel Bach, interview, December 15, 1987.

63. Visit and interviews at 4 Rehov Beeri, Tel Aviv, January 25, 1988. There is some dispute over the correct spelling of Berl Kaznelson's name. This version is as it appears in the first English supplement of the *Davar Palestine Labour Daily*, September 27, 1929. It is probably the way Kaznelson spelled it himself.

64. Ibid.

65. Ykutiel Federman, interview, January 25, 1988.

66. *Jerusalem Post*, March 26, 1972.

67. Joseph Sheiner, interview, January 26, 1988.

68. Author interview with one of the supreme court judges who sat on the Lansky case.

69. *Jerusalem Post*, September 12, 1972.

70. Ibid.

71. Translated from Supreme Court Judgements, Jerusalem, vol. 26, part 2, September 11, 1972.

72. *Jerusalem Post*, September 12, 1972.

73. Yoram Alroy, interview, December 16, 1987.

19. "A Jew Has a Slim Chance in the World"

1. *Jerusalem Post*, September 13, 1972.

2. Ibid.

3. Yoram Alroy, interview, December 16, 1987.

4. Malana Mason, interview, January 16, 1990.

5. David Landau, interview, December 16, 1987.

6. Paul Lansky, open letter to Dr. Yosef Burg, October 9, 1972. Meyer Lansky circulated copies of this letter to friends in Israel, but it is not known where, if at all, the letter was published.

7. Ibid.

8. Ibid.

9. Meyer Lansky II, interview, September 6, 1990; Malana Mason, interview, January 16, 1990; correspondence of Paul Lansky with Twilight Electronics, St. Louis, Missouri.

10. Malana Mason, interview, January 16, 1990.

11. Joseph Sheiner, interview, January 26, 1988.

12. Oded Scheiner [*sic*], interview, May 30, 1991.

13. Joseph Sheiner, interview, January 26, 1988.

14. Ibid.

15. Ibid. See also Department of State telegram, Amembassy, Asunción, to Washington, November 10, 1973 (STATE). After Lansky's attempt to enter Paraguay, President Stroessner instituted an inquiry which established that, at the instigation of the honorary consul in Tel Aviv, "'Instituto de Bienestar Rural,' the agency directly responsible for certifying Bona Fide immigrants for work in agricultural sector, had issued list of Israelis authorized to enter Paraguay, which included Meyer Lansky and family."

16. Joseph Sheiner, interview, January 26, 1988.

17. Ibid.

18. Ibid.

19. Teddy Lansky, meeting with author, July 14, 1988.

20. Joseph Sheiner, interview, January 26, 1988.

21. "Legat maintaining daily contact at high level with Israeli police to insure prompt receipt of travel information." Amembassy Tel Aviv to Washington, October 16, 1972. STATE.

22. Joseph Sheiner, interview, January 26, 1988.

23. Ibid.

24. Memo to Director, from Henry E. Petersen, Criminal Division, March 28, 1972. HEP:RJC:mab. 123–150. Stamped April 10, 1972. FBI.

25. Joseph Sheiner, interview, January 26, 1988.

26. Ibid.

27. Ibid.

28. Ibid.

29. *Miami News,* November 7, 1972.

30. Milt Sosin, interview, June 28, 1988.

31. *Miami News,* November 7, 1972.

32. *Miami Herald,* November 8, 1972.

33. Teddy Lansky, meeting with author, July 14, 1988.

34. *Miami Herald,* November 11, 1972.

35. Ibid.

36. Joseph Sheiner, interview, January 26, 1988.

37. Report for the court on Meyer Lansky's health by Dr. Edward St. Mary, Chief of Cardiology, Mercy Hospital. St. Mary to Judge Lawrence King, January 5, 1973, p. 2. *U.S. v. Lansky and Cellini,* U.S. District Court, Southern District of Florida, 72-415-CR-JE.

38. Oded Scheiner, interview, May 30, 1991.

39. Joseph Sheiner, interview, January 26, 1988.

40. Messick, *Lansky,* p. 277.

41. Milt Sosin, interview, June 28, 1988.

20. *"The Biggest Damn Crook in the Whole Wide World"*

All the Justice Department documents cited in this chapter were obtained through the Freedom of Information Act. The full testimony in the contempt of court case (*United States v. Meyer Lansky,* No. 73-2536, U.S. Court of Appeals, Fifth Circuit, June 28, 1974) is available because the case went to appeal. Only the motions and pleadings are available for the tax evasion case (*United States v. Meyer Lansky and Dino Cellini,* 72-415-CR-JE, U.S. District Court, Southern District of Florida) and for the Flamingo skimming case (*United States v. Meyer Lansky et al.,* Criminal — LV 2474, RDF, U.S. District court, Nevada). Vincent Teresa recorded his version of his testimony in his book *Vinnie Teresa's Mafia.* This has been checked against the recollections of the prosecutor, R. J. Campbell, the daily reports in the Miami newspapers, and the memories of Milt Sosin, who covered the trial for the *Miami News.*

In Nevada, Oscar Goodman kindly supplied his recollection of the Flamingo skimming case.

I am grateful for the help of those prosecuting attorneys who no longer work for the Justice Department. Those who remain in the department are precluded from commenting on their cases (see note 75).

1. William S. Lynch to Will Wilson, Assistant Attorney General, September 15, 1970. JUSTICE.

2. From seven in April 1969 to eighteen in February 1971. Mollenhoff, pp. 1–7 and 257–264.

3. Will R. Wilson, interview, March 28, 1991.

4. Mollenhoff, p. 185. Confirmed by interview with Will R. Wilson, March 28, 1991.

5. Will R. Wilson, interview, March 28, 1991.

6. R. J. Campbell, interview, April 24, 1991.

7. Ibid., April 26, 1990.

8. Ibid.

9. Ibid.

10. Ibid., May 4, 1990, and April 24, 1991.

11. Ibid., April 24, 1991.

12. Ibid.

13. Ibid.

14. *Miami Herald*, January 6, 1973.

15. *The Godfather* was released on March 15, 1972, *The Godfather, Part II* on December 12, 1974, according to the records of Paramount Pictures, Office of Communications.

16. Puzo, *Godfather Papers*, p. 31.

17. *Miami Herald*, February 27, 1973.

18. Ibid., March 1, 1973.

19. Jury selection occupied Monday, February 26, 1973. Evidence was heard on Tuesday, Wednesday, and Thursday mornings. The jury gave its verdict on the afternoon of Thursday, March 1.

20. *New York Post*, June 14, 1973.

21. Joseph Sheiner, interview, January 26, 1988.

22. *U.S. v. Lansky and Cellini*. Testimony of Dr. Grumer, July 11, 1973.

23. Buddy Lansky, interview, April 10, 1989.

24. *Miami Herald*, May 17, 1975.

25. See note 22 above.

26. *Miami News*, March 15, 1973.

27. *Miami Herald*, July 12, 1973.

28. Dr. Edward St. Mary, interview, March 2, 1990.

29. Ibid.

30. *Miami News*, July 17, 1973.

31. Ibid.

32. E. David Rosen, meeting with author, April 29, 1991.

33. *Miami Herald*, July 19, 1973.

34. R. J. Campbell, interview, May 4, 1990.

35. Ibid.

36. *Miami Herald*, July 18, 1973.

37. Milt Sosin, interview, July 28, 1988.

38. Teresa, *My Life in the Mafia*, p. 105.

39. Ibid., p. 46.

40. Teresa, *My Life in the Mafia*, p. 174.

41. *U.S. v. Lansky and Cellini*. Indictment, Count 1, Clause 3L, p. 4.

42. Ibid., Indictment, Count 2.

43. Ibid., Indictment, "Overt acts," 9, 13 (pp. 5, 6).

44. Teresa, *Vinnie Teresa's Mafia*, pp. 4, 40.

45. Ibid., p. 45.

46. Ibid., p. 45. This appears to be another example of Teresa's inability to tell a straight story. R. J. Campbell remembers it was Teresa who first told him of Cellini's involvement with junkets to the Colony Club.

47. Ibid., p. 46.

48. Ibid., p. 50.

49. *Miami Herald,* July 21, 1973.

50. Ibid.

51. Teresa, *Vinnie Teresa's Mafia,* p. 55.

52. Ibid.

53. Milt Sosin, interview, July 28, 1988.

54. Ibid.

55. *Miami News,* July 24, 1973.

56. Teresa, *Vinnie Teresa's Mafia,* p. 69.

57. R. J. Campbell, interviews, May 4, 1990, and April 24, 1991.

58. *Miami Herald,* July 26, 1973.

59. Joseph Sheiner, interview, January 26, 1988.

60. Ibid.

61. *U.S. v. Lansky,* No. 73-2536. June 28, 1974.

62. Memorandum to Deputy Chief Marvin R. Loewy, October 14, 1976, Re: Meyer Lansky, p. 3. JUSTICE.

63. *Miami Herald,* August 23, 1974.

64. Memorandum to Deputy Chief Marvin R. Loewy, October 14, 1976, Re: Meyer Lansky, p. 3.

65. IRS Criminal Reference Report, pp. 43, 44. STRIKE FORCE 18 PAPERS.

66. *U.S. v. Lansky, et al.,* LV 2474. Report of Dr. Edward St. Mary, January 5, 1973, p. 3.

67. Author interviews with former FBI and Justice Department staff.

68. Ibid.

69. *Miami Herald,* August 23, 1974.

70. *U.S. v. Lansky, et al.,* LV 2474. Hearing of September 30, 1976.

71. *Miami News,* November 4, 1976.

72. Author interview with FBI agent assigned to Lansky investigation in the early 1970s.

73. *Miami Herald,* August 23, 1974.

74. Author interviews with several members of the Nevada bar.

75. April 3, 1990, letter to author from G. Douglas Tillett, U.S. Department of Justice: "It would be inappropriate for Mr. DeFeo or any employee of the Department of Justice to comment on the Lansky trial beyond what has already been said in the court records."

76. *Seattle Times,* August 9, 1981, September 23, 1981, and February 12, 1982. Also, *New York Times,* February 25, 1990.

77. R. J. Campbell, interview, April 24, 1991.

78. Author interviews with former Justice Department attorneys. The strongest evidence in the memorandum to Loewy of October 14, 1976 (see note 62 above), is of Meyer helping an unemployed dealer to get a job at the Flamingo in the early 1960s.

79. Patton to Bork, July 23, 1974, Re: *U.S. v. Meyer Lansky* (C.A.5, No. 73-2536). JUSTICE.

80. Ibid.

81. Memoranda, Henry E. Petersen to the Solicitor General, and Peter M. Shannon to the Solicitor General, both dated October 25, 1974. JUSTICE.

82. Handwritten notes, Memorandum, William L. Patton to the Solicitor General, October 31, 1974, Re: *U.S. v. Meyer Lansky* (C.A.5, No. 73-2536), decided June 28, 1974, rehearing denied October 8, 1974. JUSTICE.

83. Office of the Solicitor General, November 21, 1974, copies to Mr. Patton, Mr. Frey, Criminal and Public Information. JUSTICE.

21. Shalom, Meyer . . .

1. Sann Interviews.

2. See, for example, *Miami News,* May 16, 1975, and October 19, 1978; *Miami Herald,* January 23, 1982. Also, *People v. Lake Elsinore Sands Casino,* Office of the District Attorney, Riverside, California, April 26, 1977.

3. Will R. Wilson, interview, March 28, 1991.

4. Truscott, "Nixon's Real Estate."

5. Kohn, "Strange Bedfellows."

6. See, for example, Hinckle and Turner, *The Fish Is Red;* Weissman, ed., *Big Brother and the Holding Company;* and Scott, *Crime and Cover-up.*

7. Joseph Sheiner, interview, January 26, 1988.

8. David Landau, interview, December 16, 1987.

9. Ibid.

10. Ibid.

11. Ibid., March 17, 1990.

12. Oded Scheiner, interview, May 30, 1991.

13. Joseph Sheiner, interview, January 26, 1988; Oded Scheiner, interview, May 30, 1991.

14. Yoram Sheftel, interview, December 15, 1987.

15. Yoram Alroy, interview, December 16, 1987.

16. The account of Aloni's trip to Miami Beach is based on Yaacov Aloni, interview, Jerusalem, January 27, 1988.

17. Ibid., and May 29, 1991.

18. *Lansky v. Lansky,* Divorce Decree documents; also Property Settlement Agreement no. 219227, *Edna P. Lansky v. Paul Lansky,* County of Pierce, Washington, February 8, 1974.

19. Meyer Lansky II, interview, September 6, 1990.

20. Ibid.

21. Ibid.

22. Ibid., September 12, 1990.

23. Ibid.

24. Ibid.

25. Ibid., May 26, 1991.

26. Ibid., September 7, 1990.

27. *Miami Herald,* July 3, 1977.

28. Ibid., July 14, 1977.

29. Joseph Sheiner, interview, January 26, 1988.

30. *Miami Herald,* July 3, 1977.

31. Buddy Lansky, interview, May 1, 1989.

32. Joseph Sheiner, interview, January 26, 1988.

33. Buddy Lansky, interview, May 1, 1989.

34. Yaacov Aloni, interview, January 27, 1988.

35. *Miami News,* August 29, 1977.

36. *Miami News* and *Miami Herald,* October 13 and October 14, 1977.

37. *Miami News* and *Miami Herald,* October 15, 1977.

38. Buddy Lansky, interview, May 1, 1989.

39. *Jerusalem Post,* September 7, 1977.

40. Ibid., September 8, 1977.

41. Meyer Lansky to Menachem Begin, November 28, 1977. Israeli government source.

42. *Jerusalem Post,* January 5, 1978.

43. Joseph Sheiner, interview, January 26, 1988.

44. Ibid.

45. *Jerusalem Post,* August 6, 1980.

46. Yoram Sheftel, interview, December 15, 1987.

47. Ibid.

48. *Jerusalem Post,* August 6, 1980.

49. Joseph Sheiner, interview, January 26, 1988.

50. Yoram Sheftel, interview, December 15, 1987.

51. Ibid.

52. (1) Having entered Israel on a tourist visa on July 27, 1970, Meyer Lansky applied for Israeli citizenship under the Law of Return in December 1970. (2) Following Dr. Burg's rejection of this under clause 2(b)(3) of the Law of Return, Lansky took the interior minister to the Israeli High Court

under an order nisi, applied for in September 1971 and argued by Lansky's lawyer, Yoram Alroy, in March 1972. (3) In August 1977, Lansky applied, with the help of his Miami Beach rabbi, for a tourist visa to visit Israel. When this was rejected on September 6, 1977, he appealed (4) to Menachem Begin — and to Dr. Burg — on November 28, 1977. These appeals were rejected by the Israeli Interior Ministry on January 4, 1978. Yoram Sheftel applied for a tourist visa on Lansky's behalf early in 1980 (5). When this was first granted, then deferred in June 1980, Sheftel applied (6) for an order nisi on Lansky's behalf in August 1980. Following the high court's decision that Dr. Burg should show cause for changing his decision, the Interior Ministry finally granted a thirty-day tourist visa — subject to the $100,000 bond and letter of guarantee — in September 1980.

53. Joseph Sheiner, interview, January 26, 1988.

54. Ibid.

22. *A Legend in His Lifetime*

1. *Miami Herald,* November 8, 1972.

2. Joseph Sheiner, interview, January 26, 1988.

3. Ibid.

4. Author interview with an associate of one of the partners in the proposed syndicate.

5. Buddy Lansky, interview, June 12, 1989.

6. Author interview with the doctor.

7. Buddy Lansky, interview, March 23, 1989.

8. Ibid.

9. Ibid.

10. Ibid.

11. Ibid.

12. Author interviews with Lansky family friends.

13. Joseph Sheiner, interview, January 26, 1988.

14. Ibid.

15. Ibid.

16. Ibid.

17. *New York Herald Tribune,* January 27, 1962.

18. Yoram Sheftel, interview, December 15, 1987.

19. Ibid.

20. The story of Sheftel's visit with Lansky and the party to watch *The Gangster Chronicles* is based on Yoram Sheftel, interview, December 15, 1987.

21. Dr. Seymour J. Gray, interview, March 1, 1990.

22. Jyll Rosenfeld, telephone conversation, October 20, 1988. Confirmed by author conversation with Jackie Mason.

23. Joseph Sheiner, interview, January 26, 1988.

24. Jyll Rosenfeld, telephone conversation, October 20, 1988.

25. Harold Conrad, interview, April 2, 1990.

26. Howard Sann, interview, March 29, 1990.

27. Sann Interviews.

28. Ibid.

29. Ibid.

30. Dr. Seymour J. Gray, interview, June 5, 1991.

31. Howard Sann, interview, March 29, 1990.

32. Ibid.

33. Sann Interviews.

34. Joseph Sheiner, interview, January 26, 1988.

35. Howard Sann, interview, March 29, 1990.

36. Sann Interviews.

37. Milton Hoff, interview, May 17, 1989.

38. Milt Sosin, interview, September 11, 1989.

39. *Miami News,* February 10, 1978.

40. Ibid.

41. Bill Roemer, interview, January 23, 1991.

42. Dr. David Russin, interview, September 25, 1989.

43. Ibid.

44. Buddy Lansky, interview, March 29, 1989.

45. Ibid.

46. Ibid.

47. Joseph Varon, interview, June 9, 1989.

48. Joseph Sheiner, interview, January 26, 1988.

49. Buddy Lansky, interview, March 23, 1989.

50. Ibid., May 8, 1989.

51. Ibid., March 27, 1989.

52. Ibid.

53. Meyer Lansky II, interview, September 7, 1990.

54. Milt Sosin, interview, September 11, 1989.

55. Buddy Lansky, interview, April 24, 1989.

56. Ibid.

57. Ibid., May 1, 1989.

58. Yaacov Aloni, interview, January 27, 1988.

59. Interview by Alison Glass Mahoney with Pet Heaven executive.

60. Buddy Lansky, interview, December 4, 1989.

61. Author interview with medical attendant.

62. Ibid.

63. Buddy Lansky, May 8, 1989.

64. Last Will and Testament of Meyer Lansky, sworn before Marilyn Shear and Lawrence N. Rosen, October 26, 1982. Filed for record, Dade County Courthouse, February 7, 1983.

65. Conrad, "Meyer Lansky," p. 60.

66. Ibid.

67. Author meeting with Teddy Lansky, July 14, 1988.

68. Buddy Lansky, interview, April 3, 1989.

69. Author interview with medical attendant.

23. *"If There's a Life After Death . . ."*

1. John Sampson, interviews, May 19, 1989, and May 22, 1991.

2. Ibid.

3. *Sunday Times* (London), January 16, 1983.

4. *New York Times*, January 16, 1983.

5. *Detroit News*, January 16, 1983.

6. *Chicago Tribune*, January 16, 1983.

7. *Omaha World-Herald*, January 16, 1983.

8. *News of the World* (London), January 16, 1983.

9. *New York Daily News*, January 16, 1983. See also *New York Times*, January 16, 1983, for references to "underworld penetration of legitimate businesses."

10. *Miami Herald*, January 16, 1983.

11. Meyer Lansky II, interview, September 10, 1990.

12. Buddy Lansky, interview, December 4, 1989.

13. Meyer Lansky II, interview, September 10, 1990.

14. Ibid.

15. Ibid.

16. Dade County Courthouse, Miami. 83/1122 Division 3.

17. Milt Sosin, interview, September 11, 1989.

18. Sann Interviews.

19. Author meeting with Teddy Lansky, July 14, 1988.

20. Sann Interviews.

21. Carl Brandt, conversation with author, July 19, 1988.

22. Buddy Lansky, interview, April 17, 1989.

23. Ibid.

24. Ibid., May 8, 1989.

25. Ibid., October 4, 1989.

26. Ibid.

27. Ibid., May 8, 1989.

28. Filed at Broward County Circuit Court, Fort Lauderdale, numbered 83-345326.

29. Author interviews with family attorneys.

30. Ibid.

31. Buddy Lansky, interview, May 1, 1989.

32. Ibid.

33. Joseph Varon, interview, August 1, 1990.

34. To be precise, $35.74 in 1981, $14.61 in 1986. "U.S. Average Well-

head Value per Barrel of Crude Oil by State," *Petroleum Industry Statistics,* vol. IX, no. 3 (September 1989), Section VI, Table 8.

35. Correspondence of December 15, 1988. Michigan Department of Natural Resources, Minerals Lease Management Section, Real Estate Division. Also, interview with Roger Nelson, Geological Survey Division, December 22, 1988.

36. Michigan Department of Natural Resources. Report 01-SW, Program G/009/11, Mineral Lease Revenue.

37. Buddy Lansky, interview, May 8, 1989.

38. Ibid., March 27, 1989.

39. Ibid.

40. Ibid., May 8, 1989.

41. Ibid.

42. Ibid.; also, March 27, 1989: "They call Jimmy Alo down. Say, 'You better come down here.' So he comes down, he went up to Sandra and says, 'Give me your brother's money.' She says, 'I don't have it.' He said to her, 'Sandra, if I had a gun, I'd kill both of you.'"

43. Myra Lansky, interview, January 16, 1990.

44. Ibid.

45. Ibid. Also Malana Mason, interview, January 16, 1990.

46. Meyer Lansky II, interview, September 10, 1990.

47. Buddy Lansky, interview, March 27, 1989.

48. Ibid.

49. Ibid., March 23, 1989.

50. Partial Assignment and Bill of Sale, Liber 496, p. 399, Michigan Department of Natural Resources, June 29, 1987.

51. *Miami Herald,* April 9, 1989.

52. Buddy Lansky, March 23, 1989.

53. Ibid., April 10, 1989.

54. *Miami Herald,* April 9, 1989.

55. Buddy Lansky, interview, October 16, 1989.

56. Ibid., December 4, 1989.

57. Buddy Lansky, interviews and meetings, November and December 1989.

58. Arch Creek nursing staff, interview, January 3, 1990.

59. Buddy Lansky, interview, April 17, 1989, and several other interviews and meetings.

60. Ibid., April 3, 1989.

61. Arch Creek nursing staff, interview, January 3, 1990.

62. Ibid.

Bibliography

Books

Albini, Joseph. *The American Mafia: Genesis of a Legend*. New York: Appleton-Century-Crofts, 1971.

Aleichem, Sholem. Introduction by Hillel Halkin. *Tevye the Dairyman*. New York: Schocken, 1987.

Allen, Steve. *Ripoff: The Corruption That Plagues America*. Secaucus, New Jersey: Lyle Stuart, 1979.

Anslinger, Harry J., and Will Oursler. *The Murderers: The Story of the Narcotic Gangs*. New York: Farrar, Straus, and Cudahy, 1961.

Asbury, Herbert. *The Gangs of New York*. New York: Dorset Press, 1989.

Barzini, Luigi. *From Caesar to the Mafia*. Freeport, New York: Library Press, Bantam Books, 1971.

Batista, Fulgencio. *Cuba Betrayed*. New York: Vantage, 1962.

Bell, Daniel. *The End of Ideology*. London: Free Press/Collier-Macmillan, 1961.

Bellow, Adam. *The Educational Alliance: A Centennial Celebration*. Arlington, Virginia: Keens Company, 1990.

Berman, Susan. *Easy Street*. New York: Dial Press, 1981.

Birmingham, Stephen. *The Rest of Us*. Boston: Little, Brown, 1984.

Blakey, G. Robert, and Richard N. Billings. *The Plot to Kill the President*. New York: Times Books, 1981.

515

Block, Alan. *East Side, West Side: Organizing Crime in New York, 1930–1950*. New Brunswick, New Jersey: Transaction Books, 1985.

———. *Masters of Paradise: Organized Crime and the Internal Revenue Service in the Bahamas*. New Brunswick, New Jersey: Transaction Publishers, 1991.

Bonanno, Joseph. *A Man of Honor*. New York: Simon and Schuster, 1983.

Bradley, Hugh. *Such Was Saratoga*. New York: Arno Press, 1975.

Bristow, Edward J. *Prostitution and Prejudice: The Jewish Fight Against White Slavery, 1870–1939*. New York: Clarendon Press, 1982.

Buck, Fred S. *Horse Race Betting*. New York: Arco Publishing, 1977.

Campbell, Rodney. *The Luciano Project: The Secret Wartime Collaboration of the Mafia and the U.S. Navy*. New York: McGraw-Hill, 1977.

Chandler, David. *Brothers in Blood: The Rise of the Criminal Brotherhoods*. New York: Dutton, 1975.

Chubb, Judith. *The Mafia and Politics: The Italian State Under Siege*. Ithaca, New York: Cornell University Press, 1989.

Clark, T. *The World of Damon Runyon*. New York: Harper and Row, 1978.

Clarke, Donald Henderson. *In the Reign of Rothstein*. New York: Vanguard Press, 1929.

Conrad, Harold. *Dear Muffo: Thirty-five Years in the Fast Lane*. Briarcliff Manor, New York: Stein and Day, 1982.

Cook, Fred J. *Mafia!* Greenwich, Connecticut: Fawcett, 1973.

Cooney, John E. *The Annenbergs*. New York: Simon and Schuster, 1982.

Crane, Milton, ed. *Sins of New York*. New York: Bono and Gaer, 1947. Reprinted from *Fortune,* July 1939.

Cressey, Donald R. *Organized Crime and Criminal Organizations*. Churchill College Overseas Fellowship Lectures, No. 7. Cambridge: W. Heffer and Sons, 1971.

———. *Theft of the Nation: The Structure and Operations of Organized Crime in America*. New York: Harper and Row, 1969.

Cuddy, Don. *Tales of Old Hollywood*. Decatur, Illinois: Spectator Books, 1977.

Demaris, Ovid. *The Director: An Oral Biography of J. Edgar Hoover*. New York: Harper's Magazine Press, 1975.

———. *The Last Mafioso: The Treacherous World of Jimmy Fratianno*. New York: Bantam, 1981.

Dewey, Thomas E. *Twenty Against the Underworld*. Garden City, New York: Doubleday, 1974.

Donohue, James A. *Illicit Alcohol*. Penn Yan, New York: Chronicle-Express, 1965.

Eisenberg, Dennis, Uri Dan, and Eli Landau. *Meyer Lansky: Mogul of the Mob*. New York: Paddington Press, 1979.

Faith, Nicholas. *Safety in Numbers: The Mysterious World of Swiss Banking.* London: Hamish Hamilton, 1982.

Feder, Sid, and Joachim Joesten. *The Luciano Story.* New York: David McKay, 1954.

Fitzgerald, F. Scott. *The Great Gatsby.* New York: Charles Scribner's Sons, 1925 (1953 edition).

Fox, Stephen. *Blood and Power: Organized Crime in Twentieth Century America.* New York: William Morrow, 1989.

Frey, James H., and William R. Eadington, eds. *Gambling: Views from the Social Sciences.* The Annals of the American Academy of Political and Social Science. Beverly Hills, California: Sage Publications, 1984.

Fried, Albert. *The Rise and Fall of the Jewish Gangster in America.* New York: Holt, Rinehart and Winston, 1980.

Friedrich, Otto. *City of Nets.* New York: Harper and Row, 1986.

Gabler, Neal. *An Empire of Their Own: How the Jews Invented Hollywood.* New York: Crown, 1988.

Gage, Nicholas. *The Mafia Is Not an Equal Opportunity Employer.* New York: McGraw-Hill, 1971.

————, ed. *Mafia, USA.* New York: Dell, 1972.

Gallagher, Dorothy. *All the Right Enemies.* London: Rutgers University Press, 1988.

Gardner, Jack. *Gambling.* Detroit: Gale Research, 1980.

Giancana, Antoinette, and Thomas C. Renner. *Mafia Princess: Growing Up in Sam Giancana's Family.* New York: Avon, 1984.

Gold, Michael. *Jews Without Money.* New York: Carroll and Graf, 1984.

Golden, Howard. *The Brooklyn Neighborhood Book.* Brooklyn: Fund for the Borough of Brooklyn, n.d.

Gordon, Lois, and Alan Gordon. *American Chronicle: Six Decades in American Life, 1920–1980.* New York: Atheneum, 1987.

Goren, Arthur A. *Kehillah Experiment, 1908–1912: New York Jews and the Quest for Community.* New York: Columbia University Press, 1970.

Hamilton, Charles. *Men of the Underworld: The Professional Criminal's Own Story.* New York: Macmillan, 1952.

Hanna, David. *Frank Costello: The Gangster with a Thousand Faces.* New York: Belmont Tower Books, 1974.

Heimer, Mel. *Fabulous Bawd: The Story of Saratoga.* New York: Henry Holt, 1952.

Hinckle, Warren, and William W. Turner. *The Fish Is Red: The Story of the Secret War Against Castro.* New York: Harper and Row, 1981.

Hindus, Milton. *The Old East Side: An Anthology.* Philadelphia: Jewish Publication Society of America, 1969.

Hobsbawm, E. J. *Bandits*. London: Weidenfeld and Nicholson, 1969.

Hofstadter, Richard. *The Paranoid Style in American Politics and Other Essays*. New York: Knopf, 1965.

Houts, Marshall. *King's X: Common Law and the Death of Sir Harry Oakes*. New York: William Morrow, 1972.

Howe, Irving. *Jewish American Stories*. New York: New American Library, 1977.

――――. *World of Our Fathers*. New York: Bantam, 1980.

Howe, Irving, and Kenneth Libo. *How We Lived: A Documentary History of Immigrant Jews in America, 1880–1930*. New York: Richard Marek, 1979.

Ianni, Francis A. J., and Elizabeth Reuss-Ianni, eds. *The Crime Society*. New York: New American Library, 1976.

――――. *A Family Business*. London: Routledge and Kegan Paul, 1972.

Irey, Elmer L., and William J. Slocum. *The Tax Dodgers*. New York: Greenberg, 1948.

Jennings, Dean. *We Only Kill Each Other: The Life and Bad Times of Bugsy Siegel*. London: John Long, 1968.

Joey, with Dave Fisher. *Killer: Autobiography of Joey, a Professional Murderer*. New York: W. H. Allen, 1973.

Joselit, Jenna Weissman. *Our Gang: Jewish Crime and the New York Jewish Community, 1900–1940*. Bloomington: Indiana University Press, 1983.

Katcher, Leo. *The Big Bankroll: The Life and Times of Arnold Rothstein*. New Rochelle, New York: Arlington House, 1958.

Katz, Leonard. *Uncle Frank: The Biography of Frank Costello*. New York: Drake, 1973.

Kefauver, Estes. *Crime in America*. London: Victor Gollancz, 1952.

Kelley, Kitty. *His Way: The Unauthorized Biography of Frank Sinatra*. New York: Bantam Books, 1986.

Kelly, Robert J., ed. *Organized Crime: A Global Perspective*. Totowa, New Jersey: Rowman and Littlefield, 1986.

Kwitny, Jonathan. *The Crimes of Patriots: A True Tale of Dope, Dirty Money, and the CIA*. New York: W. W. Norton, 1987.

――――. *Vicious Circles: The Mafia in the Marketplace*. New York: W. W. Norton, 1979.

Lacey, Robert. *Ford: The Men and the Machine*. Boston: Little, Brown, 1986.

Landesman, A. F. *Brownsville: The Birth, Development, and Passing of a Jewish Community in New York*. New York: Bloch Publishing, 1969.

Lewis, Norman. *The Honoured Society*. London: Eland Books, 1984.

Limpus, Lowell M. *Honest Cop*. New York: E. P. Dutton, 1939.

Maas, Peter. *The Valachi Papers*. New York: Putnam's, 1968.

McClellan, John L. *Crime Without Punishment*. New York: Duell, Sloan and Pearce, 1962.

McClintick, David. *Indecent Exposure*. New York: Dell, 1982.

McCoy, Alfred W. *The Politics of Heroin in Southeast Asia*. New York: Harper and Row, 1972.

McIver, Stuart. *Glimpses of South Florida History*. Miami: Florida Flair Books, 1989.

MacKenzie, Norman, ed. *Secret Societies*. New York: Holt Rinehart and Winston, 1967.

Maxtone-Grahame, John. *The Only Way to Cross*. New York: Macmillan, 1972.

Meir, Golda. *My Life*. New York: Dell, 1975.

Meskil, Paul. *Don Carlo: Boss of Bosses*. New York: Popular Library, 1973.

Messick, Hank. *Lansky*. New York: Putnam's, 1971.

———. *The Silent Syndicate*. New York: Macmillan, 1967.

———. *Syndicate Abroad*. London: Macmillan, 1969.

———. *Syndicate in the Sun*. New York: Macmillan, 1968.

Miller, R., ed. *Brooklyn U.S.A.* New York: Brooklyn College Press, 1979.

Mitgang, Herbert. *The Man Who Rode the Tiger: The Life and Times of Judge Samuel Seabury*. New York: Lippincott, 1963.

Moldea, Dan E. *The Hoffa Wars: Teamsters, Rebels, Politicians, and the Mob*. New York: Paddington Press, 1978.

Mollenhoff, Clark R. *Strike Force: Organized Crime and the Government*. Englewood Cliffs, New Jersey: Prentice-Hall, 1972.

Moore, William Howard. *The Kefauver Committee and the Politics of Crime, 1950–1952*. Columbia: University of Missouri Press, 1974.

Morgan, John. *No Gangster More Bold*. London: Hodder and Stoughton, 1985.

Morris, Norval, and Gordon Hawkins. *The Honest Politician's Guide to Crime Control*. Chicago: University of Chicago Press, 1970.

Navasky, Victor S. *Kennedy Justice*. New York: Atheneum, 1971.

Naylor, R. T. *Hot Money*. Toronto: McClelland and Stewart, 1987.

Neff, James. *Mobbed Up*. New York: Dell, 1989.

Nelli, Humbert S. *The Business of Crime: Italians and Syndicate Crime in the United States*. Chicago: University of Chicago Press, 1976.

Ness, Eliot, and Oscar Fraley. *The Untouchables*. New York: Pocket Books, 1957.

Newman, Peter C. *Bronfman Dynasty: The Rothschilds of the New World*. Toronto: McClelland and Stewart, 1978.

Nown, Graham. *The English Godfather: Owney Madden*. London: Ward Lock, 1987.

O'Brien, Lee. *American Jewish Organizations and Israel*. Alexandria, Virginia: Progressive Litho, 1986.

Ortiz, Darwin. *Gambling Scams*. New York: Dodd, Mead, 1984.

Paher, Stanley W. *Las Vegas: As It Began, As It Grew*. Las Vegas: Nevada Publications, 1971.

Pantaleone, Michele. *The Mafia and Politics*. London: Chatto and Windus, 1966.

Peterson, Virgil W. *Barbarians in Our Midst*. Boston: Little, Brown, 1952.

————. *The Mob: Two Hundred Years of Organized Crime in New York*. Ottawa, Illinois: Green Hill Publishers, 1983.

Phillips, R. Hart. *Cuba: Island of Paradox*. New York: McDowell, 1959.

Pileggi, Nicholas. *Wiseguy*. New York: Pocket Books, 1985.

Pistone, Joseph D., and Richard Woodley. *Donnie Brasco: My Undercover Life in the Mafia*. New York: NAL Books, 1975.

Plate, Thomas. *Crime Pays!* New York: Simon and Schuster, 1975.

Powell, Hickman. *Lucky Luciano: His Amazing Trial and Wild Witnesses*. Secaucus, New Jersey: Arno Press, 1975.

Powers, Richard Gid. *G-Men*. Carbondale: Southern Illinois University Press, 1983.

————. *Secrecy and Power: The Life of J. Edgar Hoover*. New York: Free Press, 1987.

Prall, Robert H., and Norton Mockridge. *This Is Costello on the Spot*. Greenwich, Connecticut: Fawcett, 1951.

Puzo, Mario. *The Godfather Papers*. London: Pan Books, 1972.

Pye, Michael. *The King over the Water*. New York: Holt, Rinehart and Winston, 1981.

Raphael, Marc Lee. *A History of the United Jewish Appeal, 1939–1982*. Decatur, Georgia: Scholars Press, 1982.

Reid, Ed. *The Grim Reapers: The Anatomy of Organized Crime in America*. Chicago: Henry Regnery, 1969.

Reid, Ed, and Ovid Demaris. *The Green Felt Jungle*. London: Cox and Wyman, 1965.

Reuter, Peter. *Disorganized Crime*. London: MIT Press, 1985.

Roemer, William F., Jr. *Man Against the Mob*. New York: Donald I. Fine, 1989.

Rosten, Leo. *The Joys of Yiddish*. New York: Pocket Books, 1968.

Runyon, Damon. *On Broadway*. London: Pan Books, 1950.

————. *From First to Last*. London: Pan Books, 1954.

Salerno, Ralph, and J. S. Tompkins. *The Crime Confederation*. New York: Popular Library, 1969.

Samuel, M. *The World of Sholem Aleichem*. New York: Knopf, 1943.

Sanders, Ronald. *The Downtown Jews: Portraits of an Immigrant Generation*. New York: Dover Publications, 1987.

Sann, Paul. *Kill the Dutchman!* New York: Popular Library, 1971.

Sasuly, Richard. *Bookies and Bettors: Two Hundred Years of Gambling*. New York: Holt, Rinehart and Winston, 1982.

Scarne, John. *The Mafia Conspiracy*. North Bergen, New Jersey: Scarne Enterprises, 1976.

———. *Scarne's Complete Guide to Gambling*. New York: Simon and Schuster, 1961.

Scheim, David E. *Contract on America: The Mafia Murders of John and Robert Kennedy*. Silver Springs, Maryland: Argyle Press, 1983.

Scott, Peter Dale. *Crime and Cover-up: The CIA, the Mafia, and the Dallas-Watergate Connection*. Berkeley: Westworks, 1977.

Short, Martin. *Crime, Inc*. London: Thames Methuen, 1984.

Silver, Isidore, intro. *The Challenge of Crime in a Free Society: A Report by the President's Commission on Law Enforcement and Administration of Justice*. New York: Avon, 1968.

Simons, Howard. *Jewish Times: Voices of the American Jewish Experience*. Boston: Houghton Mifflin, 1988.

Singer, Isaac Bashevis. *Gimpel the Fool*. New York: Fawcett Crest, 1953.

———. *Old Love*. New York: Fawcett Crest, 1966.

Skolnick, Jerome H. *House of Cards*. Boston: Little, Brown, 1978.

Smiley, Nixon. *Knights of the Fourth Estate: The Story of the Miami Herald*. Miami: E. A. Seamann, 1974.

Smith, Bradley F. *The Shadow Warriors: OSS and the Origins of the CIA*. New York: Basic Books, 1983.

Smith, Dwight C., Jr. *The Mafia Mystique*. New York: Basic Books, 1975.

Smith, Eugene. *Passenger Ships of the World, Past and Present*. Boston: George H. Dean, n.d.

Smith, Richard Harris. *OSS: The History of America's First Central Intelligence Agency*. Berkeley: University of California Press, 1972.

Smith, Richard Norton. *Thomas E. Dewey and His Times*. New York: Simon and Schuster, 1982.

Smith, Wayne S. *The Closest of Enemies: A Personal and Diplomatic Account of U.S.-Cuban Relations Since 1957*. New York: W. W. Norton, 1987.

Soares, John. *Loaded Dice*. New York: Dell, 1985.

Sondern, Frederic, Jr. *Brotherhood of Evil: The Mafia*. New York: Farrar, Straus, and Cudahy, 1959.

Strasberg, Lee. *A Dream of Passion*. Boston: Little, Brown, 1987.

Stuart, Mark A. *Gangster #2: Longy Zwillman, the Man Who Invented Organized Crime*. Secaucus, New Jersey: Lyle Stuart, 1985.

Sullivan, William C., and Bill Brown. *The Bureau: My Thirty Years in Hoover's FBI*. New York: W. W. Norton, 1979.

Swanstrom, Edward E. *The Waterfront Labor Problem*. New York: Fordham University Press, 1938.

Talese, Gay. *Honor Thy Father*. New York: Dell, 1971.

Tcherikower, Elias. *The Early Jewish Labor Movement in the United States*. Translated and Revised by Aaron Anronorsky, from the original

Yiddish edition. New York: YIVO Institute for Jewish Research, 1961.

TenEick, Virginia Elliot. *History of Hollywood, 1920 to 1950.* Hollywood, Florida: City of Hollywood, 1966.

Teresa, Vincent, with Thomas C. Renner. *My Life in the Mafia.* London: Hart-Davis, MacGibbon, 1973.

———. *Vinnie Teresa's Mafia.* Garden City, New York: Doubleday, 1975.

Thomas, Hugh. *Cuba: The Pursuit of Freedom, 1762–1969.* New York: Harper and Row, 1971.

Thompson, Craig, and Allen Raymond. *Gang Rule in New York: The Story of a Lawless Era.* New York: Dial Press, 1940.

Tobey, Charles W. *The Return to Morality.* New York: Doubleday, 1952.

Trott, Lloyd. *Mafia: A Selected Annotated Bibliography.* Cambridge: University of Cambridge, Institute of Criminology, 1977.

Turkus, Burton B., and Sid Feder. *Murder, Inc.* New York: Farrar, Straus, and Young, 1951.

Turner, Wallace. *Gambler's Money.* Boston: Houghton Mifflin, 1965.

Tyler, Gus. *Organized Crime in America: A Book of Readings.* Ann Arbor: University of Michigan Press, 1962.

Vishniac, Roman. *Polish Jews: A Pictorial Record.* New York: Schocken, 1965.

Volz, J., and P. J. Bridge. *The Mafia Talks.* Greenwich, Connecticut: Fawcett, 1969.

Waller, George. *Saratoga: Saga of an Impious Era.* Saratoga Springs, New York: Historical Society of Saratoga Springs, 1966.

Waller, Leslie. *The Swiss Bank Connection.* New York: Signet, 1972.

Warshow, Robert. *The Immediate Experience.* New York: Atheneum, 1975.

Weissman, Steve, ed. *Big Brother and the Holding Company: The World Behind Watergate.* Palo Alto: Ramparts Press, 1974.

Werner, M. R. *Tammany Hall.* New York: Greenwood Press, 1968.

Whyte, William Foote. *Street Corner Society.* Chicago: University of Chicago Press, 1943.

Wilkerson, Tichi, and Borie, Marcia. *The Hollywood Reporter.* New York: Coward-McCann, 1983.

Williams, T. Harry. *Huey Long.* London: Thames and Hudson, 1969.

Wolf, George, and Joseph DiMona. *Frank Costello: Prime Minister of the Underworld.* London: Futura, 1975.

Wright, Frank. *World War II and the Emergence of Modern Las Vegas.* Las Vegas: Nevada State Museum and Historical Society, 1991.

Zborowski, Mark, and Elizabeth Hertzog. *Life Is with People: The Culture of the Shtetl.* New York: Schocken, 1962.

Zuckerman, Michael J. *Vengeance Is Mine.* New York: Macmillan, 1987.

Articles and Theses

Ain, Abraham. "Swislocz: Portrait of a Jewish Community in Eastern Europe." *YIVO Annual of Jewish Social Science* 4 (1949).

Asbury, Herbert. "America's Number One Mystery Man." *Collier's*, April 12 and 19, 1947.

"August at Saratoga." *Fortune*, August, 1935.

Bingham, Theodore A. "Foreign Criminals in New York." *North American Review*, September 1908.

Block, Alan A. "A Modern Marriage of Convenience: A Collaboration Between Organized Crime and U.S. Intelligence." In Robert J. Kelly, ed., *Organized Crime: A Global Perspective.* Totowa, New Jersey: Rowman and Littlefield, 1986.

Conrad, Harold. "Meyer Lansky: July 4, 1902–January 15, 1983." *Rolling Stone*, March 3, 1983.

Dan, Uri. "Meyer Lansky Breaks His Silence." A three-part series, in Hebrew, in the Israeli daily newspaper *Ma'ariv*, July 2, 4, and 5, 1971.

Davis, J. Richard. "Things I Couldn't Tell Till Now." *Collier's*, July 22 and 29, August 5, 12, 19, and 26, 1939.

Dawidowicz, Lucy S. "From Past/Jewish East Europe to Jewish East Side." In Marshall Sklare, *The Jew in American Society.* New York: Behrman House, 1974.

Dubois, Larry, and Laurence Gonzales. "The Puppet: Uncovering the Secret World of Nixon, Hughes, and the CIA." *Playboy*, September 1976.

Finch, Edward R., Jr. "Hands in Your Pockets. A Survey of the Background and Work of the New York County Rackets Bureau." Senior thesis, Princeton University, 1941.

Fuentes, Norberto. "Mafia in Cuba." *Cuba International*, August 1979.

Gaby, Donald D. "What Would It Cost Today?" *South Florida History Magazine*, Winter 1991.

Gage, Nicholas. "The Little Big Man Who Laughs at the Law." *Atlantic*, July 1970.

———. "Underworld Genius: How One Gang Leader Thrives While Others Fall by the Wayside." *Wall Street Journal*, November 19, 1969.

Gomes, Dennis C. "Investigation of the Background of Alvin Ira Malnik." Audit Division, Nevada Gaming Control Board, March 5, 1976.

Haller, Mark H. "Bootleggers and American Gambling, 1920–1950." In *Gambling in America.* Commission of the Review of National Policy Toward Gambling, Appendix 1. Washington, D.C., 1976.

———. "Bootleggers as Businessmen: From City Slums to City Builders." In David E. Kyvig, ed., *Law, Alcohol, and Order: Perspectives on National Prohibition.* Westport, Connecticut: Greenwood Press, 1985.

———. "Illegal Enterprise: A Theoretical and Historical Interpretation." *Criminology* 28, no. 2 (1990).

Halpern, Irving W., et al. "The Slum and Crime: A Statistical Study of the Distribution of Adult and Juvenile Delinquents in the Boroughs of Manhattan, Brooklyn, and New York City." New York City Housing Authority, 1934.

Hammer, Richard. "Playboy's History of Organized Crime." *Playboy,* August 1973–July 1974.

Havemann, Ernest. "Mobsters Move In on Troubled Havana." *Life,* March 10, 1958.

Hawkins, Gordon, "God and the Mafia." *Public Interest,* no. 14 (winter 1969).

———. "A Nationwide Crime Syndicate: Assessing the Evidence." A paper read at the University of Chicago Law School conference on organized crime, February 26, 1970.

Hertzberg, Arthur. "Israel and American Jewry." *Commentary* 44 (August 1967).

Joselit, Jenna Weissman. "An Answer to Commissioner Bingham: A Case Study of New York Jews and Crime, 1907." YIVO *Annual of Jewish Social Science* 18 (1982).

Kaufman, Perry Bruce. "The Best City of Them All: A History of Las Vegas, 1930–1960." Ph.D. dissertation, University of California, Santa Barbara, 1974.

Klein, Claude. "The Lansky Case: Meir Lansky v. Minister of the Interior (1972) (II) 26 P.D.377." *Israel Law Review* 8, no. 2 (1973).

Kohn, Howard. "Strange Bedfellows: The Hughes-Nixon-Lansky Connection — The Secret Alliances of the CIA from World War II to Watergate." *Rolling Stone,* May 20, 1976.

Lavine, Harold. "Intellect Set Mobster Financier Apart From Underworld Figures." *Arizona Republic,* January 27, 1983.

Lippmann, Walter. "The Underworld: Our Secret Servant," *Forum,* 85, no. 2 (January 1931).

Lukas, J. Anthony. "High Rolling in Las Vegas." *More,* May 1974.

Lupsha, Peter A. "American Values and Organized Crime: Suckers vs. Wiseguys." In S. Girgus, ed., *The American Self: Myth, Culture, and American Ideology.* Albuquerque: University of New Mexico Press, 1981.

———. "Organized Crime in the United States." In Robert J. Kelly, ed., *Organized Crime: A Global Perspective.* Totowa, New Jersey: Rowman and Littlefield, 1986.

Melamed, S. M. "The Mind of the Ghetto." *The Reflex* 3, no. 2 (August 1928).

Mitler, Ernest A. "Legal and Administrative Problems in the Control of Legalised Casino Gambling: A Comparative Study." Ph.D. thesis, Oxford University, 1986.

Plissner, Martin. "Take the Numbers with a Grain of Salt." *Miami Herald,* April 9, 1978. Also *Washington Post,* March 19, 1978.

Plombeck, Charles Thelen. "Confidentiality and Disclosure: The Money Laundering Control Act of 1986 and Banking Secrecy." *International Lawyer* 22 (1988).

Rabin, Dov, ed. "Grodno," *Encyclopaedia of the Jewish Diaspora,* vol. 9. Tel Aviv: Memorial Books, 1973.

Reuter, Peter, and Jonathan B. Rubinstein. "Fact, Fancy, and Organized Crime." *Public Interest,* no. 53 (fall 1978).

Rockaway, Robert A. "The Rise of the Jewish Gangster in America." *Journal of Ethnic Studies* 8, no. 2 (summer 1980).

———. "Scoundrel Time." *Jerusalem Post,* International Edition, May 5, 1990.

Rottenberg, Dan. "Israel vs. Meyer Lansky: A Talmudic Problem." *Expo Magazines,* Winter 1979.

Rusch, Jonathan J. "Hue and Cry in the Counting House: Some Observations on the Bank Secrecy Act." *Catholic University Law Review* 37 (1988).

Schulz, William. "The Shocking Success Story of 'Public Enemy No. 1,'" *Reader's Digest,* May 1970.

Slonim, Joel. "The Jewish Gangster," *The Reflex* 3, no. 1 (July 1978).

Smith, Patterson. "Collectible Crime Literature: The American Gangster." *Antiquarian Booksellers Bookman's Weekly,* May 5, 1986.

Smith, Sandy. "The Mob: Part I, The Fix," *Life,* September 1, 1967.

———. "The Mob: Part II, Mobsters in the Market Place," *Life,* September 8, 1967.

Stamos, George, Jr. "The Great Resorts of Las Vegas." *Las Vegas Sun,* April 1, 1979, and following weeks.

Toby, Jackson. "Hoodlum or Business Man: An American Dilemma." In Marshall Sklare, *The Jews: Social Patterns of An American Group.* Glencoe, Illinois: Free Press, 1958.

Truscott, Lucien K. "Nixon's Real Estate: The Rebozo Connection." *Village Voice,* August 30, 1973.

Velie, Lester. "Suckers in Paradise: How Americans Lose Their Shirts in Caribbean Gambling Joints." *Saturday Evening Post,* March 28, 1953.

Villa, John K. "A Critical View of the Banking Secrecy Act and the Money Laundering Statutes." *Catholic University Law Review* 37 (1988).

Oral Histories and Privately Published Monographs

Binion, Lester Ben "Benny." "Some Recollections of a Texas and Las Vegas Gaming Operator." Oral History Program, University of Nevada, Reno, 1976.

Cahill, Robbins E. "Recollections of Work in State Politics, Government, Taxation, Gaming Control, Clark County Administration and the

Nevada Resort Association." Oral History Program, University of Nevada, Reno, 1977.

Cahlan, John F. "Fifty Years in Journalism and Community Development." Oral History Program, University of Nevada, Reno, 1987.

Investigative Reporters and Editors, Inc. *The Arizona Project.* School of Journalism, University of Missouri, Columbia, 1977.

Moore, William J. "Pioneer Developer on the Las Vegas Strip — Bill Moore and the Last Frontier Hotel." Oral History Program, University of Nevada, Reno, 1981.

Olsen, Edward A. "My Careers as a Journalist in Oregon, Idaho, and Nevada; in Nevada Gaming Control; and at the University of Nevada." Oral History Program, University of Nevada, Reno, 1972.

Parker, John. *Yankee, You Can't Go Home Again.* A collection of essays on Cuba before Castro, privately published. Copies were lodged by John Parker with several libraries, among them the University of Texas, Austin; Florida International University, Miami; and the University of Miami, Otto C. Richter Library.

Petricciani, Silvio. "The Evolution of Gaming in Nevada: The Twenties to the Eighties." Oral History Program, University of Nevada, Reno, 1982.

Saiger, Mort. "Recollections of Early Times on the Las Vegas Strip." Oral History Program, University of Nevada, Reno, 1985.

Government Documents

Bibliographical details compiled and checked with the help of Kathy Ireland and Peggy Walker, Government Documents Section, S. E. Wimberly Library, Florida Atlantic University, Boca Raton.

Bahamas Islands. *Report of the Commission of Inquiry into the Operation of the Business of Casinos in Freeport and Nassau.* London: HMSO, 1967.

FBI Criminal Investigative Division, Organized Crime Intelligence and Analysis Unit. "Chronological History of La Cosa Nostra in the United States: January 1920–August 1987." In U.S. Senate, *Organized Crime: Twenty-five Years After Valachi.* Hearings Before the Permanent Subcommittee on Investigations of the Committee on Governmental Affairs. 100th Congress. Washington: USGPO, 1988.

Police Guide on Organized Crime. Washington: Technical Assistance Division, Office of Criminal Justice Assistance, Law Enforcement Assistance Administration, 1974.

U.S. Senate. *Alleged Assassination Plots Involving Foreign Leaders.* Hearings Before the Select Committee to Study Government Operations with Respect to Intelligence Activities. 94th Congress. Washington: USGPO, 1975.

———. *Final Report of the Select Committee on Improper Activities in the Labor or Management Field*. 86th Congress. Published in four parts. Washington: USGPO, 1960.

———. *Organized Crime in Interstate Commerce*. Hearings Before the Special Committee to Investigate Organized Crime in Interstate Commerce. 81st Congress, 2nd Session, and 82nd Congress, 1st Session. Interim Reports, Final Report, Hearings in twelve parts and Index. Washington: USGPO, 1950–51.

———. *Organized Crime and Illicit Traffic in Narcotics*. Hearings Before the Permanent Subcommittee on Investigations of the Committee on Government Operations. 88th Congress, 1st Session. Hearings in five parts and Index. Washington: USGPO, 1965.

———. *Organized Crime — Stolen Securities*. Hearings Before the Permanent Subcommitte on Investigations of the Committee on Government Operations. 92nd Congress, 1st Session. Washington: USGPO, 1971.

———. *Transmission of Gambling Information*. Hearings Before a Subcommittee on Interstate and Foreign Commerce. 81st Congress, 2nd Session. Washington: USGPO, 1951.

Index